SEA TROUT: SCIENCE AND MANAGEMENT

SEA TROUT:
SCIENCE AND MANAGEMENT

Proceedings of the
2nd International Sea Trout Symposium

---

20 – 22 October 2016
Dundalk: Ireland

Edited by
GRAEME HARRIS

Matador
9 Priory Business Park,
Wistow Road, Kibworth Beauchamp,
Leicestershire. LE8 0RX
Tel: 0116 279 2299
Email: books@troubador.co.uk
Web: www.troubador.co.uk/matador
Twitter: @matadorbooks

ISBN 978 1788035 354

British Library Cataloguing in Publication Data.
A catalogue record for this book is available from the British Library.

Printed and bound by CPI Group (UK) Ltd, Croydon, CR0 4YY
Typeset in 11pt Aldine401 BT by Troubador Publishing Ltd, Leicester, UK

Matador is an imprint of Troubador Publishing Ltd

CONTENTS

PREFACE

This volume presents the formal proceedings of 2nd International Sea Trout Symposium on *'Sea Trout: Science & Management'* held in Dundalk, Ireland on 20th – 22nd October 2015. It now some 12 years since the 1st International Symposium on the *'Biology, Conservation and Management'* of this little understood, but increasingly important and valuable fish, was held in Wales in 2004 and much has changed over the intervening period. There have been significant advances in the development of new technologies, notable shifts in the economic and eco-political drivers for management research and the emergence of new threats and pressures that will all shape future management priorities. There is, therefore, a clear need for both the application of new knowledge and the better application of existing knowledge in furthering the sustainable management of sea trout stocks and their associated fisheries: both now and in the future.

The 2nd Symposium was convened with four main aims. Firstly, to review progress in filling those gaps in our knowledge previously identified at the 1st Symposium about the unknowns and uncertainties that restrict our ability to manage the resource efficiently and effectively. Secondly, to identify any new knowledge gaps that are now apparent. Thirdly, to recommend strategic priorities for future management research and investigation to fill those knowledge gaps. A fourth aim was to foster closer co-operation and working relationships between fishery scientists (who generate knowledge) and fishery managers (who seek to use it) by encouraging a more structured and collaborative approach in addressing those future research needs and management priorities.

Over 160 delegates from 13 sea trout producing nations throughout Europe attended the three-day event. The notable presence of representatives from various angling organisations was a very welcome development. It has become increasingly evident that the success of many scientific studies, and then the development and implementation of local management programmes based on those studies, depends on the co-operation and support of local fisheries communities as the principal end-users and beneficiaries of science-led management.

Formal papers were presented by 30 experts in their respective topic areas under 6 broad themes:

1. Understanding Anadromy
2. Populations & Management
3. Movement & Migration
4. Monitoring & Surveillance
5. Threat Assessment
6. Looking Ahead

Although tangible progress has been made since the 1ˢᵗ Symposium in several topic areas, progress in others has been less fruitful. There is a practical limit to the number of significant papers that can be accommodated into any programme for a meeting of this type. Inevitably, papers on other important topics could not be included, either because of the lack of time or because they were not offered for publication in these proceedings.

We hope to continue the momentum gained from the 1ˢᵗ Symposium in raising the profile of the sea trout so that it is no longer undervalued and taken-for-granted by respective Governments, their management agencies, fishery stakeholders and other interested groups. The adage *"The more we learn, the less we know"* frequently seems apposite when seeking to understand, and then to manage, a species as complex as *Salmo trutta* that exhibits such a remarkable range of variability in the expression of its life history and migratory behaviour throughout its natural range. As such, it is often difficult to make broad generalisations that are equally valid to all regions of Europe (and probably unwise to do so). Nevertheless, the more we learn, the more likely it becomes that we can start asking *the right questions* about the best approach for the future management of the resource at a local, national and international level. Identifying and addressing the remaining knowledge gaps so that we can ask the right questions in the future is the ultimate goal of this symposium.

The Convenors.
31ˢᵗ March 2017

ACKNOWLEDGEMENTS

Convenors

Cathal Gallagher	*Inland Fisheries Ireland*
Graeme Harris	*Fishskill Consultancy Services Ltd*
Ivor Llewelyn	*Atlantic Salmon Trust*

Steering Group

John Armstrong	Marine Science Scotland
Ronald Campbell	Tweed Foundation
Seamus Connor	Department of Culture, Arts & Leisure
Paddy Gargan	Inland Fisheries Ireland
Graeme Harris	FishSkill Consultancy Services Ltd. *(Chair)*
Petri Heinemaa	European Inland Fisheries Advisory Committee
Paul Knight	Salmon & Trout Conservation UK
Shaun Leonard	Wild Trout Trust
Nigel Milner	APEM Ltd
Art Niven	Institute of Fisheries Management
Stig Pedersen	International Council for the Exploration of the Sea
Ted Potter	Centre for Environment, Fisheries & Aquaculture Science
Robert Rosell	Agri-Food & Biosciences Institute
Ken Whelan	Atlantic Salmon Trust

Management Group

John Armstrong	Marine Science Scotland
Ronald Campbell	Tweed Foundation
Paddy Gargan	Inland Fisheries Ireland
Graeme Harris	FishSkill Consultancy Services Ltd. *(Chair)*
Nigel Milner	APEM Ltd
Stig Pedersen	International Council for the Exploration of the Sea
Ted Potter	Centre for Environment, Fisheries & Aquaculture Science
Robert Rosell	Agri-Food & Biosciences Institute

Symposium Administrator

Sandra Doyle	Inland Fisheries Ireland

We gratefully acknowledge the commitment of Inland Fisheries Ireland in the Republic of Ireland and the Department of Environment, Culture & Leisure in Northern Ireland for jointly hosting this event in the Island of Ireland and for their considerable administrative support and backing. We also thank our associate sponsors in the UK, the Atlantic Salmon Trust, Institute of Fisheries Management, Salmon & Trout Conservation UK and Wild Trout Trust, for their support and practical assistance.

We are also grateful to the members of our Steering and Management Groups for their enthusiastic encouragement and help in shaping the key elements of this Symposium. Our special thanks go to our authors and to the anonymous referees who undertook the independent expert peer reviews of the 30 papers now published in these Proceedings.

In order to promote their widest dissemination across the broadest possible range of interest groups, these proceedings were published privately to achieve a major saving in their final cost price. Thanks are due to staff at Troubador Publishing Ltd. for their help in making this possible.

The Convenors.
31st March 2017

Anadromy in brown trout (*Salmo trutta*): A review of the relative roles of genes and environmental factors and the implications for management and conservation

A. FERGUSON[1], T. REED[2], P. MCGINNITY[2] & P. PRODÖHL[1]

[1]*Institute for Global Food Security, School of Biological Sciences, Queen's University Belfast, Belfast BT9 5AG, Northern Ireland.*
[2]*School of Biological, Earth and Environmental Sciences, University College Cork, Cork, Ireland.*

ABSTRACT

While many brown trout (*Salmo trutta*) populations spend their entire life cycle in fresh water, especially as river-lake migrants, others show facultative anadromy. That is, some trout migrate to sea while other individuals of the same population remain resident within their natal river. Sea trout can give rise to river resident offspring and vice versa, although there is a strong tendency to track the parental life history. Anadromy delivers better feeding and thus larger size, which, especially for females, results in higher fecundity and enhanced mate choice. River residence, more prevalent in males, can give higher survival and avoids the energy expenditure required by anadromy. Overall, the costs and benefits of anadromy versus residency, measured in terms of survival and reproduction, are finely balanced and small changes can lead to evolutionary changes in life history. The decision to be anadromous or resident is a quantitative threshold trait, which is controlled by multiple genes and environmental factors. The binary nature of the trait is postulated to be the result of the environmentally determined physiological condition (e.g. energy status) relative to a genetically determined threshold, although this may not be the only mechanism involved. Anadromy ensues when an individual's condition fails to meet the threshold level, which varies between sexes and among individuals and populations. Environmental factors and genetic architecture may also directly influence life history, e.g., by altering gene expression. A strong genetic influence on the anadromy decision means that facultative anadromy can be altered by natural selection driven by changes such as differential exploitation, stocking, partial barriers to migration, and changes in climate, and freshwater and marine productivity, together with parasite, pathogen and predator abundance resulting in reduced marine survival and growth. Further studies of the factors determining life history choice, together with multiple population

1

estimates of heritability and differential reproductive success (fitness), are required to understand fully the impact of natural and anthropogenic environmental changes on sea trout dynamics.

Keywords: sea trout; river resident trout; quantitative threshold trait; sexual maturation; parental effects; physiological condition.

NOMENCLATURE

While many valid species names have been designated for distinct trout lineages and morphotypes (e.g. Ferguson, 2004; Kottelat & Freyhof, 2007), brown trout and *Salmo trutta* L. are still widely used as common and scientific species names for the native trout of Europe, western Asia and north Africa, and include both sea and freshwater life histories. However, it is common practice among anglers and managers to regard the term brown trout as referring only to freshwater trout, although it will be used here in the species context. Within brown trout, there are various alternative life histories in respect of migration, reproduction and feeding (Frost & Brown, 1967; Elliott, 1994; Klemetsen *et al.*, 2003). In formerly glaciated regions in NW Europe many populations have abandoned the anadromy of their postglacial colonist ancestors and have adopted a freshwater migratory or resident life history, including river-lake migration (adfluvial potamodromy), extensive migrations within rivers (fluvial potamodromy), river resident, and lake resident (Ferguson, 2006). Thus sea trout, where trout migrate to sea to feed before returning to their natal river to breed (anadromy), is just one extreme of a continuum of life histories, with some individuals pursuing more than one option within their lifetime. Many authors use the term 'freshwater resident' in the sense of river resident, while some incorrectly use it to include all freshwater forms including migratory ones, in spite of the fact that the dictionary definition of resident is "an animal that does not migrate". Because of this ambiguity, the term should not be used but river resident or lake resident specified as appropriate to account for important evolutionary differences in brown trout life history variation. Use of the general term 'migratory' has also led to some confusion with studies involving adfluvial migrants being incorrectly cited by others as referring to anadromy. Where there is likely to be confusion, the term 'migratory' should be qualified as above.

The main difference between freshwater migration and anadromy is the physiological changes required due to the different ionic strengths and osmolality experienced by sea trout. The distinction breaks down further in areas such as the Baltic Sea where salinity is around 0.1-0.4% in the far north and east compared to more than 3% in oceanic sea water (The Baltic Sea-European Environmental Agency). In the Baltic, fry and 0+ parr can migrate to the sea (Landergren, 2001) and spawning can occur in this brackish water (Landergren & Vallin, 1998). Similarly in the Burrishoole system (Western Ireland) parr migrate to the brackish Lough Furnace and appear to remain there, or in the estuary, before returning to freshwater as un-silvered trout (Poole *et al.*, 2006).

Adfluvial migration is probably similar in benefits to anadromy (see below) but lowers the relative costs. In regions such as Ireland and Scotland, with numerous freshwater lakes, an adfluvial life history for brown trout is estimated to be numerically the most common one, based on the relative abundance of such populations. Migration to lakes occurs even where there is no barrier to anadromy and in many cases both adfluvial and anadromous life histories are present in the same catchment (e.g. Poole *et al.*, 2006). In Loch Lomond (Scotland), a large freshwater lake, carbon stable-isotope analysis showed that individual brown trout appear to repeatedly move between the lake and estuarine / marine environments (Etheridge *et al.*, 2008), which concurs with angling reports of non-breeding sea trout of various sea ages in the lake (Balmaha Anglers). In this case there is only a short river (c10km) separating the loch and the River Clyde estuary. For rainbow trout (*Oncorhynchus mykiss* (Walbaum)), anadromy is also less common in river systems with large lakes (Kendall *et al.*, 2015). Holecek & Scarnecchia (2013) regard the switch in a rainbow trout population to an adfluvial life history as "exercising the next best option" when anadromy was prevented by dam construction.

Although a simple dichotomy between sea trout and freshwater trout belies the large temporal and spatial diversity of life history patterns in brown trout (Cucherousset *et al.*, 2005), it does reflect the emphasis of many studies relevant to sea trout. Thus, this review concentrates on the factors responsible specifically for adopting an anadromous life history and mainly considers only the two extremes of sea trout, and trout which spend their entire life within their natal region of a river (river resident, hereafter simply 'resident'). Due to the limited studies on the genetics of anadromy in brown trout, this review draws from work on other species in the *Salmoninae* sub-family (salmonines), especially rainbow trout, where again the species name is often used to denote freshwater life histories and steelhead its anadromous form.

BACKGROUND BIOLOGY

This section does not attempt to provide a complete overview of sea trout biology but rather to deal only with those aspects relevant to discussions below. Sea trout are found in western Europe from the River Miño (Caballero *et al.*, 2013), which forms the northern border between Portugal and Spain, northwards to Scandinavia and the Cheshkaya Gulf in NW Russia, including Iceland and the Baltic Sea (Klemetsen *et al.*, 2003), although natural stocks in Finnish rivers have largely been lost (Kallio-Nyberg *et al.*, 2010).Within this range sea trout biology varies considerably. Migration to sea as smolts varies from age 1+ in the southern part of the range to 9+ in the north with most smolts being 2+ and 3+ over large parts of the distribution area (Jonsson & L'Abée-Lund, 1993; Jonsson *et al.*, 2001). The period spent at sea ranges from a few weeks (finnock – 0SW) to eight years, with average sea residence times generally decreasing with increasing latitude (L'Abee-Lund *et al.*, 1989). In Norway, where lakes are present in a catchment, overwintering is generally in freshwater (Klemetsen *et al.*, 2003) although in small rivers with poor wintering conditions both adult and juvenile sea trout can feed at sea during the winter (Knutsen *et al.*,

2004; Jensen & Rikardsen, 2012). Overwintering can occur in rivers other than the natal one and brown trout have been recorded wintering up to four times elsewhere before returning to the natal one for reproduction (Jensen *et al.*, 2015). Where the winter is spent in freshwater, the seasonal migration to sea can be repeated annually (Jonsson, 1985; Elliott, 1994; Klemetsen *et al.*, 2003) although former sea trout can subsequently adopt a freshwater life history, a phenomenon also known in rainbow trout (Null *et al.*, 2013). It is increasingly recognised that sea trout can spend a minority of their life at sea with the rest spent in lakes or rivers.

Sea trout feed mainly in estuaries and coastal waters (Middlemas *et al.*, 2009; Davidsen *et al.*, 2014a) with most individuals in Norway staying within 100 km of the river mouth (Jonsson & Jonsson, 2005). However, tagged sea trout have crossed the North Sea from France to Scandinavia (Euzenat, 1999). It has been suggested that estuaries provide better feeding than rivers, but with reduced likelihood of predation and reduced salinity compared to the open sea (Thorpe, 1994a), although fluctuating salinity may actually produce greater physiological stress than the higher, but more stable, salinity of sea water (Jensen & Rikardsen, 2012).

FACULTATIVE ANADROMY AND POPULATION STRUCTURING

In brown trout, there is a continuum from completely freshwater populations to completely anadromous ones (Jonsson & Jonsson, 2011). However, many populations show facultative anadromy with some individuals migrating while other individuals remain resident within their natal river, sometimes referred to as 'partial migration' (Dellefors & Faremo, 1988; Jonsson & Jonsson, 1993), although 'partial' does not qualify the migration. Even for brown trout populations in close geographical proximity, the proportion of individuals showing anadromy can vary considerably (Jonsson & Jonsson, 2006a), which suggests that complex genetic and ecological factors influence the balance between anadromy and residency among populations (Kendall *et al.*, 2015). Understanding the relative importance, and interplay, of the determinants of anadromy within facultatively anadromous populations is a fundamental requirement for their effective management. Increased life history diversity potentially decreases overall population fluctuations as a result of environmental changes, in an analogous fashion to the stabilising influence of asset diversification in a financial portfolio (Schindler *et al.*, 2015).

Offspring of sea trout and resident brown trout may show different life histories to their parents, although, as discussed below, there is a tendency to track the parental life history (Jonsson, 1982). Studies using molecular genetic markers such as allozymes, microsatellites and mitochondrial DNA (mtDNA) have failed to find any genetic differentiation between samples of sea and resident brown trout obtained from exactly the same area of a river rather than adjacent ones, i.e. truly sympatric rather than parapatric (Hindar *et al.*, 1991; Cross *et al.*, 1992; Charles *et al.*, 2005, 2006) and a similar situation occurs in rainbow trout (Docker & Heath, 2003). However, in the absence of a high level of reproductive isolation, such effectively neutral markers would not be expected to reveal differentiation (Ferguson, 1994). It should be strongly emphasised that this lack of genetic differentiation between anadromous and resident salmonines based on such markers does not imply that there is not a genetic basis to anadromy because heritable traits segregate within families and lineages.

The consensus of studies carried out to date is that anadromous and resident salmonines can freely interbreed. Jonsson (1985) and Schreiber & Diefenbach (2005) noted female sea trout and resident male brown trout at the same spawning grounds and suggested that the unequal sex ratio (see below) led to resident males breeding with anadromous females. Similarly for brook charr (*Salvelinus fontinalis* (Mitchill)), Thériault *et al.*, (2007) found that interbreeding was due to resident males mating with both resident and anadromous females. In this case, the sneaking behaviour by small males prevents any genetic differentiation that could arise due to size-assortative mating (Dodson *et al.*, 2013). Courter *et al.,* (2013) found that female resident rainbow trout produce anadromous offspring that survive and return to spawn.

There are a few examples of genetic differentiation between sympatric anadromous and resident rainbow trout (Zimmerman & Reeves, 2000; Docker & Heath, 2003). In the first case, the apparent differentiation of the two forms was associated with spatial and temporal segregation of spawning activities (Zimmerman & Reeves, 2000), as was the genetic differentiation between resident and anadromous brook charr (Boula *et al.*, 2002). In another situation (Narum *et al.*, 2004), where genetic divergence between sympatric steelhead and resident rainbow occurred in one tributary of a river system but not in another, the genetic differentiation appears to have resulted from stocking with a genetically distinct steelhead stock.

Typically genetic differentiation is found between predominantly anadromous and principally resident brown trout populations within rivers where a complete or partial upstream barrier to sea trout migration is present (e.g. Skaala & Nævdal, 1989). However, such allopatric genetic differentiation is typical of brown trout populations (Ferguson, 1989) and may simply represent independent evolution rather than being correlated with life history. Where populations exist above falls there is clearly strong selection against migration, as such migrants are lost from the population, resulting in genetic differences in respect of life history determinants as well (Thrower *et al.*, 2004; Thrower & Hard, 2009).

In a few cases significant genetic differentiation has been found between parapatric/allopatric populations of brown trout and rainbow trout where no physical barrier to interbreeding occurs. In the Glenarrif River (NE Ireland) significant allozyme and mtDNA differences were found between sea trout and resident trout samples taken c1km apart in the river (Fleming, 1983; unpublished studies cited in Ferguson, 2006). The resident trout sample was taken immediately below an upstream impassable waterfall and was genetically more similar to samples from above the fall than to the downstream sea trout sample. It seems, therefore, that this resident population was formed by displaced individuals from above the falls, and has remained distinct through spatial or other reproductive isolation. Similar situations have been found for rainbow trout in small Californian rivers where above waterfalls residents sometimes descend over the falls. These remain near the base of the falls and form populations that are reproductively isolated from the below falls stocks (Pearse *et al.*, 2009; Hayes *et al.*, 2012). Berejikian *et al.*, (2013) found that below barriers the proportions of resident rainbow trout were greater in the upper reaches, suggesting that above-barrier populations may be contributing to these resident populations through ongoing migration. Hayes *et al.*, (2012) and Wilzbach *et al.*, (2012) detected movement to below a waterfall of a small proportion of rainbow trout tagged above it, with some detected near the entrance to the sea. In the Wilzbach *et al.*, (2012) study some tagged individuals were released 5km downstream of the falls and, while most remained within a few hundred metres of the release site, a few moved downstream.

WHY IS ANADROMY FACULTATIVE IN BROWN TROUT AND SOME OTHER SALMONINES?

BENEFITS OF ANADROMY

Anadromy potentially offer many benefits to individuals continuing with this postglacial ancestral life history, while at the same time these are countered by ensuing costs (Gross, 1987; Brönmark *et al.*, 2013) (summarised in Table 1). Thus anadromous and resident life histories show compromises between survival to first reproduction and the size and age at reproduction. Migration to the sea, where in temperate regions productivity and thus food availability is higher than in freshwater (Gross *et al.*, 1988), results in larger size, higher fecundity and greater energy stores at reproduction (Fleming & Reynolds, 2004; Jonsson & Jonsson, 2006a). However, it delays maturity and lowers the probability of surviving to reproduce. While sexual maturation and the choice of anadromous life history are closely interconnected, they are also conflicting strategies that need to be considered together (Thorpe, 1994b; Thorpe & Metcalfe, 1998; Sloat *et al.*, 2014).

BENEFITS OF RESIDENCY

Switching from anadromy to residency conveys many benefits, which can also be seen as the costs of anadromy. These include less risk of predation during migration and in the marine environment. In Denmark, as a result of predation by fish and birds, smolt mortality during passage through lakes and reservoirs is substantially higher than in rivers, (Jepsen *et al.*, 1998). Weirs for water offtake can also cause substantial mortalities and, together with predation, are the crucial factors responsible for smolt mortality in Danish rivers (Rasmussen, 2006). Predators may be attracted to concentrations of migrating smolts and adults (Greenstreet *et al.*, 1993; Hendry *et al.*, 2004). The number of trout predators appears to be higher at sea than in freshwater, including lakes (Jonsson & Jonsson, 2004) and predation is a major mortality factor shortly after the smolts reach the sea (Dieperink *et al.*, 2002).

In addition, residency avoids the energetic costs associated with migration. Increased mortality may result from energy depletion during upstream migration especially if there are waterfalls or other barriers that cause delays (Hendry *et al.*, 2004). Bohlin *et al.*, (2001) found a negative correlation between altitude and the extent of anadromy in Swedish trout populations, suggesting that anadromy is less common in populations where migration involves greater energy expenditure. However, altitude is also related to other factors such as water temperature and flow regimes that can have a proximate influence on migration (see below). Jonsson & Jonsson (2006b) found that the condition factor (i.e. length / mass ratio) of returning sea trout decreased as they migrated a greater distance inland.

Table 1. Potential benefits of anadromy and river residency in brown trout. Based on information in: Gross *et al.*, 1987; Elliott, 1994; Fleming, 1996, 1998; Jonsson & Jonsson, 1999; Fleming & Reynolds, 2004; Hendry *et al.*, 2004; Jonsson & Jonsson, 2006. *Note that the benefits of one tactic can be regarded as the 'costs' of the other.*

Benefits of anadromy

- Migration to more stable marine environment avoids harsh abiotic or biotic conditions in river.
- Better feeding at sea than in rivers and thus faster growth, reaching larger size.
- As growth occurs, larger food items such as fish become accessible, increasing growth further.
- Larger size results in:
    - Being able to swim / hold position against higher current velocities;
    - Wider choice of spawning gravels, for females.
    - Better dominance in competition and female choice during mating, for males.
    - Eggs being buried deeper thereby reducing risk of washout and overcutting by smaller resident females.
    - Indirect effects to traits such as mortality rate, age at maturity, fecundity and egg mass.
    - Larger eggs, which produce larger offspring with better competitive ability and higher survival.

Benefits of river residency

- Higher survival due to:
    - Less risk of predation during migration and at sea.
    - Avoidance of parasites and diseases which are more abundant at sea.
    - Less chance of capture by humans.
- Higher survival increases chance of iteroparity.
- Avoids energetic costs of migration and physiological changes required for moving from freshwater to sea.
- Able to gain access to spawning areas in small tributary rivers.
- Avoids straying and being unable to find a suitable breeding site.
- If accompanied by earlier maturity than anadromy, residency yields reduced generation time (and all else being equal, 'faster' life histories outcompete 'slower' life histories).

SEX AND FACULTATIVE ANADROMY

Often within brown trout populations, with both sea trout and residents, there is a sex bias with females predominating typically among anadromous trout and males among residents (Jonsson, 1985; Dellefors & Faremo, 1988; Elliott, 1994). In 17 coastal rivers in Norway Jonsson *et al.* (2001) found that, on average, 50% of the males but only 4% of the females spawned as residents. In the Glynn River (N. Ireland), Fleming (1983) found that above a series of impassable waterfalls the sex ratio was not significantly different from equality. However, in the section below the waterfalls, of 248 mature resident trout only two were females (0.8%) but in 111 smolts and mature sea trout that were examined 104 (94%) were female.

A sex bias would be expected from the balance of benefits of the two life histories (Hendry *et al.*, 2004). Thus, female reproductive success is generally limited by gamete production with a larger body size giving greater fecundity and egg size (Fleming, 1996; Quinn *et al.*, 2011). Larger females can potentially attract mates, acquire and defend better spawning sites in a wider range of substrate sizes, and excavate deeper nests (Fleming & Reynolds, 2004).

Compared with females, male reproductive success is typically limited by access to mates (Fleming, 1998) rather than gamete production since even small males can produce millions of sperm (Munkittrick & Moccia, 1987). While a larger size can be of benefit to males in attracting and defending mates, obtaining a large body size is less critical for male reproduction because instead of aggressive defence of females, a tactic displayed typically by larger anadromous males (Esteve, 2005), they can adopt a 'sneaking' tactic allowing successful egg fertilisation at a small size (Gross, 1985; Hutchings & Myers, 1988). Thus males more often mature as residents since they are less dependent on large body size for reproductive success and consequently mature across a much greater range of ages and sizes (Jonsson & Jonsson, 1993). Early maturity in males also results in reduced pre-reproductive mortality (Gross & Repka, 1998).

NATURAL SELECTION ON ANADROMY VERSUS RESIDENCY

Facultative anadromy and residency in brown trout and other salmonines can be explained as alternative tactics within a conditional strategy (Dodson *et al.*, 2013; Sloat *et al.*, 2014; Kendall *et al.*, 2015) with individuals within a population being able to adopt either tactic. Whichever tactic is more successful under particular environmental conditions will result in the individuals adopting that tactic leaving more offspring, that is, they will have higher Darwinian fitness (Gross, 1987; Brönmark *et al.*, 2013). Taking into consideration that there is a partial genetic basis to the life history choice (see below), positive natural selection for one or other tactic (e.g. anadromy) will tend to increase the frequency of that tactic over generations. While the expected outcome is that populations would become fixed for one tactic, the relative benefits and costs can vary temporally as a consequence of diverse factors including different environmental conditions, population density and composition. This results in many populations displaying both life

Table 2. Non-mutually exclusive hypotheses to explain why balancing selection may maintain a mix of anadromous and resident tactics in a population, rather than only one.

1. Ecological conditions vary across time

Explanation: If the relative fitness of anadromous and resident individuals varies through time, temporally fluctuating selection may favour the capacity of individuals to produce either type via phenotypic plasticity (where individuals 'choose' their tactic based on cues) or bet-hedging (where tactics develop randomly).

Examples*: In some years, or for some cohorts, relative growth and survival benefits at sea may outweigh those in the river, but in other years, the reverse may be true. Thus, neither tactic outcompetes the other in the long-run.*

2. Ecological conditions vary across space

Explanation: If the relative fitness of anadromous and resident tactics varies across habitat types within a single freely interbreeding population, this may select for individuals that are capable of producing either tactic (via plasticity or bet-hedging)

Examples*: Fry that rear in more productive parts of the river, or that obtain better feeding territories, may be better off remaining resident and maturing early, whereas fry that rear in lower-energy environments may gain more by becoming anadromous. Smaller tributaries or spawning areas with smaller gravels may select for smaller resident females, whereas larger tributaries or areas with larger gravels may favour larger anadromous females (if going to sea is the only way to get big). A relatively small amount of gene flow among habitats/tributaries within rivers will still be enough to prevent genetic differentiation.*

3. Frequency dependence favours a stable mix of tactics

Explanation: Smaller resident males may 'sneak' more fertilisations when rare, whereas larger anadromous males may obtain more fertilisations on average when small resident males are most abundant. This mechanism can act to stabilise tactic frequencies at some intermediate value or, in theory, could lead to constant cycling of tactic frequencies.

Examples: *Early maturing resident males have a spawning advantage relative to anadromous males only when rare.*

4. Sexually-antagonistic selection maintains genetic variation in anadromy

Explanation: The evolutionary interests of males and females may be in conflict, such that genes that increase the propensity for anadromy are selected for in females but against in males. This then maintains genetic variation in the propensity for anadromy.

Examples*: Females carrying genes for higher condition-thresholds are more likely to be anadromous, which increases their reproductive success, but their sons may then inherit these same genes and hence also become anadromous, which may be less optimal for males than residency. Such 'sexual conflict' may mean that neither tactic has superior fitness overall (averaged across males and females), hence both co-exist.*

5. Heterozygote advantage favours the maintenance of genetic variation in anadromy

Explanation: For a given genetic locus affecting the propensity for anadromy, two or more alleles (different copies of the same gene) can be maintained in the population if heterozygotes (individuals with two different copies) have higher fitness than homozygotes (individuals with two identical copies).

Example: *Heterozygous parents produce a mix of anadromous and resident offspring, whereas homozygous parents produce more of one type than the other. If selection on average favours some intermediate threshold for anadromy, heterozygotes may have a long-term fitness advantage over homozygotes. This mechanism could partially explain why genetic variation in anadromy thresholds is maintained, but by itself does not explain why an intermediate degree of anadromy is favoured (although the other hypotheses might).*

histories, to a greater or lesser degree (see Table 2). That is, fluctuating natural selection on alternative phenotypes is expected to lead to the evolution of flexible life history strategies such as facultative anadromy. It is also possible that frequency dependent selection plays a role where increased frequency of one life history could allow selection to favour the other until a balance is achieved (Hecht *et al.*, 2015). Thus, as the migratory fraction increases, the resident fish will have reduced competition for food. Similarly, the rarer male type may have a competitive advantage in spawning. It is worth noting that similar balancing selection mechanisms (e.g. fluctuating environments, frequency dependence, opposing selection between the sexes) are also likely to explain why some populations of brown trout are capable of producing either river residents or adfluvial migrants that use lakes (instead of the sea) to grow larger, or why yet other populations are characterised by more complex mixes of river residents, adfluvial migrants and sea trout. Variability in the extent of anadromy or migration within populations, and among geographically adjacent populations, would suggest that the relative benefits and costs are finely balanced and thus evolutionary changes may occur rapidly as a result of relatively small alterations to any of the underlying factors (see below for more detailed discussion).

If anadromy or residency is advantageous in particular situations, it would be expected that compensatory adaptations would occur to increase benefits relative to costs (Hendry *et al.*, 2004). Jonsson & Jonsson (2006b) found that sea trout body size, age at sexual maturity, relative fecundity, and the ratio of fecundity to egg mass increased with increasing distance from the sea to the spawning grounds consistent with the hypothesis that selection favours a larger body size when migratory costs are greater. Bernatchez & Dodson (1987) noted that anadromous salmonines that migrated longer distances were more efficient in energy use. Freshwater residents can have larger ova than similar sized anadromous females (Jonsson & Jonsson, 1999) and increased survival of young may compensate to some extent for lower fecundity.

Due to greater survival, residents should be more likely to show multiple spawning (iteroparity) than anadromous fish and this can increase the total lifetime fecundity. In a rainbow trout population, although female residents produced on average 1400 eggs, compared with 3500 eggs for steelhead, most of residents spawned a second time whereas this was the case for less than 5% of steelhead (Schroeder & Smith, 1989). However, repeat spawning in sea trout would appear to be more common as, in a survey of 102 European populations, Jonsson & L'Abée-Lund (1993) found that the proportion of repeat breeders in sea trout was from 30% in northern rivers to 60% in southern ones. Individual sea trout have been recorded spawning up to 11 times (Harris & Milner, 2006).

COMPONENTS OF ANADROMY

It is important to recognise that anadromy consists of a number of distinct, but interlinked, consecutive components. In particular, it is important to differentiate between the genetic and environmental factors that drive the individual's choice of anadromy or residency and the subsequent downstream changes that take place as a consequence of this decision. Thus fundamental to facultative anadromy is the decision on whether to migrate or to remain as a resident in the river and mature. This decision may involve one or more 'decision windows', which may take place a considerable time before external evidence of migration occurs (Hecht *et al.*, 2015; McKinney *et al.*, 2015) in the form of the changes associated with smoltification, i.e. the changes that occur prior to and during downstream movement to the sea as smolts. Failure to recognise this distinction between the decision process and consequential smoltification has led to misinterpretation of some studies. Examining the genetic changes that occur during smoltification primarily indicates those genes which determine the physiological and other changes outlined below.

In addition to smoltification other components of anadromy include migrations to and from the sea, which involve directed movement and precise navigation to reach appropriate feeding habitats and return to natal spawning grounds. Return migration to freshwater may be triggered by the onset of sexual maturation, although such return does not necessarily involve spawning.

SMOLTIFICATION

Smoltification involves a set of changes prior to seaward migration (Hoar, 1988), with subsequent return to freshwater involving a reversal of these. Smoltification happens in response to environmental cues (McCormick *et al.*, 1998; Jensen *et al.*, 2012) with the brain being the main integrator of this information, and thus the main regulator of the process (McKinney *et al.*, 2015). This occurs through interpretation of seasonal cycles, often via the effects of photoperiods on circadian rhythms ('biological clocks'), and through various hormones (Björnsson *et al.*, 2011).

The most obvious external aspect of smoltification is the body colouration changes that are necessary for the different camouflage requirements of bottom dwelling life in a river compared to mid-water life in the sea. In rivers, dark backs and spotted sides allow fish to blend with bottom rock and gravel patterns. Conversely, light bellies, silver sides, and dark backs help camouflage fish in a mid-water marine environment as they will not stand out against the background, irrespective of the direction from which they are viewed by predators. Similar silvering also occurs in some pelagic lake dwelling brown trout (Crozier & Ferguson, 1986; Olsson & Greenberg, 2004) as it is an adaptation for mid-water camouflage and is not specifically associated with anadromy. There are also changes in shape, which are likely associated with greater swimming efficiency, with the snout becoming more pointed, the body slimmer and more streamlined, and a lengthening of the caudal peduncle (Hard *et al.*, 1999).

Smoltification involves physiological and biochemical adjustments including changes in visual pigments, haemoglobin, olfactory sensitivity, buoyancy (swim bladder size), metabolism, and salinity tolerance (Dann *et al.*, 2003; McCormick *et al.*, 1998). Most of the ionic regulation is carried out by the gills and involves an increase in enzymes such as gill Na^+/K^+-ATPase together with a switch in its isozymes from α1a, which is most abundant in freshwater, to α1b, the dominant isozyme in seawater (McCormick *et al.*, 2009, 2013). Sea survival increases with smolt size possibly because they have better osmoregulation and are less vulnerable to predation (Klemetsen *et al.*, 2003).

Studies at the smoltification stage are the earliest at which it is possible to externally differentiate migrants from residents within a population and many comparative studies on smolts and non-smolts have been undertaken for this practical reason. To examine earlier genetic and phenotypic changes between migrants and residents currently requires the establishment of offspring lines based on populations of predominantly migrant or resident life histories. Over the past century, rainbow trout throughout their natural range in western North America have been blocked from anadromy by construction of artificial barriers and by artificial translocations above natural barriers (Thrower *et al.*, 2004; Phillis *et al.*, 2014; Pearse *et al.*, 2014). These multiple replicate 'selection experiments' have provided valuable material for the investigation of phenotypic and genetic differences between steelhead and resident rainbow trout.

DETERMINANTS OF THE ANADROMY / RESIDENCY DECISION

GENETIC FACTORS

It has been known for some time, from the results of rearing and translocation experiments, that there is a partial genetic basis for the anadromy 'decision' in brown trout. Skrochowska (1969) released reared progeny of anadromous, resident and reciprocal hybrid parentage. Subsequent recaptures indicated a propensity for offspring to follow parental life history, with hybrids being intermediate. Jonsson (1982) reciprocally transplanted juvenile brown trout between an isolated lake containing a resident population and a lake downstream containing a sea trout population, the juvenile growth rates in both populations being similar. Subsequent downstream movement was more frequent in the anadromous rather than the resident trout irrespective of the lake of release.

As with brown trout, resident rainbow trout can produce anadromous offspring and *vice versa*. However, again the predominant pattern is for offspring to track the parental life history (Zimmerman & Reeves, 2000; Seamons *et al.*, 2004; Zimmerman *et al.* 2009; Hayes *et al.*, 2012). Overall many genetic studies carried out on salmonines have confirmed that there is genetic variation for the propensity for facultative migration (reviewed by Kendall *et al.*, 2015, with emphasis on rainbow trout) but with considerable developmental plasticity. Sex associated differences in anadromy within populations under communal environmental conditions are also a clear indicator of a genetic basis to life history.

Unfortunately heritability estimates, i.e., the contribution of genetic variance to the variability of life history among individuals in a given population, have been determined in only a few studies. Thrower *et al.*, (2004) bred pure and reciprocally crossed lines of anadromous and resident rainbow trout from Sashin Creek (Alaska), the residents being from above waterfalls and were artificially established from the anadromous stock 70 years previously. After two years in a common hatchery environment they found that narrow sense heritability (h^2 – additive genetic variance only) estimates for freshwater maturation and smolting were between 0.44 – 0.51 and 0.45 – 0.56 respectively. Hecht *et al.*, (2015) found a modal h^2 estimate of 0.61 (0.39 – 0.77) for life history in the same hatchery lines but using a larger pedigree. They also found significant genetic correlations of life history with growth rate, size, condition factor, and morphological traits, which themselves showed moderate heritabilities. Heritability estimates (h^2) for anadromy in a natural population of brook charr were 0.52 – 0.56 (Thériault *et al.*, 2007). All these heritability estimates are within the range of values reported for threshold traits (reviewed by Roff, 1996). While no heritability estimates have as yet been published for sea trout, the similarity of steelhead and brook charr estimates under very different environments and, in spite of the few populations examined, may suggest heritability of a similar magnitude, Thus, approximately half of the variability in life history among individuals within a population is likely to be due to additive genetic variance for this trait, with the remainder attributed to non-additive genetic variance, parental effects and environmental influences. However, it is very important to acknowledge that heritability estimates are specific to the population and particular environmental conditions examined. Therefore, explicit estimates are required for a range of brown trout populations under different conditions before any credence is given to any estimates. What is clear, however, is that there are both strong genetic and strong environmental influences on facultative anadromy within salmonine populations.

In reciprocal common garden experiments involving steelhead from two populations, Doctor *et al.*, (2014) demonstrated that both genetics and temperature play an important role in determining growth rate, condition-factor, and proportion of age-1 smolts in steelhead. Broad-sense heritabilities (H^2 – all genetic variance and parental effects) for the two populations at different times of year and for these three traits, ranged as follows: 0.49 – 0.60; 0.07 – 0.59; 0.69 – 0.77.

Studies of the molecular genetic basis of anadromy have identified several gene markers and chromosome regions associated with alternative life histories in rainbow trout (Nichols *et al.*, 2008; Martínez *et al.*, 2011; Narum *et al.*, 2011; Hecht *et al.*, 2012). Pearse *et al.*, (2014) showed that a large region of one rainbow trout chromosome, Omy5, is strongly associated with life history in 13 resident (above a barrier) and 8 anadromous populations. The genes in this region appear to be tightly linked, possibly as the result of a chromosomal inversion or other rearrangement limiting recombination. The common genetic basis for life-history variation in a geographically varied set of populations probably results from strong parallel natural selection acting on one or more genes in this region that influence life history traits. This study supports previous suggestions (Nichols *et al.*, 2008; Hale *et al.*, 2013) that this gene group on Omy5 represents a 'master control region' influencing rainbow trout life history.

In a key study involving the offspring of wild anadromous and resident rainbow trout from Sashin Creek reared under common hatchery conditions for one year, McKinney *et al*. (2015) found differential gene expression in the brain between these lines for 1982 genes (7% of genes examined). Differences between anadromous and resident offspring were detected from hatching onwards with the greatest number of gene differences being found at eight months of age, more than a year before obvious external appearance of smolting. Patterns of gene expression during development differed between males and females, which may reflect the fact that males in the resident population mature earlier than females (McKinney *et al*., 2015). Genes showing differential expression included those involved with light sensitivity, circadian biological rhythms, growth, morphology, and olfactory imprinting, the latter being important in homing. A caveat to the use of the offspring of allopatric anadromous and resident trout is that aspects other than life history trait may differ as a result of evolutionary divergence, although their recent common ancestry (c70 years) should minimise this.

PROXIMATE ENVIRONMENTAL FACTORS

Many studies have shown that environmental influences, including those during embryo development within the egg (Jonsson & Jonsson, 2014a), collectively determine a trout's developmental and physiological state (i.e. 'condition'), which has a proximate influence on the decision on whether to migrate or remain resident. Key aspects of condition potentially include size, growth rate, and 'energy status' including lipid levels and standard metabolic rate (see references below).

Size and growth rate of migrants are the aspects of condition most easily, and thus commonly, measured in association with life history. However, the relationship is complicated by time of measurement relative to emigration time, sex, age, temperature, and potentially genetic background. For example, size at smoltification may not reflect size at decision time perhaps a year earlier (Acolas *et al*., 2012; Beakes *et al*., 2010; Sloat, 2013; McKinney *et al*., 2015). In the meantime residents may have diverted energy from growth to sexual maturation. Conversely, as survival at sea is size dependent (Klemetsen *et al*., 2003), pre-migrants may have accelerated growth during this period. Also, emigration may occur over several successive years for the same cohort. Not surprisingly then, the relationship of size and growth to life history has been found to vary (in both sign and magnitude) among studies and appears to be population specific to some extent. Body size in a brook charr population has been shown to be significantly correlated with age of migration (Thériault & Dodson, 2003), with smaller fish at age 1+ delaying migration to age 2+; however, larger 1+ fish that migrated were no different in size to 1+ fish that remained resident (Thériault & Dodson, 2003). Thériault *et al*., (2007) subsequently reported, for the same population, a negative correlation between the size of age 1+ parr and their propensity to remain in the river at that age, but these 'residents' likely included fish that would have migrated at age 2+. These results suggest that, at least for facultatively anadromous brook charr, the smallest 1+ parr are constrained from smoltifying, but this does not necessarily imply that size at age 1+ is the actual cue that triggers anadromy or residency; although it may be correlated with the true physiological cue.

Failure to account for sex of the juveniles, and even their parents, can make it difficult to evaluate effects of size and growth on migration in some studies. Males from resident rainbow trout mothers matured at smaller sizes than those from anadromous mothers (Berejikian *et al.*, 2014). McMillan *et al.*, (2012) found no difference in size between migrant and resident rainbow trout unless males and females were examined separately.

Some studies have found large size and fast growth associated with migration while others have found the opposite, suggesting that any relationship between life history and size is purely coincidental correlation. Jonsson (1985) found that the largest and fastest growing juveniles became anadromous while those with medium growth rates became residents, and the slowest growing individuals became sea trout but at an older age. Hecht *et al.*, (2015) found a significant correlation between life history and condition factor with steelhead migrants showing a lower mean condition factor than residents at 12, 15 and 24 months post-fertilisation, the last being at smoltification. This indicates that the life history decision was taken during the first year of life in this experimental population derived from Sashin Creek steelhead and residents.

Various studies suggest that brown trout become migratory due to energy limitation in natal rivers. Accordingly they remain in the river until growth starts to level off (i.e. they approach asymptotic body size), at which point they either mature or migrate to better feeding areas (Jonsson & Jonsson, 1993). It has been suggested that population asymptotic size, especially for females, is one of the best predictors of life history (Sloat & Reeves, 2014). That is, if only a small size can ultimately be reached in the river then migration occurs. Increased juvenile density can result in increased competition for food and space resulting in fewer fish reaching the necessary condition to mature as residents (Jonsson & Jonsson, 1993). Hence food limitation may be a significant factor. Olsson *et al.*, (2006) transplanted offspring of adfluvial brown trout between two sections of a river with different fish densities. Adfluvial migratory behaviour developed in the river section with high trout density and low specific growth rate, whereas residency developed in the section with the converse situation. Cucherousset *et al.*, (2005) found that life history traits varied among brown trout cohorts due to environmental variability and that trout with higher metabolic needs were more likely to migrate. Wysujack *et al.*, (2009) fed hatchery-reared offspring of adfluvial brown trout from the same population at three different levels and found that low food availability, which was associated with low growth rates, increased the proportion of migrants: more so for females than males. Although the trout were from migratory parents, at the lowest food level 17% were residents and at the highest 42%. O'Neal & Stanford (2011) found that resident brown trout dominated in smaller tributary rivers of the Rio Grande in Patagonia, where invertebrate biomass was two to three times higher than in larger tributaries. The latter either supported a mix of anadromous and resident individuals or were dominated by anadromous fish. Marco-Rius *et al.*, (2013) found strong evidence for positive density dependence determining anadromy in brown trout with migrants maximising growth by moving into the sea. It is also important to acknowledge that food quality, i.e. energy value, may be as important as food quantity (Kendall *et al.*, 2015).

Van Leeuwen *et al.*, (2015) reared brown trout offspring of allopatric (different tributaries of River Tweed) river-resident and anadromous parents for seven months under high-, mid-, or low-food availability. They were then made to compete for feeding territories in a semi-natural river channel. Parental migration trait had a significant effect on dominance status in territorial interactions, with offspring of anadromous fish being dominant over equivalent sized offspring of residents, but only when both were reared under the intermediate food regime. The results suggest that the inherited migratory tendency of the offspring interacts with the environmental conditions to potentially influence competition for feeding territories and thus the probability of migration.

Metabolism, rather than actual growth or size, may be important in determining life history, with anadromous individuals having higher metabolic costs than residents: these differences being genetically based (Sloat & Reeves, 2014). Greater metabolic costs can lead to lower energy efficiency and reduced lipid storage, the latter being an important component in maturation (McMillan *et al.*, 2012). Forseth *et al.*, (1999) found that faster growing adfluvial brown trout became migratory earlier, albeit at a smaller body size than slower growing individuals which migrated one year later. Migrants maintained higher metabolic rates and were energetically constrained (i.e. growth rate could not be sustained) at a younger age by limited food resources in the river. Under conditions of limited food availability, fish with lower metabolism will meet their metabolic requirements easier, a tendency that should lead to residency. Future migrants in brook charr also exhibit lower growth efficiencies and higher associated metabolic costs than future residents (Morinville & Rasmussen, 2003). Lipid storage, the major source of energy for maturation (Tocher, 2003) may likewise be a good predictor of life history. In rainbow trout, McMillan *et al.*, (2012) found that larger males with higher lipid levels had a greater probability of maturing as residents at age 1+.

Temperature appears to be a key factor in the migratory decision (Brannon *et al.*, 2004; Sloat & Reeves, 2014), with both absolute temperature and variation in temperature being important (Kendall *et al.*, 2015). Temperature is clearly linked to food availability, feeding activity, metabolism and lipid storage, and may also have a direct influence as a stressor on the migratory decision (Sogard *et al.*, 2012). McMillan *et al.* (2012) found an inverse relationship between individual condition and water temperature as growth was greater in warmer streams while whole body lipid content was higher in cooler streams. This observation suggests one possible mechanism whereby temperature can influence life history. In a common garden experiment at different temperatures, Sloat & Reeves (2014) found that individuals of both sexes with the fastest growth, within their respective temperature treatments, had a greater probability of freshwater maturation (i.e. residency), but higher temperatures resulted in decreased freshwater maturation despite significantly increasing growth.

Further environmental factors associated with the migration/residence decision include water flow rate, although again the relationship is complex. Female residency in rainbow trout increased with decreasing mean annual flow (Mills *et al.*, 2012), possibly because lower water conditions are unsuitable for spawning of larger steelhead females. Conversely, Berejikian *et al.*, (2013) found that steelhead were more prevalent in rivers with low flows and high temperatures. These latter factors likely operate more as indirect agents of natural selection, however, rather than as proximate drivers of individual decisions.

Expected survival in the natal river measured over the long term, which is likely determined by a combination of the factors outlined above, clearly influences what life histories should evolve there; for example, low expected survival should select for higher rates of anadromy on average. Year-to-year variation in survival in the natal river, or variation in survival across river microhabitats, may also correlate with temporal or spatial variation in anadromy within a given river, with individual parr in theory capable of basing their migratory decisions on some projection of their likely survival prospects should they not migrate (e.g. using current physiological condition as a proximal cue). However, while low survival may result in more juveniles selecting anadromy, it may not actually produce more migrants because fewer juveniles survive to the smolt stage (Railsback *et al.*, 2014).

PARENTAL FACTORS

Parental effects, especially maternal ones, can be both genetically and environmentally induced, as well as resulting from unique gene-environment interactions. A maternal environmental effect, for example, refers to situations where environmental factors (e.g. feeding opportunities) affect some aspect of the mother's phenotype (e.g. her body size), which in turn affects the life histories of her offspring. A maternal genetic effect occurs when maternal genotype affects offspring phenotypes independently of the genes she passes on to them; for example, genetically large mothers may invest in larger eggs and the resulting offspring may be more likely to adopt one or other life history tactic – not because they inherited their mother's genes for large body size, but because they hatched from large eggs. Indeed, egg size is known to have an impact on survival and growth of juveniles particularly in the early stages of life (Einum & Fleming, 1999; Kamler, 2005). Resident trout co-occurring with sea trout have larger eggs than corresponding resident only populations (Olofsson & Mosegaard, 1999). Jonsson & Jonsson (2006a) argue that this larger egg size of resident brown trout compared to sea trout of similar body size may enable the young to compete with sea trout. Although few studies have so far been undertaken, epigenetic changes in the parental genomes induced by environmental conditions, especially during early development, can be transmitted to their offspring (Burton & Metcalfe, 2014). In a study of Atlantic salmon (*Salmo salar* L.), Burton *et al.* (2013) found that maternal influences on juvenile performance could be related to the environment experienced by the mother as a juvenile, as well as to her condition at the time of breeding. Jonsson & Jonsson (2016) found that the egg size in Atlantic salmon offspring, and thus yolk availability to alevin grand-offspring, is influenced by the temperature experienced by the mother during the last two months of egg maturation.

Berejikian *et al.*, (2014) found that variation in the expression of residency or anadromy in both male and female rainbow trout was strongly influenced by maternal life history. Female offspring produced by anadromous mothers rarely expressed residency (2%), while the percentage of maturing male parr produced by anadromous mothers was much higher (41%) across a diversity of freshwater habitats. Both male and female parr that were produced by resident mothers were significantly more likely to show residency than the offspring of anadromous mothers. In an experimental stocking programme with brown trout, Marco-Rius *et al.*, (2013) found a greater sea trout return from sea with crosses involving anadromous males, but no maternal effect was observed. In cases where the sex of the offspring is unknown, distinguishing such parental effects from sex-specific patterns of gene inheritance or expression is challenging, however.

INTEGRATING GENETIC AND ENVIRONMENTAL FACTORS IN THE ANADROMY / RESIDENCY DECISION

As outlined above, there are genetic, environmental and parental influences on the life history decision in facultatively anadromous salmonines. Thus facultative anadromy is a classic quantitative trait controlled by multiple genes with the manifestation dependent on interactions between this genetic architecture and environmental factors. However, unlike continuous quantitative traits, the life history decision is a binary one with the alternatives being controlled by a threshold. While several threshold models have been proposed, an environmentally-cued genetic threshold (ET) model (based on Tompkins & Hazel, 2007) is compatible with much of what is known about the life history decision in facultatively anadromous salmonines (Kendall *et al.*, 2015). Although it may not be the precise and only mechanism involved (see below), a consideration of it provides a useful framework to understand how genetic and environmental influences operating via a threshold could result in the alternative tactics of migration or residency. If an individual's condition (as defined above) exceeds a genetically determined threshold value at a 'decision window' it will remain in the river and mature there. If it does not, it will become a sea trout, delaying maturation until a larger size (Figure 1). In practice, at least two decision windows may be necessary to account for some observations (Satterthwaite *et al.*, 2009; Dodson *et al.*, 2013). That is, there may be three decisions – migrate, mature as a resident, or wait until a later decision window. Information on condition is possibly translated into a physiological signal via hormonal changes (McCormick, 2009).

Under the ET model, individuals within a population have different thresholds values, which are likely to be continuous and follow a normal distribution within the population, as is typical of other quantitative traits (Tomkins & Hazel, 2007). Variation in threshold values means that the proportion of individuals expressing anadromy versus residency depends on both the distribution of variation in thresholds and the distribution of the condition of individuals in the population at the time. Life history frequency can change in the short term as a consequence of environmentally induced changes in condition. Evolutionary changes can arise through variations in the mean distribution of thresholds up or down, as an outcome of the environmental conditions acting as agents of selection in determining relative reproductive success of life history strategies. Accordingly if the success of anadromy is reduced due, e.g., to poorer feeding or survival at sea, then selection will result in a lowering of mean condition-threshold values, resulting in more resident fish (see below for more detailed discussion).

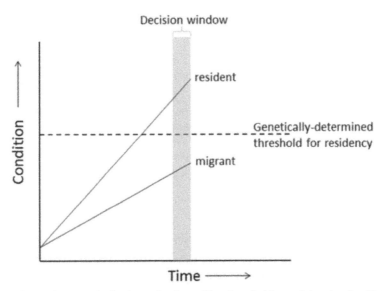

Figure 1. Illustration of how the genetically determined condition threshold can determine the life history adopted. The y-axis here represents some measure of physiological condition that triggers residency when it exceeds the hypothesised genetic threshold, or anadromy if not.

Threshold values may vary among populations and between sexes in response to differential selection (Sloat *et al.*, 2014) (Figure 2). Hence males are likely to have lower condition threshold values than females, i.e. they are less likely to be anadromous. This in turn implies that either some of the genes affecting the threshold(s) are linked to sex-determining genes, or they exhibit sex-dependent expression patterns. Populations with a lower incidence of anadromy would also have lower mean threshold values than populations with a higher incidence. In addition, populations will differ in their likelihood of their individuals achieving the condition-threshold, and this may fluctuate from year-to-year depending on environmental conditions.

Baerwald *et al.*, (2016) indicated that differential DNA methylation at gene regulatory elements may be an important molecular mechanism allowing interactions between an organism and its environment to determine life history. They propose that life history may be at least partially controlled by an epigenetic response threshold involving an integration of parentally inherited factors, environmental factors and developmental history. Interactions among these factors can influence life history choice dependent on whether the threshold is achieved or not.

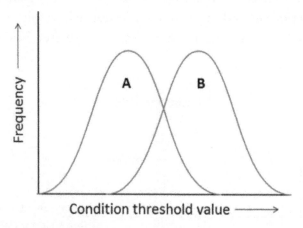

Figure 2. Possible distributions of condition threshold values in males (A) and females (B), or two populations with lower (A) and higher (B) propensities for anadromy. A single point along the x-axis here corresponds to a single threshold value, e.g. the dashed line in Figure.1.

Genes may directly influence the occurrence of anadromy, as in obligate anadromous species, irrespective of environmental influences. However, it could be that apparently obligate anadromous populations were once facultatively anadromous, but subsequently evolved very high condition thresholds such that they no longer produce residents in that environment. This raises the intriguing possibility that residency, or other freshwater life history, could re-emerge, as a result of changing environmental conditions at sea, in populations that are obligatively anadromous at present.

The fact that genetic, environmental, and parental factors are inextricably, and complexly, linked in determining life history (Figure 3) means that they cannot be considered in isolation, in either empirical or mathematical modelling studies. Not surprisingly where specific aspects have been looked at in isolation, the findings are often inconsistent with other data. Significant genetic variance in traits, such as size, growth rate, metabolic rate, and age of smoltification, may in part explain the contradiction among studies regarding the role that these traits play in the life history decision (Dodson *et al.*, 2013; Doctor *et al.*, 2014; Hecht *et al.*, 2015). Thus studies of condition and life history have often being carried out against variable genetic backgrounds where both intra-population and inter-population variability in the genetic propensity for life history occurs. It is generally well recognised that examining genetic differences between populations or other groups requires studies to be carried out in communal environmental conditions (common garden experiments), with reciprocal hybrids to control for parental effects. However, it seems less widely appreciated that investigating the influence of varying

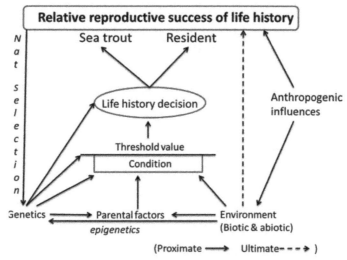

Figure 3. Summary of how genetic, environmental and parental factors could interact to determine the life history and how evolutionary changes to life history could result from environmental changes that alter the relative reproductive success of the two tactics.

environments requires either common gene pool experiments or reciprocal transfers of pure and hybrid stocks among the environments being tested.

GENETIC AND ENVIRONMENTAL INFLUENCES ON OTHER COMPONENTS OF ANADROMY

Once the decision to migrate has been made then several downstream consequential events occur. While there is clear evidence for both genetic and environmental influences on the anadromy decision, to what extent are the other components heritable and to what degree is variation in these the result of environmentally induced plasticity? Note, however, that these are not mutually exclusive alternatives as the degree of plasticity in given traits itself can be heritable. As with the decision to migrate, each of these components is also likely to involve interacting genetic and environmental factors. Furthermore, natural selection is likely to operate to maximise Darwinian fitness in each case. Thus these further components of anadromy may evolve under the action of selection and resultant, 'more efficient', anadromy may compensate for some of the costs involved in this life history as noted above.

GENETIC CORRELATES OF SMOLTIFICATION

Crosses between sympatric adfluvial kokanee and anadromous sockeye salmon (*O. nerka* (Walbaum)) indicated that there is a genetic basis for the propensity to undergo smolting

(Foote *et al.*, 1992). Hybrids between the two forms were intermediate in osmoregulatory ability in seawater, suggesting that the propensity for smoltification is the result of additive genetic variance at multiple genes. While the ecology and physiology of smoltification is well understood in salmonine fishes, relatively little was known of the genetic and molecular regulatory mechanisms underlying this process until recently. Two main molecular genomics approaches have been used to compare smolts and residents. The first comprises studies of gene expression, i.e. which genes are differentially active in the two life histories. The second involves determining genes or groups of genes (chromosome regions) that are correlated with life history through mapping quantitative trait loci (QTL) and genome wide association studies (GWAS). As emphasised above, while such studies are informative with regard to the genetic control of smoltification, they do not indicate why or how the smoltification is initiated in the first place, i.e. the decision to migrate.

Giger *et al.*, (2006) found shared differences in the genes expressed between smolts and resident brown trout from various European populations irrespective of their geographical and phylogenetic background, thus indicating common genetic pathways related to smoltification. Subsequently, Giger *et al.*, (2008) found that 21% of a random sample of screened genes were differentially expressed, which would suggest that many genes are involved in smoltification, or are indirectly affected by the process, in keeping with the genome wide distribution of gene associations found in later studies. Many other studies have shown gene expression differences, especially in the gills, between smolts and resident salmonines (e.g., Boulet *et al.*, 2012; Robertson & McCormick, 2012; Garrett, 2013; Hecht *et al.*, 2014; Sutherland *et al.*, 2014). Genes that have been found to be differentially expressed relate, in most cases, to known physiological differences between smolts and residents, i.e., those associated with circadian rhythmicity, growth, osmoregulation, metabolism, protein breakdown, innate immunity, and sexual maturation. Differences in one of the genes, *transaldolase* 1, which is involved in lipid metabolism and is expressed at a lower level in smolts, can be detected over three months prior to migration (Amstutz *et al.*, 2006).

QTL and gene markers correlated with smoltification traits in rainbow trout have been found on many chromosomes, including Omy5 as outlined above and Omy12 (Nichols *et al.*, 2008; Hecht *et al.*, 2012, 2013; Hale *et al.*, 2013; Pearse *et al.*, 2014). In a QTL analysis of osmoregulatory capacity in resident rainbow trout, Le Bras *et al.*, (2011) identified three QTL on Omy12 for traits associated with seawater adaptability. Hecht *et al.*, (2012) found the largest number of QTL associated with *Omy*12. Similarly, Hecht *et al.*, (2013) in a genome wide association study found associations between anadromy and this chromosome. Just as a gene region on Omy5 may act as a master switch for the life history decision so the genes on Omy12 may control smoltification in steelhead.

As noted above, one possible pathway that environmentally induced phenotypic plasticity could be linked to variation in life history is through epigenetic regulation determining which genes are expressed and which are silenced. One common mechanism for this is gene methylation, by which methyl groups are attached to the DNA preventing gene expression.

Different genome-wide methylation patterns between hatchery freshwater controls and seawater transferred brown trout have been identified suggesting that epigenetic mechanisms may be involved, at least partially, in gene activation or deactivation during smoltification (Morán *et al.*, 2013). Baerwald *et al.*, (2015), using F_2 siblings produced from a cross between steelhead and resident Sashin Creek rainbow trout reared in a common environment, detected 57 highly significant differentially methylated regions (DMRs) between smolts and resident juveniles. Many of the DMRs encode proteins with activity relevant to smoltification, including circadian rhythms and protein kinase activity: an enzyme to which a multitude of functions have been attributed.

INHERITED MIGRATION PATTERNS AND HOMING

Juvenile steelhead, without prior migratory experience, have been shown to be capable of responding to magnetic fields at the latitudinal boundaries of their ocean range with oriented swimming that would lead them towards appropriate foraging grounds (Putman *et al.*, 2014a). Environmental factors could still play an important role if fish calibrate their responses relative to the local magnetic field in which they develop. Two Chinook salmon (*Oncorhynchus tshawytscha* (Walbaum)) populations and their hybrids reared under identical conditions differed in their oceanic distribution, and hybrids displayed an intermediate distribution relative to the two pure populations (Quinn *et al.*, 2011). Subsequently Chinook salmon have been shown to use an inherited magnetic map that facilitates navigation during their oceanic migration (Putman *et al.*, 2014b). Similar mechanisms may exist for other salmonines.

Hatchery-reared sea trout from different populations showed distinct migration pathways when released from common sites in the Baltic (Svärdson & Fagerström, 1982; Kallio-Nyberg *et al.*, 2002) and natural sea trout populations differ in their distribution at sea (Jonsson & Jonsson, 2014b), indicating at least a partial genetic basis for their migratory behaviour. Jonsson & Jonsson (2014b) note a higher straying rate of some hatchery reared stocks from populations distant to the river of release compared to more local stocks, which indicates that homing is partly inherited.

RETURN FROM SEA

Little is known of the factors controlling the timing of sea trout return from the sea, an aspect showing considerable variation within and among populations. Norwegian populations overwintering in freshwater (Klemetsen *et al.*, 2003) may simply be a physiological response to the greater difficulty of ionic regulation in cold water. Unlike Atlantic salmon, return to freshwater is not necessarily accompanied by sexual maturation, although this may be the driving force in many cases. It is not known if timing of maturation at sea is connected to the original freshwater mature-or-migrate decision or whether these are independent aspects of the anadromous life history.

Timing of maturation in brown trout is a quantitative trait (Palm & Ryman, 1999). While age at sexual maturity in salmonines has a moderate heritability (Dodson *et al.*, 2013), it is phenotypically plastic. In Atlantic salmon, a single genome region under natural selection is associated with age of maturity (Ayllon *et al.*, 2015; Barson *et al.*, 2015). Interestingly one of the genes in this region has previously been found to be associated with the timing of puberty in humans, suggesting a conserved mechanism for timing of maturation in vertebrates. It would seem highly likely then that the same gene region may control time of maturity in brown trout.

MANAGEMENT AND CONSERVATION IMPLICATIONS OF A GENETIC BASIS TO ANADROMY

A strong genetic component to the anadromy decision in brown trout means the trait can be changed by (i.e. can evolve as a result of) natural selection. Due to the large heritabilities of growth, size and morphological traits, these characters also have substantial evolutionary potential (Hecht *et al.*, 2015). However, the significant genetic correlation between traits, including life history, means that they do not evolve independently but as a suite of coordinated characters. This genetic covariance means that the response of life history to selection cannot be examined in isolation from these other traits (Hecht *et al.*, 2015).

As noted above, facultative anadromy is the result of a balance between the benefits and costs of life history traits and these are expected to vary spatially and temporally with changes in environmental conditions, including those imposed by anthropogenic actions and climate changes (Kendall *et al.*, 2015). Environmental changes can result in: (1) a proximate effect through changing individual condition and thus the likelihood of migration; and (2) ultimate evolutionary changes to the genetic make-up including the threshold for migration, as a consequence of changes in the relative reproductive success of anadromous and resident trout. For example, reduction in the number of spawning sea trout could have a direct impact on the extent of anadromy as well as an evolutionary one. Thus reduced spawning would result in an overall reduction in juvenile density, which, as discussed above, may favour residency. In the longer term a reduced benefit to anadromy will lower the threshold for residency. The main environmental and anthropogenic changes likely to result in genetic changes are outlined below. A full consideration of the topic would require a dedicated review.

Negative changes to marine survival and feeding, and to survival and energy expenditure during migrations, will result in genetic changes in favour of residency (Hendry *et al.*, 2004). Marine survival and growth may decline as the outcome of predicted climate changes resulting in changes in food availability (see below), increased predation (Friedland *et al.*, 2012), and exploitation by commercial nets, either directly or as a by product of netting for other fishes, both of sea trout and their prey. A major problem in some areas is infestations of sea lice

(*Lepeophtheirus salmonis*) associated with Atlantic salmon farming, which have led to reduced marine survival and changes associated with migration, growth, physiology and reproduction (Skaala *et al.*, 2014; reviewed by Thorstad *et al.*, 2015). Model projections by Satterthwaite *et al.* (2009) for steelhead suggest that when sea survival rates were reduced by some 50%, anadromy no longer occurred, although the extent of the reduction required was population specific (Satterthwaite *et al.*, 2010). Taranger *et al.* (2015) note that within 15km of salmon farms in Norway sea lice levels are sufficiently high to result in 50% – 100% mortality of sea trout. Poole *et al.* (2006) found that in the Burrishoole system the mean return rate of smolts as finnock (.0SW maidens) in the years 1988-98 was one third of that prior to 1988, finnock being the predominant returning age class in this system. Sea lice emanating from salmon farms were implicated in this decline. It is not known whether the subsequent decline in sea trout smolts was the result of lower marine survival acting through natural selection to reduce anadromy or whether this decrease was the result of lowering of juvenile density due to depressed egg deposition. However, the fact that, even prior to the collapse, sea trout contributed less than 20% of the total egg deposition in the system would suggest a heritable rather than a direct density-dependent response (Poole *et al.*, 2006).

Conversely, making particular times of the year in the natal river completely inhospitable (e.g. high temperature, low flow, low food availability) will eliminate the resident life history (Satterthwaite *et al.*, 2010). However, in simulations that varied growth and survival only, Railsback *et al.*, (2014) showed that as a result of variation among habitats and individuals, the extent of anadromy within a population changed gradually instead of shifting abruptly.

Changes in survival of both downstream and upstream migrants and in the energy costs of migration can occur for a number of reasons. Changes in water flow as a result of changes in precipitation and water abstraction can delay migration thus increasing the exposure to predators and energy expenditure. These effects are increased by partial barriers to upstream migration due to water offtake and hydroelectric weirs. It should be emphasised that even where such barriers do not prevent upstream migration, they can increase the costs of facultative anadromy relative to residency. Sandlund & Jonsson (2016) reported that, following the construction of a hydroelectric power station and consequent reduced water flow, fluvial trout had ceased to migrate from a tributary to the main river due to reduced habitat quality in terms of food and shelter, which appeared to have removed the growth benefit previously associated with migration.

In many rivers more angling attention is given to sea trout than resident trout resulting in greater exploitation of the former. Since sea trout produce relatively more eggs than residents, this differential exploitation is magnified. Thériault *et al.*, (2008) present a theoretical model of how increased harvesting of anadromous brook charr reduces the probability of migration. Since cessation of fishing pressure does not produce as strong selection pressures in the opposite direction, recovery is likely to take much longer (Conover, 2000; Law, 2000).

Predicted climate changes are likely to impact on life history choice. The expected climate change in Western Europe is for warmer conditions with increased rainfall resulting in greater river flows (Harrod *et al.*, 2009). Temperature increase in the sea is predicted to reduce primary productivity (Piou & Prévost, 2012) and thus potentially reduce food availability for sea trout. As noted above, both temperature and flow rate impact on anadromy and thus changes in sea trout distribution and biological characteristics are likely to occur (reviewed by Jonsson & Jonsson, 2009). Warmer conditions and a longer feeding period, together with freshwater enrichment, may increase freshwater growth rates with a consequent decrease in anadromy (Finstad & Hein, 2012).

Stocking with fertile domesticated trout strains could result in a decrease in the genetic potential for anadromy in wild populations (Ferguson, 2007). Ruzzante *et al.*, (2004) found that although domesticated trout, which had been stocked into rivers, produced smolts, these experienced high mortality at sea and were therefore largely absent in returning spawners. This suggests that genetic changes during domestication have reduced the ability to survive in the sea and the authors conclude that sea trout of domesticated origin are unlikely to reproduce to any significant extent. As noted above, there is a genetic propensity for the ability to carry out ionic and osmoregulation at sea, which is independent of the actual seaward migration and the two aspects should not be confused. However, stocked domesticated trout that remain in freshwater have been shown to breed successfully (Hansen *et al.*, 2000) and thus may increase the proportion of freshwater trout relative to sea trout. Hatchery-produced steelhead smolts from residents above a barrier had substantially lower marine survival rates than similar smolts from the anadromous founder population below the barrier, indicating strong selection against aspects of anadromy in the above-barrier population over approximately 70 years (Thrower & Hard, 2009). The main farm strains of brown trout have been isolated from wild stocks for more than twice that time and were originally mainly derived from the adfluvial populations in Loch Leven, Scotland (Ferguson, 2007). An experimental study in Norway (Jonsson & Jonsson, 2014b) indicated that wild sea trout survived better than most hatchery produced trout, and that trout originating from populations distant to the river of release survived less well than those of local origin.

Stocking with farm trout, or the hatchery-reared offspring of non-native trout, also reduces the reproductive success of wild populations through interbreeding with the stocked fish (reviewed by Ferguson, 2007); which would reduce population density thus favouring residency. Stocking with domesticated strains of farm brown trout, other than sterile triploids, in areas with self sustaining populations is no longer permitted in England and Wales as of 2015 (Environment Agency, 2014) and will be phased out in Scotland by 2020 (Scottish Government, 2015). However, such stocking is still permitted in other jurisdictions.

Stocking with hatchery-reared offspring of sea trout parents obtained from the same river as being stocked (supportive breeding) is still widely practised in the countries surrounding the Baltic Sea. However, even if no genetic changes occur, hatchery-rearing can alter the physiological condition of the trout thus changing their likelihood of migration (Davidsen *et al.*, 2014b). In an experimental stocking programme, Marco-Rius *et al.*, (2013) found that that planting artificially fertilized eggs in nursery areas of the river, together with the selection of anadromous males as brood stock, and mate pairs with higher similarity at the MHC class II B-gene locus, increased the return of sea trout.

FUTURE PERSPECTIVES

Studies on the determinants of anadromy in brown trout, especially genetic aspects, lag substantially behind those on rainbow trout; although, even for the latter, Kendal *et al.*, (2015) consider that available information has many limitations. However, given the considerable similarities of facultative anadromy in the two species, rainbow trout studies can act as a springboard enabling rapid progress to be made in respect of brown trout. Key aspects which need to be tackled are those essential to understanding and enabling predictive modelling of the impact of changing environmental conditions on anadromy and how lost or depleted anadromous populations can be restored. Fundamental to this is the estimation of heritability of anadromy and relative Darwinian fitness of alternative life histories in a range of populations of different phylogenetic origins and biological characteristics (Ferguson, 2006). In particular, theory suggests that in order to predict changing selection on environmentally-cued threshold traits we need to measure (a) the frequency distribution of cue (e.g. condition) values and how this is affected by environmental change, and (b) how the fitness of each tactic varies as a function of the cue (Tomkins & Hazel, 2007). Heritability estimates of the various factors (e.g. growth, metabolic rate, lipid storage) contributing to individual condition are also required together with the genetic covariance of these and anadromy. In addition, detailed investigation of the genetic factors controlling the life history decision is required. It is emphasised that such studies need to target early developmental stages, as this is when the 'decision window(s)' occurs, and not focus on smolts, which are a downstream consequence of the decision. This will require making use of experimental lines derived from above (resident) and below (anadromous) barrier populations together with innovative approaches to predict the future life histories of individual fish at an early developmental stage.

Detailed studies of the influence of environmental factors on anadromy in brown trout are also required, including juvenile density, food availability, water temperature, water flow, and difficulty (cost) of migration. Variation in condition among populations as a result of variation in these factors, and how individuals respond to this, requires examination. Similar recommendations in respect of rainbow trout have been advocated by Kendall *et al.* (2015) and that review should be consulted for a more detailed exposition.

As there is clear evidence of a density dependent aspect to facultative anadromy it should be instructive to artificially manipulate juvenile densities. This could be done using sterile triploid farm trout, which would obviate the potential problems of genetic changes due to interbreeding noted above (Ferguson, 2007).

Examination of issues affecting marine survival and growth is fundamental to full life cycle understanding. Experimental studies of environmental factors must be undertaken in the context of controlling for genetic variability as outlined above. Most studies to date of sea trout have been undertaken on a few river systems. However, there is requirement for investigation of relative frequency of life histories in a much larger number of rivers, together with detailed biotic and abiotic measurements and associated riverscape features. Studies of parental influences on life history and epigenetic modifications can serve to elucidate how genetic and environmental influences interact. Although investigations of the inheritance of environmentally induced epigenetic modifications are at an early stage (Burton & Metcalfe, 2014), studies of such inheritance are likely to be fundamentally important in understanding life history choice, as well as the impact of environmental changes in general.

ACKNOWLEDGEMENTS

We thank Tom P. Quinn, John B. Taggart and Bror Jonsson for their detailed and incisive reviews of the manuscript and for many valuable suggestions.

REFERENCES

Acolas M.L., Labonne, J., Baglinière, J.L. & Roussel, J.M. (2012). The role of body size versus growth on the decision to migrate: a case study with *Salmo trutta. Naturwissenschaften,* **99**, 11-21.

Amstutz, U., Thomas Giger, T., Champigneulle, A., Day, P.J.R. & Largiadèr, C.R. (2006). Distinct temporal patterns of Transaldolase 1 gene expression in future migratory and sedentary brown trout (*Salmo trutta*). *Aquaculture,* **260**, 326-336.

Ayllon, F., Kjærner-Semb, E., Furmanek, T., Wennevik, V., Solberg, M., Sægrov, H., Urdal, K., Dahle, G., Taranger, G.L., Glover, K.A., Almén, M.S., Rubin, C.J., Edvardsen, R.B. & Wargelius, A. (2015). The vgll3 locus controls age at maturity in wild and domesticated Atlantic salmon (*Salmo salar*) males. PLOS Genetics, 11, e1005628. doi:10.1371/journal.pgen.1005628.

Barson, N.J., Aykanat, T., Hindar, K., Baranski, M., Bolstad, G.H., Fiske, P., Jacq, C., Jensen, A.J., Johnston, S.E., Karlsson, S., Kent, M., Niemelä, E., Nome, T., Næsje, T.F., Orell, P., Romakkaniemi, A., Sægrov, H., Urdal, K., Erkinaro, J., Lien, S. & Primmer, C.R. (2015). Sex-dependent dominance at a single locus maintains variation in age at maturity in Atlantic salmon. *Nature,* **528**, 405–408.

Baerwald, M.R., Meek, M.H., Stephens, M.R., Nagarajan, R.P, Goodbla, A.M., Tomalty, K.M.H., Thorgaard, G.H., May, B. & Nichols, K.M. (2016). Migration-related phenotypic divergence is associated with epigenetic modifications in rainbow trout. *Molecular Ecology,* **25**, 1785-1800.

Beakes, M.P., Satterthwaite, W.H., Collins, E.M., Swank, D.R., Merz, J.E., Titus, R.G., Sogard, S.M. & Mangel, M. (2010). Smolt transformation in two California steelhead populations: effects of temporal variability in growth. *Transactions of the American Fisheries Society,* **139**, 1263–1275.

Berejikian, B.A., Campbell, L.A. & Moore M. E. (2013). Large-scale freshwater habitat features infuence the degree of anadromy in eight Hood Canal *Oncorhynchus mykiss* populations. *Canadian Journal of Fisheries and Aquatic Sciences*, **70**, 756–765.

Berejikian, B.A., Bush, R.A. & Campbell, L.A. (2014). Maternal control over offspring life history in a partially anadromous species, *Oncorhynchus mykiss*. *Transactions of the American Fisheries Society*, **143**, 369-379.

Bernatchez, L. & Dodson, J.J. (1987). Relationship between bioenergetics and behaviour in anadromous fish migrations. *Canadian Journal of Fisheries and Aquatic Sciences*, **44**, 399-407.

Björnsson, B.T., Stefansson, S.O. & McCormick, S.D. (2011). Environmental endocrinology of salmon smoltification. *General and Comparative Endocrinology*, **15**, 290-298.

Bohlin, T., Pettersson, J. & Degerman, E. (2001). Population density of migratory and resident brown trout (*Salmo trutta*) in relation to altitude: evidence for a migration cost. *Journal of Animal Ecology*, **70**, 112-121.

Boula, D., Castric, V., Bernatchez, L. & Audet, C. (2002). Physiological, endocrine, and genetic bases of anadromy in the brook charr, *Salvelinus fontinalis*, of the Laval River (Quebec, Canada). *Environmental Biology of Fishes*, **64**, 229–242.

Boulet, M., Normandeau, É., Bougas, B., Audet, C. & Bernatchez, L. (2012). Comparative transcriptomics of anadromous and resident brook charr *Salvelinus fontinalis* before their first salt water transition. *Current Zoology*, **58**, 158−170.

Brannon, E.L., Powell, M.S., Quinn, T.P. & Talbot, A. (2004). Population structure of Columbia River Basin chinook salmon and steelhead trout. *Reviews in Fishery Science*, **12**, 199-232.

Brönmark, C., Hulthen, K., Nilsson, P.A., Skov, C., Hansson, L.A., Brodersen, J. & Chapman, B.B. (2013). There and back again: migration in freshwater fishes. *Canadian Journal of Zoology*, **91**, 1–13.

Burton, T., McKelvey, S., Stewart, D.C., Armstrong, J.D., and Metcalfe, N.B. (2013). Early maternal experience shapes offspring performance in the wild. *Ecology*, **94**, 618-626.

Burton, T. & Metcalfe, N.B. (2014). Can environmental conditions experienced in early life influence future generations? *Proceedings Royal Society B*, **281**, 20140311.

Caballero, P., Morán, P. & Marco-Rius, F. (2013). A review of the genetic and ecological basis of phenotypic plasticity in brown trout. In: *Trout: From Physiology to Conservation* (Polakof, S. & Moon, T.W. *Eds.*). Nova Science, USA, 9-26.

Charles, K., Guyomard, R., Hoyheim, B., Ombredane, D. & Baglinière, J-L. (2005). Lack of genetic differentiation between anadromous and resident sympatric brown trout (*Salmo trutta*) in a Normandy population. *Aquatic Living Resources*, **18**, 65-69.

Charles, K., Roussel, J.M., Lebel, J.M., Baglinière, J-L. & Ombredane, D. (2006). Genetic differentiation between anadromous and freshwater resident brown trout (*Salmo trutta* L.): insights obtained from stable isotope analysis. *Ecology of Freshwater Fish*, **15**, 255-263.

Conover, D.O. (2000). Darwinian fishery science. *Marine Ecology Progress Series*, **208**, 303-306.

Courter, I.I., Child, D.B., Hobbs, J.A., Garrison, T.M., Glessner, J.J.G. & Duery, S. (2013). Resident rainbow trout produce anadromous offspring in a large interior watershed. *Canadian Journal of Fisheries and Aquatic Sciences*, **70**, 701-710.

Cross, T.F., Mills, C.P.R. & de Courcy Williams, M. (1992). An intensive study of allozyme variation in freshwater resident and anadromous trout, *Salmo trutta* L., in western Ireland. *Journal of Fish Biology*, **40**, 25-32.

Crozier, W.W. & Ferguson, A. (1986). Electrophoretic examination of the population structure of brown trout, *Salmo trutta* L., from the Lough Neagh catchment, Northern Ireland. *Journal of Fish Biology*, **28**, 459-477.

Cucherousset, J., Ombredane, D., Charles K., Marchand, F. & Baglinière, J-L. (2005). A continuum of life history tactics in a brown trout (*Salmo trutta*) population. *Canadian Journal of Fisheries and Aquatic Sciences*, **62**, 1600-1610.

Dann, S.G., Allison, W.T., Levin, D.B. & Hawryshyn, C.W. (2003). Identification of a unique transcript down-regulated in the retina of rainbow trout (*Oncorhynchus mykiss*) at smoltification. *Comparative Biochemistry and Physiology*, **136B**, 849-860.

Davidsen, J.G., Daverdin, M., Arnekleiv, J.V. Rønning, L., Sjursen, A.D. & and Koksvik, J.I. (2014a). Riverine and near coastal migration performance of hatchery brown trout *Salmo trutta*. *Journal of Fish Biology*, **85**, 586–596.

Davidsen, J.G., Daverdin, M., Sjursen, A.D., Rønning, L., Arnekleiv, J.V. & Koksvik, J.I. (2014b). Does reduced feeding prior to release improve the marine migration of hatchery brown trout *Salmo trutta* smolts? *Journal of Fish Biology*, **85**, 1992–2002.

Dellefors, C. & Faremo, U. (1988). Early sexual-maturation in males of wild sea trout, *Salmo trutta* L., inhibits smoltification. *Journal of Fish Biology*, **33**, 741-749.

Dieperink, C., Bak, B.D., Pedersen, L-F., Pedersen, M.I. & Pedersen, S. (2002). Predation on Atlantic salmon and sea trout during their first days as postsmolts. *Journal of Fish Biology*, **61**, 848-852.

Docker, M.F. & Heath, D.D. (2003). Genetic comparison between sympatric anadromous steelhead and freshwater resident rainbow trout in British Columbia, Canada. *Conservation Genetics*, **4**, 227-231.

Doctor, K., Berejikian, B., Hard, J.J. & VanDoornik, D. (2014). Growth-mediated life history traits of steelhead reveal phenotypic divergence and plastic response to temperature. *Transactions of the American Fisheries Society*, **143**, 317-333.

Dodson, J.J., Aubin-Horth, N., Thériault, V. & Páez, D.J. (2013). The evolutionary ecology of alternative migratory tactics in salmonid fishes. *Biological Reviews*, **88**, 602-625.

Einum, S. & Fleming, I.A. (1995). Maternal effects of egg size in brown trout (*Salmo trutta*): norms of reaction to environmental quality. *Proceedings Royal Society London B*, **266**, 2095-2100.

Eldøy, S.H., Davidsen, J.G., Thorstad, E.B., Whoriskey, F., Aarestrup, K., Næsje, T.F., Rønning, L., Sjursen, A.D., Rikardsen, A.H. & and Arnekleiv, J.V. (2015). Marine migration and habitat use of anadromous brown trout *Salmo trutta*. *Canadian Journal of Fisheries and Aquatic Sciences*, 72, 1366 – 1378.

Elliott, J.M. (1994). *Quantitative Ecology and the Brown Trout*. Oxford University Press, New York, 286 pp.

Esteve, M. (2005). Observations of spawning behaviour in salmoninae: *Salmo*, *Oncorhynchus* and *Salvelinus*. *Reviews in Fish Biology and Fisheries*, **15**, 1-21.

Etheridge, E.C., Harrod, C., Bean, C., Adams, C.E. (2008). Continuous variation in the pattern of marine versus freshwater foraging in brown trout *Salmo trutta* L. from Loch Lomond, Scotland. *Journal of Fish Biology*, **73**, 44-53.

Euzenat, G. (1999). Sea trout (*Salmo trutta* L.) in Normandy and Picardy. In: *Biology and ecology of the brown trout and sea trout.* (Baglinière, J-L. & Maisse, G., *Eds.*). Springer-Praxis Series in Aquaculture and Fisheries, Berlin, 175–203.

Ferguson, A. (1989). Genetic differences among brown trout, *Salmo trutta*, stocks and their importance for conservation and management of the species. *Freshwater Biology*, **21**, 35-46.

Ferguson, A. (1994). Molecular genetics in fisheries: Current and future perspectives. *Reviews in Fish Biology and Fisheries,* **4**, 379-383.

Ferguson, A. (2004). The importance of identifying conservation units: brown trout and pollan biodiversity in Ireland. *Biology and Environment: Proceedings of the Royal Irish Academy*, **104B**, 33-41.

Ferguson, A. (2006). Genetics of sea trout, with particular reference to Britain and Ireland. In: *Sea Trout: Biology, Conservation & Management.* (Graeme Harris & Nigel Milner. *Eds.*). Proceedings of the First International Sea Trout Symposium, July, 2004, Cardiff, Wales, UK. Blackwell Publishing, Oxford, 155-182.

Finstad, A.G. & Hein, C.L. (2012). Migrate or stay: terrestrial primary productivity and climate drive anadromy in Arctic char. *Global Change Biology*, 18, 2487-2497.

Fleming, C.C. (1983). Population biology of anadromous brown trout (*Salmo trutta* L.) in Ireland and Britain. PhD Thesis, The Queen's University of Belfast, 475pp.

Fleming, I.A. (1996). Reproductive strategies of Atlantic salmon: ecology and evolution. *Reviews in Fish Biology and Fisheries*, **6**, 379-416.

Fleming, I.A. (1998). Pattern and variability in the breeding system of Atlantic salmon (*Salmo salar*), with comparisons to other salmonids. *Canadian Journal of Fisheries and Aquatic Sciences*, **55 (Suppl. 1)**, 59-76.

Fleming, I.A., & Reynolds, J.D. (2004). Salmonid breeding systems. In: *Evolution Illuminated: Salmon and their relatives* (Hendry, A.P. & Stearns, S.C. *Eds.*). Oxford University Press, New York, 264-294.

Foote, C.J., Wood, C.C., Clarke, W.C. & Blackburn, J. (1992). Circannual cycle of seawater adaptability in *Oncorhynchus nerka*: genetic differences in smoltification of sympatric sockeye salmon and kokanee. *Canadian Journal of Fisheries and Aquatic Sciences*, **49**, 99-109.

Forseth, T., Næsje, T.F., Jonsson, B. & Hårsaker, K. (1999). Juvenile migration in brown trout: a consequence of energetic state. *Journal of Animal Ecology*, **68**, 783-793.

Friedland, K.D., Manning, J.P., Link, J.S., Gilbert, J.R. Gilbert, A.T. & O'Connell, A.F. (2012). Variation in wind and piscivorous predator fields affecting the survival of Atlantic salmon, *Salmo salar*, in the Gulf of Maine. *Fisheries Management and Ecology*, **19**, 22–35.

Frost, W.E. & Brown, M.E. (1967). *The Trout.* Collins New Naturalist Series, London, 316 pp.

Garrett, I.D.F. (2013). Gene expression life history markers in a hatchery and a wild population of young-of-the-year *Oncorhynchus mykiss*. M.Sc. Thesis. Portland State University, Oregon.

Giger, T., Excoffier, L., Day, P.J.R., Champigneulle, A., Hansen, M.M., Powell, R. & Largiader, C.R. (2006). Life history shapes gene expression in salmonids. *Current Biology* **16**, 281-282.

Giger, T., Excoffier, L., Amstutz, U., Day, P.J.R., Champigneulle, A., Hansen, M.H., Kelso, J. & Largiadèr, C.R. (2008). Population transcriptomics of life-history variation in the genus *Salmo*. *Molecular Ecology*, **17**, 3095-3108.

Greenstreet, S.P.R., Morgan, R.I.G., Barnett, S. & Redhead, P. (1993). Variation in the numbers of shags *Phalacrocorax aristotelis* and common seals *Phoca vitulina* near the mouth of an Atlantic salmon *Salmo salar* river at the time of the smolt run. *Journal of Animal Ecology*, **62**, 565-576.

Gross, M. R. (1985). Disruptive selection for alternative life histories in salmon. *Nature*, **313**, 47-48.

Gross, M.R. (1987). Evolution of diadromy in fishes. *American Fisheries Society Symposium*, **1**, 14-25.

Gross, M.R., Coleman, R.M. & McDowall, R.M. (1988). Aquatic productivity and the evolution of diadromous fish migration. *Science*, **239**, 1291-1293.

Gross, M.R., Coleman, R.M. & McDowall, R.M. (1988). Aquatic productivity and the evolution of diadromous fish migration. *Science*, **239**, 1291-1293.

Hale, M.C., Thrower, F.P., Berntson, E.A., Miller M.R. & Nichols, K.M. (2013). Evaluating adaptive divergence between migratory and nonmigratory ecotypes of a salmonid fish, *Oncorhynchus mykiss*. *G3-Genes Genomes Genetics*, **3**, 1273-1285.

Hansen, M.M., Ruzzante, D.E., Nielsen, E.E. & Mensberg, K-L.D. (2000). Microsatellite and mitochondrial DNA polymorphism reveals life-history dependent interbreeding between hatchery and wild brown trout (*Salmo trutta* L.) *Molecular Ecology*, **9**, 583-594.

Hard, J.J., Winans, G.A. & Richardson, J.C. (1999). Phenotypic and genetic architecture of juvenile morphometry in Chinook salmon. *Journal of Heredity*, **90**, 597-606.

Harris, G. & Milner, N. (2006). Setting the scene – Sea trout in England and Wales – A personal perspective. In: *Sea Trout: Biology, Conservation & Management*. (Graeme Harris & Nigel Milner, *Eds*.). Proceedings of the First International Sea Trout Symposium, July 2004, Cardiff, Wales, UK. Blackwell Publishing, Oxford, 155–182.

Harrod, C., Graham, C. & Mallela, J. (2009). Climate change and the fishes of Britain and Ireland. *Journal of Fish Biology*, **74**, 1143-1205.

Hayes, S.A., Hanson, C.V., Pearse, D.E., Bond, M.H., Garza, J.C., Mac-Farlane, R.B. (2012). Should I stay or should I go? The influence of genetic origin on emigration behavior and physiology of resident and anadromous juvenile *Oncorhynchus mykiss*. *North American Journal of Fisheries Management*, **32**, 772-780.

Hazel, W.N., Smock, R. & Johnson, M.D. (1990). A polygenic model for the evolution and maintenance of conditional strategies. *Proceedings Royal Society London B*, **242**, 181-187.

Hecht, B.C., Thrower, F.P., Hale, M.C., Miller, M.R. & Nichols, K.M. (2012). Genetic architecture of migration-related traits in rainbow and steelhead trout, *Oncorhynchus mykiss*. *G3-Genes Genomes Genetics*, **2**, 1113-1127.

Hecht, B.C., Campbell, N.R., Holecek, D.E., Narum, S.R. (2013). Genome-wide association reveals genetic basis for the propensity to migrate in wild populations of rainbow and steelhead trout. *Molecular Ecology*, **22**, 3061-3076.

Hecht, B.C., Valle, M.E., Thrower, F.P. & Nichols, K.M. (2014). Divergence in expression of candidate genes for the smoltification process between juvenile resident rainbow and anadromous steelhead trout. *Marine Biotechnology*, 16, 638-656.

Hecht, B.C., Hard, J.J., Thrower, F.P. & Nichols, K.M. (2015). Quantitative genetics of migration related traits in rainbow and steelhead trout. *G3-Genes Genomes Genetics*, **5**, 873-879.

Hendry, A.P., Bohlin, T., Jonsson, B. & Berg, O.K. (2004). To sea or not to sea? Anadromy versus non-anadromy in salmonids. In: *Evolution Illuminated – Salmon and their relatives* (Hendry, A.P. & Stearns, S.C. *Eds.*). Oxford University Press, New York, 92-125.

Hindar, K., Jonsson, B., Ryman, N. & Ståhl, G. (1991). Genetic relationships among landlocked, resident, and anadromous brown trout, *Salmo trutta* L. *Heredity*, **66**, 83-91.

Hoar, W.S. (1988). The physiology of smolting salmonids. In: *Fish Physiology* (Hoar, W.S., Randall, D.J. & Donaldson, E.M., Eds). Academic Press, London, 275–343.

Holecek, D.E. & Scarnecchia, D.L. (2013) Comparison of two life history strategies after impoundment of a historically anadromous stock of Columbia River redband trout. *Transactions of the American Fisheries Society*, **142**, 1157-1166.

Hutchings, J.A. & Myers, R.A. (1988). Mating success of alternative maturation phenotypes in male Atlantic salmon, *Salmo salar*. *Oecologia*, 75, 169-174.

Jensen, J.L.A. & Rikardsen, A.H. (2012). Archival tags reveal that Arctic charr *Salvelinus alpinus* and brown trout *Salmo trutta* can use estuarine and marine waters during winter. *Journal of Fish Biology*, **81**, 735-749.

Jensen, A.J., Finstad, B., Fiske, P., Hvidsten, N.A., Rikardsen, A.H. & Saksgård, L. (2012). Timing of smolt migration in sympatric populations of Atlantic salmon (*Salmo salar),* brown trout *(Salmo trutta),* and Arctic char *(Salvelinus alpinus). Canadian Journal of Fisheries and Aquatic Sciences*, **69**,711-723.

Jensen, A.J., Diserud, O.H., Finstad, B., Fiske, P. & Rikardsen, A.H. (2015). Between-watershed movements of two anadromous salmonids in the Arctic. *Canadian Journal of Fisheries and Aquatic Sciences*, **72**,

Jepsen, N., Aarestrup, K., Økland, F. & Rasmussen, G. (1998). Survival of radiotagged Atlantic salmon (*Salmo salar* L.) and trout (*Salmo trutta* L.) smolts passing a reservoir during seaward migration. *Hydrobiologia*, **371/372**, 347-353.

Jonsson, B. (1982). Diadromous and resident trout *Salmo trutta*: is there difference due to genetics? *Oikos*, **38**, 297-300.

Jonsson, B. (1985). Life history pattern of freshwater resident and sea-run migrant brown trout in Norway. *Transactions of the American Fisheries Society*, **114**, 182-194.

Jonsson, B. & Jonsson, N. (1993). Partial migration: niche shift versus sexual maturation in fishes. *Reviews in Fish Biology and Fisheries*, **3**, 348-365.

Jonsson, N. & Jonsson, B. (1999). Trade-off between egg mass and egg number in brown trout. *Journal of Fish Biology*, **55**, 767-783.

Jonsson, B. & Jonsson, N. (2004). Factors affecting marine production of Atlantic salmon (*Salmo salar*). *Canadian Journal of Fisheries and Aquatic Sciences*, **61**, 2369-2383.

Jonsson, B. & Jonsson, N. (2005). Lipid energy reserves influence life-history decision of Atlantic salmon (*Salmo salar*) and brown trout (*S. trutta*) in fresh water. *Ecology of Freshwater Fish*, **14**, 296–301.

Jonsson, B. & Jonsson, N. (2006a). Life history of anadromous brown trout. 196-223. In: *Sea Trout: Biology, Conservation & Management.* (Graeme Harris & Nigel Milner. *Eds.*). Proceedings of the First International Sea Trout Symposium, July, 2004, Cardiff, Wales, UK. Blackwell Publishing, Oxford, 196-223.

Jonsson, B. & Jonsson, N. (2006b). Life history effects of migratory costs in anadromous brown trout *Salmo trutta*. *Journal of Fish Biology*, **69**, 860-869.

Jonsson, B. & Jonsson, N. (2009). A review of the likely effects of climate change on anadromous Atlantic salmon *Salmo salar* and brown trout *Salmo trutta*, with particular reference to water temperature and flow. *Journal of Fish Biology*, **75**, 2381-2447.

Jonsson, B. & Jonsson, N. (2011). *Ecology of Atlantic Salmon and Brown Trout: Habitat as a Template for Life Histories*. Fish & Fisheries Series, **33**. Springer, New York.

Jonsson, B. & Jonsson, N. (2014a). Early environment influences later performance in fishes. *Journal of Fish Biology*, **85**, 151-188.

Jonsson, B. & Jonsson, N. (2014b). Naturally and hatchery produced European trout *Salmo trutta*: do their marine survival and dispersal differ? *Journal of Coastal Conservation*, **18**, 79-87.

Jonsson, B. & Jonsson, N. (2016). Trans-generational maternal effect: temperature influences egg size of the offspring in Atlantic salmon *Salmo salar*. *Journal of Fish Biology*, **89**, 1482-1487.

Jonsson, B., Jonsson, N., Brodtkorb, E. & Ingebrigtsen, P. J. (2001). Life history traits of brown trout vary with the size of small streams. *Functional Ecology*, **15**, 310-317.

Jonsson, B. & L'Abée-Lund, J.H. (1993). Latitudinal clines in life history variables of anadromous brown trout in Europe. *Journal of Fish Biology*, **43 (Suppl. A)**, 1-16.

Kallio-Nyberg, I., Saura, A. & Ahlfors, P. (2002). Sea migration pattern of two sea trout (*Salmo trutta*) stocks released into the Gulf of Finland. *Annales Zoologici Fennici*, **39**, 221-235.

Kallio-Nyberg, I., Jutila, E., Koljonen, M-L., Koskiniemi, J. & Solaniemi, I. (2010). Can the lost migratory *Salmo trutta* stocks be compensated with resident trout stocks in coastal rivers? *Fisheries Research*, **102**, 69-79.

Kamler, E. (2005). Parent–egg–progeny relationships in teleost fishes: An energetics perspective. *Reviews in Fish Biology and Fisheries*, **15**, 399-421.

Kendall, N.W., McMillan J.R., Sloat, M.R., Buehrens, T.W., Quinn, T.P., Pess, G.R., Kuzishchin, K.V., McClure, M.M. & Zabel, R.W. (2015). Anadromy and residency in steelhead and rainbow trout (*Oncorhynchus mykiss*): a review of the processes and patterns. *Canadian Journal of Fisheries and Aquatic Sciences*, **72**, 319-342.

Klemetsen, A., Amundsen, P.-A., Dempson, J.B., Jonsson, B., Jonsson, N., O'Connell, M.F. & Mortensen, E. (2003). Atlantic salmon *Salmo salar* L., brown trout *Salmo trutta* L. and Arctic charr *Salvelinus alpinus* (L.): a review of aspects of their life histories. *Ecology of Freshwater Fish*, **12**, 1-59.

Knutsen, J.A., Knutsen, H., Olsen, E.M. & Jonsson, B. (2004). Marine feeding of anadromous *Salmo trutta* during winter. *Journal of Fish Biology*, **64**, 89-99.

Kottelat, M. & Freyhof, J. (2007). *Handbook of European Freshwater Fishes*. Kottelat, Cornol, Switzerland and Freyhof, Berlin, Germany. 646 pp.

L'Abee-Lund, J.H., Jonsson, B., Jensen, A.J., Sættem, L.M., Heggberget, T.G., Johnsen, B.O. & Næsje, T.F. (1989). Latitudinal variation in life-history characteristics of sea-run migrant brown trout *Salmo trutta*. *Journal of Animal Ecology*, **58**, 525-542

Landergren, P. (2001). Survival and growth of sea trout parr in fresh and brackish water. *Journal of Fish Biology*, **58**, 591-593.

Landergren, P. & Vallin, L. (1998). Spawning of sea trout, *Salmo trutta* L., in brackish waters–lost effort or successful strategy? *Fisheries Research*, **35**, 229-236.

Law, R. (2000). Fishing, selection, and phenotypic evolution. *ICES Journal of Marine Science*, **57**, 659-668.

Le Bras, Y., Dechamp, N., Krieg, F., Filangi, O., Guyomard, R., Boussaha, M., Bovenhuis, H., Pottinger, T.G., Prunet, P., Le Roy, P. & Quillet, E. (2011). Detection of QTL with effects on osmoregulation capacities in the rainbow trout (*Oncorhynchus mykiss*). *BMC Genetics*, **12**, 46-60.

Lehmann, M., Spoelstra, K., Visser, M.E. & Helm, B. (2012). Effects of temperature on circadian clock and chronotype: an experimental study on a passerine bird. *Chronobiology International*, **29**, 1062-1071.

Marco-Rius, F., Sotelo, G., Caballero, P. & Morán, P. (2013). Insights for planning an effective stocking program in anadromous brown trout (*Salmo trutta*). *Canadian Journal of Fisheries and Aquatic Sciences*, **70**, 1092–1100.

Martínez, A., Garza, J.C., Pearse, D.E. (2011). A microsatellite genome screen identifies chromosomal regions under differential selection in steelhead and rainbow trout. *Transactions of the American Fisheries Society*, **140**, 829-842.

McCormick, S.D. (2009). Evolution of the hormonal control of animal performance: insights from the seaward migration of salmon. *Integrative and Comparative Biology*, **49**, 408-422.

McCormick, S.D., Hansen, L.P., Quinn, T.P. & Saunders, R.L. (1998). Movement, migration, and smolting of Atlantic salmon (*Salmo salar*). *Canadian Journal of Fisheries and Aquatic Sciences*, **55 (Suppl. 1)**, 77-92.

McCormick, S.D., Regish, A.M. & Christensen, A.K. (2009). Distinct freshwater and seawater isoforms of Na+/K+-ATPase in gill chloride cells of Atlantic salmon. *Journal of Experimental Biology*, **212**, 3994-4001.

McCormick, S.D. Regish, A.M., Christensen, A.K. & Björnsson, B.J. (2013). Differential regulation of sodium–potassium pump isoforms during smolt development and seawater exposure of Atlantic salmon. *The Journal of Experimental Biology*, **216**, 1142-1151.

McKinney, G.J., Hale, M.C., Goetz, G., Gribskov, M., Thrower, F.P. & Nichols, K.M. (2015). Ontogenetic changes in embryonic and brain gene expression in progeny produced from migratory and resident *Oncorhynchus mykiss*. *Molecular Ecology*, **24**, 1792-1809.

McMillan, J.R., Dunham, J., Reeves, G.H., Mills, J.S. & Jordan, C.E. (2012). Individual condition and stream temperature influence early maturation of rainbow and steelhead trout, *Oncorhynchus mykiss*. *Environmental Biology of Fishes*, **93**, 343-355.

Middlemas, S.J., Stewart, D.C., Mackay, S. & Armstrong, J.D. (2009). Habitat use and dispersal of post-smolt sea trout *Salmo trutta* in a Scottish sea loch system. *Journal of Fish Biology*, **74**, 639-651.

Mills, J.S., Dunham, J.B., Reeves, G.H., McMillan, J.R., Zimmerman, C.E., and Jordan, C.E. (2012). Variability in expression of anadromy by female *Oncorhynchus mykiss* within a river network. *Environmental Biology of Fishes*, **93**, 505–517.

Morán, P., Marco-Rius, F., Megías, M., Covelo-Soto, L. & Pérez-Figueroa, A. (2013). Environmental induced methylation changes associated with seawater adaptation in brown trout. *Aquaculture*, **392–395**, 77–83.

Morinville, G. & Rasmussen, J. (2003). Early juvenile bioenergetic differences between anadromous and resident brook trout (*Salvelinus fontinalis*). *Canadian Journal of Fisheries and Aquatic Sciences*, **60**, 401-410.

Munkittrick, K.R. & Moccia, R.D. (1987). Seasonal changes in the quality of rainbow trout (*Salmo gairdneri*) semen: effect of a delay in stripping on spermatocrit, motility, volume and seminal plasma constituents. *Aquaculture*, **64**,147-156.

Narum, S.R., Contor, C., Talbot, A. & Powell, M.S. (2004). Genetic divergence of sympatric resident and anadromous forms of *Oncorhynchus mykiss* in the Walla Walla River, U.S.A. *Journal of Fish Biology*, **65**, 471-488.

Narum, S.R., Zendt, J.S., Frederiksen, C., Campbell, N., Matala A. & Sharp, W.R. (2011). Candidate genetic markers associated with anadromy in *Oncorhynchus mykiss* of the Klickitat River. *Transactions of the American Fisheries Society*, **140**, 843-854.

Nichols, K.M., Edo, A.F., Wheeler, P.A. & Thorgaard, G.H. (2008). The genetic basis of smoltification-related traits in *Oncorhynchus mykiss*. *Genetics,* **179**, 1559-1575.

Null, R.E., Niemela, K.S. & Hamelberg, S.F. (2013). Post-spawn migrations of hatchery-origin *Oncorhynchus mykiss* kelts in the Central Valley of California. *Environmental Biology of Fishes*, **96**, 341-353.

Olofsson, H. & Mosegaard, H. (1999). Larger eggs in resident brown trout living in sympatry with anadromous brown trout. *Ecology of Freshwater Fish*, 8, 59–64.

Olsson, I.C. & Greenberg, L.A. (2004). Partial migration in a landlocked brown trout population. *Journal of Fish Biology*, **65**, 106-121.

Olsson I.C., Greenberg L.A., Bergman E. & Wysujack K. (2006). Environmentally induced migration: the importance of food. *Ecology Letters*, **9**, 645-651.

O'Neal, S.L. & Stanford, J.A. (2011). Partial migration in a robust brown trout population of a Patagonian river. *Transactions of the American Fisheries Society*, **140,** 623-635.

Palm, S. & Ryman, N. (1999). Genetic basis of phenotypic differences between transplanted stocks of brown trout. *Ecology of Freshwater Fish*, **8**, 169-180.

Pearse, D.E., Hayes, S.A., Bond, M.H., Hanson, C.V., Anderson, E.C., Macfarlane, R.B. & Garza, J.C. (2009). Over the falls? Rapid evolution of ecotypic differentiation in steelhead/ rainbow trout (*Oncorhynchus mykiss*). *Journal of Heredity,* **100**, 515-525.

Pearse, D.E., Miller, M.R., Abadia-Cardoso, A. & Garza, J.C. (2014). Rapid parallel evolution of standing variation in a single, complex, genomic region is associated with life history in steelhead/rainbow trout. *Proceedings of the Royal Society B: Biological Sciences*, **281**. DOI:10.1098/rspb.2014.0012.

Piou, C & Prévost, E. (2012). Contrasting effects of climate change in continental vs. oceanic environments on population persistence and microevolution of Atlantic salmon. *Global Change Biology*, **19**, 711-723.

Poole, W.R., Dillane, M., DeEyto, E., Rogan, G., McGinnity, P. & Whelan, K. (2006). Characteristics of the Burrishoole sea trout population: Census, marine survival, enhancement and stock-recruitment relationships, 1971-2003. In: *Sea Trout: Biology, Conservation & Management*. (Graeme Harris & Nigel Milner. *Eds*.). Proceedings of the First International Sea Trout Symposium, July 2004, Cardiff, Wales, UK. Blackwell Publishing, Oxford, 279-306.

Putman, N.F., Meinke, A.M., & Noakes, D.L.G. (2014a). Rearing in a distorted magnetic field disrupts the 'map sense' of juvenile steelhead trout. *Biology Letters*, 10 20140169; DOI: 10.1098/rsbl.2014.0169.

Putman, N.F., Scanlan, M.M., Billman, E.J., O'Neil, J.P., Couture, R.B., Quinn, T.P., Lohmann, K.J. & Noakes, D.L.G. (2014b). An inherited magnetic map guides ocean navigation in juvenile pacific salmon. *Current Biology*, **24**, 446-450.

Quinn, T.P., Chamberlin, J. & Brannon, E.L. (2011). Experimental evidence of population-specific marine distributions of Chinook salmon, *Oncorhynchus tshawytscha*. *Environmental Biology of Fish*, **92**, 313-322.

Railsback, S.F., Harvey, B.C. & White, J.L. (2014). Facultative anadromy in salmonids: linking habitat, individual life history decisions, and population-level consequences. *Canadian Journal of Fisheries and Aquatic Sciences*, **71**, 1270-1278.

Rasmussen, G.H. (2006). Research activities and management of brown trout and sea trout (*Salmo trutta* L.) in Denmark. In: *Sea Trout: Biology, Conservation & Management*. (Graeme Harris & Nigel Milner. *Eds.*). Proceedings of the First International Sea Trout Symposium, July 2004, Cardiff, Wales, UK. Blackwell Publishing, Oxford, 342-348.

Robertson, L.A. & McCormick, S.D. (2012). Transcriptional profiling of the parr–smolt transformation in Atlantic salmon. *Comparative Biochemistry and Physiology, Part D*, **7**, 351-360.

Roff, D.A. (1996). The evolution of threshold traits in animals. *Quarterly Review of Biology* **71**, 3-35.

Ruzzante, D.E., Hansen, M.H., Meldrup, D. & Ebert, K.M. (2004). Stocking impact and migration pattern in an anadromous brown trout (*Salmo trutta*) complex: where have all the stocked spawning sea trout gone? *Molecular Ecology*, **13**, 1433-1445.

Sandlund, O.T. & Jonsson, B. (2016). Life history plasticity: migration ceased in response to environmental change? *Ecology of Freshwater Fish*, **25**, 225-233.

Satterthwaite, W.H., Beakes, M.P., Collins, E.M., Swank, D.R., Merz, J.E., Titus, R.G., Sogard, S.M. & Mangel, M. (2009). Steelhead life history on California's Central Coast: insights from a state-dependent model. *Transactions of the American Fisheries Society*, **138**, 532–548.

Satterthwaite, W.H., Beakes, M.P., Collins, E.M., Swank, D.R., Merz, J.E., Titus, R.G., Sogard, S.M. & Mangel, M. (2010). State-dependent life history models in a changing (and regulated) environment: steelhead in the California Central Valley. *Evolutionary Applications*, **3**, 221-243.

Schindler, D.E., Armstrong, J.B. & Reed, T.E. (2015). The portfolio concept in ecology and evolution. *Frontiers in Ecology and the Environment*, **13**, 257–263.

Seamons, T.R., Bentzen, P. & Quinn, T.P. (2004). The mating system of steelhead, *Oncorhynchus mykiss*, inferred by molecular analysis of parents and progeny. *Environmental Biology of Fishes*, **69**, 333-344.

Skaala, Ø., Kålås, S. & Borgstrøm, R. (2014). Evidence of salmon lice-induced mortality of anadromous brown trout (*Salmo trutta*) in the Hardangerfjord, Norway. *Marine Biology Research*, **10**, 279-288

Skaala, Ø. & Nævdal, G. (1989). Genetic differentiation between freshwater resident and anadromous brown trout, *Salmo trutta*, within watercourses. *Journal of Fish Biology*, **34**, 597-605.

Skrochowska, S. (1969). Migrations of the sea-trout (*Salmo trutta* L.), brown trout (*Salmo trutta* m. *fario* L.) and their crosses. Part1. Problem, methods and results of tagging. *Polish Archives of Hydrobiology*, **16**, 125-140.

Sloat, M.R. (2013). Born to run? Integrating individual behavior, physiology, and life histories in partially migratory steelhead and rainbow trout (*Oncorhynchus mykiss*). Ph.D. Thesis. Oregon State University, Corvallis.

Sloat, M.R. & Reeves, G.H. (2014). Individual condition, standard metabolic rate, and rearing temperature influence steelhead and rainbow trout (*Oncorhynchus mykiss*) life histories. *Canadian Journal of Fisheries and Aquatic Sciences*, **71**, 491-501.

Sloat, M.R., Fraser, D.J., Dunham, J.B., Falke, J.A., Jordan, C.E., McMillan, J.R., & Ohms, H.A. (2014). Ecological and evolutionary patterns of freshwater maturation in Pacific and Atlantic salmonines. *Reviews in Fish Biology and Fisheries*, **24**, 689-707.

Sogard, S.M., Merz, J.E., Satterthwaite, W.H., Beakes, M.P., Swank, D.R., Collins, E.M., Titus, R.G., & Mangel, M. (2012). Contrasts in habitat characteristics and life history patterns of *Oncorhynchus mykiss* in California's central coast and central valley. *Transactions of the American Fisheries Society*, **141**, 747–760.

Sutherland, B.J.G., Hanson, K.C., Jantzen, J.R., Koop, B.F. & Smith, C.T. (2014). Divergent immunity and energetic programs in the gills of migratory and resident *Oncorhynchus mykiss*. *Molecular Ecology*, **23**, 1952-1964.

Svärdson, G. & Fagerström, Å. (1982). Adaptive differences in the long-distance migration of some trout (*Salmo trutta* L.) stocks. *Report Institute of Freshwater Research Drottningholm*, **60**, 51-80.

Taranger, G.L., Karlsen, Ø., Bannister, R.J., Glover, K.A., Husa, V., Karlsbakk, E., Kvamme, B.O., Boxaspen, K.K., Bjørn, P.A., Finstad, B., Madhun, A.S., Morton, H.C. & Svåsand, T. (2015). Risk assessment of the environmental impact of Norwegian Atlantic salmon farming. *ICES Journal of Marine Science*, **72**, 997–1021.

Thériault, V. & Dodson, J. J. (2003). The role of size in determining anadromy or residency in brook charr (*Salvelinus fontinalis*). *Journal of Fish Biology*, **63**, 1-16.

Thériault, V., Garant, D., Bernatchez, L. & Dodson, J.J. (2007). Heritability of life history tactics and genetic correlation with body size in a natural population of brook charr (*Salvelinus fontinalis*). *Journal of Evolutionary Biology*, **20**, 2266-2277.

Thériault, V., Dunlop, E., Dieckman, U., Bernatchez, L. & Dodson, J. J. (2008). The impact of fishing-induced mortality on the evolution of alternative life-history tactics in brook charr. *Evolutionary Applications*, **1**, 409-423.

Thorpe, J.E. (1994a). Salmonid fishes and the estuarine environment. *Estuaries*, **17**, 76-93.

Thorpe, J.E. (1994b). An alternative view of smolting in salmonids. *Aquaculture*, **121**, 105-113.

Thorpe, J.E. & Metcalfe, N.B. (1998). Is smolting a positive or a negative developmental decision? *Aquaculture*, **168**, 95-103.

Thorstad, E.B., Todd, C.D., Uglem, I., Bjørn, P.A., Gargan, P.G., Vollset, K.W., Halttunen, E., Kålås, S., Berg, M. & Finstad, B. (2015). Effects of salmon lice *Lepeophtheirus salmonis* on wild sea trout *Salmo trutta*—a literature review. *Aquaculture Environment Interactions*, **7**, 91–113.

Thrower, F.P., Hard, J.J. & Joyce, J.E. (2004). Genetic architecture of growth and early life-history transitions in anadromous and derived freshwater populations of steelhead. *Journal of Fish Biology*, **65 (Suppl. A)**, 286-307.

Thrower, F.P. & Hard, J.J. (2009). Effects of a single event of close inbreeding on growth and survival in steelhead. *Conservation Genetics*, **10**, 1299-1307.

Tocher, D.R. (2003). Metabolism and functions of lipids and fatty acids in teleost fish. *Reviews in Fisheries Science*, **11**, 107–184.

Tomkins, J.L. & Hazel, W. (2007). The status of the conditional evolutionarily stable strategy. *Trends in Ecology and Evolution*, **22**, 522-528.

Van Leeuwen, T.E., Hughes, M.R., Dodd, J.A., Adams, C.E. & Metcalfe, N.B. (2015). Resource availability and life-history origin affect competitive behavior in territorial disputes. *Behavioral Ecology*, **27**, 385-392.

Wells, A., Grierson, C.E., Marshall, L., MacKenzie, M., Russon, I.J., Reinardy, H., Sivertsgård, R., Bjørn, P.A., Finstad, B., Bonga, S.E.W., Todd, C.D. & Hazon, N. (2007). Physiological consequences of 'premature freshwater return' for wild sea-run brown trout (*Salmo trutta*) post-smolts infested with sea lice (*Lepeophtheirus salmonis*). *Canadian Journal of Fisheries and Aquatic Sciences*, **64**, 1360-1369.

Wilzbach, M.A., Ashenfelter, M.J. & Ricker, S.J. (2012). Movement of resident rainbow trout transplanted below a barrier to anadromy. *Transactions of the American Fisheries Society*, **141**, 294-304,

Wysujack, K., Greenberg, L.A., Bergman, E. & Olsson, I.C. (2009). The role of the environment in partial migration: food availability affects the adoption of a migratory tactic in brown trout *Salmo trutta*. *Ecology of Freshwater Fish*, **18**, 52-59.

Zimmerman, C.E. & Reeves, G.H. (2000). Population structure of sympatric anadromous and nonanadromous *Oncorhynchus mykiss*: evidence from spawning surveys and otolith microchemistry. *Canadian Journal of Fisheries and Aquatic Sciences*, **57**, 2151-2167.

Zimmerman, C.E., Edwards, G.W. & Perry, K. (2009). Maternal origin and migratory history of steelhead and rainbow trout captured in rivers of the Central Valley, California. *Transactions of the American Fisheries Society*, **138**, 280-291.

ELECTRONIC REFERENCES

Balmaha Anglers. The sea trout runs on Loch Lomond. *Available at*: http://balmaha-anglers.co.uk/articles/sea-trout-runs-loch-lomond

Environment Agency (2014). Protecting wild brown trout: It's all in the genes. *Available at:* https://environmentagencyblog.gov.uk/2014/12/29/protecting-wild-brown-trout .

Ferguson, A. (2007). Genetic impacts of stocking on indigenous brown trout populations. Environment Agency Science Report SC040071/SR, 93pp. ISBN 978-1-84432-798-0. *Available at:* https://www.gov.uk/government/uploads/ system/uploads/attachment_data/file/291703/scho0707bmzi-e-e.pdf

Phillis, C., Moore, Buoro, M., S Hayes, S., Garza, C. & Pearse, D.E. (2014). Shifting thresholds: rapid evolution of migratory life histories in steelhead/rainbow trout, *Oncorhynchus mykiss*. *Available at:* https://peerj.com/preprints/361v1.pdf.

Schroeder, R.K. & Smith, L.H. (1989). Life history of rainbow trout and effects of angling regulations, Deschutes River, Oregon. *Available at*: http://agris.fao.org/agris-search/search. do?recordID=US9102167

Scottish Government (2015). Scottish Government Policy on Introductions of Fish to Scottish Inland Waters. *Available at*: http://www.gov.scot/Topics/marine/Licensing/fishintros/intadv

The Baltic Sea-European Environmental Agency. Table 2: Salinity in different part of the Baltic Sea *Available at*: http://www.eea.europa.eu/publications/report_2002_0524_154909/regional-seas-around-europe/page141.html

Understanding anadromy as an individual adaptive behaviour:
Theory and its consequences

S. F. RAILSBACK[1] & B. C. HARVEY[2]

[1]*Lang Railsback & Associates and Department of Mathematics, Humboldt State University, Arcata, California 95521, USA*
[2]*U.S. Forest Service, Pacific Southwest Research Station, Arcata, California 95521, USA*

ABSTRACT

Facultative anadromy, the apparent ability of individual fish to decide if and when to migrate to the ocean, has been addressed as a genetic tendency, a population-level adaptation and as an individual adaptive behaviour. We developed a model, *inSALMO-FA*, that represents anadromy as an individual behaviour that maximizes expected reproductive output at the next spawning. In the model, each juvenile salmonid decides if and when to migrate to the ocean by considering its current size, recently experienced growth and predation risk. The conclusions from several simulation experiments include: 1) individual variation in experience can produce both anadromous and resident individuals under many conditions, even at the same site, 2) predation risk may be more important than growth in driving anadromy, 3) habitat enhancement can produce more of both smolts and residents instead of causing one life history to dominate at a site, and 4) individuals with higher metabolic rates and dominance are not consistently more likely to smolt. Because models like *inSALMO* let us examine the consequences of alternative hypotheses about anadromy under controlled and observable conditions that still include much natural complexity, they are an important supplement to field and laboratory experiments for understanding anadromy.

Keywords: adaptive behaviour, facultative anadromy, modelling, sea trout, steelhead.

INTRODUCTION

THREE WAYS OF THINKING ABOUT FACULTATIVE ANADROMY

Understanding facultative anadromy, the apparent ability of individual fish to decide whether and when to migrate to the ocean, is an interesting and important question in managing sea trout (*Salmo trutta* L.). [The term *"partial migration"* is sometimes used for this ability, but this can be confused with other behaviours, such as migrating partway to the ocean (Secor & Kerr, 2009).] Without some understanding of what causes sea trout, or other facultative anadromous fish such as steelhead (*Oncorhynchus mykiss*) and Atlantic salmon (*Salmo salar*), to become anadromous, it is difficult to predict how management actions will affect relative numbers of anadromous and freshwater-resident fish. The question *"why do some fish become anadromous?"* has been considered in several different ways, each using different kinds of theory and raising different hypotheses. Here we briefly review three of these perspectives on facultative anadromy. While these perspectives look at the question in different ways, they are certainly not mutually exclusive and share common assumptions (as discussed in the Conclusions, below), and all three are very likely important in determining anadromy.

Perspective 1: Anadromy as a genetic tendency
This perspective assumes that anadromy is driven strongly by innate genetic tendencies. There is widespread evidence that genetics can have strong effects on anadromy (Kendall et al., (2015); Ferguson et al., (2016)). However, simply understanding that anadromy is driven in part by genetics is not useful for management because we also need to know what genetic characteristics of individual fish interact with what characteristics of the environment to trigger migration or residence (Kendall *et al.*, 2015). For example, Sloat & Reeves (2014) posed individual variation in metabolic rates as one hypothesis for a genetic trait that could drive anadromy. If one associates higher metabolic rates with boldness, athleticism and higher food demands, then it seems natural to assume that individual fish born with higher rates should be more likely to be anadromous and that the environmental conditions that also affect growth, such as temperature and food availability, could interact with metabolism in promoting or discouraging anadromy. We explore this hypothesis further below.

Perspective 2: Anadromy as a population-level adaptation
This perspective is based on the assumption that the tendencies in anadromy of local salmonid populations (e.g. the sea trout population of a particular stream) are adapted to local environmental conditions. This perspective is largely based on life history theory and assumes that life history strategies that produce highest reproductive output should dominate. Satterthwaite *et al.*, (2009; 2010) developed and implemented this approach for several California populations of *O. mykiss*. They modelled the expected reproductive output of anadromous versus resident females. By making simplifying assumptions, such as that life history decisions

are made on specific dates, they were able to apply an optimization model and identify how the best strategy depends on fish size, freshwater growth and survival conditions during juvenile rearing. For example, Satterthwaite *et al.*, (2010) showed that their theory produced predictions matching observed anadromy in two rivers differing strongly in growth and survival conditions.

Perspective 3: Anadromy as an individual adaptation

This perspective is like the second, but applies to individual fish instead of populations. It assumes that individuals have the ability to select anadromy or residence depending on their size, the time of year and on their individual experience of growth and mortality risk. Hence, individual fish in the same population can make different anadromy decisions when, because of small-scale habitat variation, competition, etc., they experience different growth and risk. We developed and explored this perspective using an individual-based model applied to steelhead trout in a California stream (Railsback *et al.*, 2014), using theory based closely on that of Satterthwaite *et al.*, (2009; 2010). We describe the theory and the model in more detail below.

OBJECTIVES

The goal of this paper is to explore the third perspective on anadromy. Thus, if we assume anadromy is an adaptive decision of individual fish, then what are the consequences for understanding and managing sea trout populations? Firstly, we introduce *inSALMO-FA,* our individual-based model, and explain its theory for individual variation in anadromy. This model is large and complex, but comes from a family of individual-based salmonid models that we have been testing and applying for over 15 years. We then use *inSALMO* as a virtual salmonid population and conduct experiments addressing two questions.

The first simulation experiment illustrates what *inSALMO* says about a typical management question: if we "restore" a spawning stream to improve juvenile survival and growth, will it produce more anadromous adults or simply cause more individuals to remain resident? The second experiment uses *inSALMO* to explore the hypothesis of Sloat *et al.*, (2014) that inherent variation in metabolic rates could explain genetic tendencies in anadromy. To do so, we simulate two artificial, competing species of trout that differ in their metabolic rate and competitive ability, and observe how many individuals of each species select residence instead of anadromy.

OUR VIRTUAL POPULATION: THE *inSALMO-FA* MODEL

Controlled manipulation of stream habitat conditions such as growth and survival, with accurate observation of the fate, such as size, survival or mortality, residence or anadromy, of individual fish is essentially impossible in the field, so we do so in a detailed individual-based model. The model, termed *inSALMO-FA* (the version of *inSALMO*, a general salmon model, that addresses facultative anadromy), is one of a family of stream salmonid models used for research and management applications (*c.f.* Railsback & Harvey (2001); Railsback *et al.*, (2005); (2009). Railsback *et al.*, (2014) provide a detailed description of *inSALMO-FA* and its application to several stream management questions. We summarize the model briefly with focus on its theory for the anadromy decision.

The primary purpose of *inSALMO-FA* is to provide a tool for understanding how river management actions, such as changing flow and temperature regimes, and habitat restoration projects, affect the spawning, rearing of the juvenile life stages and smolt production of facultative anadromous salmonids. The model represents individual fish and how they interact with the stream environment and with each other to determine survival and growth, and population characteristics emerge from the fate of individuals. Because the model's purpose is limited to freshwater management questions, many complexities of facultative anadromous life cycles, such as iteroparity and early maturing males, are neglected. Although *inSALMO* was developed for steelhead management in California, it can be applied to other regions and species of facultative and obligate anadromous salmonids.

The life stages represented in *inSALMO* start with adults arriving in spawning streams, through spawning, egg incubation, emergence, juvenile rearing and then outmigration. The model operates at a one-day time step over one year or a sequence of years. Habitat is represented as stream reaches, each a few hundreds to thousands of meters in length. Either one or several linked reaches can be simulated. Reach characteristics include daily flow, temperature and turbidity, along with parameters controlling overall food availability and predation risk. Each reach is made up of habitat cells as polygons laid out to capture variation in habitat while being no smaller than the area used by typical fish (Figure 1). Individual cells have variables for depth, velocity and food availability (which depends on daily flow), along with static variables representing the availability of spawning gravel, velocity shelter for drift feeding, and hiding cover. Predation risk depends on characteristics of both a fish and its cell and with the risk due to terrestrial animals (especially birds) represented separately from risk due to fish.

Spawning adults are represented as individuals with variables for sex, length, and weight. The simulated adults create redds when they spawn, which have variables for the number of live eggs and their developmental status. When eggs are fully developed, they "emerge" as new juveniles. Juveniles have variables for sex, length, weight, and their life history status as "juvenile", "pre-smolt", and "smolt", or as "pre-spawner" for individuals remaining resident. The model executes 11 actions on each simulated day:

1. Habitat is updated. The daily flow, temperature, and turbidity of each reach are read in, and the cells then update their flow-dependent variables.
2. Adults may 'arrive' from the ocean. They are 'created' and placed in their spawning reach.
3. Any female adults ready to spawn select a cell, create a redd in it, and then incur a weight loss that causes them to die within a few days.

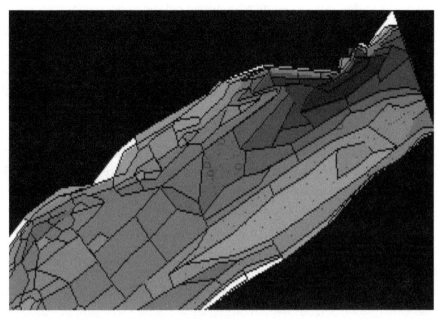

Figure 1. Example of *inSALMO*'s graphical display (part of one simulated stream reach). Habitat cells are irregular polygons, here shaded by depth. Redds appear as open ovals and juveniles as dots.

4.   Fish select their habitat by deciding which cell to occupy, with the habitat selection objective varying among life stages. A length-based hierarchy is assumed in habitat selection in that the action is executed from the largest to the smallest fish so that larger fish get first access to food and habitat.

5.   Fish grow according to the food intake and swimming costs afforded by their cell.

6.   All fish are subjected to mortality risk from terrestrial and fish predators and from starvation and disease. The probability of each kind of mortality depends on characteristics of the individual fish and their habitat cell.

7.   Juvenile fish update their life history status, with the juveniles deciding whether to become pre-smolts or pre-spawners or to remain uncommitted, and the pre-smolts deciding whether it is time to smolt and begin downstream migration.

8.   Incubating eggs are subjected to mortality due to such causes as dewatering, scour and extreme temperature.

9.   The development status of each redd is updated by a temperature-dependent amount.

10.   Eggs in fully developed redds turn into new juvenile fish.

11.   Model outputs are updated.

The primary features that set *inSALMO-FA* apart from simpler salmonid models are the two adaptive individual behaviours it represents. The first such behaviour is habitat selection (the fourth action listed above). Adults select a cell that maximizes their survival, considering both predation risk and starvation, while they do not feed; hence they select cells with low predation risk and low swimming costs. Fish in the pre-adult life stages select a cell to maximize their expected future reproductive output, which depends on survival from predation and starvation and on growth. Therefore, these fish normally select habitat where they have positive growth and relatively low risk of predation by larger fish or birds. Railsback & Harvey (2002) explored alternatives to this habitat selection assumption and found it best reproduced a variety of patterns observed in real salmonids. During an initial period after emergence, juveniles can alternatively choose "outmigration" by movement to the next downstream reach or out of the model if expected future reproductive output in their current reach is very low. (Early outmigration is typical of newly emerged juveniles that fail to find rearing habitat.) The second adaptive individual behaviour is anadromy, explained below.

ANADROMY THEORY

We adapted the theoretical approach of Satterthwaite *et al.*, (2009, 2010) to the anadromy decision of individuals for *inSALMO-FA*. In doing so, we made three simplifications and several generalizations. The first simplification was considering only two life history options: as 1) smolting within the first year after emergence and 2) remaining as a resident intending to spawn at 2-years old. Satterthwaite *et al.*, (2010) found these two options were the most commonly chosen in both model predictions and observations from two Central Valley rivers near our site. The second simplification was that mathematical optimization of the life history decision is neither realistic nor possible when simulating a population of competing individuals, so we instead used "state- and prediction-based" theory (Railsback & Harvey, 2013) by assuming individuals predict future survival and growth from their recent experience and use the predictions to estimate expected fitness under each option. In the third simplification, we neglected multiple spawning in modelling expected fitness, instead equating fitness with expected fecundity at next spawning.

The most important generalization we made was in not imposing a fixed timeline of dates for life history events, so that our simulated spawners (like the real ones at our site) arrive over many months, and juveniles reconsider anadromy every day over an extended period and could emigrate as smolts throughout the year.

Following an initial 30-day period after emergence, model juveniles decide each day whether to turn into a pre-smolt, an irreversible decision to become anadromous. If a juvenile has not become a pre-smolt by the date at which commitment to resident spawning must be made (in time to spawn the next season), it automatically becomes a pre-spawner that intends to spawn as a resident. Juveniles that decide to become anadromous begin their downstream migration after a fixed delay period during which they attempt to grow.

The decision of whether to become a pre-smolt is made by comparing the expected fitness from anadromy (F_A) to the expected fitness from residence (F_R): on any day that F_A is greater than F_R the juvenile becomes a pre-smolt. As with Satterthwaite *et al.*, (2010), we treated the fitness measures F_A and F_R as expected numbers of future offspring: the expected probability of surviving to the next spawning opportunity multiplied by the estimated number of eggs produced or fertilized at next spawning. These expected fitness measures depend on the fish's expectations of future survival and growth; expected survival and growth in freshwater are estimated as the average experienced by the individual over the past 30 days; hence, an individual's recent experience affects its decision.

For anadromy, $F_A = S_S \times S_O \times O_O$. Where S_S is the expected survival to smolting, including survival of both predation and starvation and S_O is the expected survival through the ocean life stage, from smolt outmigration through return to freshwater as an adult. Like Satterthwaite *et al.,* (2010), we modelled S_O as an increasing nonlinear function of the length at which smolts migrate downstream: S_O is low unless predicted size at outmigration is relatively high. The expected number of offspring for anadromy O_O is an assumed constant, with separate values for females and males.

Expected fitness for remaining as a resident F_R is approximated as the expected reproductive output at age 2: the product of expected survival until age-2 spawning (S_2) and the expected number of offspring at age-2 spawning (O_2). The value of O_2 is a typical fecundity relation based on expected length at spawning.

In summary, *inSALMO* represents the growth and survival of individuals as a complex function of habitat variation over time and space and competition among individuals; and the decision of whether and when to become anadromous is a complex function of date, fish size, and the growth and survival recently experienced by the individual. As parameterized for our study site, juveniles were more likely to choose anadromy when they were larger and growing more rapidly and when stream survival was lower.

Simulation Experiment 1: Effects of Habitat Restoration on Anadromy

In a previously published experiment (Railsback *et al.*, 2014), we applied *inSALMO-FA* to two study sites that represent degraded and restored habitat for spawning steelhead. As part of that study, we conducted a simple simulation experiment to predict the number of anadromous smolts emigrating from the simulated stream reach as we systematically varied both growth potential (by varying the concentration of drift food) and predation risk. The purpose was to see how the results from *inSALMO's* simulated population of unique and competing individuals differed from those of the population-level models of Satterthwaite *et al.*, (2009, 2010).

As expected from the theory for the anadromy decision, the experiment found that more juveniles *chose* anadromy when stream survival was lower and growth higher. However, the number of smolts *produced* was highest when survival was relatively high, not low – conditions that also produced high numbers of resident-spawners. The simple explanation is that when stream predation risk is high, juveniles have a stronger incentive to migrate to the ocean but fewer of them survive predation until they can migrate out. The first conclusion of this experiment was therefore that high survival should not be seen as deterrent to production of anadromous individuals; in contrast, low survival reduces production of all juveniles.

A second conclusion from this experiment was that survival was at least as important as a driver of smolt production as was growth; and that growth had very little effect on the number of residents produced. Managers may tend to place more emphasis on growth, perhaps because it is easier to observe, but *inSALMO-FA* indicates that providing a relatively safe habitat is also critical for increasing smolt production.

The third important conclusion of this experiment was that populations may not flip dramatically between being predominantly anadromous or resident as stream conditions change. Instead, habitat variability and competition among individuals, and the resulting variation among individuals in growth and risk, yielded both anadromous and resident individuals under almost all conditions.

Simulation Experiment 2: Effect of Metabolic Rate on Anadromy

Our second simulation experiment examining the consequences of *inSALMO*'s perspective of anadromy as an individual adaptation was actually to explore the first perspective, anadromy as a genetic tendency. Specifically, we explored the hypothesis of Sloat & Reeves (2014) that inherent individual variation in metabolic rates is a mechanism by which genetics can affect anadromy. Inherent metabolic differences among individuals have been documented even at the embryo life stage (Régnier *et al.*, 2010, Metcalfe *et al.*, 2016). Metabolic rates affect growth since higher metabolism reduces energy available for growth, but can also be associated with aggression and dominance because more active individuals may be more able to defend territories and dominate resources. *InSALMO-FA* contains mechanisms to link these effects of metabolism to the anadromy decision.

To explore effects of inherent differences in metabolic rate, we simulated two artificial species of steelhead-like fish. One (which we called *O. meekest*) had metabolic rates (standard plus activity respiration) set to half of *inSALMO*'s normal values. Sloat & Reeves (2014) observed that dominant, aggressive *O. mykiss* juveniles had approximately twice the metabolic rate of less-active individuals. The other species (*O. machoest*) had normal metabolic rates and higher dominance. Instead of assuming that length was the only determinant of dominance (the fish select habitat and acquire resources in order of their length), the dominance of *O. machoest* had dominance equal to 1.2 times their length (so that an *O. machoest* individual outcompetes *O. meekest* individuals up to 1.2 times its length). We initialized simulations with equal numbers of *O. machoest* and *O. meekest* spawners and then examined the number of juveniles in each species that (a) selected the anadromous life history and (b) actually smolted.

In our experiment, higher metabolism did not produce substantially higher anadromy. Fewer *O. machoest* juveniles survived long enough to decide between anadromy and residence, compared to *O. meekest* (Figure 2). The lower metabolic rate of *O. meekest* allowed them to grow more and to use safer habitat while still meeting their metabolic demands; hence, more of this species survived and they were larger. Of the individuals that survived long enough to decide between anadromy and residence, 90% of *O. machoest* chose anadromy, slightly higher than the 83% of *O. meekest*.

We drew several conclusions from this simulation experiment. Variation in metabolic rate did not seem to have strong effects on the production of smolts, apparently because the higher competitive ability that we associated with it did not compensate for the energetic costs of higher metabolism. In a sensitivity analysis experiment, we found *O. machoest* dominance to have little effect on smolt production when varied from 1.0 to 1.5. Dominance may have had little effect because low-metabolism and high-metabolism fish inherently need different kinds of habitat; with high metabolism requiring use of high-food-intake habitat even at the cost of higher predation risk, so that *O. machoest* individuals mainly competed with each other instead of with *O. meekest*.

The lower growth of *O. machoest* would discourage, not encourage, anadromy in our model where the assumed benefits of anadromy increase sharply with juvenile size and growth rate. However, field studies have found sites where anadromy appears to be associated with lower freshwater growth (Kendall *et al.*, 2015), perhaps where migration distance to the ocean is shorter and less risky than at our site. At such sites, higher metabolic rate may well promote anadromy strongly. However, high metabolic rates can have a high cost in growth and survival and so can decrease the number of fish that actually survive to the ocean.

This experiment, like the previous one, found high variation among individuals. Neither of our artificial species was consistently anadromous or resident, as both species produced both life histories.

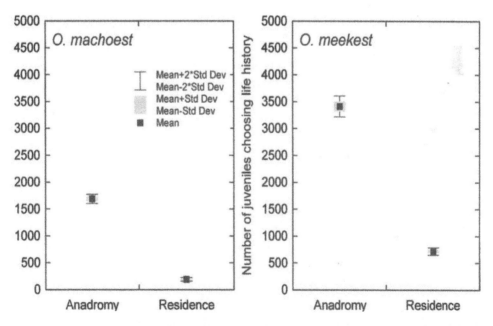

Figure 2. Results of Simulation Experiment 2. Mean and distribution over 10 replicate simulations (differing only in the random numbers that affect initial size of juveniles and mortality) in the number of juveniles selecting anadromous and resident life histories. *Left*: the artificial species with normal metabolism and high dominance. *Right*: the artificial species with low metabolism and low dominance.

CONCLUSIONS

The three perspectives on anadromy we introduced here are certainly not mutually exclusive or conflicting. For example, all three perspectives assume that anadromy is under natural selection and driven by environmental conditions and evolutionary pressures. The first and third perspectives assume that variation among individuals is important. The extent to which these perspectives have been explored so far via modelling and field studies still leaves unresolved the basic questions of how individual variation in state and experience (size; growth; perceived predation risk) interact with physiology (and perhaps individual variation in physiology) to determine anadromy. We also still have little understanding of the underlying mechanisms (e.g., metabolic rates and their effects on behaviour and growth) that link anadromy to genetics, physiology, and environment.

Understanding these questions via field and laboratory studies alone has proven very difficult, with too many variables that are too difficult to control or even measure, and it is impossible to manipulate specific characteristics of real fish. Simulation experiments of the kind we illustrate here are therefore essential as a complementary research approach. If we can capture enough essence of the real environment along with fish behaviour and physiology in computer models, we can then run completely controlled and observable simulation experiments to understand and test the consequences of alternative hypotheses. The combination of simulation and empirical experiments are a promising, yet still under-used, approach for understanding complex ecological management issues like anadromy.

Simulation experiments do still have important uncertainties, some shared with more empirical approaches. Our study, for example, assumed that individual fish are able to sense and base decisions on predation risks and growth rates, neglecting the limited ability of real fish to do so. Further, we ignore the very likely feedbacks of microevolution on behaviour (e.g., Quinn & Adams, 1996), and any interactions between such evolution and human manipulation of the environment.

Our model that implements the perspective of anadromy as an individual adaptive behaviour produced several novel and believable insights. These include the observation that survival can be as important as growth, or more so, in controlling anadromy, and that providing higher-survival habitat types can increase production of both smolts and residents. Our model indicates that individual variation in state and experience are by themselves sufficient to explain why both resident and anadromous fish are produced in the same sites.

The *inSALMO* model and the related *inSTREAM* resident trout model were developed for general use by other researchers and management biologists and are available from the authors. Publications related to the models, and some software, are available at: www. humboldt.edu/ecomodel.

ACKNOWLEDGEMENTS

The development of inSALMO-FA was funded by the U.S. Bureau of Reclamation and U. S. Fish and Wildlife Service. Simulation experiment 2 was proposed and facilitated by Jason Dunham (U. S. Geological Survey FRESC Research Group, Corvallis, Oregon, USA), with contributions from Matthew Sloat (Oregon State University) and Gordon Reeves (U. S. Forest Service Pacific Northwest Research Station, Corvallis).

REFERENCES

Kendall, N.W., McMillan, J.R., Sloat, M.R., Buehrens, T.W., Quinn, T.P., Pess, G.R., Kuzishchin, K.V., McClure, M.M. & Zabel, R.W. (2015). Anadromy and residency in steelhead and rainbow trout (*Oncorhynchus mykiss*): a review of the processes and patterns. *Canadian Journal of Fisheries and Aquatic Sciences*, **72**, 319-342.

Metcalfe, N.B., Leeuwen, T.E.V. & Killen, S.S. (*2016*). Does individual variation in metabolic phenotype predict fish behaviour and performance? *Journal of Fish Biology*, **88**, 298-321.

Quinn, T.P. & Adams, D.J. (1996). Environmental changes affecting the migratory timing of American shad and sockeye salmon. *Ecology* **77**, 1151-1162.

Railsback, S.F. & Harvey, B.C. (2001). Individual-based model formulation for cutthroat trout, Little Jones Creek, California. *General Technical Report PSW-GTR-182*, Pacific Southwest Research Station, U. S. Forest Service, Albany, California, USA, 80 pp.

Railsback, S.F. & Harvey, B.C. (2002). Analysis of habitat selection rules using an individual-based model. *Ecology* **83**, 1817-1830.

Railsback, S.F., Harvey, B.C., Hayse, J.W. & LaGory, K.E. (2005). Tests of theory for diel variation in salmonid feeding activity and habitat use. *Ecology,* **86**, 947-959.

Railsback, S.F., Harvey, B.C., Jackson, S.K. & Lamberson, R.H. (2009). InSTREAM: the individual-based stream trout research and environmental assessment model. *General Technical Report PSW-GTR-218*. Pacific Southwest Research Station, U. S. Forest Service, Albany, California, USA, 254 pp.

Railsback, S.F. & Harvey, B.C. (2013). Trait-mediated trophic interactions: is foraging theory keeping up? *Trends in Ecology & Evolution*, **28**, 119-125.

Railsback, S.F., Gard, M., Harvey, B.C., White, J.L. & Zimmerman, J.K.H. (2013). Contrast of degraded and restored stream habitat using an individual-based salmon model. *North American Journal of Fisheries Management*, **33**, 384-399.

Railsback, S.F., Harvey, B.C. & White, J.L. (2014). Facultative anadromy in salmonids: linking habitat, individual life history decisions, and population-level consequences. *Canadian Journal of Fisheries and Aquatic Sciences*, **71**, 1270-1278.

Régnier, T., Bolliet, V., Labonne, J. & Gaudin, P. (2010). Assessing maternal effects on metabolic rate dynamics along early development in brown trout (*Salmo trutta*): an individual-based approach. *Journal of Comparative Physiology B*, **180**, 25-31.

Satterthwaite, W. H., Beakes, M. P., Collins, E. M., Swank, D. R., Merz, J. E., Titus, R. G., Sogard, S. M. & Mangel, M. (2009). Steelhead life history on California's central coast: insights from a state-dependent model. *Transactions of the American Fisheries Society* **138**, 532-548.

Satterthwaite, W. H., Beakes, M. P., Collins, E. M., Swank, D. R., Merz, J. E., Titus, R. G., Sogard, S. M. & Mangel, M. (2010). State-dependent life history models in a changing (and regulated) environment: steelhead in the California Central Valley. *Evolutionary Applications*, **3**, 221-243.

Secor, D. & Kerr, L.A. (2009). Lexicon of life cycle diversity in diadromous and other fishes. *American Fisheries Society, Symposium*, **69**, 537-556.

Sloat, M.R. & Reeves, G.H. (2014). Individual condition, standard metabolic rate, and rearing temperature influence steelhead and rainbow trout (*Oncorhynchus mykiss*) life histories. *Canadian Journal of Fisheries and Aquatic Sciences*, **71**, 491-501.

Sea does matter: seascape heterogeneity influences coastal migration tactics and population connectivity in brown trout (*Salmo trutta L.*)

S. LAUNEY[1,2], E. QUÉMÉRÉ[1,2], J-L. FAGARD[3], & J-L. BAGLINIÈRE[1,2].

[1]*INRA, UMR 0985 Ecology and Health of Ecosystems, 35042 Rennes, France.*
[2]*Agrocampus Ouest, 65 rue de Saint-Brieuc, 35042 Rennes, France.*
[3]*ONEMA Station Salmonicole de Eu, Rue des Fontaines, 76260 Eu, France*

ABSTRACT

Populations of brown trout (*Salmo trutta*) from the rivers of the French Channel coast display a large continuum of migratory strategies from complete freshwater residence to anadromy. To clarify the influence of life-history strategies and natural environmental factors on population connectivity, an integrated approach was adopted that combined GIS data on marine landscape (here referred to as seascape) structure, patterns of life history variation and inferences of dispersal based on neutral genetic markers. Landscape genetics analyses showed a hierarchical genetic structure with two main genetic units corresponding to the eastern and western marine eco-regions of the English Channel delineated by the Cotentin peninsula. Within these two regions, models accounting for depth and seabed habitat type explained significantly more variance in genetic differentiation than simple isolation-by-distance models. These results indicate that the genetic structure of brown trout populations within the English Channel may be shaped by the spatial arrangement and quality of marine habitats in respect of feeding opportunities which, in turn, promote a clinal variation of migratory behaviour that determines the level of genetic exchange among neighbouring streams. This suggests that the marine environment, rarely considered in studies to date, has a role in combination with conditions in the freshwater environment in determining the levels of intra- and inter-regional gene flow among coastal brown trout populations and, also, on the evolution of migratory life-histories in *Salmo trutta*. This study also highlights the necessity for management policies to go beyond the scale of individual watersheds and incorporate knowledge of meta-population dynamics in order to protect coastal *S. trutta* populations.

Keywords: facultative anadromy; dispersal; environmental factors; micro-geographic adaptation; seascape; genetics.

INTRODUCTION

"Migration" commonly refers to the tactic that animals use to cope with adverse environmental conditions and to reach suitable areas for feeding and breeding (Nathan *et al.,* 2008; Dingle & Drake, 2007). The decision whether or not to migrate is influenced by the energetic status of the individual in its habitat, and results from a compromise between potential energy gain and survival in order to maximize its fitness (Ferguson *et al.* 2017). In various taxonomic groups, including ungulates, birds and fishes, life-history strategies are often associated with specific migration patterns that have been shown to vary considerably across the landscape in relation to ecological factors such as temperature (Nilsson *et al.,* 2006; Parn *et al.,* 2012), topography (Bohlin *et al.,* 2001; Narum *et al.,* 2008), hydromorphology (Jonsson *et al.,* 2001; Fausch *et al.,* 2002), resource shortage and climate (L'Abée-Lund *et al.,* 1989; Olsson *et al.,* 2006).

Certain species, including many salmonid fish species, can display a large gradient of migratory patterns, with strictly resident populations and strictly migratory populations being the two endpoints of the migration continuum made up of a mixture of migrants and resident individuals (Jonsson & Jonsson, 1993; Cucherousset *et al.,* 2005). Because migrants are more likely than resident individuals to contribute to genetic mixing through dispersal (Hansen & Mensberg, 1998; Knutsen *et al.,* 2001), connectivity and genetic structure among such populations strongly depends on migratory life-history traits and their spatial variation (Neville *et al.,* 2006). In particular, brown trout (*Salmo trutta*) exhibit a large plasticity of migratory variants from anadromy (sea trout), freshwater migrations between rivers and lakes and within rivers (potamodromy), to strict residency in the natal river (Baglinière & Maisse, 1999, Klemetsen *et al.,* 2003). Additionally, sea-trout populations in Northwest Europe exhibit large variations in the length of time spent at sea, ranging from a few months to several years (Ferguson, 2006). At sea, they are mostly observed in estuaries or coastal areas in shallow water where they feed on marine benthic prey (Knutsen *et al.,* 2001, Rikardsen *et al.,* 2006). They are known to stay close to the estuary (<100 km) of their natal river (Jonsson & Jonsson, 2011). However, the variation of migratory patterns between populations remains largely unexplained (Ferguson, 2006). Migratory behaviour is considered as a complex quantitative trait, expected to have evolved to a trade-off between cost and benefits. Alternative migratory tactics are considered as a threshold trait (Dodson *et al.,* 2013) with a genetic, heritable component (Thériault *et al.,* 2007) and a significant environmental trigger: but where the precise mechanisms and interactions are still largely unknown (Ferguson *et al.,* (2017).

The concept of "*landscape connectivity*" encompasses all aspects of the landscape shaping the displacement of individuals among resources or habitat patches (Baguette & Van Dyck, 2007). It describes the complex interaction between the landscape heterogeneity and the dispersal behaviour of individuals in response to this heterogeneity, leading to gene flow. Many studies have investigated the structural connectivity of landscapes, focusing on the influence of the spatial configuration of habitat patches or barriers on individual movements (Storfer *et al.,* 2007, Quéméré *et al.,* 2010). The role of landscape features in mediating gene flow across populations has been investigated in a wide range of animal and plant taxa thanks to the emergence of landscape genetics (Manel *et al.*, 2003). Landscape genetics combines molecular data and dedicated new statistical tools (Manel *et al.*, 2003; Storfer *et al.*, 2010; Perrier *et al.*, 2011) to identify landscape features that have an impact on population genetics processes, particularly those constraining or promoting gene flow (Quéméré *et al.*, 2010). In the marine environment, where direct observation of animal movements is almost impossible, this approach can be an effective tool using measures of gene flow to describe dispersal patterns. However, these studies often neglect how individual life history and especially dispersal propensity is affected by the landscape structure. Large differences in dispersal ability may be observed within and between the populations of a species according to various environmental regimes and selective pressures (Clobert *et al.*, 2004; Hanski *et al.*, 2004). Integrating knowledge on life history variation across large spatial scales would provide a more accurate assessment of landscape connectivity than only considering geographical distances or landscape heterogeneity.

It is indeed a major challenge to understand how life history, notably the migratory behavior, is affected by proximal environmental factors. Two major biogeographical gradients, namely altitude and latitude, have been shown to affect the prevalence of anadromy in species with alternative migratory tactics: but whether these gradients reflect either strict local adaptation or phenotypic plasticity is not clear. In several species, the anadromous tactic tends to decrease with altitude and/or distance from the river mouth (*see* Bohlin *et al.*, 2001 for brown trout and Narum *et al.*, 2008 for steelhead/rainbow trout). Similarly, for many salmonid species there is a latitudinal gradient in the prevalence of the anadromous form, with mostly resident populations at the southern limit of their natural range and increased anadromy to the north (Gross *et al.*, 1988 and review in Dodson *et al.*, 2013). However, some particular situations cannot be explained either by latitude or altitude gradients. For instance, there are very few or no sea trout found in the rivers in Brittany, while important sea trout populations are found to both the north and south of this region. Interestingly, this situation is similar in other species with alternative migration tactics, such as lamprey. In Brittany, only the freshwater resident species (*Lampetra planeri*) is found, while the anadromous congeneric species (*Lampetra fluviatilis)* is also found in rivers from Normandy (north) or the Atlantic coast (south). This raises the question as to whether specific environmental features could favour residency in species with a plastic life history.

Quéméré *et al.*, (2016) addressed this question by investigating the role of natural landscape features, particularly those linked to the marine environment (seascape), and life history (anadromy) in shaping the rate and patterns of migration among coastal brown trout (*Salmo trutta* L.) populations. At first, they tested the hypothesis that the pattern of connectivity and genetic structure among coastal brown trout populations reflected the spatial variation of migratory behaviour. Indeed, straying events will result in genetic exchanges between rivers and populations. Since straying rate and dispersal distance are expected to increase with the time that the fish stays away from its natal river (Ferguson, 2006), they expected intensity of gene flow between populations to increase both with the proportion of anadromous fish in the population, and with their sea age. Secondly, they tested the hypothesis that marine landscape (seascape) parameters influence gene flow between rivers. They suggest that the variability in life history is correlated with seascape heterogeneity (bottom substrate quality), so that anadromy may be promoted in rivers flowing into coastal areas with more favourable habitats, particularly in relation to feeding opportunities. We review and discuss below the main results of this work in terms of their evolutionary consequences for trout populations and for their management.

SAMPLING STRATEGY, STATISTICAL ANALYSIS & MAIN RESULTS

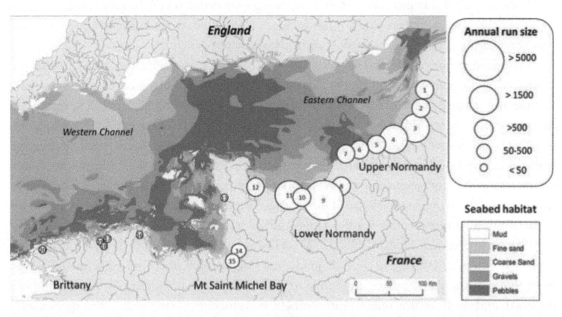

Figure 1. Map of sampled rivers with estimated annual run size of sea trouts and seabed habitats across the Channel. 1) Canche, 2) Authie, 3) Bresle, 4) Arques, 5) Saane, 6) Durdent, 7) Valmont, 8) Seine, 9) Touques, 10) Dives, 11) Orne, 12) Vire, 13) Sienne, 14) Sée, 15) Sélune, 16) Trieux, 17) Léguer, 18) Yar, 19) Douron & 20) Aber. Annual run sizes were estimated from either trapping/video counting data or from catch returns submitted by recreational fishermen (anglers' associations) (CNICS). Seabed habitats, according to the Eunis classification, were provided by the "Mapping European Seabed Habitats" (MESH project http://www.searchmesh.net). Adapted from Quéméré *et al.*, 2016.

Twenty rivers were sampled along the northern coast of France (Figure 1). These rivers flow into either the eastern English Channel or the western English Channel as delimited by the Cotentin Peninsula and the large submarine pebbly zone that extends from it. The marine habitats are characterized by contrasting hydrological, oceanographic and biogeographical conditions (Carpentier *et al.*, 2009, Figure 1), which in turn promotes important variation in primary production and trophic resources for fish. Trout populations in these rivers exhibit contrasting patterns of migratory behaviour, with a continuum from East to West. In the populations of the eastern part (Upper Normandy), the anadromous "sea trout" strategy predominates. Annual runs of several thousand fish are observed, and sea trout often spend one year at sea or very occasionally 2 years or more. In Lower Normandy (including Mont Saint Michel Bay), the populations support both resident and anadromous fish, and the proportion of 0SW finnock (= post-smolt sea trout spending only a few months at sea) is higher. In Brittany, mainly resident trout are found. Sea trout are observed in very low numbers and almost all are finnock. Rivers in Normandy and Brittany have been subjected to massive stocking from hatchery-reared strains, with hundreds of thousands of juveniles trouts released for the last 30 years. To estimate the genetic effect of this stocking on natural populations, samples were obtained from the 4 main hatcheries supplying fish to these rivers (1 in Brittany and 3 in Normandy).

Material for genetic analysis from most of the study rivers was obtained from a collection of scale samples from adult sea trout provided by recreational fishermen on a voluntary basis. These samples are stored at the Centre *National d'Interprétation des Captures de Salmonidés Migrateurs* (CNICS, ONEMA-INRA Rennes), where they were examined to estimate the juvenile river age, sea age and age at first maturity of each fish. For French sea trout population, four types of sea trout were defined according the age at first maturity (Richard & Baglinière, 1990). Type 0 corresponds to a fish which returns to freshwater to spawn after less than a year in the sea (= .0SW finnock stage). Types 1 and 2 correspond to a fish that return to spawn after one year or two years in sea respectively (as .1SW or .2SW fish). Type 3 is a fish that returns to spawn after 3 years at sea (not found in this area).

For those rivers producing only a small number of sea trout (mainly the rivers in Brittany), freshwater resident adults were sampled by electrofishing in the lower reaches of those rivers accessible to migrating sea trout. A fin clip was taken from each fish for genetic analysis. Following DNA extraction, each individual was genotyped using a set of 13 microsatellite markers (*see* Quéméré *et al.*, (2016) for details).

Standard genetic analyses were undertaken to define the patterns and rate of gene flow within and between populations in the study area and to gauge the impact of past stocking practice (*details in* Quéméré *et al.*, 2016). The main findings in respect of genetic structure were:

1. the genetic structure was best described by three main genetic units based on: a) the Eastern Channel, b) the Western Channel, c) hatchery stocks (Figure 2);
2. introgression from hatchery stocks was relatively weak in all populations (Figure 2), except for the Orne and Vire with introgression rates of 0.47 and 0.72 respectively;
3. genetic structure increased as the proportion of sea trout (and the time spent at sea) decreased: the Fst value was *a*) 0.013 (95% CI 0.0095-0.018) between rivers from Upper Normandy, *b*) 0.024 (0.0165-0.032) between rivers from Lower Normandy and *c*) 0.04 (0.034-0.048) between rivers from Brittany.

Figure 2. Individual clustering results with DAPC (Jombart et al., 2010) for K=3 (optimal number of genetic clusters) Each bar corresponds to one individual, each colour to a genetic cluster.

The influence of environmental factors (seascape) on trout dispersal between rivers was investigated using a causal modelling approach. Firstly, a least-cost path analysis was used to determine the influence of seabed-depth on sea trout dispersal. Secondly, alternative models of landscape permeability were tested based on the nature of seabed habitats (Figure 1) encountered by sea trout. The best models were selected from a multiple regression on distance matrix analysis, aimed at explaining the pair-wise genetic difference (Fst) due to different environmental variables, mainly the seabed habitat and the Cotentin barrier (*see* Quéméré *et al.*, 2016). The main findings in this respect were:

1. there was greater support for models based on least-depth distances than on shortest waterway path, indicating that sea trout disperse preferentially through shallow waters areas;
2. while geographical distance alone explained 35% of the genetic variation, this increased to 58% with the incorporation of seascape variables;
3. the best models to explain gene flow incorporated the effect of both the Cotentin barrier and the seabed habitats;
4. there was a positive correlation between the proportion of pebble/gravel areas and genetic differentiation, meaning that the least gene flow occurred with the increasing amounts of these habitat types along potential dispersal pathways.

DISCUSSION

THE DIFFERENT EFFECTS OF STOCKING PRACTICES

Intensive stocking with non-native and domesticated trout can potentially reduce the genetic diversity within and between sea trout populations and disrupt their adaptation to local conditions (Hansen *et al.*, 2002; McGinnity *et al.*, 2004; Ferguson, 2006; Perrier *et al.*, 2011). Supplementary stocking can also lead to a decrease in the genetic potential for anadromy in wild populations, hence reducing connectivity at the meta-population scale (Hansen *et al.*, 2000; Ruzzante *et al.*, 2004). Therefore, to improve population management, it is necessary to assess the impact of past and present stocking practices on the genetic integrity of wild population. Overall, the results of Quémére et al. (2016) are consistent with the extensive literature illustrating that a large majority of natural trout populations exhibit only weak evidence of any genetic influence from stocking with hatchery reared fish (*see* Ferguson, (2006) for a recent review and also Hansen *et al.*, (2010) for counter examples). Indeed, only moderate levels of admixture with hatchery-reared fish were detected in most rivers (results above, and Figure 2). For instance, all sea trout populations from the Eastern Basin of the Channel exhibited low introgression rates (Qm = 0.04-0.14) despite intensive stocking programmes with some 700,000 juveniles annually for at least 30 years. However, two notable exceptions are the Orne and the Vire populations that show high rates of admixture (Qm> 0.4) that is probably linked with their very unusual stocking history. No sea trout were reported on these rivers before an intensive stocking program began in the late 1970s (Richard, 1981) with imported stocks from Polish rivers known for their propensity to produced large multi-sea winter sea trout (Bachelier, 1966).

Interestingly, although the nearby Touques River underwent a similar stocking programme, the sea trout population remains relatively unimpacted (Qm = 0.05). This may be due to the presence of a large stock of resident wild trout prior to the stocking that were better able to out-compete hatchery-reared individuals (Araki *et al.*, 2007). The Orne and Vire Rivers were historically best known as salmon rivers, unlike the Touques River where the salmon occur only occasionally. The low impact of stocking observed in most rivers is also supported by the very small proportions of admixed individuals that was significantly lower than the expected values given the relative proportions of wild and stocked individuals (Wilcoxon signed-rank test, V=28, Pvalue<0.01). This suggested either a low survival and reproductive success of admixed individuals or some degree of reproductive isolation between wild and hatchery individuals. The introgression rates observed in this study are lower than those obtained for Atlantic salmon (*Salmo salar*) in the same area (Perrier *et al.*, 2011). In contrast, Perrier *et al.* (2011) found moderate to high levels of admixture with distant donor salmon populations in Lower Normandy (mean Qm = 0.45, range = 0.12-0.84) and Upper Normandy (mean Qm = 0.24, range = 0.05-0.57). However, it is unclear if this is due to a higher stocking intensity for salmon, or a higher resistance of brown trout to introgression. Finally, it was not possible to disentangle and identify the separate hatchery strains and thus establish the source of introgression in each wild population. However, this is not surprising since hatcheries are known to exchange eggs and young fish between culture units when their output is below local target requirements. This may have resulted in the 'homogenisation' of the hatchery strains at a regional scale.

VERY LOW GENETIC STRUCTURE IN UPPER NORMANDY: VAGRANCY OR REALITY?

Populations from Upper Normandy showed very little genetic structure. However, the samples were mostly from fish captured by fishermen in the lower reaches of the river and there is now growing evidence that sea trout can exhibit important vagrant behaviour (Chat *et al.*, (2016)). Thus, sea trout captured from the downstream part of a river may not actually reproduce in that same river and and thus not contribute genetically to the population. To address this issue, we carried out additional sampling from two major sea trout rivers from this area, the Bresle and the Arques (*see* populations 3 & 4 in Figure 1). Juveniles were obtained from several sites along a transect from the downstream to the upstream parts of the rivers, with 10 sites on the Bresle and 4 sites on the Arques (Figure 3), and then genotyped using the same set of markers as the sea trout adults sampled in the lower reaches.

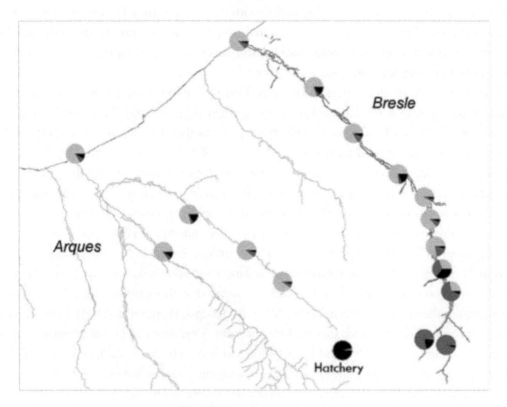

Figure 3. Genetic clustering based on STRUCTURE analysis for trout sampled along a transect in the Arques and Bresle rivers, and from the main hatchery. Each circle shows the proportions of fish from each site assigned to each of the 3 identified genetic clusters. For both rivers, the downstream site represents adult sea trout while all the other sites represent juveniles.

A clustering analysis (STRUCTURE software, Pritchard *et al.*, 2000), revealed 3 genetic units in these rivers (Figure 3). One unit (dark grey on the figure) corresponds to the uppermost sites of the Bresle River, and another unit (light grey) corresponds to all the other sites on both rivers as well as the sea trout adults. The last genetic unit (black) represented the hatchery population. This shows that the juveniles from both the Arques and Bresle rivers belong to the same genetic stock and that this is the same as the sea trout adults sampled near the river mouth. The absence of genetic structure between sea trout and resident trout in the lower reaches has also been reported on the rivers Touques, Dives and Oir (Charles *et al.*, 2005). Thus, the low genetic structure in Normandy is not an artifact caused by sea trout vagrancy but the consequence of actual gene flow between neighbouring populations. From a functional viewpoint, populations from Upper Normandy in particular can actually be considered as one large genetically inter-connected meta-population.

The only exception is the upstream portion of the Bresle River, where sea trout are not able to spawn either due to the presence of physical barriers to upstream migration (dams), or ecological restriction (spawning areas not suitable for sea trout in small streams because of width and substrate size and quality). Higher introgression from hatchery stocks was detected in two sampling sites in this area. This confirms previous reports that stocking with hatchery-reared trout results in greater introgression in the freshwater component of a river than in the anadromous component, which may be attributed to a higher mortality at sea of hatchery-reared trout that became anadromous (Ferguson 2006).

ROLE OF LANDSCAPE ON MIGRATION PATTERNS

These results show that seascape heterogeneity influences rates and patterns of gene flow, with a direct barrier effect of the Cotentin peninsula and also with the indirect effect of marine habitats on migratory strategy (*see below*), which subsequently determines the level of genetic exchange between streams.

The very low numbers of sea trout entering the rivers flowing into the Western Channel is evidenced by the low catches and biological characteristics of fish reported by the recreational fishermen (CNICS data, ONEMA-INRA Rennes). For instance, the recorded catch in the rivers located to the West of the Cotentin Peninsula from 2011-2014 was more than 10 times lower than the total sea trout catch recorded in the rivers located to the East of Cotentin (Table 1). Furthermore, the average size of each fish was much smaller in the western area than in the eastern area. This size difference is related to a shift in the proportion of the sea-age type of adult sea trout (Richard & Baglinière 1990) returning in the rivers (Table 1). In the western area, Type 0 (finnock) predominate (64.8%), while 95% of the sea trout in the eastern area are Type 1 or 2 (1 or 2 sea-winter fish). Finnock move up and down the coast near estuaries, moving in and out of freshwater with the tides. This stage can be considered as a first phase in the exploration and dispersal of the brown trout in the sea, especially since it has been shown that the fast growing resident trout juveniles could migrate into the sea without smoltification (Tanguy *et al.*, 1994). If a fish exploring the estuaries or nearby coastal zones discovers potentially rich sea feeding areas, it may remain at sea for one or more sea winters to take full advantage of the improved feeding opportunities for faster growth and associated reproductive success. Conversely, if the feeding conditions at sea are poor, the fish may restrict its sea residence period to a just a few weeks or months.

Soft-bottom habitats are very productive. They are more prevalent in the Eastern Channel, and represent essential nursery areas for sand eels, sprat and herrings (Carpentier *et al.*, 2009) on which sea trout are known to feed preferentially at sea (Knutsen *et al.*, 2001). By contrast, pebbly/rocky bottoms are more prevalent in coastal areas in the Western Channel. In addition, in the Eastern area, rivers are calcareous resulting in a faster freshwater growth rate than in the granitic rivers of Brittany. Fish with a higher growth rate in freshwater may have higher energetic needs when they arrive at sea, and thus spend more time there if they encounter favourable feeding conditions. Thus, the variability in migration behaviour observed along the French coasts of the Channel could be, at least in some part, due to micro-geographical adaptations to local gradients in food and foraging conditions in both the freshwater and marine environment. This accords with the *"food availability hypothesis"* (Gross *et al.*, 1988), which argues that aquatic productivity is the main driver in the evolution of diadromous migration.

Table 1. Number and biological characteristics of voluntary sea trout catches recorded during 2011-2014 fishing seasons (data from the French Centre of salmonid catch records – CNICS). Three types of sea trout were defined according the age at first maturity (see text).

Parameter	Rivers to the West of Contentin Peninsula	Rivers to the East of Contentin Peninsula
Reported Rod catch	82	1,073
No. Fish Sampled	70	983
Mean Length (mm)	461 (SD = 95.46)	579 (SD = 82.56)
Type 1 (= 0SW)	64.8%	6%
Type 2 (= 1SW)	35.2%	90%
Type 3 (= 2SW)	0.0%	4%

PLASTICITY IN ANADROMY AND GLOBAL CHANGE

The reality of global climate change is now widely accepted, and this may have major impacts on natural habitats and, therefore, a profound effect on population dynamics in many taxa (Parmesan & Yohe, 2003). The resilience of organisms to such changes can depend upon their ability to colonize and occupy new habitats. Species can respond to stress induced by changes in their environment in two different ways: either they can shift their geographical range by leaving hostile habitats and colonizing ones that are more favourable or they can adapt to the new conditions by plastic responses or by genetic adaptation. For species with complex life histories, response to environmental changes may be hard to predict because selection can act simultaneously but in different ways on multiple traits at different phases of their life cycles. For instance, anadromous salmonids have to respond to changes in both the river, where they reproduce, and in the ocean, where they migrate to feed. Thus, understanding the environmental constraints on phenotypic plasticity and the extent of evolutionary variation in this plasticity is crucial for predicting the effect of climate change on the persistence of natural populations. This is even more important when the trait under scrutiny is linked directly to the capacity of a species to migrate and hence escape unfavourable conditions and colonize new environments. The brown trout (*Salmo trutta*) is considered one of the most plastic of all salmonids in term of its life history variation (Elliot, 1994; Baglinière, 1999), particularly in its migratory tactics, which should make it relatively resilient as a species to the effects of climate change. However, because homing behaviour is not absolute, the anadromous form is a potential source of dispersion and gene flow for the species. Consequently, changes in the expression of anadromy could have evolutionary consequences not only for populations at a local geographical scale but also for the species at a broader spatial and temporal scale. Alternative migratory tactics reflect both phenotypic plasticity in response to environmental conditions and local adaptation at a very fine scale throughout the life cycle, which also indicates that global change may affect different populations in different ways (Jensen *et al*. 2008). Following a Workshop in Copenhagen in 2013, the report of the ICES Working Group on Sea Trout (WKTRUTTA) stressed that, although partial migration patterns and their evolution under global change and anthropogenic disturbances had major implication for stocks structuring and assessment, knowledge on the factors determining these patterns was scarce. They highlighted the need for further research to identify the genetic influences of life-history diversity and their interactions with environmental factors (ICES. 2013). Quémeré et al. (2016) findings highlight the need to take into account the marine environment in these studies, together with the freshwater environment, because environmental factors at sea (and perturbations that might occur in coastal areas) can have important impacts on the adaptive capacities of brown trout populations.

PERSPECTIVES AND IMPLICATION FOR MANAGEMENT

This study identifies the need for a more "holistic" approach to encompass the spatial variability in life history patterns and their heterogeneity at broader scales when studying the ecology and evolution of long distance migratory aquatic animals (Bisbal & McConnaha, 1998). The importance of the freshwater phase in the promotion of an anadromous strategy has been recognized through effects on growth and growth rate (high-growth-rate individuals tend to migrate (Cucherousset *et al*., 2006; Acolas *et al*., 2012) or through landscape barriers (Narum *et al*., 2008), but also see discussions in Ferguson et al., (2016). However, there is a need to take into account the role of the marine environment to understand how the trade-offs between the costs and benefits of anadromy are resolved in different rivers. Our study was restricted to the French coast of the Channel and would need to be expanded. As a first step, we need to "cross the Channel" and investigate if similar correlations between variability in migratory behaviour and seascape heterogeneity can be found in sea trout populations in the rivers in southern England.

The landscape genetics approach used here can help map the areas of marine habitat that are selected preferentially by sea trout for spatial dispersal, and thus identify the main dispersal corridors, particularly in those preferred shallow coastal areas. This will help to assess the impact of coastal development projects, such as inshore and offshore wind farms and tidal energy projects, such as estuary barrages and tidal lagoons. A marine environment of good quality, especially in terms of feeding opportunities, is crucial for the conservation and maintenance of sea trout populations. For instance, in the Bresle river, one of the most important sea trout rivers in France, it has been shown that the juvenile survival rate from egg to smolt is much lower for trout (0.21%) than for Atlantic salmon (1.24%), while the survival rate at sea (from smolt to returning adult) is four times higher for sea trout at 20.3% than for salmon at 4.9% (Euzenat et al., 2012; Baglinière & Ombredane, 2013). Clearly, any deterioration in the marine environment could have catastrophic effects on the long-term evolution of the sea trout populations.

Our study further highlights that effective management policies for protecting *S. trutta* populations should not be only at the scale of local watersheds but at larger regional scale. More data are needed, particularly long-term life history data, in order to better understand the impact of environmental factors (both in freshwater and in the marine environment) on the expression of facultative anadromy in brown trout and its consequences in terms of gene flow. In order to achieve this, standardization of monitoring practices, tagging information and the integration of data collections at national or even international level are of utmost importance.

In France, for instance, certain recommendations can be made for the better conservation of sea trout. Monitoring should continue on sea trout populations on the index rivers (Bresle and Oir), where biological data has been collected on migrating smolts and returning adults for over 30 years. This monitoring could be optimized by mark-and-recapture studies using pit-tags, but our findings also show that this monitoring should be expanded to include nearby rivers to understand how the populations are evolving at the meta-population scale, particularly in the case of the Bresle River where genetic exchanges with nearby rivers are frequent. This study used samples and biological information collected by recreational fishermen. However, while reports of rod catches are mandatory for Atlantic salmon, sea trout rod catches are currently submitted on a voluntary basis only. Thus, the available data for sea trout is, therefore, not comprehensive, and can be biased as fishermen tend to target bigger fish that have spent more time at sea. Sea trout fishermen might be motivated to declare and sample more sea trout, either by mandatory measures or through educational programs in which researchers and local management agencies can collaborate in order to raise awareness about the importance and management value of such samples. Thus, a more comprehensive database on the biological characteristics of sea trout could be accumulated. There is also available information on sea trout from video-counters and/or trapping stations that is currently not fully used and which could be incorporated into models to estimate the abundance of sea trout populations and changes in the distribution area of the species at a larger geographic scale.

ACKNOWLEDGMENTS

We wish to thank: C. Rivière, C. Le Rohic, F. Fournel, G. Euzenat, J. Normand, the SD76 (ONEMA), G. Garrot (SEINORMIGR), Y. Salaville, I. Mirkovic and H. Catroux (respectively Fédération de Pêche of Calvados, Seine-Maritime and Côte d'Armor), the Centre national d'interprétation des captures de salmonidés migrateurs (CNICS, ONEMA) and the U3E INRA unit for their valuable help in collecting scale samples and data on migratory patterns and stocking practices. We also thank A.L. Besnard for her valuable help with the lab work. Samples were genotyped at the sequencing platform of Le Rheu, France. This study was supported by a grant from ONEMA and the European Regional Development Fund (Transnational program Interreg IV, Project AARC – Atlantic Aquatic Resource Conservation).

REFERENCES

Araki, H., Waples, R.S., Ardren, W.R., Cooper, B. & Blouin, M.S. (2007). Effective population size of steelhead trout: influence of variance in reproductive success, hatchery programs, and genetic compensation between life-history forms. *Molecular Ecology*. **16**, 953-66.

Bachelier, R. (1966). Le saumon polonais. *Knowledge and Management of Aquatic Ecosytems*, **220**, 101-108

Baglinière, J-L., (1999). Introduction: The brown trout (*Salmo trutta* L.): its origin, distribution and economic and scientific significance. In: *Biology and Ecology of the Brown and Sea trout* (Baglinière, J-L. & Maisse, G. *Eds.*), Springer-Praxis, Chichester, pp. 1-12.

Baglinière, J-L. & Maisse, G. (*Eds.*). (1999). Biology and Ecology of the Brown and Sea Trout, Springer-Praxis, Chichester, 286 pp

Baglinière, J-L. & Ombredane, D. (2013). Le saumon atlantique (*Salmo salar*) et la truite commune (*Salmo trutta*) dans le Massif armoricain: éléments d'écologie et de fonctionnement des populations. *Pen Ar Bed*, **215**, 9-14

Baguette, M. & Van Dyck, H. (2007). Landscape connectivity and animal behavior: functional grain as a key determinant for dispersal. *Landscape Ecology*, **22**, 1117-1129.

Bohlin, T., Pettersson, J. & Degerman, E . (2001). Population density of migratory and resident brown trout (*Salmo trutta*) in relation to altitude: evidence for a migration cost. *Journal of Animal Ecology*, **70**, 112-121.

Carpentier, A., Coppin, F., Curet, L., Dauvin, J-C., Delavenne, J., Dewarumez, J-M., Dupuis, L., Foveau, A., Garcia, C., Gardel, L., Harrop, S., Just, R., Koubbi, P., Lauria, V., Martin, C., Meaden, G., Morin, J., Ota, Y., Rostiaux, E., Smith, B., Spilmont, N., Vaz, S., Villanueva, C-M., Verin, Y., Walton J. & Warembourg C. (2009). Atlas des Habitats des Ressources Marines de la Manche Orientale – CHARM II / Channel Habitat Atlas for marine Resource Management – CHARM II, IFREMER. 626 pp.

Charles, K., Guyomard, R., Hoyheim, B., Ombredane, D. & Baglinière, J-L (2005). Lack of genetic differentiation between anadromous and non-anadromous sympatric trout in a Normandy population. *Aquatic Living Resources*, **18**, 65-69.

Chat, J., Masson. S., Manicki, A., Geraud. F., Rives, J., Lange. F., Huchet, E., Coste. P., Aymes, J-C. & Lepais, O. (2017). In: *Sea Trout: Science a & Management*. (Graeme Harris. *Ed.*). Proceedings of the 2nd International Sea Trout Symposium, October 2015, Dundalk, Ireland. Troubador, 354–370.

Clobert, J., Ims, R. & Rousset, F. (2004). Causes, mechanisms and consequences of dispersal. In: *Ecology, genetics and evolution of metapopulation* (Hanski I, Gaggiotti O Eds.), Elsevier Academic Press, Amsterdam, 307-335.

Cucherousset, J., Ombredane, D., Charles, K., Marchand, F. & Baglinière, J-L. (2005). A continuum of life history tactics in a brown trout (*Salmo trutta*) population. *Canadian Journal of Fisheries and Aquatic Sciences*, **62**, 1600-1610.

Cucherousset, J., Ombredane, D., Baglinière, J-L. (2006). Linking juvenile growth and migration behaviour of brown trout (*Salmo trutta*) using individual PIT-tagging. *Cahiers de Biologie Marine*, **47**, 73-78.

Dingle, H. & Drake, V.A. (2007). What is migration? *Bioscience*, **57**, 113 – 121.

Dodson, J.J., Aubin-Horth, N., Theriault, V. & Paez, D.J. (2013). The evolutionary ecology of alternative migratory tactics in salmonid fishes. *Biological Reviews*, **88**, 602-625.

Elliott, J.M. (1994). Quantitative Ecology and the Brown Trout. Oxford University Press, Oxford, 286 pp.

Fausch, K.D., Torgersen, C.E., Baxter, C.V. & Li, H.W. (2002). Landscapes to riverscapes: Bridging the gap between research and conservation of stream fishes. *Bioscience*, **52**, 483-498.

Ferguson, A. (2006). Genetics of Sea Trout, with Particular Reference to Britain and Ireland. In: *Sea Trout: Biology, Conservation & Management* (Graeme Harris & Nigel Milner. *Eds.*). Proceedings of the 1st International Sea Trout Symposium, July 2004, Cardiff, Wales, UK. Blackwell Publishing, Oxford, 155-182.

Ferguson, A., Reed, T., McGinnity, P. & Prodöhl, P. (2017). Anadromy in brown trout (*Salmo trutta*): A review of the relative roles of genes and environmental factors and the implications for management and conservation. In: *Sea Trout: Science a & Management*. (Graeme Harris. *Ed.*). Proceedings of the 2nd International Sea Trout Symposium, October 2015, Dundalk, Ireland. Troubador, 1–40.

Gross, M.R., Coleman, R.M. & McDowall, R.M. (1988). Aquatic productivity and the evolution of diadromous fish migration. *Science*, **239**, 1291-1293.

Hansen, M.M. & Mensberg, K.L.D. (1998). Genetic differentiation and relationship between genetic and geographical distance in Danish sea trout (*Salmo trutta* L.) populations. *Heredity*, **81**, 493-504.

Hansen, M.M., Ruzzante, D.E., Nielsen, E.E. & Mensberg, K.L.D. (2000). Microsatellite and mitochondrial DNA polymorphism reveals life-history dependent interbreeding between hatchery and wild brown trout (*Salmo trutta* L.). *Molecular Ecology*, **9**, 583-594.

Hansen, M.M., Ruzzante, D.E., Nielsen, E.E., Bekkevold, D. & Mensberg, K.L.D. (2002). Long-term effective population sizes, temporal stability of genetic composition and potential for local adaptation in anadromous brown trout (*Salmo trutta*) populations. *Molecular Ecology*, **11**, 2523-2535.

Hansen, M.M., Meier, K. & Mensberg K.L.D. (2010). Identifying footprints of selection in stocked brown trout populations: a spatio-temporal approach. *Molecular Ecology*, **19**, 1787-1800.

Hanski, I., Eralahti, C., Kankare, M., Ovaskainen, O. & Siren H. (2004). Variation in migration propensity among individuals maintained by landscape structure. *Ecology Letters*, **7**, 958-966.

ICES. (2013). Report of the Workshop on Sea Trout (WKTRUTTA), 12-14 November 2013, ICES Headquarters, Copehagen, Denmark, ICES CM 2013/SSGEF:15. 243 pp.

Jensen, L.F, Hansen, M.M., Pertoldi, C., Holdensgaard, G., Mensberg, K.L.D, & Loeschcke, V. (2008). Local adaptation in brown trout early life-history traits: implications for climate change adaptability. *Proceedings of the Royal Society London Series B: Biological Sciences,* **275**, 2859–2868.Jombart, T., Devillard, S. & Balloux, F. (2010). Discriminant analysis of principal components: a new method for the analysis of genetically structured populations. *BMC Genetics*, **11**, 94.

Jonsson, B. & Jonsson, N. (1993.) Partial migration: niche shift versus sexual maturation in fishes. *Reviews in Fish Biology and Fisheries*, **3**, 348-365.

Jonsson, B. & Jonsson, N. (Eds.). (2011). Ecology of Atlantic Salmon and Brown Trout: Habitats as Template for Life Histories. Springer Verlag, Heidelberg, 655p.

Jonsson, B., Jonsson, N., Brodtkorb, E. & Ingebrigtsen, P.J. (2001). Life-history traits of Brown Trout vary with the size of small streams. *Functional Ecology*, **15**, 310-317.

Klemetsen, A., Amundsen, P.A., Dempson, J.B., Jonsson, B., Jonsson, N., O'Connell, M. F. & Mortensen, E. (2003). Atlantic salmon *Salmo salar* L., brown trout *Salmo trutta* L. and Arctic charr *Salvelinus alpinus*.): a review of aspects of their life histories. *Ecology of Freshwater Fish*, **12**, 1-59.

Knutsen, J.A., Knutsen, H., Gjosaeter, J. & Jonsson, B. (2001). Food of anadromous brown trout at sea. *Journal of Fish Biology,* **59**, 533-543.

Knutsen, H., Jorde, P.E., Sannaes H, Hoelzel, A. R., Bergstad, O.A., Stefanni, S., Johansen, T. & Stenseth, N. C. (2009). Bathymetric barriers promoting genetic structure in the deepwater demersal fish tusk (*Brosme brosme*). *Molecular Ecology*, **18**, 3151-3162.

L'Abée-Lund, J.H., Jonsson, B., Jensen AJ, Saettem, L.F., Heggberget, T.G., Bjorn O. Johnsen B. O. & Naesje T. F. (1989). Latitudinal variation in life-history characteristics of sea-run migrant brown trout *Salmo trutta*. *Journal of Animal Ecology*, **58**, 525-542.

Manel, S., Schwartz., MK, Luikart., G & Taberlet P. (2003). Landscape genetics: combining landscape ecology and population genetics. *Trends in Ecology & Evolution*, **18**, 189-197.

McGinnity, P., Prodöhl, P., Ó Maoiléidigh, N., Hynes, R., Cotter, D., Baker, N., O'Hea, B. & Ferguson A. (2004). Differential lifetime success and performance of native and non-native Atlantic salmon examined under communal natural conditions. *Journal of Fish Biology*, **65**, 173-187.

Narum, S.R., Zendt, J.S., Graves, D. & Sharp, W.R. (2008). Influence of landscape on resident and anadromous life history types of *Oncorhynchus mykiss*. *Canadian Journal of Fisheries and Aquatic Sciences*, **65**, 1013-1023.

Nathan, R., Getz, W. M., Revilla, E., Holyoak, M., Kadmon, R., Saltz, D. & Smouse, P. E. (2008). A movement ecology paradigm for unifying organismal movement research. *Proceedings of the National Academy of Sciences*, **105**, 19052-19059.

Neville, H., Dunham, J. & Peacock M. (2006). Assessing connectivity in salmonid fishes with DNA microsatellite markers. In: *Connectivity Conservation* (Crooks, K, Sanjayan, M. *Eds*.). Cambridge University Press. 318-342.

Nilsson, A.L.K., Lindström, Å., Jonzén, N., Nilsson, S.G. & Karlsson, L. (2006). The effect of climate change on partial migration – the blue tit paradox. *Global Change Biology*, **12**, 2014-2022.

Olsson, I.C., Greenberg, L.A., Bergman, E. & Wysujack, K. (2006). Environmentally induced migration: the importance of food. *Ecology Letters,* **9**, 645-651.

Parmesan, C. & Yohe, G. (2003). A globally coherent fingerprint of climate change impacts across natural systems. *Nature*, **421**, 37-42

Pärn, H., Ringsby, T.H., Jensen, H. & Saether, B.E. (2012). Spatial heterogeneity in the effects of climate and density-dependence on dispersal in a house sparrow metapopulation. *Proceedings of the Royal Society B*, **279**, 144-152.

Perrier, C., Guyomard, R., Baglinière, J-L. & Evanno, G. (2011). Determinants of hierarchical genetic structure in Atlantic salmon populations: environmental factors vs. anthropogenic influences. *Molecular Ecology*, **20**, 4231-4245.

Pritchard, J., Stephens, M. & Donnelly, P. (2000). Inference of population structure using multilocus genotype data. *Genetics*, **155**, 945-959.

Quéméré, E., Crouau-Roy, B., Rabarivola, C., Louis, E.E., Jr. & Chikhi, L. (2010). Landscape genetics of an endangered lemur (*Propithecus tattersalli*) within its entire fragmented range. *Molecular Ecology*, **19**, 1606-1621.

Quéméré, E., Baglinière, J-L., Roussel, J-M., Evanno, G., McGinnity, P. & Launey, S. (2016). Seascape and its effect on migratory life-history strategy influences gene flow among coastal brown trout (*Salmo trutta*) populations in the English Channel. *Journal of Biogeography*, **43**, 498–509

Richard, A. (1981). Observations préliminaires sur les populations de truite de mer (*Salmo trutta* L.) en Basse-Normandie. *Bulletin Français de la Pêche et de la Pisciculture*, **283**, 114-124

Richard, A. & Baglinière, J-L., (1990). Description et interprétation des écailles de truites de mer (Salmo trutta L.) de deux rivières de Basse-Normandie : L'Orne et la Touques. *Bulletin Français de la Pêche et de la Pisciculture*, **319**, 239-257.

Rikardsen, A.H., Amundsen, P.A., Knudsen, R. & Sandring, S. (2006). Seasonal marine feeding and body condition of sea trout (*Salmo trutta*) at its northern distribution. *ICES Journal of Marine Science*, **63**, 466-475.

Ruzzante, D.E., Hansen, M.M., Meldrup, D. & Ebert, K.M. (2004). Stocking impact and migration pattern in an anadromous brown trout (*Salmo trutta*) complex: where have all the stocked spawning sea trout gone? *Molecular Ecology*, **13**, 1433-1445.

Storfer, A., Murphy, M.A., Evans, J.S., Goldberg, C.S., Robinson, S., Spear, S.F., Dezzani, R., Delmelle, E., Vierling, L. & Waits, L.P. (2007). Putting the "landscape" in landscape genetics. *Heredity*, **98**, 128-142.

Storfer, A., Murphy, M.A., Spear, S.F., Holderegger, R. & Waits, L.P. (2010). Landscape genetics: where are we now? *Molecular Ecology*, **19**, 3496-3514.

Tanguy, J-M., Ombredane, D., Baglinière, J-L. & Prunet, P. (1994). Aspects of parr-smolt transformation in anadromous and resident forms of brown in trout (*Salmo trutta*) in comparison with Atlantic salmon (*Salmo salar*). *Aquaculture*,**121**, 51-63.

Theriault, V., Garant, D., Bernatchez, L. & Dodson, J.J. (2007). Heritability of life-history tactics and genetic correlation with body size in a natural population of brook charr (*Salvelinus fontinalis*). *Journal of Evolutionary Biology*, **20**, 2266-2277.

Population genetics and Genetic Stock Identification of anadromous *Salmo trutta* from the Irish Sea and adjacent areas, using microsatellite DNA loci

P. A. PRODÖHL[1], A. ANTONIACOMI[2], C. BRADLEY[1], J. CARLSSON[3], G. R. CARVALHO[4], J. COUGHLAN[2], J. COYNE[6], M. E. CROSS[2], M. C. CROSS[2], C. A. DAVIES[5], E. DILLANE[2], P. GARGAN[6], R. A. HYNES[1], P. McGINNITY[2], N. MILNER[4], T. REED[2], W. ROCHE[6], M. TAYLOR[7], N. TYSKLIND[8] & T. F. CROSS[2]

[1]*Institute for Global Food Security, School of Biological Sciences, Queen's University Belfast, Medical Biology Centre, 97 Lisburn Road Belfast BT9 7BL, Northern Ireland, UK.*
[2]*Aquaculture and Fisheries Development Centre, School of Biological, Earth and Environmental Sciences, University College Cork, Ireland.*
[3]*Area 52 Research Group, School of Biology & Environmental Science/Earth Institute, University College Dublin, Belfield, Dublin, Ireland.*
[4]*Molecular Ecology & Fisheries Genetics Laboratory, School of Biological Sciences, Bangor University, Deiniol Road, Bangor LL57 2UW. UK.*
[5]*Centre for Applied Marine Sciences, School of Ocean Sciences, Bangor University, Menai Bridge, Anglesey, LL59 5AB, UK.*
[6]*Inland Fisheries Ireland, 3044 Lake Drive, Citywest Business Campus, Dublin D24 Y265, Dublin.*
[7]*School of Biological Sciences, University of East Anglia, Norwich NR4 7TJ. UK.*
[8]*INRA, UMR EcoFoG, CNRS, Cirad, AgroParisTech, Université des Antilles, Université de Guyane, 97310 Kourou, France.*

ABSTRACT

The management and conservation of anadromous sea trout (*Salmo trutta* L.) during the marine phase of their life history depends on a better understanding of their ecology and migratory behaviour in the sea. To address this knowledge gap, a Genetic Stock Identification (GSI) exercise using Individual Assignment (IA) was undertaken. A panel consisting of 18 microsatellite nuclear DNA loci was used for the construction of a genetic baseline for sea trout from river systems flowing into the Irish and Celtic Seas. Sampling design involved the collection of over 5,000 juvenile fish, from putative sea trout spawning areas at 99 riverine locations. This comprehensive sampling programme of Irish, Manx, Scottish, English and Welsh rivers was designed to include the majority of the larger rivers contributing sea trout to the Irish and Celtic Seas. Genomic DNA extracted from these specimens was genotyped and analysed, to examine patterns of population structure, and produce a genetic baseline for assignment of marine-caught individuals (post smolts and adults) of unknown origin. A highly genetically-distinct trout group from SW Ireland was included as an outlier. STRUCTURE analysis of riverine genetic data revealed complex patterns of population structuring, which was best explained by nine major genetically-distinct regional groups within the Irish and British database. A self-assignment exercise, based upon identified populations, using the ONCOR algorithm, demonstrated the applicability of the database for assignment, particularly at the regional level. Assignment to regional reporting groups, rather than specific populations, was then utilised for marine-caught samples. Marine sampling, mainly in the Irish Sea, secured over 1,000 adult sea trout for individual assignment analysis, using the programme ONCOR. Marine-captured fish were used for spatial distribution mapping purposes when they could be scored for 14 or more loci, and were assignable to one of the nine regional groupings, with assignment probability scores equal or greater than 0.7. Results indicate that sea trout in the Irish Sea originate from a large number of rivers throughout the sampling area, and constitute substantially mixed marine aggregations. Individual assignment suggests that most inferred movement is region specific, the majority of fish being captured in the proximity of their natal rivers. However, there was strong evidence for long range migrations, with some fish traversing the Irish Sea or moving between the Irish and Celtic Seas.

Keywords: Celtic Sea; genetic stock identification; individual assignment; Irish sea; life history; marine distribution; microsatellite loci; sea trout.

INTRODUCTION

The anadromous sea trout (*Salmo trutta* L.) in the Irish Sea and adjacent areas, represents an important resource in terms of its social, economic and biodiversity value to local communities. The sustainability of these fisheries is currently susceptible to a range of anthropogenic pressures from estuarine barriers to migration and coastal renewable energy development to climate change. In recent years, increasing concerns about the status of sea trout has focussed attention on the need for comprehensive and sustainable research, with emphasis on its marine phase, where the species is particularly exposed to a number of threats and pressures. At all stages in their life cycle, individuals belonging to each distinct sea trout population are thought to vary in the route, distance and duration of their migrations, the timing of their return from sea, and in growth trajectories and maturation schedules, in response to local environmental conditions. As recently suggested by Hilborn *et al.* (2003) and Schindler *et al.* (2010) for anadromous Pacific salmonids, such diversity in life-history strategies plays a pivotal role in the long-term resilience and productivity of meta-populations and species in continuously shifting environments.

While a substantial body of literature is available on the phylogeography and genetic diversity of fresh water resident brown trout from Britain and Ireland (*see review in* McKeown *et al.*, 2010), to date there has been relatively little work focusing on the population genetics of sea trout (*but see reviews in* Ferguson, (2006), Ferguson *et al.*, (2017). More notably there are no genetic data from recent studies on sea trout populations that are native to the rivers flowing into the Irish or Celtic Seas. In order to have an understanding of the marine ecology of anadromous *Salmo trutta* L. in the Irish Sea and adjacent areas, it is essential to acquire stock specific information on their biology and distribution at sea. Reliable and robust identification, and characterization of population or regional population units is fundamental to ensuring informed management and long-term viability of exploited fish species. Sea trout in the Irish Sea and adjacent areas are unlikely to be a single homogenous group, but rather to consist of fish derived from many genetically different contributing populations (i.e. mixed stocks).

In contrast to many other vertebrates, a substantially larger proportion of the total genetic, phenotypic and life history variation observed in brown trout/sea trout (*Salmo trutta*) is distributed among populations and particularly among regional groupings of populations (Ferguson 1989, 2004). This makes the species ideal for GSI type studies.

Genetic stock identification (GSI) is acknowledged as a useful, reliable and cost effective method of acquiring data on intra-specific migration and geographic distribution patterns. GSI has been deployed successfully for the study of many salmonid species in marine and freshwater aggregations (*see review by* Manel *et al.*, (2005) and, more specifically, recent publications by Bradbury (2015; 2016), Ensing *et al.* (2013), Griffiths *et al.* (2010), Gauthier-Ouellet *et al.* (2009) for Atlantic salmon (*Salmo salar*) and by Swatdipong *et al.* (2013) and Mäkenin (2015) for brown trout (*S. trutta* L.) in freshwaters. However, with very few exceptions to date, (Koljonen *et al.*, 2014, King *et al.*, 2016), the application of GSI in the study of anadromous sea trout has been comparatively limited.

Among the major advantages of genetic methods over conventional physical tagging for mixed stock analyses are:

1. The ability to identify all fish sampled and not just those that have been physically tagged previously.
2. No physical marking is involved and there is no bias due to additional mortality as a consequence of handling or the presence of an external tag.
3. There is no reliance on hatchery tagged fish as surrogates of wild populations.

GSI and its more recent development, individual assignment (IA), involves setting up a genetic baseline, using assumed-neutral molecular markers, from as many populations as possible of those thought to contribute to a mixed stock aggregation. A sample is then taken from a mixed aggregation and screened for the same molecular markers. Using one of the available statistical methods e.g. ONCOR (Kalinowski *et al.*, 2007); cBAYES (Neaves *et al.*, 2005); GENECLASS (Piry *et al.*, 2004); STRUCTURE (Pritchard *et al.* 2000), the mixture is divided into proportions of each contributing population or regional population grouping (in traditional GSI approaches) or assigned individually (in IA exercises). Previous work with fish of known origin (Hauser *et al.*, 2006) and simulation studies (Paetkau *et al.*, 2004; Anderson *et al.*, 2008) has demonstrated the exceptional accuracy of these methods. However, this is provided that natal philopatry predominates in the target species, that the baseline is comprehensive and that there are statistically-significant genetic differences between the populations or groups of populations comprising the baseline. In the latter respect, the larger the genetic differences among populations or larger groupings, the more accurate the assignments. The level of genetic differentiation will invariably be a function of geographical proximity, population size and the interplay of genetic drift and levels of gene flow between populations from the same or different rivers (Ensing *et al.*, 2011). The level of inherent population genetic differentiation is also relevant for the assessment of the quality of the baseline. Thus, confident and reliable individual assignment is enhanced if contributing baseline populations or regional groups of populations are sufficiently differentiated from each other.

As part of the Celtic Sea Trout Project (see introduction and other chapters of this book), the main objectives of the present study were:

To identify the natal freshwater population or regional population grouping of putative sea trout juveniles from as many riverine locations as possible around the Irish and Celtic Seas.

To describe the distribution and the likely migration patterns of sea trout primarily in the Irish Sea, during their marine phase.

MATERIALS AND METHODS

SAMPLING APPROACH

Freshwater sampling for the genetic baseline
Based on local Fisheries Officers' knowledge and published information on the distribution of juvenile sea trout in large river catchments (Harris & Milner, 2006); freshwater sampling was prioritised in areas where sea trout were known to spawn, and likely spawning areas, within rivers entering the Irish and Celtic Seas. Sampling effort was primarily focused on larger, productive sea trout systems, which would likely be the largest contributors to sea trout marine stocks. Putative outlier samples were obtained from a geographically-distinct SW Irish catchment (Figure 1). The aim was to collect up to 50 of each of two co-occurring cohorts of juveniles at each location, i.e. 0+ fry from the previous winter's spawning and 1+ parr from the spawning of the previous year. 0+ fry were killed humanely and the whole body or part of the body stored in 99% molecular grade ethanol. A tail fin clip was recovered from previously anaesthetised larger 1+ parr, preserved in 99% molecular grade ethanol and the fish returned alive to the river.

Sampling of anadromous individuals of unknown origin in sea water

In order to secure a biologically meaningful sample set, sampling of anadromous individuals in sea water accounted for the extent of the coastline around the Irish Sea and the east of the Celtic Sea, which exceeds 6,500 km, and includes both inshore and offshore habitats. To further maximise sampling success, priority was given to areas where sea trout: 1) had previously been encountered by anglers or during previous sampling programmes; 2) had been taken on rod and line; 3) areas adjacent to existing trap and/or net fisheries; and 4) within zones where experienced commercial net fishers operated and were willing to assist with the collection of samples for the project. For inshore sampling, standardised survey benthic multi-mesh gill nets, based on standard gill net design were used. These nets are capable of capturing sea trout representing different size/age classes ranging from post-smolts (>18cm) up to larger multiple spawners. Efforts were made to sample regularly throughout the year, to ensure representation of different life stages (pre-adult and adult) and to account for potential temporal distribution patterns. Offshore sampling was carried out using a modified mid-water trawl in a series of tows between 2011 and 2012. Biopsy tissue samples were removed from captured sea trout and stored in 99% molecular-grade ethanol for subsequent genetic analysis.

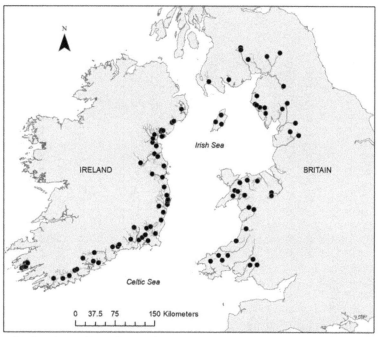

Figure 1. River sampling locations of juvenile trout for the genetic baseline.

LABORATORY ANALYSIS

Genomic DNA was extracted from tissue samples using either the Promega Wizard 96 kit, following manufacturers' instructions or a plate-wise optimised hi-salt extraction method

Table 1. Marker information for the multiplex panels used in this study, including primer sequences (with ABI labelled primer). Loci names prefixed with 'm' have been modified in this study from their original sources, for use in *S. trutta* (see Keenan *et al.,* 2013a for additional details regarding maker panels e.g. annealing temperatures, allele size range). All unlabelled primers are 'pig tailed' (i.e. prefixed with "gttt").

Locus	Forward Primer	Reverse Primer
Sea Trout-Panel - 1		
Ssa85	NED-AGGTGGGTCCTCCAAGCTAC	gtttACCCGCTCCTCACTTAATC
mOne102a & b[‡]	NED-GGGATTATTCTTACTTTGGCTGTT	gtttCCTGGTTGGGAATCACTGC
CA054565	PET-TCTGTGGTTCCCGATCTTTC	gtttCAACATTTGCCTAGCCAGA
CA053293	PET-TCTCATGGTGAGCAACAAACA	gtttACTCTGGGGCATTCATTCAG
Str2QUB	PET-CTGGGGTCCACAGCCTATAA	gtttGAGCTACAACCTGATCCACCA
Ssa416UoS	FAM-TGACCAACAACAAACGCACAT	gtttCCCACCCATTAACACAACTAT
mOne101	FAM-TGCTAAAATGACTGAAATGTTGAGA	gtttGAGAATGAATGGCTGAATGGA
Cocl-Lav-4	VIC-TGGTGTAATGGCTTTTCCTG	gtttGGGAGCAACATTGGACTCTC
Oneµ9	VIC-CTCTCTTTGGCTCGGGGAATGTT	gtttGCATGTTCTGACAGCCTACAGCT
CA048828	VIC-GAGGGCTTCCCATACAACAA	gtttGTTTAAGCGGTGAGTTGACGAGAG
Sea Trout-Panel - 2		
SsaD71	NED-AACGTGAAACATAAATCGATGG	gtTTAAGAATGGGTTGCCTATGAG
Sasa-TAP2A	gtttGTCCTGAATGTTGGCTCCCAGG	NED-GCGGGACACCGTCAGGGCAGT
MHC-I	PET-AGGAAGGTGCTGAAGAGGAAC	gtttCAATTACCACAAGCCCGCTC
Ssa410UoS	gtttGGAAAATAAATCAATGCTGCTGGTT	PET-CTACAATCTGGACTATCTTCTTCA
Str3QUB	FAM-CTGACCGCTGCACACTAA	gtttGGCTCTAATGACTGGCAGA
CA060177	FAM-CGCTTCCTGGACAAAAATTA	gtttGAGCACACCCATTCTCA
Ssa197	VIC-GGGTTGAGTAGGGAGGCTTG	gtttTGGCAGGGATTTGACATAAC

[‡] *Amplifies two independently-segregating loci*

(Aljanabi and Martinez, 1997). No differences were observed in the quality or downstream analysis of resulting DNA from the two methods.

The 18 microsatellite loci used in this study (Table 1) were chosen from the 38 loci characterised and optimised by Keenan *et al.* (2013a) for *Salmo trutta* genetic research. The criteria applied by Keenan *et al.* (2013a) in their selection of loci included; 1) reliability of amplification, 2) consistency of automated allelic calls, 3) sufficient polymorphism (≥ 2 alleles) and 4) allele size range (amenable to multiplexing). The 18 loci were resolved in two unique multiplex groups on either a 96 capillary ABI3730XL analyser (samples from Ireland) or an ABI3130 DNA analyser (samples from Britain) with genotypes scored using either GeneMapper (ThermoFisher Scientific) or Genemarker (SoftGenetics) software. Careful calibrations involving the screening of a common set of samples on both systems ensured consistency of genotypic typing and, therefore, inter-calibration between instruments. Polymerase chain reaction (PCR) and cycling conditions follow those described by Keenan *et al.* (2013a), with minor modifications (details available from authors upon request).

STATISTICAL ANALYSIS

Production of Population Baseline
Following genotyping, all individual juvenile trout which could be unambiguously scored for at least 14 of the 18 microsatellite loci were considered for inclusion in the genetic baseline. To ensure an unbiased sample for the construction of the fresh water baseline prior to further analysis, each population sample was checked for the presence of individuals with family ties (i.e. full sibs). This was done by systematically checking each of the riverine samples using the Sibling-Group Partitioning Programme (Almudevar & Field, 1999). In samples where family over-representation was identified, the effect (i.e. bias) was minimised by consecutively removing individuals from the largest families. In instances where the resulting number of individuals within a sample fell below 30, the sample was excluded from further analysis.

Intra-population sample statistics (i.e. number of alleles per locus, allelic richness (AR), observed and expected heterozygosity, conformity to HW expectations) were estimated using the programme *diveRsity* (Keenan *et al.*, 2013b). At those locations where samples were collected for 0+ fry and 1+ parr, heterogeneity of allele frequencies between temporal pairs of samples was investigated with 'Fisher's Exact tests' using the programme GENEPOP (Raymond & Rousset, 1995). Where no significant differences were observed, temporal samples were combined. Spatial samples were then compared using pairwise F-statistics (θ; Weir & Cockerham, 1984 and D_{Jost}; Jost, 2008) again using *diveRsity*. Statistical significance of estimated values (i.e. evidence for population differentiation) was determined using bootstrapping (Keenan *et al.*, 2013b).

To investigate levels of population genetic structuring within the data, the Bayesian framework developed by Pritchard *et al.* (2000) and implemented in the programme STRUCTURE V2.3 was used. This approach does not require a pre-defined hypothesis of population genetic structuring, instead, given a potentially "mixed" sample, the algorithm attempts to identify the minimum number of genetically independent entities (i.e. Mendelian genetic populations) that best explain the data, assuming HWE within inferred clusters. In this study, STRUCTURE analyses were run using a hierarchical approach (Rosenberg *et al.*, 2002). The rationale behind the hierarchical procedure is to identify major genetic groupings within the data (possibly related by phylogeographic history). At each level, the main identified groups were independently examined in subsequent STRUCTURE runs. One of the main advantages of the hierarchical approach is that it facilitates the disentangling of complex patterns of population sub-structuring (e.g. populations with different levels of genetic divergence).

For each hierarchical level, STRUCTURE analysis was carried out using the admixture model, with correlated allelic frequencies and identification of sample geographic location (Pritchard *et al.*, 2000). The latter parameter was used to account for population samples characterised by shallow levels of genetic divergence. The length of burn-in period (100,000) and the number of MCMC repetitions after burn-in (100,000) were determined empirically, following initial trial runs seeking convergence (see STRUCTURE manual for details). In each case, K (number of populations) ranged from 1 to 10 and, for each value of K, 20 iterations were carried out to ensure data concordance and reliability of results. The programme CLUMPP v 1.1.2 (Jakobsson & Rosenberg, 2007) was used to consolidate membership coefficients for the 20 iterations for each K estimate. Given the large data set, the "greedy" algorithm within CLUMPP was used, with 1,000 repeats. The most likely number of clusters present in the dataset was inferred using the Evanno method (Evanno *et al.*, 2005). The within- and among-STRUCTURE defined groups of populations (i.e. regions) θ and D_{Jost} values were calculated using *diverRsity* (Keenan *et al.*, 2013b).

Individual Assignment

a. Self-Assignment: The quality and power of the STRUCTURE-defined baseline for Individual Assignment was assessed with the leave-one out test (i.e. self-assignment test) using the programme ONCOR (Kalinowski *et al.*, 2007). The test involves genotypes from each fish of known provenance being serially removed from the baseline and then reassigned against the reconstituted baseline.

b. Marine Assignment: Assignments of marine samples (unknown origin) to the genetic baseline were also carried out using ONCOR. Sea-caught fish with an assignment P value of equal to or more than 0.7 were considered to be robust assignments. While this P value threshold is somewhat arbitrary, it was elected to be used as a conservative measure, after examining the results of actual marine assignments. Thus, assignment was found to be more consistent to region of origin above this value, whereas lower P values led to more diffuse assignments to other adjacent regions (data available on request). It is important however, to emphasise that the analyses, taking into consideration all assignments (irrespective of P value threshold), were not found to be substantially distinct (only more diffuse).

RESULTS

A total of 5,314 individual juvenile trout, collected from 99 spatially-distributed riverine sites (see Figure 1) were genotyped. While in most cases a single location was sampled from each river, for larger rivers more than one site was sampled (details on request). A proportion of these river samples consisted of both 0+ and 1+ juveniles from the same locations. After the removal of individuals with less than 14 interpretable loci (out of 18) or siblings from samples biased by excess of full kin individuals (see Materials and Methods) 4,944 individual juvenile trout (~93%) remained for subsequent analysis. Only one river population sample was dismissed on the basis of small sample size following removal of excess full kin individuals.

Within individual samples, the number of loci found to deviate from HWE following Bonferroni correction ranged from 1 to 4 (avg. 1.1). In most instances, there were no obvious geographic or locus-specific patterns for deviations from HWE, thus, these most likely reflected random genetic sampling error. A higher number of incidences, however, were observed for *Cocl*-Lav-4, MHCI and *Ssa*410UOS loci, which were found to be out of HWE for 23%, 18% and 14% of the samples respectively. In all cases, this was due to heterozygote deficiency. To test for possible bias, resulting from the three loci that show higher than average incidences of departures from HWE among samples, the STRUCTURE analysis was repeated after removing these particular loci. No major differences were observed when comparing the results including or excluding these loci. [*Complete sample summary statistics available on request from first author.*]

Pair-wise heterogeneity tests for allele frequency distributions among temporal samples indicated no significant differences. Hence, the relevant temporal samples were pooled prior to subsequent analysis. F-statistics analysis (both θ and D_{Jost} estimates) indicate that all pair-wise spatial sample comparisons, while varying in the degree of genetic divergence, were statistically-significantly different from each other (data not shown).

DETERMINATION OF REGIONAL GROUPINGS

Results of the hierarchical STRUCTURE analyses can be summarised as follows:

At the first hierarchical level (*Level 0*), sea trout from rivers entering the Irish and Celtic Sea were divided into three major groups: 1) West of Ireland (Currane tributaries); 2) south and east coasts of Ireland and 3) Britain, including the Isle of Man (Figure 2). In addition to the West of Ireland cluster, which was isolated on the basis of its demonstrated discreteness, *Level*

1 of STRUCTURE involved the separate analysis of the Irish and British samples (Figure 3). The Irish samples were clustered into four groups; Ireland-South, Ireland-Southeast, Ireland-Northeast and Ireland-North. The British samples were best explained by four groups: the Isle of Man, Britain-Solway/Morecambe, Britain-West Wales and Britain-South Wales. These clusters are mostly in concordance with their geographical locations (Figure 4). No major further structuring was apparent with additional analyses.

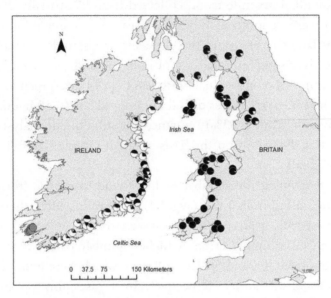

Figure 2. *Level 0* hierarchical structuring of putative anadromous *S. trutta* from the Irish and Celtic Seas, as derived from sampling of juveniles in riverine locations. Different colours on pies represent genetic membership (proportion) to particular major regional groups as follows: 'grey' –Ireland-west; 'white' –Ireland-south and east and 'black' – Britain

The results of the hierarchical STRUCTURE analyses provide good evidence for the presence of nine major regional groupings that follow a clear geographical pattern in rivers entering the Irish and Celtic Seas (Figure 4). These nine groups (1. Ireland-West, 2. Ireland-South, 3. Ireland-South East, 4. Ireland-North East, 5. Ireland-North, 6. Isle of Man, 7. Britain-Solway/Morecambe; 8. Britain-West Wales, 9. Britain-South Wales) were subsequently assessed for self-assignment (i.e. to examine the quality of the baseline) and actual assignment analyses (see below for rationale for using regional population groupings, rather than individual riverine populations for assignment).

F-statistics analyses based on the STRUCTURE-defined populations indicated substantial levels of genetic sub-structuring among the population baseline surveyed. Weir & Cockerham (1984) F_{ST} estimator (θ) was found to be 0.026 (95% C.I. 0.025 – 0.027). The equivalent adjusted statistic, accounting for the high level of alleles observed at microsatellites (i.e. D_{JOST}) was 0.111 (95% C.I. 0.108 – 0.115). Pair-wise θ and D_{Jost} values between the nine major groupings are shown in Table 2. All pair-wise comparisons were found to be significant.

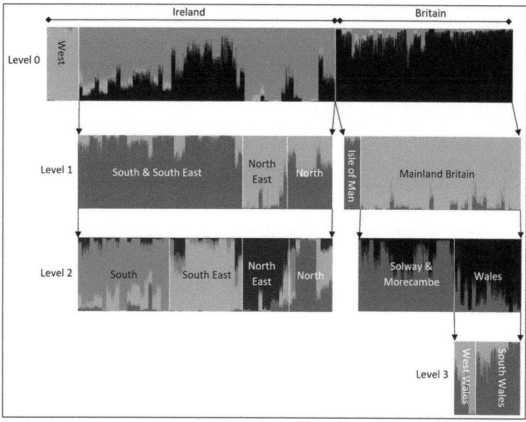

Figure 3. Summary bar plots of hierarchical STRUCTURE analysis including *Level 0*; *Level 1*, *Level 2* and *Level 3*. At *Level 0*, samples are best explained by three main genetic clusters (1. Ireland-West, 2. Ireland South and East, and 3. Isle of Man & mainland Britain). At *Level 1*, Ireland divides into three additional subgroups (1. Ireland-South & South East, 2. Ireland-North East and 3. Ireland-North) and Britain separates from Isle of Man. At *Level 2*, both Ireland South & South East and Britain can be further subdivided independently. Finally, at *Level 3*, Wales can be further split into two genetically distinct subgroups. Note that subsequent to *Level 0*, the different shades of grey and black have independent meanings in Britain and Ireland, and do not imply relationships between the two areas.

TESTING OF BASELINE QUALITY USING SELF-ASSIGNMENT

The results of the assessment of the "quality" (or power) of assignment to inferred population and regional reporting group (i.e. genetic baseline), tested with the self-assignment leave-one-out procedure, are summarized in Table 3 for both populations and regions, and in Figure 5 for regions only. Correct self-assignments are substantially higher to the nine-major regional population groups (illustrated by "grey" highlighted values in the diagonal on the right side of Table 3), in comparison to correct self-assignment to populations within regions (illustrated by "grey" highlighted average estimates in column "Avg% Assignment", Table 3). These results are not entirely unexpected, and reflect the fact that regional reporting groups (by default consisting of several population baseline rivers) capture a significantly larger diversity of alleles associated with particular regions, in comparison, to any single population baseline riverine sample within a regional group. Thus, an individual trout with a rare allele/genotype unique to a riverine site might fail to be assigned back to its home river (i.e. because population sample size is not sufficiently large to capture more than one copy of these rare genetic variants). Such a fish will, however, most likely assign to the correct home region (i.e. where the rare genetic variants are more likely to be found given larger sample size involved). Since, from a fishery management perspective, the main objective is the identification of mutually exclusive groups of populations (i.e. management units) rather than individual populations *per se* (Scribner *et al.*, 1998; Winans *et al.*, 2004), all subsequent assignments are reported to region only.

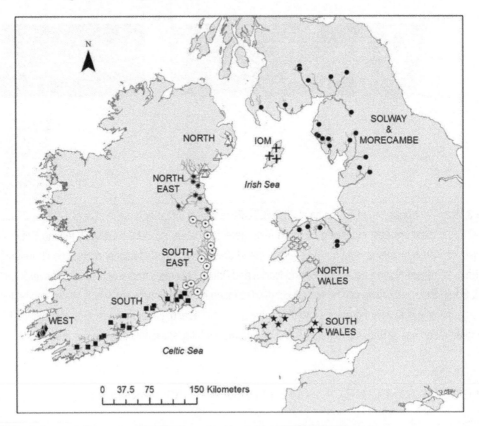

Figure 4. Final nine reporting groups identified from the hierarchical STRUCTURE analyses.

The accuracy of self-assignment to each of the nine STRUCTURE-defined regions ranged from 0.99 in the case of the Ireland-West region to 0.70 in the case of Britain-South Wales. While high accuracy for assignment (>0.9) was observed in Ireland-North East (0.98), Ireland-North (0.91) and Isle of Man (0.93), slightly lower accuracies (<0.9) were noted for Ireland-South (0.86), Ireland-South East (0.81), Britain-Solway/Morecambe (0.84) and Britain-West Wales (0.76). It is important to note that where mis-assignments occur, they are usually restricted to geographically adjacent regions (i.e. confirming the earlier assertion and emphasizing the relevance of considering broader regional groups for management). In a minority of cases, however, there were mis-assignments across the Irish Sea and particularly from Irish regions to Solway/Morecambe and *vice versa*. The latter may represent an historical phylogeographic signal, but additional work would be required to test this hypothesis.

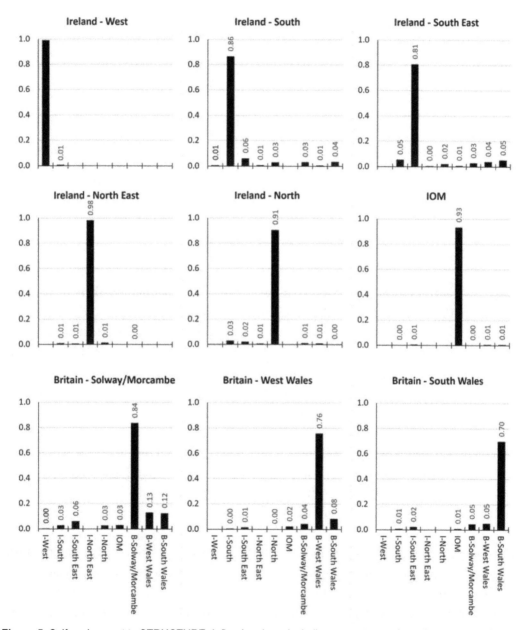

Figure 5. Self-assignment to STRUCTURE defined regions, including percentage mis-assignments to other regions. In each case, results represent a summary of average sample correct self-assignments specific to the particular region. *Note: 'I' = Ireland, 'B' = Britain, '0.00' < 0.001.*

81

Table 2. Estimates of θ (below diagonal) and D_{Jost} (above diagonal) for pair-wise regional group comparisons.

Regional Groups	Ireland					Isle of Man	Britain		
	West	*South*	*SE*	*NE*	*N*		*Sol / More*	*South Wales*	*West Wales*
Ireland-West	-	0.145	0.157	0.178	0.182	0.192	0.170	0.175	0.215
Ireland-South	0.058	-	0.024	0.066	0.049	0.084	0.037	0.051	0.063
Ireland-South East	0.066	0.009	-	0.065	0.058	0.067	0.025	0.030	0.047
Ireland-North East	0.075	0.023	0.024	-	0.069	0.146	0.088	0.105	0.113
Ireland-North	0.071	0.018	0.019	0.025	-	0.116	0.056	0.081	0.072
Isle of Man	0.077	0.034	0.030	0.055	0.043	-	0.087	0.090	0.091
Britain-Solw/More	0.064	0.012	0.008	0.031	0.018	0.034	-	0.024	0.033
Britain-West Wales	0.063	0.017	0.011	0.036	0.026	0.032	0.008	-	0.032
Britain-South Wales	0.081	0.023	0.016	0.046	0.027	0.038	0.012	0.012	-

MARINE ASSIGNMENT

Sampling in the marine environment was challenging due to the extent of the British and Irish coastline within the project area, the logistics and cost of marine sampling, the overreliance on in-kind sampling effort, and, in some cases, restrictions imposed under the terms of sampling permits. The majority of the marine samples were from inshore locations, largely within the Irish Sea. A total of 1,367 *S. trutta* from across the project area were sampled in the sea (Figure 6). Sample sizes in different locations were very variable and related to uneven regional sampling effort and opportunistic sampling. Thus, they should not be regarded as representative of local natural abundance. The largest number of sea trout were captured from the coastal areas adjacent to the Britain-Solway/Morecambe reporting region, followed by the area adjacent to Ireland-Southeast. Genomic DNA was successfully extracted from biopsy tissue from 1,213 individuals. Multi-locus genotypes ($\geq$ 14 loci) were obtained for 1,041 individuals. Of these, 569 (54.6%) were assigned to reporting regions with a P value ≥ 0.7.

A summary of the assignment of individuals captured largely in the Irish Sea (inshore and offshore areas) adjacent to the nine identified reporting regions with probability of assignment (P) values equal or greater than 0.7, is provided in Table 4 and, in all but the Ireland-West region, in Figure 7. Notwithstanding sampling bias, where both effort and successful captures varied greatly, interesting trends can be noted from the assignment analyses.

While sea trout from a variety of regions are represented in each recapture area,

Table 3. Summary results, expressed as percentages, of correct self-assignment (ONCOR) to riverine population sample within regional reporting region (grey vertical columns on the left side of the vertical line in the Table; average correct self-assignment among populations within region in addition to minimum and maximum estimates in each case), and for correct self-assignment to reporting regions (grey highlighted values in the diagonal in the right-hand side of the vertical line in the Table). Note: 'I' = Ireland; 'B' = Britain.

Regional Groups	No. Population samples	Within region θ	*Avg % Assignment	*Min % Assignment	*Max % Assignment	Ireland - West	Ireland - South	Ireland - South East	Ireland - North East	Ireland - North	Isle of Man	Britain – Solway/Morecambe	Britain – West Wales	Britain – South Wales
Ireland - West	8	0.042	78.1	67.4	91.7	99.17	0.11	–	–	–	–	–	–	–
Ireland - South	18	0.044	69.6	40.0	91.3	0.55	86.48	6.09	0.74	2.94	–	3.14	0.66	3.50
Ireland - South East	14	0.028	56.8	37.0	94.7	–	5.39	80.76	0.49	2.15	0.74	2.81	3.99	5.10
Ireland - North East	7	0.057	87.7	73.2	100	–	0.91	0.61	98.03	1.37	–	0.22	–	–
Ireland - North	9	0.062	77.7	54.3	100	–	2.95	2.19	0.74	90.61	–	1.08	1.00	0.32
Isle of Man	3	0.027	78.1	72.2	87.5	–	0.20	0.61	–	–	93.33	0.22	0.66	0.64
Britain – Solway/ Morecambe	24	0.04	62.3	27.3	83.8	0.28	2.85	6.09	–	2.74	2.96	83.68	12.96	12.42
Britain - West Wales	8	0.047	65.5	32.4	95.5	–	0.41	1.46	–	0.20	2.22	4.22	75.75	8.28
Britain - South Wales	7	0.019	46.5	28.6	68.9	–	0.81	2.19	–	–	0.74	4.54	4.98	69.75

proportions vary greatly (discernible by examining the individual columns in Table 4B). Excluding the Ireland-North East region where there were only two marine recaptures, the next lowest recovery in adjacent waters was in the case of Britain-West Wales at 13%, whereas 82% of trout from Isle of Man rivers were caught locally (Table 4 B). Probably because of variation in effort and subsequent catch, the largest contributing regional group to the sea trout in the Irish Sea and adjacent areas of the Celtic Sea are from the rivers constituting the Solway/Morecambe Bay complex. The next largest represented group are comprised by rivers in the Ireland-North region, and then the Ireland-South East region. In contrast, there were no fish assigned to the west coast of Ireland, as represented by the Lough Currane sample.

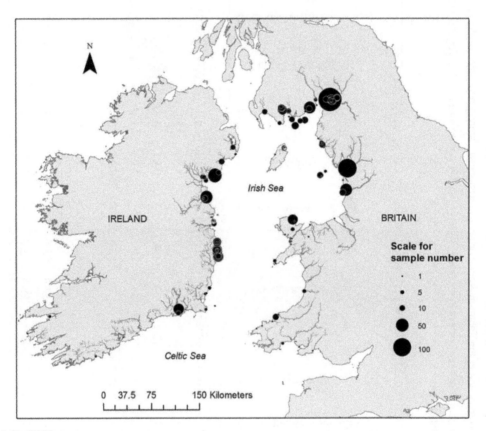

Figure 6. Location of all anadromous *S. trutta* captured in the Irish and Celtic Seas. Size of pies are proportional to number of fish captured in a given location.

DISCUSSION

Prior to the Celtic Sea Trout Project (http://celticseatrout.com/), very little was known of the biology, distribution and migratory behaviour of sea trout in the Irish Sea and adjacent Celtic

Sea. The Irish Sea in particular, is a relatively contained and discrete geographical entity, which for migrant trout, may mimic an extensive freshwater lake as opposed to the oceanic expanses of the Atlantic. Our results, however, show that some sea trout from rivers entering the Irish Sea did not confine themselves to the region during marine migrations. For the first time, molecular markers have provided an opportunity to describe the population and regional structure of sea trout from rivers entering the Irish and Celtic seas. Using these results as a genetic reference, individual sea trout sampled during their marine migrations can be assigned, with a very high degree of confidence, back to their natal region (i.e. reporting groups). Thus, the results from the CSTP project provides new insights into the biology of the sea trout in the Irish Sea and adjacent areas of the eastern Celtic Sea, which, when combined with other data, will considerably advance the knowledge of the ecology of the species in the region. Furthermore, not only is this information of key relevance for management and conservation of sea trout in the area, but it also provides guidelines for future studies. As such, one of the recommendations is for a future series of papers, combining, for example, genetics and observations of life history, age and growth data, stomach contents, parasites, geology, microchemistry and other aspects of sea trout biology.

However, the main aim of this chapter was to identify aspects of the biology of anadromous *S. trutta* that are relevant to management. Major findings in this context include:

1. The majority of sea-caught sea trout assigned to each region were caught locally. Therefore, conservation efforts in the sea should be intensified close to the mouths of the rivers within a particular region;
2. A smaller proportion of fish make long distance migrations e.g. British to Irish coasts or Irish Sea to Celtic Sea or *vice versa*. If these trout are predominantly larger and older individuals, it would be important that sustainable management be extended over the entire sea area. This question could be tested in a subsequent study;
3. The proportion of local, relative to long distance migrant fish varied among regions. For example, individual sea trout putatively spawned in Ireland-North and Isle of Man were mostly caught locally, while the Ireland-South sample contained many long distance migrants (spawned in other regions) (Figure 7). This suggests that different conservation strategies need to be enforced in different regions;
4. There is some evidence (combined distribution data; Ireland-North) of a tendency for fish to move in a northerly direction. Whether this apparent movement is in response to better feeding opportunities or other underlying reasons needs to be explored;
5. Any proposed marine developments (e.g. associated with marine renewables, aquaculture, fisheries) are likely to affect sea trout from rivers entering the sea within a particular region, but also from other regions. Therefore, all sea based activities will have an effect on multiple stocks, particularly in the Irish Sea (The Celtic sea was far more poorly sampled).

One of the potential weaknesses identified in this study was related to sampling design and its influence on the quality of the baseline. Two immediate options exist in sampling design to assemble the required baseline for sea trout; one can either utilise juvenile trout or adults returning to fresh water. One problem with the former approach is that sampling of undifferentiated juveniles can also include the progeny of resident (non-anadromous) trout in the baseline. These fish make no contribution to fish in the sea and, hence, are likely to affect the quality of the baseline and subsequent interpretation of the population structure of sea trout in the region if resident trout represent distinct populations. This issue is potentially more problematic in large river catchments, where multiple distinct populations are probable and juveniles along a river transect may represent mixtures from genetically distinct populations (Dillane *et al.*, 2008; Ferguson *et al.*, 2017). Despite this caveat, for logistic reasons, this was the strategy (i.e. sampling of juveniles) adopted in the present study. The second option, using adult fish to construct baselines, can lead to different problems, as adult trout have been shown to occur in non-natal rivers, and then move back to their natal rivers to spawn (Chat *et al.*, 2017). The extent of such behaviour has not been fully quantified but was regarded as sufficiently important so as to preclude the use of this approach in the present study. It might be more accurate to establish genetic baselines using smolts and or post spawned kelts, however, sampling either stage is not without associated complications, which, as discussed below, are primarily logistical in nature.

The extensive spatial sampling programme of trout from Irish, Manx and British rivers undertaken in this study, was designed to capture all of the major contributing sea trout rivers in the Irish and Celtic Seas (but see below). Assuming that each river should support at least one genetically distinct population, approximately one third of the estimated number of populations contributing sea trout to the Irish Sea and to the eastern Celtic Sea, were sampled, though these probably represent the larger populations. Thus, an analysis was undertaken to determine regional structuring of populations, on the assumption that populations within a defined region might be substantially more similar within regions than amongst such groups. Given the available resources, it was decided to try to achieve maximum spatial coverage at the expense of testing for temporal stability of the database. In this respect, the current study resembled, and was based on, the nature of genetic structuring in previous (Bourret *et al.*, 2013) and on-going studies (J. Gilbey, Freshwater Laboratory, Pitlochry, UK, *pers. comm.*) on Atlantic salmon *Salmo salar*, rather than the often longer term studies that have been undertaken on Pacific salmon and trout species-genus *Oncorhynchus* (*see review by* Koljonen *et al.*, 2007).

Freshwater juvenile sampling methods were designed based on life history and adequate sample size, but also while avoiding overrepresentation of small numbers of families (family effects). Also, at some locations, it was only possible to collect sufficient fry/parr from the most recent or previous spawning event, or 1+ parr, further limiting a more comprehensive assessment of the temporal stability of the genetic structure identified in this study. Notwithstanding these caveats, sea trout in the Irish and Celtic Seas have proven to be highly suitable for the application of GSI, satisfying the three criteria outlined in the introduction. This work has produced genetically-based evidence confirming philopatry in the form of significant F_{ST} differences between nearly all spatial samples. Evidence of the comprehensiveness of the freshwater database has also been produced, at least to the regional level.

Table 4. Summary of the assignments (samples with P ≥ 0.7) of the marine-caught trout adjacent to the areas defined by the nine major reporting groups identified by STRUCTURE (A – numbers; B – proportions).

4A. Numbers

Captured in & Assigned to	Ireland					Isle of Man	Britain			No. fish
	West	*South*	*SE*	*NE*	*N*		*Solway & Morecambe*	*West Wales*	*South Wales*	
Ire-West	-	1	-	-	-	-	-	-		1
Ire-South	-	13	10	5	3	1	22	1		55
Ire - SE	-	4	45	3	3	3	23	2	-	83
Ire - NE	-	-	1	-	-	-	1	-	-	2
Ire - North	-	1	51	35	24	-	18	3	-	132
IOM	-	-	1	-	-	27	3	2	-	33
Britain-Solway & Morecambe	-	6	42	1	3	2	122	5	1	182
West Wales	-	3	11	-	1	-	13	4	-	32
South Wales	-	3	12	1	2	2	18	4	7	49
Grand Total	-	31	173	45	36	35	220	21	8	569
% Recaptures	-	5%	30%	8%	6%	6%	39%	4%	1%	

4B. Proportions

Captured in & Assigned to	Ireland					Isle of Man	Britain		
	West	South	SE	NE	N		Solway & Morecambe	West Wales	South Wales
Ire-West	-	100%	-	-	-	-	-	-	-
Ire-South	-	23%	18%	9%	5%	2%	41%	2%	-
Ire - SE	-	5%	54%	4%	4%	4%	28%	2%	-
Ire - NE	-	-	50%	-	-	-	50%	-	-
Ire - North	-	1%	39%	27%	18%	-	14%	2%	-
IOM	-	-	3%	-	-	82%	9%	6%	-
Britain- Solway & Morecambe	-	4%	23%	1%	2%	1%	66%	3%	1%
West Wales	-	9%	34%	-	3%	-	41%	13%	-
South Wales	-	6%	24%	2%	4%	4%	37%	8%	14%

The evidence for a phylogeographic legacy (i.e. historical colonization patterns) of the populations comprising the baseline is interesting. As suggested from the results of the self-assignment analyses, there is some evidence for close genetic relationships between the sea trout from the British west coast, and south and south east Irish rivers. While this still needs to be confirmed, this similarity may be due to close geographic proximity over long periods, and to shared colonisation history, rather than contemporary gene flow. A future study of colonisation processes which are likely to have influenced currently observed relationships among regional groups and populations would be of great interest. However, it is also plausible that small numbers of anomalies in the baseline are a consequence of contemporary straying.

The observation that the majority of sea trout in certain regions are distributed and feed locally in the Irish Sea was not unexpected (Fahy, 1985; Potter et al., 2017a). This trend would influence the biology of the fish from diverse regions differently, since, for example, feeding opportunities would be likely to vary, so influencing marine growth. The types and location of coastal based activities e.g. aquaculture, marine renewables, shipping and recreation, that may affect sea trout of the inshore habitat should also be taken into consideration.

A key advantage of genetic "tagging" over traditional tagging methods is that a far greater number of fish can be sampled. Even applying stringent criteria (probability of assignment

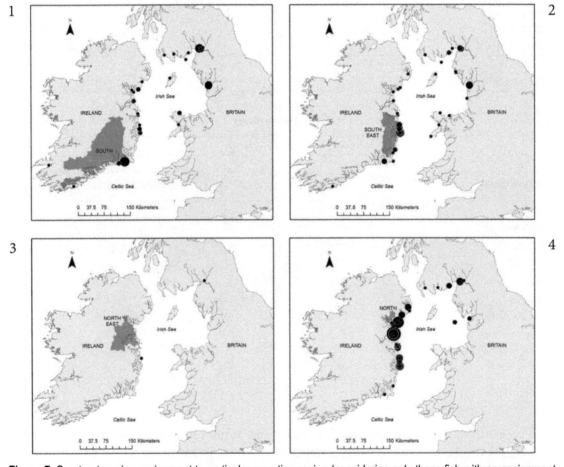

Figure 7. Sea trout marine assignment to particular reporting region (considering only those fish with an assignment value (P) of equal or greater than 0.7) as follows: 1) Ireland-South; 2) Ireland-Southeast; 3) Ireland-Northeast; 4) Ireland-North. Ireland-West is not shown (i.e. no marine fish assigned to the region). Pie size (marine samples) reflects number of fish captured in a given location.

(P) equal to or greater than 0.7) more than half the trout captured at sea could be confidently assigned (in this case, 569 fish). It is, however, important to remember (as noted in the introduction) that genetically-based assignments are not absolutes as would be obtained from physical tagging, but rather are based on statistical outputs derived within a probabilistic framework, as are many techniques used in fisheries management and, indeed, in forensic sciences. While creating minor limitations, the advantages of acquiring data for large numbers of wild fish from many rivers far outweighs any disadvantages. Furthermore, it is important to emphasise that absolute certainty in assignment is not necessary to obtain useful insights into biological phenomena such as life history variation, or migration distribution, or to produce information that may be pertinent to management e.g. the occurrence of mixed stock aggregations.

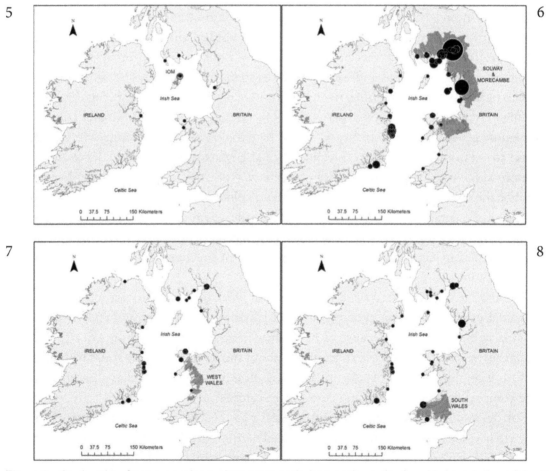

Figure 7 – Continuation. Sea trout marine assignment to particular reporting region (considering only those fish with an assignment value (P) of equal or greater than 0.7) as follows: 5) Isle of Man; 6) Britain-Solway/Morecambe; 7) Britain-West Wales; 8) Britain-South Wales.

The adopted strategy in the present study of concentrating assignment to reporting regions is well justified from a management perspective, where the main goal is to identify mutually exclusive management units (i.e. groups that need to be managed separately). Furthermore, despite the considerable sampling effort undertaken, it is unlikely that all sea trout populations within the designated area were sampled. Thus, based on prior information, samples were preferentially obtained from larger rivers, which were assumed to harbour larger sea trout populations, which would, in turn, be more likely to contribute to marine catches. Thus, small rivers and some multiple populations within large rivers may have been missed. A future study should attempt to achieve a fully comprehensive baseline, and thus achieve greatly improved efficiency in assignment to individual rivers.

The current study concentrated on sea trout from rivers flowing into the Irish Sea from the east Irish coast, the Isle of Man and central west Britain, and to a lesser extent into the Celtic Sea from the south coast of Ireland. Future studies should also consider all areas of both islands in preparing a genetic baseline either by combining with on-going studies i.e. Living North Sea (http://www.living-north-sea.eu), AARC (http://aarcproject.org/), ASAP (https://projects.exeter.ac.uk/meeg/atlantic-salmon-arc-project-asap), or by *de novo* studies; e.g. the west coast of Ireland and west coast of Scotland. In addition, consideration must be given to optimal sampling within a river (Ferguson *et al.*, 2017). Sampling of undifferentiated juveniles from single locations, particularly in large river systems where considerable population genetic sub-structuring is likely to exist, risks undermining the baseline in respect to sea trout identification (Hecht *et al.*, 2013; Martinez *et al.*, 2011). The sampling of tributary-specific sea trout smolts might be one way of overcoming this issue. Even better might be the sampling of stream-specific sea trout kelts. In addition, the long-term temporal stability of the database will need testing, as it is the norm with Pacific species. Temporal sampling might also provide genetically derived management-relevant data on population sizes in particular tributaries and rivers i.e. number of breeders (N_b), effective population size (N_e) (Waples & Yokota, 2007; Waples *et al.*, 2016).

The marine sampling described in the current work does not provide a comprehensive and spatially explicit assessment of migration and distribution of sea trout in the Irish Sea, and particularly the Celtic Sea, because of major bias in effort/catch/sampling effort. However, biologically relevant inferences can be drawn about movements, which could be considered in a future combined study of genetics and biological data. Future studies should ensure far more comparable marine effort and consequent catches.

Furthermore, future studies might utilise Single Nucleotide Polymorphisms (SNPs) (Ackerman *et al.*, 2011) in addition to, or instead of microsatellites. For instance, Ackerman *et al.* (2011) have shown that SNPs, under diversifying selection, provide increased accuracy and precision in mixed-stock analysis of sockeye salmon (*Oncorhynchus nerka*) from the Copper River in Alaska. While this approach would necessitate rescreening of both the database and marine samples, recent developments in genomics methodologies are now potentially permitting rapid screening of thousands of SNP loci, and, as demonstrated by the Ackerman *et al.* (2011) study, the choice of neutral loci or adaptive loci for analysis.

In summary, we conclude that GSI is an excellent tool for use in elucidating the biology and assisting in the management of sea trout in the Irish Sea and adjacent areas. In this particular study, due to the constraints of sampling, assignment to STRUCTURE defined regions proved far more accurate than assignment to river. It was concluded that there is strong philopatry and at least short term temporal genetic stability in sea trout in the area. In addition, there would appear to be metapopulation-like structuring in certain areas (Quémèré *et al.*, 2015). Studies of microchemistry might enable identification of the progeny of sea trout in mixed juvenile aggregations, thus simplifying baseline sampling (*pers. comm.* Ronald Campbell, River Tweed Foundation). In the present study, a threshold assignment P value of 0.7 was used, but it should be noted that this value may be region specific (i.e. the more discrete the region, the lower the acceptable threshold value). Additional analysis, taking other biological and/or ecological data into consideration would be useful in trying to validate the approach (*see also*: Potter *et al.*, 2017b; Milner *et al.*, 2017).

The genetic database used in the current study is the largest and most comprehensive assembled for the study of anadromous *Salmo trutta* in a defined ecosystem. The genetic baseline is of sufficient quality to provide information on accurate regional genetic structuring. As has been discussed throughout, the baseline could be further improved by refining the spatial and temporal extent of baseline sampling. The argument is that related benefits of such an approach easily justify costs. This is an issue, however, that will have to be considered by those responsible for the management of sea trout in this area, and will have to take into consideration priorities and the consequences of failing to possess the relevant information. From both management and evolutionary perspectives, one aspect where refinement of the baseline might be justified is to increase the confidence of assigning fish to individual regions and, ideally, to particular rivers.

ACKNOWLEDGEMENTS

This study was funded as part of the Ireland-Wales Territorial Co-operation Programme 2007-2013 (INTERREG 4A) – Celtic Sea Trout project. PP, TC, PMcG, CB, TR, ED, JC and JC were also supported by the Beaufort Marine Research Award in Fish Population Genetics funded by the Irish Government under the Sea Change Programme. Additional funding was provided by the River Annan District Salmon Fishery Board, the Nith District Salmon Fishery Board and the Galloway Fisheries Trust. The personnel at Inland Fisheries Ireland, Bangor University, the Environmental Agency, Natural Resources Wales, Dept. of Environment, Food and Agriculture, Isle of Man, Nith District Salmon Fisheries Board (NSFB), Galloway Fisheries Trust (GFT), River Annan District Salmon Fishery Board (ASFB) and Buccleuch Estate (Border Esk) are acknowledged for their considerable efforts in collecting marine samples.

REFERENCES

Ackerman, M. W., Habicht, C. & Seeb, L. W. (2011). Single-Nucleotide Polymorphisms (SNPs) under diversifying selection provide increased accuracy and precision in Mixed-Stock Analyses of sockeye salmon from the Copper River, Alaska. *Transactions of the American Fisheries Society* **140**, 865-881.

Aljanabi, S. M. & Martinez, I. (1997). Universal and rapid salt-extraction of high quality genomic DNA for PCR-based techniques. *Nucleic Acids Research* **25**, 4692-4693.

Anderson, E. C., Waples, R. S. & Kalinowski, S. T. (2008). An improved method for predicting the accuracy of genetic stock identification. *Canadian Journal of Fisheries and Aquatic Sciences* **65**, 1475-1486.

Almudevar, A. & Field, C. (1999). Estimation of single generation sibling relationships based on DNA markers. *Journal of Agricultural Biological and Environmental Statistics* **4**, 136-165.

Bourret, V., Kent, M.P., Hayes, B.J., Primmer, C.R., Vasemagi, A., Karlsson, S., Hindar, K., McGinnity, P., Verspoor, E., Bernatchez, L. & Lien, S. (2013). SNP-array reveals genome wide patterns associated with geographical and potential adaptive divergence across the natural range of Atlantic salmon (*Salmo salar*). *Molecular Ecology* 22, 532–551.

Bradbury, I. R., Hamilton, L.C., Chaput,G., Robertson, M.J., Goraguer, H., Walsh, A., Morris, V., Reddin, D., Dempson, B., Sheehan, T.F., King, T. & Bernatchez, L. (2016). Genetic mixed stock analysis of an interceptory Atlantic salmon fishery in the Northwest Atlantic. *Fisheries Research* **174**, 234-244.

Bradbury, I.R., Hamilton, L.C., Rafferty, S., Meerburg, D., Poole, R., Dempson, J.B., Robertson, M.J., Reddin, D.G., Bourret, V., Dionne, M., Chaput, G., Sheehan, T.F., King, T.L., Candy, J.R. & Bernatchez, L. (2015). Genetic evidence of local exploitation of Atlantic salmon in a coastal subsistence fishery in the Northwest Atlantic. *Canadian Journal of Fisheries and Aquatic Sciences* **72**, 83–95.

Chat, J., Masson, S., Manicki, A., Gueraud, F., Rives, J., Lange, F., Huchet, E., Coste, P., Aymes, J-C. & Lepais, O. (2017). Do sea trout migrations promote inter-basin connectivity between populations? In: *Sea trout: Science & Management.* (Graeme Harris. (*Ed.*) . Proceeding of the 2nd International Sea Trout Conference. October 2015, Dundalk, Ireland. Troubador, 354–370.

Dillane, E., McGinnity, P., Coughlan, J.P., Cross, M.C., De Eyto, E., Kenchington, E., Prodöhl, P & Cross, T.F. (2008). Demographics and landscape features determine intrariver population structure in Atlantic salmon (*Salmo salar* L.): the case of the River Moy in Ireland. *Molecular Ecology* **17**, 4786-4800.

Ensing, D., Crozier, W.W., Boylan, P., Ó Maoiléidigh , N. & McGinnity, P. (2013). An analysis of genetic stock identification on a small geographical scale using microsatellite markers, and its application in the management of a mixed-stock fishery for Atlantic salmon (*Salmo salar*) in Ireland. *Journal of Fish Biology* **82**, 2080–2094.

Ensing, D., Prodöhl, P. A., McGinnity, P., Boylan, P., Ó Maoiléidigh, N. & Crozier, W.W. (2011). Complex pattern of genetic structuring in the Atlantic salmon (*Salmo salar* L.) of the River Foyle system in north-west Ireland: disentangling the evolutionary signal from population stochasticity. *Ecology and Evolution* **1**, 359-372.

Evanno, G., Regnaut, S. & Goudet, J. (2005). Detecting the number of clusters of individuals using the software STRUCTURE: a simulation study. *Molecular Ecology* **14**, 2611–2620.

Fahy, E. (1985). The Child of the Tides. The Glendale Press, Dublin, 188 pp.

Ferguson, A. (1989). Genetic differences among brown trout, *Salmo trutta,* stocks and their importance for the conservation and management of the species. *Freshwater Biology* **21**, 35–46.

Ferguson, A. (2004). The importance of identifying conservation units: brown trout and pollen biodiversity in Ireland. *Biology & Environment: Proceedings of the Royal Irish Academy* **104B** (3), 33-41.

Ferguson, A. (2006). Genetics of sea trout, with particular reference to Britain and Ireland. In: *Sea Trout: Biology, Conservation & management.* (Graeme Harris & Nigel Milner. (Eds.). Proceedings of the First International Sea Trout Symposium, Cardiff, July 2004. Oxford: Blackwell Scientific Publications. 157-182

Ferguson. A., Reed, T., McGinnity, P. & Prodöhl, P. (2017). Anadromy in brown trout (*Salmo trutta*): A review of the relative roles of genes and environmental factors and the implications for management. In: *Sea Trout: Science & Management.* (Graeme Harris. *Ed.*). Proceedings of the 2nd International Sea Trout Symposium, October 2015, Dundalk, Ireland. Troubador, 1–40.

Gauthier-Ouellet, M., Dionne, M., Caron, F., King, T.L. & Bernatchez, L. (2009). Spatiotemporal dynamics of the Atlantic salmon (*Salmo salar*) Greenland fishery inferred from mixed-stock analysis. *Canadian Journal of Fisheries and Aquatic Sciences* **66** (12), 2040–2051.

Griffiths, A.M., Machado-Schiaffino, G., Dillane, E., Coughlan, J., Horreo, J.L., Bowkett, A.E., Minting, P., Toms, S., Roche, W., Gargan, P., McGinnity, P., Cross, T., Bright, D., Garcia-Vazquez, E. & Stevens, R. (2010). Genetic stock identification of Atlantic salmon (*Salmo salar*) populations in the southern part of the European range. *BMC Genetics* **11**, 31. doi:10.1186/1471-2156-11-31.

Harris, G. & Milner, N.J. (2006). *Sea Trout: Biology, Conservation and Management.* (Graeme Harris & Nigel Milner. (Eds.). Proceedings of the First International Sea Trout Symposium, July 2004,Cardiff,Wales. Oxford: Blackwell Scientific Publications. 499 pp.

Hauser, L., Seamons T.R., Dauer, M., Naish, K.A. & Quinn, T.P. (2006). An empirical verification of population assignment methods by marking and parentage data: Hatchery and wild steelhead (*Oncorhynchus mykiss*) in Forks Creek, Washington, USA. *Molecular Ecology* **15**, 3157–3173.

Hecht, B. C., Campbell, N. R., Holecek, D. E. & Narum, S. R. (2013). Genome-wide association reveals genetic basis for the propensity to migrate in wild populations of rainbow and steelhead trout. *Molecular Ecology* **22**, 3061–3076.

Hilborn, R., Quinn, T. P., Schindler, D. A. & Rogers, L.A. (2003). Biocomplexity and fisheries sustainability. *Proceedings of the National Academy of Sciences of the United States of America* **100**, 6564-6568.

Jakobsson, M. & Rosenberg, N.A. (2007) CLUMPP: a cluster matching and permutation program for dealing with label switching and multimodality in analysis of population structure. *Bioinformatics* **23**: 1801–1806.

Jost, L. (2008). G_{st} and it relatives do not measure differentiation. *Molecular Ecology* **17**, 4015-4026.

Kalinowski, S.T., Manlove, K.R., & Taper, M.L. (2007). ONCOR: software for genetic stock identification. *Montana State University, Bozeman, Montana, USA.*

Keenan, K., Bradley, C. R., Magee, J. J., Hynes, R. A., Kennedy, R. J., Crozier, W. W., Poole, R., Cross, T. F., McGinnity, P. & Prodöhl, P. A. (2013a). Beaufort Trout MicroPlex: A high throughput multiplex platform comprising 38 informative microsatellite loci for use in brown trout and sea trout (*Salmo trutta* L.) population genetics studies. *Journal of Fish Biology* **82**, 1789-1804.

Keenan, K., McGinnity, P., Cross, T., Crozier, W.W. & Prodöhl, P. (2013b) diveRsity: An R package for the estimation and exploration of population genetics parameters and their associated errors. *Methods in Ecology and Evolution* **4**, 782-788.

King, A., Hillman, R., Elsmere, P., Stockley, B. & Stevens, J. (2016). Investigating patterns of straying and mixed stock exploitation of sea trout, *Salmo trutta*, in rivers sharing an estuary in south-west England. *Fisheries Management and Ecology* **23**, 376–389.

Koljonen, M-L., King, T.L. & Nielsen, E.E. (2007). Genetic identification of individuals and populations. In: *The Genetics of Atlantic Salmon: Implications for Conservation*. (Verspoor, E., Nielsen, J. & Stradmeyer, L., *Eds.*). Oxford. Blackwell Scientific Publications. 270-298

Koljonen, M.-L., Gross, R. & Koskiniemi, J. (2014). Wild Estonian and Russian sea trout (*Salmo trutta*) in Finnish coastal sea trout catches: results of genetic mixed stock analysis. *Hereditas* **151**, 177-195.

McKeown, N., Hynes, R., Duguid, R. A., Ferguson, A. & Prodöhl, P. (2010). Phylogeographic structure of brown trout (*Salmo trutta*) in Britain and Ireland: glacial refugia, post-glacial colonisation, and origins of sympatric populations. *Journal of Fish Biology* **76,** 319-347.

Mäkinen, H., Niva, T., Koljonen, M-L. & Primmer, C.R. (2015). Temporal variation in lake-run brown trout (*Salmo trutta*) mixed-stock fishery catches in a large Fennoscandian lake. *Boreal Environment Research* **20**(5), 651–665.

Martínez, A., Garza, J.C. & Pearse, D.E. (2011). A microsatellite genome screen identifies chromosomal regions under differential selection in steelhead and rainbow trout. *Transactions of the American Fisheries Society* **140**, 829-842.

Manel, S., Gaggiotti, O.E. & Waples, R.S. (2005). Assignment methods: matching biological questions with appropriate techniques. *Trends in Ecology & Evolution* **20**, 136–42.

Milner, N., Potter, E., Roche, W., Tysklind. N., Davidson, I., King, J., Coyne, J. & Davies, C. (2017). Variation in sea trout (*Salmo trutta*) abundance and life histories in the Irish Sea. In: Sea Trout: Management & Science. (Graeme Harris,. Ed.). Proceedings of the 2nd International Sea Trout Symposium. October 2015, Dundalk, Ireland. Troubador, 96–128.

Paetkau, D., Slade, R., Burden, M. & Estoup, A. (2004). Genetic assignment methods for the direct, real-time estimation of migration rate: a simulation-based exploration of accuracy and power. *Molecular Ecology* **13**, 55–65.

Piry, S., Alapetite, A., Cornuet, J. M., Paetkau, D., Baudouin, L. & Estoup, A. (2004). GENECLASS2: A software for genetic assignment and first-generation migrant detection. *Journal of Heredity* **95**, 536-539.

Potter, E.C.E, Campbell, R., Sumner, K. & Marshall, S. (2017a). Marine migrations and distribution of sea trout from rivers in Great Britain. In: *Sea trout: Science & Management*. (Graeme Harris. *Ed.*). *Proceeding of the 2nd International Sea Trout Conference*, October 2015, Dundalk, Ireland. Troubador, 205–227.

Potter, E., Beraud, C., Bacon, J., Van der Molen, J. & Van Leeuwen S. (2017b). Simulation of movements of sea trout post-smolts in the Irish & Celtic Seas. In*: Sea Trout: Science & Management*. (Graeme Harris. *Ed*.). Proceedings of the 2nd International Sea Trout Symposium. October 2015, Dundalk, Ireland. Troubador, 228–252.

Pritchard, J., Stephens, M. & Donnelly. P. (2000). Inference of population structure using multilocus genotype data. *Genetics* **155**, 945-959.

Quémeré, E. Baglinière, J-L., Roussel, J.M., Evanno, G., McGinnity, P. & Launey, S. (2015). Seascape and its effect on migratory life-history strategy influences gene flow among coastal brown trout populations (*Salmo trutta*) in the English Channel. *Journal of Biogeography* **43**, 498–509.

Raymond, M. & Rousset, F. (1995). GenePop (version 1.2) – population genetics software for exact tests and ecumenicism. *Journal of Heredity,* **86**, 248–249.

Rosenberg N. A., Pritchard, J. K., Weber, J. L., Cann, H. M., Kidd, K. K., Zhivotovsky, L. A. & Feldman, M. W. (2002). Genetic structure of human populations. *Science* **298**, 2381–2385.

Schindler, D. E., Hilborn, R., Chasco, B., Boatright, P., Quinn, T. P., Rodgers, L. A. & Webster, M. S. (2010). Population diversity and the portfolio effect in an exploited species. *Nature* **465**, 609-613.

Scribner, K. T., Crane, P. A., Spearman, W. J. & Seeb L. W. (1998). DNA and allozyme markers provide concordant estimates of population differentiation: analyses of US and Canadian populations of Yukon River fall-run chum salmon (*Oncorhynchus keta*). *Canadian Journal of Fisheries and Aquatic Sciences* **55**, 1748–1758.

Swatdipong, A., Vasemägi, A., Niva, T., Koljonen, M.-L. & Primmer, C.R. (2013). Genetic mixed-stock analysis of lake-run brown trout *Salmo trutta* fishery catches in the Inari Basin, northern Finland: implications for conservation and management. *Journal of Fish Biology* **83**, 598–617.

Waples, R. S. & Yokota, M. (2007). Temporal estimates of effective population size in species with overlapping generations. *Genetics* **175**, 219–233.

Waples, R. K., Larson, W. A. & Waples, R. S. (2016). Estimating contemporary effective population size in non-model species using linkage disequilibrium across thousands of loci. *Heredity* **117**, 233–240.

Weir, B.S. & Cockerham, C.C. (1984). Estimating F-statistics for the analysis of population structure. *Evolution* **38**, 1358–1370.

Winans, G, A., Paquin, M. M., Van Doornik, D. M., Baker, B. M., Thornton, P., Rawding, D., Marshall, A., Moran, P. & Kalinowski, S. (2004). Genetic stock identification of steelhead in the Columbia River Basin: an evaluation of different molecular markers. *North American Journal of Fisheries Management* **24**, 672–685.

ELECTRONIC REFERENCES

Neaves, P.I., Wallace, C.G., Candy, J.R. & Beacham, T.D. (2005). CBayes: computer program for mixed stock analysis of allelic data [online]. *Available from*: http://www.pac.dfo-mpo.gc.ca/ science/facilities-installations/pbs-sbp/mgllgm/ apps/index-eng.html.

Variation in sea trout (*Salmon trutta*) abundance and life histories in the Irish Sea

N. MILNER[1], E. POTTER[2], W. ROCHE[3], N. TYSKLIND[4], I. DAVIDSON[5], J. KING[6], J. COYNE[4] & C. DAVIES[7].

[1]*APEM Ltd. c/o Bangor University, School of Biological Sciences, Deiniol Road, Bangor, Gwynedd, LL57 2UW, Wales.*
[2]*Cefas Fisheries Laboratory, Pakefield Road. Lowestoft, Suffolk, NR33 0HT, England.*
[3]*Inland Fisheries Ireland, Citywest Business Campus, Dublin 24, Ireland.*
[4]*INRA, UMR8172 EcoFoG, AgroParisTech, Cirad, CNRS, Université des Antilles, Université de Guyane, 97310 Kourou, France.*
[5]*Natural Resources Wales, Chester Road, Buckley Flintshire CH7 3AJ, Wales.*
[6]*CAMS, Bangor University, School of Ocean Sciences, Menai Bridge, Anglesey, LL59 5AB, Wales.*
[7]*Bangor University, Department of Chemistry, Deiniol Road, Bangor Gwynedd, LL57 2UW, Wales.*

ABSTRACT

The key traits of growth, survival and maturation during the marine phase define the phenotypes of returning adult anadromous brown trout (*Salmo trutta*) and thus their population dynamics, stock structures and the characteristics of their fisheries. This paper reviews recent and historical evidence for spatial and temporal variation in life history traits and other demographic features of sea trout around the Irish Sea and examines some of the causal factors, focussing on the marine environment. Stock abundance, indexed by rod catches, showed synchronous variation over wide areas, suggesting a response to common factor/s. Contemporary data, based on scale reading and size structures, were compared with historical information to describe variation in growth, survival and maturation (as indexed by time of first return). Spatial patterns in growth and survival were different between eastern and western seaboards, with slower growth and lower marine survival characterising several rivers of eastern Ireland. North-south variation in growth was evident on the Wales to Scotland seaboard and tentatively linked to temperature gradients, although growth opportunity will be influenced also by the variable and complex patterns of marine productivity in the Irish Sea. Previous research focus has been on the role of freshwater factors in initiating anadromy as a tactic to optimise fitness. These results show the additional influence of marine habitat on life histories and consequently the age and size structures of sea trout stocks. Long-term changes in life history traits are described that might reflect marine climate change. The results look at sea trout from a marine ecosystem perspective in the Irish Sea and are discussed briefly in the context of sea trout fisheries and conservation management.

Keywords: sea trout; life history traits; population dynamics; marine habitat; climate change.

INTRODUCTION

Life history traits govern fish population structures and dynamics. In partially migrating (Jonsson & Jonsson, 1993; Chapman *et al.,* 2012) anadromous species such as the brown trout (*Salmo trutta* L.) the marine environment increases growth opportunity which through growth, survival and return timing influences the nature and value of the fisheries. In life history terms, anadromy offers fitness benefits through increased growth and fecundity, but at the expense of additional mortality through risks from predation and migration energetic costs. Therefore, trade-offs exist that maximise fitness in the face of prevailing environmental factors governing these key traits, in both freshwater and at sea (Jonsson & Jonsson 1993; Dodson *et al.,* 2012; Ferguson *et al.,* 2017).

There has been much research interest in the genetic and environmental factors that act during the juvenile freshwater phase to determine anadromy (Forseth *et al.,* 1999; Cucherousset *et al.,* 2005; Olsson *et al.,* 2006; Wysujack *et al.,* 2009). The broad principles involve adoption of alternative migratory tactics (residency *vs* migration) according to some internal trigger when metabolic condition, approximated by size or growth energetics, passes a threshold in the first year (Dodson *et al.,* 2012). The combination of individual predisposition (the threshold) and environmental factors controlling productivity and growth, determines the probability of anadromy in individuals and thus in the population. Hence anadromy is termed a threshold quantitative trait under the control of multiple genes and environmental factors (Ferguson, 2006).

However, migration from freshwater is only part of the life cycle. Marine growth performance, survival, maturation timing and the return migration to rivers are necessary to deliver the reproductive benefits of migration to sea. Until very recently (Thorstad *et al.,* 2016; Quéméré *et al.,* 2016) the marine-phase life-history processes have received less attention than those in freshwater; although the population dynamics of anadromous salmonids can be assumed to be influenced by traits such as post-smolt survival, marine growth rate and time of first maturation in ways that maximise individual fitness and population resilience (Hutchings & Jones, 1998; Fleming *et al.,* 2014). That sea trout populations vary in average marine growth and timing of first return is well established (L'Abée-Lund *et al.,* 1989; Baglinière & Maisse, 1999; Harris & Milner, 2006; de Leeuw *et al.,* 2007; Tysklind *et al.,* 2015); but the causes of this variation and implications for population fitness are less studied and less clear. Jonsson *et al.*

(1991) concluded that in Norwegian rivers variation in longevity and body size with latitude was probably due more to conditions in freshwater than at sea; although their results indicate nevertheless a role for marine temperature.

Partial migration applies also to the marine phase, because maturation leading to first return to rivers is hypothesised to be conditional upon post-smolt growth and survival (Gross *et al.*, 1988; Marschall *et al.*, 1998). Thus, part of the marine population returns in a given year and part remains at sea to return as maiden fish in later years. Therefore variation in the marine habitat, coupled with the high phenotypic plasticity of trout, can be expected *a priori* to influence the life history characteristics of river stocks (composed of one or more populations) and the fisheries they support.

This paper describes sea trout life history variation in rivers around the Irish Sea and investigates some of its causes, drawing on the Celtic Sea Trout Project (CSTP) funded by the EU Interreg IVA Programme (http://celticseatrout.com) and historical studies. The central hypotheses tested are that key life history traits of growth, survival and time of first return (taken here as an index of first maturation) vary in the face of marine environmental spatial and temporal factors in ways that tend to optimise lifetime fitness (*sensu* Stearns, 1999).

THE IRISH SEA AS SEA TROUT HABITAT

The Irish Sea presents a wide variety of marine habitats likely to influence the ecology and life histories of sea trout. It is a partly enclosed, fully saline (32-35 ppt) sea lying between England, Wales, Scotland and the Island of Ireland, with the Isle of Man lying in the middle of the northern basin (Figure 1), and connected to the Atlantic at its southern and northern ends. Its conventional limits are the St George's Channel, lying between Pembrokeshire (southwest Wales) and Waterford in southeast Ireland, and the North Channel between Northern Island and the Mull of Kintyre in southwest Scotland (Vincent *et al.*, 2004), with dimensions of about 300 km by 70 km. In this account the rivers of South Wales (as far as the Usk) and southwest Ireland (as far as the Currane) (Figure 1) have been included to cover information from recent studies, therefore extending the area to the Celtic Sea, but the term Irish Sea is used to include all sites.

The present day structure of the Irish Sea is the result of repeated glaciations concluding about 15,000 years ago, a process that has also influenced the genetic structure of trout populations (Ferguson, 2006). Bathymetry is characterised by a deeper western channel (80-275m) and large shallow embayments (<50m, and much being <20m) on the eastern seaboard, notably Carmarthen and Cardigan Bays in Wales, Liverpool Bay in north-west England and Solway Firth on the English-Scottish border, separated by rocky coastlines often with fast tidal currents. In contrast, the western seaboard is less structured, but has offshore sand banks in its southern half and some unique features such as the enclosed Strangford Lough in the north. Prevailing southwest winds make the western seaboard more sheltered

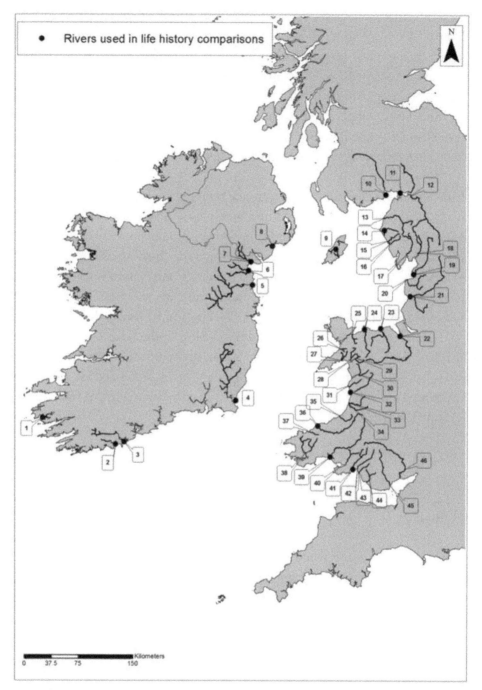

Figure 1. Map of river locations, identifying (black spot) those used in life history analysis. 1-Currane, 2-Argideen, 3-Bandon, 4-Slaney, 5-Boyne, 6-Dee(White River), 7-Castletown, 8-Shimna, 9-Isle of Man (Neb, Sulby, Glass), 10-Nith, 22-Border Esk, 12-Eden, 13-Derwent, 14-Ehen, 15-Irt, 16-Cumbrian Esk, 17-Leven, 18-Kent, 19-lune, 20-Wyre, 21-Ribble, 22-Dee, 23-Clwyd, 24-Conwy, 25-Ogwen, 26-Llyfni, 27-Dwyfawr, 28-Glaslyn, 29-Dwyryd, 30-Mawddach, 31-Dysynni, 32-Dyfi, 33-Rheidol, 34-Ystwyth, 35-Aeron, 36-Teifi, 37-Nevern, 38-East & West Cleddau, 39-Twyi, 40-Loughor, 41-Tawe, 42-Neath, 43-Afan, 44-Ogmore, 45-Taff, 46-Usk.

than the eastern. Tidal ranges vary considerably from 10m in Liverpool bay to <1m in the North Channel. A prevailing northerly residual current reflects the input of Atlantic water from both ends, being more dominant from the south. Extensive closed circulation and gyres exist in the shallow eastern bays; but seasonal fronts build up that control stratification and exchange. Sea water temperatures vary according to the latitude and bathymetry, influenced by the Atlantic intrusion in winter months that extends warm (>7°C) water northwards up the deep western channel. Annual range is greatest (warmer in summer and cooler in winter) in the shallow eastern embayments. The water is coolest in February or March and warmest in August.

The Irish Sea has numerous marine coastal sites of national conservation importance (Vincent *et al.*, 2004) and because of its comparatively large tidal range has a rapidly expanding and planned marine renewable energy industry comprising offshore wind farms, tidal stream generation and tidal energy lagoons. Freshwater input to the Irish Sea is high with most (61%) from rivers draining the eastern seaboard. The rivers are very varied in their hydrology and geomorphology. The surrounding land types range from the steep, unimproved, base-poor, mountainous uplands of western Wales and NW England, through the richer agricultural lowlands and coastal plains of SE Ireland and SW Wales, to the large estuaries of the Rivers Liffey, Welsh Dee, Mersey and Lune and Border Esk, surrounded in some cases by urbanised and industrial landscapes. Throughout there are very many small coastal streams, most of which support sea trout. For a full description of Irish Sea hydrography see reviews by Vincent *et al.* (2004) and Howarth (2006).

METHODS

DATA SOURCES

This account is based on results from historical studies in the Irish Sea, rod catches routinely recorded by the Environment Agency in England and Wales and scale sampling and reading by the Celtic Sea Trout Project (CSTP, 2016). Sampling of the post-smolt and adult phases only is described, and most of the CSTP results reported here are from a selection of 23 rivers (from 42 with scale samples) for which adequate data were available. Adult data were collected in three main ways:

1. Rod catches were the only indices of in-river stock size universally available for most rivers, although they bring problems of data quality, consistency and through the assumptions implicit in using catch as an index of stock (Shelton, 2001). Rod catch data are gathered differently in the countries around the Irish Sea and those from the Welsh and English rivers, collated from license returns and reported by the Environment Agency, are considered to be the most reliable (Harris & Evans, 2017) and are reported in this account. Catch

data have been collected consistently since 1976 in Wales, when fisheries management was transferred to regional organisations and, since 1994 in England and Wales, when the regional monitoring was consolidated nationally, reporting was enhanced by an improved reminder system and the inclusion of fishing effort into license returns began. The Environment Agency adjusts declared rod catch (C) by fixed factors to correct for changes in reporting efficiency (Environment Agency, 2003) as follows: pre-1992, C x 1.56; 1992 and 1993, C x 1.9; and post 1993, C x 1·1. For long-term trend analyses the Welsh data from 1976 and the English data from 1994 were used. The Irish and Scottish catch data (CSTP, 2016) were not used in this analysis.

2. During the CSTP, scales were collected by volunteer anglers, scientific teams and by sampling from the few remaining commercial fisheries, mostly between 2009 and 2012. Standard protocols were established for the anglers and communicated through numerous meetings, printed media and a website (www.celticseatrout.com).

3. Historical catch statistics and some life history data from scale reading provided temporal comparisons. These were drawn mainly from Nall (1930, 1931), Went (1962), Fahy (1978), Solomon (1995) and Harris (2002) and references therein. The raw data from Harris (2002) were available and these were reworked to test hypotheses on temporal and spatial variation, comparing with present day (CSTP) data.

AGE AND LIFE HISTORY SCHEDULES FROM SCALES

Scale reading procedures and protocols (Poole, 2010) were established within the CSTP to ensure consistency and quality assurance between workers in the participating laboratories in Ireland (Inland Fisheries Ireland) and Wales (Bangor University). The life history is summarised by the scale reading formula, and the nomenclature used is based on that used by most workers in the British Isles (Elliott & Chambers, 1997), being in two parts: the number before the point shows the freshwater age; and the coding after the point shows the sea age and spawning history, as exemplified by some examples below.

- 1.0+: smolted after one freshwater winter and first returned to the river before first sea winter.
- n.0+: as above, but unspecified freshwater age.
- n.1+: first returned to the river after one sea winter, with plus growth (most fish have plus growth).
- n.0+SM+: first returned to the river as a whitling, spawned, returned to sea and returned to the river a second time as a previous spawner.
- n.2+2SM+: spent two years at sea before its first return to the river, spawned and returned to sea on two occasions and has then been captured returning to the river a third time at a total sea age of 4 years.

Most information on sea trout life histories has come from scale reading on adult stocks sampled by angling in rivers and coastal and estuarine netting; but an important exception is the trap site on the Welsh Dee where a continuous stock assessment programme has operated since 1991 (Davidson *et al.*, 2006a). Because the rod catch statistics and the scale samples from traps and rod fisheries refer to the whole catchment scale, the whole river run is taken to be the basic stock unit; but in reality it is likely to comprise multiple populations and this necessary sampling regime obscures to some extent the characteristics of true populations.

Scales from 5,108 river-caught adults were read, of which 3,907 had complete readings. The others had, variously, unreadable freshwater growth, unclear outer checks, or ambiguous distinction between sea winters and freshwater return (spawning or freshwater resident phases). The results have included these partial readings where appropriate; for example, an inability to record freshwater age or failure to distinguish reliably a sea-winter check from freshwater sojourn does not prevent an estimate of total sea age (i.e. post-smolt age).

ENVIRONMENTAL DATA

Water temperature is a major determinant of fish growth (Brett, 1956) and was used in this study as an explanatory variable for fish size. Long-term variation in monthly sea surface temperature (SST) was estimated for four coastal sites in the Irish Sea (Swansea, Moelfre, Port Erin and Heysham), averaged for the period 1960-2004 using data from Joyce (2006). Correlations between these data and Central England Air Temperature (CET) were strong (unpublished data) and were used to estimate from CET data the SST values for years after 2004.

To provide data compatible with the CSTP study rivers and to enable comparison with the 1996-98 data (Harris, 2002), satellite-derived SST data (AVHRR Pathfinder Version 5: http://poet.jpl.nasa.gov/) for 2010 to 2012 were averaged for a square of approximately $20km^2$ adjacent to each river mouth. Monthly averages were derived from daily data. Temperature values used were night time SST to approximate average daily temperature at 1m depth. Latitude was taken at the tidal limit of each river.

DATA ANALYSIS

Trends in rod catch were analysed for two periods. 1) Between 1976 and 2011 adjusted annual rod catches for 12 Welsh rivers were used that were considered not to have been influenced unduly by freshwater environmental or reporting factors (Ogmore, Tawe, Tywi, Cleddau, Nevern, Teifi, Dyfi, Mawddach, Dwyfawr, Llyfni, Conwy, Clwyd). 2) Between 1994 and 2012 catch per unit effort (cpue – as catch per angler day) were available for 26 Welsh and10 English rivers. Rod catch data were transformed to z-values (z = (annual value – long-term mean) / long-term standard deviation) to compare better long-term trends amongst rivers on a standardised scale.

Two-way factorial analysis of variance was used to estimate approximate values for temporal variance. This analysis used data for the period 1994 to 2010 (only provisional data for 2010 were available at the time) for 10 English and 26 Welsh rivers that had sea trout annual rod catches >100. Annual adjusted catch (C), expressed as ln(C) and cpue and their z-scores, were analyzed by random effects two-way ANOVA using Excel. There were no missing data or zero catches. The additive model applied to natural log-transformed data, Ln(C) was:

$$Ln(C_{ij}) = \mu + s_i + y_j + e_{ij}$$

where C_{ij} = rod catch for river *i* in year *j*; s_i = effect due to river *i*; y_j = effect due to year *j*; e_{ij} = error, including recording error and interaction between site *i* and year *j*.

Variance was partitioned into three components (spatial, temporal and error). Spatial variance (V_s), temporal variance (V_t) and error variance (V_e) were estimated approximately from:

$$V_s = (MS_s\text{-}MS_e)/m$$
$$V_t = (MS_t\text{-}MS_e)/n$$
$$V_e = MS_e$$
$$\text{and } V_T = V_s + V_t + V_e$$

where V_T = total variance; MS_s = mean square (rivers); MS_t = mean square (years); MS_e = error mean square; *m* = number of years; *n* = number of rivers.

Temporal variance is that attributed to variation between years and indicates the degree of synchronous variation between rivers. Spatial variance is that deriving from differences amongst rivers. In the case of z-scores there is no spatial variance (between river) component because the data for each are standardised to their long term mean and the calculation was simplified accordingly ($V_T = V_t + V_e$).

Three life history traits were available for 23 rivers, sampled over 2009 to 2012:
1. Whitling length (as an index of first year growth),
2. Proportion of whitling (as an index of proportions of fish returning in their first post-smolt year); and
3. Proportional survival between sea age 1 and sea age 2 (as an index of post first sea-winter survival).

Three explanatory factors were considered:
1. Latitude (degrees) of the river mouth,
2. Seaboard category; thus eastern seaboard includes rivers entering Galloway, English Welsh and Isle of Man coasts, and western seaboard includes rivers entering the Island of Ireland coasts),
3. Mean sea surface temperature in: a) spring, b) summer and c) winter months.

Annual survival (S%) was estimated from loss rates based on the abundance (N_t) of sea age classes, taking whitling as year 0. $N_t = N_0 e^{-zt}$ where N_0 = start abundance, N_t = final abundance, t = the time period (years) and z = instantaneous mortality (loss) rate; then annual $S = 100.e^{-z}$. Starting abundance was taken as the abundance of sea age 1 sea trout, i.e. fish after their first sea winter. This start point was chosen because the abundance of returning whitling does not reflect the relative abundance of surviving sea age 0 fish (N_0) due to variation in the first post-smolt year return pattern among rivers. This meant that the survival estimates were in fact mean survival of fish after their first sea winter, thus after the "decision" to return as whitling or remain at sea is made; but the results are still indicative of average marine loss rates of adult fish.

Relationships amongst the life history traits and the abiotic variables were analysed by tree regression (Crawley, 2009), general linear models, ANOVA and ANCOVA using R (R Core team, 2014).

Due to small annual samples sizes and resulting inadvertent seasonal bias, the data were averaged across years prior to analysis over the CSTP sampling period, 2009 – 2012. This avoided pseudo-replication issues, but obscured between-year effects which would have been useful to examine. The relationships are therefore indicative only of the average environmental conditions and life histories obtaining over the four years of the CSTP study.

RESULTS

STOCK SIZE AND TRENDS IN ABUNDANCE

The Welsh catch data for 12 rivers showed long-term trends in adjusted catch since 1976, with V_t = 19%, V_s = 60% and V_e = 21%, indicating the levels of synchronous variation. This is evident in the z-score variation (Figure 2) in which V_t = 51%, indicating a strong degree of synchrony in the proportional changes of the catches in these rivers. The sharp decline in the late 1980s (Figure 2) matches the timing of reductions in sea trout stocks of western Ireland (Gargan *et al.*, 2006) and Scotland (Butler & Walker, 2006). However, sea lice infestation (Gargan *et al.*, 2017), to which the Irish and Scottish declines were attributed, was not likely a factor in the Welsh situation because there is no marine salmonid aquaculture in the Irish Sea. Some of the spatial variation could have been due to the rod catch adjustment applied; but assuming that the adjustments are appropriate, the data indicated some overall decline in abundance over this period overlaying common cycles amongst the rivers and of course within-river effects. The post-1990 long-term mean catch (604 in this set of larger rivers) has declined by 44% from the pre-1990 mean catch (1,067).

Variation on a wider spatial scale from 36 rivers on the eastern seaboard of the Irish Sea (26 in Wales and 10 in England) also showed high synchrony in the annual variation of cpue over the period 1994 to 2011 (Figure 3). Thus, across all 36 rivers, proportions were: V_t = 35%, V_s = 26% and V_e = 39%. Average values for the Welsh and English data were strongly correlated (Pearson's r = 0.815). The strong temporal coherence in these data is even more evident in cpue z-scores (Figure 3), which removes the spatial effect and for which, across all rivers, $V_t = 53\%$.

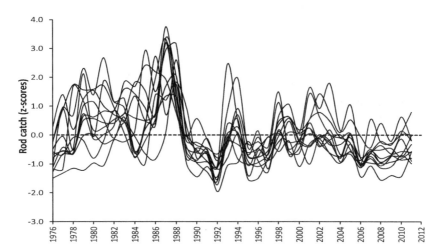

Figure 2. Long-term trends in sea trout rod catch (adjusted for reporting) in 12 Welsh rivers, standardised by z-scores, for the period 1976 to 2011.

STOCK AGE STRUCTURE

There was substantial spatial variation around the Irish Sea in the age structures, with Irish rivers being characterised by a high proportion of whitling (n.0+). Whitling incidence was also high in several rivers of the eastern seaboard, but generally less so than Ireland and, correspondingly, rivers in Isle of Man and the eastern seaboard tended to have a higher proportion of older, larger, multiple spawning adults. There are exceptions such as the Currane (in SW Ireland, not within the Irish Sea) and the River Slaney, which are explored below.

Recent surveys (CSTP, 2016) over the period 2009-2012 showed that 46 different scale formulae (analogous to alternative life histories) occurred across the 23 rivers. The numbers of different scale formulae per river ranged between 5 (Slaney) and 27 (Tywi), the mean, median and modes being 13.5, 12.0 and 10.0 respectively. The most prevalent formula (life history category) was 2.0+ at 46.9%, followed by 2.1+ (20.7%), 3.0+ (8.5%), 2.1+SM+(4.9%) and 2.0+SM1+(3.7%). There was no statistical difference in mean smolt age between the rivers of the eastern (mean = 1.98, sd = 0.062) and western (mean = 2.07, sd = 0.168) seaboards (Table 1); but sea age (yr) was significantly different, with higher mean sea age in rivers of the eastern seaboard (mean = 0.93, sd = 0.390) compared with the west (mean = 0.39, sd = 294). The most prevalent sea age was n.0+ (58.4%) followed by n.1+, n.2+, n.3+ and n.4+ at 29.0%, 8.2%, 2.8% and 1.2% respectively and the oldest sea age was n.8+.

The n.0+ fish (whitling) are small, generally <35cm, and arrived later in the year than older maiden adults. This was shown for the river Dee, north Wales, where a year-round trapping programme (Davidson *et al.*, 2006a) provided the best set of data (with minimum sampling bias) for any individual river in the Irish Sea (Table 2). In the Dee and elsewhere the older sea-winter sea trout (maidens and previous spawners) returned first, for example n.2+ maidens returned in March and April; the peak month for most groups was June and, apart from the whitling (n.0+), few fish arrived after July. In the Dee, Davidson *et al.* (2006a) recorded some fish returning to spawn up to 10 times, with 17 categories of adult life histories, compared with only 8 seen in the CSTP sample.

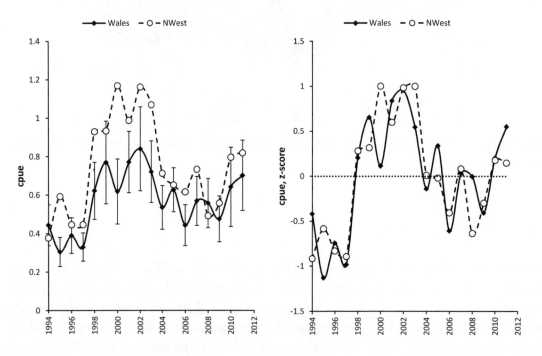

Figure 3. Long-term trends in (left-hand panel) mean annual sea trout rod catch per unit effort (catch per angler day) and (right-hand panel) z-scores of cpue in 26 Welsh and 10 English rivers for the period 1994 to 2011. Error bars (2xSE) are shown for the Welsh cpue set only, for clarity.

The parsimonious assumption that the mean size of whitling returning to rivers will increase as they grow during the year was not met. This was probably due to some combination of smolt migration timing, age and size of smolts and possibly compensatory growth. In the Dee the smallest of the 2.0+ and 3.0+ whitling arrived in August, at the end of the main whitling run (Table 1), and larger fish of the same cohorts were recorded both earlier and later. There was evidence that older smolts returned earlier and at smaller size than younger smolts, although the variance was high (Figure 4). Consequently there was no systematic trend in mean whitling size during the period of their return and the same pattern was seen in the Harris data set (1996-98) for several other English and Welsh rivers (CSTP, 2016).

Table 1. Smolt and sea age composition, whiting (2.0+) fork length, percentage of whiting and percentage marine survival (after sea winter 1) of principal Irish Sea rivers sampled in 2009 – 2012.

Country/Region	River	Sample	% smolt age (yrs 1 to 5)					Mean smolt age (yrs)	% sea age (yrs 0 to 8)									Mean sea age (yrs)	Length 2.0+ (mm)	% as n.0+	% survival post-yr1
			1	2	3	4	5		0	1	2	3	4	5	6	7	8				
Galloway	Border Esk	432	6.5	85.9	7.6	0.0	0.0	2.0	18.3	61.8	16.2	3.0	0.7	0.6	0.0	0.0	0.0	1.1	339	18	24
	Fleet	165	7.3	88.5	4.2	0.0	0.0	2.0	70.9	20.6	5.5	1.8	0.6	0.6	0.0	0.0	0.0	0.4	281	71	48
	Luce	240	3.3	89.6	7.1	0.0	0.0	2.0	35.8	46.7	11.7	3.3	1.3	1.3	0.0	0.0	0.0	0.9	288	36	42
	Nith	305	8.5	77.0	14.4	0.0	0.0	2.1	21.0	55.7	17.0	3.6	2.0	0.7	0.0	0.0	0.0	1.1	330	21	36
Isle of Man	Neb, Sulby, Glass	65	1.5	95.4	3.1	0.0	0.0	2.0	52.3	24.6	9.2	6.2	4.6	3.1	0.0	0.0	0.0	1.0	334	52	67
Ireland	Argideen	253	10.3	79.1	10.3	0.4	0.0	2.0	52.6	41.5	4.7	1.2	0.0	0.0	0.0	0.0	0.0	0.5	285	53	19
	Bandon	84	21.4	72.6	6.0	0.0	0.0	1.8	44.0	53.6	2.4	0.0	0.0	0.0	0.0	0.0	0.0	0.6	309	44	7
	Boyne	242	9.5	74.8	14.5	1.2	0.0	2.1	77.7	17.8	3.7	0.8	0.0	0.0	0.0	0.0	0.0	0.3	289	78	23
	Castletown	348	12.9	77.3	9.8	0.0	0.0	2.0	84.5	14.4	0.9	0.3	0.0	0.0	0.0	0.0	0.0	0.2	287	84	20
	Currane	376	0.3	60.4	35.9	3.2	0.3	2.4	36.2	47.9	9.6	1.9	0.8	0.8	1.9	1.1	0.0	1.0	272	36	60
	Dee White River	234	9.4	76.9	13.2	0.4	0.0	2.0	85.5	12.0	2.1	0.4	0.0	0.0	0.0	0.0	0.0	0.2	264	85	21
	Slaney	186	0.0	86.0	14.0	0.0	0.0	2.1	84.4	14.5	1.1	0.0	0.0	0.0	0.0	0.0	0.0	0.2	220	85	32
Northern Ireland	Shimna	394	10.9	71.8	16.8	0.5	0.0	2.1	85.3	9.4	4.6	0.8	0.0	0.0	0.0	0.0	0.0	0.2	271	84	11
NW England	Ehen	210	6.2	88.1	5.7	0.0	0.0	2.0	78.1	18.1	2.9	1.0	0.0	0.0	0.0	0.0	0.0	0.3	316	78	28
	Lune	323	4.3	91.0	4.6	0.0	0.0	2.0	8.0	55.1	26.9	7.7	1.9	0.0	0.3	0.0	0.0	1.4	302	8	33
	Ribble	76	9.2	89.5	1.3	0.0	0.0	1.9	15.8	55.3	25.0	3.9	0.0	0.0	0.0	0.0	0.0	1.2	285	16	30
Wales	Clwyd	84	6.0	89.3	4.8	0.0	0.0	2.0	72.6	17.9	9.5	0.0	0.0	0.0	0.0	0.0	0.0	0.4	319	73	56
	Conwy	73	12.3	83.6	4.1	0.0	0.0	1.9	46.6	42.5	9.6	0.0	1.4	0.0	0.0	0.0	0.0	0.7	348	47	35
	Dee	117	8.5	89.7	1.7	0.0	0.0	1.9	59.0	34.2	6.0	0.9	0.0	0.0	0.0	0.0	0.0	0.5	338	42	38
	Dyfi	247	6.1	88.3	5.7	0.0	0.0	2.0	8.5	65.2	20.6	2.4	2.8	0.4	0.0	0.0	0.0	1.3	365	9	34
	Tawe	32	21.9	75.0	3.1	0.0	0.0	1.8	31.3	40.6	12.5	9.4	3.1	3.1	0.0	0.0	0.0	1.2	436	31	62
	Teifi	118	3.4	91.5	5.1	0.0	0.0	2.0	28.8	48.3	12.7	6.8	1.7	0.8	0.0	0.8	0.0	1.1	349	29	54
	Tywi	394	4.3	90.1	5.6	0.0	0.0	2.0	21.3	40.1	19.0	12.7	5.6	1.0	0.0	0.0	0.3	1.5	367	21	46
	Total	4998	7.1	81.7	10.8	0.4	0.0	2.0	47.5	37.0	10.6	3.1	1.2	0.4	0.2	0.1	0.0	0.8			

Table 2. Numbers and percentage frequencies of adult sea trout life history categories for the River Dee, North Wales, data pooled for 2010-2012.

Sea Age	Mar	Apr	May	Jun	Jul	Aug	Sep	Oct	Nov	Dec	Total	% All
0+	0.0	0.0	0.2	24.6	50.0	20.5	1.6	1.4	1.6	0.2	570	41.9
0+Sm+	0.0	0.0	16.1	73.5	6.0	2.1	0.9	0.9	0.6	0.0	336	24.7
0+2Sm+	0.0	0.0	24.5	63.5	7.3	0.9	0.0	0.9	0.0	0.9	110	8.1
0+3SM+	0.0	2.8	33.3	61.1	2,8	0.0	0.0	0.0.	0.0	0.0	36	2.6
0+4SM+	0.0	0.0	53.8	38.5	7.7	0.0	0.0	0.0	0.0	0.0	13	1.0
0+5SM+	0.0	0.0	33.3	66.7	0.0	0.0	0.0	0.0	0.0	0.0	3	0.2
0+6SM+	0.0	0.0	0.0	100.0	0.0	0.0	0.0	0.0	0.0	0.0	2	0.1
0.9SM+	0.0	0.0	0.0	100.0	0.0	0.0	0.0	0.0	0.0	0.0	1	0.1
1+	0.6	0.0	9.6	68.7	14.5	1.2	2.4	3.0	0.0	0.0	166	12.2
1+SM+	0.0	1.5	18.2	74.2	3.0	0.0	3.0	0.0	0.0	0.0	66	4.9
1+2SM+	0.0	0.0	30.0	50.0	15.0	0.0	0.0	5.0	0.0	0.0	20	1.5
1+3SM+	0.0	0.0	25.0	75.0	0.0	0.0	0.0	0.0	0.0	0.0	12	0.9
1+$SM+	0.0	0.0	50.0	50.0	0.0	0.0	0.0	0.0	0.0	0.0	2	0.1
1+5SM+	0.0	0.0	0.0	100.0	0.0	0.0	0.0	0.0	0.0	0.0	2	0.1
2+	6.7	6.7	0.0	60.0	13.3	6.7	0.0	0.0	6.7	0.0	15	1.1
2.SM+	0.0	0.0	20.0	60.0	20.0	0.0	0.0	0.0	0.0	0.0	5	0.4
2.2SM+	0.0	0.0	0.0	100.0	0.0	0.0	0.0	0.0	0.0	0.0.	1	0.1
ALL	0.0	0.2	10.4	51.1	25.6	9.4	1.3	1.3	0.9	0.1	1360	

Although five smolt age classes (1 to 5yr old) have been identified previously (Went, 1962) and were seen also in the 2009-2012 surveys, most sea trout in Irish Sea rivers migrate to sea at age 2+ (Table 2). An exception is the Currane system in which a high proportion of 3-year old smolts was recorded (Table 2). The Currane is unusual in that its freshwater production is dominated by a lake system close to the sea and its adjacent marine environment is more oceanic than that of the other rivers. Fahy (1978) reported that mean smolt age (MSA) in Ireland and Wales was generally lower compared to Scottish stocks, with higher latitude being associated with longer parr life cycles (i.e. higher MSA); a pattern reported also in Scandinavia (L'Abée Lund *et al.*, 1989). However, data from more recent surveys (Harris, 2002; CSTP, 2016) did not demonstrate a statistically significant relationship over the latitude range of the Irish Sea. Taking the Fahy, Harris and CSTP sets to be representative in years 1970-80, 1996-1998 and 2010-2012 respectively (NB these samples were not from all the same rivers), the mean MSA for the periods were 2.56 (n = 8, sd = 0.391), 2.05 yr (n=10, sd = 0.038) and 2.01 (n = 21, sd = 0.122) respectively, suggesting a long-term reduction in MSA, although with less change over the later interval. 2+ smolts still dominate the sea trout populations in Irish Sea rivers. In 8 rivers (Border Esk, Lune, Ribble, Dee, Clwyd, Dyfi, Teifi and Tywi) that were sampled in both of the more recent periods MSA had decreased significantly (P < 0.001) from 2.05 (sd = 0.037) to 1.98 (sd = 0.038). In contemporary data (2010 – 2012) there was no statistical difference in MSA between the eastern (mean = 1.98, sd = 0.062, n = 15) and western (mean = 2.07, sd = 0.168, n = 8) seaboard rivers.

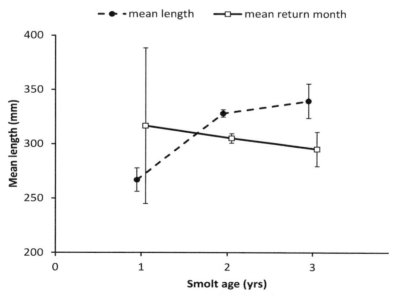

Figure 4. Size (fork length) and mean return time of whitling (n.0+) of different smolt ages, 1.0+ (N=3), 2.0+ (N=488), 3.0+ (N=42) in the river Dee 2010-2012. Error bars are +/- 95% CL.

SPATIAL AND TEMPORAL VARIATION IN GROWTH

Measurement of true growth rate in sea trout is complicated by their partial migration back to rivers, because only part of each cohort is available to be sampled by fisheries or traps, the remainder being still at sea. A resulting dichotomy of growth performance is illustrated by long-term trap data from the River Dee, north Wales (Davidson *et al.*, 2006a). Partitioning of size data (in this case, only mass in kg was available) between fish that returned as spawners and those of the same cohort that remained at sea to return subsequently as maiden fish demonstrated that remaining at sea conferred a growth advantage in most cases (Figure 5). This could be due a combination of inherent growth performance of different migrant groups, or to the reduction of feeding in freshwater (Elliott, 1997), coupled with the energy demands of migration and reproduction (Jonsson & Jonsson 2006). Comparative growth is therefore better represented by maiden fish, which have not had the freshwater growth interruption.

Fork length at 2.0+ was taken as an index of marine growth in the first post-smolt year (Table 1). The variation was examined initially by tree regression incorporating factors that were regarded as potential explanatory variables: latitude, seaboard category (east or west), sea surface temperature (SST) and river size (catchment area, km^2). Whitling size was partitioned into east and west categories with the east having a mean length of 284

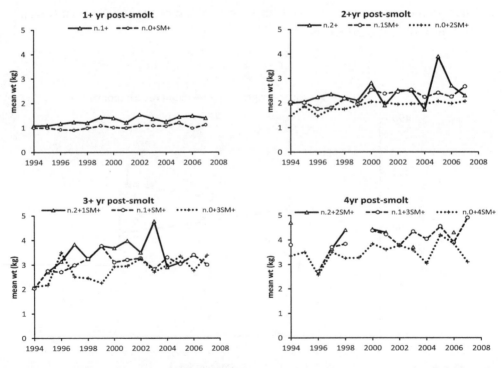

Figure 5. Annual variation in the effect of remaining at sea or returning to spawn, on mean size (kg) of sea trout in the River Dee (1994-2007). Four cohorts (1-4yr post-smolt) are shown within which, in most cases, fish that have remained at sea are larger at age than those that have previously returned to spawn.

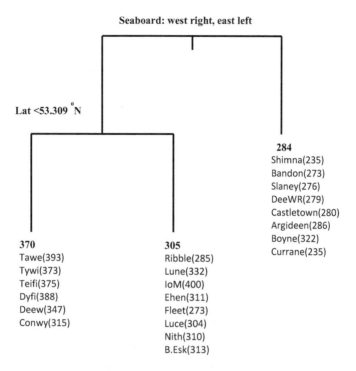

Figure 6. Tree regression model for mean fork length (mm) of whitling for 23 rivers in the Irish Sea (including the Currane). Rivers grouped in each category are shown with their mean lengths. The first node (seaboard) is either western or eastern seaboard of the Irish Sea, the second is latitude.

mm (Figure 6). The eastern rivers were further partitioned into north (north of latitude 53°, approximately north Wales) and south groups, having mean lengths of 305mm and 370mm respectively. Thus the Irish coast is typified by smaller whitling and on the eastern sea board larger mean sizes typically occur in more southerly rivers. There are important river-specific effects and within these broad categories there is further variation not revealed by the tree regression. For example, the river Currane, although grouping with the western coast, has large whitling, possibly a function of its lake system or productive oceanic marine environment. The length (L) of 2.0+ whitling was significantly related to latitude (Lat) on the eastern seaboard by: $L = -27.279 \times Lat + 1793.8$, $n = 15$, $r = 0.801$, $p < 0.01$), but not on the western seaboard (the Irish coast) where the relationship was $L = -11.572 \times Lat + 904.9$, $n = 8$, $r = 0.529$, NS).

Water temperature varies with latitude, being colder in more northerly regions (although influenced also by local bathymetry and hydrography) and with longitude (warmer in summer and cooler in the winter on the east side of the Irish Sea, CSTP, 2016). Mean annual sizes of whitling (2.0+) and 2.1+ and 2.2+ maidens were correlated negatively with latitude and positively with temperature on the east side, but less so on the west seaboard (Table 3). The

Table 3. Correlations (Pearson's r) between various growth metrics (lengths at age and annual increment up to the first sea winter of sea trout from rivers of the eastern (15 rivers) and western (8 rivers) seaboards of the Irish Sea, and latitude and annual mean sea surface temperature in the adjacent marine zones. ND = no data.

Growth metric (mm)	Latitude		Water temp (°C)	
	East	West	East	West
length 2.0+	-0.801	-0.529	0.794	0.585
length 2.1+	-0.838	-0.492	0.795	0.649
length 2.2+	-0.172	ND	0.273	ND
Δ length, n.0+ to n.1+	-0.297	-0.203	0.238	0.338
$P_{0.05 =}$	0.4973	0.664	0.4973	0.664

interaction of temperature (spring and summer) and longitude was evident, such that for a given temperature smolts were larger in the east than the west coasts (Figure 7).

Long-term climate change has caused average SST to rise in the Irish Sea by about 0.3 °C per decade between 1960 and 2004 (CSTP, 2016) and this may have been a contributory factor in long-term change in sea trout size. Historical mean size data from scale readings, mainly for river-caught sea trout, reported in reviews by Solomon (1995) and Harris (2002), were combined with the CSTP data to describe long-term change in length on the eastern seaboard (Figure 8). The sample sizes were often small and the representation of different rivers in the different periods was inconsistent. Temporal change was seen over the period (1923-2011). It has already been

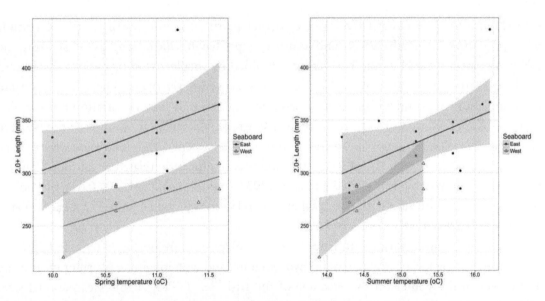

Figure 7. Relationships between whitling size (2.0+) and sea surface temperatures (Left: spring, Right: summer) on eastern and western seaboards of the Irish Sea. Shaded areas are 95% confidence limits.

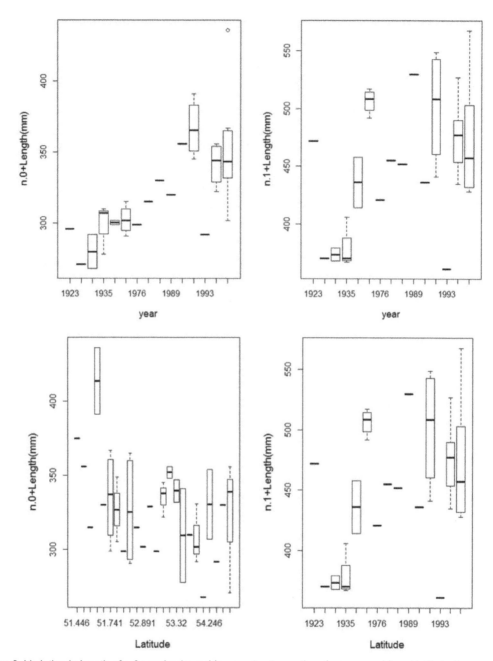

Figure 8. Variation in length of n.0+ and n.1+ maiden sea trout over time (*upper panels*) and latitude (*lower panels*). The data are based on scale readings from various studies reported in Solomon (1995) and Harris (2002).

shown that whitling size varies with latitude and the unbalanced data set (unequal representation of rivers over years and latitudes) further renders bivariate plots uncertain. However, after latitude effects were accounted for, using analysis of covariance, the n.0+ increase was still significant over time ($p < 0.05$), but the increase in n.1+ was marginally not significant.

PROPORTIONS OF WHITLING (TIMING OF FIRST RETURN)

The proportion of whitling (as mean values over the CSTP study 2009-2012) in sea trout rod catches varied considerably among the 23 rivers, ranging from 8% in the Lune to 86% on the Dee White River (Table 1). Tree regression showed primary splits at mean whitling length < 295mm: rivers with smaller whitling had higher mean proportions of whitling (62%). Of rivers in the larger whitling size group, those with annual survival > 43.9% had mean whitling proportions of 38%, and those with annual survival < 44% had the lowest proportions of whitling (mean 24%). Thus, high proportions of whitling were associated with smaller size and lower survival. There was a significantly ($p<0.01$) higher whitling proportion on the western seaboard (mean = 68.8%, sd = 20.90, n = 8) than the east (mean = 36.8%, sd = 23.16, n = 15); and on the western side the whitling proportion was statistically positively correlated with latitude (Figure 9).

Long-term variation in whitling proportions was hard to assess due to the lack of data, but some patterns were seen in rod catch size distributions from Wales. Based on size/age keys for the River Dee, it is known that the size category < 0.8kg, comprises mostly whitling. In a sample of 1,200 fish < 0.8kg trapped between 2003 and 2007, 98.6% were whitling. The proportion of this size category in rod catches has increased significantly between 1976 and 2007 in 5 rivers for which data were available (Figure 10).

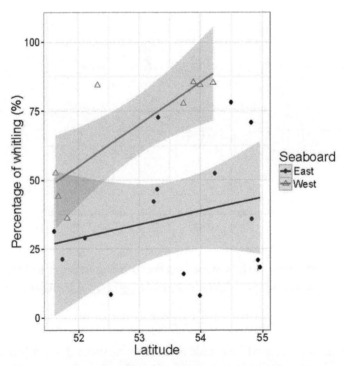

Figure 9. Relationships between percentage of whitling and latitude in 23 Irish Sea rivers on eastern and western seaboards of the Irish Sea. Shaded areas are 95% confidence limits. The relationship was significant for the western rivers (y = 15.214X + 736.14, r^2 = 0.695, n = 8), but not for the eastern group.

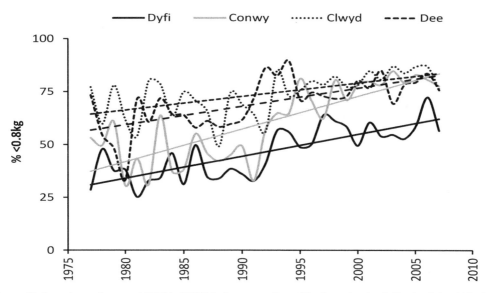

Figure 10. Long term changes (1977 to 2007) in the proportions (Y) of sea trout < 0.8kg (mainly whitling), in the rod catches of four Welsh rivers. Equations: Dyfi Y = 1.04X - 2025.2, R^2 = 0.615; Conwy Y = 1.5439X - 3015.1, R^2 = 0.640; Dee Y = 0.8681X – 1659.6, R^2 = 0.427; Clwyd Y = 0.6447 -1210.2, R^2 = 0.327.

SURVIVAL

Annual survival (S) in the second sea year averaged 39.5% (sd = 16.39) over the 23 rivers and ranged from 7% (Bandon) to 67% (Isle of Man rivers) (Table 1). Survival was positively correlated with whitling length (Figure 11), but the Currane stood out from the other Irish rivers as a stock with high survival (59%). Omitting this atypical river from the western seaboard set, the survival was significantly lower (mean = 19%, sd = 8.4, n = 7) than on the eastern side (mean = 42%, sd = 15.1, n = 15). Tree regression (Figure 12) identified a primary split at average whitling size of 295 mm; stocks with smaller mean size had mean survival of 28%. Within the larger size group, a further significant split occurred at SST of 11°C, with the lower temperature group having lower survival rates, 41% compared with 51% for the warmer group. Overall, low marine survival was associated with cooler average temperatures and smaller whitling size. It should be noted that the survivals are for fish older than whitling; this is not evidence of a direct association between whitling size and whitling survival, but merely of an index of average adult sea trout survival. Survival estimates were made for 7 rivers that were sampled in 1996-98 and 2009-2012 (Tywi, Teifi, Dyfi, Dee, Ribble, Lune and Border Esk), but there was no significant change between these periods. Although contemporary adult survival and proportion of whitling across all rivers were significantly negatively related to whitling size, survival was not significantly related to whitling proportion (Figure 11).

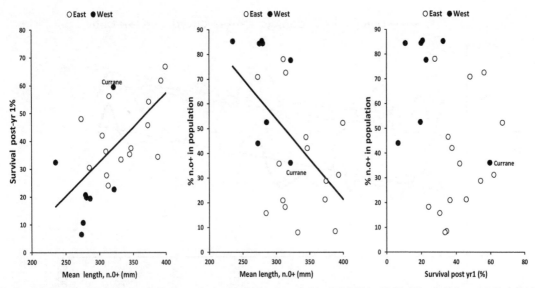

Figure 11. Relationships between (*left*) survival and whitling length (Y = 0.2472X - 42.50, R² = 0.404, p<0.01); (*middle*) proportion of whitling and whitling length (Y = -0.3257 =151.7, R² = 0.288, P<0.01); and (*right*) proportion of whitling and survival (R² = 0.074, NS) for 23 Irish Sea rivers. The Currane stands out from other Irish rivers (*see text*).

INFLUENCE OF TEMPORAL VARIATION IN MARINE ENVIRONMENT ON TRAITS

Environmental factors have been suggested above as influences on life history features. This was examined for the period 1994 to 2011 when rod catches were supported by effort data and returning stock estimates (RSE) were available for the River Dee, north Wales. Environmental change was indexed by anomalies in seasonal NAO (North Atlantic Oscillation) and mean sea surface temperature (SST) for the Irish Sea, all standardised by z-scores for comparison (Figure 13), but correlations (Table 5) were performed on the raw data. Significant correlations between cpue and RSE data gave confidence *post hoc* in the interpretation of the former as stock indices (Table 4). NAO variation was not significantly correlated with any stock metrics; but SST for April-June was significantly correlated with abundance in the eastern seaboard rivers, with the proportion of whitling in the River Dee and with the Dee RSE.

DISCUSSION

When sea trout migrate to sea to feed on their major food items of sand eel and sprat (Roche *et al*, 2017) they become part of the pelagic marine ecosystem and are subject to a completely new set of environmental variables. There is abundant evidence that sea conditions influence life history traits of sea trout (e.g. Jonsson & L'Abée-Lund, 1993; de Leeuw *et al*., 2007; Degerman *et al*., 2012; Thorstad *et al*., 2016; Quéméré *et al*., 2016), which in turn translate into variance

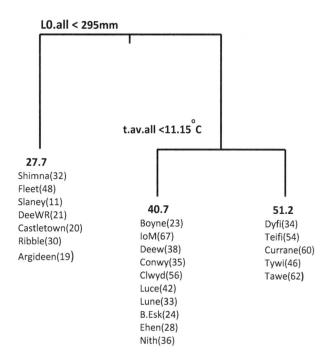

Figure 12. Tree regression model for annual % survival (post sea age 1) for 23 rivers in the Irish Sea (including the Currane). Rivers grouped in each category are shown with their mean % survivals. The first node is at whitling length 295mm and the second is at average annual sea temperature of 11°C. Note Currane grouping with South Wales rivers.

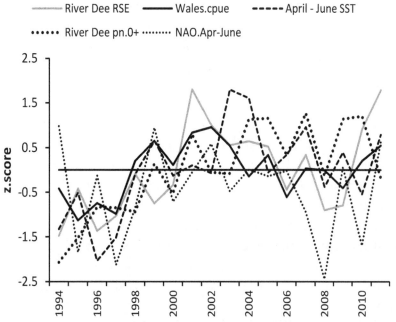

Figure 13. Long-term variation in annual stock parameters: catch per unit effort (cpue), total returning stock estimate (RSE), proportion of whitling (n.0+) in the river Dee and seasonal environmental variables: April to June North Atlantic Oscillation (NAO) and mean Irish Sea surface temperature (SST).

Table 4. Correlations (Pearson's *r*) between various annual stock parameters: catch per unit effort (cpue), total returning stock estimate (RSE), proportion of whitling (n.0+) in the river Dee and seasonal climate variables: North Atlantic Oscillation (NAO) and mean Irish Sea sea surface temperature (SST). (df = 16, $P_{0.05}$ = 0.468).

Variable	Wales cpue	NW cpue	Dee RSE	Dee propn0+
NW cpue	0.816	-	-	-
Dee RSE	0.678	0.678	-	-
Dee propn0+	0.397	0.220	0.519	-
NAO Nov-Dec	0.063	0.121	-0.143	-0.447
NAO Apr-Jun	0.409	0.234	0.161	0.047
NAO Jul -Oct	-0.247	-0.133	0.107	-0.040
SST Jan-Mar	0.385	0.472	0.192	-0.045
SST Apr-Jun	0.514	0.521	0.546	0.556
SST Jul-Sep	0.316	0.395	0.088	-0.082
SST Oct - Dec	-0.232	-0.082	-0.017	-0.400

in population dynamics parameters such as population growth rate and resilience (Tysklind *et al.*, 2015); but the results reported here are the first we are aware of to quantify the influence of marine environmental factors on sea trout life histories in British Isles coastal waters. Direct measurements could not be made for any of these features, and the various surrogates used come with uncertainties, caveats and cautions in their interpretation.

The synchronous long-term changes in abundance indicated by changes in rod catch are indicative of responses to some common factor or factors, although the mechanisms are not clear. Catch variation is partly a function of fishing effort, which could vary systematically over time; but synchronicity was seen in both catches alone and in cpue. Run size, here indexed by cpue, could also be directly affected by freshwater factors. For example, river flow is known to be an important influence on Atlantic salmon (*Salmo salar* L.) runs and catches in many rivers (Banks, 1969, Gee, 1980; Thorstad *et al.*, 2008, Milner *et al.*, 2012), but its effects are less clear for sea trout. Analysis of electronic counter data in the River Lune for example, showed that sea trout runs are far less responsive to flow variation than salmon (Milner, *unpublished*). While a river flow effect may be a contributory factor, it seems unlikely to explain the widespread synchrony observed in the Irish Sea east coast catch data.

Total adult catch may be a less precise measure of returns to freshwater if the relative abundance of different age classes alters over time. Such systematic change was observed in a subset of Welsh rivers, which showed an increase in proportions of smaller (younger) fish, which would increase total catch. Marine survival over recent years from late 1990s to 2012, has not changed detectably and the increase in proportions of small fish (< 0.8kg), dominated by whitling, is therefore thought to be probably more indicative of a shift to earlier return and first maturation than to reduced marine growth or increased marine mortality of older fish over this time period.

Marine growth estimates were based on the lengths of 2.0+ sea trout (whitling), to eliminate any effect of smolt age variation between rivers (although it was shown that this source of error was small). However, a further source of variation could be the size of smolts, which would invoke the influence of freshwater environmental conditions on parr growth, thus in turn affecting whitling size, if smolt size varied substantially and systematically with latitude. In the absence of contemporary Irish Sea data on smolt lengths, this remains a potentially confounding factor. Jonson & L'Abée-Lund (1993) found no relationship between smolt size and latitude in their description of clinal variation in European and Scandinavian sea trout traits. They did find significant relationships between latitude and parr growth (difference between year-2 and year-1 lengths) and between parr growth and smolt size. Davidson *et al.* (2006b) reported a consistent annual parr growth in the Welsh Dee of around 10-11 cm over the period between 1987 and 2000, which corresponds to mean smolt length of around 19 cm according to the results of Jonsson & L'Abée-Lund (1993). Moreover, over the latitude range of the Irish Sea (approximately 51.6° to 55.0°), their relationship predicted a range of parr growth of 9.0 to 10.8 cm at the northern and southern limits respectively. If that size difference (18mm) was translated to smolt size it would only explain 20% of the difference in 2.0+ whitling size (91 mm, as predicted by its relationship with latitude in the Irish Sea). Therefore, while some minor smolt size effect can be anticipated, it is probably insufficient to invalidate the conclusions presented here on the response of post-smolt growth to marine environmental factors.

It was not possible with the data available to estimate directly the survival of post-smolts. Instead an index of adult marine mortality (strictly, a loss rate) was derived from the relative abundance of fish older than n.1+ in the river samples, from which a mean % survival index was derived. This minimised the problem of the evidently highly variable proportion of fish returning as whitling, but it is acknowledged that this index is expected to be greater than true survival in the first post-smolt year, which like other anadromous salmonids is a period of high mortality (Thorstad *et al.*, 2016). It may nevertheless be indicative of general survival conditions in the putative marine habitats occupied by sea trout from the different rivers. The positive correlation between survival rate and whitling size (Figures 11 & 12) is therefore interpreted as evidence that marine conditions favouring high growth, principally high SST and possibly also higher food availability (although there are no data on that) are conducive to high survival in sea trout older than 1 sea winter. The hypothesis is that survival of sea trout in their first sea summer is also higher, and that high survival might therefore lower the likelihood of early return as whitling. The speculative life history argument for this is that low marine growth and survival would lead to reduced reproductive potential and lifetime fitness if such a disadvantageous marine stage was prolonged, therefore natural selection would favour an earlier return and commencement of the reproductive phase. Sea age at maturity in Atlantic salmon is positively correlated with growth rate at sea when compared across multiple populations, but negatively correlated within a population (Hutchings & Jones, 1998).

Marine growth has increased throughout the Irish Sea since the 1920s and in the River Dee specifically since around 1990 (Davidson *et al.,* 2006a); but there was no evidence of changing mortality, at least for the period from the late 1990s to 2010. However, within a river stock, an increasing tendency to return as n.0+ will *a priori* reduce the proportion of older age classes, because mortality is expected to be higher in fish that return and begin their reproductive phase earlier than those that remain at sea. Freshwater return was also seen to reduce growth compared with maiden trout remaining at sea and this effect has been reported elsewhere (Jonsson and Jonsson, 2009; Degerman *et al.*, 2012).

Marine factors are reported to influence salmon marine growth and survival (Friedland 1998; Friedland *et al.*, 2000; Beaugrand & Reid, 2003; Boylan & Adams, 2006; Todd *et al.*, 2012), and similar effects on sea trout are likely. The preliminary study here showed significant correlations between spring SST and sea trout stock abundance and composition in the Irish Sea since 1994. The mechanisms are unclear, but such major environmental drivers have been linked with marine productivity through trophodymanics (Beaugrand & Reid, 2003), although plankton changes in the Irish Sea have been limited compared with the North Sea (Edward *et al.*, 2013). Unfortunately, suitable data on the abundance of keystone prey species such as sand eel and sprat are lacking for the Irish Sea, so it was not possible to develop further the association between marine ecosystem state and sea trout feeding. Water temperature is an important determinant of fish growth that has demonstrably changed over decades and varies spatially with latitude and longitude in the Irish Sea. Significant temporal association between temperature and sea trout growth was shown, and the importance of in April to June SST on growth and abundance coincided with the early post-smolt period when growth and survival conditions are likely to be most critical (Thorstad *et al.*, 2016; Aldvén & Davidsen, 2017). However, growth-temperature models appropriate to growth in salt water and with fish-dominated diets are still lacking, so it has not been possible to link growth to temperature directly through a process mechanism. Nevertheless, the tentative conclusion is that climate-forcing has altered aspects of the Irish Sea environment, changing conditions for sea trout growth and therefore time of first return.

An important unknown factor was the actual environment occupied by sea trout in the sea. There is a continuum of use from long-term (2+yr) stay at sea to to-and-fro exchanges between sea, estuaries and rivers (Thorstad *et al.*, 2016; Aldven & Davidsen, 2017). The parsimonious assumption made here is that the majority of sea trout in the Irish Sea make comparatively restricted movements (perhaps < 100km) from their natal river mouth. This is expected to vary between rivers depending upon local coastal topography, marine productivity and residual current patterns which are likely to influence the extent of their presumed search to maximise growth opportunity. The literature shows a wide range in movements, from the extensive migrations in the North Sea, enabled in part by a wide scale circulatory current pattern, to far more local movements in lochs and fjord systems (e.g. in western Scotland and Norway), but the majority show excursions of less than 100km (Potter *et al*, 2017a; Thorstad *et al.*, 2016). Given the comparatively small size of the Irish Sea and its coastal complexity, at least on the eastern seaboard, it is felt reasonable to assume a fairly restricted migration pattern for most fish; although for any one river there is evidence of a negatively skewed distribution, with a small proportion making longer distance migrations

(Potter *et al.*, 2017b) and this would account for the level of exchange in populations evident from genetic and microchemistry data (Prodhöl *et al.*, 2017; CSTP, 2016). This is supported by hydrodynamic modelling to simulate first year migration tracks for post-smolts in the Irish Sea (Potter *et al.*, 2017b), and these simulated tracks suggest that the fish may experience temperature regimes (total degree days) that are similar to those derived from an assumption of limited movement adopted here.

The time of first return was indexed by the proportion of whitling and taken to represent time of first maturity. This is contentious because there is evidence that sea trout, whitling in particular, can enter rivers to overwinter without breeding (Thorstad *et al.*, 2016). Degerman *et al.* (2012) concluded that in Baltic stocks over-wintering may be more prevalent in areas where winter growth conditions are poor and survival probabilities are low compared with freshwater. Unfortunately, reliable maturity status data are sparse for the Irish Sea; however, for the best-studied population on the Welsh Dee, Davidson *et al.*, (2006a) found that between 1994 and 2002 an average of 76% of whitling were mature (range 58 – 95%), based on relative abundance of .0+SM+ fish in their cohort. Therefore, while some of the observed unexplained variance in whitling proportion might be explained by river-specific behaviours, the level of maturation is sufficiently high to draw conclusions about relative impact of environmental factors.

Two further constraints apply to the data. Firstly, the adult phenotype will reflect the outcome of interaction amongst marine, freshwater and genetic factors. The latter two were not available to this study, but are clearly important (Jonsson & Jonsson, 2006. Dodson *et al.*, 2013; Ferguson *et al.*, 2017). Scandinavian studies have demonstrated statistical association between river size, gradient and altitude and the traits of body size and longevity (L'Abbée-Lund *et al.*, 1989; Jonsson *et al.*, 1991; Jonsson *et al.*, 2001). An analysis of 192 rivers in the British Isles and Europe (Milner *et al.*, 2006) showed that adult body size was significantly correlated with catchment size in salmon and sea trout; but the relationship, although significant, was much more variable in sea trout. In contrast, Jonsson *et al.* (2001) reported that river size in Norway was not related to fish size in rivers with average daily flow > $1m^3s^{-1}$. One has to be cautious in accepting that such spatial patterns represent process-based effects. For example, the intuitively attractive idea that large rivers are associated with larger average anadromous salmonid size because of the greater energetic migration demands in longer, steeper rivers, has been questioned for Atlantic salmon in which large spring spawners can be limited to lowland catchments (Webb & Campbell, 1997).

Secondly, the river samples in this account are likely to represent multiple populations, because within-river genetic structuring is strong in brown trout (Ferguson, 2006) implying a high degree of reproductive isolation. Thus, some of the extensive phenotypic variation seen in migratory trout populations is probably adaptive response to freshwater environments of sub-catchments. These effects will introduce unexplained variance into studies looking at marine effects alone when, as here, they are based on catchment-scale sampling of rod catches. In the present study, catchment area as a surrogate for river size did not explain significant variance of proportions of whitling or mean sea age; but other variables, coupled with population level sampling at sub-catchment scale, might do so. An obvious future action is to design studies that incorporate marine and freshwater variables and genetics simultaneously, using data within as well as among river stocks, at appropriate spatial scales, to explain life history variance. Even with these caveats, the results showed significant spatial and temporal variation in life history features, and sufficient is known about the broad principles to conclude that marine effects play an important role in that variation.

The management implications lie in four main areas:

1. If common marine factors are influencing sea trout stock composition through life history changes, these are of common concern to cross-border marine planning. Planning decisions must take account of likely medium to long term environmental influences on the abundance and structure of sea trout stocks and other species that will be affected.

2. The potential for the multiple populations to support overall resilience of an effective metapopulation through portfolio effects (Schtickzelle & Quinn, 2007) appears to be high and asymmetric subsidies of adjacent sea trout fisheries have been reported from Canada (Veinott *et al.*, 2012) There are many more small coastal streams entering the Irish Sea than are represented in this account, and at least 500 with catchment areas <10km² (CSTP, 2016). The genetic structuring in the larger rivers seen in Irish Sea sea trout (CSTP, 2016; Prodhol *et al.,* 2017) supports the premise of tight homing and a strong degree of reproductive isolation. However, in addition to extensive non-reproductive straying, effective straying (*sensu* Quinn, 1993) does occur in sea trout and, in small streams, has been shown to homogenise their population genetic structures (Ayllon *et al.*, 2006). There is more to understand about the interdependence of these stocks and of their mixed fisheries; but they can probably be regarded as forming a wide unitary complex, within which even the smaller entities have value. Thus management should aim at their collective conservation and protection of their joint marine habitat. Moreover, non-reproductive straying into adjacent coastal zones and into rivers means that many fisheries may exploit mixed stocks and should be managed accordingly.

3. Climate change is an factor that is already affecting sea trout, although prediction of how they will respond in the future is elusive without an understanding of reaction norms (how individual genotypes respond to changing environment) and it can be erroneous to infer response to future environmental change from empirical relationships observed between populations that reflect phenotypic response (Marschall *et al.*, 1998). These evolutionary mechanisms are very important to explore further, but for assessment purposes, broad scale climate factors need to be incorporated formally and routinely into assessments to better describe stock fluctuations and trends.

4. Understanding of broad scale marine factors will only come from better, targeted long-term monitoring and collaborative research into the variation in marine ecosystem components, for example keystone prey species, and its causes. The sea is not after all a

black box into which sea trout disappear and return; but is shown to be a highly structured and dynamic habitat, exerting a strong influence on population dynamics, and the future of sea trout stocks depends as much upon understanding and protecting it as the freshwater environment.

ACKNOWLEDGEMENTS

We thank Dr Graeme Harris for access to the original data that he collected during the 1990s and the many individuals in Salmon District Fisheries Boards, Rivers Trusts and angling organisations for assistance with collecting fish and scale samples. The Celtic Sea Trout Project was funded by the Ireland-Wales Cross Border Collaboration Programme supported through Interreg IVA, the Environment Agency, Atlantic Salmon Trust, the Nith District Salmon Fisheries Board, the Galloway Fisheries Trust and the Annan District Salmon Fishery Board.

REFERENCES

Aldven, D., & Davidsen, J.G. (2017) Marine Migrations of sea trout (*Salmo trutta*). In: *Sea Trout: Science and Management*. (Graeme Harris. Ed.). Proceedings of the 2nd International Sea Trout Symposium. October 2015, Dundalk, Ireland. Troubador, 267–276.

Ayllon, F., Moran, P., & Garcia-Vasques, E. (2006). Maintenance of a small anadromous subpopulation of brown trout (*Salmo trutta* L.) by straying. *Freshwater Biology*, **51**: 351–358.

Baglinière, J-L. & Maisse, G. (1999). *Biology and Ecology of the Brown Trout and Sea Trout*. Springer Praxis Series in Aquaculture and Fisheries, Cornwall, UK, 286 pp.

Banks, J.W. (1969). A review of the literature on the upstream migration of Adult salmonids. *Journal of Fish Biology*, **1**, 85-136.

Brett, J. R. (1956). Some principles in the thermal requirements of fishes. *Quarterly Review of Biology*, **31**, 75-87.

Beaugrand, G & Reid, P.C. (2003). Long-term changes in phytoplankton, zooplankton and salmon related to climate change. Global Change Biology, **9**, 801-817.

Boylan, P. & Adams, C.E. (2006). The influence of broad scale climatic phenomena on long term trends in Atlantic salmon population size: an example from the River Foyle, Ireland. *Journal of Fish Biology*, **68**, 276–283.

Butler, J.R.A & Walker, A.F. (2006). Characteristics of the sea trout *Salmo trutta* (L.) stock collapse in the River Ewe (Wester Ross, Scotland, in 1988-2001. *In: Sea Trout: Biology, Conservation and Management*. (Graeme Harris & Nigel Milner. *Eds*). Proceedings of the First International Sea Trout Symposium. July 2004, Cardiff, Wales. Blackwell Publishing, Oxford, 45-59.

Chapman, B.B., Hulthén, K., Brodersen, J., Nilsson, P.A., Skov, C., Hansson, L-A & Brönmark, C. (2012). Partial migration in fishes: cause and consequences. *Journal of Fish Biology*, **81**, 456-478.

Crawley, M.J. (2009). The R Book. Wiley and Sons, Chichester, 942 pp.

Cucherousset, J., Ombredane, D., Charles, K., Marchand, F. & Baglinière, J-L. (2005). A continuum of life history tactics in a brown trout (*Salmo trutta*) population. *Canadian Journal of Fisheries and Aquatic Sciences,* **62**, 1600–1610.

Davidson, I.C., Cove, R.J. & Hazlewood, M.S. (2006a). Annual variation in age composition, growth, and abundance of sea trout returning to the river Dee at Chester, 1991-2003. In: *Sea Trout: Biology, Conservation and Management.* (Graeme Harris & Nigel Milner. *Eds*). Proceedings of the First International Sea Trout Symposium. July 2004, Cardiff, Wales. Blackwell Publishing, Oxford, 76 – 87.

Davidson, I.C., Hazelwood, M.S & Cove, R.J. (2006b). Predicted growth of juvenile trout and salmon in four rivers in England and Wales based on past and possible future temperature regimes linked to climate change. In: *Sea Trout: Biology, Conservation and Management.* (Graeme Harris & Nigel Milner. *Eds*). Proceedings of the First International Sea Trout Symposium. July 2004, Cardiff, Wales. Blackwell Publishing, Oxford, 410 – 414.

de Leeuw, J.J., ter Hofstede, R. & Winter, H.V. (2007). Sea growth of anadromous brown trout (*Salmo trutta*). *Journal of Sea Research,* **58**, 163-165.

Degerman, E., Leonardsson, K, & Lundqvist, H. (2012). Coastal migrations, temporary use of neighbouring rivers, and growth of sea trout (*Salmo trutta*) from nine northern Baltic Sea rivers. *ICES Journal of Marine Science,* **69**, 971-980.

Dodson, J.J., Aubin-Horth, N., Thériault, V. & Paez, D.J. (2013). The evolutionary ecology of alternative migratory tactics in salmonid fishes. *Biological Reviews,* **88**, 602-625.

Edwards, M., Bresnan, E., Cook, K., Heath, M., Helaouet, P., Lynam, C., Raine, R. & Widdicombe, C. (2013). Impacts of climate change on plankton. Marine Climate Change Impacts Partnership: Science Review. *MCCIP Science Review 2013*: 98-112.

Elliott, J.M. (1997). Stomach contents of adult sea trout caught in six English rivers. *Journal of Fish Biology.* **50**, 1129–1132.

Elliott, J.M. & Chambers, S. (1996). *A Guide to The Interpretation of Sea Trout Scales.* National Rivers Authority, R&D Report 22. National Rivers Authority, Bristol, 63 pp.

Environment Agency (2003). *Salmon Action Plan Guidelines.* Version 2, April 2003. Environment Agency, Bristol, 83 pp.

Fahy, E. (1978). Variation in some biological characteristics of British sea trout, *Salmo trutta* L. *Journal of Fish Biology*, **13**, 123-138.

Ferguson, A. (2006). Genetics of sea trout with particular reference to Britain and Ireland. In: *Sea Trout: Biology, Conservation and Management.* (Graeme Harris & Nigel Milner. *Eds*). Proceedings of the First International Sea Trout Symposium. July 2004, Cardiff, Wales. Blackwell Publishing, Oxford, 157 – 182.

Ferguson, A., Reed. T., McGinnity, P. & Prodöhl, P. (2017). Anadromy in brown trout (*Salmo trutta*): A review of the roles of genes and environmental factors and the implications for management and conservation. In: *Sea Trout: Science & Management.* (Graeme Harris. *Ed.*). Proceedings of the 2nd International Sea Trout Symposium, October 2015, Dundalk, Ireland. Troubador, 1–40.

Fleming, I.A., Bottom, D.L., Jones, K.K., Simenstad, C.A. & Craig, J.F. (2014). Resilience of anadromous and resident salmonid populations. *Journal of Fish Biology,* **85**, 1-7.

Forseth, T. Naesje, T.F., Jonsson, B. & Harsaker, K. (1999). Juvenile migration in brown trout: a consequence of energetic state. *Journal of Animal Ecology,* **57**, 672-682.

Friedland K.D. (1998). Ocean climate influences on critical Atlantic salmon (*Salmo salar* L.) life history events. *Canadian Journal of Fisheries & Aquatic Sciences,* **55** (Suppl. 1), 119-130.

Friedland, K.D., Hansen, L.P., Dunkley, D.A. & Maclean, J.C. (2000). Linkage between ocean climate, post-smolt growth and survival of Atlantic salmon (*Salmo salar*, L.) in the North Sea area. ICES Journal of Marine Science, **57**, 419-429.

Gargan, P.G., Roche, W.K., Forde, G. P. & Ferguson, A. (2006). Characteristics of the Sea trout stocks from the Owengowla and Invermore fisheries, Connemara, Western Ireland and recent trends in marine survival. In: *Sea Trout: Biology, Conservation, and Management.* (Graeme Harris & Nigel Milner. *Eds*). Proceedings of the First International Sea Trout Symposium. July 2004, Cardiff, Wales. Blackwell Publishing, Oxford, 60 – 75.

Gargan, P., Shephard, S. & Macintyre, C. (2017). Assessment of the increased mortality risk and population regulating effect of sea lice (*Lepeophtheirus salmonis*) from marine salmon farms on wild sea trout in Ireland and Scotland. In: *Sea Trout: Science & Management.* (Graeme Harris. *Ed.*). Proceedings of the 2nd International Sea Trout Symposium, October 2015, Dundalk, Ireland. Troubador, 507–522.

Gee, A.S. (1980). Angling success for Atlantic salmon (*Salmo salar*) in the River Wye in relation to effort and river flow. *Fisheries Management* **11**, 131-138.

Gowen, R.J. & Stewart, B.M (2005). The Irish Sea: nutrient status and phytoplankton. *Journal of Sea Research,* **54**, 36–50.

Graham, C.T. & Harrod, D.C. (2009). Implications of climate change for the fishes of the British Isles. *Journal of Fish Biology,* **74**, 1143–1205.

Gross, M.R., Coleman, R.M. & McDowall, R.M. (1988). Aquatic productivity and the evolution of diadromous fish migration. *Science,* **239**, 1291-1293.

Harris, G.S. (2002). Sea trout Stock Descriptions: the structure and composition of adult sea trout stocks from 16 rivers in England & Wales. Environment Agency R&D Technical Report W224. Environment Agency, Bristol, 93 pp.

Harris, G.S. & Milner. N.J. (Eds) (2006). *Sea Trout: Biology, Conservation and Management.* Proceedings of the First International Sea Trout Symposium, Cardiff, July 2004. Blackwell Scientific Publications, Oxford, 499 pp.

Harris, G.S. & Evans, R. (2017). The relative importance of sea trout and salmon to the rod fisheries in England & Wales. In: *Sea Trout: Management & Science.* (Graeme Harris. *Ed.*). Proceedings of the 2nd International Sea Trout Symposium, October 2015, Dundalk, Ireland. Troubador, 185–204.

Howarth, M.J. (2006). *Hydrography of the Irish Sea.* SEA6 Technical Report. POL Internal document 174. Geotek Ltd and Hartley Anderson Ltd Report to Department of Trade and Industry, 30 pp.

Hutchings, J.A. & Jones, M.E.B. (1998). Life history variation and growth rate thresholds for maturity in Atlantic salmon, *Salmo salar. Canadian Journal of Fisheries and Aquatic Sciences.* **55**, (Suppl. 1), 22–47.

Jonsson, B., L'Abée-Lund, J.H. & Heggberget, T.G. (1991). Longevity, body size and growth in anadromous brown trout. *Canadian Journal of Fisheries and Aquatic Sciences* **45**, 1537-1547.

Jonsson, B., L'Abée-Lund, J.H. (1993). Latitudinal clines in life history variables of anadromous brown trout in Europe. *Journal of Fish Biology,* **43**(Suppl. A), 1-16.

Jonsson, B. & Jonsson, N. (1993). Partial migration: niche shift *vs* sexual maturation in fishes. *Reviews in Fish Biology and Fisheries,* **3**, 348-365.

Jonsson, B. & Jonsson, N. (2001). Life history traits of brown trout vary with the size of small streams. *Functional Ecology,* **15**, 310-317.

Jonsson, B. & Jonsson, N. (2006). Life-history effects of migratory costs in anadromous brown trout. *Journal of Fish Biology,* **69**, 860-869.

Jonsson, B. & Jonsson, N. (2009). A review of the likely effects of climate change on anadromous Atlantic salmon *Salmo salar* and brown trout *Salmo trutta*, with particular reference to water temperature and flow. *Journal of Fish Biology,* **75**, 2381–2447.

Joyce, A.E. (2006). The coastal temperature network and ferry route programme: long-term temperature and salinity observations. Science Series. Data Report 43. Cefas, Lowestoft. 129 pp.

L'Abée-Lund, J.H., Jonsson, B., Jensen, A.J., Sættem, L.M., Heggberget, T.G., Johnsen, B. & Næsje, T.F. (1989). Latitudinal variation in life history characteristics of sea-run migrant brown trout *Salmo trutta*. *Journal of Applied Ecology*, **58**, 525-542.

Marschall, E.A., Quinn, T.P., Roff, D.A., Hutchings, J.A., Metcalfe, N.B., Bakke, T.A., Saunders, R.L. & Poff, N.L. (1998). A framework for understanding Atlantic salmon (*Salmo salar*) life history. *Canadian Journal of Fisheries and Aquatic Sciences,* **55** (Suppl.), 48-58.

Milner, N.J., Karlsson, L., Degerman, E., Jholander, A., MacLean, J.C & Hansen, L-P. (2006). Sea trout (*Salmo trutta* L.) in Atlantic salmon (*Salmo salar* L.) rivers in Scandinavia and Europe. *Sea Trout: Biology, Conservation and Management.* (Graeme Harris & Nigel Milner *Eds.*). Proceedings of First International Sea Trout Symposium, July 2004, Cardiff. Blackwell Scientific Publications, Oxford, 139-153.

Milner, N.J., Solomon, D.J. & Smith, G.W. (2012). The role of river flow in the migration of adult Atlantic salmon, *Salmo salar*, through estuaries and rivers. *Fisheries Management and Ecology,* **19**, 537-547.

Nall, G.H. (1930). The life of the Sea Trout. Seeley Service & Co. London, 335 pp.

Nall, G.H. (1931). Sea Trout of the Solway Rivers. Fishery Board for Scotland, Salmon Fisheries No. III, HMSO Edinburgh, 72 pp.

Olsson, I.C., Greenberg, L.A., Bergman, E. & Wysujack, K. (2006). Environmentally induced migration: the importance of food. *Ecology Letters,* **9**, 645-651.

Poole, R. (Ed). (2010). *Manual on Sea Trout Ageing, Digital Scale Reading and Growth Methodology.* Internal Report of the Celtic Sea Trout Project. May 2010, Burrishoole, Ireland, 48 pp.

Potter, E.C.E., Campbell, R., Sumner, K. & Marshall, S. (2017a). Movements of sea trout in the coastal waters of Great Britain. In: *Sea Trout: Science and Management.* (Graeme Harris. *Ed.*). Proceedings of the 2nd International Sea Trout Symposium. October 2015, Dundalk, Ireland. Troubador, 205–227.

Potter, E.C.E., Beraud, C., Bacon, J., van der Molen, J. & van Leeuwen, S. (2017b). Simulation of the movements of sea trout post-smolts in the Irish and Celtic Seas In: *Sea Trout: Science and Management.* (Graeme Harris. Ed.). Proceedings of the 2nd International Sea Trout Symposium. October 2015, Dundalk, Ireland. Troubador, 228–252.

Prodöhl, P.A., Antoniacomi, A., Bradley, C., Carlsson, J., Carvalho, G.R., Coughlan, J., Coyne, J., Cross, M.e., Cross, M.C., Davies, A., Dillane, E., Gargan, P., Hynes, R., McGinnity, P., Milner, N., Reed, T., Roche, W., Taylor, M., Tysklind, N., & Cross, T.F. (2017), Population genetics and Genetic Stock Identification of anadromous *Salmo trutta* from the Irish Sea and adjacent areas, using microsatellite DNA loci. In: *Sea Trout: Science and Management.* (Graeme Harris. *Ed.*) Proceedings of the 2nd International Sea Trout Symposium. October 2015, Dundalk, Ireland. Troubador, 69–95.

Quémére, E., Baglinière, J-L., Roussel, J-M., Evanno, G., McGinnity, P. & Launey, S. (2016). Seascape and its effect on migratory life history strategy influences gene flow among coastal brown trout (*Salmo trutta*) populations in the English Channel. *Journal of Biogeography,* **43**, 498-509.

Quinn, T.P. (1993). A review of homing and straying of wild and hatchery-produced salmon. *Fisheries Research,* **18**, 29-44.

Roche, W., Milner, N., Davies, C., King, J., Coyne., Gargan, P. & Hughes R. (2017). Feeding ecology of sea trout in the Irish Sea. In: *Sea Trout: Science & Management.* (Graeme Harris. *Ed.*). Proceedings of the 2nd International Sea Trout Symposium, October 2015, Dundalk, Ireland. Troubador, 371–395.

Schtickzelle, N. & Quinn, T.P. (2007). A metapopulation perspective for salmon and other anadromous fish. *Fish and Fisheries* **8**, 297-314.

Shelton, R. (2001). The Interpretation of Rod and Net Catch Data. Proceedings of a Workshop held at the Centre for Environment, Fisheries and Aquaculture Science, Lowestoft, 6-7 November 2001, 107 pp.

Solomon, D.J. (1995). Sea Trout Investigations: Phase I Final Report. National Rivers Authority. R&D Note 318, 104 pp + Appendices.

Stearns, S.C. (1999). *The Evolution of Life Histories*, Oxford University Press, Oxford. 249 pp.

Thorstad, E.B., Økland, F., Aarestrup, K., & Heggberget, T.O. (2008). Factors affecting the within river spawning migration of Atlantic salmon, with emphasis on human impacts. *Reviews in Fish Biology and Fisheries,* **18**, 345-371.

Thorstad, E.B., Todd, C.D., Uglem, I., BjornP.A., Gargan, P.G., Vollset, K.W., Halttunene, E., Kålå, M.B. & Finstand, B. (2016). Marine life of the sea trout. *Marine Biology,* **163**, 47

Todd, C.D, Friedland, K.D., MacLean, J.C., Whyte, B.D., Russell, I.C, Lonergan, M.E. & Morrissey, M.B. (2012). Phenological and phenotypic changes in Atlantic salmon populations in response to a changing climate. *ICES Journal of Marine Science,* **69**, 1686–1698.

Tysklind, N., Carvalho, G.R. & Milner, N.J. (2015). Population dynamics analysis of sea trout populations around the Celtic and Irish Seas. Report to the Atlantic Salmon Trust. AST Perth, 56 pp.

Veinott, G., Westley, P.A.H., Warner, L. & Purchase C.F. (2012). Assigning origins in a potentially mixed stocks recreational sea trout (*Salmo trutta*) fishery. *Ecology of Freshwater Fish,* **21**, 541-551.

Vincent, M.A., Atkins, S.M., Lumb, C.M., Golding, N., Lieberknecht, L.M. & Webster, M. (2004). *Marine nature conservation and sustainable development – the Irish Sea Pilot.* Report to Defra by the Joint Nature Conservation Committee, Peterborough, 176 pp.

Webb J.H. & Campbell, R.N.B. (1997). Patterns of run timing in adult Atlantic salmon returning to Scottish rivers – some new perspectives and management implications. In: *Managing Wild Atlantic Salmon New Challenges – New Techniques.* (F.G. Whoriskey & K.E. Whelan. Eds.). 5th International Atlantic Salmon Symposium, Galway. Atlantic Salmon Federation, 100-138.

Went, A.E.J. (1962). Irish sea trout, a review of investigations to date. Scientific *Proceedings of the Royal Society of Dublin*, 1A, No.10, 265-296.

Wysujack, K., Greenberg, L. A., Bergman, E., & Olsson, I. C. (2009). The role of the environment in partial migration: food availability affects the adoption of a migratory tactic in brown trout *Salmo trutta*. *Ecology of Freshwater Fish,* **18**, 52-59.

ELECTRONIC REFERENCE

CSTP. (2016). Celtic Sea Trout Project – Technical Report to Ireland Wales Territorial Cooperation Programme 2007-2013 (INTERREG 4A). (Nigel Milner, Philip McGinnity & William Roche. *Eds.,*). Inland Fisheries Ireland, Dublin. *Available at:* http://celticseatrout.com/downloads/technical-report/

R Core Team (2014). R: A language and environment for statistical computing. R Foundation for Statistical Computing, Vienna, Austria. URL http://www.R-project.org .

Catch and stock based Biological Reference Points for sea trout in England & Wales: A comparison of methods and critical examination of their potential application to stock assessment and management

I.C. DAVIDSON[1], M.W. APRAHAMIAN[2], G. PEIRSON[3], R.J. HILLMAN[4], N. COOK[5], P.S. ELSMERE[4], R.J. COVE[1] & A. CROFT[6]

[1]*Natural Resources Wales, Chester Road Buckley, Flintshire CH7 3AJ, Wales.*
[2]*Environment Agency, Richard Fairclough House, Knutsford Road, Warrington, WA4 1HG.*
[3]*Environment Agency, Mance House, Arthur Drive, Hoo Farm Industrial Estate, Worcester Road, Kidderminster, Worcestershire DY11 7RA, England.*
[4]*Environment Agency, Sir John Moore House, Victoria Square, Bodmin, Cornwall, PL31 1EB, England.*
[5]*Environment Agency, Tyneside House, Skinnerburn Road, Newcastle Business Park, Newcastle Tyne & Wear, NE4 7AR, England.*
[6]*Environment Agency, Lutra House, Dodd Way, Off Seedlee Road, Walton Summit, Preston Lancashire, PR5 8BX, England.*

ABSTRACT

The recent ICES Workshop on sea trout (WKTRUTTA) concluded that, with the exception of habitat/parr production models applied in the Baltic, there were no examples of *Biological Reference Points* (BRPs) being developed for sea trout and nothing equivalent to the use of *Conservation Limits* in salmon management. This paper explores various catch-based and stock-based methods for deriving BRPs in sea trout utilising data collected by the Environment Agency and Natural Resources Wales in England and Wales (E&W).

Catch-based methods involve the use of angling catch or CPUE as indices of stock performance and include: (i) comparisons of recent catch metrics with historic reference levels and (ii) derivation of pseudo stock-recruitment (SR) relationships and associated BRPs. Stock based methods seek to derive BRPs in more conventional ways using SR relationships generated for the index and other monitored rivers in E&W. BRPs from these systems are compared and mechanisms explored to transfer and apply them to other rivers. These different approaches to setting BRPs and their 'compliance' outcomes are compared across a subset of sea trout rivers that are broadly representative of the range of river/stock types in E&W. Their value as potential tools for sea trout stock assessment and management is critically examined and future development needs identified.

Keywords: biological reference points; *Salmo trutta* L.; sea trout; stock-recruitment.

INTRODUCTION

Biological Reference Points (BRPs) are usually associated with stock-recruitment (SR) relationships and have been used in the assessment and management of Atlantic salmon (*Salmo salar*, L.) stocks for a number of years. On the advice of the International Council for the Exploration of the Seas (ICES, 1995), the North Atlantic Salmon Conservation Organisation (NASCO, 1998) have proposed that $S_{MSY,}$ the spawning stock size generating the Maximum Sustainable Yield (or catch), should be used in the long-term to define the 'Conservation Limit' for salmon (a 'limit' reference point) (Potter, *et al.*, 2003). Also, that fisheries managers should aim to maintain stocks above the Conservation Limit and set appropriate risk-based compliance criteria in order to do so.

In England and Wales (E&W), river-specific Conservation Limits have been set for salmon on this basis since the 1990s (Wyatt & Barnard, 1997a; 1997b; Milner *et al.*, 2000). Associated compliance criteria aim to ensure that stocks exceed their Conservation Limit in 4 years out of 5 on average. This is the 'Management Objective' and the average stock level required to meet this objective equates to the 'Management Target' (a 'target' reference point) (Milner *et al.*, 2000; Environment Agency, 2003; Cefas, Environment Agency & Natural Resources Wales, 2015a; 2015b).

A recent ICES Workshop on sea trout (WKTRUTTA. 2013) concluded that, with the exception of the habitat/parr production models applied in the Baltic, there were no examples of BRPs being developed for sea trout and nothing equivalent to the use of Conservation Limits (CLs) in salmon management.

On only a few intensively monitored sea trout rivers (e.g. the 'index' rivers) have data on population abundance and composition been collected in sufficient detail and over enough years to allow SR relationships to be produced. Published examples include SR relationships for sea trout on the Black Brows Beck, England (Elliott, 1985; Elliott, 1994; Elliott & Elliott, 2006), the Bresle river in France (Euzenat *et al.*, 2006) and the Burrishoole system in Ireland (Poole *et al.*, 2006). Even here, these three systems are quite different; the Black Brows Beck is a very small sub-catchment study while the Bresle and Burrishoole are whole-catchment studies. Furthermore, the Burrishoole differs from the others as a lake dominated system with a significant non-anadromous brown trout component.

While other intensively monitored systems exist, any time-series of data are less well established than the published examples above (although tentative SR relationships are explored in this paper for the few rivers with permanent traps or fish counters in E&W), and so, particularly in view of the complex and variable sea trout life cycle, there is relatively little information available for use in developing models to 'transport' BRPs elsewhere (WKTRUTTA. 2013).

Given the shortage of population census data from trapped/counted rivers, the potential use of more widely available fishery data as a means of assessing the status of the sea trout resource has been explored in a variety of ways (WKTRUTTA, 2013). For example, the Environment Agency and Natural Resources Wales apply a fishery based procedure to their principal sea trout rivers in E&W (Aprahamian, *pers. com.*). This examines the most recent 10-year trend in angling catch rate as well as the current 3-year mean catch rate relative to a 10-year rolling average (50 and 80 percentiles); it then assigns a '*risk*' category dependent on the outcome of these assessments. While this approach aims to provide an early warning of potential problems, outputs need to be treated with caution, not least because catch-based reference levels may not necessarily reflect biological optima, such as carrying capacity. WKTRUTTA (2013) also examined the use of angling catch data to derive 'pseudo' SR curves and provides an example from the River Tweed, Scotland, where catches in year n and n+4 were used as indices of stock and recruitment for a population dominated by 2-year old smolts and .1+ maiden adults (Gardiner, *pers. com.*).

This paper seeks to develop the latter approach in particular, using angling catch and catch-per-unit-effort (CPUE) data to derive 'pseudo' SR relationships and associated BRPs for sea trout on 13 rivers in E&W. On five of these rivers, this includes comparison with SR relationships and with BRPs produced using more conventional census estimates of stock and recruitment collected from traps and counters. In all cases, the SR models of Ricker (1954) and Beverton & Holt (1957) are fitted to the data sets and compared. The validity of the various methods employed and their potential application to stock assessment and management are closely examined.

METHODS

ANGLING CATCH AND CENSUS BASED STOCK AND RECRUITMENT DATA

In England and Wales (E&W), rod catch statistics for sea trout and salmon have been collected in a consistent way since the introduction, in 1994, of a single national rod licencing and catch return and reminder system. This provides river-specific data that includes daily records of species, number and size (weight) of fish caught, and annual estimates of fishing effort (days/part-days) fished for salmon and sea trout combined (Environment & Natural Resources Wales, 2015).

National catch declaration rates from this system are estimated to be around 90% (Environment Agency, 2003). Prior to this, the licencing and catch return/reminder systems varied by region and, although time-series extend back to at least the 1970s on most rivers (Russell *et al.*, 1995), they are less accurate and comparable over the earlier part of the record. For example, effort data (other than licence sales) are absent and catch declaration rates are likely to have varied between regions (Environment Agency, 2003).

For the 13 named sea trout rivers examined in this study (Figure 1), data on angling catch and CPUE (= catch per day) from 1994 to 2013 were used to derive 'pseudo' SR relationships and associated BRPs. These rivers were considered broadly representative of the range of rivers and stock structures in E&W and included five of the six trapped/counted rivers: namely the Tyne, Tamar, Dee, Lune and Kent (Fig 1). For these named rivers, more conventional census-based stock and recruitment data were used to produce comparable SR relationships/BRPs. Data sets were limited by the availability of the biological data, such as data on sea and river age, and length and weight, required to partition Returning Stock Estimates (RSEs) into year-class components. Biological data were collected from trapping programmes and (in the case of the Tyne) from fishery/broodstock sampling programmes. For the Tyne and Lune, rod catch data were also used to estimate the abundance of .0+ maiden fish. On the Kent, the abundance of .0+ and older fish were established from counter signal size and video records (Shields *et al.*, 2006).

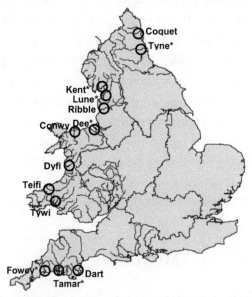

Figure 1. Selection of 13 sea trout rivers in E&W for which catch based pseudo SR relationships have been derived, including 6 trapped/counted rivers (indicated '*').

Two methods of deriving stock and recruitment variables from rod catch data were explored:

a) Use of angling CPUE data (catch per day): where *Stock* = Catch per day for all fish in year n and *Recruitment* = Catch per day for fish of weight <=1.5lbs (0.680kg) in year n+3.

b) Use of angling catch and assumed rod exploitation rates to derive Returning Stock Estimates (RSEs) and egg deposition estimates: where *Stock* = Total egg deposition for all fish returning in year n (dependent on modelled rod exploitation rates to derive RSEs from catch, as well as standard assumptions relating to sex composition, size-fecundity relationships, post-fishery survival rates, etc.) and *Recruitment* = Catch derived RSEs for fish of weight <=1.5lbs in year n+3.

Fish of weight < =1.5lbs in year n+3 were selected as indicators of recruitment because .0+ maiden fish are strongly represented in this size class to the exclusion of virtually all other sea age groups (i.e. they can be readily identified in the catch record). For example, from trapping data on the Welsh Dee (1994-2013) more than 90% of .0+ fish were in the < =1.5lbs size-class and only a small proportion of older fish fell below the 1.5lbs threshold (e.g. ~5% or less of .0+SM+ and .1+ fish). The .0+ sea age group is also a significant component (>50%) of the maiden sea trout return on many west coast rivers in E&W (Solomon, 1994; Harris, 2002), although they are a minor component on east coast rivers. (Two of the thirteen rivers examined in this study, the Coquet and the Tyne, are east coast rivers where, on average, less than 25% of the declared rod catch comprised .0+ sized fish). Finally, on most rivers in E&W, the majority (some 60-90%) of sea trout appear (from adult scales) to have emigrated as 2 year-old smolts so that recruitment as .0+ maidens occurs at n+3 years after the return of the parental spawning stock. This is assumed to be the common pattern.

EXPLOITATION RATE MODEL

Use of angling catch and assumed rod exploitation rates to derive RSEs on rivers without traps or counters has been integral to salmon CL compliance procedures for a number of years in E&W (Milner *et al.*, 2000) and Ireland (Standing Scientific Committee on Salmon, 2016; White *et al.,* 2016).

In this study, a multi-variate model was used to predict annual extant exploitation rates for sea trout on a river-by-river basis. This model was developed for both salmon and sea trout, using stepwise regression methods (Minitab 16 – *see* https://www.minitab.com/en-us/) and based on species specific extant exploitation rates (1997-2010) obtained on four rivers where common time-series of RSEs were available for both species: namely the Tamar, Fowey, Dee and Kent.

Independent variables selected in the final model were: (i) Angling effort (total days fished) per km of fishery (cubic term) and (ii) River-specific post-July in-season flow expressed as a % of mean flow in the reference period 1984-1993 – where Log_{10} Exploit rate = − 0.161 + 0.0296 Effort per km – 0.000316 Effort per km^2 + 0.000001 Effort per km^3 + 0.283 Log_{10} Post-July in-season flow; r^2 = 0.739; P<0.001. Other variables examined but not included in the model were: (i) Pre-August in-season flow expressed as a % of mean flow in the reference period 1984-1993 and (ii) Mean catch date as days from the 31st December (as a measure of run timing).

Figure 2 shows a version of the model using only angling effort (total days fished) per km of fishery as the independent variable (cubic term), and illustrating separate relationships for sea trout, salmon and both species combined (the latter being the basis for the final model). While the effort data collected from licence returns does not distinguish between the days spent fishing for sea trout and salmon separately, effort was partitioned between these species based on information provided in surveys conducted in 1992 and 2006 (Evans *pers com.*) to identify, on a river-by-river basis, the proportional split in total angling effort expended on the two species.

The exploitation rate model that combined data for both species was used in this study because (i) visually, the combined model (as presented in Fig 2) appeared to provide a reasonable fit to both data sets, and (ii) it extended the range of effort observations (= total days fished per km of fishery) beyond that available for sea trout alone. The latter was important because on some intensively fished rivers where the exploitation rate model was applied (e.g. the Tywi and Teifi), observed levels of sea trout fishing effort in some years (~60-80 days fished per km of fishery) exceeded those used in calibrating the model for sea trout alone.

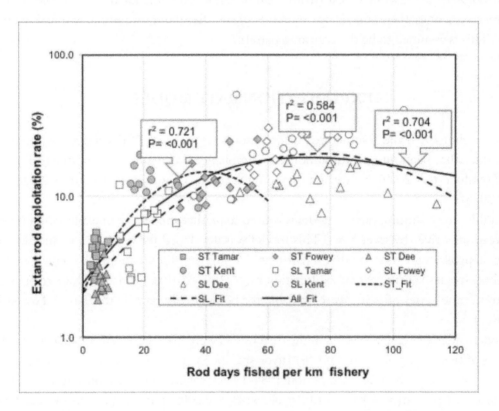

Figure 2. Cubic regression relationships between angling effort (rod days fished per km of fishery) and extant rod exploitation rates on the rivers Tamar, Fowey, Dee and Kent. (Separate relationships are shown for sea trout, salmon, and both species combined).

STOCK-RECRUITMENT (SR) RELATIONSHIPS

The Ricker (1954) and Beverton & Holt (1957) SR relationships (given below) were fitted to the data sets as the most commonly applied SR models (Hilborn & Walters, 1992), with both models widely used in sea trout population studies (e.g. Elliott, 1985; Elliott, 1994; Elliott & Elliott, 2006; Euzenat *et al.*, 2006, Poole *et al.*, 2006). Thus:

Ricker (1954):	$R = Se^{a(1-S/b)}$	*Equation 1*
Beverton & Holt (1957):	$R = aS/(b+S)$	*Equation 2*
Where: S = Stock and R = Recruits.		

The 'a' and 'b' parameters for these curves were initially derived using linear regression methods (*see* Hilborn & Walters, 1992). Thus:

Ricker model:	$Log(R/S) = a - (a/b)S$	*Equation 3*
Beverton & Holt model:	$S/R = b/a + (1/a)S$	*Equation 4*

Using these initial 'a' and 'b' parameters as starting values, Ricker and Beverton & Holt SR curves were fitted to the data sets using a combination of non-linear regression methods (e.g. Elliott, 1985; Hilborn & Walters, 1992) available for use in Minitab 16 (see https://www.minitab.com/en-us/) and Microsoft Excel – for the latter applying the method of Brown (2001).

Two null hypotheses (Ho) were tested to examine the 'goodness-of-fit' of these curves (see Elliott, 1985). Firstly, that there is no dependence of recruits (R) on stock (S), i.e. values of R vary randomly around a constant, estimated by the arithmetic mean value of R (Ho: R= meanR) and secondly that R is related to S, but only so that there is a constant proportionate survival (p), and therefore losses are due to density-independent factors (Ho: R = pS). The proportion of the variance in recruits associated with each of these null hypotheses was calculated (after Elliott, 1985) as: (i) r^2s = (sum of squares due to regression)/(total sum of squares about the mean value of R) and (ii) r^2p = (residual sum of squares)/(sum of squares about the line pS). Both hypotheses were tested for each model using F-values for the variance ratios.

RESULTS

FITTED SR CURVES

Fig 3 shows Ricker and Beverton & Holt SR curves fitted to the three stock and recruitment data sets examined in this study; i.e. based on (i) trap/counter derived RSEs/eggs (from index and other monitored rivers); (ii) rod catch derived RSEs/eggs; and (iii) rod CPUE. Parameter ('a' and 'b') estimates for these curves (Equations 1 and 2) and associated goodness-of-fit statistics (r^2 and p values) are shown in Table 1 (Ricker curve) and Table 2 (Beverton & Holt curve) for (i) the initial parameter values obtained using linear regression methods (Equations 3 and 4) and (ii) final models fitted using non-linear methods.

Table 1 (a-c) Parameter ('a' and 'b') values, goodness-of-fit (r^2, r^2s and r^2p) statistics, and Smax and Rmax values for Ricker SR curves fitted to stock (S) and recruitment (R) data from:

a) Traps/counters (S=Eggs; R=RSE .0+ fish):

River	Years	Year classes	Linear regression ln(R/S) on S:			Non-linear regression:				Smax	Rmax
			a	b	r^2	a	b	r^2s	r^2p		
Tyne	7	2005-2011	-9.271	-1130673435	0.130	-9.025	-789954852	0.175	0.240	87,533,309	3,877
Tamar	6	2005-2010	-4.438	-13767161	0.704 **	-3.777	-9378965	0.588 *	0.766 **	2,483,507	20,925
Dee	18	1992-2009	-5.920	-59933844	0.264 **	-5.878	-60089530	0.183 *	0.254 **	10,222,385	10,529
Lune	6	2005-2010	-6.586	-162533574	0.512	-6.595	-166946800	0.003	0.558 *	25,314,493	12,733
Kent	10	2000-2009	-8.084	-86323676	0.151	-8.245	-136119259	0.147	0.055	16,508,409	1,594

b) Rod catch (S=Eggs; R=RSE fish ≤1.5lbs):

River	Years	Year classes	Linear regression ln(R/S) on S:			Non-linear regression:				Smax	Rmax
			a	b	r^2	a	b	r^2s	r^2p		
Coquet	17	1995-2011	-7.573	-71184464	0.459 ***	-7.334	-62558838	0.139	0.595 ***	8,529,847	2,049
Tyne	17	1995-2011	-9.168	-1047874880	0.158	-9.183	-1172794383	0.022	0.120	127,712,808	4,828
Dart	17	1995-2011	-7.914	-390297429	0.086	-7.577	-299704629	0.067	0.215 *	39,554,942	7,452
Tamar	17	1995-2011	-5.828	-62970677	0.397 ***	-5.832	-67865449	0.002	0.362 **	11,635,999	12,547
Fowey	17	1995-2011	-5.291	-18447086	0.639 ****	-5.248	-18250371	0.123	0.626 ***	3,477,427	6,725
Tywi	17	1995-2011	-7.074	-216470972	0.397 ***	-7.080	-237960972	0.000	0.349 **	33,610,307	10,408
Teifi	17	1995-2011	-6.076	-102495232	0.419 ***	-6.086	-113438039	0.000	0.380 ***	18,639,760	15,600
Dyfi	17	1995-2011	-6.564	-200234680	0.594 ****	-6.559	-204282841	0.000	0.567 ***	31,143,810	16,233
Conwy	17	1995-2011	-6.072	-43672785	0.339 **	-5.804	-31041389	0.000	0.379 ***	5,348,201	5,932
Dee	17	1995-2011	-6.468	-99597229	0.094	-6.379	-99024169	0.128	0.101	15,522,806	9,687
Ribble	17	1995-2011	-6.400	-131450258	0.598 ****	-6.407	-138061532	0.018	0.614 ***	21,549,891	13,086
Lune	17	1995-2011	-6.604	-181898681	0.480 ***	-6.575	-188459354	0.118	0.505 ***	28,663,586	14,710
Kent	17	1995-2011	-6.547	-48471481	0.277 **	-6.499	-49763590	0.093	0.304 **	7,657,421	4,241

c) Rod CPUE data (S=Catch per day: all fish; R=Catch per day: fish ≤ 1.5lbs):

River	Years	Year classes	Linear regression ln(R/S) on S:			Non-linear regression:				Smax	Rmax
			a	b	r^2	a	b	r^2s	r^2p		
Coquet	17	1995-2011	0.263	0.0101	0.569 ****	0.321	0.0129	0.226 *	0.640 ***	0.0401	0.0204
Tyne	17	1995-2011	-1.405	-0.1939	0.299 **	-1.479	-0.2442	0.150	0.179 *	0.1651	0.0138
Dart	17	1995-2011	-0.093	-0.0374	0.141	0.047	0.0188	0.042	0.170 *	0.4030	0.1553
Tamar	17	1995-2011	0.895	0.1450	0.543 ****	0.989	0.1565	0.107	0.571 ***	0.1581	0.1565
Fowey	17	1995-2011	1.312	0.2884	0.827 ****	1.490	0.2934	0.265 **	0.788 ***	0.1969	0.3215
Tywi	17	1995-2011	0.336	0.0689	0.457 ***	0.494	0.0910	0.000	0.426 ***	0.1844	0.1111
Teifi	17	1995-2011	0.685	0.1799	0.430 ***	0.696	0.1885	0.000	0.409 ***	0.2709	0.1998
Dyfi	17	1995-2011	0.574	0.3690	0.581 ****	0.550	0.3711	0.005	0.484 ***	0.6745	0.4302
Conwy	17	1995-2011	0.496	0.1330	0.307 **	0.691	0.1542	0.255 **	0.489 ***	0.2231	0.1638
Dee	17	1995-2011	0.640	0.0257	0.334 **	0.743	0.0291	0.084	0.338 **	0.0392	0.0303
Ribble	17	1995-2011	0.212	0.0354	0.111	0.715	0.0747	0.089	0.580 ***	0.1045	0.0786
Lune	17	1995-2011	0.556	0.0832	0.532 ****	0.583	0.0898	0.035	0.493 ***	0.1539	0.1014
Kent	17	1995-2011	0.101	0.0251	0.166	0.195	0.0453	0.269 **	0.231 *	0.2328	0.1040

Where: *=0.050≤P<0.100; **=0.010≤P<0.050; ***=0.001≤P<0.010; ****=P<0.001

Table 2 (a-c). Parameter ('a' and 'b') values, goodness-of-fit (r^2, r^2s and r^2p) statistics, and Smax and Rmax values for Beverton & Holt SR curves fitted to stock (S) and recruitment (R) data from:-

a) Traps/counters (S=Eggs; R=RSE .0+ fish).

River	Years	Year classes	Linear regression ln(R/S) on S:			Non-linear regression:				Smax	Rmax
			a	b	r^2	a	b	r^2s	r^2p		
Tyne	7	2005-2011	5748	44031349	0.176	6129	42524562	0.135	0.203	∞	6,129
Tamar	6	2005-2010	*No solution*			*No solution*				∞	
Dee	18	1992-2009	14838	4755353	0.201 *	15370	4039977	0.185 *	0.256 **	∞	15,370
Lune	6	2005-2010	16331	7313654	0.445	14928	4472299	0.075	0.590 *	∞	14,928
Kent	10	2000-2009	1898	5062422	0.162	2761	9199713	0.152	0.062	∞	2,761

b) Rod catch (S=Eggs; R=RSE fish ≤1.5lbs).

River	Years	Year classes	Linear regression ln(R/S) on S:			Non-linear regression:				Smax	Rmax
			a	b	r^2	a	b	r^2s	r^2p		
Coquet	17	1995-2011	*No solution*			*No solution*				∞	
Tyne	17	1995-2011	7594	76081646	0.104	6208	34527497	0.038	0.135	∞	6,208
Dart	17	1995-2011	7840	22435204	0.051	9849	12437232	0.054	0.205 *	∞	9,849
Tamar	17	1995-2011	*No solution*			*No solution*				∞	
Fowey	17	1995-2011	*No solution*			*No solution*				∞	
Tywi	17	1995-2011	8251	331115	0.414 ***	8251	400000	0.000	0.288 **	∞	8,251
Teifi	17	1995-2011	12186	69616	0.436 ***	15788	1433457	0.006	0.398 **	∞	15,788
Dyfi	17	1995-2011	16465	3424965	0.568 ****	17037	2760145	0.020	0.580 **	∞	17,037
Conwy	17	1995-2011	6181	1238960	0.255 **	6181	1238960	0.000	0.292 **	∞	6,181
Dee	17	1995-2011	14691	9645175	0.079	15094	7129924	0.138	0.111	∞	15,094
Ribble	17	1995-2011	*No solution*			13379	1714315	0.016	0.614 **	∞	13,379
Lune	17	1995-2011	*No solution*			16910	5245948	0.037	0.459 **	∞	16,910
Kent	17	1995-2011	*No solution*			5588	2302763	0.051	0.272 **	∞	5,588

c) Rod CPUE data (S=Catch per day: all fish; R=Catch per day: fish ≤ 1.5lbs).

River	Years	Year classes	Linear regression ln(R/S) on S:			Non-linear regression:				Smax	Rmax
			a	b	r^2	a	b	r^2s	r^2p		
Coquet	17	1995-2011	*No solution*			*No solution*				∞	
Tyne	17	1995-2011	0.0173	0.0524	0.295 **	0.0208	0.0691	0.155	0.184 *	∞	0.0208
Dart	17	1995-2011	0.1266	0.0547	0.116	0.1968	0.1068	0.027	0.158	∞	0.1968
Tamar	17	1995-2011	*No solution*			*No solution*				∞	
Fowey	17	1995-2011	*No solution*			*No solution*				∞	
Tywi	17	1995-2011	0.1109	0.0414	0.415 ***	0.1164	0.0200	0.000	0.502 **	∞	0.1164
Teifi	17	1995-2011	0.2129	0.0506	0.393 ***	0.2000	0.0114	0.002	0.452 **	∞	0.2000
Dyfi	17	1995-2011	0.4866	0.1462	0.535 ****	0.4775	0.0948	0.055	0.509 **	∞	0.4775
Conwy	17	1995-2011	0.2634	0.1638	0.172 *	0.2136	0.0690	0.193 *	0.446 **	∞	0.2136
Dee	17	1995-2011	0.0326	0.0120	0.297 **	0.0372	0.0098	0.098	0.348 **	∞	0.0372
Ribble	17	1995-2011	0.0807	0.0173	0.430 ***	0.0847	0.0138	0.047	0.561 **	∞	0.0847
Lune	17	1995-2011	*No solution*			0.0992	0.0047	0.001	0.475 **	∞	
Kent	17	1995-2011	0.1309	0.0868	0.188 *	0.1775	0.1280	0.251 **	0.212 *	∞	0.1775

Where: *=0.050≤P<0.100; **=0.010≤P<0.050; ***=0.001≤P<0.010; ****=P<0.001

137

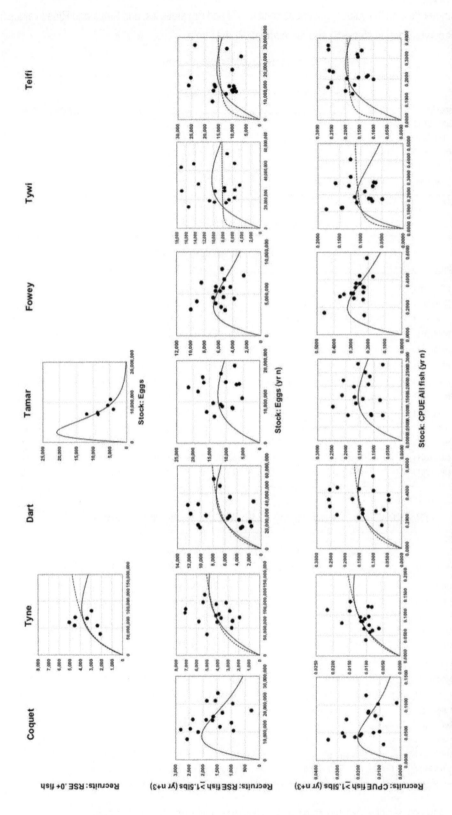

Figure 3. Ricker (solid line) and Beverton & Holt (dashed line) SR curves fitted to (i) trap/counter derived RSE/egg data (*upper tier graphs*); (ii) rod catch derived RSE/egg data (*middle tier graphs*) and (iii) rod CPUE data (*lower tier graphs*).

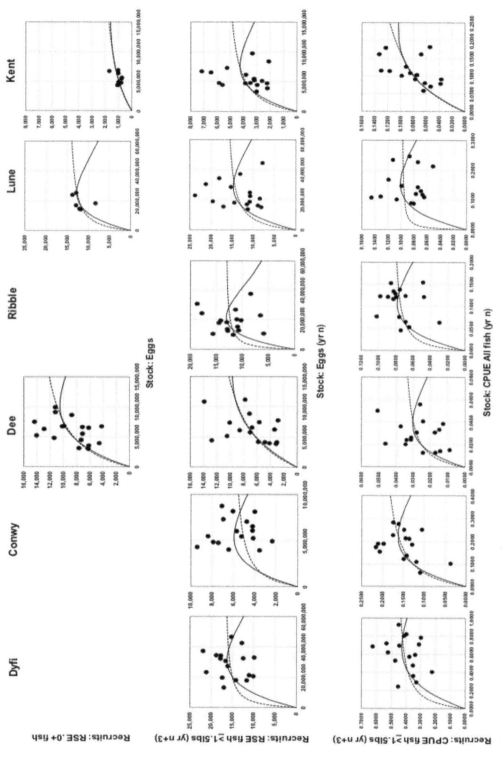

Figure 3 *(continued).* Ricker (solid line) and Beverton & Holt (dashed line) SR curves fitted to (i) trap/counter derived RSE/egg data *(upper tier graphs)*; (ii) rod catch derived RSE/egg data *(middle tier graphs)* and (iii) rod CPUE data *(lower tier graphs).*

The linear regression relationships used to provide initial 'a' and 'b' parameter estimates were statistically significant ($p < 0.05$) or near statistically significant ($0.05 \leq p < 0.10$) in most instances, and particularly so for the Ricker model. In a number of cases, the linear regression method failed to provide valid parameter estimates (i.e. produced negative 'b' values) for the Beverton & Holt model.

In the case of stock and recruitment data from trap/counter derived RSEs/eggs (5 rivers), significant or near significant linear regression relationships were present on only the Tamar (Ricker model) and Dee (Ricker and Beverton & Holt models). For this group of rivers as a whole, r^2 values were relatively high (range 0.130-0.704), but few significant relationships were present, probably because (apart from the Dee) sample sizes were small at 10 or less compared to sample sizes of 17 for rod catch derived SR data sets.

Curve fitting using non-linear regression methods resulted, for the most part, in rejection of the second null hypothesis (Ho: $R = pS$) but not the first (Ho: $R = meanR$). There were few instances where both null hypotheses could be rejected at significant or near significant levels (and none where SR data were based on rod catch derived RSEs/eggs); these are summarised below for the various data sets and SR models:

SR Model	Trap/Counter: RSE/Eggs	Rod Catch: RSE/Eggs	Rod Catch: CPUE
Ricker	Tamar, & Dee	-	Coquet, Fowey, Conway, Kent
Beverton & Holt	Dee	-	Conway & Kent

As with the linear regression approach, non-linear regression methods were able to fit the Ricker curve to all SR data sets, but failed to fit the Beverton & Holt curve in the cases of Coquet, Fowey and Tamar (Figure 3 and Tables 1 & 2). This occurred irrespective of the SR data set used (i.e. trap/counter or rod catch derived RSEs/eggs or rod CPUE data). In each of these cases, the pattern in the data tended to indicate a negative association between stock and recruitment at the higher end of the stock scale: a pattern that the asymptotic Beverton & Holt curve could not accommodate but the dome-shaped Ricker curve could. Expression of a common form of SR relationship for the three different measures of stock and recruitment used may reflect the extent to which these measures are interrelated but could also suggest a degree of consistency in underlying population processes. Where Ricker or Beverton & Holt relationships were fitted to the SR data sets, examination of the residuals associated with the fitted curves showed no systematic pattern to suggest obvious inadequacies in model choice.

Visual examination of all SR relationships in Figure 3 indicates that, in a number of cases, the ascending limb and inflection points of Ricker and Beverton & Holt curves follow very similar paths. Again, this appears to be the case irrespective of the stock and recruitment variables used (e.g. Tyne, Dart, Dee, Conwy, Kent). In other cases, the ascending limb of the Beverton & Holt curve is clearly to the left of the Ricker curve (e.g. various permutations of the

Tywi, Teifi, Ribble and Lune SR curves) and in some instances quite markedly so – sometimes with the ascending limb set at an extremely steep gradient followed by a sudden flattening out of the curve in a manner which appears unrealistic (e.g. Tywi and Teifi). The Ricker curve fitted to trap/counter data for the Tamar is also notable because all the data points (only six in total) are tightly clustered around a steeply descending right-hand limb in a way that is clearly unusual and leaves the validity of this relationship open to question.

Values for Rmax ('maximum recruitment') and Smax (the stock size resulting in Rmax) are also given in Tables 1 & 2 for the fitted Ricker and Beverton & Holt curves (note that for the latter relationship the value of Smax is always infinity). The Rmax and Smax values are provided as example reference points for comparative purposes only, i.e. their suitability as BRPs for fisheries management has not been considered in this paper.

Table 3 expresses Ricker derived Smax values as egg deposition rates (eggs per 100m2) for various stream order (Strahler, 1952) related measures of accessible wetted area. The latter range from estimates of the total accessible wetted area for all stream orders down to the accessible wetted area associated with the smallest (order 1) streams. The mean stream widths associated with each order class are also shown in Table 3. These measures were obtained from a 1:250,000 GIS and field data measurements, and were used to estimate salmon Conservation Limits in E&W (Wyatt & Barnard, 1997b). Smax egg deposition rates (Table 3) were highly variable between rivers irrespective of the wetted area used to calculate these rates, indicating that it would be very unlikely that BRP transportation methods based on a simple, common (e.g. average) egg deposition rate would prove feasible. Rather, such approaches would require a better understanding (and modelling) of the causes of this variation between rivers.

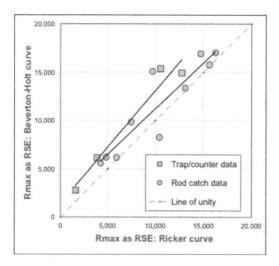 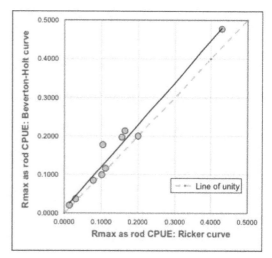

Figure 4. Comparison of Rmax values (as RSEs or CPUE) obtained with the Ricker and Beverton & Holt SR curves fitted to trap/counter and rod catch derived data sets. Solid trend lines and filled symbols indicate significant correlations (P<0.05).

Table 3 (a & b). Comparison of Smax egg deposition rates calculated for various stream order related measures of accessible wetted area and based on Smax values obtained from Ricker curves fitted to stock and recruitment data from a) traps & counters and b) rod catches:

a) Trap/counter derived stock and recruitment data:

River	Smax (Eggs)	Accessible wetted area (hectares) by stream order class:				Smax Eggs per 100m2:			
		All *Mean width (m)*	≤Order3 *Mean width (m)*	≤Order2 *Mean width (m)*	Order1 *Mean width (m)*	All	≤Order3	≤Order2	Order1
Tyne	87,533,309	541.6	312.9	168.3	77.2	1,616	2,797	5,200	11,342
		11.8	*7.5*	*4.6*	*3.1*				
Tamar	2,483,507	292.6	207.2	172.0	91.7	85	120	144	271
		6.1	*4.7*	*4.2*	*3.5*				
Dee	10,222,385	617.0	181.1	156.8	103.1	166	565	652	992
		9.9	*3.6*	*3.4*	*3.1*				
Lune	25,314,493	422.7	198.2	152.8	52.9	599	1,277	1,657	4,789
		12.2	*6.5*	*5.5*	*3.0*				
Kent	16,508,409	68.1	42.7	25.9	5.7	2,423	3,867	6,372	28,762
		8.1	*5.8*	*4.4*	*2.9*				
					Count =	5	5	5	5
					Mean =	978	1,725	2,805	9,231
					Standard deviation =	1012.1	1570.3	2805.7	11766.5
					Coefficient of variation =	1.035	0.910	1.000	1.275

b) Rod catch derived stock and recruitment data:

River	Smax (Eggs)	Accessible wetted area (hectares) by stream order class:				Smax Eggs per 100m2:			
		All *Mean width (m)*	<Order3 *Mean width (m)*	<Order2 *Mean width (m)*	Order1 *Mean width (m)*	All	<Order3	<Order2	Order1
Coquet	8,529,847	143.8	143.8	41.1	29.0	593	593	2,076	2,942
		8.2	*8.2*	*3.4*	*3.1*				
Tyne	127,712,808	541.6	312.9	168.3	77.2	2,358	4,081	7,586	16,548
		11.8	*7.5*	*4.6*	*3.1*				
Dart	39,554,942	136.7	136.7	59.9	43.3	2,894	2,894	6,606	9,129
		9.6	*9.6*	*5.6*	*4.9*				
Tamar	11,635,999	292.6	207.2	172.0	91.7	398	562	677	1,268
		6.1	*4.7*	*4.2*	*3.5*				
Fowey	3,477,427	41.5	41.5	24.9	14.4	838	838	1,396	2,419
		6.0	*6.0*	*4.5*	*3.7*				
Tywi	33,610,307	500.1	276.4	171.7	107.4	672	1,216	1,957	3,131
		8.7	*5.2*	*3.8*	*3.1*				
Teifi	18,639,760	325.9	282.9	96.9	49.7	572	659	1,924	3,748
		6.1	*5.4*	*2.3*	*1.6*				
Dyfi	31,143,810	179.1	94.7	71.7	16.1	1,739	3,290	4,345	19,316
		8.9	*5.7*	*5.2*	*3.2*				
Conwy	5,348,201	63.0	20.6	7.3	3.4	849	2,602	7,329	15,598
		9.3	*5.2*	*3.7*	*3.3*				
Dee	15,522,806	617.0	181.1	156.8	103.1	252	857	990	1,506
		9.9	*3.6*	*3.4*	*3.1*				
Ribble	21,549,891	351.1	189.7	97.3	25.5	614	1,136	2,216	8,462
		20.0	*12.8*	*8.1*	*3.1*				
Lune	28,663,586	422.7	198.2	152.8	52.9	678	1,446	1,876	5,423
		12.2	*6.5*	*5.5*	*3.0*				
Kent	7,657,421	68.1	42.7	25.9	5.7	1,124	1,794	2,956	13,341
		8.1	*5.8*	*4.4*	*2.9*				
					Count =	13	13	13	13
					Mean =	1,045	1,690	3,226	7,910
					Standard deviation =	798.3	1159.0	2431.0	6333.8
					Coefficient of variation =	0.764	0.686	0.754	0.801

Rmax values from both Ricker & Beverton & Holt SR curves were highly correlated (p<0.05) for all permutations of stock and recruitment variables (Figure 4), with, on average, Rmax values from the Beverton & Holt curve being higher than those from the Ricker curve (13-31% higher at mean levels of Rmax). For the Ricker curve, Smax values (as egg numbers) from rod catch derived RSEs were positively associated with those from trap/counter data (p=0.003); relative differences between the former and the latter ranged from 8% for the Dee to 84% for the Tyne (Figure 5). Note that the Smax values in Figure 5 result from Ricker curves re-fitted to common time-series of trap/counter and rod-catch data and so may differ from the values given in Table 1. Except for the Kent, positive associations were also evident between rod catch derived stock and recruitment variables (as RSEs/eggs or CPUE indices) and the equivalent measures from trap/counter data (Figure 6). These associations were significant (p<0.05) in all scenarios for the Dee and Tyne.

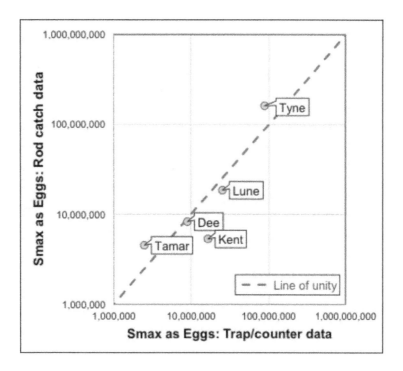

Figure 5. Comparison of Smax values (as eggs) obtained from the Ricker SR relationship fitted to trap/counter and rod catch derived data sets.

STOCK METRICS AND COMPLIANCE ASSESSMENT

SR curves have been fitted to two measures of stock and recruitment in this study: (i) RSEs/ eggs and (ii) CPUE. Stock performance for these two metrics have been compared by applying simple compliance criteria to the time-series of rod catch derived data for the 13 rivers examined here. These comprise assessment of (i) average annual deviation from the Smax egg and CPUE reference levels and (ii) the trend in stock estimates over the time-series. Both are illustrated for the River Teifi in Figure 7. Table 4 shows the results of this assessment for all 13 rivers, and indicates that, in terms of both deviation from Smax and (particularly) the long-term trend in stock estimates, the compliance outcome for the stock if measured as eggs is more severe (i.e. precautionary) than if measured as CPUE. This has implications for the choice of stock metric used to derive a reference point and how it informs management.

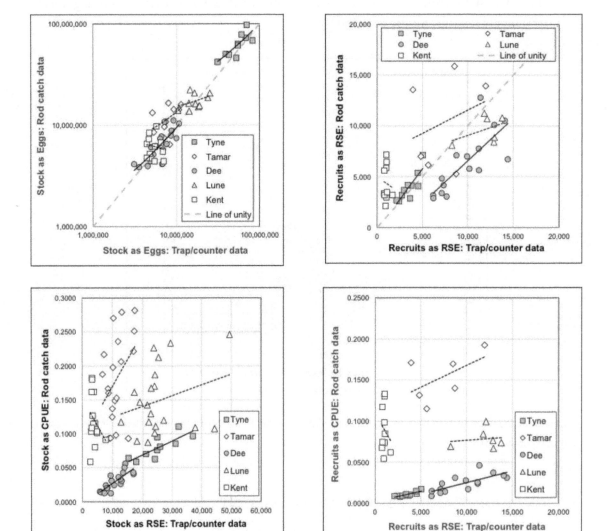

Figure 6. Associations between rod catch and trap/counter derived stock and recruitment variables for the rivers Tyne, Tamar, Dee, Lune and Kent. Solid trend lines and filled symbols indicate significant correlations (P<0.05).

Table 4. Compliance criteria applied to 17 year time-series of egg and CPUE measures of stock abundance and expressed as: (i) average deviation from Smax reference levels (i.e. the proportion (p) of Smax attained) and (ii) the trend in stock estimates. The symbol '#' highlights, on a river-by-river basis, the stock metric with the least favourable compliance outcome.

River	*Mean pSmax:*		*Trend*	
	Eggs	*CPUE*	*Eggs*	*CPUE*
Coquet	1.717	1.685 #	-0.041 #	0.005
Tyne	0.551	0.515 #	-0.007 #	-0.001
Dart	0.605 #	0.825	-0.029 #	-0.005
Tamar	1.045 #	1.143	0.005 #	0.036
Fowey	1.489 #	1.641	0.017 #	0.017
Tywi	0.795 #	1.109	-0.029 #	-0.010
Teifi	0.740 #	0.865	-0.011 #	0.004
Dyfi	1.001	0.964 #	0.039 #	0.041 #
Conway	1.204	0.839 #	0.025	0.025
Dee	0.443 #	0.805	0.019 #	0.042
Ribble	0.869 #	1.051	0.006 #	0.026
Lune	0.784	0.969	- 0.017 #	0.002
Kent	0.734	0.507 #	0.013 #	0.020

a) Stock as Eggs

b) Stock as CPUE:

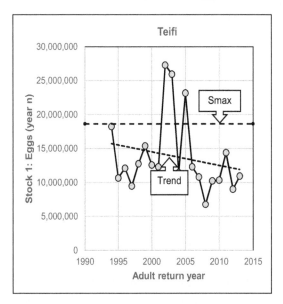

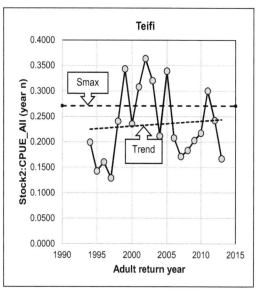

Figure 7. Compliance criteria applied to egg and CPUE stock estimates for the River Teifi and expressed as (i) average annual deviation from Smax reference levels and (ii) time-series trends in stock estimates.

DISCUSSION

Development of Biological Reference Points for the assessment and management of sea trout stocks has been an aim of the regulatory bodies in E&W for some time (Thornton, 2008). The 1st International Sea Trout Symposium in 2004 explored this theme (Elliott & Elliott, 2006; Walker *et al.,* 2006) and identified the need to *"develop and implement BRP based assessment and appropriate catchment management"* among a list of priorities for further research and investigation (Milner *et al.*, 2006). A subsequent ICES workshop on sea trout (WKTRUTTA, 2013) came to similar conclusions and recommended a follow-up workshop to focus on BRPs and related developments. This was convened in 2016 (WKTRUTTAII, *in prep.*).

This paper has focussed on the use of rod catch data to derive measures (RSEs/eggs) or indices (CPUE) of stock and recruitment, and has attempted to fit Ricker and Beverton & Holt SR curves to these data and then define associated BRPs from these curves (e.g. Smax and Rmax).

Rod catch data are widely used in stock and fishery assessments. They provide the most extensive whole catchment abundance measure for sea trout and salmon in E&W, covering more than 80 principal rivers. The data used in this study have been collected in a nationally consistent manner since 1994 and, in terms of generating RSE/egg estimates, have been treated in ways which have direct parallels with procedures well established in Atlantic salmon management to assess compliance with Conservation Limits in E&W (Wyatt & Barnard, 1997a; 1997b; Milner *et al.,* 2000) and in Ireland (Standing Scientific Committee on Salmon, 2016; White *et al.,* 2016).

Comparisons with true census data collected from the five trapped/countered rivers (Tyne, Tamar, Dee, Lune and Kent) provide some assurance that, in broad terms, rod catch derived RSE/egg estimates and CPUE data can provide reasonable measures/indicators of stock and recruitment: although this was stronger in some cases (e.g. Tyne and Dee) than others (e.g. Kent) (Figure 6).

Fitting the Ricker and Beverton & Holt SR relationships to these data sets has produced mixed results. The linear regression relationships (Equations 3 & 4) used to provide initial 'a' and 'b' parameter estimates were statistically significant ($p<0.05$) or nearly statistically significant ($0.05 \leq p < 0.10$) in most instances. However, Elliott (1985) noted that these analyses should be treated with caution, not least because measures of 'stock' feature on both sides of the equation since they are used to calculate both the dependent and independent variables. Elliott concluded that non-linear regression methods provided more realistic measures of the strength of the SR relationship. Using the latter methods, Ricker curves were fitted to all stock and recruitment data sets examined in this study, and Beverton & Holt curves to most (except Coquet, Fowey and Tamar). The Rmax values from both curves were highly correlated for all data permutations (Figure 4), as too were Smax values from Ricker curves fitted to rod-catch and trap/counter derived data sets (Figure 5).

In terms of goodness-of-fit statistics, there was widespread rejection of the second null hypothesis (Ho: R=pS), although this was not the case with first (Ho: R = meanR). There were also very few instances where both null hypotheses could be rejected at significant or near significant levels (p<0.10). Elliott (1985) refers to Bellows (1981) who suggested that the second of the null hypotheses (Ho:R = pS) is the most appropriate for testing the fit of density dependent models. However, Elliott identifies shortcomings in this test and concludes that both null hypotheses (Ho: R = meanR and Ho:R = pS) should be rejected before it can be concluded that a density dependent model is acceptable.

Among six SR models fitted to sea trout data sets from the Black Brows Beck (including the Ricker and Beverton & Holt curves), Elliott (1985) found that the second null hypothesis was widely rejected, but the first null hypothesis much less so – except in the case of the Ricker curve. In relation to the first null hypothesis, a Ricker curve fitted to egg to May/June parr census data from Elliott's study, produced an r^2 ('coefficient determination') value of 0.98 (P<0.001). However, r^2 values fell off rapidly for Ricker curves fitted to later recruit stages, including returning adults (r^2=0.31) and eggs (r^2=0.38) ($0.01 \leq P < 0.05$ in both cases). Elliott (1994) concluded that a key factor regulating population density throughout the life cycle was density-dependent survival at the newly emerged fry stage. He also noted that negative density-dependent factors are unlikely to account for more than about half of the inter-generation variation in recruitment, the remaining variation being attributable to positive density-dependent and density-independent factors.

Sea trout population studies on the Burrishoole (Poole *et al.,* 2006) reported r^2 values of 0.70-0.93 for Ricker and Beverton & Holt SR curves fitted to egg-to-smolt data. A similar study on the Bresle (Euzenat *et al.*, 2006), fitting the same SR models to data for the same life stages, reported lower r^2 values of 0.39-0.40. (In both cases, no P-values were given).

For the whole-river stocks examined in this study, recruits were expressed as .0+ maiden fish or their equivalents. Ricker curves fitted to data from the trapped/counted rivers produced r^2s values ranging from 0.003 (Lune) to 0.588 (Tamar), but only r^2s values for the Tamar and Dee (0.183) were significant or near significant (P<0.10). (Beverton & Holt curves fitted to these data sets produced similar results.)

None of the SR curves fitted to rod catch derived RSEs produced significant or near significant r^2s values, even though sample sizes were generally larger (n=17) than available for the trapped/countered rivers (Tables 1 & 2). While SR curves fitted to CPUE data fared slightly better in terms of goodness-of-fit, all rod catch derived stock and recruitment variables would be subject to additional estimation error compared to true census data. This would tend to weaken any pattern in the data that might reflect the effects of density-dependent regulation at early life stages.

Given the views of Elliott (1985) on the statistical tests that should be satisfied in determining an appropriate SR model, caution would be required if a lesser standard were to be adopted for stock assessment and management: both in terms of SR curve selection and resulting reference points. That said, the risks for management of selecting a SR model where the first null hypothesis (R=meanR) cannot be rejected may be overstated. This is likely to occur where the scatter of available observations do not lie at the extremes of the stock range (a feature of many of the data sets examined here but an indicator, at least, that very low stock levels have been avoided). While the SR relationship could be represented statistically as a horizontal line fitted through a data set at the mean level of recruitment, that would not be a fair representation of biological reality given that the true SR relationship can be expected to pass through the origin (or close to it). A fitted Ricker or Beverton & Holt curve will pass through the origin and, on the basis of numerous salmonid population studies (e.g. Milner *et al.* 2003), including some referred to here, it seems fair to assume that a best-fit Ricker or Beverton & Holt model is likely to provide a reasonable representation of the density-dependent regulatory effects underlying any set of stock and recruitment data. For example, in the case of the Burrishoole, the data set included a cluster of points close to the origin which resulted from stock collapse following a marked decline in marine survival in the late 1980s (Poole *et al.*, 2006). In the absence of these points, r^2 values (for Beverton & Holt curves) were much lower: falling from 0.93 to 0.42 for egg-to-smolt curves and from 0.62 to 0.10 for egg-to-.0+ maiden fish (WKTRUTTAII, *in prep*; Poole *pers. comm.*). Despite the reduction in goodness-of-fit in these examples, the form of the SR-curves and associated reference points changed little.

The SR data sets examined in this study have all expressed recruitment as a measure of .0+ abundance. In contrast, the more conventional approach in developing SR relationships to define freshwater carrying capacity is to express recruitment in terms of smolt output. Given that the .0+ stage is separated from the smolt stage by just a few months , it is likely that a SR relationship defined in terms of .0+ recruitment will be similar in form to the equivalent relationship for smolt recruitment, as will the values of associated stock related BRPs. However, the SR relationship for .0+ recruitment is likely to be less robust than its smolt recruitment counter-part, (i) because of a degree of dependency between the stock and recruitment variables (i.e. the abundance of .0+ fish features in the measure of stock as well as recruitment – albeit lagged by n+3 years in the former) and (ii) because the presence of any underlying trend toward increasing or decreasing marine survival could alter the form of the SR relationship overtime. While it is important to note these effects, for the latter at least, smolt return rates estimated from tagging studies on the Tamar and Dee provide no indication of any systematic change in marine survival in recent years (Davidson *et al.*, 2016).

Further comparison of SR curves and reference points derived from rod-catch based stock and recruitment data with those obtained from true census (i.e. trap/counter) data would help build confidence that the former can serve as a valid approach to sea trout stock assessment and management. The value of the comparisons made in this study has been limited because of the short time-series of census data available in most cases, e.g. only 6 or 7 years on the Tyne, Tamar and Lune. Revisiting these comparisons, say every five years, should provide increasingly more robust SR relationships from which to make judgments. The assumptions underpinning rod-catch based approaches should also be explored to better understand the effects of varying smolt age, .0+ size, and other factors (including the potential contribution of non-anadromous trout) on model outputs.

As a starting point, the procedures described here for deriving 'pseudo' SR curves and associated reference points (as RSE/eggs or CPUE) appear to have merit. They share more in common with the now well established use of Conservation Limits (CLs) in salmon management than the rod-based CPUE approach currently used to assess sea trout stocks in E&W, and could adopt the same CL compliance procedures and risk-based framework to guide management decision making. In particular, the use of RSE/egg based reference points has the advantage of already being familiar to external interests in the context of salmon management, and equates to stock units (e.g. spawner or egg numbers) that are easily understood and readily applicable to fisheries regulation (e.g. exploitation control).

RSE/egg based reference points have a stronger biological basis than CPUE equivalents and provide tangible measures of key life stages. They also incorporate size variation as well as abundance in assessment procedures, the former reflecting components of the stock such as the larger multi-sea winter/repeat spawning fish that may require targeted protection. Finally, compliance outcomes (Table 4) appear more precautionary using RSE/egg based reference points. All these factors should be considered when seeking to further develop BRPs for sea trout – including approaches involving the use of pseudo SR relationships as examined in this study.

ACKNOWLEDGEMENTS

We would like to thank all individuals from the Environment Agency, Natural Resources Wales and predecessor organisations who have contributed to the collection of the data presented here.

REFERENCES

Bellows, T.S. (1981). The descriptive properties of some models for density dependence. *Journal of Animal Ecology* **50**, 139-156.

Beverton, R.J.H. & Holt, S.J. (1957). On the dynamics of exploited fish populations. *Fisheries Investment Series* 2, Vol. 19. U.K. Ministry of Agriculture and Fisheries London.

Brown, A.M. (2001). A step-by-step guide to non-linear regression analysis of experimental data using a Microsoft Excel spreadsheet. *Computer Methods and Programs in Biomedicine.* **65** (2001), 191-200

Davidson, I.C., Cove, R.J., Hillman, R.J., Elsmere, P.S., Cook, N., & Croft, A. (2017). Observations on sea trout stock performance in the rivers Dee, Tamar, Lune and Tyne (1991-2014): The contribution of 'index river' monitoring programmes in England and Wales to fisheries management. In: *Sea Trout: Science & Management.* (Graeme Harris, *Ed.*).) Proceedings of the 2nd International Sea Trout Symposium, October 2015, Dundalk, Ireland. Troubador, 470–486.

Elliott, J.M. (1985). The choice of a stock-recruitment model for migratory trout, Salmo trutta, in an English Lake District stream. *Arch. Hydrobiol.* 104, 1, 145-168. Stuttgart, Juli, 1985.

Elliott, J.M. (1994). Quantitative Ecology and the Brown Trout. *Oxford University Press*, Oxford, xi +286 pp.

Elliott, J.M. and Elliott, J.A. (2006). A 35-year study of stock and recruitment relationships in a small population of sea trout: Assumptions, implications and limitations for predicting targets. In: *Sea Trout: Biology, Conservation and Management* (Graeme Harris & Nigel Milner. *Eds*. Proceedings of the First International Sea Trout Symposium, Cardiff, July 2004.. Blackwell Publishing, Oxford, 257-278.

Environment Agency (2003). *Salmon Action Plan Guidelines, Version 2*. Environment Agency, April 2003.

Euzenat, G., Fournel, F. & Fagard, J-L. (2006). Population dynamics and stock-recruitment relationships for sea trout in the River Bresle, Upper Normandy, France. In: *Sea Trout: Biology, Conservation and Management*. (Graeme Harris & Nigel Milner. *Eds*.). Proceedings of the First International Sea Trout Symposium, Cardiff, July 2004. Blackwell Publishing, Oxford, 307-323.

Hilborn, R. & Walters, C.J. (1992). *Quantitative Fisheries Stock Assessment: Choice, Dynamics and Uncertainty*. Kluwer Academic Publishers, Massachusetts.

Harris, G.S. (2002). Sea Trout Stock Descriptions: The Structure and Composition of Sea Trout Stocks from 16 Rivers in England and Wales. Environment Agency, Bristol. R&D Technical Report W224, 93 pp.

ICES. (1995). Report of the North Atlantic Salmon Working Group. International Council for the Exploration of the Sea, Doc C.M.1995/Assess 14, Ref: M, 191 pp.

ICES. (2014). *Report of the Workshop on Sea Trout (WKTRUTTA); 12-14 November 2013;* ICES Headquarters, Copenhagen, Denmark. SCICOM Steering Group on Ecosystem Functions; ICES CM 2013/SSGEF:15; Ref. WGBAST, WGRECORDS, SCICOM.

Milner, N.J., Davidson, I.C., Wyatt, R.J., & Aprahamian, M.A. (2000). *The use of spawning targets for salmon fishery management in England and Wales*. In: *Management and Ecology of River Fisheries*. (Cowx, I.G. *Ed*.). Fishing News Books, Blackwell Science, Oxford, 361–372.

Milner, N.J., Elliott, J.M., Armstrong, J.D., Gardiner, R., Welton, J.S., & Ladle, M. (2003). The natural control of salmon and trout populations in streams. *Fisheries Research* **62** (2003), 111-125.

Milner, N.J., Harris, G.S., Gargan, P., Beveridge, M., Pawson, M.G., Walker, A. and Whelan, K. (2006). Perspectives on sea trout science and management. In: *Sea Trout: Biology, Conservation and Management*. (Graeme Harris & Nigel Milner. *Eds*.). Proceedings of the First International Sea Trout Symposium, Cardiff, July 2004. Blackwell Publishing, Oxford, 480-490.

NASCO. (1998). Agreement on the adoption of a precautionary approach. Report of the Fifteenth Annual Meeting of the Council. NASCO, Edinburgh, 167–172.

Poole, W.R., Dillane, M., DeEyto, E., Rogan, G., McGinnity, P. & Whelan., K. (2006). Characteristics of the Burrishoole sea trout population: Census, marine survival, enhancement and stock-recruitment relationship, 1971-2003. In: *Sea Trout: Biology, Conservation and Management*. (Graeme Harris & Nigel Milner. *Eds*.). Proceedings of the First International Sea Trout Symposium, Cardiff, July 2004. Blackwell Publishing, Oxford, 279-306.

Potter, E.C.E., MacLean, J.C., Wyatt, R.J. and Campbell, R.N.B. (2003). Managing the exploitation of migratory salmonids. *Fisheries Research* **62** (2003), 127-142.

Ricker, W.E. (1954). Stock and recruitment. *J. Fish. Res. Bd. Can.* **11**:559-623

Russell, I.C., Ives, M.J., Potter, E.C.E., Buckley, A.A. & Duckett, L. (1995). Salmon and migratory trout statistics for England and Wales. *Fisheries Report Data Report*, No. 38, MAFF Lowestoft, 1995, 252 pp.

Shields, B.A., Aprahamian, M.A., Bayliss, B.A., Davidson, I.C., Elsmere, P.& Evans, R. (2006). Sea trout (*Salmo trutta*, L.) exploitation in five rivers in England and Wales. In: *Sea Trout: Biology, Conservation and Management* (Graeme Harris & Nigel Milner. *Eds.*). Proceedings of the First International Sea Trout Symposium, Cardiff, July 2004. Blackwell Publishing, Oxford, *417-433*

Solomon, D.J. (1994). *Sea trout investigations. Phase I – Final Report. R&D Note 318,* National Rivers Authority. 434-440.

Strahler, A. N. (1952). Hypsometric (area-altitude) analysis of erosional topology. *Geological Society of America Bulletin 63 (11), 1117–1142.*

Standing Scientific Committee on Salmon. (2016). The Status of Irish Salmon Stocks in 2015 with Precautionary Catch Advice for 2016. *Independent Scientific Report to Inland Fisheries Ireland:* February 2016.

Thornton, L. (2008). Evaluating options for sea trout and brown trout biological reference points. *Environment Agency Science Report, SC060070.*

Walker, A.M., Pawson, M.G. & Potter, E.C.E. (2006). Sea trout fisheries management: Should we follow the salmon? In: *Sea Trout: Biology, Conservation and Management* (Graeme Harris & Nigel Milner. *Eds.*). Proceedings of the First International Sea Trout Symposium, Cardiff, July 2004. Blackwell Publishing, Oxford, *466-479*.

White, J., Ó Maoiléidigh, N., Gargan, P., de Eyto, E., Chaput, G., Roche, W., McGinnity, P., Crozier, W.W., Boylan, P., Doherty, D., O'Higgins, K., Kennedy, B., Lawler, I., Lyons, D. & Marnell, F. (2016). Incorporating natural variability in biological reference points and population dynamics into management of Atlantic salmon (*Salmo salar* L.) stocks returning to home waters. *ICES Journal of Marine Science,* Advance Access published March 16, 2016.

WKTRUTTA. (2013). Report of the Workshop on Sea Trout (WKTRUTTA). *ICES WKTRUTTA Report 2013*, 12-14 November 2013, ICES Headquarters, Copenhagen, Denmark. SCICOM Steering Group on Ecosystem Functions, ICES CM 2013/SSGEF: 15, Ref. WGBAST, WGRECORDS, SCICOM.

Wyatt, R.J., Barnard, S. (1997a). Spawning escapement targets for Atlantic salmon. *Environment Agency, R&D Technical Report ,*W64.

Wyatt, R.J., Barnard, S. (1997b). The transportation of the maximum gain salmon spawning target from the River Bush (N.I.) to England and Wales. *Environment Agency, R&D Technical Report W65.*

ELECTRONIC REFERENCES

Cefas, Environment Agency & Natural Resources Wales (2015a). Annual assessment of salmon stocks and fisheries in England and Wales 2014: Standing report on methods, approaches and wider stock conservation and management considerations. *Available at*: https://www.gov.uk/government/uploads/system/uploads/attachment_data/file/437977/BackgroundSalmonReport-2014.pdf

Cefas, Environment Agency & Natural Resources Wales (2015b). *Annual assessment of salmon stocks and fisheries in England and Wales 2014*: Preliminary assessment prepared for ICES, March 2015: *Available at:* https://www.gov.uk/government/uploads/system/uploads/attachment_data/file/450982/ SalmonAssessmentReport-2014-finalrevised.pdf

Environment Agency & Natural Resources Wales (2015). *Salmonid and Freshwater Fisheries Statistics for England & Wales, 2014.* Version 4 September 2015. *Available at: https://www.gov.uk/government/ uploads/ system/uploads/attachment_data/file/459174/FishStatsReport2014.v4.pdf*

Trout recruitment, production and ova seeding requirements on a small coastal river: A case study from the Shimna River, Northern Ireland.

R. J. KENNEDY[1,] W. W. CROZIER[1], R. ROSELL[1], M. ALLEN[1] & P. PRODÖHL[2]

[1] *Agri-Food and Biosciences Institute, Newforge Lane, Belfast, N. Ireland, BT9 5PX.*
[2] *Queens University Belfast, University Road, Belfast, N. Ireland, BT7 1NN.*

ABSTRACT

The Shimna River is a small coastal catchment in Northern Ireland with a locally significant sea trout (*Salmo trutta* L.) fishery. A salmonid monitoring programme was initiated on the system in 2003. Cross correlation analysis of 0+ recruitment and survival against a range of potential biological and environmental explanatory factors indicated that low survival was associated with high spring discharge conditions. A significant negative relationship was also evident between 0+ trout survival and both sea trout rod catch and CPUE in the previous year, indicating lower relative survival following high ova deposition years and suggestive of functional density dependent regulation. Further analysis showed a stock-recruitment relationship between both the Shimna sea trout rod catch and CPUE and resultant 0+ fry recruitment. The Ricker model produced the best fit and explained 63% and 70% of the variance in recruitment when plotted against rod catch and CPUE respectively. The recruitment potential of late summer 0+ trout on the Shimna (above the fish counter station) was modelled using electric fishing and habitat data and ranged between 15,830 – 17,908 fish; which corresponded to an estimated ova deposition requirement of 175,890 – 596,926 ova or 3.3 – 11.2 ova m^{-2} of the total available habitat. The potential ova contribution from the resident brown trout and the sea run component of the stock was estimated; with the majority (> 85%) of the annual ova deposition contributed by ≥1 sea winter sea trout. Larger mature sea run trout are particularly important for the viability of the Shimna stock and the potential implications for future management practices are considered.

Keywords: sea trout; stock-recruitment; survival; finnock; effective population size.

INTRODUCTION

The Shimna River is a small coastal spate stream in North-East Ireland noted for its stock of sea trout. The current Irish rod caught record (7.43 kg) was caught there in 1983 (Irish Specimen Fish Committee, 2014). A fishery monitoring programme was initiated in 2003 with an annual, semi-quantitative (SQ) electric fishing survey (Crozier & Kennedy, 1994) conducted at 25 sites throughout the migratory range of sea trout in the river. Fully quantitative (FQ), depletion, electric fishing surveys have also been conducted at various sites. Detailed rod catch returns have been compiled by the local angling association for sea trout (including finnock), resident brown trout (>20 cm) and salmon and these data included raw catch and a simple Catch per Unit Effort (CPUE) metric (mean catch angler^{-1} yr^{-1}). A three channel crump weir with resistivity fish counter (Aquantic 2100C) and CCTV validation equipment was installed c. 300 m upstream from the head of tide in 2010/11.

The Shimna River is around 12 km in length; it rises in the Mourne mountains at an elevation of 430m and has one major tributary, the Burren river (Figure 1). The river is relatively acidic, nutrient poor and adjacent land use is dominated by rough upland grazing and coniferous forestry. A natural obstacle to fish migration is present c. 6.5 km upstream from the sea (c.150m elevation). This extensive waterfall/cascade is thought to be passable under only certain flow conditions.

The total wetted area available to migratory salmonids throughout the catchment is 9.9 ha with 5.3 ha available upstream of the Shimna fish counter. The river is dominated by shallower (<1m deep) habitats which account for c. 90% of the total wetted area.

The local time series were interrogated with the following objectives: 1) to investigate the recruitment dynamics of 0+ trout in the Shimna catchment, 2) to estimate the productive

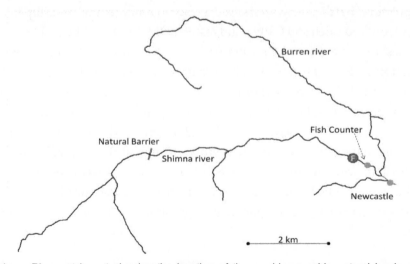

Figure 1. Shimna River catchment showing the location of the semi-impassable natural barrier and the annual quantitative electric fishing site (= F) on the Lower Shimna.

capacity of the Shimna River for juvenile (0+) trout and determine the ova deposition levels needed to attain productive capacity, 3) to estimate the relative contribution of resident and sea trout to total ova production,

JUVENILE 0+ TROUT RECRUITMENT DYNAMICS.

Juvenile (0+) trout recruitment, monitored by the SQ survey programme and expressed as a relative abundance index (mean no. 0+ trout 5 mins^{-1}), has varied from 3.8 0+ (2004) – 10.2 0+ trout 5 mins^{-1} (2010) across the time series (Figure.2).

Annual 0+ trout recruitment and a relative index of survival (SQ /Adult CPUE yr-1) were investigated against a panel of potential explanatory biological and environmental variables.

Explanatory biological variables included sea trout catch (catch and CPUE) from the previous year (yr-1), resident trout catch from the previous year (yr-1), >2+ age class resident trout density from the previous year (yr-1) and SQ indices of >0+ trout parr abundance in the same year (yr). Salmon data were also considered and included adult catches (catch and CPUE yr-1) and SQ 0+ and >0+ abundance indices (yr). Discharge data measured at a flow gauging station on the Shimna were also considered and mean daily flow records were tabulated to determine Mean Monthly Flow (MMF), mean flow during the adult migratory season (Aug – Oct) and mean flow over the ova to fry development phase (Nov– Apr) prior to each 0+ monitoring year. The number of high flood events (>Q 1 flows) that occurred during the development of each 0+ cohort (previous Nov – Apr) were also considered as a potential explanatory variable.

A cross correlation analysis was conducted to investigate the various factors potentially influencing juvenile trout recruitment and survival on the Shimna river. The analysis was programmed through GENSTAT and initially scanned each time series for autocorrelation

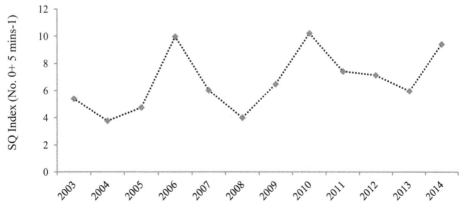

Figure 2. Mean 0+ trout recruitment (No. 5 min^{-1}) derived from semi-quantitative (SQ) electric fishing on the Shimna River (2003 – 2014).

and partial autocorrelation before conducting a cross-correlation interrogation of input against explanatory variables.

Each time series was identified as stationary and no transformations were required. A significant negative correlation was evident between 0+ trout survival and MMF in February, MMF in March and with mean flow during Nov – Apr, which may suggest that survival was reduced at higher flows in the late winter/early spring perhaps due to washout of eggs or alevins. The influence of density independent factors has been demonstrated for stream dwelling brown trout populations in France, with high flows during emergence significantly reducing subsequent 0+ densities (Cattaneo *et al.*, 2002).

A significant negative relationship was also evident between 0+ trout survival and both adult sea trout catch and CPUE in the previous year, suggestive of lower relative survival following higher adult abundance and indicating density dependent regulation. Trout recruitment (annual SQ index) was further investigated for possible density dependent relationships against measures of adult sea-trout abundance (annual catch and CPUE). A strong stock-recruitment (SR) relationship was evident between both the Shimna sea trout rod catch and sea trout CPUE (yr-1) and resultant 0+ fry recruitment (yr). The Ricker model, ($R = a$ S exp $^{-bS}$ *where* S and R are breeding stock [catch or CPUE yr-1] and recruitment [SQ index yr] respectively, and a and b are constants), produced the best fit and explained 63% and 70% of the respective variance against rod catch and CPUE for the Shimna stock (Figure 3). The main outlier from the model (2004) was subject to exceptional discharge conditions which were thought to have compromised recruitment in that year.

Dome-shaped (Ricker) curves have provided the optimum description of the stock-recruitment dynamics for a range of other sea trout populations in Europe (Nicola *et al.*, 2008) with egg density explaining 30-50% of variation of 0+ fry density in French stocks

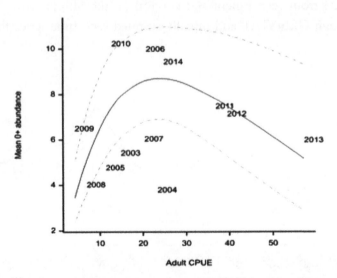

Figure 3. Ricker Stock-Recruitment relationship between sea trout CPUE (stock) and 0+ recruitment index (recruits) on the Shimna River (r^2 =0.70, S_{MAX} 23.8)

(Nicola *et al.*, 2008) and 72% of 0+ fry density in an English stock (Elliott & Elliott, 2006).

The good fit of the Ricker model to the Shimna data was surprising given the modest time series (12 years), however, several factors perhaps account for this. Critically, the adult rod catches (S) were considered likely to provide a good representation of adult stock abundance on the river, with virtually complete reporting from anglers. Angling effort was thought to be fairly steady between years, most catches were taken by the same core group of dedicated anglers and the main angling stretch was located in the tidal portion of the river which tends to provide more consistent year on year angling opportunities. In addition the catch data exhibited considerable variation over the time series with sea trout catches varying from 33 (2008) to 914 (2012) reflecting both high and low stock abundance. The monitoring of R (recruitment) has consistently occurred at the 0+ fry stage to represent the earliest audit point in the life-cycle and to reflect recruitment as soon as possible after the critical post-emergence regulatory density dependant period of between 33 – 70 days (Elliott, 1989). This early audit point may therefore reflect the underlying SR dynamic more closely than in later life stages after density independent influences have exerted further effects on the recruiting cohort.

0+ TROUT PRODUCTION & OVA DEPOSITION REQUIREMENTS

The upper productive potential of 0+ trout in the Shimna river was estimated using data from recent habitat and electric fishing surveys. The production estimates were focused on the habitat upstream of the fish counter and three different methods were used and compared: – 1) a simple model based on FQ electro-fishing data and accessible wetted habitat area; 2) a production model based on SQ electric fishing data, altitude and wetted habitat area; 3) a production estimate based on the Shimna stock recruitment model.

The 0+ fry production estimates were then converted into a respective ova requirement assuming a standard range of egg to 0+ fry (summer) survival. Elliott (1989) indicated that maximum production of late summer sea trout fry (c. 167-183 0+ /100m^{-2}) occurred at ova deposition levels of c. 3333-5000 ova 100m^{-2} representing ova to summer 0+ survival of c. 3-6% around the carrying capacity of the habitat. Kennedy *et al.*, (2012) indicated that ova to 0+ (summer) survival of Atlantic salmon *S. salar* L. in a N. Irish spate stream averaged around 9%, although in this instance the population was generally below carrying capacity. Mills *et al.* (1999) suggested that ova to end-of-year fry survival (*S. salar*) was around 7%. Local data collected on another migratory trout stream in N. Ireland (Sixmile) has suggested ova to 0+ (summer) survival of c. 5-10% (*unpublished data*). A survival range of 3-9% was therefore assumed in the back-calculation of 0+ fry to respective ova requirements.

Method 1 – Habitat/Reference Site Model
A number of FQ electric fishing sites, enclosed by barrier nets and subject to a minimum of

157

three passes (*see* Kennedy *et al.*, 2014 for methodology) were undertaken on the Shimna river (n=18) and on adjacent coastal rivers accessible to sea trout (n=65). The sites were selected to be representative of a section of river and usually contained a mix of macro-habitats ranging from holding water ($\leq$1.2 m) to shallow nursery habitat (<20cm). The mean density of 0+ fry in sea trout accessible sites across N. Ireland was 28.0 100m^{-2} whilst the mean density in the Shimna River was 21.0 100m^{-2}. The lower 0+ densities in the Shimna river may be associated with local acidic, oligotrophic conditions. The Shimna 0+ density was representative of a local group of rivers draining the Mourne mountains which exhibited an average mean summer density of 21.0 0+ 100m^{-2}: this was, perhaps, a consequence of similar geological and trophic status.

A simple model was produced to scale the average density of 0+ trout sampled in the Shimna river against the total quantity of available accessible habitat upstream of the fish counter. These estimates attempted to reflect the *upper productive capacity* of the river, and thus the upper 95% Confidence Interval (C.I.) of the mean density value was utilised (i.e. Mean 20.97 + 8.75 *U 95% C.I.*; Shimna = 29.7 0+ 100m^{-2}) and applied to the total wetted area (53,297 m^{2}).

The estimated upper recruitment potential of 0+ trout from Method 1 was **15,830** 0+ fish. The 0+ production target was then back-transformed into an estimated ova requirement assuming a standard egg to 0+ summer parr survival within the range of 3-9% (mid-point = 6% survival). The estimated ova requirement to attain this calculated target production for 0+ summer parr was 175,890 – 527,670 ova (3.3 – 9.9 ova/m^{2}) at 3 – 9% survival respectively: or 263,833 ova (4.95 ova/m^{2}) at 6% median survival.

Method 2 – Habitat/Altitude Model

The accessible habitat above the fish counter on the Shimna was categorized by altitude using GIS and the quantity of habitat available (total wetted area) was estimated (Table 1).

The average abundance of trout fry within each altitude section was determined across the 12-year time series. Lower fry densities were generally evident in the upper portion of the river >150m. This area is above the suspected natural barrier to upstream migration and in this part of the catchment production may be more reliant on river resident trout. The 50-100m altitude section was also characterised by lower fry densities, perhaps due to the extensive coniferous tree coverage evident along this section.

The relative abundance of trout fry for each altitude section (mean No. 0+ site^{-1}) derived from SQ surveys were back-transformed into density estimates (Crozier & Kennedy, 1994; Kennedy *et al.*, 2012) using data specifically derived from migratory trout rivers in N. Ireland. The relationship between SQ values (x) and density (y) was described by linear regression (n = 39, r^{2}=0.87; y = 3.054x + 7.044). The upper confidence interval of the mean 0+ abundance value (mean +1 std. dev.) in each altitude band was transformed into an estimate of 0+ density (no. 0+/100m^{2}) to reflect the mean *upper productive capacity* of habitat within the different sections. Density estimates were then scaled by the total wetted area within each altitude band and the summation of the discrete bands subsequently produced an estimate of the total 0+ production (Table 1).

Table 1. Availability of accessible habitat, electric fishing sites and 0+ (upper) production estimates by altitude on the Shimna River (above fish counter).

Altitude	Total Wetted Area (m^2)	No. annual SQ Sites	No. years	Mean No. 0+ fry per $site^{-1}$ (Std Dev)	Estimated 0+ fry Production
0-50m	20,138	3	12	5.9 *(4.7)*	7,902
51-100m	13,987	2	12	3.2 *(3.3)*	3,741
101-150m	7,083	4	12	6.0 *(4.0)*	2,668
150 m+	12,089	6	12	3.3 *(3.7)*	3,451
TOTAL	53,297	15	12		17,762

The estimated upper recruitment potential of 0+ trout ranged from 31.3 0+ $100m^{-2}$ (50-100m) to 43.8 0+ $100m^2$ (0-50m), the mean density across the river was 33.1 0+ $100m^{-2}$ and the total target production of 0+ trout for accessible habitat upstream of the Shimna counter was determined to represent **17,762** fish. The estimated ova requirement to attain this target for 0+ summer parr production was 197,358 – 592,075 ova (3.7 – 11.1 ova/m^2) at 3 – 9% survival respectively: or 296,037 ova (5.55/ova m^2) at 6% median survival).

Method 3 – Stock Recruitment Model

Stock-recruitment (SR) curves have been used to set biological reference points for the management of salmonid populations (Wyatt & Barnard, 1997). In sea trout populations, SR relationships can be confounded by the unknown effect of river resident brown trout spawners. Although resident brown trout may contribute to fry production at monitoring sites on the Shimna, the SQ assessment covers areas potentially accessible to sea trout and hence anadromous females probably contribute significantly to the recruitment measured across the survey network. Milner *et al.,* (2006) suggested that migrant female sea trout were likely to be the dominant source of total egg production in most rivers with a migratory trout component.

A strong SR relationship was evident between catches of adult sea trout and subsequent 0+ production on the Shimna river with the Ricker curve, producing the best fit ($r^2 = 0.70$) (Figure 2). The asymptote of the SR curve (S_{MAX}) was taken to reflect the *upper productive capacity* of habitat and corresponded to a mean CPUE of 23.8 sea trout $angler^{-1}$ yr^{-1} and a recruitment value of 8.7 0+ trout 5 $mins^{-1}$.

Back-calculation of the relative spatial density of 0+ trout from the SQ value generated a target of 33.6 0+ $100m^2$. Application of this density reference against the total accessible habitat area of 53,297m^2 produced an overall 0+ target of **17,908 fish**. The estimated ova requirement to attain this target for 0+ summer parr production was 198,976 – 596,926 ova (3.7 – 11.2 ova/m^2) at 3 – 9% survival respectively: or 298,463 ova (5.6 ova/m^2) at 6% median survival).

The fry production estimates (15,830 – 17,908 0+) generated by the three different methods were similar and reflected the upper productive capacity of the stock during the current time series. The mean ova deposition requirement, assuming 6% ova survival, was *286,112 ova*.

OVA DEPOSITION REQUIREMENT FOR THE SHIMNA:
COMPARISON WITH OTHER STUDIES

SR relationships have been reported across a range of other north European sea trout rivers including the Black Brows Beck in England (Elliott & Elliott, 2006), the Bresle River in France (Euzenat *et al.*, 2006) and the Burrishoole catchment in Ireland (Poole *et al.*, 2006). Ova seeding rates (ova m²) have been identified for these stocks; but the transport of ova deposition rates between rivers presents serious challenges due to differences in physical characteristics and productivity of source and the catchments where they are applied. Additionally, the potential variability in life history and the influence of river resident trout, which may freely interbreed with anadromous trout, add complexity between sea trout stocks and confound the transport of SR relationships between rivers. Ova deposition requirements derived locally for the wetted area of the Shimna river (5.3 ha) were compared with estimates based on the application of target ova seeding rates described for other sea trout rivers (Table 2).

Table 2. Comparison of the ova deposition requirement for the Shimna River from the present study with estimates derived from other sea trout stock-recruitment relationships.

Reference	Catchment	Ova Target	Habitat Area m²	Ova Requirement
Present study	Shimna River	3.3 – 11.2	53,297	175,890 – 596,926
Crisp (1993)	Pennines	6.0	53,297	319,782
Euzenat *et al.*, (2006)	Bresle River	8.75	53,297	466,349
Elliott & Elliot (2006)	Black Brows Beck	17.0	53,297	906,049

The ova deposition requirement estimated from locally derived data of 3.3-11.2 ova m² were within the range of those determined in other river studies (Table 2). Ova deposition estimates for the Shimna using the Black Brows Beck target rate (Elliott & Elliott, 2006) were much higher and this may be a consequence of generally less productive habitat on the Shimna or it may also reflect the differing spatial scale of assessment between the two situations.

RESIDENT TROUT OVA PRODUCTION ESTIMATES FOR THE SHIMNA RIVER

The potential ova production of the resident brown trout stock in the Shimna river was estimated using locally derived data (density, sex ratio and maturity) in conjunction with published fecundity estimates for river trout (Crisp & Beaumont, 1995). Biological examinations of Shimna trout have shown that female residents can first mature at c. 17cm L_F (c. 3+), and that the sex ratio increases in favour of males in older residents. At FQ survey sites, ova production was estimated by L_F class for trout >17cm L_F with reference to density, maturation and sex ratio estimates (*see* Table 3).

Table 3. Estimated ova deposition level per unit area (No. ova 100m²) for resident brown trout quantitatively sampled at a survey site in the Lower Shimna River in 2011.

Length Class (cm)	Density (100m⁻²)	Mean Length (cm)	♀ Maturity Factor	Fecundity Estimate	Ova Deposition (100m⁻²)
17	0.91	17.3	0.07	$F= 0.082Lt^{2.642}$	10
18	0.36	18.3	0.14	$F= 0.082Lt^{2.642}$	9
19	0.18	19.2	0.14	$F= 0.082Lt^{2.642}$	5
20	0	-	0.14	$F= 0.082Lt^{2.642}$	0
21	0	-	0.14	$F= 0.082Lt^{2.642}$	0
22	0.69	22.4	0.14	$F= 0.082Lt^{2.642}$	29
23	0.18	23.8	0.14	$F= 0.082Lt^{2.642}$	9
24	0	-	0.14	$F= 0.082Lt^{2.642}$	0
Total					62

One FQ site on the lower Shimna (Altitude c. 30m) was surveyed consistently from 2005. Estimated ova deposition (ova 100m⁻²) for the resident brown trout population in this area of the river was fairly stable and averaged 54 ova/100m⁻², ranging from 18 – 81 ova/100m⁻² in 2013 and 2005 respectively. The annual rod catch of resident trout from the Shimna was also relatively stable (1999 – 2014) with a mean catch of 67 resident trout yr⁻¹ (±16 @ 95% C.I.).

The overall production of ova by the resident trout stock upstream of the fish counter was modelled. Data across all years were pooled with ova production assumed to be consistent. The model divided the river into four altitudinal sections (Table 4) and used pooled FQ data (across all years) to reflect the density of mature trout (>17cm) and pooled biological data to reflect sex ratios and maturity factors within each altitudinal such that;

$$\text{OVAFQ} = \sum_{dLci=i}^{dLcin} dLci \cdot x(0.082FLci^{2.642})$$

Where: Ova_{FQ} is the total resident ova deposition at a FQ site, $dLci$ is the spatial density of trout in length class i (no m⁻²), x is the ♀ maturity factor and $FLci$ is the mean fork length of length class i (cm). The fecundity estimator was adapted from Crisp & Beaumont (1995) as:

$$Ova_{Sj} = [(\Sigma Ova_{FQ})n^{-1}]h_j$$

Where: Ova_{Sj} is total ova production in altitudinal section j, n is the number of available FQ sites and hj is the area of habitat available in section j.

Table 4. Habitat resources and ova production estimates for resident trout by altitude on the Shimna River (*above fish counter*).

Altitude	Total wetted Area (m^2)	No. Fully Quantitative Survey Sites	Mean Resident Ova Production (ova $100m^{-2}$)	Estimated Ova Production.
0-50m	20,138	11	52	10,472
51-100m	13,987	2	52	7,273
101-150m	7,083	3	36	2,550
150 m+	12,089	4	355	42,916
TOTAL	53,297			63,211

Resident trout ova deposition was greater at higher altitude sections (>150m) of the river (Table 4). This was due to higher densities of larger resident fish in upstream areas (>150m). Above 150m, 11.3% of the sampled resident trout population (n=230) was >17cm L_F compared with only 3.2% of the sampled population (n=2,745) >17cm L_F at lower altitudes (<150m pooled). Sex ratio also differed, with 66% of upstream (>150m) and 14% of downstream (<150m pooled) >18cm resident trout identified as female. A natural migratory obstacle at c. 150m may have increased reliance on resident ova production in upstream areas. Bohlin *et al*., (2001) also suggested that altitude influences sea trout production, with the recruitment contribution of anadromous stocks often dominant below 150m.

The resident trout component produced 63,211 ova or c.11 – 36% of the total estimated ova requirement for the Shimna (Table 5). This represents a minimum estimate of resident brown trout ova production. Although the data used in the model was sampled from a range

Table 5. Estimated ova deposition from various components of the trout stock in the Shimna River and relative compliance against estimated total ova requirement (*the contribution from ≥ 1SW sea trout is shown in brackets*).

Stock Component	2011	2012	2013	2014
Resident Trout	63,211	63,211	63,211	63,211
.0SW Finnock	n/a	n/a	n/a	n/a
≥ 1SW Sea Trout	227,810	397,362	611,388	518,539
% Ova from ≥ 1SW Sea Trout	78	86	91	89
% Total Ova Requirement	102 (79)	161 (139)	236 (214)	203 (181)

of habitats, the deep habitats >1.2m were not sampled. These may hold a greater proportion of mature resident brown trout and the model may reflect a conservative ova production estimate. After accounting for resident trout production, the ova requirement from sea trout on the Shimna was estimated to range from 112,679 – 533,715 ova or 2.1 – 10.0 ova m². It is important to note, however, that while young trout often follow the life history of their parents (*see* Ferguson *et al.*, (2017), sea trout can produce resident trout offspring and *vice-versa*. Thus, any independent estimates of ova production must allow for a certain degree of uncertainty.

SEA TROUT OVA PRODUCTION ESTIMATES FOR THE SHIMNA RIVER.

Migratory fish were counted at a resistivity fish counter with validation and species differentiation based on CCTV imagery, length frequency analysis and an adult sampling programme. Adult sampling work was based on targeted electric fishing surveys of known holding habitats and monitored angling returns. Calibration work indicated the counter did not register sea trout <40 cm L_F, which effectively excluded finnock (.0SW sea trout) from the count. Biological characteristics of sea trout sampled in the tidal portion of the Shimna (below the counter) were compared with those sampled further upstream (above the counter) adjacent to spawning habitats. These data indicated a dominance of finnock in the tidal areas during summer (>80% of sampled population), but revealed a much lower abundance of finnock around spawning habitats closer to spawning time (<30% of sampled population) when mature maiden 1SW sea trout (modal L_F 48-49 cm) dominated (Figure 4). The apparent abundance of finnock in the tidal areas, but their relative lack above the fish counter, may indicate that they are mostly immature and so do not ascend to the upstream spawning habitats. Additionally, finnock

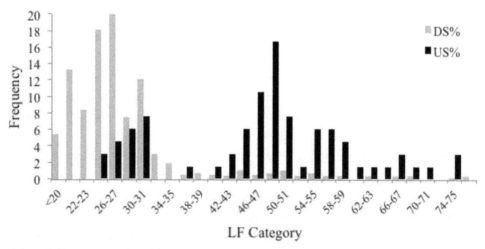

Figure. 4. Length-Frequency profile of Shimna River sea trout sampled in downstream, tidal sections (DS) and from upstream spawning habitats (US).

may be subject to higher rates of '*vagrancy*' with 'additional' immature fish present in the tidal stretches that may originate from other rivers.

The estimated sea trout run (> 40cm) over the counter from 2011 – 2014 was 221 (range 89 in 2011 to 300 in 2013). These estimated numbers are well in agreement with figures derived from ongoing genetic investigation involving juvenile trout recruits (0+ and 1+) taken across the Shimna and Burren rivers in 2012 and 2014, which indicate an effective population size (i.e. number of breeding adult fish N_e) of c. 200 spawners (P. Prodöhl, *pers. com.*). The ova production from sea trout was estimated from the fish counter in combination with local annual biological characteristics (sex ratio, L_F) and published length-based fecundity relationships (Solomon, 1997). The annual ova production from sea trout (>40cm) was tabulated (Table 5) for comparison against an estimated total ova seeding requirement – taken as 286,112 ova for illustration. Compliance against the ova requirement ranged from 102% (2011) to 236% (2013), with mature female sea trout (≥1 SW) contributing on average >85% of the estimated ova deposition each year.

CONCLUSIONS

The Shimna stock demonstrated a strong Ricker type SR relationship between indices of sea trout abundance and subsequent 0+ fry recruitment. This form of density dependant population regulation has been observed in a range of other European trout stocks (Nicola *et al.*, 2008) and suggests that sea trout drive productivity in the Shimna population. Ova production models further indicated that larger (>40cm) sea trout, produced the majority (c. 85%) of eggs deposited in the river each year. The large mature component of the sea run stock represented the main driver of productivity in the Shimna and should be subject to *precautionary management*. Given the strong SR relationship on the Shimna, a rod harvest may be sustainable in years of increased adult abundance, although the identification or prediction of such conditions presents a challenge for fishery managers. Alternatively, future recreational harvests could be limited (in a controlled fashion with appropriate bag limits) to the more abundant finnock component of the stock (<40cm fish). The harvest of finnock, although affording protection to larger spawners, may also present particular challenges for fishery managers. Recent genetic work has suggested that finnock can move between rivers particularly in the lower tidal sections (King *et al.*, 2016). If finnock from other stocks were present in the tidal section of a river it would effectively represent a mixed stock fishery with inherent management risks. More research on the movements of finnock and the extent of between river vagrancy is required before the widespread adoption of a finnock based management strategy could be considered.

The estimated ova deposition requirement for the Shimna trout stock (3.3 – 11.2 ova m²) was within the range of other European studies (Nicola *et al.*, 2008), but this should, however, be treated with caution as uncertainty persists around the relatively short time series of data and the assumption of temporal stability in the freshwater resident stock component.

Further research is needed to develop the Shimna work. This includes investigating the relationship between stock size and rod catch metrics as the fish counter dataset matures. The estimation of in-river mortality rates for sea trout prior to spawning and annual assessments of resident brown trout ova production would also be useful. The investigation of the origin, behaviour, ova production capacity and biological characteristics of finnock, both during the season and in different river sections (i.e. estuary and upstream habitats), is needed. Population genetics work examining patterns of population structuring within the Shimna river catchment, including the relationships between resident and migratory sea trout, the relative fitness of both life histories, the levels/patterns of finnock straying and contribution to spawning are currently underway.

ACKNOWLEDGEMENTS

Particular thanks are extended to the committee and members of the Shimna Angling Club for their interest, support and practical help over the years. Thanks also to Kieran McOscar, Gavin Marshall and Patrick Quinn and to the staff from the Department of Culture, Arts and Leisure based at the Castlewellan office.

REFERENCES

Bohlin, T., Pettersson, J. & Degerman, E. (2001). Population density of migratory and resident brown trout in relation to altitude: evidence for a migration cost. *Journal of Animal Ecology, 70*, 112-121.

Cattaneo, F., N. Lamouroux, P. Breil & Capra, H. (2002). The influence of hydrological and biotic processes on brown trout *(Salmo trutta)* population dynamics. *Canadian Journal of Fisheries and Aquatic Sciences, 59*, 12-22.

Crisp, D.T. (1993). Population densities of juvenile trout (*Salmo trutta*) in five upland streams and their effects upon growth, survival and dispersal. *Journal of Applied Ecology 30*, 759–771.

Crisp, D. T. & Beaumont, W. R. C. (1995). The trout (*Salmo trutta*) population of the Afon Cwm, a small tributary of the Afon Dyfi, mid-Wales. *Journal of Fish Biology, 46*, 703–716.

Crozier, W.W. & Kennedy, G. J. A. (1994). Application of semi-quantitative electrofishing to juvenile salmonid stock surveys. *Journal of Fish Biology, 45*, 159–164.

Elliott, J. M. (1989). The critical-period concept for juvenile survival and its relevance for population regulation in young sea trout, *Salmo trutta*. *Journal of Fish Biology, 35*, 91–98.

Elliott, J.M. & Elliott, J.A. (2006). A 35 year study of stock-recruitment relationships in a small population of sea trout: assumptions, implications and limitations for producing targets. In: *Sea trout: Biology, conservation and Management.* (Graeme Harris & Nigel Milner. *Eds.*). Proceedings of the 1st International Sea Trout Symposium, July 2004, Cardiff, Wales, UK. Blackwell Publishing, Oxford; 257 – 278.

Euzenat, G., Fournel, F. & Fagard, J-L. (2006). Population dynamics and stock-recruitment relationship of sea trout in the River Bresle, Upper Normandy, France. *In*: *Sea trout: Biology, conservation and*

Management. (Graeme Harris & Nigel Milner. *Eds*.). Proceedings of the 1st International Sea Trout Symposium, July 2004, Cardiff, Wales, UK. Blackwell Publishing, Oxford, 307-323.

Ferguson, A., Reed, T., McGinnity, P. & Prodöhl, P. (2017). Anadromy in brown trout (*Salmo trutta*): A review of the relative roles of genes and environmental factors and the implications for management and conservation. (2016). In: *Sea Trout: Science & Management*. (Graeme Harris. *Ed*.). Proceeding of the 2nd International Sea Trout Symposium, October 2015. Dundalk, Ireland. Troubador, 1–40.

Kennedy, R.J., Crozier, W.W. & Allen, M. (2012). The effect of stocking 0+ year age-class Atlantic salmon fry: a case study from the River Bush, Northern Ireland. *Journal of Fish Biology,* **81**, 1730-1746.

Kennedy, R.J., Johnston, P. & Allen, M. (2014). Assessment of a catchment-wide salmon habitat rehabilitation scheme on a drained river system in Northern Ireland. *Fisheries Management and Ecology,* **21**, 275–287.

King, A., Stockley, B., Hillman, R., Elsmere, P. & Stevens, J. (2017). Managing mixed stocks of sea trout (*Salmo trutta* L) straying between rivers sharing a common estuary on Southwest England: a genetic approach. *In: Sea Trout: Science & Management*. (Graeme Harris. *Ed*.). Proceeding of the 2nd International Sea Trout Symposium, October 2015. Dundalk, Ireland. Troubador, 308–327.

Milner, N.J., Harris, G., Gargan, P., Beveridge, M., Pawson, M., Walker, A. & Whelan, K. (2006). Perspectives on sea trout science and management. In: *Sea trout: Biology, Conservation and Management*. (Graeme Harris & Nigel Milner. *Eds*.). Proceedings of the 1st International Sea Trout Symposium, July 2004, Cardiff, Wales, UK. Blackwell Publishing, Oxford. 480-489.

Mills, D.H., Hadoke, G.D.F. & Read, J.B.D. (1999). Atlantic Salmon Facts. The Atlantic Salmon Trust, Pitlochry. 24 pp.

Nicola, G. Almodovar, A., Jonsson, B. & Elvira, B. (2008). Recruitment variability of resident brown trout in peripheral populations from southern Europe. *Freshwater Biology* **53**, 2364 – 2374.

Poole, R., Dillane, M., Deeyto, E., Rogan G., McGinnity, P. & Whelan, K. (2006). Characteristics of the Burrishoole sea trout population: census, marine survival, enhancement & stock recruitment, 1971-2003. In: *Sea trout: Biology, conservation and Management*. (Graeme Harris & Nigel Milner. *Eds*.). Proceedings of the 1st International Sea Trout Symposium, July 2004, Cardiff, Wales, UK. Blackwell Publishing, Oxford. 279 – 306.

Solomon, D.J. (1997). Review of Sea Trout Fecundity. R&D Technical Report W60, Environment Agency, Bristol, 22 pp.

Estimating salmonid angling exploitation rates from systems monitored by fish counters, and potential application to fisheries management in Ireland

M. MILLANE[1], S. SHEPHARD[1], J. WHITE[2], N. Ó MAOILÉIDIGH[2],
K. O'HIGGINS[1], P. O'MALLEY[1], W. ROCHE[1], R. POOLE[2], G. ROGAN[2],
N. BOND[2] & P. GARGAN[1]

[1]*Inland Fisheries Ireland, 3044 Lake Drive, Citywest Business Campus, Dublin 24, Ireland.*
[2]*Marine Institute, Rinville, Oranmore, Co. Galway, Ireland.*

ABSTRACT

Long-term angling catch records and fish counter data for anadromous salmonid populations from many freshwater systems are now becoming available. These provide an opportunity to evaluate more comprehensively angling exploitation rates for sea trout, and Atlantic salmon, including the spring salmon component, with the inclusion of a greater number of freshwater systems than was previously available. This paper examines angling exploitation rates in different types of freshwater system, (e.g. river or lake-dominated), under varying fisheries management strategies (e.g. 'open for harvest' or 'open for catch-and-release-only' fisheries), fish counter types (full or partial counter), and for salmon, changes in regulatory measures. A modelling exercise was undertaken to establish angling exploitation bands for migratory salmonid stocks and found to be of use for the first two of these categories.

The overall median angling exploitation rate on sea trout stocks across all systems was 13.3% with the highest exploitation rates for individual systems recorded on Ballynahinch (33.3%), Dee (35.7%), Eany (40.8%) and Owenmore (24.6%) stocks and the lowest exploitation (<10%) occurring on stocks in the Burrishoole, Carrowmore and Maine catchments. The majority of exploitation rates on sea trout stocks were < 18% across all categories examined. The overall angling exploitation rate on salmon stocks was 10.8% with only three systems out of 25, all river-dominated, having exploitation rates > 20%. Median exploitation rates were < 14% across all categories examined. For spring salmon, the overall exploitation rate was 15.6% with exploitation rates < 19% across all categories examined.

The modelling exercise indicated that exploitation bands could be identified for salmon stocks in river and lake-dominated systems, under either open for harvest or open for catch-and-release-only angling regimes. It is envisaged that further development of the model output presented may facilitate refinement of the exploitation bands currently applied by fishery scientists and better inform the sustainable management of salmon (and potentially sea trout) stocks, notably in systems where no direct measure of total population abundance is currently available.

Keywords: *Salmo trutta*; *Salmo salar*; fish counters; angling; exploitation rate; modelling; Ireland.

INTRODUCTION

Angling catch records in association with known information on fish population size can provide a valuable measure of the fishing exploitation pressure experienced by salmonid stocks in a freshwater system (Gargan *et al.*, 2001; Shields *et al.*, 2006; Thorley *et al.*, 2007). Such angling exploitation rates (*i.e.* the catch divided by the known population and often expressed as a percentage) and associated ranges can be applied to similar systems where fish population data are lacking in order to provide an estimate of total stock abundance (SSCS, 2015). In addition, angling exploitation rates are useful to assess inter-annual variability in angling pressure on fish stocks in a system and provide such comparison between systems (Crozier & Kennedy, 2001; Milner *et al.*, 2001). In Ireland, only single-catchment studies on salmonid angling exploitation rates have been conducted, with a predominant focus on Atlantic salmon (Crozier & Kennedy 2001; Gargan *et al.*, 2001; Whelan *et al.*, 2001). There is a paucity of such information available for sea trout (Burrishoole exploitation rates; Anon., 1970-2014), although CPUEs have been more widely reported (Gargan *et al.*, 2006a, 2006b; Poole *et al.*, 2006). Long-term angling catch records and fish counter data from multiple freshwater systems are now available to elucidate more comprehensively angling exploitation rates for anadromous salmonid populations in freshwaters in Ireland, under a variety of categories and management regimes. This paper presents an evaluation of salmonid angling exploitation rates in Irish freshwaters. In addition, the paper explores their applicability to refine the exploitation rates currently applied to Irish salmon rivers by the Standing Scientific Committee on Salmon (SSCS) in their annual assessments of Conservation Limit (CL) attainment.

Atlantic salmon and sea trout populations are widely distributed throughout Ireland with 141 freshwater systems designated as salmon rivers (SSCS, 2015), a large proportion of which also have sea trout present. There are an additional 88 systems primarily classified as sea trout only rivers which do not have significant salmon runs (McGinnity *et al.*, 2003; NASCO, 2005). Many of the salmon and sea trout stocks in these systems have experienced periods of substantial declines in both angling catch and abundance over the last three decades (Gargan *et al.*, 2006b; Anon., 2008; SSCS, 2015). Sea trout stocks notably suffered a catastrophic population collapse in the west of Ireland in the late 1980s to early 1990s (reviewed in Gargan *et al.*, 2006a), while the abundance of Atlantic salmon in Ireland has been estimated to have decreased by 75% in recent decades (Anon., 2008). In response to these declines, a series of regulatory measures on angling were introduced progressively since the 1990s. These include: a) bag limits on catch, b) restrictions on fishing gear and fishing season, c) a carcass tagging and log book scheme, d) mandatory catch-and-release (C&R) bye-laws for sea trout fishing in the west of Ireland and e) the introduction of Conservation Limits (CLs) to better manage salmon stocks (Ó Maoiléidigh *et al.*, 2000). [For a full description of the salmon and sea trout angling management system and the rules governing when rivers are open for harvest, open for C&R-only angling or closed, the reader is referred to the Inland Fisheries Ireland (IFI) website: http://fishinginireland.info/salmon/salmontagging.htm and to SSCS (2015).]

Atlantic salmon stock management in Ireland is largely guided by the SSCS. This independent body provides scientific advice to IFI as the competent state authority to guide management decisions and policy development concerning the conservation and sustainable exploitation of Ireland's salmon stocks (SSCS, 2015). Since 2007, annual stock status has been assessed with reference to catchment-specific CLs (Ó Maoiléidigh *et al.*, 2004; White *et al.*, 2016). These are defined as the stock level that will achieve long-term average maximum sustainable yield (NASCO, 1998; SSCS, 2015). The outcome of this assessment determines if individual river systems will be open for harvest, open for C&R-only angling or closed, in the following year. No such assessments based on CLs have been developed to manage sea trout fisheries in Ireland; and stocks are principally managed through regulatory measures that control fishing effort and limit catch.

The SSCS assessment forecasts salmon returns for individual systems primarily from fish counter, angling catch and exploitation rates, and commercial catch data taken from the most recent five-year time series available. In systems without fish counters and limited or no catch data, a juvenile salmon abundance threshold is employed to determine whether systems can be opened for C&R-only fishing (SSCS, 2015). Rod-catch exploitation rates are applied to systems where quantitative population data from fish counters are not available in order to provide a measure of population size and thus determine CL attainment (Table 1). These exploitation bands were derived in 2006 using observed values from 18 Irish rivers with fish counters. The rates for other rivers were assigned to these bands using '*expert judgment*' within standardised bands based on 'high', 'medium' and 'low' fishing intensities for salmon and additional 'high' and 'low' bands in systems where significant populations of spring salmon are present (SSCS, 2015).

Table 1. Salmon angling exploitation rates used by the Standing Scientific Committee on Salmon since 2006 which are applied to Irish river systems where quantitative population data are not available in order to provide a measure of stock size and thus determine conservation limit attainment. These are based on observed values from 18 Irish rivers with fish counters and angling catch information.

Taxa	Intensity	Min	Midpoint	Max
Salmon	Low	1	5	12
	Medium	7	15	35
	High	10	33	50
Spring salmon	Low	6	12	27
	High	15	31	46

The number of fish counters in operation in salmonid catchments in Ireland has increased from 18 in 2006, when the exploitation rates currently used by the SSCS were devised, to 32 in 2014 (SSCS, 2015). The resulting information is now valuable for examining angling exploitation rates in different freshwater system types (e.g. river or lake-dominated) under varying management regimes (e.g. open for harvest or open for C&R-only fisheries). It is envisaged that a refinement of the rates currently applied by the SSCS has the potential to better inform the sustainable management of salmon stocks, notably in systems where no measure of total population abundance is directly available.

METHODS

OVERVIEW

Annual angling catch records of Atlantic salmon and sea trout and corresponding run data from freshwater systems in Ireland where fish counters are present were collated in order to estimate angling exploitation rates in fished waters categorised by system type (river-dominated, lake-dominated or river and lake) and management strategy (open for harvest or open for C&R-only angling). In addition, the data were examined to ascertain whether exploitation rates differed before and after the commencement of nationwide regulatory angling measures which were introduced in 2007 (and included a cessation of the large marine fishery for salmon), and between freshwater systems where full or partial fish counters were present. Data on the larger spring (MSW) salmon, considered as those fish that entered a freshwater system between January and May of each year, were also examined in this regard. Regression models applied to the collated dataset were used to define angling exploitation bands for each system type and management strategy combination. The modelling was undertaken to evaluate their applicability in refining the ranges currently applied to salmon catchments by the SSCS (Table 1) as well as exploring their potential value to predict angling exploitation rates for sea trout fisheries in order to inform population estimates where run data are absent or incomplete. For the model, systems were categorised as either river-dominated (*river*) or lake-dominated (*lake*).

ANGLING AND FISH COUNTER RECORDS

Angling catch records of Atlantic salmon were principally taken from the *Salmon and Sea Trout Carcass Tagging and Logbook Scheme* (CTLS) as reported in annual reports produced by IFI and its predecessors for the years 2001–2014 (CFB 2004, 2005a, 2005b, 2008, 2009, 2010; IFI 2011, 2012, 2013, 2014). The sea trout angling records used were annual estimates of system-specific catch as supplied by regional fisheries inspectors and local fisheries managers. This is because sea trout ≤ 40 cm fork length are not legally required to be reported by anglers for the CTLS. The majority of the angling catch data and run data used in this study are from the period 2002-2014 as fish counters were progressively installed on an increasing number of salmonid waters during this time. A longer time series of catch and run / population data were available for both species for the freshwater section of the Burrishoole system (total trap) from 1971, and from the Erriff system from 1986 for salmon and from 1998 for sea trout. More robust records of sea trout angling catch from both fisheries were available as such catches have typically been recorded on a daily or weekly basis during the angling season. It should be noted that some resident brown trout catches may have erroneously been reported as sea trout in the Burrishoole records in the 1993/1994 period. A literature review was undertaken to identify salmonid recapture rates in systems, similar to those in Ireland, which could be applied to the reported angling catch to account for fish which may have been re-caught following the introduction of C&R. From this, a recapture rate of 5% was assigned to salmon based on Webb (2001) *as cited in* Bilsby (2006) and Thorley *et al.*, (2007) (from the Rivers Dee and Spey, Scotland, respectively); and a 12% recapture rate was assumed for spring salmon. As there was a paucity of information available on the recapture rates of sea trout (reviewed in Olsen *et al.*, 2010), this was also assumed to be 5% for sea trout, based on the salmon recapture rate.

Annual counts of salmon and sea trout were taken from fish counters of which there are two types in operation in Ireland, namely resistivity (Logie) and optical infra-red (Vaki) counters

Figure 1. Location of fishery systems with fish counters referred to in the study (*note*: a total upstream trap operates on the Burrishoole fishery).

(Figure 1). Detected fish were initially separated into salmon and sea trout based on the signal strength generated by a fish passing the counting electrodes or optical sensors. Each year, the numbers of each fish species detected were validated by examining a proportion of the counter data (usually 15 to 20%) in relation to contemporaneous video footage (resistivity counters) or infrared images (infrared counters). From this, a correction factor was applied to the remainder of the counter data. All downstream counts from January to May were considered to represent out-migrating fish. To correct for fish counted upstream but which may then come back downstream, or the temporary incursion of vagrant sea trout from other systems, the downstream count from June to December was subtracted from the upstream count over the same period. The estimated upstream run of fish was corrected to include fish caught and killed downstream of the counter and excluded fish caught and killed above the counter (SSCS, 2015). System-specific raising factors were applied to fish counts in systems where partial counters were present, to account for fish moving over a weir without being counted. Raising factors were based on those used by the SSCS to determine annual salmon stocks in Irish catchments (SSCS, 2015).

A data screening and validation exercise was initially undertaken on the assembled dataset to assess the reliability of the collated angling catch and fish counter information. This was conducted with reference to the angling catch and fish counter reports (CFB, 2004, 2005a, 2005b, 2008, 2009, 2010; IFI, 2011, 2012, 2013, 2014; IFI Consolidation Fish Counter Reports, 2011–2014) and in consultation with fisheries inspectors and fisheries managers. Any data considered to be incomplete (e.g. in years where a fish counter was reported to be periodically inoperable) were excluded from the analyses. In addition, information on sea trout runs from counter infrastructure primarily calibrated to record salmon was also excluded because

Table 2. Number of water bodies used to calculate salmonid angling exploitation rates by system type, management strategy, counter type and in the periods pre and post the introduction of regulatory measures. The number of data years used to calculate median exploitation rates for each category and sub-category is indicated in brackets. Pre- and post measures refer to regulations introduced in 2007, including major fishery closures and other fishing restrictions.

Category	Sub-category	Salmon	Spring salmon	Sea trout
No. of systems	---	25 (258)	10 (76)	12 (107)
System Type	River	14 (121)	7 (51)	7 (33)
	Lake	4 (60)	2 (17)	2 (41)
	River-lake	7 (77)	1 (8)	3 (35)
Management strategy	Open for harvest	25 (232)	10 (65)	7 (48)
	Catch & release-only	8 (26)	2 (11)	7 (61)
Counter	Full	18 (189)	5 (37)	10 (99)
	Partial	7 (69)	5 (39)	2 (10)
Regulatory	Pre-measures (<2007)	15 (94)	6 (11)	4 (40)
	Post measures (>2006)	25 (164)	10 (65)	12 (69)

of concerns with their reliability to count smaller sea trout. Further to this, only two partial counters were used for sea trout in the analyses, one where a minor raising factor of 12% was employed (R. Eany) and the second where the recorded count was doubled (R. Dee). The final validated dataset comprised 25 freshwater systems with salmon, of which 10 had spring salmon, and 12 freshwater systems for sea trout (Table 2).

DATA ANALYSES AND MODELLING

Angling exploitation rates were calculated for each year as the total rod catch (killed plus C&R fish) / total run of fish, and expressed as percentages. Median exploitation rates per system and their associated percentile range (PR, 2.5–97.5%) were calculated by system, category and sub-category. Wilcoxon Rank Sum (WR) or Kruskal-Wallis (KW) tests (or their parametric equivalents, where appropriate) were used to compare differences in categories. For sea trout in the Erriff and Burrishoole systems, Spearman's Rank correlations were used to explore associations in returns (counter or trap data) with exploitation and angling catch, respectively.

Salmonid exploitation rates (for salmon and sea trout separately) were modelled using a binomial GLMM (Generalized Linear Mixed Model) using the lme4 package (Bates *et al.*, 2015) in R (R Core Team, 2015). To avoid relying on inference from a single best fitting model, multi-model inference (Burnham & Anderson, 2002) was performed on a global model and six *a priori* defined subset models, where subset models were specified by sequentially removing interactions and then covariates from the global model. It is assumed that the counts of fish caught in year j, in water i, of Run_{ij} followed a binomial distribution with the probability π_{ij}.

$$Caught_{ij} \sim Bin(\pi_{ij}, Run_{ij})$$
$$E(Caught_{ij}) = Run_{ij} \times \pi_{ij}$$
$$Var(Caught_{ij}) = Run_{ij} \times \pi_{ij} \times (1\text{-x}\,\pi_{ij})$$

The probability that a running fish was caught (exploitation rate) was specified in the global model as

$$\text{Logit}\,(\pi_{ij}) = \eta_{ij}$$
$$\eta_{ij} = \beta_1 + \beta_2 \times system \times \beta_2 \times status + \beta_3 \times latitude + \beta_4 \times expert + r_i + y_j + \varepsilon_{ij}$$
$$r_i \sim N(0,\sigma^2_{river})$$
$$y_j \sim N(0,\sigma^2_{year})$$
$$\varepsilon_{ij} \sim N(0,\sigma^2_{\varepsilon})$$

where: *system* is type of water (river or lake), *status* is management strategy (open for harvest or open for C&R-only angling), *latitude* is geographic latitude in decimal degrees and *expert* is an expert opinion on annual fishing intensity (light, medium or heavy). y_j and r_i are random effects on the intercept of year and individual water respectively, and ε_{ij} is an observation level random effect, applied to address over-dispersion.

All models were compared based on the Akaike Information Criterion (AIC), where all models within two AIC units of the best fitting subset model were included into a set for reporting. The effect of individual terms in the models was determined using a Chi Square test in the R 'drop1' command. Model validation used residual plots to check for heterogeneity of residuals and linearity of relationships. Predicted salmonid exploitation rates by system and status were visualised using the R package "Effects" (Fox, 2003).

RESULTS

ANGLING EXPLOITATION RATES FOR SEA TROUT & SALMON

The overall median angling exploitation rate on sea trout stocks across all systems (n=12) was 13.3% (PR 2–43). The highest exploitation rates for individual systems were recorded on the Ballynahinch (33.3%), Dee (35.7%), Eany (40.8%) and Owenmore (24.6%) stocks with the lowest exploitation (<10%) occurring on stocks in the Burrishoole, Carrowmore and Maine catchments (Table 3). Median exploitation rates on sea trout stocks were < 18% across all four categories examined (i.e. *system type*, *catch regime*, *counter type* and *regulatory measures*) with the exception of waters where *partial* fish counters (37.9%) were in operation (Table 4). *River* systems (17.7%) had a notably higher exploitation rate than *lake* systems (7.1%) (KW$_2$, H = 25.3, p < 0.001, post-hoc WR, p < 0.05) and there was a moderately, but non-significant, higher exploitation rate when waters were solely restricted to *catch & release (C&R)* angling (13.2%) over those where harvesting was permitted (11.2%) (WR, U = 1557, Z = 0.6, p > 0.05). Waters with *partial* fish counters had a 27% higher exploitation rate than those where *full* counters were operational (WR, U = 78, Z = -4.4, p <0.01), although, data from only two sites was available for comparison in the former case. Three subset models (M5, M6 and M7) were within two Akaike Information Criterion (AIC) points. None of the tested covariates had a significant effect on sea trout exploitation rate (Table 5).

Sea trout exploitation on the Burrishoole and Erriff systems
Median angling exploitation rates on sea trout in the Burrishoole and Erriff systems were 6.7% (PR 0.4–28.5) and 10.9% (PR 5.2–30.5), respectively, over the available time-series (Table 3). Both systems have been mandatory C&R fisheries since 1990 and no angling occurred on the Burrishoole between 1997 and 2007. No consistent overall trends in exploitation are evident for either time series, including before and after the implementation of mandatory C&R on the Burrishoole system in 1990 (t-test$_{30}$ = 0.46, p > 0.05). Annual exploitation rates were relatively high in some years in both systems when low numbers of returning fish were recorded (Figure 2). This is reflected in a significant negative association between exploitation

rates and population size for the Erriff system (Spearman, r_s = -0.52, $p < 0.05$), although no such significant statistical relationship was evident for the Burrishoole between 1971 and 1989 (Spearman, r_s = 0.43, $p > 0.05$) or over the available time series (Spearman, r_s = 0.18, $p > 0.05$). For both systems, angling catch was significantly highly correlated with population size (Spearman, r_s = 0.7 (Erriff) and 0.89 (Burrishoole), $p < 0.05$).

Table 3. Median angling exploitation rates (%) for salmon, spring salmon, and sea trout per system (2.5% – 97.5% percentile range in brackets). The number of data years used to calculate median exploitation rates for each system per taxon is respectively indicated in column *n*.

System	System type	n	Salmon	Spring salmon	Sea trout
Ballynahinch	River-lake	9, –, 5	4.4 (1.8–8.6)	-	33.3 (20.1–43.5)
Ballysadare	River	12, 10, –	15.5 (9.6–48)	18.9 (9.5–56.7)	-
Bandon	River	12, 7, –	20.2 (9.7–35.4)	17.9 (5.7–39.2)	-
Blackwater	River	13, –,–	8.7 (2.2–16.3)	-	-
Boyne	River	10, 8, –	6.2 (3.3–13.6)	5.2 (2.2–7.7)	-
Bunowen	River	5, –, 7	15.3 (3.5–18.6)	-	14 (7.8–28.5)
Burrishoole	Lake	32, –, 32	4.4 (0.8–14.2)	-	6.7 (0.4–28.5)
Carrowmore	Lake	8, 8, 9	14.2 (6.4–34.6)	12 (5.9–29.7)	9.3 (4.1–31.1)
Cashla	River-lake	13, –,13	6.1 (3–12.6)	-	15 (6.1–27.7)
Clifden	River	5, –,5	29.6 (9.2–40.7)	-	13.6 (3.6–23.8)
Corrib	River-lake	8,8, –	10.7 (8.1–14.4)	13.8 (4.8–53.8)	-
Culfin	River-lake	6, –, –	4.4 (0.7–10.3)	-	-
Dawros	River-lake	6, –,–	11.8 (3.3–18.5)	-	-
Dee	River	5, –,5	8.2 (5.3–16.1)	-	35.7 (14.6–39.6)
Eany	River	12, –,5	16.8 (8.9–33.8)	-	40.8 (22–50.9)
Erriff	River-lake	29, –,17	17.9 (7.3–38.6)	-	10.9 (5.2–30.5)
Eske	River-lake	6, –,–	7.4 (3.5–13)	-	-
Feale	River	13,10, –	12.1 (5.4–29.2)	16.8 (6.9–26.8)	-
Inagh	Lake	8, –,–	7.4 (5–14.2)	-	-
Maine	River	6, –,3	8.4 (3.3–10.8)	-	6.2 (4.3–11.1)
Mulkear	River	7, –,–	18.4 (2.9–26.3)	-	-
Owenduff	River	7,6,4	12 (6.4–12.8)	18.2 (6.3–24.5)	21.2 (13.7–26.6)
Owenmore	River	5,4,4	29.4 (25.1–37.1)	6.8 (0–14.4)	24.6 (7.5–32)
Slaney	River	9,6, –	17.8 (2.1–37.5)	26.7 (7.2–44.2)	-
Waterville	Lake	12,9, –	15.4 (4.2–33.1)	19.2 (5.9–28.2)	-

ANGLING EXPLOITATION RATES FOR SALMON

Across all systems, the overall median angling exploitation rate on salmon stocks was 10.8%

Table 4. Median angling exploitation rates (%) for salmon, spring salmon, and sea trout by system type, management strategy, counter type and in the periods pre and post the introduction of regulatory measures (with 2.5% – 97.5% percentile range in brackets).

Category	Sub-category	Salmon	Spring salmon	Sea trout
	River	13.6 (2.9–37.1)	15.9 (2.2–50.4)	17.7 (3.6–50.9)
System type	Lake	6.2 (1–33)	18.4 (5.9–29.7)	7.1 (1.3–30.6)
	River-lake	10.7 (1.8–26.7)	13.8 (4.8–53.8)	14.7 (5.2–43.5)
Management strategy	Open for harvest	11.3 (2.9–35.4)	17.3 (4.2–53.8)	11.2 (2.6–42.8)
	Catch & release-only	6.2 (0.7–30.4)	6.3 (2.2–35.6)	13.2 (2.0–40.8)
Counter	Full	9.9 (1.8–34.6)	17.8 (0–56.7)	11.3 (2.0–33.3)
	Partial	13.7 (3.3–35.4)	12.1 (2.2–53.8)	37.9 (14.6–50.9)
Regulatory	Pre-measures (<2007)	10.1 (2.9–37.5)	18 (5–56.7)	10.8 (0.4–28.5)
	Post measures (>2006)	10.9 (1.8–32.5)	15 (2.2–50.4)	14.3 (2.0–43.5)

Table 5. Outputs from three selected statistical models (binomial GLMM) of sea trout exploitation rate in Irish systems (rivers and lakes) managed as open for harvest or open for C&R-only fisheries. Estimate gives the direction of the effect (positive or negative), the z value is the Wald test statistic and Pr(>|z|) is a p-value for a two-tail test (ns = not significant).

Model	Parameter[1]	Estimate	SE	Z value	Pr(>|z|)
	Intercept	-1.839	0.304	-6.061	<0.001
M5	System	0.373	0.421	0.887	ns
	Status	-0.066	0.371	-0.177	ns
M6	Intercept	-1.850	0.292	-6.358	<0.001
	System	0.345	0.387	0.892	ns
M7	Intercept	-1.678	0.254	-6.606	<0.001
	Status	0.046	0.354	0.129	ns

[1]*refer to methods section for a definition of each parameter.*

(PR 1.8–34.6) with only three waters out of 25, all river-dominated systems, having exploitation rates > 20% (Bandon 20.2%, Clifden 29.6% and Owenmore 29.4%). Median exploitation rates were < 14% across all four categories examined. As with sea trout stocks, the exploitation rate on salmon stocks was greater on *rivers* (13.6%) than *lakes* (6.2%) (KW$_2$, H = 31.6, $p < 0.001$, post-hoc WR, $p < 0.001$) and higher in systems with *partial* fish counters installed (13.7%) over those where *full* counters (9.9%) operated (WR, U = 4617, Z = -3.6, $p < 0.001$). The rate was higher however, where harvesting was allowed (11.3%) in comparison to systems restricted to *C&R* (6.2%) (WR, U = 1782, Z = 3.4, $p < 0.001$). Exploitation was moderately higher after the introduction of regulatory measures (10.9%) than in the preceding period (10.1%). The full model (M1) had an AIC = 1976.4, while for model M3 the AIC = 1976.7; no other

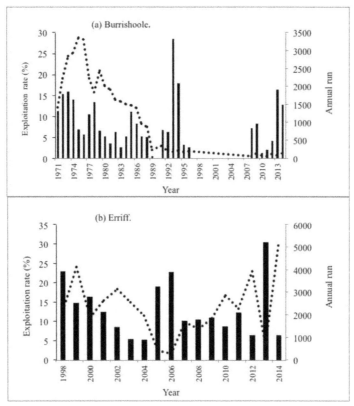

Figure 2. Angling exploitation rate (■) and annual run (•••) of sea trout populations in (a) the Burrishoole system from 1971 to 2014 (trap data); and (b) in the Erriff system from 1998 to 2014 (counter data).

candidate models were within two AIC points. Both final models showed significant effects on angling exploitation rate of the interaction between system type and status ($p < 0.01$) M1 showed a significant effect of expert opinion on angling intensity ($p < 0.05$). The effect of latitude was not significant (Table 6). The finding that angling exploitation rates were higher in systems with an 'open for harvest' rather than a 'open for C&R-only' management strategy is also evident in the model output (Figure 3).

ANGLING EXPLOITATION RATES FOR THE SPRING SALMON COMPONENT

The overall median angling exploitation rate across all systems (n=10) on the spring salmon component of salmon stocks was 15.6% (PR 2.2–54). Median exploitation rates were < 19% across all four categories examined. A higher exploitation rate occurred in *lake* (18.4%) than *river-lake* systems (13.8%) (WR, U = 1782, Z = 3.4, $p < 0.001$) with *river* systems (15.9%) intermediate to these (KW$_2$, H = 0.98, $p > 0.05$). As with the whole salmon stock, the angling exploitation of spring salmon was also notably significantly higher in open waters where

177

Table 6. Outputs from two selected statistical models (binomial GLMM) of salmon exploitation rate in Irish systems (rivers and lakes) managed as open for harvest or open for C&R-only fisheries. Estimate gives the direction of the effect (positive or negative), the z value is the Wald test statistic and Pr(>|z|) is a p-value for a two-tail test (ns = not significant).

Model	Parameter[1]	Estimate	SE	Z value	Pr(>/z/)
	Intercept	-3.647	0.528	-6.539	<0.001
	System	1.722	0.442	3.901	<0.001
	Status	1.440	0.433	3.328	<0.001
M1	Latitude	-0.147	0.094	-1.565	ns
	Expert/low	-0.746	0.341	-2.190	<0.05
	Expert/medium	-0.086	0.282	-0.303	ns
	System : status	-1.324	0.456	-2.900	<0.01
	Intercept	-3.647	0.529	-6.891	<0.001
	System	1.833	0.454	4.036	<0.001
M3	Status/open for harvest	1.524	0.446	3.421	<0.001
	Expert/low	-0.654	0.341	-1.902	ns
	Expert/medium	-0.010	0.282	-0.036	ns
	System : status	-1.349	0.474	-2.850	<0.01

[1]*refer to methods section for a definition of each parameter.*

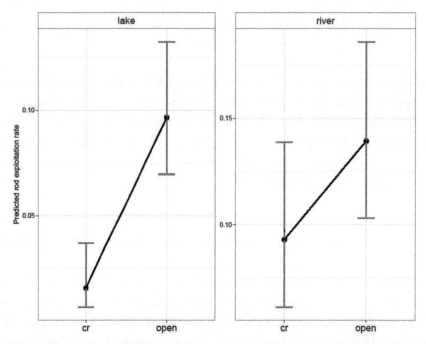

Figure 3. Predicted salmon angling exploitation rate by system type and management strategy (cr = only catch-and-release angling: open = open to angling harvest).

harvesting was permitted (17.3%) over those designated solely for *C&R* (6.3%) (WR, U = 174, Z = 2.7, p < 0.01). In addition, exploitation was moderately higher after the introduction of regulatory measures (18%) than in the preceding period (15%), but not significantly so (WR, U = 307, Z = -0.74, p > 0.05). Unlike the whole salmon stock however, there was no significant difference in the exploitation of spring salmon between systems with *full* fish counters (17.8%) and those with *partial* fish counters (12.1%) (WR, U = 565, Z = 1.62, p > 0.05).

DISCUSSION

This paper represents the first such study to comprehensively examine angling exploitation rates on salmonid populations in Ireland from multiple systems and system types, under different management strategies and counting regimes, and for salmon, to explore any changes to exploitation as a result of the introduction of regulatory measures on catch. In addition, the study presents an updated assessment of sea trout angling pressure on stocks in the Burrishoole and Erriff systems, building upon previous investigations in these fisheries (Gargan *et al.*, 2006a; Poole *et al.*, 2006). Further to this, modeling of the output has offered a potential mechanism to better inform any future refinement of the angling exploitation rates currently used by the SSCS in their annual assessments of salmon stocks (SSCS, 2015). Direct comparisons of angling exploitation rates between published studies are somewhat limited by the mid-point chosen by the authors (median, mean etc.) to report rates. Nevertheless, where appropriate, the results of this study are placed in the context of the available comparable literature.

Large variation is evident between median angling exploitation rates on sea trout stocks in the individual systems examined (6.2–40.8 %), a number of which (*e.g.* Ballynahinch, Dee and Eany) may be considerably higher than those known for British freshwaters. Here, long-term mean exploitation rates were reported to range from 2.7–20.5% (Davidson *et al.*, 2006; Shields *et al.*, 2006). It is notable that a significant negative association between sea trout stock sizes and exploitation rates was found in the Erriff. This indicates that as stock size decreases, the exploitation rate increases. Similar trends were also observed in three British rivers, albeit two other systems in the same study displayed no such relationship (Shields *et al.*, 2006). Negative associations between salmon stock size and angling exploitation have also been reported (Peterman & Steer, 1981; Mills *et al.*, 1986; Beaumont, 1991; Gargan *et al.*, 2001; Hansen, 2001). Other studies have found no such evident relationship (Crozier & Kennedy, 2001; Whelan *et al.*, 2001). Despite this, sea trout angling catch on both the Erriff and Burrishoole were highly positively associated with stock size. This has commonly been reported for salmon (*e.g.* Beaumont, 1991; Solomon & Potter, 1992; Crozier & Kennedy, 2001; Gargan *et al.*, 2001; Hansen, 2001), further supporting the cautionary use of angling catch to approximate adult salmonid stock abundance for management purposes. Investigations by Shields *et al.*, (2006) however, suggested that this relationship is less clear for sea trout, indicating that further study may be required to establish such a link for this species.

A wide range of angling exploitation rates on Atlantic salmon stocks and their stock components have been reported in the literature. In Irish catchments, long-term studies on angling exploitation have reported mean rates as 19.3% on the Erriff (Gargan *et al.*, 2001), 15% on the Burrishoole (grilse only, Whelan *et al.*, 2001) and 11% on the River Bush (Crozier & Kennedy, 2001). The calculated rates from this study are generally consistent or lower than the reported rates, with only three waters out of the 25 systems examined having exploitation rates > 20% (Bandon 20.2%, Clifden 29.6% and Owenmore 29.4%). The exploitation rate on the Erriff system (17.9%) was in line with that previously reported (Gargan *et al.*, 2001). However, the current exploitation rate reported for the Burrishoole system on the total stock (4.4%, Percentile Range 0.8–14.2%), is much lower than historic estimates of exploitation on the grilse stock (Whelan *et al.*, 2001), taking into account that the grilse component represents around 90% of the annual run of fish into this fishery (Whelan *et al.*, 2001).

Overall, median exploitation rates for the spring salmon component were found to be higher (15.6%) than that for the whole salmon stock (10.8%). Exploitation rates on early running stock components, notably multi-sea winter fish, are generally reported to be higher than that experienced by the whole stock (Solomon & Potter, 1992; Crozier & Kennedy, 2001; reviewed in Thorley *et al.*, 2007); however, no clear trend in this regard was evident for corresponding exploitation rates from the individual systems examined. This may highlight a reduced accuracy of assigning a fish to a particular stock component using the time of year caught, rather than more specific age information (e.g. scale analyses), which is more difficult to collect systematically, in order to elucidate exploitation rates on a sub-population. This is recognised in the SSCS assessment format, where salmon stocks with a sizeable multi-sea winter component may be identified by additional factors such as fish weight to separately evaluate their CL attainment (SSCS, 2015).

There is a paucity of information on angling exploitation rates in the literature to compare against values as reported in this assessment under the various categories examined. The notably higher exploitation rate in river-dominated over lake-dominated systems, for both sea trout and salmon stocks, may reflect a relatively increased probability of catch in rivers. Lake systems may well offer more refuge from encounters with anglers and thus decrease angling pressure on residing stocks. It is unclear why both stocks also had significantly higher exploitation rates in systems where partial rather full counter facilities were present. It should be noted that partial counters are typically installed in relatively wider channels where the operation of full counters is not feasible. The output may indicate an undercounting of returning adults in some systems, which would manifest itself in a higher exploitation rate than that occurring. Neither trend was evident for the spring salmon component. There was no significant difference detected between exploitation rates on salmon stocks in the periods before and after the introduction of regulatory measures in 2007. As the rates were calculated on both harvested and C&R fish, this may mask any substantial changes to the harvested component. Indeed, C&R fishing has increasingly been adopted by anglers in Irish salmon fisheries since 2007, compared to the preceding time period examined. In England, mean rod exploitation on salmon stocks in the River Lune substantially decreased from 26.4% to 14.8% after the introduction of regulations on catch (Aprahamian *et al.*, 2006).

The generation of a large dataset of angling exploitation rates, based on information from multiple systems and years, has facilitated the exploration of their applicability to refine the broader rate bands (low, medium and high) as currently employed by the SSCS in their annual assessments of salmon stocks (SSCS, 2015). The modeling exercise indicated that exploitation bands could respectively be identified for river and lake-dominated systems under either open for harvest or open for C&R-only angling regimes. With further development, this approach could be applied to better evaluate the attainment of CLs for individual salmon stocks under system type and fisheries management strategy where quantitative population data are lacking. The model output suggests lower exploitation rates in both river and lake-dominated systems, where harvesting is permitted, than that currently applied by the SSCS. This is also the case for fisheries designated as C&R in lake-dominated systems (with river-dominated systems having a comparable exploitation rate for C&R to that currently used). The inclusion of additional variables in the model, such alkalinity, pH, water levels, fishing gear permitted, age classes and more detailed classification of system type, or by using a Bayesian Framework approach, may further inform the designation of exploitation bands under each category. Indeed, it is likely that fishing gear used may exert an influence on angling exploitation rates through an increased probability of catch, notably in some systems open for harvest where a wider variety of methods (e.g. worm and prawn) are permitted than more restrictive methods (e.g. single barbless hooks) prescribed in waters open for C&R-only angling. In addition, it would be informative to further examine the model approach to define exploitation bands for the spring salmon component as more data becomes available.

The angling exploitation rates on sea trout stocks presented here, and the model approach successfully applied for salmon, may prove valuable as part of any wider process initiated to establish biological reference points for Irish sea trout populations and measure their attainment in future. The overall process undertaken highlights the need to continue to systematically collect reliable multi-annual data on angling catches and population size, and improve this where necessary, in order to better evaluate the status of these species that are of major conservation and socio-economic importance.

ACKNOWLEDGMENTS

The contribution of Inland Fisheries Ireland staff nationally in providing fish counter data and sea trout catch data are gratefully acknowledged. The Marine Institute is also acknowledged for provision of additional fish counter and trap data and Burrishoole rod catch data. Returns of angling catch information by anglers and private fishery owners are further acknowledged.

REFERENCES

Anon. (2008). The Status of EU Protected Habitats and Species in Ireland. *Conservation status in Ireland of habitats and species listed in the European Council Directive on the Conservation of Habitats, Flora and Fauna 92/42/EEC.* National Parks and Wildlife Service. Department of Environment, Heritage and Local Government, The Brunswick Press, Dublin, 136 pp.

Anon. (1970-2014). Annual Reports of the Salmon Research Trust of Ireland, Salmon Research Agency of Ireland and Marine Institute for the Burrishoole Fish Census and Rod Fishery (*various pages*).

Aprahamian, M.W., Wyatt, R.J. & Shields, B.A. (2006). Use of biological reference points for the conservation of Atlantic salmon, *Salmo salar*, in the River Lune, North West England. *Fisheries Management and Ecology*, **13**: 21–30.

Beaumont, W.R.C., Welton, J.S. & Ladle, M. (1991). Comparison of rod catch data with known numbers of Atlantic salmon (*Salmo salar*) recorded by a resistivity fish counter in a southern chalk stream. In: *Catch Effort Sampling Strategies: Their Application in Freshwater Fisheries Management* (Cowx, I.G., *Ed*.). Fishing News Books, Oxford, 49–60.

Bilsby, H. (2006). The River Dee: stock component review 2006. The River Dee Trust, 124 pp.

Burnham, K.P. & Anderson, D.R. (2002). Model Selection and Multimodel Inference: A Practical Information-Theoretic Approach, 2nd edn. Springer-Verlag, New York, 488 pp.

CFB. (2004). 2001-2003 Wild Salmon and Sea Trout Tagging Scheme Fisheries Statistics Report. Central Fisheries Board, Dublin, 40 pp.

CFB. (2005a). 2003-2004 Wild Salmon and Sea Trout Tagging Scheme Fisheries Statistics Report. Central Fisheries Board, Dublin, 31 pp.

CFB. (2005b). Irish Angling Catch Statistics 2004. Central Fisheries Board, Dublin, 36 pp.

CFB (2008). 2006-2007 Wild Salmon and Sea Trout Statistics. Central Fisheries Board, Dublin, 36 pp.

CFB. (2009). Wild Salmon and Sea Trout Statistics Report 2008. Central and Regional Fisheries Boards, Ireland, 81 pp.

CFB. (2010). Wild Salmon and Sea Trout Statistics Report 2009. Central and Regional Fisheries Boards, Ireland, 76 pp.

Crozier, W.W. & Kennedy, G.J.A. (2001). Relationship between freshwater angling catch of Atlantic salmon and stock size in the River Bush, Northern Ireland. *Journal of Fish Biology*, **58**: 240–247.

Davidson, I., Cove, R.J. & Hazlewood, M.S. (2006). Annual Variation in Age Composition, Growth and Abundance of Sea Trout Returning to the River Dee at Chester, 1991–200. In: *Sea Trout: Biology, Conservation and Management.* (Graeme Harris & Nigel Milner. *Eds.*). Proceedings of the 1st International Sea Trout Symposium, Cardiff, July 2004. Blackwell Scientific Publications, Oxford, 76–87.

Gargan, P., Stafford, J. & Ó Maoiléidigh, N. (2001). The Relationship between Salmon Rod Catch, Stock Size, Rod Exploitation and Rod Effort on The Erriff Fishery, Western Ireland. In: *The Interpretation of Rod and Net Catch Data.* (Shelton, R., *Ed*.). The Atlantic Salmon Trust, Pitlochry, 68–75.

Gargan, P., Poole, R. & Forde, G. (2006a). A Review of the Status of Irish Sea Trout Stocks. In: *Sea Trout: Biology, Conservation and Management.* (Graeme Harris & Nigel Milner. *Eds*). Proceedings of the 1st International Sea Trout Symposium, Cardiff, July 2004. Blackwell Scientific Publications, Oxford, 25–44.

Gargan, P., Roche, W., Forde, G. & Ferguson, A. (2006b). Characteristics of the Sea Trout (*Salmo trutta* L.) Stocks from the Owengowla and Invermore Fisheries, Connemara, Western Ireland, and Recent Trends in Marine Survival. In: *Sea Trout: Biology, Conservation and Management.* (Graeme Harris & Nigel Milner. *Eds.*). Proceedings of the 1st International Sea Trout Symposium, Cardiff, July 2004. Blackwell Scientific Publications, Oxford, 60–75.

Hansen, L.P. (2001). Relationship between Catches, Rod Exploitation and Total Run of Atlantic Salmon in the River Drammenselv, Norway. In: *The Interpretation of Rod and Net Catch Data.* (Shelton, R.G.J. *Ed.*). Atlantic Salmon Trust, Moulin, Pitlochry, 85–90.

IFI. (2011). Wild Salmon and Sea Trout Statistics Report 2010. Inland Fisheries Ireland, Dublin, 74 pp.

IFI. (2012). Wild Salmon and Sea Trout Statistics Report 2011. Inland Fisheries Ireland, Dublin, 107 pp.

IFI. (2013). Wild Salmon and Sea Trout Statistics Report 2012. Inland Fisheries Ireland, Dublin, 112 pp.

IFI. (2014). Wild Salmon and Sea Trout Statistics Report 2013. Inland Fisheries Ireland, Dublin, 110 pp.

IFI. (2011-2014). Consolidation Fish Counter Reports (2011-2014). Inland Fisheries Ireland, Dublin, (*various pages*).

McGinnity, P., Gargan, P., Roche, W., Mills, P. & McGarrigle, M. (2003). Quantification of the freshwater salmon habitat asset in Ireland using data interpreted in a GIS platform. *Irish Freshwater Fisheries, Ecology and Management Series: Number 3*, Central Fisheries Board, Dublin, Ireland.

Mills, C.P.R., Mahon, G.A.J. & Piggins, D.J. (1986). The influence of stock levels, fishing effort & environmental factors on angler's catch of Atlantic salmon and sea trout. *Aquaculture and Fisheries Management*, **17**: 289–97.

Milner, N.J., Davidson, I.C., Evans, R.E., Locke, V. & Wyatt, R.J. (2001). The use of rod catches to estimate salmon runs in England and Wales. In: *The Interpretation of Rod and Net Catch Data.* (Shelton, R.G.J., *Ed.*). Atlantic Salmon Trust, Moulin, Pitlochry, 46-67.

NASCO. (1998). Agreement on the adoption of a precautionary approach. In: *Report of the 15th Annual Meeting of the Council*, CNL(98)46. North Atlantic Salmon Conservation Organisation, 4 pp.

NASCO. (2005). Development of the NASCO Database of Irish Salmon Rivers – Report on Progress, CNL(05)45. North Atlantic Salmon Conservation Organisation, 20 pp.

Olsen, R.E., Næsje, T.F., Poppe, T., Sneddon, L. & Webb, J. (2010). Risk Assessment of Catch and Release. Opinion of the Panel on Animal Health and Welfare of the Norwegian Scientific Committee for Food Safety, 79 pp.

Ó Maoiléidigh, N., McLaughlin, D., Cullen, A., McDermott, T. & Bond, N. (2000). Carcass Tags and Logbooks for Managing Irish Salmon Stocks. Trinity College, Dublin. (Moriarty, C. *Ed.*), 40–48.

Ó Maoiléidigh, N., McGinnity, P., Prévost, E., Potter, E.C.E., Gargan, P., Crozier, W.W., Mills, P. & Roche, W. (2004). Application of pre-fishery abundance modelling and Bayesian hierarchical stock and recruitment analysis to the provision of precautionary catch advice for Irish salmon (*Salmo salar* L.) fisheries. *ICES Journal of Marine Science*, **61**: 1370–1378.

Peterman, R.M. & Steer, G.J. (1981). Relation between sportfishing catchability coefficients and salmon abundance. *Transactions of the American Fisheries Society*, **114**: 436–440.

Poole, W.R., Dillane, M., de Eyto, E., Rogan, G., McGinnity, P. & Whelan, K. (2006). Characteristics of the Burrishoole Sea Trout Population: Census, Marine Survival, Enhancement and Stock–Recruitment

Relationship,1971–2003. In: *Sea Trout: Biology, Conservation and Management.* (Graeme Harris & Nigel Milner. *Eds.*). Proceedings of the 1st International Sea Trout Symposium, Cardiff, July 2004. Blackwell Scientific Publications, Oxford, 279–306.

Shields, B.A., Aprahamian, M.W., Bayliss, B.D., Davidson, I.C., Elsmere, P. & Evans, R. (2006). Sea trout (*Salmo trutta* L.) exploitation in five rivers in England and Wales. In: *Sea Trout: Biology, Conservation and Management.* (Graeme Harris & Nigel Milner. *Eds.*). Proceedings of the 1st International Sea Trout Symposium, Cardiff, July 2004. Blackwell Scientific Publications, Oxford, 417–433.

Solomon, D.J. & Potter, E.C.E. (1992). The Measurement and Evaluation of the Exploitation of Atlantic Salmon. Atlantic Salmon Trust, Moulin, Pitlochry, 38 pp.

SSCS. (2015). The Status of Irish Salmon Stocks in 2014 with Precautionary Catch Advice for 2015. Report of the Standing Scientific Committee on Salmon to Inland Fisheries Ireland, 88 pp.

Thorley, J.L., Youngson, A.F. & Laughton, R. (2007). Seasonal variation in rod recapture rates indicates differential exploitation of Atlantic salmon, *Salmo salar*, stock components. *Fisheries Management and Ecology*, **14**: 191–198.

Webb, J.H. (2001). Development, implementation and biological implications of the catch and release policy for early running Atlantic salmon in the Aberdeenshire Dee, 1995–1999. In: *Catch and Release: Atlantic salmon in the UK.* (Lyndon, A.R., *Ed.*). IFM Scottish Branch Catch and Release Conference 2001. Institute of Fisheries Management, Edinburgh, 18–23.

Whelan, K.F, Whelan, B.J., & Rogan, G. (2001). Catch as a Predictor of Salmon Stock in the Burrishoole Fishery, Co. Mayo, Western Ireland. Paper presented at the Atlantic Salmon Trust Working Group on Catch Data, Lowestoft, November 2001.

White, J., Ó Maoiléidigh, N., Gargan, P., de Eyto, E., Chaput, G., Roche, W., McGinnity, P., Crozier, W.W., Boylan, P., Doherty, D., O'Higgins, K., Kennedy, B., Lawler, I., Lyons, D. & Marnell, F. (2016). Incorporating natural variability in biological reference points and population dynamics into management of Atlantic salmon (*Salmo salar* L.) stocks returning to home waters. *ICES Journal of Marine Science*, doi:10.1093/icesjms/fsw015.

ELECTRONIC REFERENCE

Bates, D., Maechler, M., Bolker, B. & Walker, S. (2015). lme4: Linear mixed-effects models using Eigen and S4. R package version 1.1-9. *Available from:* https://CRAN.R-project.org/package=lme4

Fox, F. (2003). Effect Displays in R for Generalised Linear Models. *Journal of Statistical Software*, 8(15), 1–27. URL http://www.jstatsoft.org/v08/i15/.

R Core Team (2015). R: A language and environment for statistical computing. R Foundation for Statistical Computing, Vienna, Austria. URL https://www.R-project.org/.

The relative importance of sea trout and salmon to the recreational rod fisheries in England & Wales

G. HARRIS[1] & R. EVANS[2]

[1]Fishskill Consultancy Services, Greenacre, Bwlch, Brecon, Powys, LD3 7PZ, Wales.
[2]Natural Resources Wales, Ty Cambria, Newport Road, Cardiff CF24 0TP, Wales.

ABSTRACT

The historical approach to the management of migratory fisheries in England & Wales since the seminal Salmon Fisheries Acts of the 1880s has traditionally attached far greater importance to the management of the Atlantic salmon than to the congeneric and co-dwelling sea trout. The widespread and significant decline in the abundance and composition of salmon stocks throughout much of the British Isles in recent years has promoted a far greater awareness of the importance and value of sea trout as the mainstay of the recreational rod fisheries on many rivers. The long time-series of robust catch statistics for salmon and sea trout from each of the 80 principal migratory fish rivers in England and Wales is analysed to compare their relative importance to the rod fisheries in different geographical regions and rivers. This examines their contribution to a) the total annual catch, b) the catch in each month of the annual fishing season, c) the catch-per-unit of rod fishing effort and d) the rod fishing effort targeted specifically at salmon and/or sea trout as the preferred choice of anglers. An example from Wales is given to illustrate the cumulative importance of small, often neglected, 'minor streams' in contributing to the catch of sea trout and salmon to that region.

Keywords: sea trout; salmon; rod fisheries; relative importance; catch records; minor rivers.

INTRODUCTION

The management of migratory salmonid fisheries in the British Isles over much of the last century was driven by the far greater importance and value attached to maintaining and protecting Atlantic salmon fisheries by Governments, their management agencies and fishery stakeholder interests. As such, the existence of co-dwelling, congeneric stocks of sea trout in many rivers was largely overlooked in the development and implementation of fisheries management strategies and programmes (Scott, 1969). Because they both exhibited similar life histories in the marine and freshwater environments and had almost identical habitat requirements while in freshwater, this historical neglect was based on the general presumption that *"provided we looked after the more important and valuable salmon, then the sea trout would look after themselves"*. Consequently, very little direct management action occurred to benefit sea trout stocks and their associated recreational and commercial fisheries so that they remained largely undervalued and taken-for-granted. This traditional and seemingly complacent perspective of the general importance of sea trout in many fisheries began to change from the late 1970s in response to two separate developments identified by Harris & Milner (2006) as:-

1. The outbreak of the pandemic disease *'ulcerative dermal necrosis'* (UDN) that ravaged salmon and sea trout stocks throughout much of the British Isles from the late 1960s until the mid-1970s. However, while sea trout stocks steadily recovered to something like their former levels of abundance during the 1980s, salmon stocks have continued to decline to the present day. This decline in salmon stocks then focussed attention on the importance of the sea trout as an alternative to salmon in maintaining the rod fisheries on many rivers.

2. The dramatic growth of commercial salmon farming on the west coasts of Scotland and Ireland from the late 1970s, where salmon were reared in cages moored in estuaries and sheltered coastal bays. The parallel and dramatic collapse of the runs of sea trout in neighbouring rivers resulted from the increased mortality of post-smolts during their early feeding in coastal waters. This was attributed to massive infestations of the salmon louse (*Lepeophtheirus salmonis*) originating from salmon held at very high densities in the cage farms (c.f. Gargan *et al.*, 2003; Butler & Walker, 2006; 2002 Gargan *et al.*, 2017). These remote parts of Scotland and Ireland are characterised by many small, lake-fed river systems with only small runs of salmon but reasonable stocks of sea trout. In the absence of any significant salmon stocks to support the rod-fisheries, the collapse of their sea trout stocks had a major impact on the social and economic value of many fisheries to the local economy.

One of the over-arching aims of the 1st International Sea Trout Symposium was *'to raise the status and profile of the sea trout at home and abroad'* so that it was no longer neglected, overlooked or taken-for-granted by Governments, their state management agencies and fishery stakeholders when developing their management strategies for migratory fish (Harris & Milner, 2006). In this important context, one of the six principal recommendations from the Symposium stated:

"Sea trout offer socio-economic benefits that may be more widely distributed and in total may be greater than salmon, but studies and developments of these have been largely ignored. It is crucial that research in this area is commissioned to encourage and inform sustainable developments to maximise these benefits".

Several authoritative studies on the social and economic value of fisheries in the British Isles have reported a range of monetary values for salmon and sea trout fisheries (Radford & Hatcher, 1991; Radford *et al.*, 2001; Spurgeon *et al.,* 2001). By way of example, these included an estimated value of £8 million annually to the Welsh Economy (Nautilus, 2000) and a gross annual expenditure by anglers fishing the River Teifi (West Wales) of £1 million in that single catchment alone (Spurgeon *et al.,* 2001). The most recent study on the economic impact of freshwater angling in England & Wales (Radford *et al.,* 2007) reported that, for all regions of England & Wales combined, anglers fishing specifically for salmon and sea trout during the 2006 season made 429,000 fishing trips and their expenditure of £36.9 million generated £28.6 million in household income and supported 1,179 jobs. However, as noted by O'Reilly & Mawle (2006), one of the principal limitations of past economic studies was that any derived value attributable to sea trout became subsumed into a combined value that also included salmon; so that separate values were not available for either species.

In the absence of any comparable information that separates the economic value of salmon from sea trout, this paper, by default, falls back on a review of the published catch statistics to compare the relative importance of their respective contributions to the rod fisheries in E&W that support and sustain any underlying economic benefits to society.

BACKGROUND

Evans & Harris (2017) describe the methodology adopted throughout England & Wales for obtaining detailed catch records from individual anglers based on a dual system of statutory rod licensing and mandatory catch returns for each angler fishing for salmon and sea trout in any year. This system has been in place without material change since 1994 and now provides a dataset covering 21 years of robust, consistent and directly comparable data for each of salmon and sea trout rivers in England & Wales.

Figure 1 shows the location of the 80 'principal' migratory fish rivers in England & Wales that sustain significant recreational rod fisheries for salmon and sea trout. Note that the majority of these fisheries are located on the west and southwest coast. Catch data from each of these rivers has been published since 1994 by the Environment Agency for E&W in the series of annual reports on "Salmonid & Freshwater Fisheries Statistics for England & Wales" (*available from* http://publications.environment-agency.gov.uk).

Annual rod catches are linked initially to the length of the statutory fishing season and to the strength and timing of the annual runs of fish within that season that determine their availability to anglers. Other factors, principally river flow levels affecting run patterns and fishing effort, then act to influence annual rod capture rates and angling success. Few salmon rivers in E&W now maintain any significant runs of MSW 'spring' salmon in the early months of the season (normally February – May). Several of the larger rivers in the north of England still retain reasonable runs of MSW 'autumn' salmon from September until the start of the spawning season in late November/December. However, the salmon rod catch on most rivers is very dependent on the runs of 1SW 'grilse' salmon that normally appear from July through to September. Sea trout rivers are not noted for producing early or late runs of fish. The annual

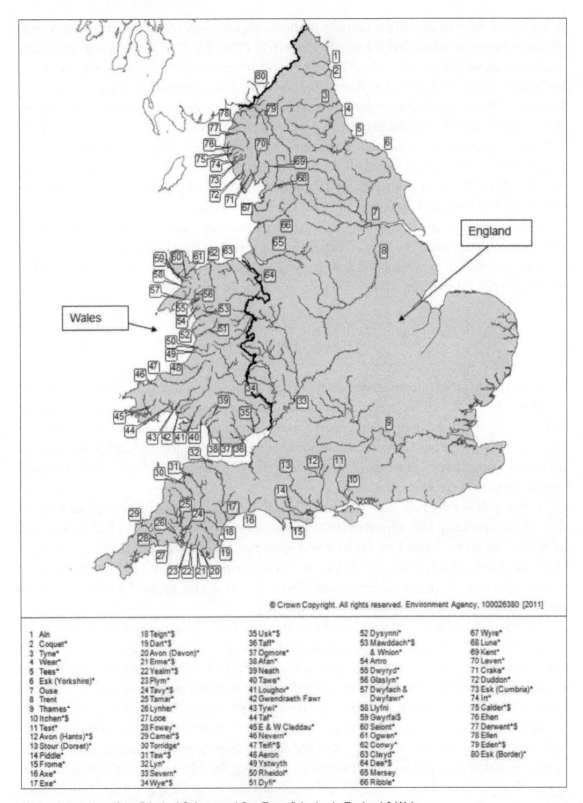

1 Aln	18 Teign*$	35 Usk*$	52 Dysynni*	67 Wyre*
2 Coquet*	19 Dart*$	36 Taff*	53 Mawddach*$	68 Lune*
3 Tyne*	20 Avon (Devon)*	37 Ogmore*	& Wnion*	69 Kent*
4 Wear*	21 Erme*$	38 Afan*	54 Artro	70 Leven*
5 Tees*	22 Yealm*$	39 Neath	55 Dwyryd*	71 Crake*
6 Esk (Yorkshire)*	23 Plym*	40 Tawe*	56 Glaslyn*	72 Duddon*
7 Ouse	24 Tavy*$	41 Loughor*	57 Dwyfach &	73 Esk (Cumbria)*
8 Trent	25 Tamar*	42 Gwendraeth Fawr	Dwyfawr*	74 Irt*
9 Thames*	26 Lynher*	43 Tywi*	58 Llyfni	75 Calder*$
10 Itchen*$	27 Looe	44 Taf*	59 Gwyrfai$	76 Ehen
11 Test*	28 Fowey*	45 E & W Cleddau*	60 Seiont*	77 Derwent*$
12 Avon (Hants)*$	29 Camel*$	46 Nevern*	61 Ogwen*	78 Ellen
13 Stour (Dorset)*	30 Torridge*	47 Teifi*$	62 Conwy*	79 Eden*$
14 Piddle*	31 Taw*$	48 Aeron*	63 Clwyd*	80 Esk (Border)*
15 Frome*	32 Lyn*	49 Ystwyth*	64 Dee*$	
16 Axe*	33 Severn*	50 Rheidol*	65 Mersey	
17 Exe*	34 Wye*$	51 Dyfi*	66 Ribble*	

Figure 1. Location of the Principal Salmon and Sea Trout fisheries in England & Wales.

run normally begins in April, reaches a peak in July/August before tailing off from September to the start of the spawning season in November/early December.

The system of statutory fishery byelaws and voluntary regulations imposed by fishery owners or their tenants to protect salmon and sea trout stocks from over-exploitation by anglers varies widely between regions and rivers and is highly complicated. However, for present purposes, the salmon fishing season on most rivers begins in March and ends in early or late October. It may start and end a few weeks earlier or later on those rivers with early 'spring' and/or late 'autumn' runs of MSW salmon. The fishing season for sea trout is generally shorter than salmon, effectively starting in April and ending in September or early October. While a few sea trout may run before and after the end of this period, the fishing season for sea trout broadly covers all, or almost all, of the annual run.

REGIONAL COMPARISONS

TOTAL ANNUAL CATCH

Information on the total annual catch provides a basic perspective of the relative contribution and importance of sea trout and salmon to the rod fisheries over time. Table 1 shows the aggregated mean annual catch of each species over the 21-year period (1994-2014) for the 80 principal migratory fish river in England and Wales in each of the five main geographical 'statistical reporting regions' with significant migratory fisheries.

Table 1. Aggregated Mean Annual Rod Catches of Sea Trout & Salmon for the main Reporting Regions in England & Wales (1994 – 2014).

Reporting Region	No. Rivers[2]	Mean Annual Catch			% Sea Trout
		Sea Trout	Salmon	Combined	
North East England	6	4,225	4,593	8,818	47.9
North West England	14	6,447	6,050	12,497	51.6
South West England	22	7,048	2,190	9,238	76.3
South East England	8	807	243	1,050	76.9
*All England**	*50*	*18,527*	*13,076*	*31,603*	*58.6*
Wales	30	17,345	4,269	21,614	80.2
All England & Wales*[1]	80	35,872	17,345	53,217	67.4

*[1]*Excludes the very small rod catches from the Midland and Anglian Regions of England.* *[2]The number of rivers in the regional totals has remained fairly constant throughout the study period.*

Table 2. Mean Annual Rod Catch from Principal Sea Trout & Salmon Rivers in Wales (2004-2014).

River Name	Length (km) *[1]	Mean Catch		Combined Rod catch	Sea trout as % of catch
		sea trout	salmon		
Aeron	28.9	177	4	181	97.8
Afan	18	121	10	132	92.3
Cleddau*[2]	38.8	481	57	538	89.4
Clwyd	50.3	973	94	1068	91.2
Conwy	42.1	459	175	634	72.4
Dee	107.4	372	690	1062	35.0
Dwyfor*[3]	40.2	407	14	421	96.7
Dwyryd	28.3	51	13	64	79.7
Dyfi	44.3	1670	133	1803	92.6
Dysynni	20.3	389	3	393	99.1
Glaslyn	28.1	615	27	642	95.8
Gwendraeth*[4]	23.9	50	0	50	100.0
Llyfni	15.3	152	3	156	98.0
Loughor	33.9	258	31	289	89.2
Mawddach	32.5	628	105	733	85.7
Neath	37.9	435	64	499	87.2
Nevern	32.3	557	35	592	94.0
Ogmore	28.9	445	55	499	89.0
Ogwen	21.2	164	82	246	66.5
Rheidol	45.1	428	31	459	93.2
Seiont	24.6	56	35	90.7	61.4
Taf	38.5	276	98	374	73.7
Taff	49.3	66	35	102	65.3
Tawe	47.3	211	138	349	60.5
Teifi	103.2	2342	553	2895	80.9
Tywi	81.8	2613	580	3194	81.8
Usk	109.2	147	796	943	15.6
Wye	122.1	45	703	748	6.1
Ystwyth	34.9	169	7	176	96.1

*[1] Approximate length of main river from source to sea. *[2] Includes Eastern & Western Branches.
*[3] Includes Dwyfawr & Dwyfach. *[4] Includes Gwendraeth Fawr & Gwendraeth Fach.

The proportion of sea trout in the combined catch of the 50 rivers in England was 58.6% overall. The proportions of sea trout in the English North East and North West regions were similar at 48% and 52% respectively, and broadly equal to the proportions of salmon. However, the proportion of sea trout increased to approximately 76% in each of Southwest and South East regions and was even higher at 80% in the Welsh Region. The Welsh Region, with a mean annual catch of 17,345 sea trout produced 48% of the total catch of 35,872 sea trout for all regions of England & Wales compared with only 25% (4,269) of the total salmon catch (17,345).

Annual rod catch data are frequently summarised and reported as an aggregated total for all the rivers in a geographical region. Harris & Winstone (1990) observed that this common practice may undervalue and misrepresent the relative importance of sea trout if the regional total includes the catch from a small number of the larger and most productive salmon fisheries within that region. This is evident in the Northeast Region, where the Tyne and Tees are two of the most productive salmon rivers in E&W. Their combined catch of 3,869 fish in 2014 represented 48% of the total salmon catch of 8,145 fish for the 50 rivers in England and 36% of the total salmon catch of 10,307 fish reported for all 80 rivers in E&W for that year. In 2014, they also produced more salmon than the combined catch of 2,961 fish reported for all 52 rivers in Wales and Southwest England. Similarly, for the same year in the Welsh region, the two most productive salmon rivers are the Wye and Usk. Their combined catch of just 860 salmon represented 33% of the total catch of 2,630 salmon for all 30 rivers in the region. These two rivers are notable for the absence of any significant run of sea trout. Their combined catch of 102 fish represented only 0.35% of the total catch of 29,560 sea trout for all 30 rivers in the Welsh region in 2014.

Not surprisingly, the relative proportions of sea trout and salmon vary widely for each river within each reporting region. Table 2 summarises the mean annual catch for each of the 30 principal rivers in Wales. With the notable exception of the Wye and Usk (as salmon rivers with few sea trout), the proportion of sea trout in the annual catch exceeded salmon on all other Welsh rivers, ranging from 60 – 99% of the combined catch of both species. It is relevant to note here that the rivers with the highest proportion of sea trout were all short rivers with a main river length of < 50 km.

With the notable exception of the three longest Welsh rivers (Wye, Usk and Dee), where the relative proportions of sea trout were 6.1%, 15.6% and 35% respectively, the sea trout catch dominated the salmon catch on all other rivers: ranging from 60 – 70% on 4 rivers, 70 – 80% on 3 rivers, 80 – 90% on 7 rivers and from 90 – 100% on 12 rivers. Even on the Tywi and Teifi, where the salmon catch was 580 and 553 fish respectively, the proportion of sea trout was >80% of the combined catch of both species.

MONTH OF CAPTURE

The total rod catch at the end of each season does not provide a clear measure of the relative importance of each species to the rod fishery in the different months of the year. A more indicative assessment of importance is provided by a breakdown of the relative contribution of sea trout and salmon to the pattern of rod catches for each species in each month of the annual fishing season. Table 3 summarises the aggregated mean monthly catches of sea trout and salmon for the last 21 years and Figures 2[A-C] provides an example of the main differences in the monthly pattern of catches in three different regions.

The contribution of sea trout to the rod catch in all regions of E&W was greater than salmon in each month of the effective angling season except October (Figure 2^A), when salmon dominated the catch. At a regional level, the sea trout dominated the salmon catch (often by a very large margin) in all months of the season in Wales (Figure 2^B), Southwest England and Southeast England. This general pattern changed in Northeast and Northwest England (Figure 2^C) where sea trout were dominant in the late spring and summer months (March – August) while salmon were dominant in September and October. The increased contribution and importance of salmon in these two northern regions in the last two months of the season reflects their stronger late runs of 'autumn' salmon.

Table 3. The Aggregated Mean Monthly Rod Catch of Sea Trout & Salmon for the Main Reporting Regions of England & Wales (1994 – 2014).

| Reporting Region | Species | Mean no. fish caught in each month of fishing season*[1] | | | | | | | | Total No |
		Mar	Apr	May	Jun	Jul	Aug	Sep	Oct	
Northeast	Sea Trout	0	39	93	368	704	791	897	1219	4110
England	Salmon	62	96	148	258	299	562	1087	1988	4501
Northwest	Sea Trout	13	41	199	838	1608	1578	1271	780	6328
England	Salmon	38	51	97	261	497	891	1803	2315	5953
Southwest	Sea Trout	17	156	477	960	1904	1681	1161	383	6738
England	Salmon	38	61	135	195	260	333	587	283	1893
Southeast	Sea Trout	4	6	20	72	153	200	242	109	805
England	Salmon	1	2	13	34	86	119	118	13	386
Wales	Sea Trout	44	298	742	2601	4646	4250	2966	1082	16629
	Salmon	39	89	238	548	619	696	1076	845	4149
All E&W	Sea Trout	78	540	1807	4838	9015	8500	6537	3572	34885
Regions	Salmon	177	300	631	1297	1761	2601	4671	5445	16883

*[1] *Length of statutory fishing season may vary within and between regions by a few weeks at the start and/or end the year. The sea trout season is generally shorter than the salmon season on most rivers.*

CATCH-PER-UNIT-EFFORT

Catch-Per-Unit-Effort (CPUE) is the number of fishing trips (days or part-days) required to catch a given number of fish. The average number of sea trout and salmon caught by each angler over the fishing season provides a further measure of the relative importance each species. This can expressed as the number of fish caught on each fishing trip or the number of trips required to catch *either* one sea trout *or* one salmon. The number of fish caught by an angler on any one fishing trip represents a measure of 'angler satisfaction' that defines the general attraction and appeal of a fishery.

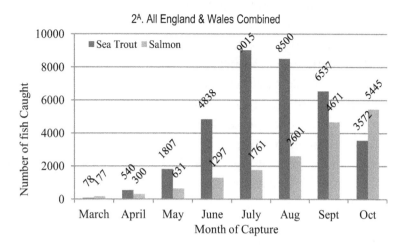

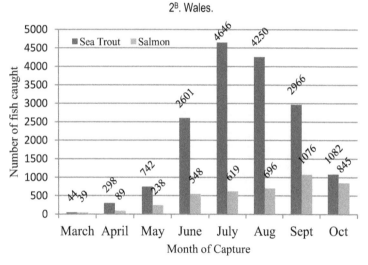

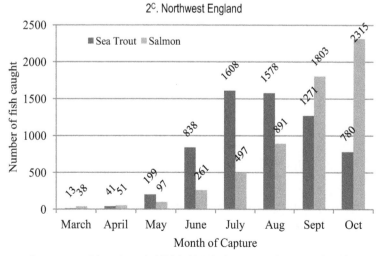

Figure 2 [A-C]. Aggregated mean monthly rod catch (1994–2014) of sea trout & salmon for: 2[A] = rivers in England & Wales combined, 2[B] = Wales and 2[C] = Northwest England.

The average number of fishing trips required to catch one salmon or one sea trout (Table 4) was similar in the Northeast and Northwest regions at approximately 8 days for each species. By contrast, it required fewer days to catch sea trout than salmon in Southwest and Southeast England and in Wales, with anglers spending between 5.4 – 15.9 days to catch one salmon compared with only 2.6 – 4.1 days to catch one sea trout.

A breakdown of angler CPUE for each month of the fishing season would show that the likelihood of catching each species was greatest in the summer months for sea trout while salmon angling improved in the autumn.

Not surprisingly, the aggregated regional CPUE data for all the rivers in each region incorporated a wide range of variability between years. For Wales (Table 5), this ranged from 6.9 – 20.7 days to catch one salmon and 3.3 – 8.9 days to catch one sea trout and, on average for all years, it took twice as long to catch one salmon than one sea trout. However, in no year was the likelihood of catching salmon greater than that for sea trout.

Table 4. Fishing Effort, Annual Rod Catch and CPUE for Reporting Regions in England & Wales (1994-2014).

Reporting Region	Total no. days fished in season	Mean. fishing trips per angler	Mean annual reported rod catch		Mean rod catch per angler fishing trip		No. Days required to catch one fish of either species	
			Salmon	Sea Trout	Salmon	Sea Trout	Salmon	Sea Trout
North East England	36,122	11.4	4,594	4,225	0.127	0.118	7.9	8.4
North West England	50,018	10.3	6,050	6,447	0.125	0.136	8.0	7.4
South West England	24,897	9.2	2,199	7,043	0.088	0.292	11.4	3.4
South East England	2,202	9.0	387	847	0.184	0.391	5.4	2.6
Wales	72,017	12.9	4,461	17,344	0.063	0.246	15.9	4.1
All Regions E&W	192,278	11.2	18,029	36,027	0.096	0.193	10.4	5.2

Days includes full and part days.

TARGETED FISHING EFFORT

Although the mandatory annual catch return form requires each angler to provide details of the number of trips (days or part-days) that were fished on a named river (or rivers) over the annual fishing season, it does not include a breakdown of the amount of that effort that was targeted at *either* salmon *or* sea trout. The inherent assumption that anglers target their fishing effort equally to catch both species at the same time on each fishing trip is basically flawed as each angler would normally adopt a certain style and method of fishing to target either salmon or sea trout in accordance with their personal preferences, weather and water conditions, time of year, the availability of fish and the greater likelihood (= 'reward') of capturing one or another species on any occasion.

Table 5. Annual Fishing Effort, Rod Catch and catch-per-unit-efort (CPUE) for the 30 Principal Migratory Fish Rivers in Wales (1994 – 2014).

Year	Total No. Days*[1] Fished	Reported Rod Catch		Reported Catch per Day fished		No trips required to catch one fish	
		Salmon No.	Sea Trout No.	Salmon	Sea Trout	Salmon	Sea Trout
1994	296,053	24,891	45,759	0.084	0.155	11.9	6.5
1995	245,218	16,006	27,335	0.065	0.111	15.3	9.0
1996	233,313	17,444	29,685	0.075	0.127	13.4	7.9
1997	269,705	13,047	30,142	0.048	0.112	20.7	8.9
1998	236,705	17,109	48,309	0.072	0.204	13.8	4.9
1999	186,977	12,505	47,786	0.067	0.256	15.0	3.9
2000	177,307	17,596	41,322	0.099	0.233	10.1	4.3
2001	133,726	14,383	40,374	0.108	0.302	9.3	3.3
2002	181,557	15,282	49,796	0.084	0.274	11.9	3.6
2003	171,621	11,519	45,101	0.067	0.263	14.9	3.8
2004	188,972	27,332	36,104	0.145	0.191	6.9	5.2
2005	184,330	21,418	40,319	0.116	0.219	8.6	4.6
2006	147,017	19,509	24,269	0.133	0.165	7.5	6.1
2007	164,292	19,984	29,398	0.122	0.179	8.2	5.6
2008	171,827	23,512	27,707	0.137	0.161	7.3	6.2
2009	179,358	15,561	30,359	0.087	0.169	11.5	5.9
2010	188,235	24,826	37,543	0.132	0.199	7.6	5.0
2011	195,963	23,008	35,564	0.117	0.181	8.5	5.5
2012	173,059	18,455	30,700	0.107	0.177	9.4	5.6
2013	168,744	14,920	29,427	0.088	0.174	11.3	5.7
2014	143,856	10,307	29,560	0.072	0.205	14.0	4.9
Mean	*192,278*	*18,029*	*36,027*	*0.096*	*0.193*	*10.4*	*5.2*

[1] Days = full days or part-days fished.

The only information on targeted fishing effort and angler preferences for either salmon or sea trout is available from a pioneer study undertaken by the Environment Agency England & Wales in 2007 (Table 6). This was based on a questionnaire survey of the 22,000 anglers who obtained a licence to fish for salmon and sea trout during the 2006 fishing season. Each angler was asked to cross-reference the details on rod catch and fishing effort (as number of days or part days fished) entered on their mandatory catch return and then provide a breakdown of that effort targeted directly at *either* salmon *or* sea trout on up to three named rivers that they fished that year. The results from the 8,357 completed questionnaires (Robert Evans – *pers comm.*)) provided information on targeted fishing effort from 65 named rivers under the following headings:

    a. night-time fishing for sea trout-only,
    b. day-time fishing for sea trout-only,
    c. day-time fishing for salmon-only,
    d. day-time fishing for both species at the same time.

It is to be noted that night fishing during the period from dusk to dawn is an increasingly popular feature of sea trout angling in England & Wales. It entails fly-fishing during periods of low river levels in the late spring and summer months: when it can be particularly rewarding. In practice, night fishing is unproductive and unsafe when the river is coloured and above normal summer levels. Because it is very rare for anglers to catch salmon during the hours of darkness, it is reasonable to assume that all night fishing is specifically targeted at sea trout.

Table 6. Targeted Angling Effort at Sea Trout & Salmon by Day and Night in England & Wales on 'Priority Rivers'. (2005 Fishing Season).

Reporting Region	All Fishing Effort (Day + Night)	Sea Trout-Only Effort				Day Time Fishing Effort			
		At Night		By Day		Salmon-Only		Both Species*[1]	
		No	%	No	%	No	%	No	%
North East England	15,285	2,595	17.0	574	3.8	4,499	29.4	7,617	49.8
North West England	20,262	4,007	19.8	949	4.7	11,288	55.7	4,018	19.8
South West England	8,643	3,145	36.4	769	8.9	3,217	37.2	1,512	17.5
Welsh Region	32,485	11,881	36.6	2,293	7.1	9,144	28.1	9,167	28.2
All Regions E&W*[2]	76,675	21,628	28.2	4,585	6.0	28,148	36.7	22,314	29.1

*[1] Fishing for both species at the same time on any one fishing trip. *[2] Excludes some rivers and regions with insufficient data.

Night fishing for sea trout-only represented 28.2% of all targeted effort throughout E&W and was most popular in the Southwest of England (36.4%) and Wales (36.6%) compared with the Northeast and Northwest of England at slightly less than 20%. The daytime fishing effort targeted at salmon-only averaged 36.7% overall and ranged from 28.1% in Wales to 55.7%

in Northeast England. Fishing effort targeted at both species together on the same fishing occasion ranged from 17.5% in the Southwest region to 49.8% in the Northeast region and was 29.1% overall. The combined day and night effort targeted at sea trout-only was 20.8% in the Northeast Region compared with 43.7% in Wales. The higher proportions of anglers fishing by day for both species together in the Northeast England, where 12,116 trips (79.9%) out of the total of 15,285 reported trips reflects the strength of the salmon runs in 5 rivers covered by the survey.

Not surprisingly, the results for individual rivers within each region show a wide range of differences in the nature of the targeted effort linked to the likelihood (probability) of catching a salmon or a sea trout on any occasion. In very simple terms, the various rivers covered in the survey could be split into three broad categories based on the nature of the targeted fishing effort. Thus:-

1. *Large rivers producing good salmon catches but very few sea trout.* This is shown by the Wye, where in the absence of sea trout, anglers targeted 78.5% of their effort at daylight fishing for salmon-only with very little night fishing for sea trout-only. Targeted effort at sea trout-only by day (4.3%) and at night (0.9%) was 5.2%, while daytime effort targeted at both species together was 16.4%.

2. *Medium sized rivers producing good catches of both salmon and sea trout.* This is shown by the Tywi, where targeted effort at salmon-only by day was 8.6% compared with 64.6% % targeted at sea trout by both day (9.7%) and night (54.9%). The effort targeted at both species together in daylight was 26.4%: which probably reflects the greater likelihood of catching either species on the same occasion.

3. *Small rivers producing reasonable catches of sea trout but very few salmon.* Total fishing effort on the Rheidol of 1,221 trips was targeted almost entirely at sea-trout-only at 83.7% by day (1.3%) and night (82.4%), with only 0.3% of all daytime trips targeted at sea-trout-only and just 16.0% of effort targeted at fishing for both species on the same occasion. This general picture is common for most of the shorter rivers surveyed.

THE IMPORTANCE OF MINOR RIVERS

Very many of the migratory fish rivers in the British Isles are relatively short streams that generally produce only small runs of salmon and depend largely on the contribution of the stronger runs of sea trout to maintain their recreational rod fisheries. Individually, these minor streams produce only a very small proportion of the rod catch for a given geographical regions and, as such, they are generally considered to be of lesser importance and value than the larger, more productive fisheries when determining management needs and priorities. However, their collective contribution to the social and economic value of the fisheries in any region may be significant, especially in those regions of the British Isles where they are widespread: notably the West of Ireland and the Western Highlands & Islands of Scotland.

This general observation is illustrated by a comparison of the relative importance of sea trout and salmon to the rod catch from of 8 minor Welsh streams. They all flow into Cardigan Bay (West Wales) along a 120 km length of coastline and are located in remote rural areas where general tourism is vital to the local economy. They are less than 30 km in length and almost all of the worthwhile fishing is controlled by local angling clubs that issue angling permits to both local and visiting anglers at a very modest cost.

TOTAL ANNUAL CATCH

Figure 3 shows the aggregated annual catch reported for each river over the 21-year study period and Table 7 provides a breakdown in each year for each river. It is clear that all 8 rivers are essentially '*sea trout rivers with an occasional salmon*' and that the rod fishery is largely, if not entirely, dependent on the presence of moderate runs of sea trout. All streams contain a small, self-sustaining runs of salmon, but salmon catches were rare and a '*nil*' catch occurred in some years over the 21-year period of the record. The relative proportions of sea trout to salmon ranged from 88.9% (Dwyryd) to 98.5% (Dysynni) and was a remarkable 97.1% for all rivers in all years.

MONTH OF CAPTURE

The vital importance of sea trout in sustaining the rod fisheries on these minor streams is

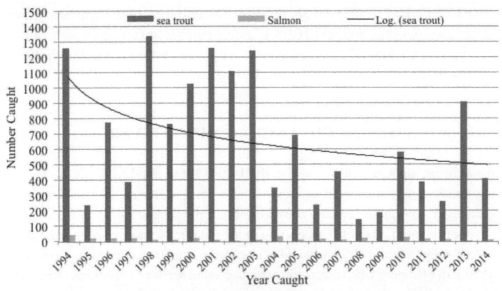

Figure 3. Mean Annual Rod Catch of Sea Trout & Salmon from 8 Minor Streams in Wales (2004 – 2014).

Table 7. Reported Total Annual Rod Catch for Sea Trout & Salmon in 8 Minor Rivers in West Wales (2004-2014)

Relative importance of sea trout & salmon

Year	Dwyfor Salmon	Dwyfor Sea Trout	Dwyryd Salmon	Dwyryd Sea Trout	Glaslyn Salmon	Glaslyn Sea Trout	Dysynni Salmon	Dysynni Sea Trout	Rheidol Salmon	Rheidol Sea Trout	Ystwyth Salmon	Ystwyth Sea Trout	Aeron Salmon	Aeron Sea Trout	Nevern Salmon	Nevern Sea Trout
1994	45	1,261	29	191	47	536	16	670	46	717	23	218	8	537	69	1,182
1995	18	228	21	294	51	491	2	221	50	772	9	50	3	54	56	414
1996	20	775	20	200	32	491	7	499	59	536	10	49	2	152	22	598
1997	23	389	20	101	40	553	8	552	44	390	23	150	3	196	14	180
1998	11	1,337	20	153	21	393	11	729	34	431	32	593	1	481	17	756
1999	12	765	10	181	11	436	2	464	27	927	11	259	6	568	18	893
2000	18	1,027	6	124	9	383	7	435	25	473	18	211	6	280	27	584
2001	11	1,261	17	367	11	240	2	406	30	693	11	223	7	364	31	1,078
2002	8	1,111	33	381	19	1,096	5	343	15	703	8	256	12	777	19	846
2003	7	1,246	16	147	4	534	1	688	12	961	1	83	0	422	34	1,125
2004	31	347	42	70	30	567	5	471	50	551	9	276	18	396	45	606
2005	11	691	17	50	9	592	2	502	38	741	3	107	0	205	27	722
2006	14	23	22	57	17	489	2	284	27	744	5	19	2	35	65	539
2007	9	455	10	48	29	682	2	410	31	587	10	376	1	306	46	415
2008	18	145	21	78	43	520	3	315	62	231	3	132	3	151	36	674
2009	4	187	5	60	22	533	5	420	16	238	5	166	2	96	17	488
2010	26	557	4	26	22	826	4	396	18	197	11	185	3	126	43	755
2011	16	295	8	25	29	680	0	439	31	354	10	261	0	144	22	500
2012	10	248	3	34	26	455	8	371	22	428	9	171	10	313	22	573
2013	6	909	4	37	47	863	5	429	33	355	7	50	1	60	33	345
2014	9	411	4	78	24	562	1	246	16	283	3	115	4	111	31	505
Mean	16	651	16	129	26	568	5	442	33	539	11	188	4	275	33	656

199

Table 8: Mean number of Sea Trout & Salmon Caught each Month of Fishing Season in 8 Minor Rivers (1994-2014)

River Name	Species	Mean Number of fish Reported in Month*[2]								Annual Rod Catch
		Mar	*Apr*	*May*	*Jun*	*Jul*	*Aug*	*Sep*	*Oct*	
Dwyfor	Sea trout	0	2	5	56	159	234	155	30	641
	Salmon	0	0	0	1	1	2	6	5	15
Dwyryd	Sea trout	0	0	0	7	19	50	40	11	127
	Salmon	0	0	0	1	1	3	5	5	15
Glaslyn*[1]	Sea trout	21	111	91	78	82	71	70	23	452
	Salmon	0	1	2	5	4	4	5	4	25
Dysynni	Sea trout	4	28	35	51	98	102	85	19	422
	Salmon	0	0	0	1	1	1	1	1	5
Rheidol	Sea trout	0	2	7	63	155	163	98	32	520
	Salmon	0	1	1	2	4	4	9	11	32
Ystwyth	Sea trout	0	1	3	22	45	60	42	13	186
	Salmon	0	0	0	1	1	1	4	4	11
Aeron	Sea trout	0	2	9	52	87	70	39	13	272
	Salmon	0	0	0	0	0	1	1	2	4
Nevern	Sea trout	0	1	18	106	205	170	96	28	624
	Salmon	0	0	0	2	4	7	11	7	31
All Rivers	Sea trout	25	147	168	435	732	920	629	168	3,224
	Salmon	0	2	3	13	16	23	42	39	138

*[1] Rod catches on the Glaslyn are affected by the tidal sluices to control flooding that delay the normal pattern of downstream migration of smolts and kelts. *[2] Length of annual fishing season was similar on each river and for both species over study period.

further highlighted from the breakdown of the annual catch of sea trout and salmon into their month of capture over the fishing season (Table 8). With perhaps the notable exception of the Glaslyn, over 50% of the very small catch of salmon was taken in the last few weeks of the season (September/October) while sea trout supported the rod fishery in all months from April/May until the end of the season in October. In the absence of worthwhile stocks of salmon, it is evident that these locally important fisheries would cease to exist in the absence of sea trout.

ROD CATCH & FISHING EFFORT

Table 9 shows the mean number of salmon and/or sea trout caught by each angler on each fishing trip over the season and the average number of fishing trips required to catch one salmon or one sea trout. For all rivers, the number of trips required to catch one sea trout ranged from 1.5 days (Dwyfor and Glaslyn) to 2.6 days (Dwyryd) with a combined mean of 1.9 days. By contrast, the number of trips required to catch one salmon ranged from a low of 18 trips (Dwyryd) to a staggering 165 trips on the Aeron and an even higher 267 trips on the Dysynni. Based on the all-rivers average of 14.2 annual trips by each angler, they would each catch an average of 7.5 sea trout a year compared with almost three years required to catch a single salmon at the same level of fishing effort.

The mean annual fishing effort on each river ranged from 326 days (Dwyryd) to 1,265 days (Rheidol) with an aggregated mean for the 8 rivers of 848 days (Table 9). While their individual contribution to the total fishing effort for all 30 principal fisheries in Wales is relatively small, their combined annual fishing effort of 6,781 days represented 13.8% of the total of 49,186 fishing trips made on all 30 Welsh rivers in 2014 and was greater than the 5,640 days spent fishing on four of the top-ten migratory fish rivers in Wales: namely the Dyfi (1,364), Mawddach (1,614), Conway (1,213)and Clwyd (1,449). As such, the collective contribution of these small minor streams to the social and economic benefits of the Welsh region is clearly of considerable local and regional importance.

STOCK ASSESSMENT

By their very nature, small rivers are more vulnerable to the negative effects of relatively minor, small-scale, environmental and man-made impacts that would normally have little tangible effect on larger rivers with more abundant stocks, more extensive spawning and nursery areas and greater stream flows. Figure 4 shows the combined rod catches of sea trout (and salmon) for the 8 minor streams over the last 21 years. It shows a steady decline for sea trout over the period that is most evident since 2003 when the catch decreased steadily from a peak of 698 fish to 288 fish in 2014. Too few salmon were caught to illustrate any trend.

The most recent formal assessments for 2015 of the status of salmon and sea trout in Wales by Natural Resources Wales (Ian Davidson – *pers. comm.*) for these 8 minor streams is cause for some concern about their future ability to sustain attractive and worthwhile fisheries. Salmon stocks were judged to be '*at risk*' in the Dwyfor and Rheidol, '*probably at risk*' in the Dwyryd, Dysynni and Nevern and '*probably not at risk*' in the Glaslyn. [The Ystwyth and Aeron were not assessed for salmon.] For sea trout, the Dwyfor, Dwyryd, Glaslyn and Rheidol were judged to be '*not at risk*', but the Dysynni and Nevern were '*probably not at risk*' while the Ystwyth and Aeron were both '*at risk*'.

Table 9. Mean Annual Rod Catch, Fishing Effort & CPUE for 8 Minor Streams (1994 – 2014).

River	Total. Days*¹ Fished	No. Days fished per angler	Rod Catch Salmon No.	Rod Catch Sea Trout No.	Reported Catch per Day fished Salmon	Reported Catch per Day fished Sea Trout	No. days of effort required to catch one fish Salmon	No. days of effort required to catch one fish Sea Trout
Dwyfor	1,006	13.5	15	667	0.018	0.678	56.5	1.5
Dwyryd	326	14.9	16	129	0.054	0.382	18.5	2.6
Glaslyn	958	14.4	26	568	0.029	0.689	34.3	1.5
Dysynni	1,044	12.7	4	442	0.004	0.464	267.3	2.2
Rheidol	1,265	16.9	33	539	0.028	0.442	36.4	2.3
Ystwyth	395	11.1	9	188	0.025	0.486	40.8	2.1
Aeron	606	16.7	4	275	0.006	0.427	165.0	2.3
Nevern	1,180	13.1	33	648	0.029	0.551	34.0	1.8
Mean	*848*	*14.2*	*18*	*432*	*0.024*	*0.515*	*41.6*	*1.9*

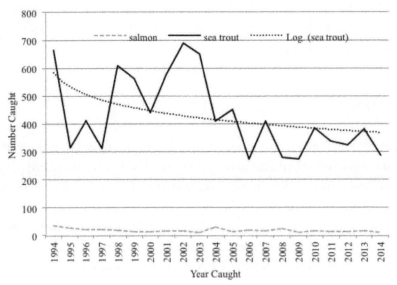

Figure 4. Aggregated Mean Annual Rod Catch of Salmon & Sea Trout for 8 Minor Welsh Rivers (1994-2014).

GENERAL PERSPECTIVE

The decline in salmon stocks (and catches) throughout England & Wales over recent years has increased the status and importance of sea trout in supporting the recreational fisheries at a national, regional and local level. The sea trout has now become the mainstay of the rod fisheries on all but a few of the 80 principal migratory salmonid rivers, with an importance that is equal to or greater than that of the salmon in terms of its greater contribution to a) the total annual catch, b) the monthly pattern of catches over the season and c) its greater likelihood of capture on any fishing trip over the annual season. It is also the preferred target species of anglers fishing by day and at night where the probability of catching a salmon is considered as 'low' or 'unlikely'.

The majority of rivers in most regions of E&W are short 'minor streams' that produce reasonable rod catches of sea trout but sustain only very limited stocks of salmon. While the individual contribution of these minor streams is small in relation to the catch for a region, they are each important at a local community level and their collective contribution to the regional catch may be significant and equivalent to that from several of the larger, more productive and prestigious rod fisheries.

The rod fisheries on these minor rivers are highly or entirely dependent on continued presence sea trout throughout the season. In the absence of sea trout, they would cease to exist as attractive and worthwhile rod fisheries and their social and economic benefits to their local communities and to the region would be lost. These small streams are often low in the order of management priorities. They are particularly vulnerable to damage and degradation of their aquatic environments and their management needs are often overlooked. They should not be neglected.

ACKNOWLEDGMENTS

Part of this work was undertaken as an integral part of Task 2 of the EU-funded Interreg 4A Celtic Sea Trout Project. Our thanks are due Marine Science Scotland, the Environment Agency and Natural Resources Wales for support in accessing and interpreting the catch records stored in their respective statistical databases.

REFERENCES

Butler, J.R.A. & Walker A.F. (2006). Characteristic of the sea trout Salmo trutta (L.) in the River Ewe (Wester Ross, Scotland), in 1888-2001. In: *Sea Tout: Biology, Conservation and Management.* (Graeme Harris & Nigel Milner. *Eds*). Proceedings of the 1st International Sea Trout Symposium, July 2004, Cardiff, Wales. Blackwell Publishing, 45 – 59.

Evans. R. & Harris, G.S. (2017). The Collection of Rod Catch Statistics for Sea Trout & Salmon in England & Wales. (2017). In: *Sea Trout: Science & Management.* (G.S. Harris, *Ed.*). Proceedings of the 2nd International Sea Trout Symposium. October 2016. Dundalk, Ireland. Troubador, 487–506.

Gargan, P.G., Tully, O. & Poole, R. (2003). The relationship between sea lice infestation, sea lice production and sea trout survival in Ireland, 1992 – 2001. In: *Salmon at the Edge.* (D. Mills Ed.).

Proceedings of the 6th International Atlantic Salmon Symposium. July 2002, Edinburgh, Scotland. Atlantic Salmon Trust/Atlantic Salmon Federation, 119 – 135.

Gargan, P.G., Shephard, S., MacIntyre, C. & Finstad, B. (2017) Assessment of the increased mortality risk and population regulating effect of sea lice (*Lepeophtheirus salmonis*) from marine salmon farms on wild sea trout in Ireland and Scotland. In: Sea Trout: Science & Management. (Graeme Harris. *Ed.*). Proceedings of the 2nd International Sea Trout Symposium. October 2015, Dundalk, Ireland. Troubador, 507–522.

Harris, G.S. & Winstone, A.J. (1990). The sea trout fisheries of Wales. In: *The sea trout in Scotland*. (M.J. Picken & W.M. Shearer *Eds*.). Proceedings of a Symposium held at Dunstaffnage Marine Research Laboratory, June, 1987. Scottish Marine Biological Association & Department of Agriculture & Fisheries for Scotland. 25 – 33.

Harris, G. & Milner, N. (2006). Setting the Scene – Sea Trout in England and Wales – A Personal Perspective. In: *Sea Trout: Biology Conservation & Management*. (Graeme Harris & Nigel Milner. *Eds*.). Proceedings of the 1st International Sea Trout Symposium, July 2004, Cardiff, Wales. Blackwell Publishing. 1 – 8.

Milner, N.J., Harris, G.S., Gargan, P., Beveridge, M.., Pawson, M.G., Walker. A. & Whelan, K. (2006). Perspectives on Sea Trout Science and Management. In: *Sea Trout Biology, Conservation & Management*. (Graeme. Harris & Nigel Milner. *Eds*.). Proceedings of the 1st International Sea Trout Symposium, July 2004, Cardiff Wales, Blackwell Publishing. 480 – 490.

Nautilus, (2000). Study into inland and sea fisheries ion Wales. Report prepared for National Assembly for Wales. Nautilus Consultants Ltd., 120 pp.

O'Reilly, P. & Mawle, G. (2006). An Appreciation of the Social and Economic Values of Sea Trout in Wales. In: *Sea Trout Biology, Conservation & Management*. (Graeme Harris & Nigel Milner *Eds*.). Proceedings of the 1st International Sea Trout Symposium, July 2004, Cardiff Wales, Blackwell Publishing. 457 – 465.

Radford, A.F., Hatcher, A.C. & Whitmarsh, D.J. (1991). An economic evaluation of salmon fisheries in Great Britain. Volume1. *Principles, Methodology and Results for England & Wales*. A report prepared for the Ministry of Agriculture, Fisheries & Food. Centre for Marine Resource Economics, Portsmouth Polytechnic. 290 pp.

Scott, J. (1969). *Sea Trout Fishing*. Seeley, Service & Co., London, 216 pp.

Radford, A., Riddington, G. & Gibson, H. (2007). Economic Evaluation of Inland Fisheries: The Economic Impact of Freshwater Angling in England & Wales. Environment Agency Science Report SC050026/SR2. Environment Agency, Bristol, 166 pp.

Spurgeon, J., Colarullo, G., Radford, A.F. & Tingley, D. (2001). Economic evaluation of inland fisheries. Environment Agency R&D Technical Report. Project W2-057. Environment Agency, Bristol. 100 pp.

Marine migrations and distribution of sea trout from rivers in Great Britain

E. POTTER[1], R. CAMPBELL[2], K. SUMNER[3] & S. MARSHALL[4]

[1] Cefas, Pakefield Road, Lowestoft, Suffolk, NR33 0HT, England.
[2] The Tweed Foundation, The Tweed Fish Conservancy Centre, Drygrange Steading, Melrose, Roxburghshire, TD6 9DJ, Scotland.
[3] Environment Agency, Horizon House, Deanery Road, Bristol, BS1 5AH, England.
[4] West Sutherland Fisheries Trust, Gardeners Cottage, Scourie By Lairg, Sutherland, IV27 4PA, Scotland.

ABSTRACT

Tagging and marking have been widely used to study the migratory behaviour, distribution and population dynamics of sea trout. Studies have been conducted around Great Britain (England, Wales and Scotland) for more than 150 years and, although patchy, provide a broad understanding of the migration and distribution of the species in the sea. The studies reveal three broad categories of migratory behaviour. Most fish from rivers in the west and north of Scotland appear to remain in the sea lochs in the neighbourhood of their home river for at least three to four months, and many do not venture further out to sea. Sea trout from rivers in eastern Scotland and around much of the coast of England and Wales, except the north-east, exhibit the second migration pattern. These fish disperse along the coast in both directions from the river of origin, although few migrate more than 150 km away, and many enter neighbouring rivers but do not necessarily spawn there. The third pattern is shown by the sea trout from the River Tweed and rivers in north-east England. The majority of these fish undertake relatively long migrations (>300 km) into the southern North Sea, where conditions are warmer in the summer months and prey species are abundant, but very few appear to enter other rivers. While the majority of tag recaptures have been reported from rivers and coastal fisheries, there is evidence that sea trout from all areas move offshore and that the distribution of recaptures in coastal waters reflects only the edge of the marine distributions of these stocks.

Keywords: sea trout; marine migrations; tagging; Scotland; England; Wales.

INTRODUCTION

Anadromy is an important life-history strategy for trout (*Salmo trutta*) enabling all or part of a population to make use of better growth opportunities in the sea and thereby produce more gametes (Forseth *et al.*, 1999; Thorstad *et al.*, 2016). However, migration into the marine environment may bring with it greater risks associated with increased energetic costs and predation losses (Wysujack *et al.*, 2009). The life history strategies adopted by different populations will therefore be affected by conditions both in freshwater (Olsson *et al.*, 2006) and in the sea in the areas to which the fish may migrate (Thorstad *et al.*, 2016). This in turn will affect stock characteristics, such as the size of the fish, the fisheries in which the stock is exploited and the potential impacts of anthropogenic activities such as salmon farming (Gargan *et al.*, 2012) and renewable energy developments (Malcolm *et al.*, 2010). Understanding the marine migrations of sea trout is therefore of great importance for stock conservation and management.

Tagging has been used for many years to investigate the behaviour and distribution of fish, their population dynamics and their vulnerability to anthropogenic activities, particularly fisheries (e.g. Anon 1867; Calderwood 1922). Many studies have been conducted on migratory salmonids because of their complex life cycles and because these species are particularly amenable to tagging studies as they can be caught and tagged with relative ease as they leave or return to freshwater. This paper brings together available information on the marine migrations of sea trout from rivers around Great Britain (i.e. England, Wales and Scotland) derived from tagging studies conducted in the last 160 years. It draws on original data sources where these are available, published records and reviews, in particular those of Solomon (1995) for England & Wales and Malcolm *et al.* (2010) for Scotland. There are numerous inconsistencies in the reports of the historic tagging studies, and where original data are no longer available, it is very difficult to determine which records are correct; best judgement has therefore been used to identify the most complete data sets.

SEA TROUT TAGGING STUDIES IN GREAT BRITAIN

Table 1 provides a list of tagging studies conducted in the past 160 years to investigate the marine migratory behaviour of sea trout in Great Britain. Brief overviews of those studies in which there were recoveries outside the river or estuary where the fish were tagged are presented below, starting with rivers in the north-east of Scotland and moving in a clockwise direction around Great Britain. The positions of rivers/estuaries in which tagging was undertaken and key recapture locations referred to in the text and tables are shown in Figure 1. Distances between tagging and recapture locations provided in the text are expressed as approximate straight line swimming distances in the sea.

For many of the studies reported here, few details are available of the capture and handling procedures, and although all the studies appear to have employed numbered tags, several different tag types were used. Few details have been found of the tags used prior to the 1950s, but in the 1950s and 1960s, smolts are known to have been marked with small plastic (ivorine) or darkened (oxidised) silver plates attached with silver wire (Anon, 1953; Swain, 1959), and it is likely that similar tags were used in the earlier studies. Subsequently, these tags were replaced by Carlin-type tags which were employed on both smolts and adults (Swain, 1971), until they in turn were replaced in many studies by coded-wire tags (CWTs) for smolts and anchor tags for adults (e.g. ICES, 2008).

A large smolt-tagging programme was undertaken on the Rivers Coquet, Wear and Esk on the English northeast coast between 1985 and 1995 to investigate the exploitation of the salmon and sea trout stocks in specific fisheries (Table 1). Results from these studies are not included below because the smolts were marked with CWTs and tags were generally recovered only from markets where targeted scanning programmes were conducted, principally the fishery on the English northeast coast. A small number of acoustic telemetry studies have also been undertaken on sea trout in estuaries and coastal waters around Great Britain, and where these provide information on fish movements beyond the immediate vicinity of the river, they have been included.

NORTH-EAST & EAST SCOTLAND NORTH OF THE RIVER TWEED

Many of the tagging studies in this area were conducted between about 1913 and 1937 and reported in the Fishery Board for Scotland, Salmon Fishery annual reports (Table 1). Fish generally appear to have been caught using fine-meshed seine nets operated at net and coble fishing stations in estuaries or near river mouths outside the commercial fishing season. Few smolts were tagged at this time, and some of the studies were conducted in the winter months to investigate the behaviour of fish, particularly whitling, that appeared to be over-wintering in estuaries. Later studies which included parr or smolt tagging were conducted on the Rivers North Esk and Tay.

River Conon: In March and Aug-Sept 1936, 622 whitling, 47 adult sea trout (one to three sea winter (1SW – 3SW)) and 10 kelts were tagged in the lower reaches of the River Conon (Nall, 1937). All but one of the recaptures was reported from nets operated in the lower Conon, and the remaining fish was recaptured the following year on the north side of the entrance to the Firth of Tay (over 300 km to the south).

Black Isle, Moray Firth: Nall (1935) describes a small number of recaptures of sea trout that were tagged in the open sea off the Black Isle, to the north of the Inner Moray Firth in 1913 and 1914; these came from the Rivers Conon (45 km east/south), Ness (12 km south), Beauly (24 km south/west) and Don (200 km east/south).

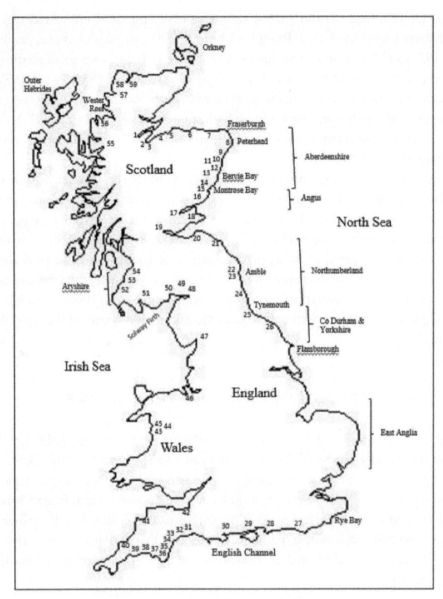

Key to rivers:	13 R. Bervie	25 R.Wear	37 Rs.Tavy, Tamar	48 R.Esk (Border)
1 R. Conon	14 R. N.Esk	26 R.Esk (Yorkshire)	& Lynher	49 R.Annan
2 R. Beauly	15 R. S.Esk	27 R.Ouse	38 R.Looe	50 R. Nith
3 R. Ness	16 Rs. Lunan, Elliot	28 Washbrook Creek	39 R.Fowey	51 R.Cree
4 R. Nairne	and Dighty Burns	29 R.Itchen	40 R.Camel	52 R.Stincha
5 R. Findhorn	17 Rs. Tay & Earn	30 R.Avon (Hants)	41 Rs.Taw & Torridge	53 R.Girvan
6 R. Spey	18 Rs. Eden & Leven	31 R.Axe	42 R.Parrett	54 R.Doon
7 R. Deveron	19 R. Forth	32 R.Otter	43 R.Dyfi	55 Lochs Torridon
8 R. Ugie	20 R. Esk	33 R.Exe	44 R.Dysynni	and Sheildaig
9 R. Ythan	21 R. Tweed	34 R.Teign	45 R.Mawddach	56 Loch Ewe
10 R. Don	22 R.Aln	35 R.Dart	46 R.Dee	57 R.Laxford
11 R. Dee	23 R.Coquet	36 Rs.Avon, Erme,	47 R.Leven, Keer, Sprint	58 R.Polla
12 R. Cowie	24 R. Tyne	Yealm & Plym	and Sambrigg Beck	59 Loch Hope

Figure 1. Map of Great Britain showing rivers (numbered – key below) and place names referred to in the text and tables.

Table 1. Summary of sea trout tagging studies with recaptures outside the river of origin undertaken in Great Britain from 1850 to 2015 *(na = information not available)*

Sampling Location	Dates	Number of fish tagged					Recaptures elsewhere	Reference
		Smolts	Finnock	Sea-trout	Kelts	Total		
Kyle of Sutherland	1934-35		190	148		338	0	Nall 1936
R. Conon	1936		622	47		595	1	Nall 1938
Black Isle, Moray Firth	1913-14					na	4	Nall 1935
Beauly Firth	1921-22		189	69		258	30	Calderwood 1922; Nall 1929
R. Beauly	1921-23		556	350		906	14	Calderwood 1922; Nall 1929
R. Ness	1921-24		248	144		392	13	Calderwood 1922; Nall 1929
R. Findhorn	1925-26		475	15		490	2	Nall 1928a
R. Spey	1925-26	*487*		*73*		560	5	Nall 1928b
R. Ugie	1926-27		217	35		252	1	Nall 1928a
R. Ythan	1926-27					264	6	Nall 1927 & 1935
R. Don	1925	*1044*		*55*		1099	18	Nall 1927
R. Bervie	1933-34		184	2	1	68	9	Nall 1935
Bervie Bay	1933-34					119		
R. North Esk	1933-34		838	90	12	940	94	Nall 1935
	1976-80	7223	2198	303		9724	743	Pratten & Shearer 1983
R. South Esk	1933-34		1053	155	232	1440	63	Nall 1935
R. Tay	1986	400 parr					8	Walker 1987
R. Forth & R. Teith	1915-19					~300	0	Menzies 1919; Nall 1935
R. Tweed	1851-54		406			406	)	Anon 1867; Nall 1935
	1860-64	3967	60		936	4963	) 13	Anon 1867; Nall 1935
	1870-76					na	)	Anon 1876; Nall 1935
	1928-29		301	121	165	596	14	Nall 1930 & 1935
	1937-38		99	182	701	982	7	Nall 1955
	1951-54	18 504				18 504	47	Balmain &. Shearer 1956
	1994-ongoing		710	252		962	4	Tweed Foundation unpub. data
R. Coquet	1951-57	39 350			3936		538	Potter 1987
	1985-94)	7000 CWT				7000	-	Pawson 2008
Amble (nets)	1983-84		439			439	134	Cefas unpublished data
Tynemouth (nets)	1984		186			186	24	Cefas unpublished data
R. Wear	1985-96	57 000+ CWT				57 000+	-	Pawson 2008
R.Esk (Yorkshire)	1979-83	8123					37	Cefas unpublished data
	1994-95	15 000+ CWT				15 000+	-	Pawson 2008
Flamborough (nets)	1983		188			188	45	Cefas unpublished data
East Anglia	1949-55	*1114*		*197*		1311		Potter 1987
Rye Bay	1978					63	8	Cefas unpublished data
R. Axe	1959-66	29 440				29 440	51	Cefas unpublished data
	1959-66				6514	6514	136	Cefas unpublished data
R. Fowey	1978-84					1684	6	Solomon 1995
Rs Dyfi, Dysynni & Maddach	1970s					na	na	Harris & Morgan 1989
Rs Dyfi & Marlais	1980s					na	na	Solomon 1995
R. Dee (Wales)	1990s-ongoing					na	2	Ian Davidson pers. comm.
Rs Leven, Keer, Sprint & Sambrigg Beck	na					na	2	Solomon 1995
R. Esk (Border)	1930-31					901	30	Nall 1935
R. Annan	1931-32					10	0	Nall 1935
R. Nith	1931-32					30	0	Nall 1935
R. Cree	1931-32					64	1	Nall 1935
R. Stinchar	1931-32					387	1	Nall 1935
R. Girvan	1931-32					170	0	Nall 1935
R. Doon	1931-32					562	2	Nall 1935
Wester Ross	1997-98					na	0	Wester Ross Rivers Trust
Lochs Torridon & Sheildaig	2009					48	telemetry	Middlemas *et al* 2009
Loch Ewe	1924-25					77	0	Nall 1935
	1995					12	telemetry	Johnstone *et al* 1995
R. Laxford (Lochs Stack & More)	1925					69	0	Nall 1935
Rs Laxford & Polla	1997-ongoing					4350		Marshall, unpublished data
R. Hope & Loch Hope						na	0	Nall 1925
Outer Hebrides	2014-15					112	0	Paul Hopper pers. comm.
Orkney	1931-32					546	1	Nall 1933

Rivers Beauly and Ness, and Beauly Firth*:* Studies undertaken in the 1920s suggested that whitling, and to a lesser degree adult sea trout, gathered in the Beauly Firth at various times of year to feed (Nall, 1927). There was particular interest in investigating the movements of non-spawners into the rivers flowing into the Firth, including the Rivers Ness and Beauly, and determining whether fish bred in one river spawned in another. Between January 1921 and November 1923, 926 sea trout (60% whitling, 33% older maiden sea trout and 6% kelts) were tagged in the River Beauly (Nall, 1929). The distribution of recaptures was similar for all age groups, and of a total of 31 recaptures, 17 were caught in the River Beauly itself, seven in the Ness (11 km east), six in the Beauly Firth and one in the River Conon (65 km north by sea). During this period, a further 268 fish (73% whitling, 22% older maiden sea trout and 5% kelts) were tagged in the Beauly and Inverness Firths, of which 26 were recaptured in the Beauly Firth, nine in the River Beauly and 17 in the River Ness (Nall, 1929). In a further investigation of stocks around the Beauly Firth, 401 sea trout (64% whitling, 32% older maiden sea trout and 4% kelts) were tagged at the mouth of the River Ness between January 1921 and January 1924 (Nall, 1929). Only 13 of the 133 recaptures were reported from outside the River Ness, one in the River Beauly (11 km west), 11 in the Beauly Firth and one in the River Nairn (43 km east).

River Findhorn*:* As part of a general investigation of the River Findhorn sea trout stock, 475 whitling and 15 adult fish were tagged at the tidal limit between October 1925 and September 1926 (Nall, 1928a). All recaptures (105) were made in the Findhorn or its tributaries, except for two fish caught in the River Spey (35 km east) and one in the River Nairn (17 km west), both about 10 months after tagging.

River Spey*:* Nall (1928b) reported that 560 sea trout (87% whitling and the remainder older sea trout and kelts) were tagged on the River Spey in September 1925 (496) and January 1926 (64). Only 20 recaptures were reported, 15 in the Spey after intervals of one to 21 months. Three of the remaining fish were caught in the lower Findhorn (35 km west), and the other two were caught to the east/south, one in the Ythan (120 km) and one in a bagnet near Peterhead (~95 km).

Rivers Ugie, Ythan and Don*:* Nall (1927; 1928a) describes tagging conducted on the Rivers Ugie, Don and Ythan to investigate the movements of mixed shoals of younger sea trout which were thought to cruise up and down the shore on the east coast, running in and out of estuaries seeking prey and shelter. A total of 217 whitling and about 35 older sea trout were marked in the estuary of the River Ugie in January 1926 and January 1927 (Nall, 1928a). All but four of the recaptures were made in the River Ugie. The other four fish were caught between one and six months after tagging, one each off Peterheard near the mouth of the Ugie itself, at the mouth of the Philorth Burn near Fraserburgh and in the Philorth Burn (both ~25 km north), and in the River Spey (90 km north/west).

Over the same period, 264 sea trout were tagged in the River Ythan (Nall, 1928a; 1935), and out of 42 recaptures, 36 were made in the Ythan, three in the Dee (20 miles south), two in coastal nets about 5 km south of the Ythan and one well upstream in the River Teith over 250 km to the south.

On the River Don, 95% of the 1099 sea trout that were marked at the mouth of the river in January-February 1925 (633) and mid-November 1925 (466) were whitling (Nall, 1927). Thirty of these fish were recaptured, all of which were whitling or parr approaching smolt condition at the time of tagging. Twelve fish were recaptured in the estuary of the Don, but no recaptures were reported from the upper Don, suggesting that many of the fish may have originated from other rivers. Of the remaining 18 recaptures, nine were caught to the south, five in or around the Dee (4 km), one on the coast about 27 km south of the Don, two in the lower reaches on the North Esk (55 km) and one in the River Lunnan (80 km). There were also nine recaptures to the north, six in the Ythan (15 km), one in the Ugie (44 km) and one near Fraserburgh, about 80 km north of the Don.

River Bervie: A total of 68 sea trout were caught and tagged in the lower reaches of the river Bervie between spring 1933 and January 1934, and a further 119 fish were tagged in the sea close to the mouth of the river (Nall, 1935). One fish was recaptured in the River Bervie, seven in Bervie Bay and two in Montrose Bay, just to the south. One of the remaining recaptures was reported from the River Beauly (280 km north), and six fish were caught to the south, three in the Rivers North Esk (14 km), two in the South Esk (19 km) and one in the Forth (~150 km).

River North Esk: There was particular interest in investigating sea trout stocks in the area around Montrose Bay because they supported the most valuable commercial sea trout fisheries in Scotland (Nall, 1935). Netting was undertaken in the lower reaches and estuary of the River North Esk between spring 1933 and January 1934, and 940 sea trout, mainly whitling, were caught and tagged. The majority (83%) of the 149 recaptures were caught in the River North Esk (50) and the River South Esk (58), both of which flow into Montrose Bay about 6 km apart, and in nets within about 6 km (18). Ten of the remaining recaptures had moved to the south, one being reported from the Lunan Water (13 km), seven from netting stations in the Tay (~75 km) and two from the River Forth (~140 km). A further eight recaptures were reported to the north, three in Bervie Bay (15 km), one in the Don (55 km), and one each close to the mouths of the River Don and River Spey (190 km).

Sea trout were also tagged on the River North Esk between 1976 and 1980, over which period 7,223 smolts, 2,198 whitling and 303 adult sea trout were marked (Pratten & Shearer, 1983). Fish tagged as both smolts and whitling were recaptured as far north as the River Spey (190 km) and as far south as the River Tweed (one whitling) (110 km) and the Northumbrian coastal fishery (one smolt) (~160 km), and one smolt was caught in Egersund, Norway (>500 km) in the year after tagging. The full distribution of recaptures is shown in Table 2. The recaptures of adults were mainly distributed along the coast from the River Don (55 km north) of the River Tay (~75 km south) (Table 2), but three fish undertook much longer migrations to the River Barvas, Lewis, on the west coast of Scotland (~460 km), Limfjorden (Denmark) (~650 km) and Kullen (Sweden) (>1000 km) km), all in the year after tagging.

Table 2. Recaptures of sea trout tagged at different life stages in the Rivers North Esk, Tweed and Coquet outside the river where they were tagged (shaded).

Recapture location	North Esk				River Tweed				River Coquet		
	Smolts		Whiting	Adults	Smolts		Kelts	Post-smolts	Smolts		Kelts[1]
	Year of tagging	>=one year after tagging	All recaptures	All recaptures	Year of tagging	>=one year after tagging	All recaptures	All recaptures	Year of tagging	>=one year after tagging	All recaptures
River Spey	1	1	1								
River Deveron			1								
River Ugie	1										
River Ythan	1	1									
River Don			1					1			
River Dee	5	11	4	5				1			
Aberdeenshire		6	5	3				1			1
River Cowie	1	1									
River Bervie	20		4								
River N.Esk								2			
Montrose & Bervie Bay	61	71	20	25							
River S Esk		254	69	80				1			
Angus	1	27						1			
River Lunan/Elliot & Dighty Burns	10	2	3	6							
River Tay		5	3	4			1	5			
Rivers Eden & Leven	11	3	2								
River Forth			2					8			2
River Esk			2								
River Tweed	1	2	2							2	11
River Coquet											
Northumbria	2	2	1		1	1	6		3	84	242
Yorkshire & Durham						2	3		1	6	28
East Anglia					33	1	3		85	8	15
Netherlands					4		4		4	1	1
Germany					1						1
Denmark						2	1		2	2	4
Norway & Sweden		1							2	2	
Offshore					0		1		2	1	14

River South Esk: A total of 1,440 sea trout, mainly whitling, were caught and tagged in the lower reaches and estuary of the River South Esk between spring 1933 and early 1934 (Nall, 1935). Three quarters of the 230 recaptures were reported from the River South Esk and nets at the river mouth (155), the River North Esk (15) or nets within 10 km of the South Esk (23). Of the remaining 25 recaptures, 12 had moved south, three to the Tay estuary (75 km), five to the River Earn (75 km), two to the River Forth (140 km), one to the Northumberland coast (>150 km), and one was caught by a trawler north of the Dogger Bank (about 250 km). A further 13 fish were caught to the north, nine in coastal nets between 20 km and 60 km north, two in the River Dee (55 km) and one each in the River Don (60 km) and River Deveron (160 km).

River Tay: Walker (1990) tagged 400 trout parr and 1,262 adult sea trout prior to spawning in tributaries of the River Tay. Most of the recaptures were in the burns in which the fish were tagged, but five of the parr were caught in the River Earn, two as brown trout and three as sea trout. Three of the adult sea trout were also caught outside the Tay, one near Montrose (~75 km north), one just south of Peterhead (~150 km north) and one off the River Coquet (~180 km south).

RIVER TWEED AND EASTERN ENGLAND

Tagging studies in this area were initiated in the 1950s to investigate the movements of sea trout on the east coast of England and in the southern North Sea. This included some of the first large-scale smolt tagging programmes, which were conducted on the Rivers Tweed and Coquet,

River Tweed: Between 1951 and 1954, staff of the Scottish Home Department (SHD) caught up to 5000 smolts per year (total 18,504) by seine netting in the lower reaches of the River Tweed and marked them with darkened silver or celluloid plate tags (Anon, 1953). All the recaptures outside the River Tweed itself were reported from coastal fisheries to the south in north-east England, East Anglia and subsequently in Netherlands and Germany. There were no recaptures as whitling in the Tweed or other rivers (Table 2). In the year after tagging recaptures were reported off the coasts of Norfolk (1) and Denmark (2), and maturing fish were caught off Durham (2) and Northumberland (1).

A number of studies have also been conducted to mark maiden whitling and kelts on the River Tweed since the 1850s (Table 1) (Anon. 1867 & 1876; Nall, 1930). There are records of 19 recaptures of kelts with a distribution similar to that for smolts in the year after tagging (Table 2), and only one recapture was reported from north of the Tweed, in the River Tay. The pattern of recoveries of maiden whitling, however, is quite different, with all 20 recaptures being reported from north of the Tweed between the Rivers Forth and Don (Table 2).

River Coquet: In 1951, the Ministry of Agriculture, Fisheries and Food (MAFF) installed a fixed Wolf grid trap in the pool and traverse fish pass around the Warkworth Dam at the tidal limit of the River Coquet to catch downstream migrating fish. A total of 39,350 sea trout smolts was tagged between 1951 and 1957 using similar tags to those employed on the River Tweed, and between 1951 and 1956, 3,936 sea trout kelts were tagged using Einar Lea hydrostatic tags (Anon, 1953; Potter, 1990). Apart from 16 fish caught in freshwater which were thought to be resident trout, the smolt tagging yielded 99 recaptures before the first sea-winter (Table 2). As for the Tweed, post-smolts were recaptured moving southwards along the coast after leaving freshwater, with small numbers caught on the Northumbrian (3) and Yorkshire (1) coasts in the following few weeks, 85 reported from the East Anglian coast between June and August, and recaptures later in the year on the Dutch (4), Danish (2), and Swedish and Norwegian coasts (2); two tags were also returned from trawlers fishing in the southern North Sea. A further 149 recaptures were made after at least 1SW, mainly on the north-east coast of England (90) and in the River Coquet itself (43), but also on the coasts of East Anglia (8) Netherlands (1), Denmark (2), Sweden (1), Norway (1) and offshore (1). Only two recaptures were reported north of the River Coquet, both 1SW fish caught in the River Tweed. No post-smolt or 1SW recaptures were reported from other rivers to the south.

A total of 406 of the kelts were recaptured in the year of tagging and 157 in subsequent years, with 115 (28%) and 127 (81%) being caught in the River Coquet itself in the same and subsequent years respectively. As with the smolts, the majority of the recaptures outside the Coquet were made to the south on the coasts of East Anglia, Netherlands and Denmark, and 270 were caught on the English north-east coast as returning spawners, predominantly in the year of tagging. Only 15 fish (2.6%) were caught to the north of the Coquet; 11 in the River Tweed, and the others in the River Forth (2), the River Tay (1) and on the Aberdeenshire coast (1).

River Esk (Yorkshire): Between 1979 and 1983, 8,123 sea trout smolts and 176 kelts were tagged at a fish trap operated at Ruswarp Weir on the River Esk (Yorkshire). Recaptures of the smolts were reported on the East Anglian coast (6) in the year of tagging, and then, in the following year, to the south of the Esk (10) and close to the mouth of the Esk (18). Similar results were obtained from the kelt tagging with recaptures on the East Anglian coast (2), to the south of the Esk (8), close to the mouth of the Esk (10) and in the Esk itself (3).

English north-east coast: Adult sea trout were tagged at Flamborough, Tynemouth and Amble on the English north-east coast during 1983 and 1984, to investigate the origin of the fish being exploited by the coastal fixed nets (Cefas, *unpublished data*). A total of 813 sea trout on their spawning migration were tagged at the three locations (Table 3). Of the 203 recaptures, 82 (40%) were made local to the tagging area, 21 (10%) to the south and 100 (49%) to the north, thus confirming the generally northward movement of returning adult sea trout along this coast.

Table 3. Recaptures in the year of tagging of sea trout tagged in coastal fisheries on the east coast of England.

Netting Area (North to South)	Years of tagging	Total Tagged	Recapture Locations (Relative to Netting Area				
			To South	Local Area	To North (England)	To North (Scotland)	Total
Amble	1983 - 84	439	11	68	52	3	134
Tynemouth	1984	186	9	7	8	0	24
Flamborough	1983	188	1	7	37	0	45
East Anglia	1949 - 55	1281	1	50	21	0	72

East Anglian coast: In addition to the smolt and kelt tagging conducted on the Tweed and English north-east rivers in the 1950s, complementary studies were undertaken by MAFF and SHD to tag sea trout caught off the East Anglian coast (Potter, 1990). Sea trout were tagged between June and August in 1949 (79), 1950 (444) and 1955 (788) (Table 3) and included post-smolts (~85%) and older maiden fish and previous spawners (~15%), as estimated from the bimodal size distribution. All but one of the recaptures of fish tagged in 1949 and 1950 were caught locally within a short period of tagging, but no recapture details are available. From the 1955 tagging, 58 fish were recaptured in the same year, 50 in local fisheries on the East Anglian coast soon after the fish were released, one in the River Ouse, in southeast England, six on the English northeast coast between Flamborough and Amble, and two in the River Coquet. No tagged fish were recaptured on the East Anglian coast in the years after tagging, although recoveries were reported from the coastal fishery between Whitby and the Scottish border (5) and in the Rivers Esk (1), Coquet (1), Aln (1) and Tweed (4).

SOUTHERN ENGLAND

Information is available from three sea trout tagging studies that have been undertaken on the south coast of England, in Rye Bay in the south-east and on the Rivers Axe and Fowey in the south-west.

Rye Bay: A tagging study was conducted in Rye Bay in 1978 to investigate the stocks of sea trout that were being exploited as by-catch in a local net fishery for bass (cefas, *unpublished data*). A total of 63 sea trout were tagged, ranging in length from 380 mm to 625 mm. Eight fish were recaptured, all within Rye Bay between one and 21 days after tagging. There were no recoveries in fresh water, and so no information was obtained on the potential origin of these fish.

River Axe: In 1959, the MAFF constructed a counting fence at the tidal limit on the River Axe in south Devon with the objective of monitoring all salmonid movements in and out of the river to investigate their population dynamics (Allan, 1964). Between 1960 and 1966, 29,440 emigrating sea trout smolts and 6,514 kelts were marked using a variety of different tags, including darkened silver and Carlin tags (Swain, 1959; 1971). A total of 51 of the smolts were recaptured outside the River Axe, 40 as whitling and 11 as older sea trout. Most of the recaptures were made by rod fisheries, whitling generally being too small to be caught in most estuary nets. Half of the recaptures (25) were reported from the River Otter (20 km west) and eight were reported from rivers further to the west, two in each of the Exe (28 km), Teign (30 km) and Dart (55 km) and one each in the River Fowey (140 km) and the River Camel, the latter being over 300 km by sea on the north side of the peninsular. A further nine of the smolts were caught to the east, eight in the Hampshire Avon (105 km) and one in the Fishbourne Creek at Chichester (165 km).

Although the 136 kelts recaptured outside the River Axe were distributed over a similar range to the smolts, many more were caught to the west (116) than to the east (17). Half the recaptures came from the three closest rivers, the River Otter (19), the River Exe (11) and the River Teign (37). Recaptures were also reported from many of the rivers to the west of the River Teign, including the Rivers Dart (7), Devon Avon (7), Erme (1), Yealm (1), Plym (4), Tavy (3), Tamar (3), Lynher (4), Looe (1), and Fowey (4) on the south coast, and 13 recaptures came from the north side of the peninsular, including 11 from the Rivers Taw and Torridge (380 km) and one fish from the River Parrett (450 km by sea). Twice as many of these recaptures were reported by rods (120) compared with nets (58), suggesting that many of the fish had moved up into freshwater. The majority of the recaptures to the east were taken in coastal nets (13), with the remaining four being taken in rivers between the River Axe and the Itchen. Three kelts were recaptured on the French coast along the Cherbourg peninsular.

River Fowey: Between 1978 and 1984 studies were conducted to investigate the impacts of the Colliford Reservoir scheme on the River Fowey sea trout stock (Solomon, 1995). A total of 1,684 adult sea trout (whitling or older) were tagged at traps near the tidal limit and on a spawning tributary, most on their upstream migration. Only six recaptures were reported outside the River Fowey, one by an angler on the West Looe River (15 km east), and five in coastal nets between 10 km west and 180 km east (Solomon, 1995 – *reporting undated information from Sambrook*).

WALES AND NORTH-WEST ENGLAND

Welsh rivers: There have been relatively few recorded sea trout tagging studies conducted in Wales and the north-west of England. Harris & Morgan (1989) refer to studies conducted on the neighbouring Rivers Dyfi, Dysynni and Mawddach during the 1970s in which large numbers of sea trout were tagged, but the original data are no longer available (Graeme Harris, *pers. comm.*). However, Harris & Morgan (1989) report that several fish tagged as smolts were recaptured off the east and south east of Ireland within a few weeks of tagging, a number of fish tagged as kelts were recovered in the vicinity of Arklow (Co. Wicklow, Ireland) (~150 km) and one adult fish from the River Dyfi was recaptured in Co. Kerry, on the south-west coast of Ireland (>450 km).

Tagging was also reported to have been conducted in several Welsh rivers in the early 1980s (Solomon, 1995). Most of the recaptures came from the rivers of tagging, but one fish tagged in the River Dyfi was recaptured in the River Mawddach and a further two were recaptured off the Irish coast in the year after tagging, one off Dungavon, Co. Wicklow (eastern Ireland) and one off Cod Head, Co. Cork (southwest Ireland). A tagging study was also conducted in the estuary lagoon of the River Glaslyn, known as the Cob (Solomon, 1995). Of the 780 sea trout tagged, 110 were recaptured, mainly in the Cob (102) and in the River Glaslyn itself (4). In addition, one fish was taken in the River Mawddach (55 km south), one at the mouth of the River Dwyfawr and two in this river (18 km north/west).

Sea trout have been tagged on the River Dee as part of the Dee Stock Assessment Programme, which has been ongoing since 1990 (Ian Davidson, *pers. comm.*). For the first three years of the programme, sea trout were tagged with anchor tags, but since then marking has been with visible implant (VI) tags placed under the skin behind the eye; these marks are difficult to see and so are rarely reported by fishermen. Two fish tagged as adults or kelts recoveries have been reported from outside the Dee, one in the River Conwy (60 km west) and one in the Border Esk (over 200 km north).

Cumbrian rivers: Solomon (1995) also reported details of fish tagged after stripping, having been collected for broodstock on the Rivers Leven, Keer, Sprint and Sambrigg Beck in north-west England. Although all fish were released into the River Kent, four were recaptured in the river from which they were collected. Two others were recaptured on the River Lune (20 km south) and at the mouth of the River Dee, Wales (100 km south).

WEST AND NORTHWEST SCOTLAND AND ORKNEY

A number of tagging studies were conducted in rivers flowing into the Solway Firth and on the west and north of Scotland in the 1930s, and further tagging and telemetry investigations have been conducted in more recent years.

Solway Firth: Nall (1932) reported that 901 sea trout were tagged in the lower part of the Border Esk in north-west England in 1930 (340) and 1931 (561). Of the 52 recorded recaptures, 22 were made in the River Esk or its tributaries, 20 in the coastal nets on the north side of the Inner Solway Firth and two in the nets on the south side of the Firth. In addition, three fish were recaptured in the River Eden and one each in the Rivers Sark, Annan and Urr, all of which flow into the Firth. There were only two recaptures outside the Solway area, one at the mouth of the River Calder, 90 km to the south, and one on the west side of the Irish Sea near Dublin after a year at sea. Sea trout were also tagged in the Rivers Annan (10), Nith (30) and Cree (64) in the spring of 1930 (Nall 1935). One fish from the Cree was recaptured in the inner Solway (85 km east) but no others were caught outside the river where they were tagged.

Ayrshire rivers: In 1931 and 1932, sea trout were marked on the Rivers Doon (562), Girvan (170) and Stinchar (387) (Nall 1933a). One fish from the Stinchar was recaptured 10 km to the south and two fish from the Doon were caught in the Ayr estuary (4 km north) and well up the River Stinchar (35 km south) respectively.

Upper Loch Torridon and Loch Shieldaig: Middlemas *et al.* (2009) marked 48 sea trout post-smolts with acoustic tags in Upper Loch Torridon and Loch Shieldaig and used logging acoustic receivers to follow their movements. The fish generally dispersed slowly into the marine environment in the weeks following emigration from fresh water, with only 36% of them being detected >6 km from their release site. Five left the study area to move further out to sea and two re-entered fresh water.

Rivers Laxford and Polla: A tagging programme has been operating in west Sutherland since 1997 (Marshall, *unpublished data*). Sea trout have been caught, primarily by seine net, within the estuaries of two rivers, the River Laxford on the west coast and the River Polla on the north coast, and 4,350 fish have been tagged using VI tags inserted behind the eye. Few recaptures have been reported other than in the Rivers Laxford and Polla, although this is likely to be partly due to the difficulty in identifying marked fish. One kelt from the River Laxford was recaptured 6 weeks after tagging about 60 km away in Loch Hope, and other post-smolts and kelts have been recaptured in the River Laxford, after being tagged in the River Polla (5), or vice versa (1), also a distance of about 60 km

Orkney: In 1931 and 1932, sea trout were tagged in and around Graemshall Loch (287) and St Mary's Loch (259) and all recaptures were made within about 3 km of the tagging site (Nall, 1933b). In 1927 and 1928 sea trout were tagged on South Uist in the Howmore (618), Kildonan (182) and Bharp (77) systems. All but one of the 16 recaptures was in the system where the fish was tagged; one fish tagged in the Howmore River was recaptured in the Lower Kildonan Loch about 10 km to the south.

DISCUSSION

While tagging studies can provide invaluable data on the behaviour and distribution of fish, recapture data must be interpreted with care. The tagging studies described above were undertaken over a period of more than 100 years using a variety of different experimental procedures and tags. The equipment used to capture and handle fish, including the lack of anaesthetics, in the earlier studies may have caused more mortalities than modern techniques. While few details are available of the tags used, it is quite likely that the early tags made little allowance for the growth of the fish, a problem addressed in the development of Carlin-type tags in the 1960s (Swain, 1971), and so they may not have been very easy to see once the fish had grown for a few months. In addition, disseminating information on tagging studies to anglers and netsmen may have been more difficult, and Menzies (1919), for example, reports tags being discarded by some anglers as being of no value.

The studies were also conducted at different times of year, often targeting different age groups of sea trout which would not have been representative of a particular river stock. Recaptures were mainly reported from fisheries targeting migratory salmonids and so will have been biased by the locations and times that fishing took place. Coastal and estuarine recaptures were generally made by net fisheries which operated in restricted areas for limited periods in the summer (mainly May – August), and these fisheries were often targeting salmon and so were likely to be selective for larger sea trout. Most of these fisheries operated very close to the shore, apart from the English north-east coast drift net fishery, and so recaptures offshore were largely limited to bycatch in fisheries for marine species. River recaptures were mainly made by rod fisheries which had a longer fishing season than the nets but which may also have targeted particular groups of fish. The level of exploitation by both nets and rods varies significantly between different rivers and coastal areas, and salmonid net fisheries in particular have been greatly reduced in the past 50 years. As a result, comparison of recapture rates in different fisheries must be interpreted with care.

These caveats mean that it is only possible to draw general conclusions about the migration of sea trout around the coast of Great Britain from the tags recaptures. Nevertheless, the tagging studies show three distinct patterns of movement and distribution: (1) local movements mainly within estuaries and sea lochs; (2) coastal dispersal with little evidence of directed migration and only a few long distance movements; and (3) longer distance directed migrations.

The first migration pattern is exhibited by stocks on the west and north coast of Scotland, where both conventional tagging and telemetry studies suggest that many of the fish remain within the sea lochs in the neighbourhood of the river in which they were tagged and do not move further out into coastal waters. The locally constrained movements of these stocks have been noted by other workers (Nall, 1935; Pemberton, 1976). Pemberton (1976) undertook seine netting surveys in a number of sea lochs during the summer and concluded that post-smolts remained there for three to four months before moving to the open sea in late June and July. Similar behaviour has been observed for sea trout post-smolts in Norwegian Fjords (Finstad *et al.* 2005; Thorstad *et al.*, 2007). Finstad *et al.*, (2005), for example, reported that only four (23%) out of 15 sea trout smolts acoustically tracked at the mouth of the River Eira were detected moving into the outer part of the fjord system, while the rest of the fish seemed to remain in the inner fjord.

The dispersal of sea trout in these circumstances may be restricted because they are protected from strong coastal currents by the topography of the coast and because the sea lochs provide good feeding for the early post-smolts. Potter *et al.* (2017) suggest that the movements of sea trout post-smolts in the Irish and Celtic Seas may be explained largely by passive movements with the prevailing currents tempered by a tendency to remain close to the shore. If sea trout emigrating from Scottish west coast rivers adopt the same behaviour, they would be likely to remain in the sheltered sea lochs close to their river of origin as seen in these tagging studies.

However, as noted by Nall (1935), the opportunities for recapture of tagged fish on the west coast of Scotland may be limited outside of the river of origin. Thus while the early post-smolt movements have been confirmed by the telemetry studies of Johnstone *et al.* (1995) and Middlemas *et al.* (2009), the duration of the studies was quite short, and it is not possible to say whether any of the fish moved offshore subsequently.

The second pattern of migration is that more commonly recognised for sea trout around the coast of Great Britain. Fish disperse along the coast in both directions from the river of origin, with relatively few being recaptured more than 150 km away and many entering neighbouring rivers but not necessarily spawning there. This behaviour is seen for stocks on the east coast of Scotland, from the River Forth northwards and for most stocks in England and Wales, except those in the north-east; it is well illustrated by sea trout from the River North Esk (Pratten & Shearer, 1983) (Table 2). The distribution of recaptures from this river is similar for all life-history stages, with fish moving both north and south along the coast. The large tagging study on the River Axe also demonstrates this pattern of migration, with both smolts and kelts being recaptured to the east and west, most in the lower reaches of other rivers supporting stocks of sea trout. In this case, the distribution of recaptures was skewed to the west of the Axe, particularly for kelts. It is unclear whether this represents a significant bias in the movements of the fish, because there are many more rivers supporting stocks of migratory salmonids to the west, and these provide more opportunities for recaptures in the rod and net fisheries targeting these species. The smaller-scale studies on other rivers along the east coast of Scotland to the north of the R. Forth and in England also show fish dispersing in both directions along the coast, and similar behaviour has been reported from other areas such as the Baltic (Degerman *et al.*, 2012).

The River Tweed and north-east English stocks exhibit the third pattern of migration, with the majority of the fish appearing to migrate relatively long distances into the southern North Sea. The two large tagging studies based on the Rivers Tweed and Coquet illustrate this migration pattern (Table 2). In both of these studies, nearly all recaptures of fish tagged as smolts or kelts were made to the south. Many fish were recaptured in the southern North Sea (> 300 km south) in the year of tagging, and small numbers were recovered further round the North Sea rim in the same or following years. Adult fish from these rivers were also recaptured on their spawning migrations, returning northwards along the north-east coast of England, and tagging of adult fish in East Anglia and on the north-east coast has confirmed the directed return migration of sea trout to these rivers with very few recaptures being reported to the north of their river of origin. The recaptures of fish tagged as kelts on the Rivers Tweed and Coquet show similar distributions as those tagged as smolts, and similar patterns were observed for other sea trout stocks on the English north-east coast (Rivers Wear and Esk (Yorkshire)). Unlike the first two patterns of movement, there do not appear to be any other published accounts of sea trout stocks where the majority of the fish make long directed migrations of this type. However, there is limited information available on the movements of many sea trout stocks and a wider review would be merited.

Care must be taken in interpreting the recoveries of fish tagged as whitling or adults in estuaries because these fish may not originate from that river. Thus post-smolts tagged during the winter in the estuary of the Tweed show a distribution that contrasts with that of smolts tagged on the Tweed and Coquet and which derives from the Tweed's position at or near the boundary between the two types of migration (Table 2). Some of the fish tagged as smolts on more northerly rivers (e.g. North Esk) come as far south as the Tweed, and such fish from the north are likely to have been caught and tagged as post-smolts in the Tweed estuary, along with some Tweed fish that were remaining in the local coastal area. These fish from the north were then recaptured back in or on route to their home rivers, including the Forth, Teith, Tay, South Esk, North Esk, Don and Dee (Table 2). As some fish from these northern rivers will survive to spawn again, this may also account for the recapture to the north of a few kelts tagged in the Tweed estuary. This example shows the importance of knowing the origin of any sea-trout tagged. Only emigrating smolts can be assumed to be within their home rivers; this cannot be assumed for kelts, post-smolts and adults tagged on the lower stretches of rivers or in estuaries.

The rather abrupt change between stocks on the east coast of Great Britain exhibiting the second migration pattern (River Forth northwards) and the third migration pattern (River Tweed southwards) has been described previously by Potter (1990) and Solomon (1995) and requires some consideration, as the River Tweed is only about 70 km south of the Firth of Forth. The southern part of the North Sea (off East Anglia) is shallower than the northern part (off eastern Scotland) and provides a larger feeding area for sea-trout than the narrow coastal strip of shallow water along the east coast of Scotland (European Environment Agency, 2009). There is also a high abundance of prey species such as sprat and sandeel in the southern area (ICES FishMap), and, during the summer months, sea temperatures are at least 5°C higher throughout the water column compared with the Scottish east coast (Paramor *et al.*, 2009). These conditions should provide significantly better growth opportunities than local coastal waters for stocks from east coast rivers, but the advantages will differ among stocks and must outweigh the risks if fish are to undertake the longer migrations.

The coastal current that runs down the whole of the east coast of Britain, from the north of Scotland to the English Channel, and then continues in an anti-clockwise direction around the southern North Sea, the continental and Scandinavian coasts (European Environment Agency, 2009) should facilitate the southerly movement of sea-trout post-smolts from all east coast rivers. The timing of the post-smolt recaptures from the Tweed and Coquet suggest that these fish may move with this current around the southern North Sea. Thus post-smolts from the Tweed and Coquet were caught off Yorkshire after 30 days (1), East Anglia after an average of 68 days (30) and the coasts of Netherland and Germany after an average of 114 days (6), with subsequent recoveries of older fish on the North Jutland coast after an average of 552 days (2). However, there is a back-circulation into the Firth of Forth that breaks the southerly current into two parts (Ecomare, 2015) and may affect the ability of fish from the more northerly river to utilise it to migrate easily southwards.

Another clear distinguishing feature between these two groups of stocks is that while a large proportion of the sea trout exhibiting the second migration pattern make their first return to fresh water as whitling, many of which do not spawn, individuals from the third group make their first return almost exclusively as mature older fish. Thus the long distance migration is associated with the fish returning at a significantly larger size than the locally migrating stocks and also possibly having a higher rate of repeat spawning. This is demonstrated by the size distribution of the largest sea-trout reported daily to the FishPal angling websites (http://www.fishpal.com) for the Rivers Tweed and Tyne (southerly migrating fish) and the Rivers Dee and Tay (locally migrating fish to the north of the Tweed) (Figure 2). In addition, very few fish from the Tweed and Coquet were recaptured in rivers other than the one in which they were tagged.

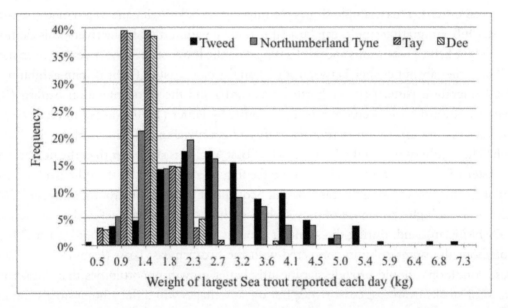

Figure 2. The largest sea-trout reported daily to the FishPal angling websites for the Rivers Tweed, Northumberland Tyne, Tay and Dee. Sea trout from the first two of these rivers can make a long southward migration, while almost all the fish from the other two rivers make only local, coastal, migrations.

While there are no net fisheries for migratory salmonids in the estuaries of the English north-east coast rivers and runs of these species were severely depleted in several of these rivers (e.g. Rivers Tyne and Wear) in the mid-20th Century, recaptures might have been expected in rod fisheries in the lower reaches of rivers such as the Aln, Coquet and Esk (Yorkshire) if the fish entered them. The absence of these recaptures indicates another marked difference in the behaviour of the fish in these two groups. This contrasts with the behaviour of fish exhibiting the second migration pattern, many of which enter other estuaries and rivers as whitling and overwinter there without spawning (Nall, 1927; Degerman *et al.*, 2012). Koed *et al.* (2007) tested the hypothesis that hypo-osmoregulatory capacity is compromised by low temperature and concluded that overwintering in freshwater was partly driven by this physiological effect.

It is possible, therefore, that warmer winter temperatures in the southern North Sea allow the fish to remain out at sea during the winter, thereby providing further improved growth opportunities for the long distance migrants.

It is unlikely to be possible to attribute the third migratory pattern to a single specific cause because many factors will affect the risks and benefits of adopting different life-history strategies. Nevertheless, the marked difference in behaviour between the two groups of stocks that are separated by only a relatively small distance on the east coast of Great Britain is surprising. While the third migration pattern may be consistent with the largely passive dispersal mechanisms described by Potter *et al.* (2017) for stocks in the Irish Sea, it is not clear that the markedly different behaviour of fish from the North Esk and the Tweed could be accounted for by the same simple behavioural rules, and this deserves further investigation.

While the great majority of the recaptures in the above tagging studies were made in coastal fisheries around Great Britain, there is evidence of offshore movements in most areas. Thus, fish from the River Axe in south west England were recaptured on the French coast, fish from Welsh and north west English rivers were recaptured on the Irish coast, and fish from English and Scottish east coast rivers were caught on the coast of Scandinavia. There are too few recaptures in most studies for meaningful comparison of the rates of offshore movement or the distances travelled. Evidence of offshore movements has also been obtained from incidental catches in marine fisheries. Balmain & Shearer (1956) compiled information on catches of approximately 160 sea trout, including some recaptures of tagged fish, taken at sea between about 1850 and 1950. Most of these reports were from the Scottish east coast up to 100 km offshore, but small numbers came from west and south-west Scotland. There was also a programme to record sea-trout caught offshore by trawlers in the southern North Sea between 1955 and 1957 (Potter, 1990). This yielded 168 reports, nearly all of which came from an area about 100 km wide and extending about 250 km north east of the East Anglian coast, with the majority being taken between 50 and 150 km offshore. Most of the catches were reported to have been made between May and September, although a few were reported in April and one in December. While these catches will have been biased by the distribution of marine net fisheries, they support the idea that the fish are not confined to coastal areas as might be suggested by the majority of the tag recaptures but disperse much more widely as suggested by the particle tracking simulations conducted by Potter *et al.* (2017).

CONCLUSIONS

Tagging has been undertaken for well over 100 years to investigate the movements of sea trout in the sea, and although methods have changed significantly over time, the results provide a good overview of the movements of stocks around the coast of Great Britain. The results suggest that there are three broad patterns of behaviour:

1. Stocks on the west and north coasts of Scotland tend to remain in the sea lochs and estuaries close to their river of origin for several months and many fish may not move further out into the sea at all.

2. Stocks on the Scottish east coast north of the River Forth and around most of England and Wales, except the north-east, disperse away from their home river in both directions along the coast, often entering neighbouring estuaries and rivers but not necessarily spawning there. While the majority of these fish remain relatively close to their home river small numbers may migrate more than 150 km.

3. Stocks from the English north-east coast rivers and the River Tweed, undertake much longer directed migrations to the southern North Sea and, as a result, very few return to their home river as whitling. This behaviour is likely to be driven to some extent by the warmer conditions and better feeding opportunities in this area.

The patterns of tag recaptures in coastal and estuary fisheries is likely to be just the edge of the total distribution of the stocks because many studies have revealed extensive offshore movements. This could be investigated further by particle tracking simulations.

ACKNOWLEDGEMENTS

We would like to acknowledge the work of the many unnamed scientists and volunteers who have assisted with the capture and tagging of many thousands of sea trout over the years and the assistance of both commercial and recreational fishermen in reporting recaptures. Preparation of this paper was funded in part by the Department for the Environment, Food and Rural Affairs (Defra), U.K. Government, under contracts C6165 and SA001.

REFERENCES

Allan, I.R.H. (1964). The salmon and sea trout stocks of the R. Axe, Devon. *Annals of Applied Biology*, **53**, 3, pp 497-498

Anon. (1867). Reports on the Natural History and Habits of Salmonids in the Tweed and its Tributaries. Appendix, Section XX, Extracts from Reports to the Tweed Fishery Commissioners by their Experimental Committee. The Tweed Fishery Commissioners, William Blackwood & Sons, Edinburgh & London. 110-120

Anon. (1876). Report of the Experimental Committee of the River Tweed Commission. History of the Berwickshire Naturalists Club, 1876. Berwick upon Tweed. 572pp.

Anon. (1953). A guide to fish marks. *Journal du Conseil International pour l'Exploration* de la Mer. **19**(2), 242-289.

Balmain, K. H. & Shearer, W.M. (1956). Records of Salmon and Sea-trout caught at sea. *Scottish Home*

Dept. Freshwater and Salmon Fisheries Research No. 11. HMSO Edinburgh, 7 pp

Calderwood, W. L. (1922). Results of Salmon and Sea-trout marking in sea and river. *Fisheries Board for Scotland 1922 No. I.* HMSO Edinburgh. 20pp.

Degerman, E., Leonardsson, K. & Lundqvist, H. (2012). Coastal migrations, temporary use of neighbouring rivers, and growth of sea trout (*Salmo trutta*) from nine northern Baltic Sea rivers. *ICES Journal of Marine Science,* **69**: 971–980.

Finstad, B., Økland, F., Thorstad, E.B., Bjørn, P.A. & McKinley, R.S. (2005). Migration of hatchery-reared Atlantic salmon and wild anadromous brown trout post-smolts in a Norwegian fjord system. *Journal of Fish Biology,* **66** (1) 86-96.

Forseth, T., Naesje, T.F., Jonsson, B. & Harsaker, K. (1999). Juvenile migration in brown trout: a consequence of energetic state. *Journal of Animal Ecology,* **68**, 783–793.

Gargan, P.G., Forde, G., Hazon, N., Russell, D.J. & Todd, C. D. (2012). Evidence for sea lice-induced marine mortality of Atlantic salmon (Salmo salar) in western Ireland from experimental releases of ranched smolts treated with emamectin benzoate. *Canadian Journal of Fish and Aquatic Sciences,* **69**: 343-353.

Harris, G.S. & Morgan, M.J. (1989). Successful Sea Trout Angling. ISBN 0 7137 17610. London: Blandford Press. 400 pp.

ICES. (2008). ICES Compilation of Microtags, Finclip and External Tag Releases 2007 by the Working Group on North Atlantic Salmon, April 1–10 2008, Galway, Eire. *International Council for the Exploration of the Sea, C.M. 2008/ACOM:18* Addendum. 32 pp.

Johnstone, A.D.F., Walker, A.F., Urquhart, G.G. & Thorne, A.E. (1995). The movements of sea trout smolts, Salmo trutta L., in a Scottish west coast sea loch determined by acoustic tracking. *Scottish Fisheries Research Report,* **56**, 1995.

Koed, A., Nielson, C., Madsen, S.S. & Thomsen, D.S. (2007). Overwintering of sea trout (Salmo trutta) in freshwater: escaping salt and low temperature or an alternate life strategy? *Canadian Journal of Fisheries and Aquatic Sciences,* **64**(5), 793-802

Malcolm, I.A., Godfrey, J. & Youngson, A.F. (2010). Review of migratory routes and behaviour of Atlantic salmon, sea trout and European eel in Scotland's coastal environment: implications for the development of marine renewables. *Scottish Marine and Freshwater Science,* **1**(14), 72pp.

Menzies, W.J.M. (1919). Sea-trout of the R. Forth. *Fishery Board for Scotland 1919, Salmon Fisheries No. I.* HMSO Edinburgh. 45pp.

Middlemas, S. J., Stewart, D.C., Mackay, S., & Armstrong, J.D. (2009). Habitat Use and dispersal of post-smolt sea trout *Salmo trutta* in a Scottish sea loch system. *Journal of Fish Biology,* **74**(3), 639-651.

Nall, G.H. (1925). Report on a collection of Sea-trout Scales from the R. Hope and Loch Hope in Sutherland. *Fishery Board for Scotland, Salmon Fisheries 1925 No. I.* HMSO Edinburgh. 26pp.

Nall, G.H. (1927). Sea-trout from the tidal waters of the Don and the Ythan. *Fishery Board for Scotland, Salmon Fisheries 1927 No. II.* HMSO Edinburgh. 46pp.

Nall, G.H. (1928a). Sea-trout from the Broom of Moy waters of the Findhorn and from the tidal waters of the Ugie. *Fishery Board for Scotland, Salmon Fisheries 1928 No. VI.* HMSO Edinburgh. 26pp.

Nall, G.H. (1928b). Sea-trout of the R. Spey. *Fishery Board for Scotland, Salmon Fisheries 1928 No. X.*

HMSO Edinburgh. 32 pp.

Nall, G.H. (1929). Sea-trout from the Beauly Firth and from the tidal waters of the Beauly and Ness rivers. *Fishery Board for Scotland, Salmon Fisheries 1929 No. III.* HMSO Edinburgh. 44pp.

Nall, G.H. (1930). Sea Trout of the River Tweed. *Fishery Board for Scotland, Salmon Fisheries 1929 No. V.* HMSO Edinburgh. 66pp.

Nall, G.H. (1932). Sea trout of the Solway Rivers. *Fishery Board for Scotland, Salmon Fisheries 1932, No. III.* HMSO Edinburgh. 72pp.

Nall, G.H. (1933a). Sea trout of the Ayrshire Rivers Doon, Girvan, and Stinchar. *Fishery Board for Scotland, Salmon Fisheries 1932, No. II.* HMSO Edinburgh. 25pp.

Nall, G.H. (1933b). Orkney Sea-trout. *Fishery Board for Scotland, Salmon Fisheries 1932 No. VIII.* HMSO Edinburgh. 44pp.

Nall, G.H. (1935). Sea-Trout of the Montrose District, Part III, The Migrations of Sea-trout. *Fishery Board for Scotland, Salmon Fisheries 1935 No. III.* HMSO Edinburgh. 24pp.

Nall, G.H. (1936). Sea-trout of the Kyle of Sutherland 1934-35. *Fishery Board for Scotland Salmon Fisheries 1936 No I.* HMSO Edinburgh. 31pp.

Nall, G.H. (1937). Sea-trout of the River Conon. *Fishery Board for Scotland, Salmon Fisheries 1937 No. IV.* HMSO Edinburgh. 23pp.

Nall, G.H. (1955). Movements of Salmon and Sea Trout, chiefly Kelts, and of Brown Trout Tagged in the Tweed between January and May, 1937 and 1938. *Freshwater and Salmon Fisheries Research 10,* Scottish Home Dept. Edinburgh. 19pp.

Olsson, I.C., Greenberg, L.A., Bergman, E. & Wysujack, K. (2006). Environmentally induced migration: the importance of food. *Ecology Letters*, **9**, 645–651.

Paramor, O.A.L., Allen, K.A., Aanesen, M., Armstrong, C., Hegland, T., Le Quesne, W., Piet, G.J., Raakær, J., Rogers, S., van Hal, R., van Hoof, L.J.W., van Overzee, H.M.J., & Frid C.L.J. (2009). MEFEPO North Sea Atlas. University of Liverpool. ISBN 0 906370 60 4

Pemberton, R. (1976). Sea trout in North Argyll sea lochs: population, distribution and movements. *Journal of Fish Biology*, **9**(2), 157-179.

Potter, E.C.E. (1990). Movements of sea trout in the central and southern North Sea: In: *The Sea-trout in Scotland.* (Picken M.J. & Shearer W.M. *Eds.*). Scottish Marine Biological Association, Oban. 47-57.

Potter, E.C.E., Beraud, C., Bacon, J., van der Molen, J. & van Leeuwen, S. (2017) Simulation of the movements of sea trout post-smolts in the Irish and Celtic Seas. In: *Sea trout: Science & Management.* (Graeme Harris. *Ed.*) Proceeding of the 2nd International Sea Trout Conference. October 2016, Dundalk, Ireland. Troubador, 228–252.

Pratten, D & Shearer, W. M. (1983). Migrations of North Esk sea trout. *Journal of the Institute of Fisheries Management,* **14**, 99-114.

Solomon, D.J. (1995). Sea Trout Stocks in England and Wales. National Rivers Authority R&D Report 25. National Rivers Authority, Bristol. 102 pp.

Swain, A. (1959). The efficiency of various types of tags. *Rapport et Proces-Verbaux des Reunions, Conseil International pour l'Exploration* de la Mer. **148**, *1959*, 23-25.

Swain, A. (1971). The efficiency of certain types of smolt tags and tagging techniques adopted by the Ministry of Agriculture, Fisheries and Food. *International Council for the Exploration of the Sea, C.M. 1971/M:10*, 7pp.

Thorstad, E.B. Okland, F. Finstad, B. Silvertsgard, R. Plantalech Manel-la, N. Bjorn, P.A. & McKinley, R.S. (2007). Fjord migration and survival of wild and hatchery reared Atlantic salmon and wild brown trout post-smolts. *Hydrobiologia*, **582**, 99-107.

Walker, A.F. (1990). The Sea Trout and Brown Trout of the River Tay. In *The Sea-trout in Scotland*. (Picken M.J. & Shearer W.M. *Eds*.). Scottish Marine Biological Association, Oban, 5-12.

Wysujack K., Greenberg, L.A., Bergman, E. & Olsson, I.C. (2009). The role of the environment in partial migration: food availability affects the adoption of a migratory tactic in brown trout *Salmo trutta*. *Ecology of Freshwater Fish*, **18**, 52–59.

ELECTRONIC REFERENCES

European Environment Agency, (2009). North Sea physiography (depth distribution and main currents). *Available at*: http://www.eea.europa.eu/data-and-maps/figures/north-sea-physiography-depth-distribution-and-main-currents .

Ecomare. (2015). Supply of Water for the North Sea. *Available at*: http://www.ecomare.nl/en encyclopedia/natural-environment/water/water-currents/sea-currents/

Thorstad, E.B., Todd, C.D., Uglem, I., Bjørn, P.A., Gargan, P.G., Vollset, K.W., Halttunen, E., Kålås, S., Berg, M., & Finstad, B. (2016). Marine life of the sea trout. *Marine Biology,* **163**: 47, 19 pp. doi: 10.1007/s00227-016-2820-3

Simulation of the movements of sea trout post-smolts in the Irish and Celtic Seas

E. POTTER, C. BERAUD, J. BACON, J. VAN DER MOLEN & S. VAN LEEUWEN

Centre for Environment Fisheries and Aquaculture Science, Pakefield Road, Lowestoft, Suffolk, NR33 0HT

ABSTRACT

Hydrodynamic modelling was undertaken to investigate the possible patterns of movements of sea trout post-smolts from different regions around the Irish and Celtic Seas. The hydrodynamics of the Irish and Celtic seas were modelled using the three-dimensional General Estuarine Transport Model/General Ocean Turbulence Model (GETM/GOTM), which simulates the most important hydrodynamic and thermodynamic processes in natural waters, taking account of seasonal variations and the effects of weather conditions. A particle tracking module was used to evaluate scenarios for the possible movements of sea trout post-smolts during the first year in the sea. These scenarios were compared with information on the distribution of sea trout in the Irish and Celtic Seas derived from the genetic assignment of fish sampled at sea back to their region of origin. The results indicate that a significant proportion of the fish remained relatively close to their river of origin. Where fish undertook longer migrations, the direction of movement appeared to be strongly influenced by the prevailing currents, although the fish were still dispersed quite widely. Temperature is likely to be important in affecting growth in the sea and life-history variation among stocks, and so the simulated tracks were also used to estimate the temperature conditions that may have been experienced by fish from the different rivers. Simulated fish from rivers in the north of the study area experienced about 10% fewer degree-days over a given period in the first year at sea than fish from the southern rivers, while stocks from rivers in the south and south-east of Ireland, experienced cooler conditions than those from Welsh rivers at the same latitude.

Keywords: Genetic assignment; hydrodynamic modelling; particle tracking; post-smolt; sea trout.

INTRODUCTION

It is believed that access to marine feeding areas, offering a higher lipid and protein diet (e.g. of sandeel or sprat), enables sea trout to grow faster and, in the case of females, to produce more and larger eggs, relative to resident trout, potentially allowing them to increase their lifetime fitness. However, these advantages must be balanced against the greater risks associated with the transition to and life in the marine environment, including higher energy expenditure and predation risks (Forseth *et al.*, 1999; Olsson *et al.*, 2006; Wysujack *et al.*, 2009). It may be expected therefore that the proportion of the fish in any population that adopts the anadromous habit will be influenced in part by conditions in the sea in the areas to which they migrate. These conditions may also be expected to influence whether sea trout mature and return to freshwater for the first time as 0SW whitling (also termed finnock) or as older sea-winter fish. Such differences among the life history strategies of different stocks have implications for fisheries management, as they affect the nature and value of the fisheries exploiting them.

Tagging studies conducted on the east and south coasts of the UK have shown large differences in the marine migratory behaviour of sea trout from different rivers. However, very few tagging or tracking studies have been undertaken on the movements of trout around the Irish and Celtic Seas (Potter *et al.*, 2017). This paper employs an alternative approach to investigate the movements of sea trout in the sea using hydrodynamic and particle tracking modelling. The work was undertaken as part of the EU Celtic Sea Trout Project (CSTP, 2016) and formed part of the programme aimed at developing a better understanding of the marine ecology of sea trout, their movements within the Irish and Celtic Seas, the conditions they may experience and the potential effects of this on the life history variation both within and between river stocks.

In this study, hydrodynamic modelling coupled off-line with a particle tracking module were employed to simulate the possible patterns of dispersal of sea trout from different rivers entering the Irish and Celtic Seas (Figure 1). The first phase involved the development and running of a hydrodynamic model of the currents, temperatures and salinity throughout the Irish and Celtic Seas. The outputs of this model were then used in a particle tracking module to simulate possible migration trajectories for sea trout from different rivers/regions by combining passive movements with the currents with simulated behavioural rules. The simulated movements were compared with information on the distribution of sea trout originating from different rivers around the Irish and Celtic Seas derived using genetic stock identification of fish sampled at sea (Prodöhl *et al.* 2017). In the final stage of the study, data were extracted on the temperature conditions that would have been experienced by each simulated fish during its migration in order to assess differences in growth opportunities for the populations originating from different rivers and the possible consequences for population growth and structuring.

HYDRODYNAMICS AND PARTICLE TRACKING MODEL

HYDROGRAPHY OF THE IRISH AND CELTIC SEAS

Residual current patterns in the Celtic and Irish Seas are complex. Ramster & Hill (1969) deduced, from seabed drifter returns and moored current meters, that there was a general northward transport across the Irish Sea basin. Modelling studies and high frequency observations have since shown the extent to which the residual flow in Irish Sea in the winter is strongly dominated by wind-driven transport (Young *et al.*, 2001). In contrast, in the summer, the establishment of thermal stratification in the Celtic Sea and a strong thermal front in the St George's channel (Figure 1) results in little or no transfer of water into the Irish Sea at depth and relatively little surface exchange (Hill *et al.*, 2008). This also limits the net movement of water out of the Irish Sea through the North Channel, although there are weak northerly currents on the eastern side and southerly currents on the western side.

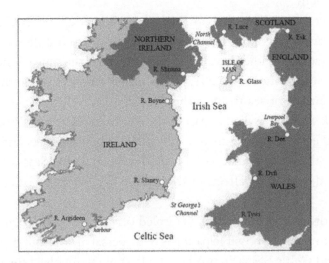

Figure 1. Main topographical features of the Irish and Celtic Seas and rivers used for particle track simulations of the movements of sea trout post-smolts.

HYDRODYNAMIC MODEL OF THE IRISH AND CELTIC SEAS

The three-dimensional General Estuarine Transport Model (GETM) (www.getm.eu : Burchard & Bolding, 2002) was used to model the patterns of currents, temperatures and salinity throughout the Irish and Celtic Seas for specific years. GETM simulates the most important hydrodynamic and thermodynamic processes in natural waters. The model solves the three-dimensional shallow-water equations, which mathematically describe the water motion in coastal seas and also solves advection-diffusion equations to model seasonal changes in temperature and salinity. The resolution of the GETM was approximately 3.5 km in the horizontal direction, and the water column was divided into 25 non-equal layers, which are organised to enhance resolution near the surface and the seabed to better catch wind effects and interactions with the seabed, respectively.

The GETM was run on a spherical grid, and the model domain extended from Latitude 9.6°W to 2.5°W and Longitude 48.8°N to 56.8°N. The model was forced with realistic winds, temperature and humidity data derived from the European Centre for Medium-Range Weather Forecast's operational reanalysis obtained through the British Atmospheric Data Centre (badc. nerc.ac.uk). The open boundaries were forced with tidal elevations and with depth-averaged velocities which were derived from a barotropic shelf-wide model set-up using Flather boundary conditions (Flather, 1976; Carter & Merrifield, 2007). The shelf-wide model was forced with tidal elevations derived from gridded harmonic constituents based on Topex Poseidon satellite altimetry. In addition, the open boundaries were forced with depth-resolved climatological boundary conditions for temperature and salinity based on the World Ocean Database (www. nodc.noaa.gov). Fresh water was introduced into the model at river mouth locations based on gauged observations. UK data were processed into daily flow rates from raw data provided by the Environment Agency (for England and Wales), the Scottish Environment Protection Agency (for Scotland), the Rivers Agency (for Northern Ireland) and the National River Flow Archive. Irish flow data were provided by Hydrodata and the Environment Protection Agency (Hydronet). Short gaps in the observed time series were filled by interpolation, whereas longer gaps were filled using climatic trends based on the surrounding data. The model was run on the Cefas High Performance computing cluster at Cefas, Lowestoft.

Once run for a specific year, the hydrodynamic model can provide estimates of the temperature and salinity at any point in the study area, at any depth and at hourly intervals through the year. For the purpose of this study, a subset of the full geographic domain was used (9.6°W to 2.8°W and 51.0°N to 56.8°N).

PARTICLE TRACKING MODULE

The results of the hydrodynamic computations can be used to drive a separate particle-tracking model (General Individuals Tracking Model (GITM)) to simulate possible migration trajectories for sea trout from different rivers. The GITM is an Individual Behaviour Model which reads the hydrodynamic model (GETM) outputs. When the GETM hydrodynamic model is run, the three-dimensional flow fields, temperatures and salinities are stored every hour; these are then used off-line by the GITM to calculate particle advection and diffusion taking account of the biological development and behaviour of the simulated fish. The advection-diffusion elements of the GITM were based on a re-coded version (Nagai *et al.*, 2003) of the Lagrangean advection-diffusion method developed by Wolk (2003). The method uses a semi-analytical advection method, which ensures that particles follow stream lines exactly, and a random walk method with advective correction (Visser, 1997) to simulate diffusion (Hunter *et al.*, 1993), which uses a constant diffusion coefficient in the horizontal and a variable diffusion coefficient in the vertical that is based on the vertical diffusivity obtained from the turbulence closure model in the GETM. Particles that cross an open boundary of the subset of the domain used for the particle tracking calculations were removed from the computation.

The biological development and behaviour module of the GITM allows particles (i.e. the fish being simulated) to progress through a user-defined number of development stages (eggs, larvae, etc). Development can be linear, temperature-dependent or size-dependent. For each stage, particles are subject to a growth rule that defines their progression to the next stage, potentially using local environmental characteristics derived from the hydrodynamic model (e.g. water temperature). Mortality can also be introduced as a constant daily rate or a temperature-dependent rate.

The particles can display various forms of vertical migratory behaviour (e.g. constant buoyancy, diel or tidally cued vertical migration), which may affect their horizontal dispersion. The speed of horizontal migration can be related to environmental parameters (e.g. swimming faster in deeper water or warmer temperature) while the horizontal direction of migration can be purely random or oriented with or against the current direction. Finally, particles can display various forms of holding or settling behaviour based on local physical conditions (e.g. temperature, salinity) or user-defined spatially varying parameters (e.g. sedimentary environment, depth, adult distributions).

VALIDATION AND TESTING OF THE HYDRODYNAMIC MODEL

The use of multivariate data from a three-dimensional density-resolving model such as the GETM necessitates a validation procedure to gain a quantitative measure of the model's performance against quality checked and accredited observations. Validation was run on the GETM model for the Irish and Celtic Seas for 2008. The observations used to validate the model performance were taken from the ICES databases for 'Surface', 'Underway', 'Temperature and Salinity' and 'CTD' data (www.ices.dk/marine-data/Pages/default.aspx); and observational data collected during Cefas cruise deployments. Each observation within the spatial and temporal limits of the 2008 GETM model was matched with its corresponding modelled point at the nearest node (latitude and longitude position) and layer (depth) of the modelled area.

A suite of statistical tests (Nash Sutcliffe model efficiency, percentage model bias, cost function, skewness and correlation) was used to evaluate the performance of the GETM hydrodynamic model over the Irish Sea domain for the year 2008 applying the validation criteria described by Allen *et al.* (2007). The model performed differently with respect to temperature and salinity (Table1). A high overall correlation was achieved ($R^2 = 0.943$) based on 29,231 temperature observations in the domain area matched against corresponding modelled values. The model efficiency, bias and cost function all fell in the 'excellent' categories from the application of the validation criteria (Allen *et al.,*2007). The positive skew of 0.457 indicated that the model tended to make more underestimations than overestimations. For salinity, the results had greater variance and two groups of outliers were identified from 29,899 observations. The performance of the model was still classified as 'excellent' in respect of model efficiency, bias and cost function, but the dataset was further skewed as a result of the outliers and the overall correlation value was reduced ($R^2 = 0.507$). There were 204 (0.68%) salinity measurements, taken at 74 positions adjacent to the Isle of Mull, where modelled values were significantly less than those observed. This was outside the main study area, and so this error is unlikely to have affected the application of the model in this study. There were also 24 (0.08%) observations from Liverpool Bay, Cork harbour and the Firth of Clyde where salinity was observed to be lower than the modelled result, and this again would have had very little effect on the results.

Hydrodynamic models are less reliable in a strip of several grid cells along any open boundary because of mismatches between the open-boundary forcing and the internal model response, and results in this area should not be used. For the particle tracking experiments discussed here, this applies only to the northern and western boundaries, as the southern boundary of the hydrodynamic model was well beyond the subset of the geographical domain used for the calculations. The northern (56.8°N) and western (9.6°W) open boundaries are well outside the principal area of interest in this study, which is centred on the Irish and Celtic Seas, and so movements of particles at these boundaries have very little effect on the study conclusions. As these boundaries are typically characterised by outflow, particles that end up in their vicinity may be regarded as having left the study domain.

Table 1. Irish Sea Model Validation – Temperature and salinity. The classifications for % Efficiency, % Bias and Cost Function are based on the criteria of Allen *et al.*, 2007.

Model Test	Temperature (n =29,931)		Salinity (n = 29,899)	
	Test Result	Classification	Test Result	Classification
% Efficiency	0.838	Excellent	-0.248	Good
% Bias	3.544	Excellent	-0.359	Excellent
Cost Function	0.206	Excellent	-0.137	Excellent
Skew	0.457		8.72	
Correlation R²	0.943		0.507	

PARTICLE TRACKING SIMULATIONS

PARAMETER SELECTION

Hydrodynamic conditions in the Irish and Celtic Seas were modelled for the period from January until December 2011 from which the tracks of individual particles could be simulated.

The dispersal of sea trout post-smolts was simulated in the numerical model by releasing particles at a specified time and location, and assigning the particles a size, growth rate and specific behaviour. Where possible, the various parameters required to run the particle tracking model were based upon published data, however, there have been relatively few detailed studies of sea trout migratory behaviour in the sea. While complex behaviour patterns could be proposed and implemented in the model, it was considered more appropriate to define the simplest behavioural rules that might be expected to simulate the observed behaviour of post-smolts after leaving freshwater. The following parameters are included in the model:-

Release locations: Particles were released at the mouths of ten rivers around the Irish Sea to provide examples of the simulated tracks of emigrating smolts from each region (Figure 1, and see Table 4 for release positions).

Release dates and times: Sea trout smolts in UK and Ireland generally emigrate between March and May, with the peak runs being associated with periods of increased river temperatures and elevated flows during April. The larger, older smolts tend to emigrate earlier than the smaller, younger fish. Moore *et al.* (1998) tracked wild sea trout smolts emigrating from the River Conwy, North Wales and reported that emigration in freshwater was predominantly nocturnal but that there were changes in this pattern in the lower reaches of the estuary, with fish moving during both the day and night. All the smolts migrated seawards on an ebb tide, but migration in the lower portion of the estuary was indicative of active swimming and quickly became independent of the tide. More recent tracking studies in Poole Harbour (southern England) have also shown sea trout smolts emigrating at all states of the tide (Andy Moore, *pers. comm.*). Particles were therefore released at hourly intervals over a period from 1st to 28th April to cover all possible emigration behaviour and all stages of a lunar cycle.

Depth: Rikardsen *et al.* (2007) reported that sea trout in their first 40 days at sea in Alta Fjord in north Norway, spent >50% of their time at depths between 1 and 2 m depth and >90% at less than 3 m. Lyse *et al.* (1998) also showed sea trout mainly occupying the upper 1-3 m of the water column in a Norwegian fjord, and Sturlaugsson & Johannsson (1998) reported that sea trout tagged with archival tags in southeast Iceland, spent 91% of the time in the top 7 m during their marine migration. Post-smolts were also caught further offshore during the CSTP marine sampling programme using a surface trawl, suggesting that even in deeper waters they remain relatively close to the surface. On the basis of these data, the particles were released at a depth of 2 m.

Vertical movements: Although vertical movements were reported by Moore *et al.,* (1998) for smolts passing through an estuary, this appeared to be associated with tidal transport on the ebbing tide, and the behaviour did not continue once the fish left the estuary. In the absence of any evidence of systematic vertical movements, these were not included in the simulations, and the simulated fish were retained at a depth of 2 m.

Length: The mean length of emigrating smolts was estimated to be 180 mm, based on data provided from the sampling studies during the CSTP programme.

Growth: Growth is included in the model because swimming speed is expressed in relation to length. A growth rate of 0.5 mm per day was used based on estimates provided from the CSTP sampling programme.

Swimming speed: Many studies have been conducted on the swimming speeds of salmonids. Most of these have estimated critical and burst speeds as a basis for investigating movements around obstructions and through fish passes, but some authors have estimated the optimal and preferred swimming speeds of fish. Kawabe *et al.* (2003) used the relationship between tail-beat frequency and swimming speed to estimate the 'preferred' swimming speed of trout to be between 0.48 and 0.58 body lengths per second (bl s^{-1}). Tudorache *et al.* (2011) estimated the preferred swimming speed of brook char to be between ~ 0.78 ± 0.02 bl s^{-1} and 0.95 ± 0.03 bl s^{-1}, and Taylor *et al.* (1996) reported that the mean (± se) speeds recorded for maximal sustainable aerobic exercise were 0.52±0.02, 0.81±0.06 and 0.39±0.02 bl s^{-1} for rainbow trout swimming at their acclimatisation temperatures of 4, 11 and 18 °C, respectively. As this study was simulating the behaviour of free swimming sea trout that would be searching for food, a mean swimming speed of 0.5 bl s^{-1} was used.

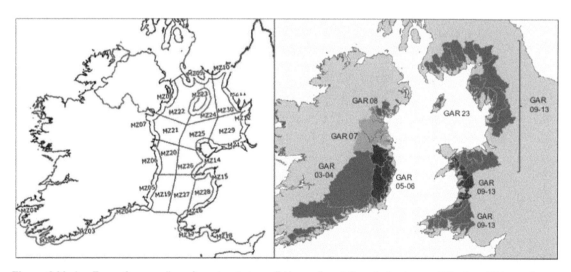

Figure 2 Marine Zones for sampling of sea trout at sea (LH panel) and Genetic Assignment Regions (RH panel).

Migratory behaviour: Little information is available on the behaviour of sea trout in the marine environment. It is generally believed that sea trout smolts do not move offshore as quickly as salmon smolts, and a number of studies have suggested that they remain relatively local to their river of origin for extended periods (e.g. Finstad *et al.*, 2005; Middlemas *et al.*, 2009). While some of these studies have observed sea trout remaining very close to the shore, they were caught at greater distances offshore during the marine sampling of the CSTP (e.g. in MZ 29 and 30; Figure 2), and tagging studies have shown some sea trout undertaking much longer migrations including fish from Welsh rivers crossing the Irish Sea (Potter *et al.*, 2017). Thorstad *et al.* (2004) also observed that the movements of sea trout post-smolts in a Norwegian fjord system were random relative to the direction of the water current.

Options were considered that would simulate this range of behaviours in the model as simply as possible, giving a tendency for fish to delay their movement away from the coast, while allowing a proportion of the fish to disperse more quickly. In view of the added complication of modelling currents very close to the shore, an option was included which simulates a fish having a preference for a specific water depth; the 'preferred water depth' was entered as a mean and standard deviation. A new variable was introduced in the code, "depth experienced by particle", calculated from the bathymetry and the free surface elevation. These parameters define a velocity coefficient which equals zero at the preferred depth and increases to one as the difference between the observed depth and the preferred depth increases (Figure 3); the fish swims in a random direction at a speed equal to the velocity coefficient multiplied by 0.5 bl s⁻¹. Thus if a fish is not at its preferred water depth, it will try to find other locations by swimming at a velocity of up to 0.5 bl s⁻¹ in a random direction. If the fish finds its preferred water depth, it will slow its swimming speed but remain moving in a random direction. Fish swimming speed will thus range from 0 to 0.5 bl s⁻¹. Fish will also be transported by the prevailing currents.

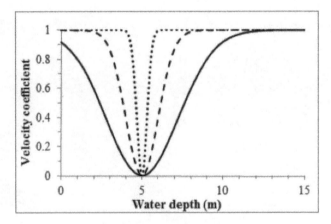

Figure 3. Examples of the velocity coefficient used in the depth related swimming behaviour where the preferred swimming depth is 5m with s.d. of 0.1m, 1m or 5m.

SIMULATED TRACKS

Simulations were run for 'smolts' emigrating and dispersing from the 10 rivers (Figure 1) using the parameter values specified above and the depth related swimming behaviour (with mean preferred swimming depth = 20 m; s.d. = 20 m). Up to 10 particles were released per hour over 28 days to investigate the patterns of distribution, but Figures 4a and 4b provide the results for one particle released per hour (i.e. 672 particles in total) in order to show differences in the distribution densities more clearly. The distributions are shown for the end of May, July and September of the first year at sea. The simulations did not attempt to model the return migration of whitling due to lack of data on the behaviour of the fish at this stage. For all rivers, the simulated fish remained relatively close to their river of origin for at least two to three months (April to June). There were then different regional patterns of movement in the summer months (July to September). Later in the year, after the breakdown of the thermal front in the St Georges channel (Figure 1), the simulated fish from most rivers showed strong northerly movements, and a large proportion were transported out of the Irish Sea.

The simulated fish from the River Argideen remained in the Celtic Sea until the end of the summer, spreading out from the Irish coast, and many of the tracks were 'lost' at the edge of the study area (Figure 4a). Between October and December, the remaining fish were transported northwards into the Irish Sea. This is in marked contrast to the simulated fish from the River Slaney which moved progressively northwards throughout the year, with the majority remaining on the western side of the Irish Sea, but small numbers entering the eastern Irish Sea (Figure 4a). Very few of the River Slaney fish went in a southerly direction, unlike the simulated fish from the Rivers Boyne and Shimna, the majority of which moved gradually southwards along the Irish coast between June and August (Figure 4a) before being transported northwards again later in the year, in October to December.

Simulated fish from the River Glass moved both to the southeast of the Isle of Man towards the English coast and northwest towards the North Channel (Figure 4a), with some of the latter group then being transported southwards along the Irish coast. From September onwards there was a general northerly movement of these fish, although significant numbers remained close to the English coast. The tracks of fish from the River Luce showed a similar pattern of movement to those from the River Glass but with fewer fish moving into the eastern Irish Sea (Figure 4b).

A large proportion of the simulated fish from the River Esk were retained in the shallow waters close to the Solway Firth (Figure 4b). Fish moving out of the Solway Firth during the summer were then transported northwards through the North Channel or southwards along the English coast; no tracks crossed to the Irish coast. In a similar way, the majority of the simulated fish from the River Dee remained in Liverpool Bay, with those fish that moved away mainly being transported northwards along the English coast (Figure 4b). The simulated fish from the River Dyfi dispersed more rapidly, with the majority moving northwards and spreading out widely in the eastern Irish Sea (Figure 4b). Finally, the simulated fish from the River Tywi were mainly retained within the Bristol Channel until the summer; small numbers then moved out into the Irish Sea, spreading out as they moved northwards (Figure 4b).

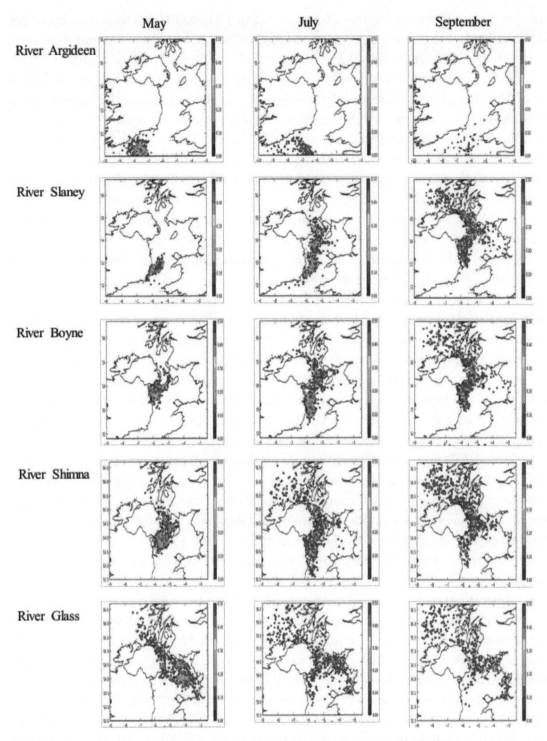

Figure 4a. Simulated tracks of 672 sea trout smolts emigrating from the rivers Argideen, Slaney, Boyne, Shimna & Glass at hourly intervals from 00:00 on 1st April 2011 until 23:00 on 28th April. Panels show estimated positions at the end of May, July and September, 2011.

238

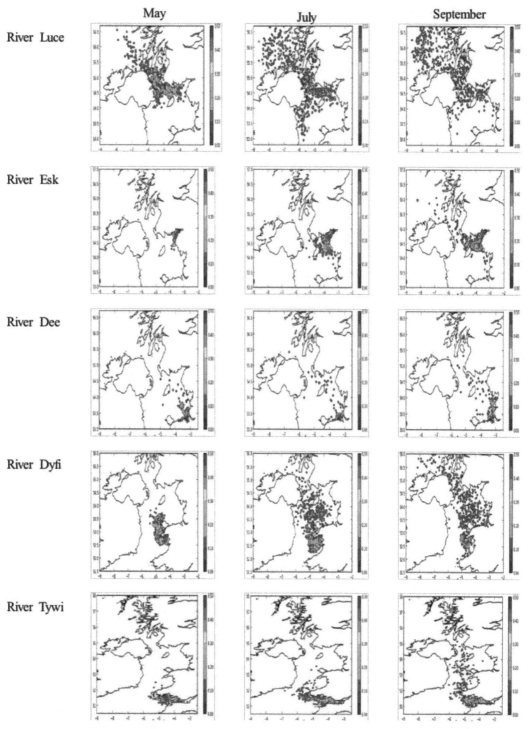

Figure 4b. Simulated tracks of 672 sea trout smolts emigrating from the rivers Luce, Esk, Dee, Dyfi & Tywi at hourly intervals from 00:00 on 1st April 2011 until 23:00 on 28th April. Panels show estimated positions at the end of May, July and September, 2011.

VALIDATION OF SIMULATIONS

The development of the genetic dataset which was used to tune and validate the particle tracking results was conducted under separate parts of the CSTP (CSTP, 2016; Prodöhl *et al.*, 2017). A genetic baseline was developed for over 100 sea trout river stocks around the Celtic and Irish Seas and used to identify regional groupings, based on genetic differences and geographic areas (Figure 2, RH panel). Survey programmes were then undertaken to sample post-smolt and adult sea trout in various 'marine zones' around the Irish Sea (Figure 2, LH panel) using a number of different fishing methods (CSTP, 2016). Tissue samples were taken from all fish sampled at sea and were used to identify their origin, by means of the Geneclass and ONCOR genetic assignment methods; the results used here are based on the preliminary analysis of the genetic data undertaken for the CSTP. Further details of these programmes are provided by CSTP (2016) and Prodöhl *et al.* (2017). The assignment results must be interpreted with care because there are no unique markers for individual river stocks, and both methods can assign fish incorrectly. In addition, fish originating from rivers that are not in the baseline dataset will be assigned to the most likely river within the baseline. Assignments to regions may therefore be expected to be more reliable than to rivers, and, since they provide a convenient way to group the data, have been used in the validation of the particle tracking results. It is not possible to determine which of the Geneclass or ONCOR assignments is more reliable, and so where fish were assigned to different regions by the two methods, they were excluded from the subsequent analyses in this study.

When combined with age data, the genetic assignments can provide an approximate picture of the dispersal of fish originating from different regions over the months after they leave freshwater. The age is first required to identify fish that have not returned to freshwater between emigrating as smolts and their capture in the sampling programme (i.e. maiden fish) by excluding fish with spawning marks on their scales; a total of 460 maiden fish were identified in this way. A sequential picture of the distribution of fish in the sea was then obtained by assuming that all fish emigrated in the same year, and the time at sea was estimated from the month of capture plus the sea age in months (where sea age 0 = 0 months, sea age 1 = 12 months, etc); this is referred to below as a 'lagged capture date'. Applying the above approach revealed anomalies in separation of 0/0+ and 1/1+ age groups based on scale reading. The *mixdist* package in R (R Development Core Team, 2008; Macdonald & Green, 1988) was therefore used to estimate the size distributions of each age group from the length frequency distributions of the total sample for each month, or for groups of months when there were few samples. The length splits derived from this analysis were used to re-assign the maiden sea trout into sea age 0 and 1 groups and determine the 'lagged capture date' values.

There were 384 maiden sea trout in the marine samples which had the same genetic assignments by the Geneclass and ONCHOR methods; 140 of these were estimated to be 0/0+, and 244 were 1/1+. The genetic assignments provide the estimated origin of the

Table 2. Numbers of samples caught in each Marine Zone assigned to different regions by genetic analysis for 3 month periods (Feb-Apr to Aug-Oct) in the year of smolt emigration. Boxed cells indicate where the Genetic Assignment Region and the Marine Zone are approximately the same.

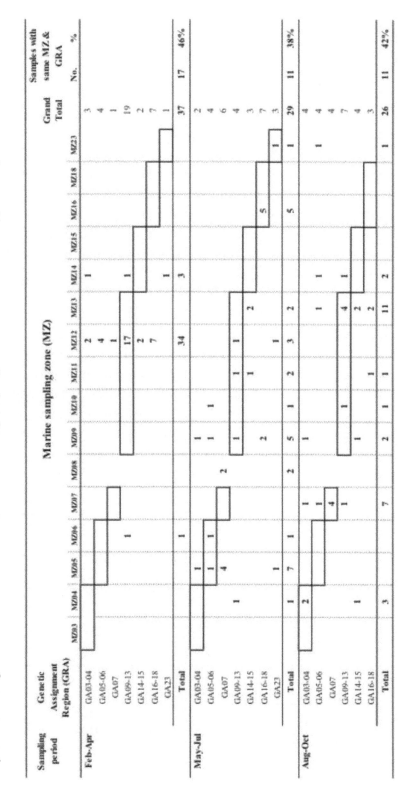

Sampling period	Genetic Assignment Region (GRA)	MZ03	MZ04	MZ05	MZ06	MZ07	MZ08	MZ09	MZ10	MZ11	MZ12	MZ13	MZ14	MZ15	MZ16	MZ18	MZ23	Grand Total	Samples with same MZ & GRA No.	%
Feb-Apr	GA03-04		1								2							3		
	GA05-06										4							4		
	GA07				1													1		
	GA09-13							1			17	1						19		
	GA14-15										2							2		
	GA16-18										7							7		
	GA23												1					1		
	Total				1						34		3					**37**	**17**	**46%**
May-Jul	GA03-04			1				1										2		
	GA05-06			1	1			1		1								4		
	GA07			4			2											6		
	GA09-13							1	1	1	1							4		
	GA14-15									1		2						3		
	GA16-18							2			1				3		1	7		
	GA23										1				2		1	3		
	Total			7	1	7	2	5	1	2	3	2			5		1	**29**	**11**	**38%**
Aug-Oct	GA03-04		2									2						4		
	GA05-06				1							3						4		
	GA07					4												4		
	GA09-13							2	1	1		2	1					7		
	GA14-15		1									2	1			1		4		
	GA16-18											2					1	3		
	Total		2		1	4		2	1	1		11	2			1	1	**26**	**11**	**42%**

sea trout sampled at sea, and the capture locations (Marine Zones) indicate where they had migrated to at the time of sampling. In order to make it easier to match the Genetic Assignment Regions (GAR) to which fish were assigned with the marine zones in which the sampling was undertaken, the GARs were given the appropriate numbered code; thus GAR03-04 covers approximately the same area as Marine Zones 03 and 04, etc (Figure 2). When tabulated for successive periods, these results give an indication of the progressive migration or dispersal of the fish over time (Table 2). A small number of fish that were genetically assigned to parts of England outside the study area, probably the south-west, have been omitted from the table.

The uneven distribution of sampling in both space and time and relatively small numbers of samples make it difficult to detect clear patterns of movement. However, out of the 140 sea age 0/0+ post-smolts, 70 (52%) were caught in the same area to which they were genetically assigned, 54 (40%) were caught to the north of their assignment area, 10 (7%) were caught to the south and 8 (6%) were caught at approximately the same latitude on the opposite side of the Irish Sea (Table 3). This pattern was similar for each of the three 3-month sampling periods during which 0/0+ fish were caught (as: 1) Feb-Apr; 2) May-Jul; 3) Aug-Oct). This is consistent with the majority of the fish having a tendency to remain in the location of their river of origin or being transported with the residual tidal currents. However, a small numbers of fish appeared to have migrated quite long distances very quickly. For example, some fish caught in Morecambe Bay during the smolt emigration period (February-April) were genetically assigned to the south coast of Ireland and southwest England. While such migrations are possible, it would probably be necessary for post-smolts to swim in a directed fashion from the time they left freshwater to cover these distances. Given the distribution of the remaining fish, this seems unlikely, and these fish may have been genetically assigned to the wrong regions.

Table 3 Marine zones (MZ) in which sea trout post-smolts were caught relative to the genetic assignment region (GAR) from which they were estimated to have originated.

Sampling Period	MZ relative to GAR				
	Same Area	North	South	East/West	Total
Feb - April	17	10	1	9	37
	46%	27%	3%	24%	
May - Jul	12	11	4	2	29
	41%	38%	14%	7%	
Aug - Oct	11	9	1	5	26
	42%	35%	4%	19%	
Total 0/0+	**40**	**30**	**6**	**16**	**76**
	53%	**39%**	**8%**	**21%**	

ENVIRONMENTAL CONDITIONS EXPERIENCED BY POST-SMOLTS

The conditions experienced by sea trout in the sea, in particular the temperature, may be expected to affect growth and fitness, and so differences in the conditions experienced by different stocks may account for differences in life-history strategies. The GETM hydrodynamic model was therefore used to estimate the temperature experienced by the simulated fish from each river over the course of their tracks. Figure 5 shows the median (and 25th and 75th percentiles) of the mean daily temperatures experienced by each simulated fish on each day between 1st May, after all 'particles' had been released, and 31st December. This has been compared with the mean daily temperature at a fixed location 10 km off the mouth of the river at a depth of 2 m over the same period, also estimated from the hydrodynamic model (Figure 5).

The mean temperatures for the tracks were generally a little lower than the temperatures at the fixed locations in the early months and then higher than for the fixed locations after September. Thus, the total cumulative degree-days experienced by the simulated fish tended to be lower than that at the fixed locations for the period from May to August, but was more similar over the whole period from May to December (Table 4, Figure 6). The Argideen appeared anomalous because the mean temperature of the simulated fish was significantly higher than at the fixed location, but the results were biased because a large proportion of the simulated fish were lost at the edge of the area bounded by the model.

There was a general trend for degree-days of both the simulated fish and at the fixed locations to decrease with latitude (Table 4, Figure 6), although the Argideen and Esk did not conform to this trend. Temperatures experienced by the simulated fish and at the fixed location

Table 4 Total degree-days between May 1st and (a) August 31st and (b) December 31st, 2011 at fixed locations 10 km off the mouth of 10 rivers around the Irish and Celtic Sea and median number of degree-days (with 25th and 75th percentiles) experienced by simulated post-smolts emigrating from those rivers.

River	Location of river mouth (Lat°/Long°)		Degree-days between May 1st and August 31st				Degree-days between May 1st and December 31st			
			Fixed location	Simulated fish			Fixed location	Simulated fish		
				25%ile	Median	75%ile		25%ile	Median	75%ile
Argideen	51° 38' 42"	08°45'48"W	1,359	1,453	1,591	1,702	2,695	2,927	3,256	3,522
Slaney	52° 21' 37"	06°32'44"W	1,767	1,647	1,692	1,726	3,132	3,060	3,161	3,245
Boyne	53° 43' 52"	06°15'38"W	1,658	1,475	1,576	1,654	3,154	2,991	3,162	3,294
Shimna	54° 12' 37"	05°53'26"W	1,516	1,434	1,513	1,607	2,997	2,908	3,072	3,236
Glass	54° 13' 48"	04° 34' 12" W	1,623	1,438	1,574	1,658	3,212	2,827	3,111	3,278
Luce	54° 51' 50"	04°48'39"W	1,634	1,396	1,469	1,594	3,130	2,823	2,984	3,209
Esk	54° 58' 07"	03°02'00"W	1,781	1,745	1,778	1,796	2,886	3,108	3,288	3,384
Dee	53° 16' 38"	03°10'09"W	1,782	1,734	1,757	1,775	3,098	3,120	3,179	3,240
Dyfi	52° 32' 40"	04°00'20"W	1,875	1,597	1,662	1,826	3,367	3,117	3,274	3,487
Tywi	51° 46' 15"	04°22'27"W	1,839	1,699	1,753	1,787	3,326	3,319	3,432	3,522

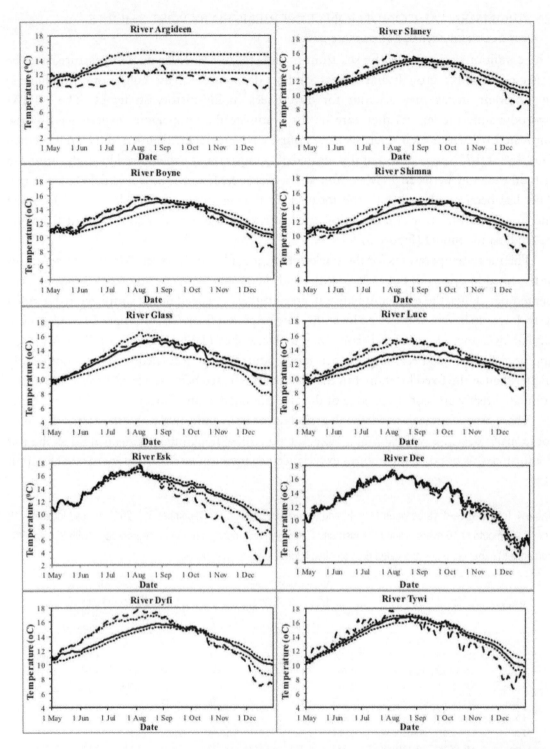

Figure 5 Temperature at fixed locations 10 km off the mouths of 10 rivers (dashed lines) and median temperature (solid lines) with 25th and 75th percentiles (dotted lines) of the mean daily temperatures experienced by all simulated post-smolts leaving the rivers, from May 1st to December 31st.

were lower than expected for the latitude in the Argideen and higher than expected in the Esk. This probably reflects the fact that the Argideen simulated tracks move offshore to the south, while a large proportion of the Esk fish were retained close to the Solway Firth. The results also suggest that fish from some rivers (e.g. Rivers Slaney and Shimna) may experience a much wider range of degree-days than those from other rivers (e.g. Rivers Dyfi and Luce). In general, the more widely dispersed the simulated tracks, the greater the variation was in the number of degree-days experienced by each individual fish.

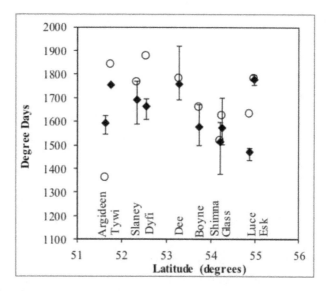

Figure 6. Total degree-days between May 1st and December 31st at fixed locations 10 km off the mouth of 10 rivers around the Irish and Celtic Sea (circles) and median of temperatures experienced by simulated fish leaving those rivers (diamonds) (bars show 25th and 75th percentiles) plotted against latitude of river.

DISCUSSION

There are very limited records of substantive sea trout tagging or tracking studies having been undertaken around the Irish and Celtic Seas, and so very little is known about the movements of these fish in this area (Potter *et al.*, 2017). In this study, we have used hydrodynamic modelling with particle tracking as an alternative approach to investigate possible patterns of migration and distribution of sea trout post-smolts emigrating from 10 different rivers. It is important that any such simulations should be validated as far as possible, and this has been attempted using genetic assignment analysis of fish caught in marine sampling programmes. While the simulated distribution patterns for the 10 river stocks for the first few months after they emigrate as smolts were broadly consistent with the genetic assignments of the fish sampled at sea, it was not possible to compare the results statistically. Not only were the samples of sea age 0/0+ fish used in the genetic analysis very small, but also the sampling varied markedly between regions. Surveys were undertaken using a range of different fishing methods with different selective properties, and the timing and extent of sampling varied greatly between areas (CSTP, 2016). Furthermore, the probability of fish from a particular region being caught in any sample will have depended, in part, on the relative size of the stocks in that region which could only be estimated very approximately. A further uncertainty arises from the probable incorrect assignment of some of the samples in the genetic analysis. The accuracy of Geneclass and ONCOR assignment scores depend ultimately on the quality of the baseline, measured in terms of how well it reflects all the 'true' populations which are contributing to the mixture. Thus, fish originating from rivers or parts of rivers that are not represented in the baseline dataset will be assigned to the most likely river in the baseline. Incorrect assignments may also be biased towards particular rivers or regions if the quality of the baseline varies or due to the relative heterogeneity in the baseline samples from different regions.

Nevertheless, the results suggest that, at least within the study area, the movements of sea age 0/0+ sea trout in the sea are strongly influenced by the prevailing currents but that this dispersal is modulated by an additional tendency to remain in shallower, coastal waters. This behaviour was simulated simply in the particle tracking model by means of the 'preferred water depth', but it is possible that the fish use alternative behaviours and navigational cues to achieve the same end. For the simulations, it was also assumed that emigrating sea trout post-smolts generally swim in a random direction relative to the current, as reported by Thorstad *et al.* (2004). More directed movements tend to reduce the rate and extent of dispersal of the simulated tracks, and so do not account so well for the widespread distributions observed in the genetic results.

The movements of sea trout observed in a number of tagging and tracking studies in UK are consistent with these results. Some of these studies have shown only very short marine migrations. For example, Johnstone *et al.* (1995) used active tracking to monitor the movements of 12 sea trout post-smolts in Loch Ewe in north-west Scotland. Three fish returned quickly to fresh water, while the other nine were tracked for periods ranging from 1 to 68 h. These fish mainly remained in the inshore littoral zone, with some extensive and directed movements; the maximum distance that a fish moved from the release point was 1.5 km. In a similar study, Middlemas *et al.* (2009) used logging acoustic receivers to track the movements of sea trout post-smolts in Loch Torridon, focussing on two connected sea loch basins within the wider Loch Torridon area, Upper Loch Torridon and Loch Shieldaig. Out of a total of 48 tagged fish, five left the study area to move further out to sea and two re-entered fresh water. In general, the post-smolts dispersed slowly into the marine environment in the weeks following emigration from fresh water, with only 36% of fish detected >6 km from their release site.

Similar studies have been conducted in Norway. Berg & Berg (1987) reported on the recaptures of sea trout smolts tagged in the Vardnes river in northern Norway. Of the 2,122 recaptures in the sea, 52.8% were reported within 3 km of the river mouth, compared to only 0.7% more than 80 km away. Similar observations have been reported from more recent telemetry studies. Finstad *et al*. (2005) followed the movements of 15 wild sea trout post-smolts tagged with acoustic tags in a Norwegian fjord. Only four post-smolts were recorded more than 9 km from the release site, taking an average of 18 days to cover the distance. No sea trout were recorded as far as 77 km from the release site (still within the fjord) during the course of the study (May to September). Thorstad *et al*. (2007) similarly tagged and released 34 sea trout smolts with acoustic tags in a Norwegian fjord system between May and early June. Eight fish were detected at a receiver located 9.5 km from the release location and three 37 km from the release point; no fish were detected at 65 km.

All the above studies were conducted in relatively protected lochs or fjords, where fish may not be subject to strong currents along the coast. In contrast, studies of sea trout smolts leaving the rivers in north east England using both conventional tags (Potter, 1990; Potter *et al*., 2017) and acoustic tags (Barry Bendall, *pers.comm.*) show that the fish migrate rapidly to the south, covering a distance of over 300 km to the East Anglian coast in about 6-8 weeks, and some continue onto the Belgium and Dutch coast. Long distance migrations have also been reported for hatchery-reared sea trout released into nine Swedish rivers in the Baltic between 1998 and 2007 (Degerman *et al*., 2012). The majority of the recaptures (61.4%) were still caught within 50 km of their river of origin, 14.2% were caught >150 km from the river of release, 2.2% >500 km away and 0.2% >1000 km away.

While the above results indicate quite varied patterns of distribution for sea trout originating in different rivers, the simulation results suggest that such variation may still be the result of the fishes' movements being largely dictated by the currents, modulated by a simple generic behavioural rule that tends to keep them in coastal waters. For example, the simulated fish from the Rivers Argideen and Slaney in southern Ireland showed quite different patterns of dispersal as a result of the different current patterns in the Celtic and Irish Seas respectively, and simulated fish from the Rivers Dyfi and Glass dispersed more rapidly and widely than those from the Rivers Esk, Dee and Tywi, where simulated fish spent longer within the estuary or nearby. The differences in dispersal were thus heavily dependent upon the topography of the estuaries and coastlines around the rivers as well as the prevailing currents. However, where the marine conditions experienced by fish from different rivers result in different selective pressures, they may lead to different behavioural responses. Such differences have been reported in the tendency for two different hatchery-reared stocks of sea trout to remain near the coastline rather than migrating further offshore (Kallio-Nyberg & Ahlfors, 2002).

The simulation results suggest that it may be possible to account for the distribution of 0/0+ sea trout from rivers all around the Irish and Celtic Seas by means of generic behavioural rules. This would imply that fish from different rivers have not adopted different migratory strategies to optimise their chances of finding food. This could be because prey species are sufficiently abundant throughout the area or because adopting different strategies, such as swimming against the current to get to particular feeding areas, may carry additional risks or costs that negate any benefits. Nevertheless, it is possible that fish may adopt different migratory strategies when the benefits are greater, and this may account for some of the longer distant migrations that have been observed (e.g. in the North Sea (Potter *et al.*, 2017)). It is also possible that older fish that are less affected by the prevailing currents may adopt more distinct behaviours.

The return migration of fish to their river of origin has also not been included in the simulations because no information was available on when fish may start their return migration or how they navigate back to their home river. Sea trout maturing at different ages are likely to adopt different migratory strategies, and it is likely that the return migration is more directed and rapid than the outward migration, and the fish may feed less at this time. If this is the case, then this phase may have relatively little effect on the growth potential of the fish over the total period in the sea. However, it is also likely that maturation begins some months before the fish return to freshwater, and this may affect their behaviour over a longer period. Clearly, including fish that are on their return migration will affect the overall distribution of the stock in the sea by increasing the numbers estimated to be closer to their river of origin. While it would be possible to use the hydrodynamic and particle tracking models to simulate and test more complex migratory scenarios, in the absence of more detailed data against which to validate the results, these would be highly speculative. Much more extensive tracking of sea trout in coastal waters will be required to improve our understanding of these behaviours.

The fish length, growth rate and swimming speed parameters mainly affect the speed of dispersal rather than the patterns of distribution. While these parameters were not subject to an extensive sensitivity analysis, they are not expected to have had a significant effect on the overall conclusions of this study. Few data are available on mortality rates for sea trout post-smolts during the first few months at sea, and so natural mortality has not been incorporated in the particle tracking model. Inclusion of mortality would not affect the estimated distribution of the fish, unless mortality rates vary significantly between areas, but it would reduce the numbers of simulated tracks in the later months. Similarly, investigations of the number of degree-days experienced by the fish are based on survivors at the end of any time period and will not be affected by including mortality unless survival is affected by the temperature experienced.

The temperatures experienced by post-smolts appear to be strongly influenced by the nature of the estuary from which they emigrate and its latitude. Where the fish are retained for longer in a large estuary, they may experience higher temperatures (e.g. River Esk), whereas on the more exposed coastline in the south of Ireland, fish may experience lower temperatures than in the more protected waters at similar latitudes in Wales. Jensen *et al.* (2014) suggested that sea trout may actively seek the warmest temperatures in a Norwegian fjord. Such behaviour might have resulted in fish tending to swim in a southerly direction against the prevailing currents in the Irish Sea, but this was not evident in the genetic results and so was not introduced in the simulations. While the simulated fish have been kept at a constant depth of 2 m, post-smolts are known to make some large vertical movements, albeit only for a small proportion of the time (Rikardsen *et al.*, 2007; Middlemas *et al.*, 2009; Sturlaugsson & Johannsson, 1998). Such movements may result in them experiencing different temperatures, depending upon whether or not there is a thermocline.

The results of this study clearly demonstrate the value of using hydrodynamic and particle tracking modelling to explore the possible behaviour and distribution of sea trout in the sea and the conditions (e.g. water temperatures) that they may experience. However, as with any modelling, the results must be treated with caution because they will only ever be as good as the data used to run the models. It is therefore most important that any simulations are validated as far as possible with alternative observations, which may be obtained by various means including conventional tagging, telemetry and genetic stock assignment.

ACKNOWLEDGEMENTS

The authors are very grateful to Phil McGinnity and Paulo Prodohl for providing a preliminary interpretation of genetic data from the EU InterReg Celtic Sea Trout Project for use in the validation of the particle tracking simulations, prior to the formal publication of these results. For a full analysis of the genetic results the reader should refer to Prodöhl et al., (2017). This study was funded as part of the Celtic Sea Trout Project and by the Department for the Environment, Food and Rural Affairs (Defra), U.K. Government, under contract SF0257.

REFERENCES

Allen, J.I., Holt, J.T., Blackford, J. & Proctor, R. (2007). Error quantification of a high-resolution coupled hydrodynamic-ecosystem coastal-ocean model: Part 2. Chlorophyll-a, nutrients and SPM. *Journal of Marine Systems*, **68** (3-4). 381-404.

Berg O.K. & Berg M. (1987). Migrations of sea trout, *Salmo trutta* L., from the Vardnes River in northern Norway. *Journal of Fish Biology*, **31**, 113-121.

Burchard, H. & Bolding, K. (2002). GETM – a general estuarine transport model. Scientific documentation, Tech. Rep. EUR 20253 EN, European Commission.

Carter, G.S. & Merrifield, M.A. (2007). Open boundary conditions for regional tidal simulations. *Ocean Modelling*, **18**, 194-209.

Degerman, E., Leonardsson, K., & Lundqvist, H. (2012). Coastal migrations, temporary use of neighbouring rivers, and growth of sea trout (*Salmo trutta*) from nine northern Baltic Sea rivers. *ICES Journal of Marine Science*, **69**: 971–980.

Finstad, B., Økland, F., Thorstad, E.B., Bjørn, P.A. & McKinley, R.S. (2005) Migration of hatchery-reared Atlantic salmon and wild sea trout post-smolts in a Norwegian fjord system. *Journal of Fish Biology*, **66**, 86-96.

Flather, R.A., (1976). A tidal model of the north-west European continental shelf. *Memoires de la Societe Royale des Sciences de Liege*, **6**(10), 141–164.

Forseth T., Naesje, T.E., Jonsson, B. & Harsaker, K. (1999). Juvenile migration in brown trout: a consequence of energetic state. *Journal of Animal Ecology*, **68**, 783–793.

Hill, A.E., Brown, J., Fernand, L., Holt, J., Horsburgh, K.J., Proctor, R., Raine, R. & Turrell, W.R. (2008). The thermohaline circulation of shallow tidal seas. *Geophysical Research Letters,* **35**(11), art no L11605.

Hunter, J. R., Craig, P.D. & Philips, H.E. (1993). On the use of random walk models with spatially variable diffusivity. *Journal of Computational Physics, 106*, 366–376.

Johnstone, A.D.F., Walker, A.F., Urquhart, G.G. & Thorne, A.E. (1995). The movements of sea trout smolts, *Salmo trutta* L., in a Scottish west coast sea loch determined by acoustic tracking. *Scottish Fisheries Research Report*, **56**, 21pp.

Kawabe, R., Kawano, T., Nakano, N., Yamashita, N., Hiraishi, T. & Naito, Y. (2003). Simultaneous measurement of swimming speed and tail beat activity of free-swimming rainbow trout *Oncorhynchus mykiss* using an acceleration data-logger. *Fisheries Science*, **69**(5), 959–965.

Kallio-Nyberg, I. & Ahlfors, P. (2002). Sea migration pattern of two sea trout (Salmo trutta) stocks released into the Gulf of Finland. *Annales Zoologici Fennici,* **39**, 221-235.

Lyse, A.A., Stefansson, S.O. & Fernö, A. (1998). Behaviour and diet of sea trout post-smolts in a Norwegian fjord system. *Journal of Fish Biology*, **52**, 923-936.

Macdonald, P.D.M. & Green, P.E.J. (1988). User's Guide to Program MIX: An interactive Program for Fitting Mixtures of Distributions. Ichthus Data Systems, Hamilton, Ontario.

Middlemas, S. J., Stewart, D. C., Mackay, S. & Armstrong J. D. (2009). Habitat use and dispersal of post-smolt sea trout *Salmo trutta* in a Scottish sea loch system. *Journal of Fish Biology,* **74**, 639–651.

Moore, A., Ives, M., Scott, M., & Bamber, S. (1998). The migratory behaviour of wild sea trout *(Salmo trutta* L.) smolts in the estuary of the River Conwy, North Wales *Aquaculture,* **168** (1), 57-68.

Nagai, T., Yamazaki, H., & Kamykowski, D. (2003). A Lagrangian photoresponse model coupled with 2nd-order turbulence closure. *Marine Ecology Progress Series,* **265**, 17-30.

Olsson, I.C., Greenberg, L.A., Bergman, E. & Wysujack, K. (2006). Environmentally induced migration: the importance of food. *Ecology Letters*, **9**, 645–651.

Potter, E.C.E., Campbell, R., Sumner, K. & Marshall, S. (2017). Movements of sea trout in the coastal waters of Great Britain. In: *Sea Trout: Science and Management*. (Graeme Harris. *Ed.*) Proceedings of the 2nd International Sea Trout Symposium. October 2015, Dundalk, Ireland. Troubador, 205–227.

Potter, E.C.E. (1990) Movement of sea trout (*Salmo trutta* L.) in the central and southern North Sea. In: Picken and Shearer (Eds), Proceedings of the Symposium on the Sea Trout of Scotland. Dunstaffnage Marine Research Lab. 18-19 June 1987, NERC, 47 – 52.

Prodöhl, P.A., Antoniacomi, A., Bradley, C., Carlsson, J., Carvalho, G.R., Coughlan, J., Coyne, J., Cross, M.E., Cross, M.C., Davies, A., Dillane, E., Gargan, P., Hynes, R., Mcginnity, P., Milner, N., Reed, T., Roche, W., Taylor, M., Tysklind, N., & Cross, T.F. (2017) Population genetics and Genetic Stock Identification of anadromous *Salmo trutta* from the Irish Sea and adjacent areas, using microsatellite DNA loci. In: *Sea Trout: Science and Management*. (Graeme Harris. *Ed.*) Proceedings of the 2nd International Sea Trout Symposium. October 2015, Dundalk, Ireland. Troubador, 69–95.

Ramster, J.W. & Hill, H.W. (1969). Current systems in the northern Irish Sea. *Nature,* **224**, 59-61.

Rikardsen, A. H., Diserud, O.H., Elliott, J.M., Dempson, J.B., Sturlaugsson, J.B. & Jensen, A.J. (2007). The marine temperature and depth preferences of Arctic charr (*Salvelinus alpinus*) and sea trout (*Salmo trutta*), as recorded by data storage tags. *Fisheries Oceanography,* **16**(5), 436–447

Sturlaugsson, J. & Johannsson, M. (1998). Migration study of wild sea trout (*Salmo trutta* L.) in SE-Iceland: Depth movements and water temperature recorded by data storage tags in freshwater and marine environment. Proceedings of Fifth European Conference on Wildlife Telemetry. Strasbourg, France 25-30 August 1996. 12pp.

Taylor, S.E., Egginton, S. & Taylor, E.W. (1996). Seasonal temperature acclimatisation of rainbow trout: cardiovascular and morphometric influences on maximal sustainable exercise level. *Journal of Experimental Biology,* **199**, 835–845.

Thorstad, E., Økland, F., Finstad, B., Sivertsgård, R., Bjørn, P. & McKinley, R. (2004). Migration speeds and orientation of Atlantic salmon and sea trout post-smolts in a Norwegian fjord system. *Environmental Biology of Fishes,* **71**(3), 305-311.

Thorstad, E., Økland, F., Finstad, B., Sivertsgård, R., Plantalech, N., Bjørn, P. & McKinley, R.S. (2007). Fjord migration and survival of wild and hatchery-reared Atlantic salmon and wild brown trout post-smolts. *Hydrobiologia,* **582**(1), 99-107.

Tudorache, C., O'Keefe, R.A. & Benfey, T.J. (2011). Optimal swimming speeds reflect preferred swimming speeds of brook charr (*Salvelinus fontinalis* Mitchill, 1874). *Fish Physiology and Biochemistry,* **37**(2), 307–315.

Visser, A. W. (1997). Using random walk models to simulate the vertical distribution of particles in a turbulent water column. *Marine Ecology Progress Series,* **158**, 275–281.

Wolk, F. (2003). Three-dimensional Lagrancian tracer modelling in Wadden Sea areas. Diploma Thesis. Carl von Ossietzky University Oldenburg, Hamburg, Germany, 85 pp.

Wysujack, K., Greenberg, L.A., Bergman, E. & Olsson, I.C. (2009). The role of the environment in partial migration: food availability affects the adoption of a migratory tactic in brown trout *Salmo trutta*. *Ecology of Freshwater Fish*, **18**, 52–59.

Young, E.F., Brown, J. & Aldridge, J.N. (2001). Application of a large area curvilinear model to the study of the wind-forced dynamics of flows through the North Channel of the Irish Sea. *Continental Shelf Research,* **21**, 1403–1434.

ELECTRONIC REFERENCES

CSTP (2016), (Milner, N., McGinnity, P. & Roche, W. *Eds.*). Celtic Sea Trout Project – Technical Report to Ireland Wales Territorial Co-operation Programme, 2007-2013 (INTERREG 4A0. [Online.] Dublin, Inland Fisheries Ireland. *Available at* http://celticseatrout.com/downloads/technical-report/

Jensen, J. L. A., Rikardsen, A. H., Thorstad, E. B., Suhr, A. H., Davidsen, J. G. & Primicerio, R. (2014). Water temperatures influence the marine area use of *Salvelinus alpinus* and *Salmo trutta*. *Journal of Fish Biology*, doi:10.1111/jfb.12366

R Development Core Team. (2008). R: A language and environment for statistical computing. R Foundation for Statistical Computing, Vienna, Austria. ISBN 3-900051-07-0. *Available at:* http://www.R-project.org.

Genetic structure and tracking of sea trout (*Salmo trutta* L.) in the Rhine and Meuse estuary in the Netherlands

D. ENSING[1] & A.K. BREUKELAAR[2]

[1]*Agri-Food & Biosciences Institute, Northern Ireland, 18a Newforge Lane, Belfast BT9 5PX, Northern Ireland.*
[2]*Rijkswaterstaat, WNZ, Boompjes 200, 3011XD Rotterdam, The Netherlands.*

ABSTRACT

This study combines both telemetry and genetics on sea trout from the River Rhine and Meuse delta in the Netherlands. Sea trout entering freshwater through the Haringvliet Dam discharge sluices were fitted with a telemetric transponder and then followed using a network of detection stations on their upstream migration through the Rhine and Meuse Rivers. The aims of the study were to establish the origin of a large group of tagged fish that were never detected again after release at the seaward side of the Haringvliet dam and if certain genetic groups were associated with specific rivers. Genetic clustering analysis established the existence of one cluster that probably originated from outside the Rhine and Meuse catchments. The majority of fish in this cluster were never detected again after release: but so were the majority of fish from all four genetic clusters detected. A second genetic cluster contained a large proportion of fish ascending the River Meuse. This could indicate that this group originated from the Meuse. Fish ascending the Rhine River were present in small proportions in all four clusters. This study shows how basic management questions can be answered by combining genetic and telemetric data.

Keywords: genetics; River Meuse; River Rhine; *Salmo trutta*; sea trout; telemetry

INTRODUCTION

Unlike Atlantic salmon (*Salmo salar* L.), sea trout and freshwater resident trout (*S. trutta* L.) were never extirpated in the Rhine and Meuse river systems. Atlantic salmon disappeared from these rivers in the middle of the 20th century because of the construction of migration barriers, over-exploitation, river channelisation, sand and gravel extraction, and pollution (de

Groot, 2002). Although sea trout stocks were negatively impacted by these same factors, they remained present in both Rhine and Meuse rivers, other inland waters, and in Dutch coastal and transitional waters (de Groot, 2002).

A major pollution incident of the Rhine near Basel, Switzerland, in 1986 was the direct cause for the design and implementation of an international plan for the ecological restoration of the Rhine (ICPR). In addition to achieving improvements in water quality, the aim was to reintroduce Atlantic salmon in the Rhine catchment (Bij de Vaate *et al.*, 2003). A similar reintroduction project for Atlantic salmon was initiated in the Meuse catchment in 1987 (Philippart *et al.*, 1994). The Dutch involvement in both reintroduction programmes was focused on improving the ability of anadromous fish to enter freshwater from the sea, as well as increasing connectivity of the Rhine/Meuse delta, through the Lower Rhine and Meuse, with the upstream spawning areas of species such as Atlantic salmon and sea trout. To improve understanding of the upstream migration routes of anadromous salmonids through the Rhine/Meuse delta, the Dutch government funded several projects from 1996 onwards to monitor and study migrating salmonids by using a telemetric tracking system (Bij de Vaate *et al.*, 2003, Breukelaar *et al.*, 1998). Although these projects answered many questions on the spatial and temporal use of the various Dutch waterways by upstream migrating salmonids, they also generated further questions, including the origin of sea trout entering freshwater at the main entry point to the Rhine/Meuse delta for anadromous fish, the Haringvliet Dam discharge sluices. At this location, where Atlantic salmon and sea trout are intercepted and released after having been fitted with a transponder, many such tagged fish are released at the seaward side of the dam and never detected again by the nationwide network of receivers. Tagging mortality, malfunctioning of receivers, and poor tag retention cannot account for the apparent 'disappearance' of these fish (Bij de Vaate *et al.*, 2003), nor can freshwater entry at a different point due to the nationwide coverage by receivers. This raised the question if these 'disappearing' fish were in fact Rhine or Meuse origin sea trout. As tissue samples collected by means of clipping the adipose fin were available from each tagged individual sea trout (and Atlantic salmon) from 1999 to 2013, genetic techniques were used to determine if the 'disappearing' sea trout formed a discrete genetic group that was separate from other such groups that re-entered freshwater. In addition to this first aim of the study, the same genetic techniques were applied to the individuals that re entered freshwater after release and combined with the telemetric data from previous studies to determine if there was any association of discrete genetic groups with specific rivers.

MATERIALS & METHODS

STUDY AREA

About 90% of the Netherlands is part of the combined Rhine and Meuse catchments, with the Rhine alone making up 60%. The Rhine and Meuse river systems follow a complex course in the Netherlands (Figure. 1), that has been much altered by human intervention since the Middle Ages. The Rhine splits into two main braches (Pannerdensch Kanaal and River Waal) a few kilometres after entering the eastern Netherlands from Germany. The Pannerdensch Kanaal splits into a north flowing branch (River IJssel) and a west flowing branch (River Nederrijn). The IJssel empties into Lake IJsselmeer through Lake Ketelmeer. The Nederrijn is known as River Lek further downstream. The River Meuse enters the Netherlands in the south east from Belgium and flows north, before flowing west towards the combined Rhine/Meuse delta. In the pre-delta area, a complex network of natural river branches and artificial canals connect the Rivers Lek, Waal, and Meuse. From this point the access to the sea is via a natural estuary (Haringvliet), or via the artificial waterway that links the port of Rotterdam with the North Sea (Nieuwe Waterweg). The Nieuwe Waterweg is the only open connection to the sea. The Haringvliet and Lake IJsselmeer are dammed off from the sea and connected with the North Sea and Wadden Sea respectively though a complex of sluices. In addition to these barriers, multiple dams and weirs exist on the rivers Meuse and Lek/Nederrijn.

SEA TROUT SAMPLES

A total of 960 tissue samples (fin clips) from telemetrically tagged sea trout collected at the Haringvliet Dam area between 1999 and 2013 were available for genetic analysis. The samples were obtained from commercial fishermen using fyke nets in the Haringvliet, near the Haringvliet Dam (Fig. 1).

GENETIC ANALYSIS OF SEA TROUT SAMPLES

All samples taken were stored in absolute ethanol (99%) at 4°C. until DNA extraction. Genomic DNA was extracted from an adipose fin clip using the high quality/high yield 96-well DNeasy Blood & Tissue Kit (Qiagen) according to the manufacturer's instructions. Random checks were performed on some samples using a 0.8% 0.5 X TBE agarose gel for DNA quality, and subsequently stored at -20°C. in 96 well plates.

All samples were genotyped for a suite of 34 microsatellite loci in four multiplexes. Multiplex one consisted of Ssa85 (O'Reillly *et al.*, 1996), mOne102a/mOne102b§ (Olsen *et al.*, 2000), Ssa406UoS (Cairney *et al.*, 2000), MHC-1 (Grimholt *et al.*, 2002), CA048302 (Vasemägi *et al.*, 2005b), Ssa419UoS (Cairney *et al.*, 2000), Ssa416UoS (Cairney *et al.*, 2000), Sssp2201 (Paterson *et al.*, 2004), CA048828 (Vasemägi *et al.*, 2005b), Cocl-lav-4 (Rogers *et al.*, 2004). Multiplex 2 consisted of Oneµ9 (Scribner *et al.*, 1996), SsaD157 (King *et al.*, 2005), Sssp2216 (Pterson *et al.*, 2004), Str2QUB (Keenan *et al.*, 2013), Str3QUB (Keenan *et al.*, 2013), Ssa420UoS (Cairney *et al.*, 2000), mOne104 (Olsen *et al.*, 2000), Ssa197 (O'Reilly *et al.*, 1996), and mOki10 (Smith *et al.*, 1998). Multipex 3 consisted of BG935488 (Vasemägi *et al.*, 2005b), SsD71 (King *et al.*,

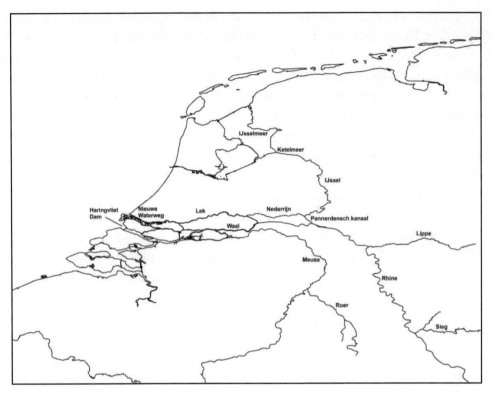

Figure 1. Map of the study area for the Lower River Rhine and Meuse catchments and delta. Geographic locations mentioned in the text are shown.

2005), SasaTAP2A (Gromholt *et al.*, 2002), CA053293 (Vasemägli *et al.*, 2005b), SSa410UoS (Cairney *et al.*, 2000), SSa422UoS (Cairney *et al.*, 2000), CA060208 (Vasemägli *et al.*, 2005b), abd MHC-I-UTR (Vasemägli *et al.*, 2005a). Finally, multiplexc four consisted of SsaD170 (King *et al.*, 2005), Sasa-UBA (Grimholt *et al.*, 2002), Ssa413UoS (Cairney *et al.*, 2000), CA054565a/CA054565b§ (Vasemägi *et al.*, 2005b), and mOne101 Olsen *et al.*, 2000). Details on primer sequences, labelling allele size range and number of alleles are given in Table 1.

PCR reactions consisted of 1 μl of template DNA, 0.15μM of each primer, 1.75 μl of PCR mastermix (Qiagen Multiplex PCR Kit, Qiagen) and DNAase free H_2O (Gibco) to make a final volume of 3.5 μl. PCR amplifications were carried out on Techne TC-PLUS thermocyclers (Techne). The PCR consisted of the following amplification cycles: For all four multiplexes the cycle started with a denaturation step at 95°C./15min followed by 5 cycles of 95°C./45sec, 55°C./60sec, 72°C./60sec followed 22 cycles of 95°C./45sec, 57°C./90sec, 72°C./60sec, finished with a final cycle of 60°C./30min.

Samples were screened on an Applied Biosystems 3130 genetic analyser (Life Technologies). Allele detection and binning was carried out on the fully automated allele scoring software Genemapper v5.0 (Life Technologies). All genotyping was subsequently manually checked and verified.

Table 1. Microsatellite multiplex panels, primer sequences, and literature references for all 34 microsatellites used in the study.

Panel/locus	Forward primer	Reverse primer
Multiplex 1		
Ssa85	NED-AGGTGGGTCCTCCAAGCTAC	gtttACCCGCTCCTCACTTAATC
mOne102a	NED-GGGATTATTCTTACTTTGGCTGTT	gtttCCTGGTTGGGAATCACTGC
mOne102b§	–	
Ssa406UoS	NED-ACCAACCTGCACATGTCTTCTATG	gtttGCTGCCGCCTGTTGTCTCTTT
MHC-I	PET-AGGAAGGTGCTGAAGAGGAAC	gtttCAATTACCACAAGCCCGCTC
CA048302	PET-TTGCCACCTCTAAACGCTTC	gtttAAATGAACCCCAGCCATACA
Ssa419UoS	PET-GGTCGTATCGCGTTTCAGGA	gtttGCTGCAATAAAGAGATGCTTGTT
Ssa416UoS	FAM-TGACCAACAACAAACGCACAT	gtttCCCACCCATTAACACAACTAT
Sssp2201	FAM-TTTAGATGGTGGGATACTGGGAGGC	gtttCGGGAGCCCCATAACCCTACTAATAAC
CA048828	VIC-GAGGGCTTCCCATACAACAA	gtttGTTTAAGCGGTGAGTTGACGAGAG
Cocl-lav-4	VIC-TGGTGTAATGGCTTTTCCTG	gtttGGGAGCAACATTGGACTCTC
Multiplex 2		
Oneµ9	NED-CTCTCTTTGGCTCGGGGAATGTT	gtttGCATGTTCTGACAGCCTACAGCT
SsaD157	NED-ATCGAAATGGAACTTTTGAATG	gtttGCTTAGGGCTGAGAGAGGAATAC
Sssp2216	PET-GGCCCAGACAGATAAACAAACACGC	gtttGCCAACAGCAGCATCTACACCCAG
Str2QUB	PET-CTGGGGTCCACAGCCTATAA	gtttGAGCTACAACCTGATCCACCA
Str3QUB	FAM-CTGACCGCTGCACACTAA	gtttGGCTCTAATCGACTGGCAGA
Ssa420UoS	FAM-GCAGGAGAGTCGCTACAG	gtttGATCTATGCCCACAAACAG
mOne104	FAM-GGGTACCCACTGACGCTATG	gttTCTGGTACTTCCCTGATGC
Ssa197	VIC-GGGTTGAGTAGGGAGGCTTG	gttTGGCAGGGATTTGACATAAC
mOki10	VIC-ATGCAATTTCCAAACTCGTGT	gtttCCCCTTTCTCCCCTTTCTCTAC
Multiplex 3		
BG935488	gttTGACCCCACCAAGTTTTTCT	NED-AAACACAGTAAGCCCATCTATTG
SsaD71	NED-AACGTGAAACATAAATCGATGG	gtTTAAGAATGGGTTGCCTATGAG
Sasa-TAP2A	gtttGTCCTGATGTTGGCTCCCAGG	NED-GCGGGACACCGTCAGGGCAGT
CA053293	PET-TCTCATGGTGAGCAACAAACA	gtttACTCTGGGCATTCATTCAG
Ssa410UoS	gttttGGAAAATAATCAATGCTGCTGGTT	PET-CTACAATCTGGACTATCTTCTTCA
Ssa422UoS	gtTTATGGGCGTCCACCTCTGACA	FAM-CACCCCAGCCTCCTCAACCTTC
CA060208	VIC-GCAACAATTCCCTTTTGACC	gtttCGTGCAGTAGGAAAGGGGTA
MHC-I-UTR	VIC-TGCCCAGATGACTTGAGAGAC	gtttCCAACCTCCTGTGTTGTGTG
Multiplex 4		
SsaD170	NED-GGAGGCAGTTAAGAGAACAAAAG	gttTCACCTACCCTTCTCATTCAAG
Sasa-UBA	NED-GGAGAGCTGCCCAGATGACTT	gtttCAATTACCACAAGCCCGCTC
Ssa413UoS	PET-GTAGACGCCATCGGTATTGTG	gtttCGTGATGCCGCTGTAGACTTG
CA054565a	VIC-TCTGTGGTTCCCGATCTTTC	gtttCAACATTTGCCTAGCCCAGA
CA054565b§	–	–
mOne101	VIC-TGCTAAATGACTGAAATGTTGAGA	gtttGAGAATGAATGGCTGAATGGA

DESCRIPTIVE STATISTICS

Basic descriptive statistics, including number of alleles (N_A), number of effective alleles (N_E), observed (H_o) and expected (H_E) heterozygosity, were computed using the program GenAlEx v6.5 (Peakall and Smouse, 2006), as were deviations from Hardy-Weinberg equilibrium (HW). Corrections to account for multiple tests (e.g. sequential Bonferroni correction, Rice (1989)) were only carried out to address the specific question being considered.

POPULATION STRUCTURE

Population structure in the samples was estimated using the program STRUCTURE v2.3.4 (Pritchard *et al.*, 2000) which defines clusters of individuals based on their genotypes at multiple loci using a Bayesian algorithm. The ΔK statistic (Evanno *et al.*, 2005) based on the rate of change in the log probability of data was used to infer the likely number of clusters. Initial Burn-in-Length was set at 50000 with 20000 iterations. 20 runs of $K=1$ to $K=10$ were executed. As STRUCTURE is optimised to finding the most basic level of clustering, a hierarchical approach was implemented here: individual clusters detected during the first run of the software were subjected to subsequent runs at the same basic programme settings until the most likely number of clusters present in the dataset had been established. Individual membership of a cluster was accepted at scores >0.75. Samples that scored below this number for membership of any cluster were omitted from further analysis.

QUALITY CONTROL

Microchecker v2.2.3 (Van Oosterhout *et al.*, 2004) was used to test for the possible presence of null-alleles and allele scoring errors. To further check for genotyping errors, 96 individuals (10 % of the total data) were genotyped again following the same protocols as in the original analysis. The genotypes were compared to the previous ones and allelic mismatches were counted to establish an error rate for the genotyping in this study.

TELEMETRIC DATA

A detailed description of the inductive coupling radio telemetric tracking system (NEDAP Trail System; http://www.nedaptrail.com/) infrastructure in the Netherlands is available in Bij de Vaate *et al.*, (2003). Fish were collected at the Haringvliet dam, surgically fitted with a transponder, adipose fin clipped for genetic analysis, and subsequently released on the seaward side of the Haringvliet dam. Fixed detection stations, constructed on the banks of watercourses that were identified as part of a likely migration route for migratory salmonids in the Rhine and Meuse catchments (Figure. 2), picked up the transponder signal, unique for each fish, when it passed. The migration route of each fish was derived from sequential passages of the detection stations.

The battery ensures a minimum lifetime of between 18 and 24 months, depending on the number of registrations. In water a transponder weights approximately 17 g. Field tests have shown that the detection system functions properly in both fresh and salt water. Maximum tolerable conductivity of the system in river water was not tested. Calculations showed however that a conductivity of less than 6 000 μS cm^{-1} does not affect transmission when the distance between the antenna and the transponder is less than 15 m.

The maximum antenna length at which a transponder still detects is 3 000 m at a mean depth of 6 m. The maximum water depth tested was 30 m using an antenna length of 700 m. The maximum passing velocity still allowing successful detection was 5-6 m s^{-1}. Effects of ship engine noises on detection were found to be negligible. However, when the transponder is close to the hull of a vessel (less than 10 cm) the signal detection is interrupted. When a tagged fish passes a detection station its unique ID-number (amongst other information) is logged onto a data storage system.

The telemetric detection data used in this study was pooled to represent four categories indicating the extent of the upstream migration in the Rhine and Meuse river systems. This established that:-

a. Category I did not re-enter freshwater after release,
b. Category II re-entered freshwater and was detected as far upstream as the delta area,
c. Category III re-entered freshwater, moved through the delta area and migrated up the River Rhine or one of its branches,
d. Category IV re-entered freshwater, moved through the delta area, and migrated up the River Meuse.

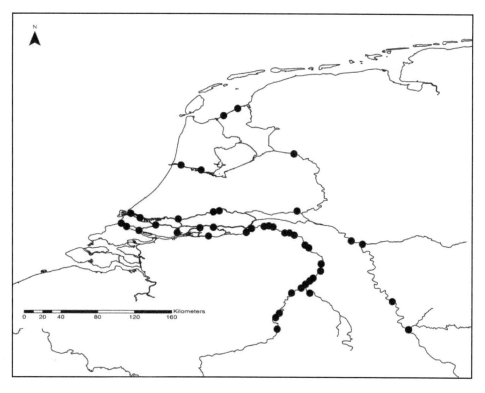

Figure 2. Map of telemetric detection sites (as closed circles) in the River Rhine and Meuse catchments and delta.

COMBINING GENETIC CLUSTERING AND TELEMETRIC DATA

If a genetic baseline for the Rhine and Meuse catchment trout had been available, a genetic assignment or stock identification study would have been possible assigning the Haringvliet samples to putative populations of origin within these catchments. Previously genetic assignment studies for example have been successfully undertaken on both sea trout (e.g. Koljonen *et al.*, 2014) and Atlantic salmon (e.g. Ensing *et al.*, 2013), highlighting the potential of the technique. In the absence of any such baseline, the association of genetic clusters with upstream migration categories is the only method available to hypothesise on the origin of different stocks present in the Haringvliet sample. A Chi-squared text was used to determine if the proportions of migration categories were similar in all genetic clusters.

RESULTS

GENETIC ANALYSIS SEA TROUT SAMPLES

Out of the 960 samples obtained, 120 samples were rejected at various stages before statistical analysis of the genotypes for reasons such as degraded DNA, poor amplification success, or the sample being an Atlantic salmon or Atlantic salmon x trout hybrid. This left 840 samples for further analysis.

DESCRIPTIVE STATISTICS

The descriptive genetic statistics are given in Table 2. Depending on locus, between 2 (mOne102a) and 70 (Sssp2201) alleles were segregating, with an overall mean of 24 alleles over all 34 loci. The number of effective alleles varied between 1.4 (Ssa416UoS) and 23.6 (Sssp2201), with a mean of 8.3 over all loci. Observed heterozygosity (H_o) was lowest at the CA054565a (H_o=0.26) and highest at the Ssa406UoS locus (H_o=0.90). Mean observed heterozygosity averaged across loci was 0.70. Expected heterozygosity (H_E) is a theoretical measure of the heterozygosity that might be expected given the number of alleles and numbers sampled. Expected heterozygosity (H_E) was lowest at the CA054565a locus (H_E=0.24) and highest at loci Ssa406UoS and Sssp2201 (H_E=0.96). The expected heterozygosity value averaged over all loci was H_E=0.77 compared with a mean observed heterozygosity across loci of 0.70. These figures do not differ greatly, suggesting that there is random mating within populations and that they were adequately sampled.

Tests for conformance to Hardy-Weinberg (HW) equilibrium were used to detect whether putative populations show significant differences from a theoretical distribution of heterozygote and homozygote genotypes expected under a theoretically large random breeding group that was stable with respect to immigration and emigration. This test is often used to infer inbreeding (if fewer heterozygous individuals than expected occur) and/or population admixtures, where two or more differentiated populations are mistakenly treated as a single group (the '*Wahlund effect*'). All but two loci (CA053293, mOne101) were found to significantly deviate from HW equilibrium (initial α=0.05) following a sequential Bonferroni correction for multiple tests indicating the sample was comprised of individuals from multiple discrete genetic populations.

POPULATION STRUCTURE

The population structure in the sea trout stocks of the Rivers Rhine and Meuse delta area in the Netherlands, supported by the results from the STRUCTURE analysis, suggests four genetic

Table 2. Descriptive genetic data for all 34 loci generated with GENALEX 6.5 (Peakall & Smouse, 2006); number of alleles (N_A), number of effective alleles (N_E), Observed heterozygosity (H_O), and expected heterozygosity (H_E). Asterisks (*) denote locus out of Hardy-Weinberg equilibrium (HW).

Locus	N_A	N_E	H_O	H_E	HW
Oneμ9	15	2.9	0.58	0.66	*
Ssa197	14	5.0	0.81	0.80	*
Ssa420UoS	38	18.6	0.88	0.95	*
SsaD157	48	19.7	0.89	0.95	*
Sssp2216	9	4.1	0.70	0.75	*
Str2QUB	67	11.5	0.86	0.91	*
Str3QUB	11	3.6	0.68	0.72	*
mOki10	30	17.6	0.88	0.94	*
mOne104	35	3.7	0.59	0.73	*
Ssa85	15	3.1	0.67	0.68	*
mOne102a	2	1.5	0.28	0.31	*
mOne102b	21	11.4	0.87	0.91	*
Ssa406UoS	60	23.3	0.90	0.96	*
MHC1	23	8.4	0.84	0.88	*
CA048302	19	2.3	0.54	0.56	*
Ssa419UoS	6	3.5	0.53	0.71	*
Ssa416UoS	4	1.4	0.25	0.28	*
Sssp2201	70	23.6	0.85	0.96	*
CA048828	44	18.6	0.88	0.95	*
Cocl-lav-4	12	4.6	0.61	0.78	*
BG935488	15	6.3	0.79	0.84	*
CA053293	12	4.2	0.76	0.76	
CA060208	12	2.8	0.59	0.64	*
MHC-1-UTR	27	9.5	0.85	0.89	*
Sasa-TAP2A	13	4.1	0.57	0.76	*
Ssa410UoS	47	18.5	0.89	0.95	*
Ssa422UoS	27	6.0	0.75	0.83	*
SsaD71	18	8.8	0.86	0.89	*
CA054565a	10	1.3	0.21	0.24	*
CA054565b	20	2.8	0.58	0.64	*
Sasa-UBA	28	9.3	0.67	0.89	*
Ssa413UoS	19	4.7	0.72	0.79	*
SsaD170	24	11.7	0.89	0.91	*
mOne101	9	3.5	0.67	0.71	

clusters present (not shown). The hierarchical approach to infer the number of clusters puts the most likely number in the samples at $\Delta K=2$ (Clusters A/B) for the initial run. A subsequent STRUCTURE runs suggested further sub-structuring existed in Cluster B (Clusters C, D, and E). In a third round of STRUCTURE, no clear sub-structuring was detected in Clusters A, C, D, and E.

QUALITY CONTROL

No evidence for either large allele dropout or scoring errors was detected by Micro-Checker. In the re-genotyping exercise of the 6 912 alleles 46 genotyping errors were found; a genotyping error rate of 0.67%. The error rate in this study is therefore unlikely to have notably influenced results from any analysis of the data set (Bonin *et al.*, 2004).

COMBINING GENETIC CLUSTERING AND TELEMETRIC DATA

The Chi-square test rejected the null hypothesis that the proportion of migration route categories was the same in the four genetic clusters. Therefore, the alternative hypothesis that the proportion of migration route categories was not the same in the four genetic clusters was accepted. From the percentage of migration categories that members were assigned to in each of the four genetic clusters (Table 3) it is clear that cluster D had the highest proportion of River Meuse migrants (32%), and cluster A the lowest (2%). Rhine migrants had the highest proportional presence in cluster E (12%) and the lowest in cluster A (2%). Fish that were detected only in the delta area and not upstream in either Rhine or Meuse rivers had the highest proportion in cluster E (22%) and the lowest in cluster C (9%). Fish that were not detected again after tagging were proportionally the largest group in all clusters, with cluster A having the highest percentage (84%) and cluster D the lowest (41%). It should be noted that none of the cluster A Rhine and Meuse migrants was detected as far upstream as the spawning areas on both rivers.

DISCUSSION

The results from the hierarchical genetic clustering analysis suggest the existence of four discrete genetic groups present in the sample. Members of all four clusters were observed in the four migration categories, but not in equal proportions.

The first round of STRUCTURE analysis suggested the existence of two distinct genetic groups at the most basic level; a large Cluster B and a smaller cluster A. Cluster A had by far the lowest percentage of members that ascend the Rivers Rhine and Meuse proper (4%) compared with the range of 20-40% found in the three clusters (C, D, and E) that were detected in a second round of STRUCTURE analysis in cluster B. Furthermore, none of the 4% of

Meuse and Rhine ascending individuals in cluster A went far enough upstream to reach the region where the spawning areas are located. This cluster also had the highest proportion of all clusters for fish not detected again after tagging (84%). This, in combination with the fact that this cluster is genetically most separate from the other three clusters, makes it most likely that it consists of fish that do not originate from either the Meuse or Rhine rivers, but from outside these catchments. A classic genetic assignment study might have resolved the origin of these fish, but the lack a comprehensive genetic baseline for trout in the Rhine, Meuse and adjacent catchments prevented this. Despite probably not originating from the Rhine and Meuse catchments, fish from cluster A do enter the delta area of these rivers. It is only possible to speculate on the reasons why, but feeding and natural straying might be a plausible explanation.

Clusters C, D, and E had a higher proportion of Rhine and Meuse ascending members compared to cluster A. When all three clusters are compared, cluster D is noticeable for the high proportion of fish that ascended the River Meuse (31%). Many of these individuals were detected in the upstream areas of this river system, where spawning would be possible. Therefore, it is tentatively suggested, that this group could comprise of individuals that originate from the River Meuse. The fact that a small proportion of cluster D members have been detected migrating upstream on the River Rhine might be explained by straying behaviour or, possibly, by opportunistic upstream migratory behaviour. Such opportunistic upstream migration patterns were observed in some individuals in this study, where fish migrated far upstream on one river, only to stop at a migration barrier before moving downstream and ascending a second river. Such behaviour is known to occur in Atlantic salmon (*pers. comm.* R. Kennedy), but in this case it could be an indicator of the difficulty anadromous salmonids have in reaching the spawning areas of the River Rhine and Meuse. These difficulties are also illustrated by the fact that only 8% of the tagged fish in this study were detected in the regions where spawning tributaries are located on either Meuse or Rhine.

Table 3. Percentage of members of the four genetic clusters (A, C, D, & E) that were detected at the four upstream migration categories. Category I did not re-enter freshwater after release. Category II re-entered freshwater and was detected as far upstream as the delta area. Category III re-entered freshwater, moved through the delta area and migrated up the River Rhine or one of its branches. Category IV re-entered fresh water, moved through the delta area and migrated up the River Meuse.

Migration Category.	*I*	*II*	*III*	*IV*
Cluster A	84	12	2	2
Cluster C	71	9	6	14
Cluster D	41	19	8	32
Cluster E	54	22	11	12

None of the clusters had more than 11% (cluster E) of sea trout ascending the Rhine. Fish detected upstream in the Rhine were the smallest category in all four genetic clusters: in real numbers, Rhine ascending fish (78) were outnumbered by Meuse ascending fish (128). This might suggest that the Meuse sea trout stock is the larger of the two. The Rhine has never been noted for having a large stock of sea trout in historical times (de Groot, 2002) and this could well be the situation today.

Another notable result from this study was the large number of fish that were never detected again after tagging and release. In all four genetic clusters this was the dominant category, and 592 out of 960 (62%) tagged fish in the entire sample in real numbers were not detected again. This figure is very similar to the 51% reported by Bij de Vaate *et al.*, 2003. This can be explained in part by the presence of a group of fish in the Rhine/Meuse delta not originating from either Rhine or Meuse: but this does not account for all of these fish. Suggestions that the 'disappearing' fish from category I are sexually immature and therefore do not undertake a full migration to the spawning sites would be plausible if it could be proven that fish from category I are significantly smaller than fish that move further upstream. This was not the case. It is probable that a combination of factors is the cause for these observations; with fish originating from outside the Rhine and Meuse systems using the delta for feeding, sexually non-mature fish entering freshwater on a 'dummy run', and other factors of an unknown nature. This study provides only an insight of the possibilities that a combined telemetric and genetics study can offer to the management of sea trout populations in general and the Meuse and Rhine stocks in particular. Despite the obvious limitations of the genetic component of this study in the absence of a genetic baseline, it was successful in answering some basic questions that benefit sea trout management in the Netherlands. Knowing that the sea trout that enter the Rhine/Meuse delta consist of several discrete genetic groups originating from both outside and inside the Rhine and Meuse is of particular value to management. It suggests the Rhine/Meuse delta is a feeding area for both native and non-native sea trout stocks and that, with better accessibility to sea trout and other anadromous fish, the Rhine/Meuse delta area could increase in importance as a feeding area in future years and so assist in the recovery of local and regional sea trout stocks.

It would be advisable to undertake a more comprehensive study in the future, using a genetic baseline comprising all Rhine and Meuse populations and those from other river systems that are likely to be using the delta area for feeding. This would give much greater resolution than the study presented here and could, for example, inform management on the success of sea trout recovery and restoration actions in both catchments.

ACKNOWLEDGEMENTS

The authors wish to thank Rijkswaterstaat (RWS) for the financial support to facilitate this study. The fishers and people involved in sampling and telemetry work are acknowledged for their help, as is Peter Irvine at AFBINI for sample extraction and genotyping.

REFERENCES

Bij de Vaate, A., Breukelaar, A. W., Vriese, T., De Laak, G. & Dijkers, C. (2003). Sea trout migration in the Rhine delta. *Journal of Fish Biology* **63**, 892-908.

Bonin, A., Bellemain, E., Eidesen, P. B., Pompanon, F., Brochmann, C. & Taberlet, P. (2004). How to track and assess genotyping errors in population genetics studies. *Molecular Ecology* **13**, 3261-3273.

Breukelaar, A. W., Bij de Vaate, A. & Fockens, K. T. W. (1998). Inland migration study of sea trout (*Salmo trutta*) into the rivers Rhine and Meuse (The Netherlands), based on inductive coupling radio telemetry. *Hydrobiologia* **371/372**, 29-33.

Cairney, M., Taggart, J. B. & Høyheim, B. (2000). Characterization of microsatellite and minisatellite loci in Atlantic salmon (*Salmo salar* L.) and cross-species amplification in other salmonids. *Molecular Ecology* **9**, 2175–2178.

de Groot, S. J. (2002). A review of the past and present status of anadromous fish species in the Netherlands: is restocking the Rhine feasible? *Hydrobiologia* **478**, 205-218.

Ensing, D., Crozier, W. W., Boylan, P., Ó Maoiléidigh, N. & McGinnity, P. (2013). An analysis of genetic stock identification on a small geographical scale using microsatellite markers, and its application in the management of a mixed-stock fishery for Atlantic salmon Salmo salar in Ireland. *Journal of Fish Biology* **82**, 2080-2094.

Evanno, G., Regnaut, S. & Goudet, J. (2005). Detecting the number of clusters of individuals using the software STRUCTURE: a simulation study. *Molecular Ecology* **14**, 2611-2620.

Grimholt, U., Drabløs, F., Jørgensen, S., Høyheim, B. & Stet, R. J. M. (2002). The major histocompatibility class I locus in Atlantic salmon (*Salmo salar* L.): polymorphism, linkage analysis and protein modelling. *Immunogenetics* **54**, 570–581.

International Commission for the Protection of the Rhine (ICPR). (1987) Aktionsprogramm Rhein. Report of the International Commission for Protection of the Rhine River against Pollution. Koblenz: ICPR.

Keenan, K., Bradley, C. R., Magee, J. J., Hynes, R. A., Kennedy, R. J., Crozier, W. W., Poole, R., Cross, T. F., McGinnity, P. & Prodöhl, P. A. (2013). Beaufort trout MicroPlex: a high-throughput multiplex platform comprising 38 informative microsatellite loci for use in resident and anadromous (sea trout) brown trout *Salmo trutta* genetic studies. *Journal of Fish Biology* **82**, 1789-1804.

King, T. L., Eackles, M. S. & Letcher, B. H. (2005). Microsatellite DNA markers for the study of Atlantic salmon (Salmo salar) kinship, population structure, and mixed-fishery analyses. *Molecular Ecology Notes* **5**, 130-132.

Koljonen, M-L., Gross, R. & Koskiniemi, J. (2014). Wild Estonian and Russian sea trout (Salmo trutta) in Finnish coastal sea trout catches: results of genetic mixed-stock analysis. *Hereditas* **151**, 177-195.

Olsen, J. B., Wilson, S. L., Kretschmer, E. J., Jones, K. C. & Seeb, J. E. (2000). Characterization of 14 tetranucleotide microsatellite loci derived from sockeye salmon. *MolecularEcology* **9**, 2155–2234.

O'Reilly, P. T., Hamilton, L. C., McConnell, S. K. & Wright, J. M. (1996). Rapid analysis of genetic variation in Atlantic salmon (Salmo salar) by PCR multiplexing of dinucleotide and tetranucleotide microsatellites. *Canadian Journal of Fisheries and Aquatic Sciences* **53**, 2292-2298.

Paterson, S., Piertney, S. B., Knox, D., Gilbey, J. & Verspoor, E. (2004). Characterization and PCR multiplexing of novel highly variable tetranucleotide Atlantic salmon (Salmo salar L.) microsatellites. *Molecular Ecology Notes* **4**, 160-162.

Peakall, R. & Smouse, P. E. (2006). GENALEX 6: genetic analysis in Excel. Population genetic software for teaching and research. *Molecular Ecology Notes* **6**, 288-295.

Philippart, J. C., Micha, J.C., Baras, E., Prignon, C., Gillet, A. & and Joris, S. (1994). The Belgian Project "Meuse Salmon 2000". First Results, Problems and Future Prospects. *Water Science & Technology* **29**, 315-317.

Pritchard, J. K., Stephens, M. & Donnelly, P. (2000). Inference of population structure using multilocus genotype data. *Genetics* **155**, 945-959.

Rice, W. R. (1989). ANALYZING TABLES OF STATISTICAL TESTS. *Evolution* **43**, 223-225.

Rogers, S. M., Marchland, M. H. & Bernatchez, L. (2004). Isolation, characterization and cross-salmonid amplification of 31 microsatellite loci in the lake whitefish (*Coregonus clupeaformis*, Mitchell). *Molecular Ecology Notes* **4**, 89–92.

Scribner, K. T., Gust, J. R. & Fields, R. L. (1996). Isolation and characterization of novel salmon microsatellite loci: cross-species amplification and population genetic applications. *Canadian Journal of Fisheries and Aquatic Sciences* **53**, 833–841.

Smith, C. T., Koop, B. F. & Nelson, R. J. (1998). Isolation and characterization of coho salmon (*Oncorhynchus kisutch*) microsatellites and their use in other salmonids. *Molecular Ecology* **7**, 1614.

Van Oosterhout, C., Hutchinson, W. F., Wills, D. P. M. & Shipley, P. (2004). MICRO-CHECKER: software for identifying and correcting genotyping errors in microsatellite data. *Molecular Ecology Notes* **4**, 535-538.

Vasemägi, A., Gross, R., Paaver, T., Koljonen, M. L., Säisä, M. & Nilsson, J. (2005a). Analysis of gene associated tandem repeat markers in Atlantic salmon (*Salmo salar* L.) populations: implications for restoration and conservation in the Baltic Sea. *Conservation Genetics* **6**, 385–397.

Vasemägi, A., Nilsson, J. & Primmer, C. R. (2005b). Seventy-five EST-linked Atlantic salmon (*Salmo salar* L.) microsatellite markers and their cross-amplification in five salmonidspecies. *Molecular Ecology Notes* **5**, 282–288.

Marine migrations of sea trout (*Salmo trutta*)

D. ALDVÉN[1] & J. G. DAVIDSEN[2]

[1]Department of Biological and Environmental Sciences, University of Gothenburg, Box 463, SE-405 30, Gothenburg, Sweden. [2]NTNU University Museum, Norwegian University of Science and Technology, NO-7491 Trondheim, Norway.

ABSTRACT

The brown trout species complex (*Salmo trutta* L.) exhibits facultative anadromy whereby a variable proportion of the juvenile trout may either spend their entire life history in the freshwater environment (as resident trout) or migrate into marine environment (as sea trout). The richer feeding conditions in the sea allows the migrants to grow faster and attain a larger size and greater fecundity on returning to freshwater to spawn so that they are 'fitter' in terms of reproductive success than the smaller resident trout from the same river. This review provides a brief synopsis of current knowledge of the migratory behaviour and habitat use of sea trout in the marine environment and identifies some critical knowledge gaps that currently limit the adoption of effective strategies for the conservation and management of the sea trout resource.

Keywords: anadromy, brown trout, marine mortality, post-smolts, kelts survival, telemetry, veteran migrants.

INTRODUCTION

Anadromy in brown trout (*Salmo trutta* L.) is an important life-history strategy. By exploiting better feeding conditions in the marine environment, migration enables individual sea trout to achieve higher growth rates, larger size-at-age and higher fecundity (Hendry *et al.,* 2004) and, therefore, provides increased benefits for fitness and survival compared with resident trout that do not undertake such migrations. The penalty costs of migration may include physiological adjustments to the allocation of energy for swimming and a greater probability of mortality from the increased risks of predation, parasitism and diseases during migration (Gross *et al.,* 1988; Jonsson & Jonsson, 1993). Although a strategy of seaward migration is widespread in populations located in watercourses with access to the sea, the biology and ecology of the anadromous sea trout is poorly understood (Drenner *et al.*, 2012; ICES, 2013). In general terms, the existing knowledge of the marine phase in the life cycle of sea trout is broadly restricted to inshore coastal areas such as estuaries and fjords (e.g. Moore & Potter, 1994; Koed *et al.*, 2006; Thorstad *et al.*, 2007; Aarestrup *et al.*, 2014; Eldøy *et al.*, 2015; Aldvén et al., 2015).

The marine movement and migration of sea trout are generally confined to near coastal areas (Jonsson & Jonsson, 2011) and therefore the species may be sensitive to negative impacts in these areas. Unaffected, natural, coastal marine ecosystems are now rare in Europe and conflicts of use between nature conservation and anthropogenic interactions, such as urbanization, aquaculture, fisheries and recreational activities are increasingly common (Bulleri & Chapman, 2010). The increasing use of near coastal areas for aquaculture may negatively influence anadromous salmonids that also provide important ecosystem services in many countries. For example, the salmon lice (*Lepeophtheirus salmonis*) in areas where salmon are farmed intensively in sea cages has negatively affected the status of wild sea trout populations by reducing growth and increasing marine mortality (Poole *et al.*, 1996; Thorstad *et al.*, 2015).

This review provides a synopsis of current knowledge on sea trout movements and habitat use in marine environments and identifies some strategic gaps in our knowledge that need to be filled to improve the design and implementation of good conservation and management practices.

POST-SMOLT MIGRATION

Out-migrant smolts are termed 'post-smolts' from the life stage when the leave the river and enter the sea as smolts until the middle of their first sea-winter (Aas *et al.*, 2011). Initial downriver migration through estuaries and into the sea has been observed as principally nocturnal (Moore & Potter, 1994; Moore *et al.*, 1998; Koed *et al.*, 2006; Thorstad *et al.*, 2007; Aarestrup *et al.*, 2014; Aldvén *et al.*, 2015; Flaten *et al.*, 2016), but it may also take place in daylight (Moore *et al.*, 1998; Aarestrup *et al.*, 2014). Seaward movement has been shown to follow tidal cycles, with post-smolts moving through estuaries at ebbing tides or during the period of slack water between two high tides (Moore & Potter, 1994; Thorstad *et al.*, 2007). The transition from fresh to salt water is often associated with high mortalities for post-smolts, ranging from 12 – 49% (Koed *et al.*, 2006; del Villar-Guerra *et al.*, 2013, Aldvén *et al.*, 2015). Post-smolts may exhibit either active movement through estuaries with directed swimming (Thorstad *et al.*, 2007; Moore *et al.*, 1998; Aldvén *et al.*, 2015; but see Davidsen *et al.*, 2014a) or passive downstream movement similar to that of a drifting object (Moore & Potter, 1994). Post-smolts utilize the top surface layer of the water column (0.6-7 m) independent of the depth at the locality (Lyse *et al.*, 1998; Ruud, 2015) and they tend to stay close to their natal rivers after initial sea entry. However, they later display a variety of dispersal behaviours, with some travelling large distances (over 30 km) while others remain closer to their natal rivers (Berg & Berg, 1987; Finstad *et al.*, 2005; Thorstad *et al.*, 2007; Middlemas *et al.*, 2009; Manel-la *et al.*, 2011; del Villar-Guerra *et al.*, 2013; Davidsen *et al.*, 2014a; Aldvén *et al.*, 2016; Flatten, *et al.*, 2016).

As the post-smolts progress further out from estuaries and fjords, the nocturnal movement pattern breaks down and the diel migration pattern seems to disappear (Thorstad *et al.*, 2007, Aldvén *et al.*, 2015). Post-smolts within fjords have been shown to stay close to the shoreline in the fastest moving section of the water column (Lyse *et al.*, 1998; Thorstad *et al.*, 2007). A tendency for post-smolts to avoid areas with narrow channels and tidal flats along the shoreline was reported also by del Villa Guerra *et. al.*, (2014). Post-smolt migration speeds within fjord systems often vary within and between study sites, with a range from 0.003 to 0.56 body lengths per second (Thorstad *et al.*, 2004; Finstad *et al.*, 2005; Thorstad *et al.*, 2007; Aarestrup *et al.*, 2014; Aldvén *et al.*, 2016). Although Finstad *et al.*, (2005) recorded a gradual increase in the migration speed of sea trout as they moved out to sea, Aarestrup *et al.*, (2014) and Aldvén *et al.*, (2016) found a gradual decrease in migration speeds as the post-smolts moved seawards. This behaviour could reflect different migration strategies related to habitat use during the marine migrations. In Sweden and Denmark, it was found that some 47 – 83% of post-smolts, remained within the brackish fjord systems, while others migrated through the fjord to the more open and saline sea (del Villar-Guerra *et al.*, 2014; Aldvén *et al.*, 2016).

Downstream migration into the sea is associated with high mortalities. Mortality during initial marine migrations have been shown to range generally from 21 – 65% (Thorstad *et al.*, 2007; Aarestrup *et al.*, 2014; Aldvén *et al.*, 2015; Flaten *et al.*, *2016*); with mortality losses ranging from 0.63 – 2.08 % per km reported by Aarestrup *et al.*, (2014) and Aldvén *et al.*, (2015).

Marine residence times vary widely between populations and latitudes. Studies from Norway showed that the time spent at sea of first-time (maiden) migrants varied from 68 ± 21 days in northern Norway to 6 – 9 months in central Norway (Berg & Berg ,1987; Jonsson & Jonsson, 2009; Davidsen *et al.*, 2014a; *but see* Flaten *et al.*, (2016). Jonsson & Jonsson (2011) stated that the time spent at sea varied from 1 month to 5 years; but gave no further information.

Return rates to freshwater after first migration to sea can also vary widely between populations. Long-term studies in Western Norway by Jonsson & Jonsson, (2009) for the River Imsa from 1976 –2005 and from Northern Norway by Jensen *et al.*, (2015) for the River Halselva from 1994 – 2007 reported mean yearly return rates of 15% and 27%, respectively. Davidsen *et al.*, 50 fish in each year (fork length, LF , 158-288 mm (2014a) found that 16% of tagged hatchery-reared post-smolts released into a river in central Norway returned to the river after the first summer at sea, while Flaten *et al.*, (2016) observed a return rate of 65% of wild post-smolts in a neighbouring system. In the Burrishoole system, Ireland, marine survival rates ranged from 1.8 – 66% for sea trout smolts from 1975 -1994 (Poole *et al.*, 1996). In some of the Norwegian systems, survival was considered to be adversely affected by a mismatch in the timing of marine entry and available food abundance, with a lower survival observed for fall migrants that arrive in the sea when prey items were scarce (Jonsson & Jonsson, 2009). In the Irish Burrishoole system, the large variation in sea survival was caused by the establishment of salmon sea-cage farms that increased the abundance of sea lice (*Lepeophtheirus salmonis*) and caused higher post-smolt mortality rates (Poole *et al.*, 1996).

VETERAN MIGRANTS

Individual sea trout that survive their first return to freshwater to spawn can return to the sea (as kelts) to feed and recover their physical condition before returning to spawn again in freshwater. The downstream migration of kelts may occur immediately after spawning or several months later (Bendall *et al.*, 2005; Östergren & Rivinoja, 2008; Kraabøl *et al.*, 2008; Davidsen *et al.*, 2014b). In larger rivers, the outward migration of veteran migrants often takes place during the following spring and early summer (Berg & Berg, 1989; Klemetsen *et al.*, 2003; Östergren & Rivinoja, 2008; Aldvén *et al.*, 2015), but in smaller (shorter) rivers they may migrate downstream immediately after spawning; particularly in rivers with poor over-wintering habitat (Davidsen *et al.*, 2014b). As with smolts, the transition between fresh and salt water occurs mainly at night (Bendall *et al.*, 2005, Davidsen *et al.*, 2014b, Aldvén *et al.*, 2015). Residency time within estuaries in some areas may be short, often with a rapid progression rate out to sea (Bendall *et al.*, 2005, Aldvén *et al.*, 2015). This progression rate becomes slower as the fish migrate further away from the river (Aarestrup *et al.*, 2015; Aldvén *et al.*, 2015). The kelts spend >90% of their time at sea in the upper 3m of the water column, and may occasionally undertake deeper dives (Rikardsen *et al.*, 2007; Eldøy *et al.*, 2014). They are more often found in the littoral zone than in pelagic areas (Jensen *et al.*, 2014; Eldøy *et al.*, 2015). During their marine migration period, the veteran migrants are opportunistic feeders, with an increasing diet of marine prey fish by the larger sea trout (Grønvik & Klemetsen, 1987; Knutsen *et al.*, 2001; Rikardsen *et al.*, 2007). As with post-smolts, the duration of marine residency varies between study sites and can range between 1 to 366 days (Berg & Berg, 1989; Berg & Berg, 1993; Klemetsen *et al.*, 2003; Rikardsen *et al.*, 2007; Jonsson & Jonsson, 2009; Jensen & Rikardsen, 2012; Aarestrup *et al.*, 2015; Eldøy *et al.*, 2015). The time spent at sea was positively correlated to body length and smolt age, but negatively correlated to the time of sea entry (Eldøy *et al.*, 2015). However, at northern latitudes the period of residency can be prolonged by high sea temperatures (Berg & Berg, 1989). In fjord systems in central Norway, it has been reported that veteran migrants from smaller watercourses with unpredictable and harsh winter conditions over-wintered in the marine fjord or in neighbouring watercourses, while individuals from rivers within the same fjord system where there was access to a larger lake overwintered in the lake (Davidsen *et al.*, 2014b).

Veteran migrants display a large variety of migration patterns within the sea in terms of migration distance. Eldøy *et al.*, (2015) found that kelts spent 68% of their marine residence time within 4 km of the river mouth and that individuals with a poorer body condition prior to migration travelled longer distances, used pelagic areas more often and returned earlier to freshwater when compared with short distance migrants. However, migration distance can vary between populations. This may be as little as a few kilometres from their native rivers in the Bothnian Bay compared with sea trout migrating from the most southern parts to the Baltic Bay that may travel over a thousand kilometres and even enter the North Sea (Svärdson & Anheden, 1963; Kallio-Nyberg *et al.*, 2002; Bartel *et al.*, 2010; Degerman *et al.*, 2012). Long distance migrants have also been reported from Scotland and Sweden, where fish from both regions were recaptured off the Norwegian west coast and, in the former case, at the inlet to the Baltic Sea (Bernttsson & Johansson, 1977; Pratten & Shearer, 1983). Marine survival for kelts is generally higher than for smolts, ranging from 18 – 50% (Berg & Jonsson, 1990; Bendall *et al.*, 2005; Aarestrup *et al.*, 2015).

SUMMARY & KEY ISSUES

The available information in the scientific literature on sea trout movement in the marine environment is currently limited and mainly focused on fjord systems. Much of the information was derived from hydro acoustic studies on post-smolts and veteran migrants and, to some extent from data storage tags and mark-recapture experiments. The results show the spatial preferences of sea trout in relation to features such as the use of specific areas within fjords, migration pathways, depth preferences, migration distances away from their rivers of origin and the duration of their marine feeding migration. A few studies on marine feeding ecology have provided information about food preferences for different size groups of fish and several studies have shown that initial marine mortality losses can be very high. However, few attempts have been made to understand the underlying causes of this mortality and, to our knowledge, the reasons why the observed mortality rates differ significantly between marine areas has not been investigated. Possible causes might be important local differences in predation pressure, anthropogenic impacts such as salmon farms, the location of marine renewable energy projects, and food depletion. Future research should address these important knowledge gaps and should include the following topic areas and questions:

1. *Movements in other estuary types*: Most investigations to date have focused on rocky, deep, fjordic estuaries and inlets. How do fish behave in other types of outlets into the sea, such as the long, shallow and sandy estuaries in low-lying flood-plains with fast-flowing inter-tidal regimes? Is the migratory behaviour significantly different from a fjord system for example?

2. *Conventional tagging*: Is there an ongoing case to continue conventional tagging studies to overcome the practical limitations of hydro-acoustic studies (notably, short battery life, limited detection range, high operating costs) in order to determine recaptures in more distant waters outside the local study area.

3. *Long-term studies*: Most investigations to date were essentially short-term and opportunistic studies that provide only limited local 'snapshots' of behaviour. Is there a case for long-term tagging and tracking studies on selected (index-type) rivers to provide a better understanding of the range of temporal and spatial variability in behaviour?

4. *Mortality and predation*: Many studies have found a low survival during the initial marine migration. What are the causes (predation or stress induced) for the high mortality?

5. *Differentiation in migration strategy*: Several studies have reported different migrations strategies in terms of migration distance and timing, but very few have investigated the underlying mechanism (e.g. physiological, genetic, behavioural etc.) for this differentiation. What are those mechanisms?

6. *Food and feeding*: Can the habitat use in the sea be determined by the food availability in a certain habitat and if so does the habitat preference then vary with the size and age of the fish?

7. *Seascape*: Sea trout utilize different environments (pelagic and littoral) in the sea. Why is a certain habitat favoured over other available options?

8. *Anthropogenic impacts*: Human impacts on the marine environment are common (e.g. fishing, aquaculture and urbanization). How and to what extent do these affect sea trout migration strategies?

Answering these questions would greatly increase our understanding of sea trout migration, which is crucial for successful management and conservation of sea trout stocks.

REFERENCES

Aarestrup, K., Baktoft., H, Koed, A., del Villar-Guerra, D. & Thorstad, E. (2014). Comparison of the riverine and early marine migration behaviour and survival of wild and hatchery-reared sea trout *Salmo trutta* smolts. *Marine Ecology Progress Series* **496,** 197-206.

Aarestrup, K., Baktoft. H., Thorstad. E., Svendsen, J., Höjesjö. J. & Koed, A. (2015). Survival and progression rates of anadromous brown trout kelts *Salmo trutta* during downstream migration in freshwater and at sea. *Marine Ecology Progress Series,* **535,** 185–195.

Aas, Ø., Einum, S., Klemetsen, A. & Skurdal, J., (*Eds*) (2011). *Atlantic Salmon Ecology*. Wiley Blackwell, 467.

Aldvén, D., Hedger. R., Økland, F., Rivinoja, P. & Höjesjö, J. (2015). Migration speed, routes and mortality rates of sea trout *Salmo trutta* during outward migration through a complex coastal habitat. *Marine Ecology Progress Series,* **541**, 151-163.

Aldvén, D., Závorka, L., Aarestrup, K. & Höjesjö, J. (2017). Migration pathways in a fjord of two populations of sea trout (*Salmo trutta L.*) smolts. In: *Sea Trout: Science & Management.* (Graeme Harris. *Ed.*).Proceedings of the 2nd International Sea Tout Symposium. October 2015. Dundalk, Ireland. Troubador, 277–291.

Bartel, R., Pachur, M. & Bernaś, R. (2010). Distribution, migrations, and growth of tagged sea trout released into the Vistula River. *Archives of Polish Fisheries,* **18**, 225–237.

Bendall, B., Moore, A. & Quayle, V. (2005). The post-spawning movements of migratory brown trout Salmo trutta L. *Journal of Fish Biology,* **67**, 809–822.

Berg, O.K. & Berg, M. (1987). Migrations of sea trout, *Salmo trutta* L, from the Vardnes river in northern Norway. *Journal of Fish Biology* **31**, 113–121.

Berg, O.K & Berg, M. (1989). The duration of sea and freshwater residence of the sea trout, *Salmo trutta*, from the Vardnes River in northern Norway. *Environmental Biology of Fishes,* **24**, 23–32.

Berg, O.K, & Berg, M. (1993). Duration of sea and freshwater residence of Arctic char (*Salvelinus alpinus*), from the Vardnes River in northern Norway. *Aquaculture* **110**, 129–140.

Berg, O.K. & Jonsson, B. (1990). Growth and survival rates of the anadromous trout, *Salmo trutta*, from the Vardnes River, northern Norway. *Environmental Biology of Fishes* **29**, 145–154.

Bernttsson, K-E, & Johansson, R. (1977). Havsöringsundersöknar i Anråsån. *Meddelande från Havsfiskelaboratoriet,* **230**, 19 p.

Bulleri, F. & Chapman, M.G. (2010). The introduction of coastal infrastructure as a driver of change in marine environments. *Journal of Applied Ecology,* **47**, 26-35.

Cucherousset, J., Ombredane, D., Charles, K., Marchand, F. & Bagliniere. J-L. (2005). A Continuum of Life History Tactics in a brown trout (*Salmo trutta*) population. *Canadian Journal of Fisheries and Aquatic Sciences,* **62**, 1600–1610.

Davidsen, J.G., Daverdin, M., Arnekleiv, J.V., Rønning, L., Sjursen, A.D. & Koksvik, J.I. (2014a). Riverine and near coastal migration performance of hatchery brown trout *Salmo trutta. Journal of Fish Biology* **85**, 586–596.

Davidsen, J.G., Eldøy, S.H., Sjursen, A.D., Rønning, L., Thorstad, E.B., Næsje, T. F., Uglem, I., Aarestrup, K., Whoriskey, F.G., Rikardsen, A.H., Daverdin, M. & Arnekleiv, J.V. (2014b). Habitatbruk og vandringer til sjøørret i Hemnfjorden og Snillfjorden. *In: NTNU Vitenskapsmuseet naturhistorisk rapport,* 55 pp.

Degerman, E., Leonardsson, K. & Lundqvist, H. (2012). Coastal migrations, temporary use of neighbouring rivers, and growth of sea trout (*Salmo trutta*) from nine northern Baltic Sea rivers. *ICES Journal of Marine Science,* **69**, 971–980.

del Villar-Guerra, D., Aarestrup, K., Skov, C. & Koed, A. (2014). Marine migrations in anadromous brown trout (*Salmo trutta*). Fjord residency as a possible alternative in the continuum of migration to the open sea. *Ecology of Freshwater Fish* **23**, 594–603.

Drenner, S.M., Clark, T.D., Whitney, C.K., Martins, E.G., Cooke, S.J. & Hinch, S.G. (2012). A synthesis of tagging studies examining the behaviour and survival of anadromous salmonids in marine environments. *Plos One,* **7(3)**, e31311.

Eldøy S.H., Davidsen, J.G., Thorstad, E.B,, Whoriskey, F., Aarestrup, K., Næsje, T.F., Rønning, L., Sjursen, A.D., Rikardsen, A.H. &Arnekleiv, J.V. (2015). Marine migration and habitat use of anadromous brown trout (*Salmo trutta*). *Canadian Journal of Fisheries and Aquatic Sciences,* **72**, 1366–1378.

Flaten, A.C., Davidsen, J.G., Thorstad, E.B., Whoriskey, F., Rønning, L., Sjursen, A.D., Rikardsen, A.H. & Arnekleiv, J.A. (2016). The first months at sea – marine migration and habitat use of sea trout *Salmo trutta* post-smolts. *Journal of Fish Biology.***89**,1624-1640. Doi:10.1111/jfb.13065.

Finstad, B., Økland, F., Thorstad, E.B., Bjorn, P.A., & McKinley, R.S., (2005). Migration of hatchery-reared Atlantic salmon and wild anadromous brown trout post-smolts in a Norwegian fjord system. *Journal of Fish Biology,* **66**, 86–96.

Gross, M.R., Coleman, R.M. & McDowall, R.M. (1988). Aquatic productivity and the evolution of diadromous fish migration. *Science* (Washington), **239**, 1291–1293.

Grønvik, S. & Klemetsen, A. (1987). Marine food and diet overlap of co-occuring Arctic charr (*Salvelinus alpinus* L.), Brown trout (*Salmo trutta* L.) and Atlantic salmon (*S. salar* L.) off Senja, N. Norway. *Polar Biology*, **7**, 173-177.

Hendry, A.P., Bohlin, T., Jonsson, B. & Berg, O.K. (2004). To sea or not to sea? Anadromy versus non-anadromy in salmonids. In: *Evolution Illuminated: Salmon and Their Relatives* (Hendry, A.P. & Stearns, S. C., (*Eds*.). Oxford University Press, New York: 92-125

ICES, (2013). Report of the Workshop on Sea Trout (WKTRUTTA), 12–14 November 2013, ICES Headquarters, Copenhagen, Denmark. 280 p.

Jensen, A.J., Diserud, O.H., Finstad, B., Fiske, P. &Rikardsen, A.H. (2015). Between-watershed movements of two anadromous salmonids in the Arctic. *Canadian Journal of Fisheries and Aquatic Sciences* **72**, 855–863.

Jensen, J.L.A. & Rikardsen, A.H. (2012). Archival tags reveal that Arctic charr *Salvelinus alpinus* and brown trout *Salmo trutta* can use estuarine and marine waters during winter. *Journal of Fish Biology* **81**, 735–749.

Jensen J.L.A., Rikardsen, A.H., Thorstad, E.B., Suhr, A.H., Davidsen, J,G. & Primicerio, R. (2014). Water temperatures influence the marine area use of *Salvelinus alpinus* and *Salmo trutta*. *Journal of Fish Biology* **84**, 1640–1653.

Jonsson, B. (1985). Life history patterns of freshwater resident and sea-run migrant brown trout in Norway. *Transactions of the American Fisheries Society* **114**, 182–194.

Jonsson, B. & Jonsson, N. (1993). Partial migration: niche shift versus sexual maturation in fishes. *Reviews in Fish Biology and Fisheries* **3**, 348-365.

Jonsson, B. & Jonsson, N. (2006). Life-history effects of migratory costs in anadromous brown trout. *Journal of Fish Biology* **69**, 860–869.

Jonsson, B. & Jonsson, N. (2009). Migratory timing, marine survival and growth of anadromous brown trout *Salmo trutta* in the River Imsa, Norway. *Journal of Fish Biology* **74**, 621–638.

Jonsson, B. & Jonsson, N. (2011). *Ecology of Atlantic salmon and brown trout: habitat as a template for life histories*. London: Springer Science Business Media B.V., 680 pp

Kallio-Nyberg, I, Saura, A. & Ahlfors, P. (2002). Sea migration pattern of two sea trout (*Salmo trutta*) stocks released into the Gulf of Finland. *Annales Zoologici Fennici* **39**, 221–235.

Klemetsen, A., Amundsen, P.A., Dempson, J.B., Jonsson, B., Jonsson, N., O´Connell, M.F., and Mortensen, E. *et al.* (2003). Atlantic salmon *Salmo salar* L., brown trout *Salmo trutta* L. and Arctic charr *Salvelinus alpinus* (L.): a review of aspects of their life histories. *Ecology of Freshwater Fish* **12**, 1–59.

Koed, A., Baktoft, H. & Bak, B.D. (2006). Causes of mortality of Atlantic salmon (*Salmo salar*) and brown trout (*Salmo trutta*) smolts in a restored river and its estuary. *River Research and Applications* **22**, 69–78.

Kraabøl, M., Arnekleiv, J.V. & Museth, J. (2008). Emigration patterns among trout, *Salmo trutta* (L.), kelts and smolts through spillways in a hydroelectric dam. *Fisheries Management and Ecology* **15**, 417–423.

Knutsen, J. A., Knutsen, H., Gjøsæter, J. & Jonsson, B. (2001). Food of anadromous brown trout at sea. *Journal of Fish Biology* **59**, 533-543.

Lyse, A.A,, Stefansson, S.O. & Fernö, A. (1998). Behaviour and diet of sea trout post-smolts in a Norwegian fjord system. *Journal of Fish Biology* **52**, 923–936.

Manel-la, N.P., Chittenden, C.M., Okland, F., Thorstad, E.B., Davidsen, J.G., Sivertsgard, R., McKinley, R.S,, Finstad, B., (2011). Does river of origin influence the early marine migratory performance of *Salmo salar? Journal of Fish Biology* **78,** 624–634.

Middlemas, S.J., Stewart, D.C., Mackay, S. & Armstrong, J.D. 2009. Habitat use and dispersal of post-smolt sea trout *Salmo trutta* in a Scottish sea loch system. *Journal of Fish Biology* **74,** 639–651.

Moore, A., Ives, M., Scott, M. & Bamber, S. (1998). The migratory behaviour of wild sea trout (*Salmo trutta* L.) smolts in the estuary of the River Conwy, North Wales. *Aquaculture* **168**, 57–68.

Moore, A. & Potter, E.C.E. (1994). The movement of wild sea trout, *Salmo trutta* L., smolts through a river estuary. *Fisheries Management and Ecology* **1**, 1–14.

Myers, R.A. & Hutchings, J.A. (1987). Mating of anadromous Atlantic salmon, *Salmo salar* L, with mature male parr. *Journal of Fish Biology* **31**, 143–146.

Northcote, T.G. (1978). Migratory strategies and production of freshwater fishes. *In:*Ecology of freshwater fish production. (Gerking, S. *Ed*.). Blackwell Scientific, Oxford. 325-359 pp.

Östergren, J. & Rivinoja, P. (2008). Overwintering and downstream migration of sea trout (*Salmo trutta* L.) kelts under regulated flows-northern Sweden. *River Research and Applications* **24**, 551–563.

Poole, W.R., Whelan, K.F., Dillane, M.G., Cooke, D.J. & Matthews, M. (1996). The performance of sea trout, *Salmo trutta* L., stocks from the Burrishoole system western Ireland, 1970-1994. *Fisheries Management and Ecology* **3**, 73–92.

Pratten, D.J. & Shearer, W.M. (1983). The Migrations of North Esk Sea Trout. *Aquaculture Research* **14**, 99–113.

Rikardsen, A.H., Diserud, O.H., Elliott, J.M., Dempson, J.B., Sturlaugsson, J. & Jensen, A.J. (2007). The marine temperature and depth preferences of Arctic charr (*Salvelinus alpinus*) and sea trout (*Salmo trutta*), as recorded by data storage tags. *Fisheries Oceanography* **16**, 436–447.

Svärdson, G. & Anheden, H. (1963). Långvandrande skånsk havsöring. *Svensk Fiskisketidskrift*: 109-113.

Thorstad, E., Økland, F., Finstad, B., Sivertsgrd, R., Bjorn, P. & McKinley, R. (2004). Migration speeds and orientation of Atlantic salmon and sea trout post-smolts in a Norwegian fjord system. *Environmental Biology of Fishes* **71**, 305–311.

Thorstad, E. B., Økland, F., Finstad, B., Sivertsgård, R., Plantalech, N., Bjørn, P.A. & McKinley, R.S. (2007). Fjord migration and survival of wild and hatchery-reared Atlantic salmon and wild brown trout post-smolts. *Hydrobiologia* **582**, 99–107.

Thorstad, E.B., Todd, C.D., Uglem, I., Bjørn, P.A., Gargan, P.G., Vollset, K.W., Halttunen, E., Kålås, S., Berg, M. & Finstad, B. (2015). Effects of salmon lice *Lepeophtheirus salmonis* on wild sea trout *Salmo trutta* – a literature review. *Aquaculture Environment Interactions* **7**, 91–113.

ELECTRONIC REFERENCES

Eldøy, S.H. (2014). Spatial and temporal distribution and habitat use of sea trout *Salmo trutta* in a fjord system in Central Norway. Masters Thesis: NTNU University Museum, Norwegian University of Science and Technology. *Available at*: http://www.diva- portal.org/smash/get/diva2:762888 FULLTEXT01.pdf.

Ruud T. (2015). Space use and harvest selection of sea trout (*Salmo trutta*) living in a marine protected area. Masters Thesis: Norwegian University of Life Sciences. *Available at*: http://hdl.handle.net/ 11250/293744 .

Migration pathways in a fjord of two populations of sea trout (*Salmo trutta L.*) smolts

D. ALDVÉN[1], L. ZÁVORKA[1], K. AARESTRUP[2] & J. HÖJESJÖ[1]

Department of Biology and Environmental Sciences, University of Gothenburg, Box 463, SE-405 30, Gothenburg, Sweden.
[2]Technical University of Denmark, National Institute of Aquatic Resources, Vejlsøvej 39, DK-8600 Silkeborg, Denmark.

ABSTRACT

Anadromous migration in fishes is viewed as an adaptive strategy, it entails migration to a more favourable habitat for feeding and growth opportunities that ultimately increases their reproductive output (Bagenal, 1969). One example is the anadromous brown trout (sea trout) which utilise the coastal sea as its feeding grounds (Pemberton 1976; Rikardsen *et al.*, 2006). This study followed the downstream migration of anadromous brown trout (*Salmo trutta* L.) smolts from two small coastal rivers (the Bodeleån and the Kärraån) on the west coast of Sweden into an open fjord system. Its aims were to investigate if faster growing parr smoltified and emigrated from the fjord before slower growing parr and if the migration pathways differed between the two rivers. The downstream migration occurred in two distinct clusters, with one early and one late migratory group in both rivers. No significant difference was detected in size or growth rate between the two groups. Migration pathways were similar in the two rivers, although residence time within the inner fjord was affected by an interaction between river of origin and time of sea entry. Smolts from the River Kärraån entered the sea later and also stayed for a shorter period within the inner fjord and were therefore delayed during their migration through the outer fjord. The underlying causes and consequences of the two different migration tactics for individual smolts is unknown and future research should focus on resolving these issues.

Keywords: *Salmo trutta*; telemetry; survival; growth rate; loss rate; residency time.

INTRODUCTION

Anadromy in fish is an adaptive strategy where migration to a more favorable habitat for feeding and growth increases their reproductive output (Bagenal, 1969). This is demonstrated in sea trout, the anadromous form of brown trout, which utilize the coastal sea as its feeding grounds (Pemberton, 1976; Rikardsen et al., 2006). Berg & Berg (1987) concluded, using a mark-recapture approach, that the majority of sea trout remained within 100 km from the mouth of their native river whereas other studies (Bartel *et al.*, 2010; Svärdson & Fagerström, 1982) reported the recapture of migrants up to 1,000 km away from their native rivers of origin. However, little information exists about their actual movements in the sea (del Villar-Guerra *et al.*, 2014; Eldøy *et al.*, 2015), and the few available studies report different results in that the sea trout in Norway remain within the fjords (Thorstad *et al.*, 2007) whereas in Denmark they exhibit two migration tactics where they either remain within the fjord or migrate to sea (Aarestrup *et al.*, 2014; del Villar-Guerra *et al.*, 2014). In Sweden, a similar migration pattern was observed with two groups in an open coastal system: one of which stayed for longer in the estuary and one that left the system directly (Aldvén, 2015). However, the environmental and/or physiological factors determining these two tactics in terms of how long they stay in the estuary or if they remain in the fjord is unknown (Jonsson, 1985; Nielsen *et al.*, 2003). The existing data suggest that sea trout populations within a fjord system overlap in their habitat usage, and perhaps their migration pathways also, as there are often several rivers draining into a fjord but where the sea trout remain within the fjord. However, this has never been investigated. Also, the timing of migration should be similar between these rivers as the environmental conditions should be similar; with the exception of water temperature which is affected by the different upstream sources.

The anadromous strategy of sea trout involves a physiological, morphological and behavioural transformation from the parr to the smolt stage in its life history that pre-adapts the fish from life in freshwater to life in sea water. This smolt transformation (smoltification) is stimulated by photoperiod and temperature (Björnsson et al., 2011; McCormick *et al.*, 1987). Smoltification and the subsequent downstream migration of smolts are believed to be important for initial marine survival (Hvidsten *et al.,* 2009). The timing of migration is governed by age, size and growth rate (Jonsson & Jonsson, 2011). However, there are often variations in migration tendency within a population and in the timing of downstream migration and entry into the sea within a river system (Nielsen *et al.*, 2003). These variations may be governed by differences in the smoltification status of individual fish (Aarestrup *et al.,* 2000; Aldvén *et al.*, 2015) that determines the response of the individual fish to environmental cues, (temperature and discharge). Some studies suggest that smoltification is governed by growth rate so that fast growing parr become smolts at a smaller size and younger age than slower growing parr (Jonsson, 1985; Økland *et al.*, 1993). Evidence also suggests that larger individuals migrate to sea earlier than smaller fish of the same cohort (Bohlin *et al.*, 1993; Jonsson *et al.*, 1990).

This study employed acoustic telemetry to examine the behaviour of sea trout smolts within a fjord system consisting of two rivers (Bodeleån and Kärraån), an estuary and a coastal fjord environment draining to the Kattegat Sea, NE Atlantic. We predicted that fast growing parr would smoltify earlier and consequently enter the sea earlier in the season compared with slower growing individuals. We also hypothesised that the populations from the two river systems would adopt similar migration strategies, in terms of migration pathways through the different areas in the fjord, similar migration timing from the river and similar migration speeds.

MATERIALS AND METHODS

STUDY AREA

This study was conducted in two rivers, the Bodeleån (N 58° 19.745'; E 11° 54.891') and the Kärraån (N 58° 21.407'; E 11° 50.302') draining to Byfjorden, a fjord on the west coast of Sweden (Figure 1). The rivers are similar in morphology and size, varying from 3 – 6 m in width and they are bordered mainly by deciduous trees. The drainage area of the rivers is 18 km² for the Bodeleån, 25 km² for the Kärraån and the mean annual discharge for both rivers is 0.25 m³ s⁻¹. The distances from the mouth of the river to their souce is 9 km for the Bodeleån and 8 km for the Kärraån: with respective elevations of 45m and 55 m from estuary to source. The temperature varies between the rivers and the Kärraån is on average 2 °C warmer than Bodeleån (with a mean ±SD for the Kärraån of 13.1 ±4.4 °C compared with 11.3 ±3.7 °C for the Bodeleån).

ENVIRONMENTAL PARAMETERS

Water temperature and depth within each stream was measured on an hourly basis using a depth data logger (Onset, HOBO U20-001-04-Ti Data Logger). Water flow was calculated from several water velocities at different water depths. Rainfall data was obtained from the Swedish metrological and hydrological institute. Surface salinity (1 m below surface), temperature measurements and depth data within the sea were obtained from a nearby research station of University of Gothenburg (Kristineberg, N 58° 14.974'; E 11° 26.742').

TAGGING AND CAPTURE OF SEA TROUT

Sea trout were captured by electric fishing at the beginning of the smolting period (3-4th April). Electric fishing started 200 metres upstream from the PIT-antenna (Figure 1) in both rivers (at distances from the river mouth of 600 m in the Bodeleån and 800 m in the Kärraån) and continued upstream to the first impassable migration barrier (1,700 m in the Bodeleån and 2,800 m in the the Kärraån). A total of 80 parr showing visual signs of smoltification and

279

with a minimum fork-length of 130 mm (mean ± SD: 140.2 ±9.1 mm in the Bodeleån and 140.8 ±9.6 in the Kärraån) were tagged. Of these, 40 from each river,were randomly selected and equipped with VEMCO V7 transmitters (VEMCO Ltd., V7-4x-069k-3, diameter; 7mm; length; 18 mm, pulse interval 20/60 seconds; minimum battery life 89 days) and also with 23mm PIT-tags (HDX ISO 11784/11785, Oregon RFID, Portland, OR). Individual fish were anesthetized prior to surgical insertion of tags by emersion in a bath of 0.7 ml l⁻¹ benzocaine. An incision was made in the ventral surface in front of the pelvic girdle through which both tags were inserted and gently pushed into the body cavity. The incision was then closed with a single polyfilament suture (Ethicon Prolene 5-0, Ethicon Inc., Somerville, NJ, U.S.A.). Fish length (mm) and weight (g) were measured and scale samples were taken for age and growth rate determination. The fish were then left in a recovery tank along with untagged smolts caught in the same area for 4 hours before being released into the river. Smolts were released along with the untagged smolts to decrease the potential risk of predation. No smolts died and all fish appeared to be in good physical condition prior to release.

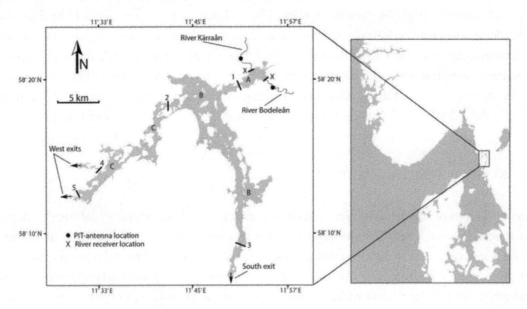

Figure 1. The study system Byfjorden. With the fjord divided up into sections (A, B and C), where numbers (1-5) represent the receiver line locations, X marks river hydrophones, and rings the within-river PIT-tag antennas. Arrows indicates the exits from the fjord.

TRACKING

Fish tracking was performed using 22 automatic acoustic listening stations (VEMCO VR2 and VR2W) deployed in fixed double-line arrays to monitor direction of the fish and to ensure detection. A double line of PIT-tag antennas was also installed in the streams (Figure 1). Range tests throughout the study period established that the receiver lines maintained overlapping coverages of 15–50 m at the river mouths and then, respectively, 300–440 m; 200–300 m; 300–400 m; 200–300 m and 100–200 m at receiver lines 1–5. Therefore, each smolt was likely to be detected when passing a receiver line. The overall efficiency of the system was subsequently estimated at 100% as no fish were detected on a receiver line further out in the fjord system without first being detected at a previous receiver line. Data collection was made on a monthly basis from deployment in March to the end of the study in August, after which no detections had been recorded for a three week period. False detections (0.13% of all detections) were removed using the method outlined by VEMCO (Vemco 2012). Manual tracking with a mobile PIT-tag antenna (Oregon RFID) was performed in both rivers at the beginning of June to assess predation, natural mortality and the desmoltification of fish that did not leave the river.

AGE AND GROWTH RATE

Age and relative growth rate (RGR) were determined using the protocol outlined by Závorka *et al.* (2014). The scales were photographed using a stereo microscope (Sagitta Pedagog AB) and the distance between annuli was measured by image analysis software (THSCSA ImageTool 3.0, http://compdent.uthscsa.edu/dig/itdesc.html, USA). Age was calculated from the number of annuli present on the scale and growth rates were back calculated using the Fraser-Lee equation (Lee 1920).

STATISTICAL ANALYSIS

Residence time within the river was determined between first detection at a stationary PIT-tag antenna within the rivers and first detection at the mouth of each river (Figure 1). Similarly, first detection at the respective river mouth receivers to the first detection at receiver line 1 was used to determine residency time within within area A. For area B this was first detection at receiver line 2 or 3 from previous detection at receiver line 1. The time from last detection at receiver line 2 and first detections at receiver line 4 or 5 was used for area C. The effects of growth rate, length and stream of origin on residency time in the different areas were analyzed using generalized linear models (GLM).

Ground speeds were calculated by dividing the residence time by the distances covered in each respective area. If multiple distances existed, the shortest possible distance between receiver lines, alternatively the Euclidean distance, was assumed if a fish was detected at receiver line 3 before 2 or *vice versa*. Loss rates of smolts within the fjord, the river and in areas A to C (Figure 1), were calculated as the percentage of smolts not leaving the area. Mortality within the rivers was quantified as the percentage of fish that were not detected in area A and not found to be alive within the rivers at the subsequent electrofishing in June. This was validated by locating the fish with a portable PIT-tag antenna (Oregeon RFID), followed by targeted electro fishing to determine rates of mortality and desmoltification.

RESULTS

ENVIRONMENTAL PARAMETERS

During the study period (April to September), surface water temperature in the fjord ranged from 6.3 to 23.2 °C. Mean tidal variation over the study period was 20 cm from highest to lowest reading. During the period of downstream migration (beginning of April to end of May, 2014) water discharge was 0.20 ± 0.18 m^{3}s^{-1} in the Kärraån and 0.13 ± 0.08 m^{3}s^{-1} in the Bodeleån. Respective temperatures were 9.1 ± 3.1 °C (range: 3.2 to 14.5 °C) in the Kärraån and 7.8 ± 2.7 °C (range: 2.9 to 12.9 °C) the Bodeleån.

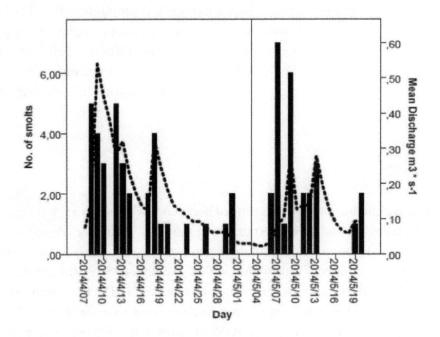

Figure 2. Number of migrating smolts and discharge plotted over time. Dates are pooled from both rivers (n~63), for a clearer view of the two migration clusters. The vertical line indicates the separation between the two migration clusters

MIGRATION AND GROWTH RATE

Of the 80 tagged smolts, 13 scale samples were unreadable and 67 samples were included in the final analysis of growth rate: two of these were from 3+ smolts and therefore excluded in the third years growth rate as the final growth season of these was a further full year compared with 1-2 months for 2+ smolts. River flow discharge strongly affected the timing of the downstream migration as a majority of the fish migrated out during increases in flow rates (Figure 2). A total of 76.25 % of all smolts were detected by the receivers at the river mouths. Downstream migration occurred at increases in flow discharge as two distinct clusters: with one batch of early migrants and one with late migrants (Two step Cluster analysis: Figure 2). No effect of RGR (1st, 2nd or 3rd year) or in the length of the fish was found at the onset of migration (Wilks' Lambda = 0.437, F = 2.32, p = 0.129) or the on the residence time within the different areas (Area A: Wilks' Lambda = 0.437, F = 2.32, p = 0.129; Area B: Wilks' Lambda = 0.780, F = 0.226, p = 0.933; Area C: Wilks' Lambda = 0.188, F = 1.44, p = 0.534). However, the stream of origin had a significant effect on residence time in area A (Wilks' Lambda = 0.204, F = 9.39, p = 0.001) as well as a significant influence on the interaction between stream of origin and migration group in the same area (Wilks' Lambda = 0.423, F = 3.28, p = 0.043) as smolts from the Bodeleån showed a longer residence time and entered the sea earlier.

Overall, the smolts that migrated early displayed a longer residency time in the fjord compared with those migrating later (Figure 3) and the smolts from the Bodeleån migrated earlier from the river than those from the Kärraån (Figure 4). The late group showed a tendency to delay their rate of progress rate through the system, and more individuals in the early group had migrated from the system at the end of the study compared with the late group (Figure 5). A difference in migration speed was found in the rivers, where the smolts from the Bodeleån showed an overall faster migration speed than the Kärraån (Kruskal-Wallis test: Chi-sq: 4.07, p = 0.044). No difference was found in the other areas (Figure 6). Overall migration speeds varied throughout the system, with a lower ground speed in the river (0.12 ±0.1 body lengths [BL] s^1, 0.84±0.28 km day^{-1}) compared with Area A (0.25 ±0.12 BL s^1, 3.03 ±0.69 km day^{-1}: Kruskal-Wallis test: Chi-sq = 13.56, p = 0.001) This was then followed by a gradual decrease in speed as the smolts emigrated through the system; thus Area 2 = 0.16±0.04 BL s^1, 1.81±0.31 km day^{-1} and Area 3 = 3: 0.14±0.07 BL s^1, 1.68±0.83 km day^{-1}. [*See* Figure 6.]

SURVIVAL

There was no difference between the survival rates of 82.5% (33 smolts) in the Karraan and 70.8% (28 smolts) in the Bodelean. (Chi-square test: 1.73, p > 0.05). Manual tracking within the rivers revealed that three tags remained in the Bodeleån and a further 9 were not detected. Of the three detected tags, the fish were considered dead as they were found either on the river bank or in shallow water with mud as substrate and remained unresponsive (did not move) during electrofishing. None of the smolts or tags remaining in the Kärraån were detected during the manual tracking and their fate was unknown. Loss rates between rivers and receiver

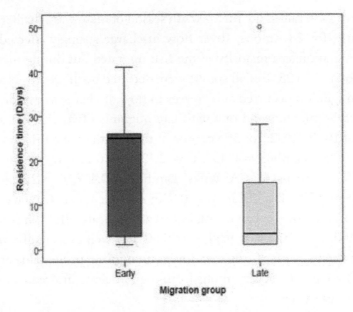

Figure 3. Residency time between early and late migration in area A.

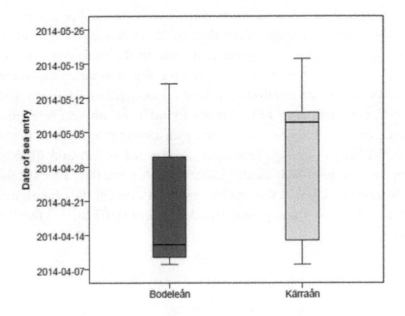

Figure 4: Day of sea entry between rivers.

line 1 was 18% (11 smolts), and the progressive loss rate, in area B, from receiver line 1 to the subsequent receiver lines (2 & 3), was 34% (17 smolts). Loss rates in area C from receiver line 2 to lines 4 & 5 was 57% (12 smolts). At the end of the study, 9 individuals had left the study area; 7 smolts (3 to the west 4 to the south) from the Bodeleån and 2 smolts (1 to the south and 1 to the west) from the Kärraån (Figure 7).

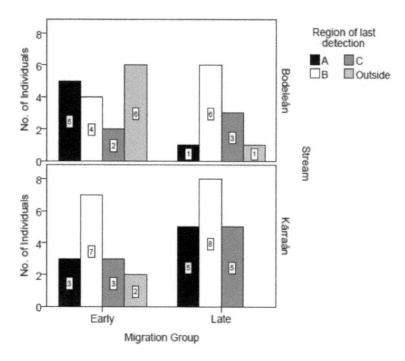

Figure 5. Region of last detection for early and late migrants in each stream.

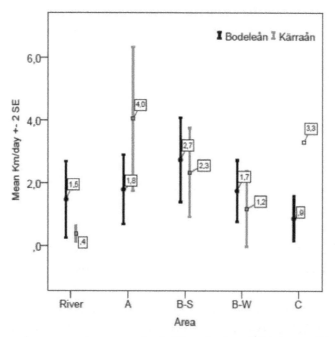

Figure 6. Ground speeds across regions, according to Figure 1; where B-S is in area B to the south exit, and B-W is in area B to Area C), for smolts from both streams. Grey represents Bodeleån and black represents Kärraån. Numbers represent mean velocities in km day⁻¹.

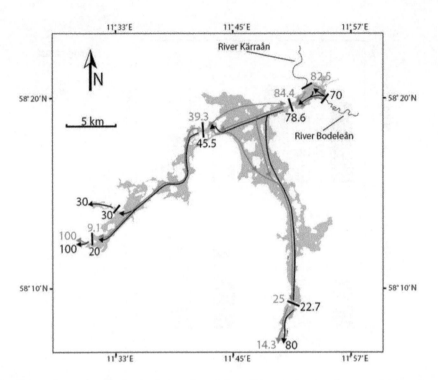

Figure 7. Migration routes and survival rates across the system. Grey numbers and arrows represent percentage of smolts survival and migration pathways through the fjord from river Kärraån, and black numbers and arrows represent smolts from Bodeleån. Numbers outside receiver arrays (to the south and west) are percentages of smolts detected at the outer receiver lines, from each river, that were last observed outside the study system.

DISCUSSION

MIGRATION AND GROWTH RATE

The timing of downstream migration and sea entry differed between the two rivers. Smolts from the Bodeleån revealed an overall earlier migration and entered the sea earlier than smolts from the Kärraån. This could not be explained by length and contrasted with previous studies which showed that the larger individuals migrated earlier than smaller fish (Bohlin *et al.*, 1993; Jonsson *et al.*, 1990). The findings from previous studies might be due to beeficial relationship between predation and growth (P/G); where larger fish migrate earlier as they are able to exploit food items better or had a lower predation risk in the sea (Brönmark *et al.*, 2008, Skov *et al.*, 2011). There is a chance that many of the larger smolts had already left the system earlier during the season. Taken together, these two factors could lead to these observations. However, the presence of both small and large fish in both groups suggests that this is not the case. Furthermore, the two observed groups could not be distinguished by RGR. Hence, our hypothesis that growth rate could explain the timing of downstream migration and that the

286

two rivers would reveal similar migration timing were rejected. RGR differences were very similar, with both low and high RGR observed in both groups. Therefore, it seems that RGR differences are too small to play any important role in the timing of migration within a year class in this system. Consequently factors other than size and RGR must affect the differences in timing of smoltification and migration within a year class. Differences in temperature between the two rivers would suggest that smolts from the Kärraån migrated earlier than smolts from the Bodeleån as the temperature in the Kärraån was 2 °C higher on average, and promoted a faster development rate at higher temperatures (Solbakken *et al.*, 1994). However, the opposite growth pattern was observed and it is unlikely that these differences are caused by differences in environmental factors. A more likely cause is a difference in the status of smoltification between the migration groups (e.g. gill Na^+, K^+ -ATPase activity), which could explain the bimodality found in this study. This factor has been shown to explain the bimodal pattern between stationary and migratory brown trout (Nielsen *et al.*, 2003; Nielsen *et al.*, 2006). Similarly, Jonsson (1985) observed no genetic effect for this differentiation and proposed an endocrine response to environmental variables for any difference.

MIGRATION ROUTES AND SPEED

The early migrants also revealed a larger variation in residence time in area A compared to later migrants (Figure 3). As a consequence of the difference in migration timing, smolts from the Kärraån seemed to be delayed in their progression through the system so that more individual from the Bodeleån had left the system at the end of the study. However, migration speeds did not differ between smolts from the Bodeleån and Kärraån. Migration routes were broadly similar between the two river systems and no favoured route to the west or to the south was detected. Only the in-river migration speed was found to differ between the rivers but no difference was found within the fjord, which concurs with our hypothesis. The difference in migration speed within rivers could be caused by smolts from the Kärraån spending a longer time within the river, resulting in a lower ground speed, than smolts from the Bodeleån. The characteristics of the lower reaches of the Kärraån over the 300 m section to the mouth of the river are more channel-like than in the Bodeleån, which had riffle areas for about 100 m above the river mouth. This section in the Kärraån has a saltwater intrusion, and is perhaps similar to an estuary in the abundance of food so that the smolts may be less likely to emigrate (Nixon *et al.*, 1968). Smolts from the Kärraån exhibited a higher migration speed in area A than the Bodeleån. This could result from the later arrival of Kärraån smolts in the sea and their higher calculated groundspeed and shorter residence time within that area. The greater residency time in area A for Bodeleån smolts may reflect the quality of the habitat outside the river mouth. This area of the Bodeleån is a large sand flat with some vegetation and although the area outside the Kärraån has similar characteristics it is smaller in extent. Similar areas have been shown to support numerous invertebrates food species, such as amphipods and polychaetes (Rasmussen, 1973). The latter species have been observed by anglers to be an important food source during early spring for returning adult migrants (Kristensen, 1984; Svärdson *et al.*, 1985). Throughout the rest of the fjord system, groundspeeds were similar between the two rivers and corresponded well with groundspeeds observed in previous studies on sea trout smolts; where there was a gradual reduction in swimming speed as they progressed towards the open sea (Aarestrup *et al.*, 2014; Thorstad *et al.*, 2004). The implication of the difference between migration timing and progression rate is hard to predict as the overall marine survival in the system seems to be very high (up to 70% Aldvén unpublished data), hence it is unlikely that these differences would have any larger impact on population numbers at the moment. There could however, still be e.g. fittness differences between the two strategies that are not visable here as the number of sea trout is very high (Unpublished elecrofishing data). Hence, the fitness consequences of these strategies needs to be evaluated.

SURVIVAL

In-river survival was similar between the two rivers. The fate of smolts within the rivers was hard to determine as only three smolts were detected in the Bodeleån and none in the Kärraån during manual tracking in June. However, the loss rates within rivers are similar to the findings from previous studies, and it is possible that some smolts were taken by avian or other land based predators (Aarestrup *et al.*, 2014; Finstad *et al.*, 2005; Koed *et al.*, 2006). It is also possible that other smolts had desmoltified (reverted) and remained within the river, hiding in deep pools or under piles of debris so that they could not be readily detected by scanning or electrofishing. However, it is more likely that these '*lost*' smolts died from predation or natural causes (Aldvén *et al.*, 2015; Jepsen *et al.*, 1998). Loss rates in the downstream sections of the fjord system corresponded well with previous studies on both smolts and kelts (Aarestrup *et al.*, 2014; Finstad *et al.*, 2005; Thorstad et *al.*, 2007).

CONCLUSIONS

In line with previous studies, we observed two migration groups during downstream migration, early and late, along with both fjord residency and migration to the open sea. The sea trout from Bodeleån migrated earlier than the sea trout in Kärraån. The trout from Bodeleån had a larger proportion of fish that had left the system in the end of the study, whereas fish from Kärraån seemed to be delayed in their migration through the system. The reasons for these two different migration strategies could not be explained by either size or growth rate. We therefore hypothesise that the difference in migration timing between the two groups is controlled by each individual's inner physiological condition. These differences in smoltification status are probably conditioned by differences in the expressed hormone levels of individual fish

(Björnsson *et al.*, 2011) reflecting differences in their life-history strategy (Réale *et al.*, 2010). Future studies should focus on the link between the individual's physiological condition and the timing of migration and investigate the fitness consequences of the two strategies and the underlying mechanism causing these differences.

ACKNOWLEDGEMENTS

D.A., K.A., and J.H. were financed by the Swedish Research Council for Environment, Agricultural Sciences and Spatial Planning (FORMAS). D.A. was also funded by Helge Ax:son Johnsons foundation, Wilhelm & Martina Lundgrens science foundation and Rådman and Mrs. Ernst Collianders foundation for charitable purposes. Thanks to Barbara Koeck, Daniel Simonsson, David Lidholm, Niclas Åberg, Markus Lundgren and Eli Niklaus for assistance during the study. Thanks to Ingvar Lagenfelt at the county board, for lending us the VR2 receivers. The experiment was approved by the Ethical Committee for Animal Research in Göteborg (license 54/2014), and complied with current laws in Sweden.

REFERENCES

Aarestrup, K., Baktoft, H., Koed, A., del Villar-Guerra, D.D & Thorstad, E. B. (2014). Comparison of the riverine and early marine migration behaviour and survival of wild and hatchery-reared sea trout Salmo trutta smolts. *Marine Ecology Progress Series* **496,** 197-206.

Aldvén, D., E. Degerman & Höjesjö, J. (2015). Environmental cues and downstream migration of anadromous brown trout (Salmo trutta) and Atlantic salmon (Salmo salar) smolts. *Boreal Environmental Research* **20**, 35–44.

Bagenal, T., 1969. The relationship between food supply and fecundity in brown trout Salmo trutta L. *Journal of Fish Biology*, **1**, 167-182.

Bartel, R., Pachur, M., & Bernas, R. (2010). Distribution, migrations, and growth of tagged sea trout released into the Vistula River. *Archives of Polish Fisheries* **18**, 225-237.

Berg, O. K. & Berg, M. (1987). Migrations of sea trout, Salmo-trutta-L, from the Vardnes river in northern Norway. *Journal of Fish Biology*, **31**, 113-121.

Björnsson, B. T., Stefansson S. O., & McCormick, S. D. (2011). Environmental endocrinology of salmon smoltification. *Gen Comp Endocrinol* **170**, 290-298.

Bohlin, T., Dellefors, C., & Faremo, U. (1993). Optimal time and size for smolt migration in wild sea trout (Salmo trutta). *Canadian Journal of Fish and Aquatic Sciences*, **50**, 224-232.

Brönmark, C., Skov, C., Brodersen, J., Nilsson, P.A., and Hansson, L.A. (2008). Seasonal Migration Determined by a Trade-Off between Predator Avoidance and Growth. *PLoS One*, **3**, 1-6.

del Villar-Guerra, D., Aarestrup, K., Skov C., & Koed, A. (2014). Marine migrations in anadromous brown trout (Salmo trutta). Fjord residency as a possible alternative in the continuum of migration to the open sea. *Ecology of Freshwater Fish*, **23**, 594-603.

Eldøy, S.H., Davidsen, J.G., Thorstad, E.B., Whoriskey, F., Aarestrup, K., Næsje, T.F., Rønning, L., Sjursen, A. D., Rikardsen, A.H., & Arnekleiv, J.V. (2015). Marine migration and habitat use of anadromous brown trout Salmo trutta. *Canadian Journal of Fish and Aquatic Sciences*, **72**, 1366-1378.

Finstad, B., Økland, F., Thorstad, E.B., Bjorn, P.A., & McKinley, R.S. (2005). Migration of hatchery-reared Atlantic salmon and wild anadromous brown trout post-smolts in a Norwegian fjord system. *Journal of Fish Biology*, **66**, 86-96.

Hvidsten, N.A., Jensen, A.J., Rikardsen, A.H., Finstad, B., Aure, J., Stefansson, S., Fiske P., & Johnsen, B.O. (2009). Influence of sea temperature and initial marine feeding on survival of Atlantic salmon Salmo salar post-smolts from the Rivers Orkla and Hals, Norway. *Journal of Fish Biology*, **74**, 1532-1548.

Jepsen, N., Aarestrup, K., Okland F., & Rasmussen, G.1998. Survival of radio-tagged Atlantic salmon (Salmo salar L.) and trout (Salmo trutta L.) smolts passing a reservoir during seaward migration. *Hydrobiologia*, **372**, 347-353.

Jonsson, B. (1985). Life history patterns of freshwater resident and sea-run migrant brown trout in Norway. *Transactions of the American Fisheries Society*, **114**, 182-194.

Jonsson, B., & Jonsson, N. (2011). Ecology of Atlantic salmon and brown trout: habitat as a template for life histories, Fish & Fisheries series, Volum 33, Dordrecht, Netherlands, Springer-Verlag, Dordrecht, 708 pp.

Jonsson, N., Jonsson B., & Hansen, L.P. (1990). Partial segregation in the timing of migration of Atlantic salmon of different ages. *Animal Behavior*, **40**, 313-321.

Koed, A., Baktoft H., & Bak, B.D. (2006). Causes of mortality of Atlantic salmon (Salmo salar) and brown trout (Salmo trutta) smolts in a restored river and its estuary. *River Research and Applications*, **22**, 69-78.

Kristensen, E. (1984). Life cycle, growth and production in estuarine populations of the polychaetes Nereis virens and N. diversicolor. *Ecography*, **7**, 249-250.

Lee, R. M. (1920). A review of the methods of age and growth determination in fishes by means of scales. *Fisheries investigations, series 2. Marine fisheries, Great Britain Ministry of Agriculture, Fisheries, and Food*, **4**, 1-32.

McCormick, S.D., Saunders, R.L., Henderson E.B., & Harmon, P.R. (1987). Photoperiod control of parr-smolt transformation in Atlantic salmon (Salmo-salar) – changes in salinity tolerance, gill Na+,K+-atpase activity, and plasma thyroid-hormones. *Canadian Journal of Fisheries and Aquatic Sciences*, **44**, 1462-1468.

Nielsen, C., Aarestrup, K., & Madsen, S.S. (2006). Comparison of physiological smolt status in descending and nondescending wild brown trout (Salmo trutta) in a Danish stream. *Ecology of Freshwater Fish*, **15**, 229–236.

Nielsen, C., Aarestrup, K., Nørum, U., & Madsen, S. (2003). Pre-migratory differentiation of wild brown trout into migrant and resident individuals. *Journal of Fish Biology*, **63**, 1184-1196.

Nixon, S.W., Oviatt, C.A., Frithsen, J., & Sullivan, B. (1986). Nutrients and the productivity of estuarine and coastal marine ecosystems. *Journal of the Limnological Society of Southern Africa*, **12**, 43-71.

Økland, F., Jonsson, B., Jensen A., & Hansen, L. (1993). Is there a threshold size regulating seaward migration of brown trout and Atlantic salmon? *Journal of Fish Biology*, **42**, 541-550.

Pemberton, R. (1976). Sea trout in North-Argyll-Sea lochs, population, distribution and movements. *Journal of Fish Biology*, **9**, 157-179.

Rasmussen, E. (1973). Systematics and ecology of the Isefjord marine fauna (Denmark). *Ophelia*, **11**, 1-507.

Réale, D., Garant, D., Humphries, M.M., Bergeron, P., Careau, V., & Montiglio, P-O. (2010). Personality and the emergence of the pace-of-life syndrome concept at the population level. *In Philosophical transactions of the Royal Society of London. Series B: Biological Sciences*, **365**, 4051-4063

Rikardsen, A.H., Amundsen, P.A., Knudsen R., & Sandring, S. (2006). Seasonal marine feeding and body condition of sea trout (Salmo trutta) at its northern distribution. *ICES Journal of Marine Science: Journal du Conseil*, **63**, 466-475.

Skov, C., Baktoft, H., Brodersen, J., Bronmark, C., Chapman, B., Hansson, L.A., & Nilsson, P.A. (2011). Sizing up your enemy: individual predation vulnerability predicts migratory probability. *Proceedings of the Royal Society of London B: Biological Sciences*. **278**, 1414–1418.

Solbakken, V.A., Hansen, T., & Stefansson, S.O. (1994). Effects of photoperiod and temperature on growth and parr-smolt transformation in Atlantic salmon (*Salmo salar* L.) and subsequent performance in seawater. *Aquaculture*, **121**, 13–27.

Svärdson, G., & Fagerström, Å. (1982). Adaptive differences in the long-distance migration of some trout (Salmo trutta L.) stocks. *Report-Institute of Freshwater Research, Drottningholm*, **60**, 51-80.

Svärdson, G., Nilsson, N-A., Fürst C., & Gustafson, K-J. (1985). Fiskebiologi. LTs-förlag, Stockholm, 135-136.

Thorstad, E.B., Økland, F., Finstad, B., Sivertsgard, R., Bjorn, P.A., & McKinley, R.S. (2004). Migration speeds and orientation of Atlantic salmon and sea trout post-smolts in a Norwegian fjord system. *Environmental Biology of Fishes*, **71**, 305-311.

Thorstad, E.B., Økland, F., Finstad, B., Sivertsgard, R., Plantalech, N., Bjorn, P.A., & McKinley, R.S. (2007). Fjord migration and survival of wild and hatchery-reared Atlantic salmon and wild brown trout post-smolts. *Hydrobiologia*, **582**, 99-107

Závorka, L., Slavík O., & Horký, P. (2014). Validation of scale-reading estimates of age and growth in a brown trout *Salmo trutta* population. *Biologia*, **69**, 691-695

ELECTRONIC REFERENCES

Vemco (2012). False Detections: What They Are and How to Remove Them from Detection Data. Document #: DOC-004691 Version 03. Available at: http://www.vemco.com/pdf/false_detections.pdf . (Accessed: 2016-01-27).

Migration behaviour and loss rate of trout smolts in the transitional zone between freshwater and saltwater

R. B. LAURIDSEN[1], A. MOORE[2], S.D. GREGORY[1], W. R.C. BEAUMONT[1], L. PRIVITERA[2] & J. A. KAVANAGH[1]

[1]*Game & Wildlife Conservation Trust, Salmon and Trout Research Centre, The River Laboratory, Wareham, BH20 6BB, UK.*
[2]*The Centre for Environment, Fisheries and Aquaculture Science, Lowestoft Laboratory, Lowestoft, NR33 0HT, UK*

ABSTRACT

Migration between freshwater nursery grounds and saltwater feeding areas is a critical event in sea trout life history. During their seaward migration, smolts encounter both natural and man-made obstructions as well as increased exposure to predators. This is particularly true in the transition zone between freshwater and saltwater where smolts enter a new environment, change their behaviour and encounter new predators. Over two years (2013-14), 81 trout smolts were trapped and acoustically tagged 17 km upstream of the tidal limit in the River Frome in Dorset, UK. Smolt migrations were then tracked by acoustic receivers deployed throughout the lower river and its estuary and the detected movements were used to estimate loss rate and migration behaviour. A Bayesian State Space model was applied to separate detection and transition probabilities. More than 90% of the in-river detections occurred at night whereas detections at the saline limit and throughout the estuary were spread evenly between day and night. Median migration speed in the river was 65-70 km day^{-1} in both years, whereas the migration speed was slower through the estuary with median speeds of less than 10 km day^{-1}. The loss rate was similar across the study zones (range 0.5-1.1 % km^{-1}); hence there was no pronounced increase in mortality in any particular part of the transition zone as reported by a number of similar studies from other systems. Even though no individual study zone displayed a particularly elevated loss rate, the cumulative loss of tracked trout smolts through the 33 km section was 24%, demonstrating a significant cost in terms of loss associated with smolt migration.

Keywords: trout smolts; acoustic tags; loss rate; migration behaviour; transition zone; Bayesian state space model.

INTRODUCTION

Many animal species undertake migration during their lifetime. Reasons for migration include seasonal changes in habitat and food resources, longer-term changes in habitat and/or dietary needs associated with the growth and development of the individual and for reproduction. Pursuing resources in space and time is among the most common reasons for migration, but individuals must reconcile the costs and benefits incurred, such as energy expenditure and increased mortality risk, with the decision to migrate.

Migration for some species is a fixed behaviour whereby environmental cues trigger synchronous migrations. A number of species, however, undertake partial migration whereby some individuals migrate and others do not. Partial migration occurs in a range of animal groups, such as mammals, birds, and fishes (e.g. pronghorn antelope, European robin, great white shark). A number of hypotheses have been proposed to explain why partial migration occurs and persists and among the most commonly cited, are *'dominance'* and *'endurance'*. The dominance hypothesis states that when food resources are scarce, the larger and more dominant individuals can outcompete the smaller subdominant individuals so that it is beneficial for subdominant individuals to migrate to richer feeding grounds (Gauthreaux, 1982). The endurance hypothesis states that individuals of larger body size are better able to endure adverse conditions during periods with low food availability and reduced temperature so that smaller individuals are more likely to migrate to avoid hardship (Ketterson & Nolan, 1976).

Among salmonids, brown trout (*Salmo trutta*) exhibit one of the most polytypic life histories: with some individuals migrating to the marine environment before returning to spawn (anadromy), some staying in their freshwater natal stream all their life (residency), with others 'doing something in between' (Thorstad *et al.*, 2016). Anadromous trout encounter richer feeding grounds and attain greater final body size than their freshwater resident counterparts, Because fecundity is intrinsically linked to body size, particularly for females, anadromous individuals enjoy greater lifetime fecundity (Jonsson, 1985). However, migration is energetically costly, not only in terms of the actual energy expenditure during migration, but also during the physiological, morphological and behavioural transformation from parr to smolt (Sheridan *et al.*, 1983). Exposure to predation also increases during migration as the smolts move through the lower river, the estuary and into the marine environment (Mather, 1998; Klemetsen *et al.*, 2003).

The freshwater phase of migratory salmonid life history is well described. However, the marine phase is less well understood due largely to the technical issues involved in conducting studies at sea. A reduction in marine survival of Atlantic salmon (*Salmo salar*) over the last three decades, combined with technological advances, has led to increased interest and resulting improvement in our ability to collect migration data from the marine environment (ICES, 2015). Consequently, there has been a recent focus on the behaviour and loss of smolts in the near-shore environment to predators, such as European sea bass (*Dicentrarchus labrax*), cod (*Gadus morhua*) and cormorants (*Phalacrocorax carbo*) (Dieperink *et al.*, 2002, Riley *et al.*, 2011, Thorstad *et al.*, 2012a). The transition zone, where the smolts migrate from the unidirectional flowing freshwater environment of the river into a saltwater environment affected by tides and waves, is thought to be a critical phase in their migration (Thorstad *et al.*, 2012b). Trout behaviour in this transition zone changes from being a benthic predator with a small territory to becoming a pelagic nomad actively exploring larger areas, as well as a complete change in diet. These physiological and behavioural changes in smolts in this zone may render them particularly vulnerable to other external stressors (Halfyard *et al.*, 2012). The transition zone of many rivers is heavily influenced by anthropogenic activity, such as dredging, netting, boat traffic and pollution; all with a potentially negative impact on smolt behaviour and survival. In summary, migrating smolts encounter new predators and physiological and anthropogenic stressors in the transition zone, and the combined effect of these stressors might be super-additive and greater than their individual effects (Brook *et al.*, 2008).

The decision whether to migrate or not is therefore a cost-benefit trade-off where the potential fecundity gain by migrating to sea is weighed against increased energy expenditure and mortality risk incurred by migration. Fecundity gain by returning anadromous individuals is relatively easy to estimate from the size of returning individuals. In this study we aim to quantify the more elusive risk associated with migration. In particular, we investigate migration behaviour and loss rate through individual zones of the lower river and the transition zone. We hypothesise that the highest loss rate occurs in the transition zone where smolts enter a new environment, change their behaviour and encounter new predators.

Fecundity gain is the obvious driver for migration. However, it is common for some anadromous individuals to return to their native river before their first winter in saltwater. These 0SW individuals that return early from their marine migration have various local names in the British Isles (notably, finnock, whitling, herling and school peel). Why do some individuals that have incurred energetic costs and increased risk during migration return to the poorer feeding grounds of the river after such a short period at sea? Some of these anadromous individuals even return to the river in the middle of summer only a few weeks after their outward migration as post-smolts several months before their first potential spawning season. We hypothesise that individuals returning to the river before their first sea winter remain in the estuary so that they experience a lower energy cost in terms of migration and potentially avoid predation in the open sea.

MATERIAL AND METHODS

STUDY SITE

The river Frome in Dorset, Southern England, is a chalk stream receiving most of its discharge directly from the cretaceous chalk aquifer. It rises in Evershot and flows approximately 70 km to the tidal limit near Wareham Bypass Bridge. Immediately downstream of Wareham the river enters Poole Harbour, a large natural estuary (36 km²) with a narrow exit (300 m wide) into the English Channel (Figure 1). This study took place in the lower part of the river Frome and its estuary, Poole Harbour.

TRAPPING, TAGGING & TRACKING

Trout smolts were trapped on an eel rack at East Burton, some 16.8 km upstream of the tidal limit. The trap was built to catch emigrating silver eels (*Anguilla anguilla*) and consisted of inclining metal slats, situated downstream of undershot sluices in the river, that allowed the passage of water but retained fish and diverted them to a holding tank. Smolts were trapped at night in the spring of 2013 and 2014. In 2013, 30 trout smolts were trapped on the eel rack from 10th – 15th of April. Their average length was 182 mm (range 123-247 mm) with an average weight of 70 g (19-177 g). In 2014, 51 smolts were trapped from 28th March – 16th April. Their average length was 213 mm (163-273 mm) and their average weight was 105 g (44-199 g). The trapped smolts were anesthetised in 2-phenoxy ethanol before surgically implanting a 16.5 x 6 mm, 180 KHz acoustic transmitter (V6, Vemco Ltd.) and a 12 x 2 mm passive integrated transponder (PIT) tag (Wyre Micro Design Ltd.) into the peritoneal cavity. The fish were allowed to recover fully after surgery before they were released immediately downstream of the trap. [All tagging was carried out in compliance with the UK Animal (Scientific Procedures) Act 1986 under Home Office licences PPL30/2732 and 70/7588.] The Vemco V6 transmitters were programmed to transmit with a nominal delay of 30 seconds and with a transmission rate varying randomly ±50% of the nominal delay (the variation in delay avoided two tags transmitting in synchrony and causing a loss of data). In the second year (2014), the nominal delay was programmed to increase from 30 to 60 seconds two weeks after release to increase the battery life of the transmitters (>90% of the fish observed exiting the estuary in 2013 did so within two weeks). This increased the battery life of the transmitters from 43 to 105 days.

Vemco VR2W receivers were positioned at three locations in freshwater: namely at a) Bindon Mill, b) East Stoke and c) the tidal limit – at distances of 5.5, 8.3 and 16.8 km downstream of the trap respectively (Figure 1). Receivers were placed in the saltwater zone at a) the saline limit, b) in Wareham Channel and c) at the exit of the estuary – at distances of 21.1, 23.4 and 32.9 km from the trap respectively (Figure 1). At the mouth of the estuary (=Exit), three receivers were deployed with the first two covering the exit and the third receiver just outside the exit. When estimating the transition probability, the receiver outside the exit informed the model about the detection probability of the two receivers at the exit (*see* statistical methods below). In the second year (2014), a further four receivers were deployed in potential feeding areas of the estuary (Figure 1).

A low head Archimedes hydro-turbine was installed at Bindon Mill in 2012 and acoustic receivers were placed by the turbine during this study to detect smolt using this route (*see*

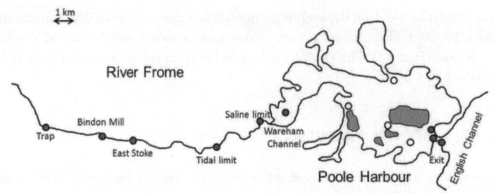

Figure 1. Map of the lower River Frome and its estuary at Poole Harbour. Grey circles indicate location of trap and acoustic receivers deployed in both 2013 & 2014. Open circles indicate estuary receivers deployed in 2014 only.

Moore *et al.*, 2017). Any smolts detected at the turbine were removed from the analysis because of the potentially adverse effect of passage through the turbine on their subsequent behaviour and survival.

An array of PIT-antennae covering the full width of the river at East Stoke detected the upstream and downstream migration of PIT-tagged fish (Welton *et al.*, 2002).

DATA ANALYSIS

Migration speed through individual zones was calculated using the time difference between the first observation at one receiver station and the first observation at the next downstream receiver station. Variation in migration speed between zones and the effect of year and smolt size was analysed using an ANOVA with a Tukey's *post hoc* test of between-zone differences.

Telemetry data has the inherent problem that detection is imperfect; a passing tag is not always detected and so it is unknown if (a) the tag did not pass a receiver or (b) if was not detected when it passed. This problem can, and should, be addressed statistically.

To estimate the risks to trout smolts associated with migrating through different zones, a Bayesian State Space models (BSSM) was applied. Other have used BSSM in this context: Gimenez *et al.* (2007) explain clearly the theory of BSSM for marked individuals and Holbrook *et al.* (2014) present an illustrative example of BSSM implementation for acoustically tagged lamprey (*Petromyzon marinus*). In essence, BSSM estimates jointly the probability that a tag is detected at a particular location and the probability that it completed the transition to that location successfully. Individuals may not complete the transition from one receiver to another for a variety of reasons including mortality, tag failure, taking up residence etc. Acoustic tracking alone cannot determine the underlying reason for an incomplete transition. To avoid invoking any particular reason for an incomplete transition, the term '*Stopped migration*' was used.

In this study, it was assumed that all tagged smolts shared the same detection and transition probabilities (i.e. that physical or behavioural differences between individuals were unimportant and that individuals travelled independently). Making these assumptions enabled the use of the simple (CJS) model (Cormack, 1964; Jolly, 1965; Seber, 1965) given by:

$$Y_t | X_t \sim Binomial(X_t - u_t, p_t)$$
$$X_{t+1} | X_t \sim Binomial(X_t, \phi_t) + u_{t+1}$$

Where: X_t is the total number of survivors from time t, including u_t, which is the number of newly marked individuals at time t; Y_t is the total number of previously marked individuals encountered at time t; p_t is the probability of detecting a tagged individual at time $t(t=2, ...,T)$ and ϕ_t is the probability that a tagged individual transitions to time $t+1$ given that it is alive at time $t(t=1, ..., T-1)$. This formulation separates the nuisance parameters (the detection probabilities, p_t) from the parameters of interest (the transition probabilities, ϕ_t) because the latter are found only in the second or "state" equation.

Values of p_t and ϕ_t were estimated from this model using the Monte Carlo Markov Chain (MCMC) method implemented in JAGS (www.mcmc-jags.sourceforge.net). JAGS uses Gibbs sampling to explore the joint probability distribution of p_t and ϕ_t. Through an iterative process, weakly informative *Beta*(1,1) prior distributions on p_t and ϕ_t were updated with increasingly credible values until, after sufficient iterations, the best stationary estimated values of p_t and ϕ_t were taken to be the median of their posterior distributions.

JAGS was run from within R using functions from the package dclone (www.cran.r-project.org/web/packages/dclone/index.html). The MCMC chains were run for 30,000 iterations, of which the first 10,000 was discarded as burnin.

RESULTS

DETECTIONS

Tags were detected at all receiver stations and the detection efficiency was >80% at all stations, although no station was 100% efficient (Table 1). Receiver efficiency and transition probability was estimated using a Bayesian State Space model (*see methods*). It was discovered that some individuals at Bindon Mill migrated through a relief channel which was not covered by receivers (*see* Moore *et al.*, 2017). Individuals that might have taken this unmonitored route were not available to be detected at Bindon Mill. Consequently, estimates of detection and transition probabilities for the section between the trap and Bindon Mill were subject to an unknown bias. To overcome this, we estimated detection and transition probabilities for the total section between the trap and East Stoke (i.e., encompassing Bindon Mill and the relief channel).

More than 80% of the first detections of individual smolts at any receiver station in the freshwater zone occurred in the hours of darkness (Table 1). There was no such nocturnal detection pattern at the saltwater stations, but 70% of the first detections at the saline limit were made during ebbing tides.

Table 1 Number of tags observed and time of day of first observation at the receiver stations. A Bayesian approach was used to estimate the detection probability at each station. CI used here denotes credible interval which is similar to, but not identical to, confidence interval. * In both 2013 and 2014, two tags were detected at the turbine at Bindon Mill: these four fish were removed from the analysis and are not included in the count of tags.

`Station	Distance from trap (km)	Year	No. Tags detected *	Detection probability (95% CI)	Day time obs.	Night time obs.
Bindon Mill	5.4	2013	20	N/A	0%	100%
		2014	36	N/A	14%	86%
East Stoke	8.2	2013	25	0.93 (0.86-0.95)	0%	100%
		2014	42		10%	90%
Tidal Limit	16.7	2013	24	0.99 (0.95-1.00)	8%	92%
		2014	45		18%	82%
Saline Limit	21.1	2013	21	0.96 (0.90-0.99)	43%	57%
		2014	42		48%	52%
Wareham Channel	23.4	2013	20	0.81 (0.70-0.84)	40%	60%
		2014	37		62%	38%
Exit	32.9	2013	22	0.84 (0.72-0.87)	68%	32%
		2014	36		56%	44%

MIGRATION SPEED

With one exception, variation in migration speed between the two years was negligible within zones (Figure 2). Initial analysis showed a highly significant interaction between zone and year that was driven purely by differences between years in the Trap – Bindon Mill zone. When this zone was removed from the analysis, the zone x year interaction was no longer significant and while there was a significant effect of zone ($F_{5,194} = 111$, $P < 0.001$) there was no effect of year. The migration speed of the smolts was highest in the middle and lower river sections where the median speed varied from 62.2 km day^{-1} in the middle river (Bindon Mill – East Stoke) to 69.1 km day^{-1} in the lower river (East Stoke – Tidal limit), both in 2014 (Figure 2). The lowest migration speed was in the upper river (Trap – Bindon Mill) where the median speed was 5.2 and 1.7 km day^{-1} in 2013 and 2014 respectively. Migration speed in the tidal section of the river and within the estuary was considerably slower than in the middle and lower river. Results of the Tukey's *post hoc* test of between-zone differences are given in Figure 2. There was a significant effect of size ($F_{1,194}$ = 5.4, P = 0.02) indicating that migration speed increases slightly with smolt size.

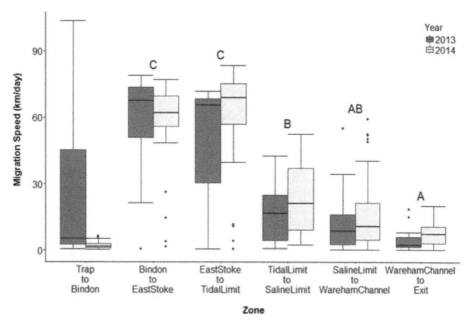

Figure 2. Migration speed in the six different zones in 2013 (grey boxes) and 2014 (open boxes). Migration speed in those zones that share the same letter are not significantly different ($F_{5,194}$, Tukey's; P > 0.05).

STOPPED MIGRATION

The transition probability within individual zones was practically identical between years (Figure 3) allowing data from the two years to be combined and the estimation of a single transition probability for each individual zone. The zone with the lowest transition probability and, therefore, the highest probability of stopped migration (10%) was observed in the outer part of the estuary from Wareham Channel to the exit of the estuary, whereas the lowest probability of stopped migration (1.5%) was observed in the zone from the tidal limit to the saline limit (Figure 4). After considering zone length, the highest probability of stopped migration was observed in outer estuary at 1.1% km^{-1} followed by the zone from the trap to East Stoke at 1.0% km^{-1}, whereas the probability of stopped migration was 0.5-0.7% km^{-1} in all other zones (Figure 5). The cumulative stopped migration rate from the trap to the exit of the estuary was 24%.

LOSS RATE BY SIZE

There was no difference between years (P>0.05) in the probability of recording the smolts at

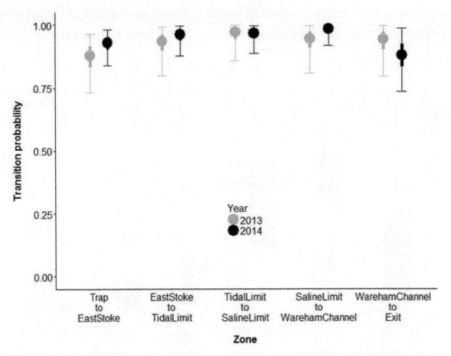

Figure 3. Transition probability by zone and year with 95% credible intervals. Credible intervals are similar to confidence intervals but not the same.

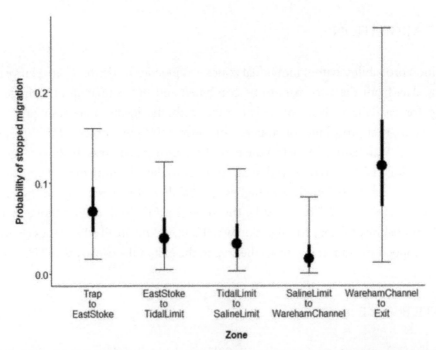

Figure 4. Probability of stopped migration within individual zones years combined with 95% credible intervals.

the exit of the estuary, but there was a small effect of size on the probability of being recorded at the exit (Logistic regression, odds multiplier $e^{0.02}$, Z = 2.1, P = 0.03).

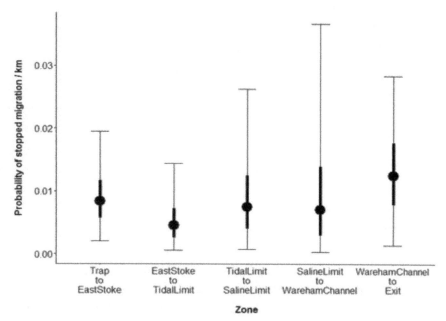

Figure 5. Probability of stopped migration within individual zones divided by the length of the zone (km) years combined with 95% credible intervals.

SUMMER OBSERVATIONS AND RETURNING ADULTS

In 2013, 4 of 22 smolts observed leaving the estuary were detected migrating into and out of the estuary exit several times between first leaving the estuary and the end of the battery life of the acoustic tags (battery life = 43 days). In 2014, when the battery life of the acoustic tags was extended to 105 days, the last observation in the estuary was made on the 15th May. No further tags were detected until the 22nd July when the first individual was detected re-entering the estuary. A further 4 individuals were detected re-entering the estuary between July 22nd and the end of the lifespan of the batteries (= August). All 5 individuals were observed entering the freshwater zone of the river within 20 hours of being observed at the mouth of the estuary. A further 6 individuals were observed returning to the river by the PIT-tag system at East Stoke. The first observed returns to the river of the 11 returning adults were made as 0SW finnock for 5 fish, a further 5 fish returned after 1SW and 1 fish was recorded as a 2SW fish.

DISCUSSION

The hypothesised increase in the loss rates of smolts in the transition zone was not observed as the loss rate of the fish tracked through the lower river and estuary in this investigation was evenly spread. A number of studies have reported very high loss rates in the transition zone for sea trout and salmon smolts (Hvidsten & Lund, 1988; Dieperink *et al.*, 2001; Dieperink, 2002). However, other studies have reported loss rates in the transition zone similar to the 0.7 – 1.1% km^{-1} observed here: Thorstad *et al.* (2007) reported 1.8% km^{-1} and Aarestrup *et al.* (2014) reported 0.6 – 0.9% km^{-1} for wild sea trout smolts in the transition zone. High loss rates in the transition zone are therefore not inherent and it appears that the wild smolts tagged in this study were fully adapted for the physiological and behavioural changes experienced in the transition zone. Studies reporting high loss rates were linked to very high predation rates that will be highly variable depending on the predator populations in different estuaries.

Larger trout were more likely to make the transition from the trapping location to the exit of the estuary. This size-dependent transition probability may be linked to the observed positive correlation between size and swimming speed because the predator avoidance potential increases with both speed and size: an observation also made in a number of other studies (Dieperink *et al.*, 2001; Finstad *et al.*, 2005).

The cumulative loss of sea trout smolts through the 33 km section where the smolts were tracked in the lower river Frome and its estuary was 24%. Similar loss rates have been reported for wild trout smolts from Scandinavia. Thorstad *et al.* (2007) reported a 35% loss over 37 km of the transition zone of a Norwegian river and Aarestrup *et al.* (2014) reported a 23% loss over 46 km of combined river and estuary from a Danish river. This indicates that there is a significant cost associated with the seaward migration of smolts in terms of loss. However, because all these studies were conducted with acoustic tags, these losses effectively represent stopped migration. Stopped migration could be caused by fish mortality, but there are other possible explanations, such as tag failure or the fish taking up residence between receivers, as observed by del Villar-Guerra *et al.* (2014).

The in-river median migration speed was >60 km day^{-1} in the zones between East Stoke and the tidal limit. This is higher than the 36.8 km day^{-1} migration speed reported for wild trout smolts by Aarestrup *et al.* (2014). The high migration speed indicates an active migration; however, as the vast majority of the observations in this zone were made at night, the smolts must have held station during the day, indicating an in-river 'start-and-stop' pattern of migration behaviour. Similar nocturnal freshwater migration patterns have been observed elsewhere and it has been suggested that nocturnal migration is an adaptive behaviour to avoid visual predators (Solomon, 1978; Moore & Potter, 1994; Moore *et al.*, 1995).

Entry into the saline zone was associated with ebbing tides, thus saving energy while progressing through the transition to saltwater by following the freshwater plume into the transition zone; a behaviour reported in a number of previous studies (Moore *et al.*, 1995; Lacroix *et al.*, 2004). Once in the estuary, there was no diel pattern in migration behaviour and the migration speed of the smolts was significantly lower than in freshwater. The migration speed was particularly low from Wareham Channel to the exit of the estuary (2.5–7.3 km day^{-1}). While this is considerably slower than the in-river migration, the water velocity in this section was much slower than in the river and it is unlikely that the smolts followed the shortest route through estuaries (Thorstad *et al.*, 2004). The observed migration speed through the estuary was similar to the 3.2 km day^{-1} reported by Aarestrup *et al.* (2014), but was significantly slower than the 31.9-42.2 km day^{-1} reported for the outer zone of a Norwegian fjord by Finstad *et al.* (2005).

No fish were detected foraging in the estuary during the summer of the second study year (2014) when the battery life of the acoustic tags had been extended and extra receivers were placed in the estuary. Furthermore, of the 11 adults observed returning to the river, all but one were recorded by the acoustic receivers at the exit of the estuary as smolts and the first in-river observation of the individual not recorded by the exit was as a 1SW fish. It appears that the anadromous individuals of river Frome all leave the estuary and seek inshore or offshore feeding areas in the English Channel. There was no support for the hypothesis that the individuals returning to the river before their first winter at sea remained in the estuary to reduce energy expenditure and exposure to predators. The marine migration distances undertaken by these individuals before returning to the river is not clear, but all anadromous individuals migrated >12 km (furthest receiver) from the river mouth. This contrasts findings by Berg & Berg (1987) from a Norwegian river where 53% of tagged fish were recaptured within 3 km of the river mouth but it concurs with generally longer migration distances observed for sea trout from the UK (Pratten & Shearer, 1983).

Handling fish during capture and tagging induces stress. Lower *et al.* (2005) showed this by measuring excretion of the well-established stress indicator, cortisol, from roach and carp undergoing different treatments. They showed that tagged fish excreted significantly higher levels of cortisol than control fish although the cortisol levels returned to pre-stress levels within 24 hours after tagging. Therefore, the impact of capture and handling on the behaviour of smolts is most likely to occur in the first day or two after tagging. Increased post-tagging stress may explain the large variation in migration speed observed in the zone immediately downstream of the trap (Figure 2). Reduced migration speed in the zone immediately downstream of tagging has been observed in a number of other smolt tagging studies (Finstad *et al.*, 2005; Aarestrup *et al.*, 2014). Alternatively, individuals merely drifting downstream in the early, slower, passive stage of smolt migration prior to active migration may also have been trapped and these would be likely to exhibit slow migration speeds immediately after tagging. Both scenarios highlight the importance of experimental design when planning studies that involve handling fish because the tagged fish will need time and space to recover before it may be assumed that normal behaviour is being observed. Even though the main effect of tagging is likely to occur within the first couple of days of handling, the vulnerability of tagged fish to delayed physiological stress and predation may continue for longer so that the estimates of loss rate may be greater among tracked smolts. Eleven of the 81 tagged fish (14%) were observed returning to the river as adults. This return rate is similar to the 20% reported for wild untagged trout from River Bresle, a French chalk stream (Euzanat *et al.*, 2004), the 21% reported from Burrishoole in the west of Ireland (Poole *et al.*, 2006) and the 19% reported for River Tamar in the southwest of England (Simon Toms, *pers. comm.*), but it is considerably lower than the 37% reported from a Norwegian river (Berg & Jonsson, 1990). There is currently no measure of the return rate of untagged sea trout from the Frome but it seems likely that any impact that tagging and handling on the survival of tagged smolts in this study fish was small so that the reported loss rates in the lower river and estuary were probably close to the natural mortality.

We established a significant cost-penalty in terms of the cumulative loss associated with the outward migration of smolts through the lower river and the transition zone. Although this study does not indicate if this mortality rate is outweighed by benefits in growth and fecundity, it contributes to our understanding of near-shore mortality in relation to the cost-benefit analysis that must underpin the life-history strategy choices of sea trout.

CONCLUSIONS

This study demonstrated a significant cost in terms of cumulative loss associated with smolt migration through the lower river and the transition zone. However, as none of the sections within the transition zone of this study displayed a particularly elevated loss rate, there was no pronounced increase in mortality during migration through the transition zone specifically as reported by similar studies elsewhere.

The reduced migration speed in the zone immediately below the trap emphasised the importance of handling and tagging early enough in space and time so that the tagged individuals then behave "normally" when they enter the section of interest for a given study.

The trout smolts migrated quickly through the freshwater zone primarily at night but no such nocturnal movement pattern was observed in the saline zone.

Individuals returning to the river before their first winter at sea did not take up residence within the estuary so that there was no evidence to suggest that this life-history strategy was associated with a shorter marine migration.

ACKNOWLEDGEMENTS

We thank Dr Anton Ibbotson for his help planning this study and Barry Bust for help deploying the receivers in Poole Harbour. We thank Pool Harbour Commissioners for permission to attach acoustic receivers to their buoys, the Weld Estate for access to the river and Defra, Clay Brendish, Anthony Daniell, Winton Capital and Sir Chips Keswick for their support in financing the project.

REFERENCES

Berg, O.K., Berg, M. (1987). Migrations of sea trout, *Salmo trutta* L., from the Vardnes River in Northern Norway. *Journal of Fish Biology* **31**,113–121.

Berg, O.K. & Jonsson, B. (1990). Growth and survival rates of the anadromous trout, *Salmo trutta*, from the Vardnes River, northern Norway. *Environmental Biology of Fish* **29**, 145–154.

Brook, B.W., Sodhi, N.S. & Bradshaw, C.J. (2008). Synergies among extinction drivers under global change *Trends in Ecology and Evoution* **23**, 453-60.

Cormack, R.M. (1964) Estimates of survival from the sighting of marked animals. *Biometrika* **51**, 429-438.

del Villar-Guerra, D., Aarestrup, K., Skov, C. & Koed, A. (2014) Marine migrations in anadromous brown trout (*Salmo trutta*). Fjord residency as a possible alternative in the continuum of migration to the open sea *Ecology of Freshwater Fish* **23**, 594–603.

Dieperink, C., Pedersen, S. & Pedersen, M.I. (2001). Estuarine predation on radio-tagged wild and domesticated sea trout (*Salmo trutta* L.) smolts *Ecology of Freshwater Fish* ,**10**, 177–183.

Dieperink, C., Bak, B.D., Pedersen, L.-F., Pedersen, M.I. & Pedersen, S. (2002). Predation on Atlantic salmon and sea trout during their first days as post-smolts *Journal of Fish Biology,* **61**, 848–852.

Gauthreaux, S.A. Jr. (1982). The ecology and evolution of avian migration systems. *In*: Farner, D. S. *et al*. (Eds), *Avian Biology*. Academic Press, 93 – 168.

Euzanat, G., Fournel, F. & Fagardet J-L. (2004) Population Dynamics and Stock–Recruitment Relationship of Sea Trout in the River Bresle, Upper Normandy, France. In: *Sea Trout: Biology, Conservation and Management*. (Graeme Harris & Nigel Milner. *Eds.*), Proceedings of the 1st International Sea Trout Symposium, July 2004, Cardiff, Wales, UK. Blackwell Publishing, Oxford. 307-326.

Finstad, B., Økland, F., Thorstad, E.B., Bjørn, P.A. & Mckinley, R.S. (2005). Migration of hatchery-reared Atlantic salmon and wild anadromous brown trout post-smolts in a Norwegian fjord system *Journal of Fish Biology* **66**, 86–96.

Gimenez, O., Rossi, V., Choquet, R., Dehais, C., Doris, B., Varella, H., Vila, J.P. and Pradel, R., 2007. State-space modelling of data on marked individuals. *Ecological Modelling,* **206**, 431-438.

Halfyard, E.A., Gibson, A.J.F., Ruzzante, D.E., Stokesbury, M.J.W. & Whoriskey F.G. (2012). Estuarine survival and migratory behaviour of Atlantic salmon *Salmo salar* smolts. *Journal of Fish Biology,* **81**, 1626-1645.

Holbrook, C. M., Johnson, N. S., Steibel, J. P., Twohey, M. B., Binder, T. R., Krueger, C. C. & Jones, M. L. (2014). Estimating reach-specific fish movement probabilities in rivers with a Bayesian state-space model: application to sea lamprey passage and capture at dams. *Canadian Journal of Fisheries and Aquatic Sciences,* **71**, 1713-1729.

Hvidsten, N.A. & Lund, R.A. (1988). Predation on hatchery-reared and wild smolts of Atlantic salmon, *Salmo salar* L., in the estuary of River Orkla. *Journal of Fish Biology,* **33**, 121–126.

ICES (2015). Report of the Working Group on North Atlantic Salmon (WGNAS), 17–26 March, Moncton, Canada. ICES CM 2015/ACOM:09, 332 pp.

Jonsson, B. 1985. Life history pattern of freshwater resident and sea-run migrant brown trout in Norway. *Transactions of the American Fisheries Society,* **114**, 182–194.

Jolly, G.M. (1965) Explicit estimates from capture-recapture data with both death and immigration – Stochastic model. *Biometrika* **52**, 225-247.

Ketterson, E.D. & Nolan, V. Jr. (1976). Geographic variation and its climatic correlates in the sex ratio of eastern-wintering dark-eyed juncos (*Junco hyemalis hyemalis*). *Ecology*, **57**, 679 – 693.

Klemetsen, A, Amundsen, P-A, Dempson, J.B., Jonsson, B., Jonsson, N., O'Connell, M.F. & Mortensen, E. (2003). Atlantic salmon *Salmo salar* L., brown trout *Salmo trutta* L. and Arctic charr *Salvelinus alpinus* (L.): a review of aspects of their life histories. *Ecology of Freshwater Fish*, **12**, 1–59.

Lacroix, G.L., McCurdy, P. & Knox, D. (2004). Migration of Atlantic salmon post-smolts in relation to habitat use in a coastal system. *Transactions of the American Fisheries Society*, **133**, 1455–1471.

Lower, N., Moore, A., Scott, A.P., Ellis, T., James, J.D. & Russell, I.C. (2005). A non-invasive method to assess the impact of electronic tag insertion on stress levels in fishes. *Journal of Fish Biology* **67**, 1202-1212.

Mather, M.E. (1998). The role of context-specific predation in understanding patterns exhibited by anadromous salmon. *Canadian Journal of Fisheries and Aquatic Sciences*, **55**, 232–246.

Moore, A., Lauridsen, R.B., Privitera, L. & Beaumont, W.R.C. (2017). The impact of a small hydropower scheme on the migratory behaviour of sea trout (*Salmo trutta* L.) smolts in the River Frome, southern England. In: *Sea Trout: Science & Management*. (Graeme Harris *Ed*.). Proceedings of the 2nd International Sea Trout Symposium, October 2015, Dundalk, Ireland. *(Troubador insert full reference at page-proof stage)*.

Moore, A. & Potter, E.C.E. (1994). The movements of sea trout *(Salmo trutta* L.) smolts through the estuary of the River Avon, Southern England. *Fisheries Management and Ecology*, **1**, 1-14.

Moore, A., Potter, E. C. E., Milner, N. J. & Bamber, S. (1995). The migratory behaviour of wild Atlantic salmon (*Salmo salar*) smolts in the estuary of the River Conwy, North Wales. *Canadian Journal of Fisheries and Aquatic Sciences*, **52**, 1923–1935.

Poole, W.R., Dillane, M., DeEyto, E., Rogan, G., McGinnity, P., & Whelan, K. (2006). Characteristics of the Burrishoole sea trout population: census, marine survival, enhancement and stock-recruitment relationship, 1971–2003. In: *Sea trout: Biology, Conservation and Management*. (Graeme Harris & Nigel Milner. *Eds*.), Proceedings of the 1st International Sea Trout Symposium, July 2004, Cardiff, Wales, UK. Blackwell Publishing, Oxford, 107–114.

Pratten, D.J., & Shearer, W.M. (1983). The migrations of North Esk sea trout. *Fisheries Management*, **14**, 99–113.

Riley, W.D., Ibbotson, A., Beaumont, W.R.C., Pawson, M.G., Cook, A.C. & Davison, P.I. (2011). Predation of the juvenile stages of diadromous fish by sea bass (*Dicentrarchus labrax*) in the tidal reaches of an English chalk stream Aquatic Conservation *Marine and Freshwater Ecosystems*, **21**, 307–312.

Seber, G.A.F. (1965) A note on the multiple recapture census. *Biometrika* **52**, 249-259.

Sheridan, M.A., Allen, W.V. & Kerstetter, T.H. (1983). Seasonal variations in the lipid composition of the steelhead trout, *Salmo gairdneri* Richardson, associated with the parr-smolt transformation *Journal of Fish Biology*, **23**, 125–134.

Solomon, D.J. (1978). Migration of smolts of Atlantic salmon (*Salmo salar* L.) and sea trout (*Salmo trutta* L.) in a chalk stream. *Environmental Biology of Fishes* **3**, 223-229.

Thorstad, E.B., Økland, F., Finstad, B., Sivertsgard, R., Bjørn, P.A. & McKinley, R.S. (2004). Migration speeds and orientation of Atlantic salmon and sea trout post-smolts in a Norwegian fjord system. *Environmental Biology of Fishes*, **71**, 305–311.

Thorstad, E.B., Økland, F., Finstad, B., Sivertsgard, R., Plantalech, N. Bjørn, P.A. & McKinley, R.S (2007). Fjord migration and survival of wild and hatchery-reared Atlantic salmon and wild brown trout post-smolts *Hydrobiologia*, **582**, 99–107.

Thorstad, E.B., Whoriskey, F., Uglem, I., Moore, A., Rikardsen, A.H. & B. Finstad (2012b). A critical life stage of the Atlantic salmon *Salmo salar*: behaviour and survival during the smolt and initial post-smolt migration *Journal of Fish Biology,* **81**, 500–542.

Thorstad, E.B., Uglem, I, Finstad, B., Chittenden, C.M., Nilsen, R., Økland, F. & Bjørn, P.A. (2012a). Stocking location and predation by marine fishes affect survival of hatchery-reared Atlantic salmon smolts *Fisheries Management and Ecology*, **19**, 400–409.

Thorstad, E.B., Todd, C.D., Uglem, I., Bjørn, P.A., Gargan, P.G., Vollset, K.W., Halttunen, E., Kålås, S., Berg, M. & Finstad, B. (2016). Marine life of the sea trout. *Marine Biology,* **163**,(47), DOI 10.1007/s00227-016-2820-3.

Welton, J.S., Beaumont, W.R.C. & Clarke, R.T. (2002). The efficacy of air, sound and acoustic bubble screens in deflecting Atlantic salmon, Salmo salar L., smolts in the River Frome, UK. *Fisheries Management and Ecology* **9**, 11–18.

Managing mixed stocks of sea trout (*Salmo trutta L.*) straying between rivers sharing a common estuary in southwest England: a genetic approach

R. A. KING[1], B. STOCKLEY[2], R. HILLMAN[3], P. ELSMERE[4] & J. R STEVENS[1]

[1] *Department of Biosciences, College of Life and Environmental Sciences, Stocker Road, University of Exeter, Exeter, EX4 4QD.*
[2] *Westcountry Rivers Trust, Kyl Cober Parc, Stoke Climsland, Callington, Cornwall, PL17 8PH.*
[3] *Environment Agency, Sir John Moore House, Victoria Square, Bodmin, Cornwall, PL31 1EB.*
[4] *Environment Agency, Unit 19/26 Pennygillam Industrial Estate, Launceston, Cornwall, PL15 7ED.*

ABSTRACT

Information on the stock composition of a fishery is essential for effective management. Here, we highlight the utility of a genetic baseline for resident trout to determine the origins of sea trout entering the Rivers Tamar, Tavy and Lynher in southwest England – all share a common estuary and have locally important runs of sea trout. Molecular characterisation of resident fish from rivers in southwest England identified a high degree of geographical structuring of the genetic variation in the baseline. Testing with simulated and real datasets showed fish can be assigned to different reporting groups and in some cases to individual rivers, with a high degree of accuracy. Mixed stock analysis of over 1,000 sea trout showed that fish entering the Tamar and Tavy constituted mixed stocks. Significantly, in the Tamar, sea trout of non-natal origin were restricted to the lower catchment. As well as providing insight into sea trout behaviour, this study also has important implications for the management of estuarine net fisheries and recreational rod-and-line fisheries.

Keywords: sea trout; fisheries management; genetic stock identification; mixed stocks: microsatellite; recreational fishery.

INTRODUCTION

In this paper the terms 'brown trout' and 'trout' refer to the species *Salmo trutta*; additionally, resident forms of brown trout are termed *'resident trout'* and those individuals that adopt an anadromous life history are termed *'sea trout'*.

The perceived wisdom is that anadromous species such as salmon and trout, after spending time feeding at sea, return to their natal river to spawn. This homing fidelity can lead to reduced gene flow between rivers and gives rise to the strong genetic structure found in many salmonid species (Dionne *et al.,* 2008; Lohmann *et al.,* 2008). However, straying is known to occur and is thought to be an important evolutionary feature of salmonids, playing an adaptive role over both short and long time scales. Straying is especially important in colonization, re-colonization and range expansion (Quinn, 1984; Tallman & Healey, 1994; Griffiths *et al.,* 2011), may help in reducing inbreeding depression within populations (Keefer & Caudill, 2014) and can give rise to spatially structured metapopulations (Schtickzelle & Quinn, 2007). However, the extent of straying is often difficult to determine, especially straying into established populations. In the case of sea trout, tagging studies have shown that, while the majority of fish may remain in coastal waters close to their natal rivers in many regions, some smolts and adults can make long distance movements (Pratten & Shearer, 1983; Fournel *et al.,* 1990; Potter *et al.,* 2017).

Straying, therefore, is an important part of salmonid behaviour and, as such, can have consequences for the management of coastal, estuarine and in-river fisheries. However, what is not clear is whether recoveries of tagged individuals from non-natal rivers represent temporary straying (sometimes referred to as *'vagrancy'*) or potentially true reproductive straying leading to spawning (Keefer & Caudill, 2014).

Traditionally, the presence of various external (i.e. Carlin tags) or internal (i.e. Coded-wire Tags (CWTs)) tags has been used to determine both the marine spatial distribution of different salmonid stocks and the mixed stock nature of fisheries (Potter & Moore, 1992; Hansen & Jacobsen, 2003). While tagging approaches are 100% successful in assigning fish back to their river of origin, such studies have some major drawbacks. Typically: a) they involve fish from only a small number of rivers, b) they often include fish of hatchery origin (that may behave differently to wild fish) and c) they generally suffer from low levels of reported recapture, despite the often large numbers of fish that are tagged (Candy & Beacham, 2000; Trudel *et al.,* 2009: Degerman *et al.,* 2012).

Since the late 1990s, there has been an increase in the use of DNA markers in fisheries research as an alternative to traditional tagging studies. Extensive microsatellite DNA baseline databases now exist for genetic stock identification (GSI) of Pacific salmonid species (e.g. Beacham *et al.,* 2006; 2014) and for Atlantic salmon (e.g. Griffiths *et al.,* 2010; Ellis *et al.,* 2011a; Bradbury *et al.,* 2015). DNA approaches have the advantage over tagging studies, in that all fish can potentially be included as any captured fish can be screened for the genetic markers being used. However, molecular approaches also have some potential drawbacks and the success of DNA-based assignments is dependent on a number of factors, including the number of microsatellite loci utilized and their levels of polymorphism and levels of genetic differentiation between populations (Hansen *et al.*, 2001). Additionally, due to the metapopulation structure of many salmonid species, assignment is usually more successful to regional groupings of rivers than to a single river of origin (*e.g.* Beacham *et al.*, 2006; Griffiths *et al.*, 2010). Despite these potential drawbacks, DNA-based approaches have become the method of choice in mixed stock fishery studies (Ensing *et al.*, 2013). However, while there have been extensive studies on the mixed stock nature of commercial offshore, coastal and estuarine salmonid net fisheries (Griffiths *et al.*, 2010; Ensing *et al.*, 2013; Koljonen *et al.*, 2014), there have been few such studies on recreational in-river fisheries (Warnock *et al.*, 2011).

The River Tamar (Figure 1), in southwest England, is one of three Environment Agency *'Index Rivers'* and shares a common estuary with two other rivers, the Tavy and the Lynher. The Tamar is subject to intensive monitoring programmes in order to develop an understanding of salmonid stock and fishery processes, and to improve the wider management of sea trout and salmon. The Tamar monitoring programme includes extensive juvenile electrofishing surveys, trapping and tagging smolts during their spring migration and then trapping the returning adults in a trap immediately below a fish pass adjacent to a weir (at Gunnislake) at the tidal limit of the river. Harris (2002) has provided a detailed description of the rod-caught sea trout stock within the River Tamar. Tamar sea trout typically smolt after two years in the river. The majority of the rod catch represents fish that returned to the river in the same year that they smolted (as 0SW maidens and known variously as school peal, finnock or whitling). Of the repeat spawning fish, some were found to have spawned up to four times; however, the majority had only a single spawning mark (Harris, 2002). There is also temporal variation in the composition of the sea trout run, with repeat spawning fish entering the river early in the year, while finnock start to return in July.

One of the stated aims of the 2nd International Sea Trout conference in Dundalk in 2015 was to address the perceived disconnection between pure scientific research into sea trout biology with the tangible needs of fisheries managers. In this paper, we demonstrate the connection between genetic analysis of trout populations in river catchments in southwest England and the management of these populations, particularly their anadromous sea trout component.

The biology and life cycle of brown trout leads to the formation of local populations (Ferguson, 1989; Ferguson *et al.*, 2017), which may contain adaptations to the local environment, such as metal tolerant fish in some rivers in Cornwall (Durrant *et al.*, 2011; Paris *et al.*, 2015). For the management of these local populations we adopt the term *'stock'*. Whilst many definitions of wild fish stocks are used in fisheries science, in this paper we assign the status of 'stock' to genetically distinct populations. In particular, we are concerned with the detection of Evolutionary Significant Units (ESUs) (Waples, 1991), which will be used to define our management stocks. Whilst ESUs have a variety of definitions (Moritz, 1994), their most important features of relevance to fisheries management of anadromous species are:

1) ESUs are the minimal unit of conservation. If we ensure that all the ESUs of a species

are maintained at a healthy level in a defined number of river catchments, then we can be confident that we have preserved the underlying genetic diversity of the species in that area. Consequently, we can assume that we have also preserved any valuable local

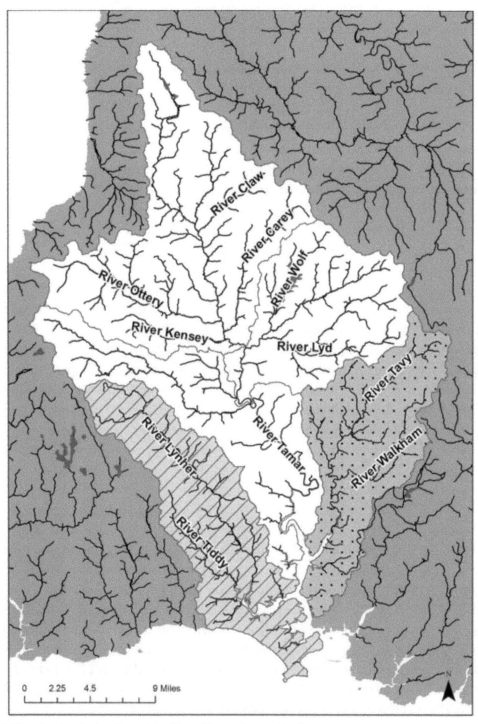

Figure 1. Map showing the locations of the Rivers Tamar, Tavy and Lynher.

adaptations that those ESUs will host, whether or not they are currently expressed phenotypically.

2) ESUs are reflections of real historical and current migratory patterns. Therefore, if we manage according to ESUs, then we are managing according to the intrinsic migratory and breeding patterns of the stocks of interest.

In this study, we utilize an extensive resident trout microsatellite baseline of rivers in southwest England to address two key questions:

1. *Do the rod and line fisheries within the Rivers Tamar, Tavy and Lynher represent mixed stock fisheries capturing straying fish from other rivers?*
2. *If strays are present, can we distinguish if they are transient/temporary or is their position of capture within the river suggestive of an intention to spawn?*

MATERIALS AND METHODS

For the initial genetic baseline, individual resident trout were sampled from 82 populations from 29 rivers in Devon and Cornwall, southwest England (Table 1). Fish were caught during routine electrofishing surveys between 2010 and 2014. The sampling scheme was designed to reduce the collection of potentially related individuals by targeting 1+ or older fish. An additional sample from the River Tamar consisted of smolts caught in a rotary screw trap during their downstream migration in April 2007. Sea trout scales were obtained from a fish trap at Gunnislake weir at the tidal limit of the River Tamar, as well as from fish caught by anglers in the recreational rod fisheries within the Tamar, Lynher and Tavy.

Samples were screened for variation with 18 nuclear microsatellite primer sets; five loci showed non-overlapping size ranges in trout and Atlantic salmon (*Salmo salar* L.) and were therefore useful for the identification of salmon and of trout x salmon hybrids. Polymerase chain reactions (PCRs) and genotyping were performed as described in Paris *et al.* (2015). Microsatellite data were checked for genetic anomalies, e.g. large allele dropout, and readability, e.g. stutter peaks and null alleles, at each locus, and for non-random associations between alleles (i.e. linkage disequilibrium, LD) and deviations from Hardy-Weinberg Equilibrium (HWE) at each locus and population. Each population was also tested for the presence of full-sib families using the program COLONY v 2.0 (Jones & Wang, 2010). Only a single individual of each full-sib group was retained in the data set for subsequent analyses. Baseline reporting groups were identified from population groupings determined from a neighbour-joining dendrogram based on Cavalli-Sforza & Edwards (1967) chord distance (D_{CE}). Mixed stock analysis (MSA) was conducted using the Bayesian procedure of Pella & Masuda (2001) as implemented in cBayes (Neaves *et al.*, 2005).

The baseline was tested using simulated mixtures and by assignment of samples

Table 1. Details of rivers sampled for resident trout and smolts.

Reporting Group	River	No. Sites	Code in Fig 1	n_1	n_2
Taw/Torridge	Taw	3	TAW.XXX	122	114
Taw/Torridge	Torridge	3	TOR.XXX	126	112
Camel	Camel	4	CAM.XXX	186	175
Land's End Complex	Gannel	2	GAN.XXX	100	99
Land's End Complex	Hayle	2	HAY.XXX	92	82
Land's End Complex	Trevaylor	2	TREV.XXX	99	99
Land's End Complex	Crowlas	1	CRO.XXX	49	45
Land's End Complex	Kennal	2	KEN.XXX	91	82
Carrick Roads	Allen	1	ALL.XXX	50	47
Carrick Roads	Tresillian	1	TRE.XXX	48	45
Carrick Roads	Fal	2	FAL.XXX	83	77
Carrick Roads	Caerhays	1	CAE.XXX	50	48
Land's End Complex	Par	1	PAR.XXX	41	36
South Cornwall	Fowey	6	FOW.XXX	271	246
South Cornwall	Lerryn	1	LER.XXX	50	49
South Cornwall	Looe	2	LOO.XXX	99	95
Tamar Estuary	Seaton	2	SEA.XXX	71	69
Tamar Estuary	Lynher	3	LYN.XXX	138	125
Tamar	Tamar*	8	TAM.XXX	341	325
Tamar Estuary	Tavy	5	TAV.XXX	183	165
South Hams	Plym	2	PLY.XXX	99	84
South Hams	Yealm	2	YEA.XXX	61	61
South Hams	Erme	2	ERM.XXX	60	52
South Hams	Avon	2	AVO.XXX	72	66
Dart/Teign	Dart	6	DAR.XXX	285	250
Dart/Teign	Teign	4	TEI.XXX	199	186
East Devon	Exe	8	EXE.XXX	316	282
East Devon	Otter	2	OTT.XXX	76	62
East Devon	Axe	3	AXE.XXX	143	118

* - sample includes smolts caught during downstream migration. n_1 = sample size.
n_2 = sample size after removal of full-sibs and salmon x trout hybrids

not included in the genetic baseline. Simulated mixtures can sometimes lead to over-confidence in the accuracy of assignment, as they only consider the allele frequencies of the sampled baseline populations. A more realistic assessment of baseline accuracy can be obtained from the analysis of real fish of known origins (Ensing *et al.* 2013). Samples were available for resident trout from 11 of the rivers in our baseline (Table 2). These samples were chosen to represent the major sea trout rivers in the region, but were collected from sites on each river that were not included in the baseline sample for each river. The data for resident trout caught in the Tamar was augmented with genotypes for

Table 2. Details of 11 baseline test samples.

Reporting Group	River	Sub-catchment	Site	Code	n	Year
Taw/Torridge	Taw	Mole	Heasley Mill	TAW.BLT	23	2006
	Torridge	East Okement	A30 bridge	TOR.BLT	21	2003
		Okement	Monkokehampton		10	2012
Camel	Camel	Allen	Lamellen	CAM.BLT	21	2003
South Cornwall	Fowey	Warleggan	Maidenhead	FOW.BLT	24	2003
		Main River	Palmersbridge		10	2015
	Looe	West Looe	Trussel Bridge	LOO.BLT	22	2003
Tamar	Tamar	Main river	Rods	TAM.BLT	23	2010-14
		Penpont Water	Trerithick		10	2010
Tamar estuary	Tavy	Main river	Creasons	TAV.BLT	19	2003
South Hams	Avon	Main river	Hatch Bridge	AVO.BLT	17	2012
Dart/Teign	Dart	East Webburn	Cockingford	DAR.BLT	23	2014
East Devon	Exe	Bathern		EXE.BLT	10	2013
		Lowman			6	2013
	Axe	Yarty	Longbridge	AXE.BLT	14	2012

n = sample size

60 sea trout caught in the trap at Gunnislake (n=54) and in the Tamar rod fishery (n=6). These fish possessed either microtags or had their adipose fins clipped, indicating that they had been trapped as smolts in a rotary screw trap in the lower Tamar during their outbound migration.

Two sources of scales were used to investigate the origins of sea trout entering each of the focal rivers. Scale samples were obtained from sea trout caught in the trap at Gunnislake Weir from 2010 (April to October, n=479) and 2011 (June to August, n=286). Collections represented both repeat spawning fish and within-year (0SW) returnees. Anglers also provided scales from sea trout caught in the recreational rod fishery of the Lynher, Tamar and Tavy between 2010 and 2014. The majority of rod-caught fish were caught between June and August in all years. For the Tamar, collections represented fish caught in the lower main river and also from a tributary, the Lyd, in the upper catchment. On the Tavy, fish were caught between the tidal limit and the confluence of the main river and the River Walkham. See King *et al.*, (2016) for full details of genetic analyses and testing of the baseline.

RESULTS

A total of 3,601 resident trout and smolts were sampled from 83 sites from 29 rivers in Devon and Cornwall. The number of sample sites per river ranged from one to eight. Hybrid individuals (n=31) were collected from 16 sites and were removed from the dataset. A further 274 individuals belonging to full-sib families were also removed. Due to high levels of linkage disequilibrium, a sample of fish from the River Torridge was also removed from the final dataset. The final baseline comprised 3,265 fish from 82 sample sites. See King *et al.* (2016) for full details.

There was a high degree of genetic structuring of the baseline samples, with geographically proximate rivers being genetically similar (Figure 2). This allowed populations from the 29 rivers to be clustered into ten groups (= reporting groups) for assignment purposes. Two of the reporting groups contained only a single river (Camel and Tamar). The number of rivers in the remaining reporting groups ranged from 2 – 6 (Figure 2). This analysis also suggested a high degree of temporal stability in the baseline, as all temporal samples used in baseline testing grouped with the baseline samples from the same river and in many cases the same tributary (Figure. 2).

Mixed stock analysis of simulated mixtures showed a high degree of self-assignment, especially to reporting group. For simulated single-river samples, the average correct assignment to river and group of origin was 98.20% and 98.61%, respectively. Likewise, simulated single reporting group mixtures generally showed high levels of self-assignment, especially to reporting group (mean = 98.29%). Analysis of multi-reporting group mixtures, concentrating on the three focal rivers, showed that it was possible to assign complex mixtures to the baseline reporting groups with a high degree of accuracy; see King *et al.* (2016) and associated appendices for full details.

Simulated data sets can give a good idea of baseline accuracy only if the populations sampled from each river to construct the baseline are representative of these catchments as a whole. Assignment of the fish of known origin to river of origin showed that, in general our baseline samples were representative of their catchments with self-assignments generally in excess of 90% (King *et al.,* 2016). There were however some clear exceptions to this. For example, self-assignment to river of origin for samples from the Taw and Torridge was 86.39% and 57.66%, respectively. However, self-assignment of these samples to a Taw/Torridge reporting group was over 92% in both cases. For nine of the 11 test samples, assignment to the correct reporting group was greater than 90%. Importantly, incorrect assignment to our three focal rivers and their corresponding reporting groups was uniformly very low (river average 0.26%, range 0.08% – 0.89%, group average 0.46%, range 0.08% – 0.91%).

Results indicate that there was a high degree of straying for fish entering the River Tamar. A significant proportion (>10%) of the sea trout caught in the Gunnislake trap were strays, mainly from the Lynher and Tavy, but also from other rivers in south Devon and Cornwall (Fig. 3). This result was consistent across the two years and also when considering whether the fish were repeat spawning sea trout or within-year returnees (King *et al.,* 2016). However, there

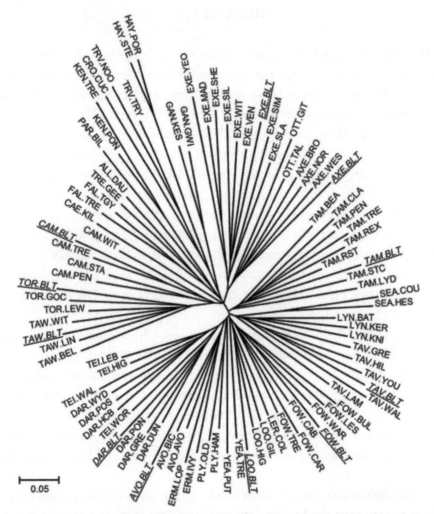

Figure 2. Unrooted neighbour-joining dendrogram, based on Cavalli-Sforza and Edwards' chord distance (D_{CE}), showing relationships between the resident trout populations sampled for the genetic baseline. The 11 baseline test samples (XXX.BLT, Table 2) are underlined.

was considerable variation in the levels of straying across each individual year. Contributions of non-Tamar fish to the monthly totals ranged from virtually zero in June 2010 to almost 50% in October 2010.

The assignments of fish from the in-river rod fisheries also showed varying degrees of straying. For the Lynher, there was a high degree of self-assignment with minor contributions from rivers in the South Cornwall and South Hams reporting groups (Figure 4).

Within the Tamar, straying appears to be restricted to the lower catchment with non-natal fish not penetrating into the upper catchment. For the tidal limit trap and lower catchment samples, there was a ~10% contribution from the Lynher and Tavy with small contributions from the South Cornwall, South Hams and Dart/Teign reporting groups (Figure 4). However,

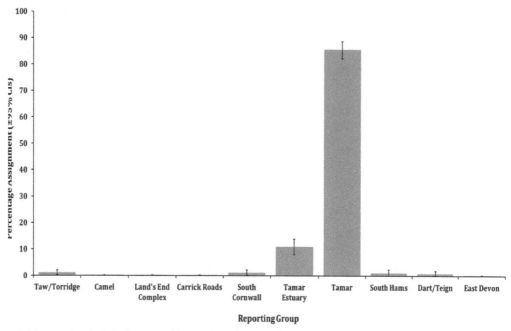

Figure 3. Mean estimated stock composition assigned to reporting group of origin, with 95% confidence intervals, jor 765 sea trout caught entering the River Tamar at Gunnislake weir.

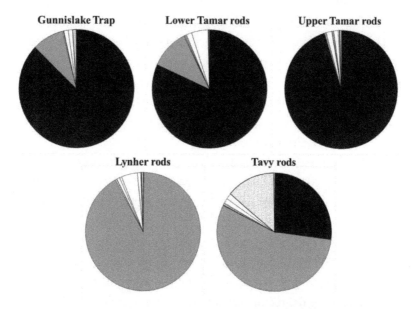

Figure 4. Mean estimate stock composition of sea trout caught in the Rivers Tamar, Lynher and Tavy. Pie-charts show proportions of sea trout trapped at Gunnislake weir caught in four rod fisheries assigned to reporting group. Black segments represent assignment to the River Tamar with grey segments assignment to the Tamar Estuary and stippled segments assignment to the Dart/Teign reporting groups. For clarity, all other reporting regions are white.

for the upper catchment sample, there is virtually no contribution from the Lynher and Tavy (0.20% and 0.29%, respectively), with the majority of fish being assigned to the Tamar.

For the Tavy, assignment of rod-caught fish to other rivers exceeded 70% (Figure 4) with significant numbers of Tamar and Lynher sea trout being caught. Interestingly, there was a high contribution of fish from the Dart/Teign group (13.6%) to the rod fishery of the lower Tavy, despite a marine separation of their river mouths of more than 80 km.

DISCUSSION

ASSESSING THE POWER AND ACCURACY OF THE GENETIC BASELINE

The power and accuracy of assignment to genetic baselines depends on a number of factors. One of the key aspects is that a baseline is representative of the set of populations likely to contribute to the mixtures to be assigned (Pella & Masuda, 2006). The Environment Agency, based on rod catches, has designated 18 principal and 6 minor sea trout rivers in the area covered by this genetic baseline. Of these rivers, samples are included from all except one minor river. Another potential source of bias is that the populations sampled for the baseline may not, in terms of allele frequencies, be representative of the catchments from which they are taken (Koljonen *et al.,* 2007). This includes both temporal stability of allele frequencies and accounting for the presence of different genetic groupings within catchments. We tested for both these potential sources of bias by querying the baseline with fish of known origin, including samples contemporary with the baseline samples but from sites/tributaries not included in the baseline, and by the use of temporal samples. Overall, the baseline proved to be both representative of the catchments studied and temporally stable over a time scale of at least one to three generations. This finding agrees with other studies in salmonid species that have shown temporally stable patterns of genetic diversity and population structure over short- (Griffiths *et al.,* 2009), medium- (Van Doornik *et al.,* 2011) and long-term (Charlier *et al.,* 2012) time scales.

The accuracy of assignment is also dependent on the levels of genetic divergence between populations (Araujo *et al.,* 2014) and is typically assessed using the F_{ST} statistic (a measure of population differentiation). The average pairwise F_{ST} found in this study was 0.028 and is comparable to other similar studies of resident trout populations (e.g. Carlsson *et al.,* 1999; Griffiths *et al.,* 2009; Paris *et al.,* 2015), though markedly greater than values detected between Atlantic salmon populations in the Tamar catchment (Ellis *et al.,* 2011b). Testing of the baseline with samples of known origin showed that, in general, we were able to assign fish to their reporting group of origin with a higher degree of certainty than to river of origin. This was highlighted by several of the test samples, *i.e.* the Torridge and Exe, where assignment to river of origin was poor, while assignment to reporting group was over 90% in both cases (King *et al.,* 2016).

Additionally, several other factors may account for the poor assignment to river of origin in some of the baseline test samples. Some rivers and reporting groups had small sample sizes. For example, the South Hams region, comprising the rivers Plym, Erme, Yealm and Avon, would benefit from additional sampling. In general, small sample sizes result in reduced accuracy of assignment (Griffiths *et al.*, 2010), with only modest gains in accuracy with sample sizes greater than 150-200 (Beacham *et al.*, 2006), though this is dependent on the size of the geographic region(s) from which samples are taken.

STRAYING IN SEA TROUT

These results highlight an interesting aspect of sea trout biology, namely that non-natal fish frequently entered the freshwater reaches of the three focal rivers. Straying appears to be an integral part of salmonid biology, but it is unclear whether straying is a failure of fish to home accurately or whether it is an innate exploratory behaviour developed to ensure that fish correctly locate, select and spawn in their river of origin; ultimately, such behaviour may lead to a dispersal strategy with broader long-term evolutionary advantages that facilitate range expansion and re-colonisation of suitable habitat (McDowall, 2001). When at sea, sea trout are generally assumed to stay close to their natal rivers but tagging and genetic studies have shown that sea trout readily move away over both short- and long-distances and can stray into non-natal rivers. For example, Jensen *et al.*, (2015) showed that sea trout from the River Halselva in northern Norway strayed more readily into neighbouring watersheds than sympatric Arctic char (*Salvelinus alpinus*). Data on tagged sea trout smolts from the River Axe (Devon, UK) showed that the majority of captures outside of the Axe were from the River Otter (20km west of the Axe), with some fish being caught as far west as the River Camel and as far east as the Hampshire Basin rivers (Solomon, 1994). Similarly, some tagged River Axe kelts made longer distance movements with recoveries from rivers entering the North Sea and the Bristol Channel (Solomon, 1994). In the Baltic, genetic assignments to a baseline comprising trout from rivers flowing into the Gulf of Finland found that significant numbers of Russian and Estonia sea trout were caught in commercial net fisheries on the south coast of Finland (Koljonen *et al.*, 2014).

One possible explanation for the occurrence of high numbers of non-natal sea trout in the lower reaches of the Tamar and Tavy is that the fish may be choosing to overwintering in freshwater. For instance, Degerman *et al.* (2012) found a peak in temporary straying of tagged sea trout of hatchery origin to rivers in the northern Baltic during September to December. Similarly, using genetic assignments, Moore *et al.* (2013) found high numbers of Arctic char overwintering in non-natal rivers. The sea trout stock in southwest Britain is dominated by fish that have spent less than a year at sea (known as 'finnock'; Harris, 2002). The reason why these fish should spend such a short time at sea is not fully understood, but is a common feature of many sea trout stocks (Degerman *et al.*, 2012). It may be that the propensity for trout to move away from their natal rivers on migrating to sea, coupled with the apparent 'need' (particularly in the case of finnock) to return to freshwater during the winter, could account for the high levels of straying found in this and other studies.

Significantly, for the Tamar, straying fish do not appear to migrate into the upper catchment and presumably do not contribute to the spawning population of the river. Thus, for the Tamar at least, we are able to distinguish vagrancy from true reproductive straying. Moore *et al.* (2013) also found that the majority of Arctic char strays were non-reproductive individuals. However, Degerman *et al.* (2012) found that it was older fish that were more likely to overwinter in freshwater. The majority of the sea trout entering the Tamar from June onwards will have spent only a few months in the marine environment and it is likely that the majority of these fish are not yet mature. Indeed, for the River Axe, it was found that only 14% – 31% of finnock had spawned when trapped migrating downstream the following spring (Solomon, 1994).

It is interesting to note the very high levels of straying of non-natal sea trout into the lower Tavy, with significant contributions from both the Tamar and the Dart/Teign reporting group. Natal homing fidelity is recognised as being driven by multiple processes, including olfaction, with fish recognizing the chemical signature of the water on which they imprinted as juveniles (Keefer & Caudill, 2014). It is possible that Tamar and Dart/Teign fish are being 'misdirected' into entering their non-natal river by chemical cues. The sources of the Tavy, Dart and Teign rise on same area of Dartmoor, with the headwaters of the Tavy and Dart being less than 1 km apart, meaning that the two rivers are likely to have similar water chemistry and some olfactory cues in common. This may be attracting Dart sea trout into the lower reaches of the Tavy. The situation is also complicated in the Tamar due to the discharge of water from a hydroelectric power station at Morwhellam Quay into the upper Tamar estuary during periods of higher flows. The water for this power station is taken from a tributary of the River Tavy and a plume of water with Tavy 'olfactory cues' may be further confusing returning fish.

The high levels of straying found in this study demonstrate that the rod fisheries in the Tamar and Tavy rivers constitute mixed stock fisheries (MSFs). Up until now, much of the focus of GSI in salmonid species has been the stock composition of commercial fisheries in the high seas and in estuarine areas (Griffiths *et al.*, 2010., Ensing *et al.*, 2013, Beacham *et al.*, 2014, Koljonen *et al.*, 2014, Bradbury *et al.*, 2016) and little attention has been paid to the stock composition of recreational rod fisheries. Warnock *et al.* (2011) found that two of five bull trout (*Salvelinus confluentus* (Suckley)) rod fisheries on the Oldman River (Alberta, Canada) were catching fish from more than one stock. Similarly, Bott *et al.* (2009) showed the presence of non-targeted and numerically depressed stocks in a sport fishery for lake sturgeon (*Acipenser fulvescens*) in Lake Michigan. The presence of non-target stocks has implications for the management of these recreational fisheries. Moreover, in the case of the Tamar, substantial monthly variations in straying rates further complicate management.

Recognition of the sea trout rod fisheries in the lower Tamar, Tavy and Lynher as forming part of a MSF would represent an extension of the current management practice for the estuary net fisheries, which are managed to protect the weakest of the three main contributing river stocks, in line with NASCO guidance for salmon (NASCO 2009, 2014). Our microsatellite data support this approach by demonstrating that they are genetically distinct entities, highlighting the need to take account of genetic evidence in current MSFdefinitions.

RELATIONSHIP BETWEEN MIGRATORY AND NON-MIGRATORY FISH STOCKS

It is of major importance to managers of rivers that contain recreational trout fisheries to understand the relationship between the migratory and resident forms of trout. Whilst there is no reliable evidence that resident trout and sea trout are genetically distinct, significant in-river genetic variation is apparent in the species in some catchments (e.g. Griffiths *et al.*, 2009; Paris *et al.*, 2015). Critically, however, as can be seen in this study, some smaller catchments, typical in southwest England, such as the Tamar, are not characterised by genetically or geographically distinct sub-populations (stocks); this finding accords with previous research on Atlantic salmon in the Tamar (Ellis *et al.*, 2011b). Thus, it appears that gene flow throughout these smaller catchments may prevent the formation of any distinct 'sea trout' sub-populations. This has a number of important implications for the managers of such rivers:

1. If we wish to protect or enhance the sea trout variant of a trout population, we do not need to protect or enhance particular geographically defined sub-populations;
2. The output of sea trout smolts versus resident trout production will be predominantly controlled by environmental factors, and management of environmental conditions in the river and river access will therefore be the priorities for management;
3. Should a manager be tasked to carry out environmental compensation/restoration of a damaged section of such a river catchment, work can be carried out for the benefit of trout anywhere in the catchment, without compromising the genetic integrity of the population;
4. Variations in indicators of fish stock health (e.g. fish counter data, rod catch, electrofishing results) relate to a single catchment-wide population, which can then be managed as such.

RELATIONSHIPS BETWEEN DIFFERENT ESUS OPERATING IN A SHARED ESTUARINE ENVIRONMENT

The Tamar estuary (Figure 1) shares inputs from a number of different rivers, in particular, the rivers Lynher, Tavy and Plym, in addition to the river Tamar itself. The immediate proximity of river outflows into a shared estuary can be hypothesized to enhance the likelihood of mixed stock fisheries. It is a well-established concern of managers that netting in such a shared estuary context is likely to operate as a mixed stock fishery (Ensing *et al.*, 2013; King *et al.*, 2016). Further exploration of this issue in the Tamar is planned and scale samples from the net fishery will be collected by the Environment Agency for further analysis.

The presence of a shared estuarine environment also raises the little considered issue of fish migration into the lower freshwater reaches of these rivers. Whilst it can be expected that netting in a shared estuary will result in mixed stock catches, it has traditionally been assumed that all fish caught in the freshwater part of a river are part of the local stock and native to the river. Similarly, adult run assessments based upon rod catch or fish-counter data collected on the lower reaches of a river catchment are based upon this assumption. Consequently, any calculations of potential breeding capacity and reproductive success based on these lower river run estimates will be inaccurate in proportion to the number of fish 'visiting' the lower reaches from neighbouring rivers. The results of this study show that this is very much the case in the rivers flowing into the Tamar estuary, and, because straying rates are asymmetrical, information on the propensity for straying will be beneficial to such estimations in differing proportions according to the incidence of straying.

In addition to complicating assessments of run numbers, the presence of fish temporarily straying from neighbouring rivers complicates management of these stocks. Accordingly, consideration will also need to be given to the impact of catching straying fish as well as to the native stock. Any management action should reflect the possibility that these visiting fish are not part of the breeding stock of the river in which they are caught, but would normally exit the river and could then be expected to return to their natal river to spawn, either in this or future years.

Assessment of anadromous trout mixed stock fisheries is complicated by the well-recognised issue of a current lack of established Biological Reference Points (BRPs) for sea trout against which to compare stock health (Davidson *et al.*, 2017). Currently, sea trout fisheries are assessed in England according to the 'sea trout performance assessment'. This assessment is based wholly on rod catch data and is at best relative, without a BRP. Therefore, whilst useful from a fishery perspective, it is not an appropriate reference against which to assess if sea trout stocks are biologically healthy or otherwise. Therefore, quantitative assessment of both resident and sea trout stocks (e.g. Goodwin *et al.*, 2016) is essential to accurately infer the health of the trout stocks in the rivers in question.

Currently, critical concerns as to the stock status of resident trout and sea trout from the Tamar, Lynher and Tavy are not apparent, with all rivers supporting generally healthy trout populations. Given that these rivers are not currently identified as having threatened stock status, there is no justification at this time for applying a catch-and-release policy to these rod fisheries on the basis that they operate as a mixed stock fishery. However, should the status of any of these stocks become a cause for future concern, then the mixed stock fishery element of the rod catch of the lower river will need to be reconsidered. For example, if the Tavy experienced a declining sea trout run sufficient to require the introduction of exploitation control measures, then control measures on the lower reaches of neighbouring rivers should also be considered in order to protect Tavy fish whilst they stray temporarily into the Lynher and Tamar.

This paper represents a collaborative approach to the management of sea trout. The initial genetic baseline against which results were tested was developed as part of the Atlantic Aquatic Resource Conservation (AARC) project, a collaboration between the University of Exeter, Westcountry Rivers Trust, the Environment Agency, local angling groups and several European partners. In investigating the issue of mixed stock sea trout fisheries, this study has highlighted a number of management-relevant issues that have not been previously examined. On a national and transnational level, it raises the question as to whether these issues are particular to the Tamar (and its shared estuary), or whether such issues are relevant to other similar estuaries where fish from multiple rivers re-enter in close proximity? Additionally, it will be important to determine if non-reproductive straying (vagrancy) is a feature only of such shared estuaries, or if it is a feature common to all rivers, driven by sea trout migration life-history patterns. Therefore, we recommend that further studies be carried out in similar estuaries, and also in river systems without other river mouths in near proximity. Prime candidates for such investigations in the southwest of England would be the Dart and Teign, and the Taw and Torridge systems, which, as well as having regionally important rod fisheries, also have estuarine net fisheries taking large numbers of sea trout annually (Environment Agency, 2014).

The AARC genetic database is unusual in that it has a relatively high baseline sample density compared to similar previous and contemporary data sets (e.g. Griffiths *et al.*, 2010), and includes many smaller streams, and multiple sample sites within medium sized rivers, such as the Tamar. However, the robustness of the database could be further improved by the inclusion of samples from additional small stream populations, which are common in the southwest of England. Indeed, additional research is ongoing, with the aim of adding more small stream trout populations into the AARC genetic database; we anticipate that this will continue to increase its resolution and assignment power, allowing hitherto difficult questions regarding sea trout movements to be addressed. Of particular benefit would be to formally link and calibrate the AARC data set with those generated by other contemporary genetic studies of trout, e.g. the Celtic Sea Trout Project. This would be especially valuable for study fish in rivers flowing into the Bristol Channel as it would allow elucidation of sea trout movements between the rivers of north Devon and Cornwall with rivers along the coast of south Wales, and vice versa.

ACKNOWLEDGEMENTS

This research forms part of the Atlantic Aquatic Resource Conservation (AARC) project, and was funded via the European Union 2007-2013 Atlantic Area Programme, an INTERREG III B initiative. Additional funding from the Atlantic Salmon Trust is gratefully acknowledged. We would like to thank Simon Toms (EA) for co-ordinating the collection of samples through the Environment Agency Southwest Region electrofishing teams and the Westcountry Rivers Trust for the collection of additional samples. We are grateful for the early project input of Dylan Bright (formerly of the Westcountry Rivers Trust) – we dedicate this chapter to his memory.

REFERENCES

Araujo H.A., Candy J.R, Beacham T.D., White B. & Wallace C. (2014). Advantages and challenges of genetic stock identification in fish stocks with low genetic resolution. *Transactions of the American Fisheries Society,* **143**, 479-488.

Beacham T.D., Candy J.R. Jonsen K.L. Supernault J., Wetklo M., Deng L., Miller K.M. Withler R.E. & Varnavskaya N. (2006.) Estimation of stock composition and individual identification of Chinook salmon across the Pacific Rim by use of microsatellite variation. *Transactions of the American Fisheries Society,* **135**, 861-888.

Beacham T.D., Beamish R.J., Candy J.R., Wallace C., Tucker S., Moss J.H. & Trudel M. (2014). Stock-specific migration pathways of juvenile Sockeye salmon in British Columbia water and in the Gulf of Alaska. *Transactions of the American Fisheries Society,* **143**, 1386-1403,

Bott K., Kornely G.W., Donofrio M.C., Elliott R.F. & Scrinber K.T. (2009). Mixed-stock analysis of lake sturgeon in the Menominee River sport harvest and adjoining waters of Lake Michigan. *North American Journal of Fisheries Management,* **29**, 1636-1642,

Bradbury I.R., Hamilton L.C., Rafferty S., Meerburg D., Poole, R., Dempson J.B., Robertson M.J., Reddin, D.G., Bourret V., Dionne M., Chaput G., Sheehan T.F., King T.L., Candy J.R. & Bernatchez L. (2015). Genetic evidence of local exploitation of Atlantic salmon in a coastal subsistence fishery in the Northwest Atlantic. *Canadian Journal of Fisheries and Aquatic Sciences,* **72**, 83-95

Bradbury I.R., Hamilton L.C., Chaput G., Robertson M.J., Goraguer H., Walsh A., Morris V., Reddin, D.G., Dempson J.B., Sheehan T.F., King T.L., Candy J.R. & Bernatchez L. (2016). Genetic mixed stock analysis of an interceptor Atlantic salmon fishery in the Northwest Atlantic. *Fisheries Research,* **174**, 234-244

Candy J.R. & Beacham T.D. (2000). Patterns of homing and straying in southern British Columbia coded-wire tagged chinook salmon (*Oncorhynchus tshawytscha*) populations. *Fisheries Research,* **47**, 41-56

Carlsson J., Olsén K.H., Nilsson J., Øverli Ø. & Stabell O. B. (1999). Microsatellites reveal fine-scale genetic structure in stream-living brown trout. *Journal of Fish Biology,* **55**, 1290–1303

Cavalli-Sforza L.L. & Edwards A.W.F. (1967). Phylogenetic analysis: models and estimation procedures. *American Journal of Human Genetics,* **19**, 233–257

Charlier J., Laikre L. & Ryman N. (2012). Genetic monitoring reveals temporal stability over 30 years in a small, lake-resident brown trout population. *Heredity,* **109**, 246-253

Davidson, I., Aprahamian,M., Peirson, G., Hillman, R., Cook, N. & Croft, A. (2017). Catch and stock based Biological Reference Points for sea trout in England & Wales: A comparison of methods and critical examination of their potential application to stock assessment and management. In: *Sea trout: Science & Management.* (Graeme Harris. *Ed.*). Proceedings of the 2nd International Sea Trout Symposium, October 2015, Dundalk, Ireland. (*Troubador & pages at page-proof stage.*)

Degerman E., Leonardsson K. & Lunqvist H. (2012). Coastal migrations, temporary use of neighbouring rivers, and growth of sea trout (*Salmo trutta*) from nine northern Baltic Sea rivers. *ICES Journal of Marine Science,* **69**, 971-980

Dionne M., Caron F., Dodson J.J., & Bernatchez L. (2008). Landscape genetics and hierarchical genetic structure in Atlantic salmon: the interaction of gene flow and local adaptation. *Molecular Ecology,* **17**, 2382–2396

Durrant C.J., Stevens J.R., Hogstrand C. and Bury N.R. (2011). The effect of metal pollution on the population genetic structure of brown trout (*Salmo trutta* L.) residing in the River Hayle, Cornwall, UK. *Environmental Pollution,* **159**, 3595-3603.

Ellis J.S., Gilbey J., Armstrong A., Balstad T., Cauwelier E., Cherbonnel C., Consuegra S., Coughlan J., Cross T.F., Crozier W., Dillane E., Ensing D., García de Leániz C., García-Vázquez E., Griffiths A.M., Hindar K., Hjorleifsdottir S., Knox D., Machado-Schiaffino G., McGinnity P., Meldrup D., Nielsen E.E., Olafsson K., Primmer C.R., Prodohl P., Stradmeyer L., Vähä J.-P., Verspoor E., Wennevik V. and Stevens J.R. (2011a). Microsatellite standardization and evaluation of genotyping error in a large multi-partner research programme for conservation of Atlantic salmon (*Salmo salar* L.). *Genetica,* **139**, 353–367

Ellis J.S., Sumner K.J., Griffiths A.M., Bright D.I. & Stevens J.R. (2011b). Population genetic structure of Atlantic salmon, *Salmo salar* L., in the River Tamar, southwest England. *Fisheries Management and Ecology,* **18**, 233–245

Ensing D., Croxier W.W., Boylan P., O Maoiléidigh N. & McGinnity P. (2013). An analysis of genetic stock identification on a small geographical scales using microsatellite markers, and it's application in the management of a mixed-stock fishery for Atlantic salmon *Salmo salar* in Ireland. *Journal of Fish Biology,* **82**, 2080-2094.

Ferguson, A. (1989). Genetic differences among brown trout, *Salmo trutta*, stocks and their importance for the conservation and management of the species. *Freshwater Biology,* **21**, 35–46.

Ferguson, A., Reed, T., Mcginnity, P. & Prodöhl, P. (2017). Anadromy in brown trout (*Salmo trutta*): a review of the relative roles of genes and environmental factors and the implications for management and conservation. In: *Sea Trout Science & Management.* (Harris, G.S. *Ed.*). Proceedings of the 2nd International Sea Trout Symposium, October 2015, Dundalk, Ireland. (Troubador *& pages at page proof stage*)

Fournel F., Euzenat G. & Fagard J.L. (1990). Evaluation des taux de recapture et de retour de la truite de mer sur le basin de la Bresle (Haute Normandie/Picardie). *Bulletin Français de la Pêche et de la Pisciculture,* **318**, 102-114

Goodwin, J.C.A., King, R.A., Jones, J.I., Ibbotson, A. & Stevens, J.R. (2016). A small number of anadromous females drive reproduction in a brown trout (*Salmo trutta*) population in an English chalk stream. *Freshwater Biology*, 61: 1075–1089.

Griffiths A.M., Machado-Schiaffino G., Dillane E., Coughlan J., Horreo J.L., Bowkett A.E., Minting P., Toms S., Roche W., Gargan P., McGinnity P., Cross T., Bright D., Garcia-Vazquez E. & Stevens J.R. (2010). Genetic stock identification of Atlantic salmon (*Salmo salar*) populations in the southern part of the European range. *BMC Genetics,* **11**, 31

Griffiths A.M., Ellis J.S., Clifton-Dey D., Machado-Schiaffino G., Bright D., Garcia-Vazquez E. & Stevens J.R. (2011). Restoration versus recolonisation; the origin of Atlantic salmon (*Salmo salar* L.) currently in the River Thames. *Biological Conservation,* **144**, 2733–2738

Griffiths A.M., Koizumi I., Bright D. & Stevens J.R. (2009). A case of isolation by distance and short-term temporal stability of population structure in brown trout (*Salmo trutta*) within the River Dart, southwest England. *Evolutionary Applications* 2, 537-554

Hamsen M.M., Kenchington E. & Nielsen E.E. (2001). Assigning individual fish to populations using microsatellite DNA markers. *Fish and Fisheries,* **2**, 93-112

Hansen L.P. & Jacobsen J.A. (2003). Origin and migration of wild and escaped farmed Atlantic salmon, *Salmo salar* L, in oceanic areas north of the Faroe Islands. *ICES Journal of Marine Science,* **60**, 110-119

325

Harris, G. (2002). Sea Trout Stock Descriptions: The Structure & Composition of Adult sea Trout Stocks from 16 Rivers in England & Wales. R&D Technical Report W224. Environment Agency, Bristol, 93 pp.

Jensen A.J., Diserud O.H., Finstad B., Fiske P. and Rikardsen A.H. (2015). Between-watershed movements of two anadromous salmonids in the Arctic. *Canadian Journal of Fisheries and Aquatic Sciences,* **72**, 855-863

Jones O.R. & Wang J.L. (2010). COLONY: a program for parentage and sibship inference from multilocus genotype data. *Molecular Ecology Resources,* **10**, 551-555

Keefer M.L. & Caudill C.C. (2014). Homing and straying by anadromous salmonids: a review of mechanisms and rates. *Reviews in Fish Biology and Fisheries,* **24**, 333-368

King R.A., Hillman R., Elsmere P., Stockley B. & Stevens J.R. (2016). Investigating patterns of straying and mixed stock exploitation of sea trout (*Salmo trutta* L.) in rivers sharing an estuary in southwest England. *Fisheries Management and Ecology,* **23**, 376 – 389.

Koljonen M-L., King T.L. & Nielsen E.E. (2007). Genetic identification of individuals and populations. In:Verspoor E., Stradmeyer L. & Nielsen J.L. (eds) *The Atlantic Salmon: genetics, conservation and management.* Blackwells Publishing, Oxford, UK,. 270-298

Koljonen M-L., Goss R. & Koskiniemi J. (2014). Wild Estonian and Russian sea trout (*Salmo trutta*) in Finnish coastal sea trout catches: results of genetic mixed-stock analysis. *Hereditas,* **151**, 177-195

Lohmann K.J., Putman N.F. & Lohmann C.M.F. (2008). Geomagnetic imprinting: a unifying hypothesis of long-distance natal homing in salmon and sea turtles. *Proceedings of the National Academy of Sciences of the United States of America,* **105**, 19096-19101

McDowell R.M. (2001). Anadromy and homing: two life-history traits with adaptive synergies in salmonid fishes? *Fish and Fisheries,* **2**, 78-85

Moore J-S., Harris L.N., Tallman R.F. & Taylor E.B. (2013). The interplay between dispersal and gene flow in anadromous Arctic char (*Salvelinus aplinus*): implications for potential for local adaptation. *Canadian Journal of Fisheries and Aquatic Sciences,* **70**, 1327-1338

Moritz C. (1994). Defining 'Evolutionarily Significant Units' for conservation. *Trends in Ecology & Evolution,* **9**, 373-375.

NASCO. (2009). Guidelines for the Management of Salmon Fisheries NASCO Council Document CNL(09)43, Edinburgh. 8pp

NASCO. (2014). Implementation Plan for the period 2013-18 – EU – UK (England and Wales) (Updated 1 December 2014) NASCO Council Document CNL(14)71, Edinburgh. 27pp.

Paris J.R., King R.A. & Stevens J.R. (2015). Human mining activity across the ages determines the genetic structure of modern brown trout (*Salmo trutta* L.) populations. *Evolutionary Applications,* **8**, 573-585

Pella J. & Masuda M. (2001). Bayesian methods for analysis of stock mixtures from genetic characters. *Fishery Bulletin,* **99**, 151-167

Pella J. & Masuda M. (2006). The Gibbs and split–merge sampler for population mixture analysis from genetic data with incomplete baselines. *Canadian Journal of Fisheries and Aquatic Sciences,* **63**, 576-596

Potter E.C.E. & Moore A. (1992). *Surveying and tracking salmon in the sea.* The Atlantic Salmon Trust, Pitlochry, Perthshire.

Potter, E., Campbell, R., Malcolm, I., Marshall, S. & Sumner, K. (2017). Marine migrations & distribution of sea trout from river in Great Britain. In: *Sea Trout: Science & Management* (Harris, G.S. *Ed.*). Proceedings of the 2nd International Sea Trout Symposium, October 2015, Dundalk, Ireland. (Troubador & *pages at page proof stage*)

Pratten D.J. & Shearer W.M. (1983). The migrations of North Esk sea trout. *Fisheries and Management,* **14**, 99-113

Quinn T.P. (1984). Homing and straying in Pacific salmon. In: J.D. McCleave, G.P. Arnold, J.J. Dodson & W.H. Neill (eds) *Mechanisms of Migration in Fishes.* New York: Plenum. pp. 357–362

Schtickzelle N. & Quinn T.P. (2007). A metapopulation perspective for salmon and other anadromous fish. *Fish and Fisheries,* **8**, 297-314

Solomon D.J. (1994). Sea Trout Investigations – Phase 1 Final Report. National Rivers Authority R&D Note 318, 102 pp.

Tallman R.F. & Healey M.C. (1994). Homing, straying, and gene flow among seasonally separated populations of chum salmon (*Oncorhynchus keta*). *Canadian Journal of Fisheries and Aquatic Sciences,* **51**, 577–588.

Tamura K., Stecher G., Peterson D., Filipski A. & Kumar S. (2013). MEGA6: Molecular Evolutionary Genetics Analysis Version 6.0. *Molecular Biology and Evolution,* **30**, 2725-2729

Trudel M., Fisher J., Orsi J.A., Morris J.F.T., Thiess M.E., Sweeting R.M., Hinton S., Fergusson E.A. & Welch D.W. (2009). Distribution and migration of juvenile Chinook Salmon derived from coded wire tag recoveries along the continental shelf of western North America. *Transactions of the American Fisheries Society,* **138**, 1369-1391

Van Doornik D.M., Waples R.S., Baird M.C. Moran P. & Berntson E.A. (2011). Genetic monitoring reveals genetic stability within and among threatened Chinook salmon populations in the Salmon River, Idaho. *North American Journal of Fisheries Management,* **31**, 96-105

Waples R.S. (1991). Pacific salmon, *Oncorhynchus* spp., and the definition of "species" under the Endangered Species Act. *Marine Fisheries Review,* **53**, 11-22.

Warnock W.G., Blackburn J.K. & Rasmussen J.B. (2011). Estimating proportional contributions of migratory Bull Trout from hierarchical populations to mixed-stock recreational fisheries using genetic and trapping data. *Transactions of the American Fisheries Society,* **140**, 345-355

ELECTRONIC REFERENCES

Environment Agency. (2014). Salmonid and freshwater fisheries statistics for England and Wales. *Available at*: http://www.gov.uk/government/collections/salmonid-and-freshwater-fisheries-statistics.

Neaves P.I., Wallace C.G., Candy J.R. & Beacham T.D. (2005). cBayes: computer program for mixed-stock analysis of allelic data, version v5.01. [Free program distributed by the authors.] *Available at*: http://www.pac.dfo-mpo.gc.ca/sci/mgl/Cbayes_e.htm.

The Marine Migration & Swimming Depth of Sea Trout (*Salmo trutta L.*) in Icelandic Waters

J. STURLAUGSSON

Laxfiskar, Hradastadir 1, 271 Mosfellsbaer, Iceland.

ABSTRACT

Information on the life history and migratory behaviour of sea trout (*Salmo trutta* L.) in Icelandic waters is scarce. This paper summarises the results of 11 years of detailed observations on the swimming depth and timing of marine residency of adult sea trout during their annual feeding migration in the sea. Over this period, 41 fish were fitted with data storage tags to monitor the timing of their marine migration and their movements in relation to swimming depth, ambient water temperature and, in three years, salinity. The typical sea migration period started in May-June and finished in July-September. The duration of the annual sea feeding migration period monitored for all 46 round-trips by fish aged from 4 – 11 years varied from 23-183 days for individual fish and averaged 59 days overall. In addition, one 12 year old fish was captured after 188 days at sea. The main sea residence period corresponded closely with the non-darkness period in this area from 20th May to 23rd July. Similar patterns of swimming behaviour during the period of sea residence were observed across all years: with swimming at depths at 0 – 5 metres for 72 – 93% of the time, at 5.1 – 10.0 metres for 6 – 25% of the time and at 10.1 – 15.0 metres for 0.4 – 2.2% of the time. Very limited time (an average of less than 0.5%) was spent at depths greater than 15 metres. The aggregated annual mean depth recorded from all fish ranged from 2.0 – 3.8 metres, confirming the pelagic nature of their feeding behaviour. Measurement of temperature and salinity indicated that the fish moved in close proximity to the coast, where lower salinities and higher temperatures occurred. A maximum depth recorded from any one fish was 70 metres. Some of the depth profiles for individual fish showed sudden rapid dives into deeper water and occasional fast upward movements from the bottom in shallow water close to the shoreline. A comparison of swimming depth in relation to fish length and maturity status showed no major variation in mean swimming depth between individual fish with regard to those parameters. Fastest recorded vertical movement of sea trout were 2.2 body length/sec.

Keywords: sea trout; Iceland; sea migration; swimming depth; risk assessment: marine residence.

INTRODUCTION

The first study using Data Storage Tags (DSTs) to obtain a continuous record of the behaviour of sea trout during their feeding migrations in the sea was undertaken in 1995 (Sturlaugsson & Johannsson 1996). Since then, the same methodology was used by Sturlaugsson in various investigations to obtain a detailed record of swimming depth and related biological and environmental data in the coastal waters of South Iceland. This paper provides a summary of the results of those investigations over the period 1996-2011, on swimming depth, marine residence time and on the life history features of the tagged fish. The principal findings presented here are abstracted from the detailed analysis of the raw data on the swimming depth of individual sea trout between 1996–2008 requested by the Scottish Government for use in risk assessment models for future tidal power schemes to generate marine renewable energy in Scotland (Sturlaugsson, 2016).

METHOD & MATERIALS

STUDY AREA

The investigation was centred on two rivers, the Tungulaekur and Grenlaekur in South Iceland (Figure 1). This is an area where the sea trout is the most abundant salmonid and both rivers are noted for their strong runs of sea trout (Antonsson & Johannsson, 2012). The rivers are mainly spring-fed and discharge at a mean rate of about 2 m^3s^{-1} during the summer months. The Tungulaekur feeds into a large glacial river (the Skafta) with a mean discharge of 120 m^3s^{-1}, while the Grenlaekur shares a common estuary with the river Skafta. The coastline is unsheltered and has extensive areas of sand that extend well out into the sea from the shoreline.

Hydrographical data from the Marine Research Institute, Reykjavik (http://www.hafro.is) shows that there is a thermocline in this area that is approximately 20 m deep during the summer that extends 2–27 km from the shore. This coastal area is influenced by a massive input of fresh water from glacial rivers in the summer for several hundred kilometres along the coast. Consequently, it is probable that sea trout experience low salinities close to the shore without entering brackish estuarine waters to feed. There is some limited information on the prey species of sea feeding sea trout (Antonsson & Johansson, 2012; Sturlaugsson & Agustsson, 2012; Sturlaugsson, *unpublished data*). Sand eels are the predominant prey with herring and capelin becoming important when available. Smaller prey species, such as amphipods and polychaetes, also occur in the diet but are quantitatively less important.

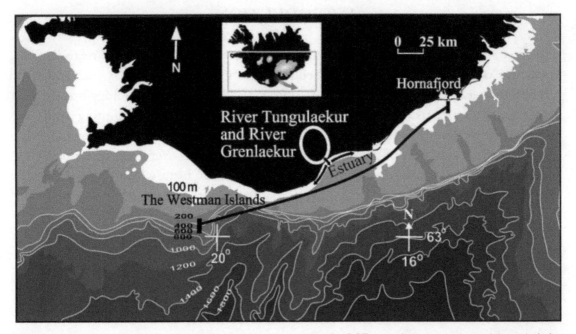

Figure 1. Map of the coast of South Iceland, showing the area that the DST tagged sea trout migrated through during the monitoring in 1996-2011. The white circle shows the area where the two home rivers of the monitored sea trout are located (Tungulaekur and Grenlaekur). Also marked is the estuary Veidios where River Grenlaekur enters the sea as well as River Skafta, the glacial river into which River Tungulaekur flows. Black arrows indicate the feeding area of the sea trout closest to the estuary. The black line stretching from Hornafjord to Westman Islands shows the coastal area used by foraging sea trout from the two rivers. These known outer limits of their distribution during sea migration are of approximately 160 km east and west of their home estuary, Veidios. The map also shows water depth intervals by bottom depth isolines (100 m, 200 m etc.). The waters are relatively shallow along the coast with water of depth 20 m or less extending 1-2 km out from shore.

SOURCE OF FISH

The adult sea trout monitored in this study were captured initially in the two rivers and generally tagged and released the same day. Most of the fish were caught by anglers in the spring prior to their annual seaward migration, although some were tagged and released on their spawning grounds in the autumn after being captured at night with a dip net. Since the behaviour of the fish could be influenced by differences in their life history features, the following biological details were obtained as an aid in identifying and interpreting any apparent aberrant or atypical behaviour exhibited by individual fish: a) length and weight at capture and recapture, b) sex (where possible), c) maturity status and d) smolt-age, sea-age and previous spawning history from scales samples taken at time of first tagging or recapture.

DATA STORAGE TAGS

The investigation used data storage tags (DSTs) manufactured by Star-Oddi (http://www.star-oddi.com/). The tags were pre-programmed to log information at different recording frequencies ranging from 5 seconds to 2 hours on the depth and ambient water temperature experienced by each fish throughout the duration of their residence in the sea during the 11 year period. Some tags were also equipped with salinity (conductivity) sensors in three of the years.

The programmed frequency of sampling for individual fish varied within and between years depending on tag type, tag memory and the specific aim of the annual sampling programme. The most detailed measurements (with the highest recording frequency) were collected over short periods during summer months, when recording intervals as frequent as every 5 – 10 seconds were used to obtain highly detailed information on vertical distribution and swimming movements between different depth layers. Table 1 gives the number of fish tagged in each year and the frequency of the uniform recording intervals throughout the sea migration period for a given year and the number of recordings obtained from that uniform sampling.

Although most of the DST tags were attached externally (modified Carlin method), a few were implanted into the peritoneal cavity. The manufacturers declared accuracy for the depth measurements of the tags was +/- 0.4% of the selected depth range – which was 50 m in all years. The accuracy for the temperature and salinity measurements was +/- 0.1^0C and +/- 1 psu respectively.

It should be noted that it was essential to recover each fish to retrieve the tag and access the stored data. This depended on their recapture during their subsequent return the rivers; either by anglers or on the spawning grounds. Consequently, not all the fish originally tagged were recovered.

Table 1. Overall mean swimming depth of sea trout in each year of the study period showing mean, SD and maximum recorded depth. The number of fish monitored in each year, the recording interval and the total number of uniform annual recordings for determining mean depth are also given.

Study Year	Fish Depth (uniform measurements during sea migration period)			Fish monitored in year	Recording Interval & number of recordings in year	
	Mean	SD	Max	No.	Intervals	No.
1996	2.6	2.73	46.5	14	1 hour	18,228
1997	3.4	2.60	21.5	10	2 hours	6,878
1998	3.3	2,41	17.0	5	2 hours	3,123
1999	3.8	2,59	26.9	7	30 min	19,676
2004	3.4	2.11	32.8	1	5 min	19,262
2006	2.5	2.57	45.2	2	1 hour	2,925
2007	2.5	1.97	13.4	2	2 hours	1,107
2008	2.6	3.25	38.3	3	30 min	7,476
2009	2.5	2.10	20.6	1	1 hour	2,024
2010	2.5	4.72	70.4	1	2 hours	2,190
2011	2.0	3.28	70.2	1	2 hours	2,259

RESULTS

Sturlaugsson (2016) provided comprehensive information on the temperature, salinity and depth profiles of individual fish in relation to their sexual maturity, size, different life history features and biological characteristics for different years. [Appendix Figure A/1 illustrates an example of the highly detailed nature of the information on depth, temperature and salinity retrieved from the DST from a single fish over one complete return migration between fresh water and the sea. Appendix Figure A/2 is an example of an occasional sudden rapid dive into deeper water obtained from high frequency recording intervals of 5-10 seconds.]

DATABASE

A total of 41 sea trout were tagged and monitored during their sea feeding migration periods. Of these, three fish made either 2 or 3 return visits between fresh water and the sea to spawn and/or over winter in the rivers. Some fish were subsequently recaptured, retagged and monitored for a second migration period. This gave continuous datasets for 47 completed marine migration periods: with a total of 85,149 separate recordings of individual fish depth and ambient water temperature at uniform recording intervals throughout the sea migration for any given year. In addition, monitoring the same parameters included 176,378 separate recordings from sub-sampling of the same tags at a more frequent measuring interval: providing a grand total of 261,527 separate recordings for the entire 11 year monitoring programme.

LIFE HISTORY FEATURES

The age of fish at tagging ranged from 4 – 10 years and their lengths ranged from 32-76 cm when captured and 47-81 cm when recaptured. Of these, 17 fish were immature 'maiden' fish and 24 had matured and spawned previously on 1-3 separate occasions before tagging. Of the 36 fish where sex could be determined when tagged or recaptured, 16 were females and 20 males. Life histories shown from scale reading established that the fish spent 2 – 5 years in fresh water before their first migration into the sea to feed and grow. They then made repeated annual return migrations between the river and the sea, with up to 8 separate sea migrations observed. Scale reading established that first spawning occurred after the second or, more commonly, the third return migration, with one example of four return migrations before first spawning. The total number of spawning occasions observed among monitored individuals ranged from 1 – 5 years. Sturlaugsson (2016) provides more detailed life history information for each individual fish. They broadly reflected the typical life history pattern of sea trout in the local area (Antonsson & Johannsson, 2012).

SEA RESIDENCE

The DST monitoring programme generated detailed information on the actual sea residence periods for adult fish; with resolution frequencies between entering the sea and returning to the river ranging from 5 minutes to 2 hours (Figure 2). Based on all 46 completed round trips for 1996 – 2010, the aggregated mean proportions of fish entering the sea to start their marine residence period were – 41.3% in May, 54.3% in June, 2.2% in July, and 2.2% % in August. Likewise, the monthly pattern of return to the river at the end of the sea residence period was: 2.2% in June, 56.5% in July, 32.6% in August, 6.5% in September and 2.2% in November. The average duration of the annual period of marine residence for all sea trout monitored throughout whole sea migration period (1996–2010) was 59 days (SD = 14.3 days) and ranged from 23-183 days. In addition, one fish monitored in 2011 was captured in sea after 188 days of sea migration. Sea trout that finished their sea migration showed that 76% of the fish started their period of sea residence within the 4 weeks from 20th May to 16th June and returned to fresh water within the 4 weeks from 15th July to 11th August (Figure 2). The main sea residence periods corresponds closely with the non-darkness period (sun altitude ≥ -6°) in this area from 20th May to 23rd July.

A large male sea trout monitored over 3 seasons (2009 – 2011) was the oldest fish studied. The results on this fish suggested that older fish may exhibit different patterns of behaviour in different years. It was first tagged in spring 2009 when aged 10 years. Its period of sea residence was 23rd May–28th August in the first year and 19th May–17th November in the second year. It then remained in fresh water until 29th December before returning to sea for the third monitored migration. This was the eighth migration between fresh water and the sea for this fish. It was finally recaptured at sea on 5th July after 188 days at sea by a trawl net used in fishing for mackerel some 35 km southeast of Surtsey Island (a distance of about 160 km west of its home estuary) when twelve years old.

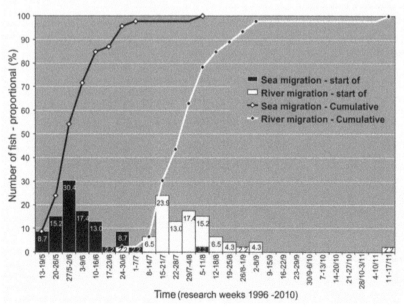

Figure 2. The mean weekly and cumulative proportions of sea trout starting and ending their period of marine residence in each research week based on 46 completed return migrations (1996 – 2010).

SWIMMING DEPTH AT SEA

The aggregated data on swimming depth from the main set of 85,149 recordings for 1996 – 2011 is summarised in Table 2. This information is transposed in Figure 3 to show the annual proportion of time that the monitored fish spent at each 5 metre depth interval between the sea surface and 70m depth. On average, the proportion of time spent at different depths was: 85% at 0–5 metres, 13.09% at 5.1–10 metres, 1.3% at 10.1–15 metres and only 0.52% of the time at depths below 15 metres. Although there was some variability in the general patterns of depths observed in different years, the time spent below 20 m was 1.1% or less in all years.

The mean values and 95% CL for overall depth in each of the 11 years of the study period are shown in Figure 4. Although the variation is significant between some years, the absolute difference is small.

The highly detailed information obtained by sub-sampling high frequency recordings (Sturlaugsson 2016) showed the same general distribution pattern given in Figure 3. Although the recording periods were usually for very short periods and highly clustered at different times in the summer, they were consistent with a generally uniform pattern of swimming depth. The most frequent measurements allowed approximate observations of the actual recorded vertical movement of sea trout, where the fastest vertical movements were 1.56 m/sec (2.2 body-length/sec).

Table 2. Aggregated proportions of sea residence time spent at given depth intervals in each year over the 11-year study period.

Depth Interval (metres)	Proportion of time at each depth interval in each year over the period of marine residence											% Mean Time
	1996	1997	1998	1999	2004	2006	2007	2008	2009	2010	2011	
0 – 5.0	85.44	78.24	80.37	72.21	81.5	85.58	88.98	87.68	89.58	90.19	93.23	85.10
5.1 -10	12.54	19.34	17.64	25.37	17.6	9.33	10.57	9,03	9.19	7.75	5.53	13.09
10.1 - 15	1.45	2.22	1.83	2.19	0.56	1.64	0.45	1.67	1.09	0.73	0.40	1.29
15.1 - 20	0.43	0.22	0.16	0.21,	0.09	0.31	*	0.95	0.10	0.32	0.44	0.29
20.1 - 25	0.07	0.03	*	0.01	0.03	0.10	*	0.40	0.05	*	0.18	0.08
25.1 - 30	0.02	*	*	0.01	0.07	*	*	0.17	*	0.27	0.04	0.05
30.1 - 35	0.02	*	*	*	0.02	*	*	0.07	*	0.18	*	0.03
35.1 - 40	*	*	*	*	*	*	*	0.03	*	0.05	0.04	0.01
40.1 - 45	0.02	*	*	*	*	*	*	*	*	0.14	*	0.01
45.1 - 50	0.01	*	*	*	*	*	*	*	*	0.09	0.04	0.02
50 - 70	*	*	*	*	*	*	*	*	*	0.27	0.09	0.18

* = No records

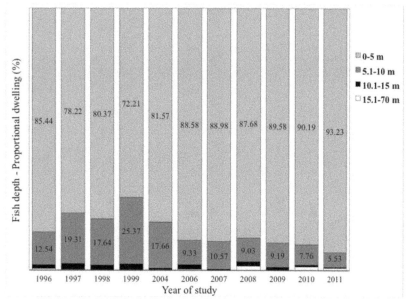

Figure 3. The aggregated mean proportion of time that sea trout spent within 5 m depth intervals during their sea residence period in each year

The aggregated data on swimming depth for all fish in all years showed that sea trout spent between 72–93% of their marine residence time in the upper 5 metres of the water column layer. They occupied the next 5 – 10 metre depth zone for 6 – 25% of their time and spent very little time in deeper water. The time spent at depths below 20 metres was 1.1% or less over the entire study period. Although some fish were recorded at a depth of 70 metres in deeper waters, such movements were very rare.

DISCUSSION

Comparable investigations into the marine feeding migrations of sea trout from other geographical regions are scarce. Rikardsen *et al.* (2007) monitored eight sea trout fitted with DSTs in Alta Fjord in Northern Norway in 2002. The fish were recaptured after 1 – 40 days and had spent 50% of the time at depths of 1 – 2 metres and more than 90% of time in water no deeper than 3 m. However, deeper dives down to 28 m were also recorded, usually at the end of the sea residence period. Hantke *et al.* (2011) monitored the swimming depth of sea trout in the coastal waters of the Baltic Sea in Germany. They observed that 64% of the fish migrated in the upper water layer at a depth of about 1.5 m, but with occasional dives to a depth of 13 metres. Davidsen *et al.* (2014) studied sea trout in a fjord in central Norway and concluded that the average swimming depth of 1.87 m in the period from April to September varied significantly in different types of coastal habitat. The mean swimming depth in littoral habitats (2.11 m) and in cliff habitats (2.53 m) was significantly deeper than in pelagic areas (1.28 m)

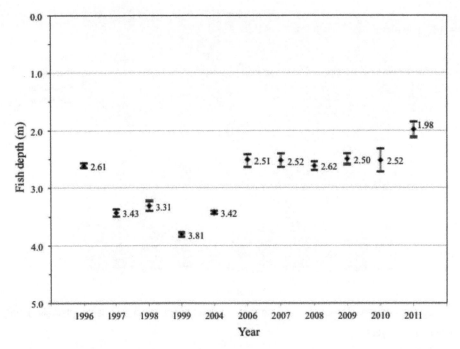

Figure 4. Aggregated annual mean values for swimming depth (with 95% CL) during marine migration within the overall study period 1996-2011. The values are based on all sea trout monitored in each year from measurements that were recorded with same uniform interval throughout the sea migration period by all the fish.

and that the average swimming depth was significantly deeper during the day (1.98 m) than at night (1.28 m). The progressively deeper swimming pattern from April into late summer was positively correlated with water temperature, suggesting that sea trout actively sought cooler, deeper water.

These studies all support the general conclusion from this investigations that sea trout feed close to the surface for most of time during their period of marine residence and that differences in the local environment or in the age, length and maturity status of individual sea trout do not materially influence this typical pattern of pelagic feeding behaviour. Although feeding fish were observed to remain close to the surface for most of the time, this could imply that they were also feeding close to the seabed when in shallow water.

Information on the swimming depths of sea trout during their marine feeding migrations has practical application for risk assessment. As noted in the introduction, one important use for such information is to serve as a basis for informing decisions on tidal stream electricity generating turbines in coastal waters. Another, more general application, would be in informing decisions for the regulation of commercial fishing with pelagic nets for marine fish species in coastal waters used as feeding areas and as migration pathways for sea trout and other diadromous fishes.

ACKNOWLEDGEMENTS

The author wishes to acknowledge the assistance of river owners, anglers and colleagues. Monitoring was partly supported by grants received from the Research Council of Iceland, the Icelandic Salmonid Enhancement Fund and the Republic Fund of Iceland. The Scottish Government funded analysis of the raw data on swimming depth of sea trout for the period 1996-2008.

REFERENCES

Antonsson, T & Johannsson, M. (2012). Life history traits of sea trout in two Icelandic Rivers. *Iceland Agricultural Sciences* **25**, 67 – 78.

Davidsen, J.G., Eldøy., S.H., Sjursen, A.D., Rønning, L., Thorstad, E.B. Næsje, T.F., Whoriskey, F., Aarestrup, K., Rikardsen, A.H., Daverdin, M. & Arnekliev, J.V. (2014). Marine migration and habitat use of sea trout Salmo trutta in a fjord in Central Norway, NTNU Vitenkapsmuseet Naturhistorisk Rapport 2016-6. [In Norwegian with summary in English.] *Available online at*: https://www.ntnu.no/documents/10476/401393002/2014-6+Rapport+Hemnfjorden.pdf.

Hantke H., Jennerich H.J. & Schulz, N. (2011). Optimierung des Bestandsmanagements für Meerforellen (*Salmo trutta trutta* L.) in den Küstengewässern Mecklen-burg-Vorpommerns durch Ermittlung vertikaler und horizon-taler Wanderwege. *Beiträge zur Fischerei* **45**, 1-11. [In German with abstract in English.] *Available online* at: http://www.landwirtschaft-mv.de/cms2/LFA_prod / LFA/content_downloads/Hefte/Heft_45/Beitrge_zur__Fischerei_Heft_45.pdf#page=5

Rikardsen, A.H., Diserud. O.H., Elliott, J.M., Dempson, J.B., Sturlaugsson, J. & Jensen, A.J. (2007). The marine temperature and depth preferences of Arctic charr (*Salvelinus alpinus*) and sea trout (*Salmo trutta*), as recorded by data storage tags. Fisheries Oceanography **16**, 436 – 447.

Sturlaugsson, J. & Johannsson, M. (1996). Migratory Pattern of Wild Sea Trout (*Salmo trutta* L.) in SE-Iceland Recorded by Data Storage Tags. International Council for the Exploration of the Sea. C.M. 1996/M:5. 16 pp. *Available online at*: http://star-oddi.com/Home/Aquatic-Fisheries-Research/Fish-and-Marine-Animal-Tagging/migratory-pattern-of-wild-sea-trout-in-se-iceland/

Sturlaugsson, J. (2016). Swimming depth of sea trout. *Scottish Marine and Freshwater Science* **17**, No.13, 35 pp.

ELECTRONIC REFERENCES

Sturlaugsson, J. & Agustsson, G.K. (2012). Sjobirtingur I Hornafirdi og Skardsfirdi. [Sea trout in Hornafjord and Skardsfjord Iceland – *In Icelandic.*] Laxfiskar. Poster. *Available at*: http://laxfiskar. is/images/stories/greinar/Sjobirtingur_i_Hornafirdi_og_Skardsfirdi-JohannesSturlaugsson_og _Gisli_Karl_Agustsson_Laxfiskar_mars2012.pdf

337

APPENDIX

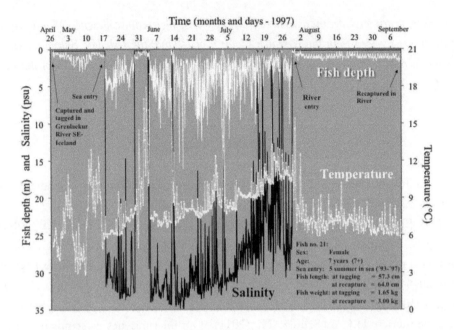

Figure A/1. Individual pattern of riverine and marine movements of sea trout No.21 in relation to swimming depth and ambient water temperature and salinity shown for measurements taken every 2 hours from April to September 1997. Salinity values lower than 5 psu are not real values, but are within the interval 0 – 5 psu. Information on the fish is given.

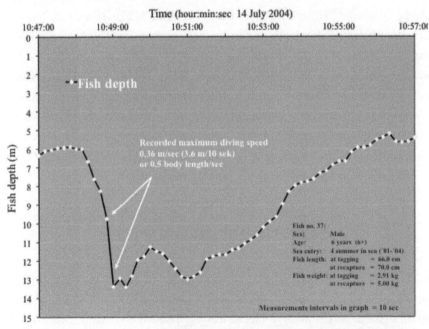

Figure A/2. 'Snapshot' of a sudden depth change of sea trout No.37 monitored at 10 second intervals over a 10 minute period on 14th July 2004.

Dispersal of post-smolt Atlantic salmon and sea trout within a Scottish sea loch system

S. J. MIDDLEMAS[1], D. C. STEWART[1], J. I. HENRY[1], M. WYNDHAM[1],
L. BALLANTYNE[2] & D. BAUM[2]

[1]*Marine Scotland Science, Freshwater Fisheries Laboratory, Faskally, Pitlochry,
Perthshire PH16 5LB, Scotland.*
[2]*Lochaber Fisheries Trust, Torlundy Training Centre, Torlundy,
Fort William PH33 6SW, Scotland.*

ABSTRACT

While both salmon (*Salmo salar* L.) and sea trout (*S. trutta* L.) spend part of their life cycle in the marine environment, salmon migrate to the open ocean, while sea trout are thought to have a more coastal distribution. Few studies have collected information simultaneously for the two species during the crucial period when they leave fresh water and first enter the sea. In 2011, the initial movements of salmon and sea trout smolts migrating from the River Lochy on Scotland's west coast were tracked using a network of moored acoustic receivers. Of 50 salmon and 20 sea trout tagged in the river, 38 salmon and 14 trout were subsequently detected at sea, with no evidence that the tagged fish formed shoals during the study period. Smolts of both species tended to leave the river during darkness and with an ebbing tide. Salmon dispersed more quickly towards the open sea, whereas sea trout tended to remain within the study area. This mirrors comparable work undertaken in Norway and highlights that sea trout are exposed to coastal issues for a longer period than salmon. Data on the usage of the inshore environment by the two species, such as that presented here, is a prerequisite to understanding and potentially mitigating the impacts of human activities.

Keywords: Salmo trutta; anadromous brown trout; smolts, migration; telemetry.

INTRODUCTION

Atlantic salmon and sea trout spend part of their lives in fresh water before transforming into smolts and migrating to sea to exploit improved feeding opportunities. However, once in the sea, salmon migrate towards the open ocean, while sea trout tend to remain in the coastal environment (Hansen *et al.,* 2003; Thorstad *et al.,* 2007; Middlemas *et al.,* 2009).

Salmon and sea trout face a number of challenges when they first enter the marine environment and this is generally considered a critical period for the fish due to losses that occur in the transition from fresh to sea water (Diepernick *et al.,* 2002; Thorstad *et al,.* 2012). In addition, survival of post-smolts of both species may be influenced by a variety of human activities, including aquaculture, energy generation, commercial fishing and pollution (Gill, 2005; Thorstad *et al.,* 2012, 2014). Understanding how these different activities may impact on salmon and sea trout, and how such interactions may be prevented or mitigated against, first requires information on the use of inshore areas made by the two species.

Advances in the application of acoustic telemetry have provided valuable information on the early marine phase of both salmon (e.g. Moore *et al.,* 1995; Lacroix *et al.,* 2004a; Davidsen *et al.,* 2009) and sea trout (e.g. Middlemas *et al.,* 2009; del Villar-Guerra *et al.,* 2013; Davidsen *et al.,* 2014). However, direct comparisons of the two species are scarce (Thorstad *et al.,* 2004, 2007; Finstad *et al.,* 2005; Sivertsgard *et al.,* 2007). For Scottish waters, there is some information on the initial migratory behaviour of sea trout (Pemberton, 1976; Johnstone *et al.,* 1995; Middlemas *et al.,* 2009) but no such information exists for salmon. The aim of the present study was, therefore, to compare the simultaneous movements of salmon and sea trout post-smolts within a Scottish west-coast sea loch system.

METHODS

STUDY AREA

The study was undertaken in a fjordic sea loch system in northwest Scotland comprising two distinct basins: Upper Loch Linnhe and Loch Eil. The study area was defined by the extent of an acoustic receiver network. The network comprised 29 moored acoustic listening stations (Vemco VR2/VR2W) which remotely monitored the movements of the tagged fish (Figure 1). Each receiver covered a radius of approximately 180m, although ranges varied with sea conditions. The receivers were spread throughout the study area, with some deployed as gates (Heupel *et al.,* 2006) to detect passage out of Upper Loch Linnhe and others placed at the major freshwater inputs to the study area (Figure 1). The receivers continuously scanned for tag output signals and recorded the date, time and a unique code for each pulse detected.

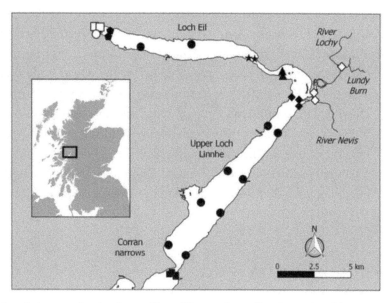

Figure 1. Map of the study area showing the position of the receivers. Receivers placed in sea water are shown as black symbols while those placed in fresh water are shown in white. The different colour/symbol combinations indicate the groupings of receivers used in the analysis, with circles indicating groups consisting of single receivers (*see text for details*).

SMOLT TRAPPING/TAGGING

Salmon and sea trout smolts were trapped as downstream migrants in two tributaries of the River Lochy, the River Nevis and the Lundy burn during April and May 2011 (Figure 1). There are no recent records of stocking in these areas and the trapped smolts were assumed to have originated from natural spawning. On the Nevis, smolts were taken from samples caught in a 6 foot diameter rotary screw trap (RST – Key Construction Ltd) and on the Lundy, smolts were selected from migrants caught in a modified fyke net spanning the width of the river. The traps were operated to commence fishing approximately one hour before sunset and were either removed from the river (Lundy) or disabled the following morning (Nevis) after they had been checked for fish.

Fish selected for tagging showed signs of smolting (silver appearance, darkened fins) and were selected on length (minimum fork length 135 mm for salmon or 140 mm for sea trout), and overall body condition (no obvious wounds, damage to fins or scale loss). Using aseptic procedures, each fish was first anaesthetised (MS222, 80 ppm) until sufficiently immobilised and then placed ventral side uppermost on a V-shaped board. An incision approximately 8-10 mm long was made with a scalpel, anterior to the pelvic fins and c. 3 mm from the mid-ventral line. An individually-coded acoustic transmitter (salmon: Vemco V7-1L, 18 mm length/1.4g in air/0.7g water, ping rate nominal 60 sec, expected life 43 days; sea trout: Vemco V7-2L, 20 mm/1.6g air/0.75g water, nominal ping rate 30 sec, expected life 52 days) that had been sanitised in alcohol, then rinsed in sterile saline solution, was inserted through the incision into the body cavity. In all cases tags were below the 8% of body weight (2.5-6.5%) and 16% of body length (10.5-14.0%) recommended for tracking Atlantic salmon smolts (Lacroix *et al.*, 2004b). The wound was closed with two discontinuous sutures (Ethicon, Coated Vicryl, W9521T). Following surgery, fish were held for 6-14 hours recovery, either in a covered plastic mesh box within the rotary screw trap (Nevis) or in a knotless, small-meshed keep net secured to the river bank (Lundy). Tagged fish were released on the evening of the day of capture between 30 minutes and one hour before darkness (c. 21:00 hours for the duration of the study).

ANALYSIS OF TRACKING DATA

Although data from fish tags are often treated as independent this may not be valid if the individuals are part of a single shoal. In order to examine this possibility, the co-occurrence of all possible pairs of tags was examined. For each pair of tags the number of available occasions was defined as those hours when at least one of the tags was detected. The proportion of available occasions where both tags were detected was calculated for each pairing. This information was then used to examine whether fish were part of a shoal or were acting independently.

MIGRATION FROM FRESH WATER

For those individuals subsequently detected at sea the time of their final detection in fresh water was examined in relation to time of day and state of tide. High tide times were taken from a water level recorder situated close to the mouth of the Lochy (Salama & Rabe, 2013) and were used to define high tide as 0/360 degrees in a circular distribution, allowing the final detections to be expressed in relation to the tidal cycle. Differences between groups, e.g. species, were examined using a Watson two-sample test of homogeneity, while a Watson one sample test was used to test the hypothesis that for a single sample the final detections in fresh water were uniformly distributed in relation to time of day and state of tide. For both tests, p-values were estimated using a bootstrapping approach (Pewsey *et al.*, 2013).

LENGTH OF TIME IN THE STUDY AREA

The length of time each fish was present in the study area was bound by the time it migrated from fresh water and the time of its final detection. A fish was assumed to have been lost to the study on its last detection, although due to the relative scarcity of receivers, it was possible that some fish could be alive within the area without being detected on the receiver network. Where the last detection was at the Corran narrows (Figure 1) the fish were assumed to have moved southwards from Upper Loch Linnhe towards the open sea and differences between these fish, and those last heard elsewhere in the study area were examined. Two sample Wilcoxon tests were used to compare the length of time spent in the study area between groups of fish. Watson tests were used to determine uniformity of the final detections at Corran narrows with respect to time of day and state of tide (Pewsey *et al.,* 2013).

DISPERSAL

Individual detections from receivers cannot be considered as independent data points as it is possible for the same tag to be detected on more than one receiver at a given time (e.g. if a fish was mid-way between two receivers). Examination of dispersal and habitat use was therefore performed using the geographically isolated groups shown in Figure 1 rather than individual receivers. In order to examine the dispersal of fish from the Lochy over time, the mean distance from the river was calculated for each fish in 6 hourly blocks from the time of their last detection in fresh water. For blocks when individuals were not detected distances were taken as the last recorded distance until they were known to leave the study area. For each period with a minimum of 10 active salmon or sea trout, the median, 75% quantiles and range were calculated.

HABITAT USE

The habitat use of salmon and sea trout in the study was investigated using the presence of tags at the different receiver groups in each hour of the study. As there was variation among fish in the periods of time detected, the analysis was undertaken using the proportion of detected hours belonging to each receiver group for each individual (Middlemas *et al.,* 2009). Hierarchical cluster analysis was performed on these data to determine if there was any evidence that fish could be categorised into groups with similar patterns of habitat use. Clustering was performed in R (R Core Team, 2013) using ward linkage, with the number of clusters determined by the largest change in distance between consecutive branches (Everitt & Hothorn, 2011). In order to allow comparisons of the initial habitat use of the two species the analysis was restricted to data from the first 7 days after the fish entered the study area. Only data with at least detections in 5 separate hours were used in the analysis, although using 2-10 hours gave the same number of clusters.

Table 1. Summary information on the salmon and sea trout smolts tagged during the study

Detail	Salmon	Salmon	Sea Trout
Release site	Lundy	Nevis	Lundy
Number tagged	15	35	20
Tagging period	27/4-29/4	27/4-28/4	29/4-10/5
Length in mm (range)	139 (136-143)	142 (135-155)	155 (140-163)
No. detected (proportion)	14 (0.93)	29 (0.83)	18 (0.9)
No. in sea (proportion)	12 (0.8)	26 (0.74)	14 (0.7)

RESULTS

A total of 70 fish was tagged during April and May 2011: 50 salmon and 20 sea trout (Table 1). The receiver network recorded a total of 137,871 individual detections during the study. Of the 70 fish, 61 were detected on the receiver network with 52 subsequently detected in the sea (Table 1). The 52 tags gave a total of 1,326 possible pairs of individuals. For 1,255 (0.95) of these combinations there were no occasions when both tags were detected together. There was no good evidence of fish shoaling in the study (Figure 2) and removal of either one of the tags which gave rise to the figure of 0.4, did not alter the results. For the rest of the analyses, the individual tags are therefore treated separately.

MIGRATION FROM FRESH WATER

There was no significant difference between species in the times that salmon and sea trout were last detected in the River Lochy with respect to either state of tide or time of day (Watson two sample test: tide, $U=0.162$, $p=0.084$; time, $U=0.1$, $p=0.301$). However, the combined final freshwater detections showed a non-uniform distribution with respect to both tide and time of day (Watson one sample test: tide, $U=0.318$, $p=0.005$; time, $U=0.363$, $p=9.99 \times 10^{-4}$), with final detections being more prevalent on an ebbing tide and during the evening (Figure 3).

LENGTH OF TIME IN THE STUDY AREA

Of the 38 salmon detected in the sea, 26 (0.68) were last detected at the Corran narrows and were assumed to have then migrated towards the open sea. Significantly fewer sea trout were last detected at Corran narrows, with only 1 out of 13 (0.08) fish detected at sea last recorded there (Fisher's Exact Test for Count Data, $p<0.001$). There was also a significant difference in the number of days until the final detection between salmon (median: 1.3 days) and sea trout

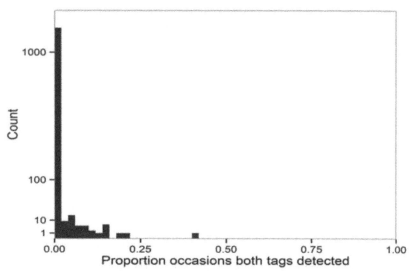

Figure 2. Histogram showing the proportion of available occasions when two tags were present together for the 1326 possible combinations of two individuals in the study. Note the y axis is square root transformed.

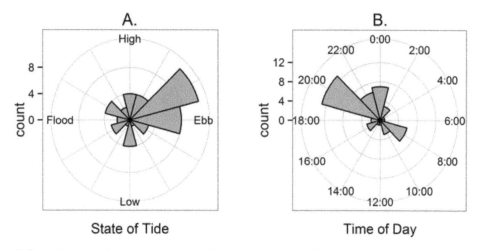

Figure 3. Rose diagrams showing the number of salmon and sea trout leaving the river in relation to A. the state of tide and B. the time of day.

(median: 31.9 days) (Wilcoxon rank sum test, W=156, p = 0.001; Figure 4). However, there was no significant difference between those salmon that left the study through the Corran narrows and those not detected there (Wilcoxon rank sum test, W=151, p = 0.889; Figure 4).

There was a non-random distribution of when salmon were last detected at the Corran narrows (Watson one sample test: tide, U=1.124, p=9.999 × 10^{-5}; time, U=0.194, p=0.0445) with the final detections being more restricted to an ebbing tide and more prevalent during the morning and evening (Figure 5).

345

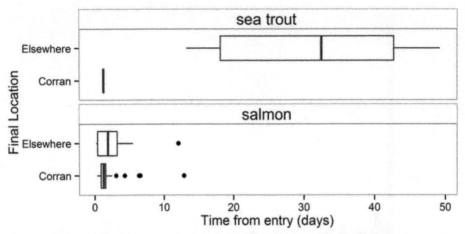

Figure 4. Box plot summarising the length of time individual salmon and sea trout spent in the study area. Results are presented separately for fish which were last heard at the Corran narrows and were therefore assumed to have migrated further out to sea and those that were last heard elsewhere.

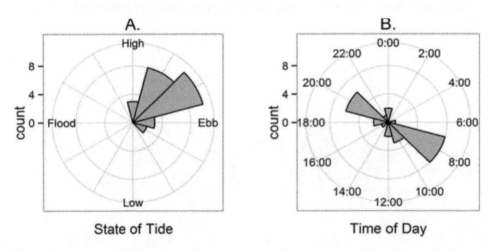

Figure 5. Rose diagrams showing the last detections of salmon at the Corran narrows in relation to A. the state of tide and B. the time of day.

DISPERSAL

Salmon and sea trout showed different patterns of dispersal from the River Lochy (Figure 6). The majority of salmon dispersed quickly southwards from the River Lochy heading towards the Corran narrows, although examination of the full range of movements showed some individuals heading away from the open sea. For those salmon that migrated through Corran narrows the median migration speed was 0.50 km h^{-1} (range 0.05-1.81) equivalent to 1.00 (0.09-3.48) body lengths s^{-1}. Sea trout tended to disperse throughout the study area, although there was a general movement north and into Loch Eil, away from the open sea.

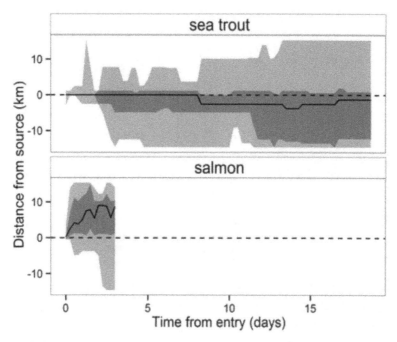

Figure 6. The relationship between time of sea entry and detected distance from the river mouth for salmon and sea trout in Upper Loch Linnhe and Loch Eil. The solid line indicates the median value calculated across individuals, the dark area the 75% quantile, the light area the range of distances. The broken line indicates the mouth of the River Lochy; negative distances indicate travel west towards Loch Eil; positive distances south through Upper Loch Linnhe towards the Corran narrows (Figure 1).

HABITAT USE

Sufficient data were collected on 20 salmon and 8 sea trout to allow an in-depth assessment of their habitat use in their first 7 days in the marine environment. The analysis suggested the presence of two different habitat-use clusters in the data collected during the study. The two clusters represent a geographic split in habitat use with cluster 1 being detected mainly in Upper Loch Linnhe and cluster 2 mainly in Loch Eil (Figure 7). There was a significantly higher proportion of salmon in cluster 1 (0.9) compared to cluster 2 (0.29) (Fisher's Exact Test for Count Data, p=0.005). However, there was no significant difference when fish from either cluster were last detected in the River Lochy with respect to either the state of tide or time of day (Watson two sample test: tide, U=0.056, p=0.72; time, U=0.046, p=0.824). Although the data supported two broad clusters of habitat use there was considerable variation among individuals belonging to the same cluster with, for example, no evidence of a set migration route shown by salmon as they moved towards the Corran narrows.

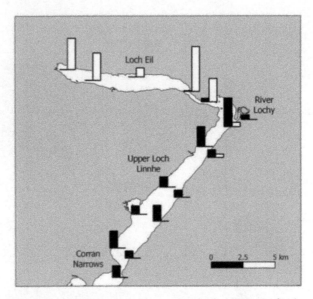

Figure 7. Results of the hierarchical cluster analysis to examine the habitat use of salmon and sea trout in Loch Eil and Upper Loch Linnhe. Bar charts are presented for each of the two clusters identified in the analysis (black = cluster 1, white = cluster 2), with the heights reflecting the mean proportion of detections at each location (max height = 0.31). The receiver groups are taken from Figure 1.

DISCUSSION

The study is the first direct comparison of the initial marine migrations of post-smolt salmon and sea trout in Scottish waters. It therefore adds to the small number of studies, which have compared the two species in their initial marine migrations in Norway (Thorstad *et al.*, 2004, 2007; Finstad *et al.*, 2005; Sivertsgard *et al.*, 2007). It also adds to the growing evidence base on the habitat use and behaviour of salmon and sea trout in the coastal zones of Scotland (Pemberton, 1976, Johnstone *et al.*, 1995, Middlemas *et al.*, 2009, Godfrey *et al.*, 2014) and more widely (Dempsen *et al.*, 2011; Thorstad *et al.*, 2012).

The general findings of the study confirm previous work, which has shown that after entry into the sea post-smolt salmon migrate towards the open ocean while post-smolt sea trout tend to remain in the coastal environment (e.g. Hansen *et al.*, 2003; Thorstad *et al.*, 2007). Early netting work on Loch Etive, which flows into lower Loch Linnhe, by Pemberton (1976) suggested that sea trout remain in inshore areas for the first few weeks following emigration to the sea before moving to the open sea during June and July. The sea trout tagged in this study did not display comparable movements to the open sea with only one individual being detected exiting the study area through the Corran narrows before the end of June. This sea trout left the study after 30 hours while others were still present over 45 days after sea entry with this upper limit determined by the battery life of the tags. Such differences between studies may reflect differences in the behaviours of sea trout from different locations within Scotland

(Middlemas *et al.*, 2009). They may also reflect the different methodologies used as netting studies are necessarily limited and due to their site-specific nature do not cover all individuals or allow for changes in behaviour that may impact on catchability. Recent tracking work in Scotland, Denmark and Norway has shown a gradual dispersal of sea trout from their natal rivers, with generally limited directional dispersal and the fish remaining in the coastal zone (Finstad *et al.*, 2005; Thorstad *et al.*, 2007; Middlemas *et al.*, 2009; del Villar-Guerra *et al.*, 2013; Davidsen *et al.*, 2014).

In contrast to sea trout, salmon spent much less time in the study area, with a median of 31 hours and the last detection occurring 13 days after entry to the sea. Salmon showed a strong preference for moving towards the open sea, with a median migration speed of 0.50 km h^{-1} (1 body length s^{-1}) over the 15.4km of the study area. This does not equate directly to the swimming speed of the tagged fish as it does not correct for the direction and speed of the water current nor did the fish migrate by the shortest possible route to reach Corran narrows. Nevertheless, the range of migration speeds is similar to those reported for salmon smolts tagged in other areas (Thorstad *et al.*, 2004, 2007; Finstad *et al.*, 2005; Sivertsgard *et al.*, 2007; Hedger *et al.*, 2008).

Salmon and sea trout post-smolts are known to form shoals (Lyse *et al.*, 1998; Shelton *et al.*, 2007): although the permanency of such shoals is unknown. The fish tracked in this study were shown not to be travelling in shoals and the overall results were not impacted by this potential form of pseudo replication. It is not clear whether the lack of shoaling within the tracked fish is due to the small number of individuals tracked or is a function of the makeup of such shoals (Pitcher & Parrish, 1993).

Despite differences in their broad movement patterns, there were no differences in the time when salmon and sea trout were last detected in fresh water. Individuals were last detected during the evening and during an ebbing tide, similar to findings of previous work on migrations of smolts and post-smolts (Thorpe & Morgan, 1978; Moore *et al.*, 1995; Riley *et al.*, 2014). Movements of salmon are known to be influenced by tidal currents with outwards migrations in the inshore environment often being assisted by transport on an ebbing tide (Moore *et al.*, 1995; Lacroix *et al.*, 2004a; 2005). Due to the current speed at the Corran narrows (up to 2.5kms^{-1}) it seems likely that tide rather than time was the main factor in controlling outwards movements and the relationship found with time was potentially due to the time of the ebb tides when salmon were migrating through the area. Nocturnal smolt migrations, which were shown by fish leaving the Lochy, are thought to be an adaptive response by the fish to the presence of certain predators that are more active during daylight (Moore *et al.*, 1995).

Within the broad patterns shown during their initial migration, it is clear that individual salmon and sea trout can exhibit a variety of behaviours, illustrated by the spread of dispersal distances shown in Figure 6. As in other areas, while the majority of sea trout remained inshore some (one fish) migrated towards the open sea (Middlemas *et al.*, 2009; del Villar-Guerra *et al.*, 2013; Davidsen *et al.*, 2014). Just as brown trout in general are known to show a great deal of plasticity in their habitat use throughout their range (Elliott, 1994; Crisp, 2000), the differences in initial marine migration shown by individuals in this study further highlights flexibility in their behaviour at sea (del Villar-Guerra *et al.*, 2013). Although there was less variability within salmon, there were still differences among individuals (Figures 5 & 6). Differences between individual salmon in their migrations have been shown in a number of studies (Lacroix *et al.*, 2005; Økland *et al.*, 2006; Hedger *et al.*, 2008). Such individual variation, and the differences shown elsewhere between migrations in different parts of the inshore environment (e.g. Hedger *et al.*, 2008; Dempsen *et al.*, 2011), highlight the need for careful extrapolation of these result to other areas.

The study demonstrates that in common with other areas, sea trout tracked in this study generally spent the majority of time in coastal areas during the first few months of the marine phase of their lives, while salmon moved rapidly to the open sea (e.g. Thorstad *et al.*, 2004, 2007; Finstad *et al.*, 2005;). This highlights that sea trout may be more likely to be affected by coastal issues such as the localised presence of marine renewable energy devices, predators and sea lice (Gill, 2005; Middlemas *et al.*, 2006, 2013; Thorstad *et al.*, 2014). However, due to their relatively local distribution it may also be easier to target management action to protect sea trout than salmon where offshore migration routes are still poorly characterised (Hansen *et al.*, 2003; Thorstad *et al.*, 2012).

ACKNOWLEDGMENTS

We wish to thank the Lochaber District Salmon Fishery Board for supporting the work and Forestry Commission Scotland, the River Lochy Association and Ewen Cameron for permitting access to trap sites. We also acknowledge assistance given by Paul MacDonald and his crew with installing and recovering moorings, Mr Fergie MacLean for advice on locations for moorings and Alan and Lawrie Byrne of Fassfern Mussels Ltd for allowing us to use existing moorings in Loch Eil. Funding was provided by Scottish Government, the Tripartite Working Group and Lochaber Fisheries Trust. Tagging was undertaken under Home Office licence 60/4251.

REFERENCES

Crisp, D.T. (2000). Trout & Salmon: Ecology, Conservation and Rehabilitation: John Wiley & Sons. 212 pp.

Davidsen, J.G., Daverdin, M., Arnekleiv, J.V., Ronning, L., Sjursen, A.D. & Koksvik, J.I. (2014). Riverine and near coastal migration performance of hatchery brown trout *Salmo trutta*. *Journal of Fish Biology*, **85**, 586-596.

Davidsen, J.G., Rikardsen, A.H., Halttunen, E., Thorstad, E.B., Okland, F., Letcher, B.H., Skardhamar, J. & Naesje, T.F. (2009). Migratory behaviour and survival rates of wild northern Atlantic salmon *Salmo salar* post-smolts: effects of environmental factors. *Journal of Fish Biology*, **75**, 1700-1718.

del Villar-Guerra, D., Aarestrup, K., Skov, C. & Koed, A. (2014). Marine migrations in anadromous brown trout (*Salmo trutta*). Fjord residency as a possible alternative in the continuum of migration to the open sea. *Ecology of Freshwater Fish*, **23**, 594-603.

Dempson, J.B., Robertson, M.J., Pennell, C.J., Furey, G., Bloom, M., Shears, M., Ollerhead, L.M.N., Clarke, K.D., Hinks, R. & Robertson, G.J. (2011). Residency time, migration route and survival of Atlantic salmon *Salmo salar* smolts in a Canadian fjord. *Journal of Fish Biology*, **78**, 1976-1992.

Dieperink, C., Bak, B.D., Pedersen, L.F., Pedersen, M.I. & Pedersen, S. (2002). Predation on Atlantic salmon and sea trout during their first days as postsmolts. *Journal of Fish Biology*, **61**, 848-852.

Elliott, J.M. (1994). Quantitative ecology and the brown trout: Oxford University Press, Oxford, 286 pp.

Everitt, B. & Hothorn, T. (2011). An introduction to applied multivariate analysis with R: Springer. 273 pp.

Finstad, B., Okland, F., Thorstad, E.B., Bjorn, P.A. & McKinley, R.S. (2005). Migration of hatchery-reared Atlantic salmon and wild anadromous brown trout post-smolts in a Norwegian fjord system. *Journal of Fish Biology*, **66**, 86-96.

Gill, A.B. (2005). Offshore renewable energy: ecological implications of generating electricity in the coastal zone. *Journal of Applied Ecology*, **42**, 605-615.

Godfrey, J.D., Stewart, D.C., Middlemas, S.J. & Armstrong, J.D. (2015). Depth use and migratory behaviour of homing Atlantic salmon (*Salmo salar*) in Scottish coastal waters. *ICES Journal of Marine Science*, **72**, 568-575.

Hansen, L., Holm, M., Holst, J., Jacobsen, J. & Mills, D. (2003). The ecology of post-smolts of Atlantic salmon. In: *Salmon at the Edge*: (Mills, D., Ed.). Oxford: Blackwell Science Ltd., Oxford, 25-39.

Hedger, R.D., Martin, F., Hatin, D., Caron, F., Whoriskey, F.G. & Dodson, J.J. (2008). Active migration of wild Atlantic salmon *Salmo salar* smolt through a coastal embayment. Marine Ecology-Progress Series, **355**: 235.

Heupel, M.R., Semmens, J.M. & Hobday, A.J. (2006). Automated acoustic tracking of aquatic animals: scales, design and deployment of listening station arrays. *Marine and Freshwater Research*, **57**, 1-13.

Johnstone, A., Walker, A., Urquhart, G. & Thorne, A. (1995). The movements of sea trout smolts, *Salmo trutta* L., in a Scottish west coast sea loch determined by acoustic tracking: Scottish Office Agriculture, Environment and Fisheries Department, 1995. 56 pp.

Lacroix, G., Knox, D. & Stokesbury, M. (2005). Survival and behaviour of post-smolt Atlantic salmon in coastal habitat with extreme tides. *Journal of Fish Biology*, **66**, 485-498.

Lacroix, G.L., McCurdy, P. & Knox, D. (2004a). Migration of Atlantic salmon post-smolts in relation to habitat use in a coastal system. *Transactions of the American Fisheries Society*, **133**, 1455-1471.

Lacroix, G.L., Knox, D. & McCurdy, P. (2004b). Effects of implanted dummy acoustic transmitters on juvenile Atlantic salmon. *Transactions of the American Fisheries Society*, **133**, 211-220.

Lyse, A.A., Stefansson, S.O. & Ferno, A. (1998). Behaviour and diet of sea trout post-smolts in a Norwegian fjord system. *Journal of Fish Biology*, **52**, 923-936.

Middlemas, S.J., Stewart, D., Mackay, S. & Armstrong, J. (2009). Habitat use and dispersal of post-smolt sea trout *Salmo trutta* in a Scottish sea loch system. *Journal of Fish Biology*, **74**, 639-651.

351

Middlemas, S.J., Barton, T.R., Armstrong, J.D. & Thompson, P.M. (2006). Functional and aggregative responses of harbour seals to changes in salmonid abundance. Proceedings of the Royal Society B-Biological Sciences, **273**, 193-198.

Middlemas, S.J., Fryer, R.J., Tulett, D. & Armstrong, J.D. (2013). Relationship between sea lice levels on sea trout and fish farm activity in western Scotland. *Fisheries Management and Ecology*, **20**, 68-74.

Moore, A., Potter, E.C.E., Milner, N.J. & Bamber, S. (1995). The migratory behavior of wild Atlantic salmon (*Salmo salar*) smolts in the estuary of the River Conwy, North Wales. *Canadian Journal of Fisheries and Aquatic Sciences*, **52**, 1923-1935.

Økland, F., Thorstad, E., Finstad, B., Sivertsgård, R., Plantalech, N., Jepsen, N. & McKinley, R. (2006). Swimming speeds and orientation of wild Atlantic salmon post-smolts during the first stage of the marine migration. *Fisheries Management and Ecology*, **13**, 271-274.

Pemberton, R. (1976). Sea trout in North Argyll sea lochs, population, distribution and movements. *Journal of Fish Biology*, **9**, 157-179.

Pewsey, A., Neuhäuser, M. & Ruxton, G.D. (2013). Circular statistics in R: Oxford University Press. 183 pp.

Pitcher, T. & Parrish, J. (1993). Functions of shoaling behaviour in teleosts. In: TJ, P., ed. Behaviour of Teleost Fishes. Chapman & Hall, London, pp. 363-439.

RCoreTeam. (2014). R: A Language and Environment for Statistical Computing. (2013). Vienna, Austria: R Foundation for Statistical Computing.

Riley, W.D., Ibbotson, A.T., Maxwell, D.L., Davison, P.I., Beaumont, W.R.C. & Ives, M.J. (2014). Development of schooling behaviour during the downstream migration of Atlantic salmon *Salmo salar* smolts in a chalk stream. *Journal of Fish Biology*, **85**, 1042-1059.

Salama, N.K.G. & Rabe, B. (2013). Developing models for investigating the environmental transmission of disease-causing agents within open-cage salmon aquaculture. *Aquaculture Environment Interactions*, **4**, 91-115.

Shelton, R., Turrell, W., Macdonald, A., McLaren, I. & Nicoll, N. (1997). Records of post-smolt Atlantic salmon, *Salmo salar* L., in the Faroe-Shetland Channel in June 1996. *Fisheries Research*, **31**, 159-162.

Sivertsgard, R., Thorstad, E.B., Okland, F., Finstad, B., Bjorn, P.A., Jepsen, N., Nordal, T. & McKinley, R.S. (2007). Effects of salmon lice infection and salmon lice protection on fjord migrating Atlantic salmon and brown trout post-smolts. *Hydrobiologia*, **582**, 35-42.

Thorpe, J. & Morgan, R. (1978). Periodicity in Atlantic salmon *Salmo salar* L. smolt migration. *Journal of Fish Biology*, **12**, 541-548.

Thorstad, E., Finstad, B., Sivertsgård, R., Bjorn, P., & Mckinleyd., R. (2004). Migration speeds and orientation of Atlantic salmon and sea trout post-smolts in a Norwegian fjord system. Environmental Biology of Fishes, **71(3)**, 305-311.

Thorstad, E. B., Økland, F., Finstad, B., Sivertsgård, R., Plantalech, N., Bjorn, P. A., & Mckinley, R. S. (2007. Fjord migration and survival of wild and hatchery-reared Atlantic salmon and wild brown trout post-smolts. Hydrobiologia, **582(1)**, 99-107.

Thorstad, E. B., Whorisky, F., Uglem, I., Moore, A., Rikardsen, A. H. & Finstad, B. (2012). A critical life stage of Atlantic salmon *Salmo salar*: behaviour and survival during the smolt and initial post-smolt migration. Journal of Fish Biology, **81(2)**, 500-542.

Thorstad, E. B., Todd, C. D., Uglem, I., Bjørn, P. A., Gargan, P. G., Vollset, K. W., Halttunen, E., Kålås, S., Berg, M. & Finstad, B. (2015). Effects of Salmon lice *Lepeophtheirus salmonis* on wild sea trout *Salmo trutta*—a literature review. *Aquaculture Environment Interactions*, 7, 91-113.

Thorstad, E. B., Todd, C. D., Uglem, I., Bjorn, P. A., Gargan, P. G., Vollset, K. W., Halttunen, E., Kålås, S., Berg, M. & Finstad, B. (2016). Marine life of the sea trout. *Marine Biology*, **163(3)**, 1-19.

Do sea trout migrations promote interbasin connectivity between populations?

J. CHAT, S. MASSON, A. MANICKI, F. GUERAUD, J. RIVES,
F. LANGE, E. HUCHET, P. COSTE, J-C. AYMES
& OLIVIER LEPAIS

*INRA, UMR 1224 Ecobiop, Aquapôle, St Pée sur Nivelle, France. Université de Pau & Pays Adour,
UMR 1224 Ecobiop, UFR Sciences et Techniques Côte Basque, Anglet, France.*

ABSTRACT

Gene flow is one of the most important factors influencing evolution in structured populations. Effective dispersal (i.e. movement followed by reproduction) affects patterns of neutral genetic diversity and influences metapopulation dynamics. Understanding the factors shaping gene flow and population connectivity is vital to improve management and conservation practices. Facultative anadromy in brown trout (*Salmo trutta* L.) offers a good opportunity to assess the impact of sea trout migration on inter-basin gene flow and population structure. We genotyped 11 microsatellite loci from more than 900 juveniles and 615 sea trout collected, respectively, by electrofishing and trapping, in southwestern France. Using juvenile genotypes as a reference for the background population genetic structure, we were able to quantify and dissociate sea trout movement from effective dispersal, i.e. movement followed by reproduction. We found that homing and straying behaviors of sea trout vary greatly depending on the source population. We observed a source-sink dynamic of migratory sea trout with asymmetric movements from south to north, which does not necessarily translate into effective dispersal and gene flow. These findings have important implications for regional management practice and broader understanding of brown trout population functioning.

Keywords: *Salmo trutta*; dispersal; gene flow; migration routes; sea trout; straying; vagrancy.

INTRODUCTION

The brown trout (*Salmo trutta* L.) has a large native distribution centred on Europe, extending from North Africa in the south to Norway and Russia in the north, and from Iceland in the west to the Aral Sea river drainage basins in the east (Elliott, 1994. On the Atlantic coast, this species exhibits a partial anadromy with two phenotypically distinct ecotypes: freshwater trout (resident) and sea trout (anadromous). The first spends its entire life in freshwater, whereas the second leaves freshwater, migrates to sea and returns to freshwater to spawn. Sea trout are not as extensively distributed as resident trout (Nall, 1930. Although common along the Atlantic coast, they are more frequent in the North than in the South. Sea trout live in sympatry with resident trout, albeit in varying proportions depending on the river. The mouth of the river Lima in the Iberian Peninsula just south of the 42°N parallel appears to be the present southern limit of anadromy (Antunes *et al.*, 2006). Nevertheless, this has not always been the case. The most southerly limit of anadromy has probably varied dramatically in the past due to climate changes that forced several waves of Atlantic sea trout to migrate south during the last ice age. This southward expansion is evidenced by the present day occurrence of brown trout of the Atlantic lineage in the Mediterranean basin, in North-West Africa (Snoj *et al.*, 2011) and in Sicily (Schöffmann *et al.*, 2007).

The distance covered by sea trout during their marine migration is variable, but seems far less extensive compared to its congeneric Atlantic salmon. Most sea trout reside in seawater in the vicinity of their natal river mouth (Skrochowska, 1969; Berg & Berg 1987). Sea trout move frequently between river, estuary and sea (Etheridge *et al.*, 2008; Jensen & Rikardsen, 2012), even in winter (Jensen & Rikardsen, 2012), and they may stay in non-natal estuaries (Degerman *et al.*, 2012).

Their propensity to visit non-native streams during marine migration (= *vagrancy*) is substantial (Jensen *et al.*, 2015) and appears to be more common among sea trout originating from small streams (Degerman *et al.*, 2012). Long-distant marine migration is also observed, as exemplified by the few sea trout captured several hundred kilometers away from the point they enter the sea (Skrochowska, 1969; Euzenat *et al.*, 1991). Despite several recent advances, many uncertainties remain about sea trout marine migration; notably the migration routes and the timing of upstream migration with respect to the reproductive season. The current lack of knowledge about sea trout marine migration is even more pronounced and critical, given global environmental changes, for sea trout populations located at the southern limit of their anadromous distribution range.

Effective dispersal, i.e. movement followed by reproduction, plays a major role on both the dynamics and the genetics of living organisms. Effective dispersal of sea trout, here synonymous with *straying*, is of particular importance for both conservation and sustainable fisheries management. It contributes to the resilience of the populations, conditions the probability of colonizing new habitats and is the unique means to exchange individuals and genes for two resident populations otherwise isolated by sea. Straying is supposed to be limited in salmonids, a group renowned for its *homing* behavior during spawning migration (reviewed in Quinn, 1993), and contrasts with the widespread vagrancy of sea trout reported in literature. Vagrancy and straying both refer to sea trout entering a non-natal river but they differ in that straying, unlike vagrancy, also requires additional spawning. In this regard, it should be noted that it is theoretically possible, although surprising, for a species to exhibit limited straying despite a widespread vagrancy.

In the present study, we tried to qualify and quantify vagrancy in conjunction with straying in Bay of Biscay trout populations comprising both resident and sea trout ecotypes. Fieldwork sampling was facilitated by a number of features associated with the study area and the biological model in that: 1) sea trout can be readily sampled during their upstream migration since they are spatially constrained by the dendritic shape of river systems, 2) they can be selectively sampled since they differ in appearance from the resident trout by several obvious phenotypical traits (Baglinière *et al.*, 2001) and 3) the study area included three major salmonid migratory corridors where traps have operated over a long period. We also benefitted from a particularly favourable context to dissociate vagrancy from straying since rivers draining into the south-eastern corner of the Bay of Biscay host trout populations that are genetically differentiated among rivers (Cortey *et al.* 2009) and even among tributaries for the large Adour river (Aurelle & Berrebi, 2001; Aurelle *et al.*, 2002). Finally, we used a genetic baseline data consisting of a large juvenile sampling programme in freshwater to accurately assign the origin of sea trout captured in each migratory corridor and confidently detect and estimate signs of contemporary gene flow between trout populations.

MATERIAL AND METHODS

SAMPLING SITES AND STRATEGIES

All river systems in southwest France contain at least some sea trout. They are particularly abundant in Adour, a large river of more than 300 km long that rises in the Pyrénées mountains and drains a basin covering almost 17000 km^2. For instance, over the last three years, more than three thousands of sea trout were captured annually in the monitoring stations (http://www.migradour.com/vflash/). Commercial catch of sea trout is allowed by small-scale commercial fisheries employing drift nets in the lower part of the Adour river (approximately 40 km inland). Several hundreds of sea trout are caught between March and July each year (Adam *et al.*, 2009). There are four widely renowned Atlantic salmon and sea trout rivers in the region, the Nives, Gave d'Oloron and Gave de Pau, which are each major tributaries of Adour river system, and to a lesser extent, the Nivelle, a coastal river of approximately 40 km long with a basin area less than 300 km^2 (Figure 1^A). Commercial fishing for sea trout is illegal in nearby French coastal waters but a by-catch of salmonids in marine fisheries located to the north of the mouth of Adour is known to be significant, although not precisely estimated.

The study area, identified hereafter as the '*in-group*', includes four river basins located in the Bay of Biscay (Figure 1[A]): the large river Adour with its numerous tributaries (including Nives, Gave d'Oloron, and Gave de Pau) and three coastal rivers (Uhabia, Untxin, Nivelle). The distance between the most northerly (Adour) and most southerly (Untxin) river mouths along the Basque coast is about 21 km. The '*out-group*' (Figure 1[B]) consists of trout originating from rivers that are geographically distant from the 'in-group'. The Urrumea and Bidasoa are Basque rivers located immediately to the south of the study area. The Leyre (a small river of 116 km long that drains into the Arcachon Bay and with a basin area covering 1700 km²), and the Garonne (a large river basin of more than 600 km long and with a basin area of 55,000 km²) have their estuary respectively located 140 km and 240 km to the north of the Adour mouth. Further north still, the Scorff and Oir are two rivers located in Brittany and Normandy respectively. Finally, two upstream tributaries of the Ebro, a Spanish river which originates in the Pyrénées but flows into the Mediterranean basin, were included to account for a phylogenetically distant lineage, the so-called Adriatic lineage. This lineage also occurs in the upper part of the Gave de Pau, although its presence in an Atlantic river system is unexpected and unexplained.

Two strategies of sampling were adopted (*see* Figure 1 & Table 1). Firstly, for the '*in-group*', juvenile samples (mostly 0+) were obtained by electrofishing in more than 80 sites spread over the study area and sampled over a period of three successive years (2011-2013). Whenever possible, a dozen juveniles were collected at each site and a sample of fin tissue (non-lethal sampling) was taken from each anaesthetized fish and stored in 95 % ethanol. The '*in-group*' was composed exclusively of juvenile trout, but the Scorff, Oir and the *Salmo salar* samples may include some mature individuals. Secondly, sea trout were collected during their upstream migration at 7 different fish traps (Figure 1[A]). The sea trout sampled included both finnock and adult sea trout *sensu* Pratten & Shearer (1983). Three of the four salmonid migratory corridors were equipped with fish traps used to catch, count and sample all or part of the ascending runs of fish. The fourth corridor, Gave de Pau, although not regularly monitored with regard to fish migration was where some ascending sea trout were occasionally captured and sampled. A total of seven fish traps provided us with representative samples from sea trout populations entering the four salmonid migratory corridors of the study site (Figure 1[A]).

DNA ISOLATION AND MICROSATELLITE GENOTYPING

DNA extraction was performed on fin clips using a modified NaCl / chloroform based protocol (Gauthey *et al.,* 2015) and from dried scales using a Qiagen DNAeasy Tissue kit. A total of 10 microsatellite markers were amplified using two multiplexed amplification protocols (Masson *et al., in press*), namely: Ssa85 (O'Reilly *et al.,* 1996), MST-60 and MST-73 (Presa & Guyomard 1996), Ssa408Uos and Ssa410Uos (Cairney *et al.,* 2000), SsoSL438 and SsoSL417 (Slettan, 1995), Str541 (Estoup *et al.,* 2000), SsaD71 (King *et al.,* 2005) and OmyFGT2TU (Sakamoto *et al.,* 1994, 1996). These were genotyped using ABI 3110 Avant (Life Biotechnology) capillary

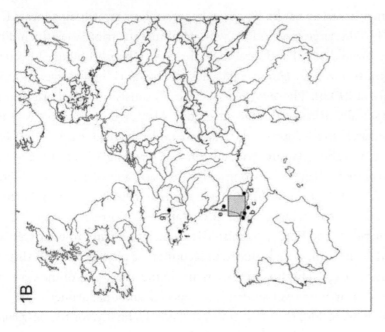

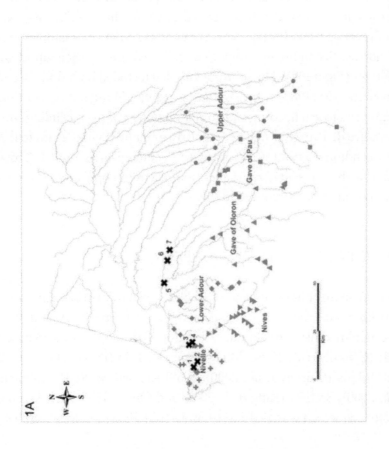

Figure 1[A & B]. Geographic distribution of juveniles and sea trout samples. Figure 1[A] = *'in group' samples*. Electrofishing sites were positioned on the map with symbols in grey according to their geographical coordinates. A different symbol has been adopted according to each main river basin or sub-basin. The numbered crosses in black indicate the position of the fish traps where sea trout were captured: *1* = Uxondoa and *2* = Olha for the Nivelle, *3* = Chopolo , *4* = Halsou for the Nives and *5* = Sorde-l'Abbaye for the Gave d'Oloron. The location of the two hydropower dams is shown as *6* = Puyoo and *7* = Baigts for the Gave de Pau. The distance between the traps and the coast at each site was 12, 18, 22, 25, 44, 58 and 67 km, respectively. Figure 1[B] = *'out-group' samples*. A = Urrumea, b = Bidasoa, c = Ebre, d = Garonne, e = Leyre, f = Scorff and g = Oir.

sequencer with raw data processed using STRand software (Toonen & Hughes, 2001) and MSatAlleles R package (Alberto, 2009; R Development Core Team, 2014).

Table 1: Origin and sample size (after removing full sibs) of the trout used in the present study.

Area or Basin(s)	Sub-basins	Juvenile No.	Sea Trout	Year(s)
Salmo trutta				
Spanish coastal rivers	Urumea, Bidasoa	51	-	
French coastal rivers	Nivelle, Uhabia, Untxin	77	110	2011-2013
Adour	Nives	130	55	2011
Adour	Lower Adour sub-basins	46	-	
Adour	Gave d'Oloron	78	302	2011
Adour	Gave de Pau	84	148	2002
Adour	Upper Adour sub-basins	91	-	
Garonne	Neste d'Aure	27	-	
Leyre	Leyre	10	-	
Brittany/Normandy	Scorff, Oir	18	-	
Ebro		12	-	
Salmo salar				
Nivelle		5		
Adour	Nives, Gaves	19		
Brittany/Normandy	Scorff, Oir	12		
Total		660	615	

*Sea trout sampled in the Nivelle River. All fish traps on the Gave d'Oloron were replaced by video cameras from 2012 and biological samples are no longer collected from sea trout.

STATISTICAL ANALYSIS

IDENTIFICATION AND REMOVAL OF FULL SIB INDIVIDUALS

The electrofishing method used to sample juveniles might result in the capture of individuals from the same family leading to high genetic relatedness among individuals and causing a bias in the estimation of the underlying population genetic structure (Anderson & Dunham, 2008; Rodriguez-Ramilo & Wang, 2012). To avoid this potential bias, Colony software version 2 (Wang & Santure, 2009; Jones & Wang, 2010) was run within each juvenile population to identify full sib individuals and thereafter keep only one family member for subsequent analysis.

DISTANCE BASED ANALYSIS

Juvenile and sea trout genotypes were used to compute Cavalli-Sforza and Edwards chord distance (Cavalli-Sforza & Edwards, 1967) between the rivers sampled and to build an unrooted neighbour-joining tree with Populations software (Langella 1999). The resulting genetic tree has been plotted and edited using TreeView version 1.6.6. (Page, 1996).

GENETIC CLUSTERING

Genetic structure was further described using the individual-based Bayesian genetic clustering method implemented in Structure version 2.3.3 (Pritchard *et al.,* 2000; Falush *et al.,* 2003). This software uses individual genotypes only, without *a priori* knowledge about sampling location of individuals, to infer the most likely number of genetic clusters (K) and compute the probability of individuals to belong to each of the defined clusters. Juveniles and sea trout were analysed jointly and an iterative hierarchical procedure using the delta K method (Evanno *et al.,* 2005) has determined that 11 genetic clusters was the most likely number of genetic groups. The averaged individual admixture coefficient of the 11 genetic clusters has been computed over rivers for juveniles and sea trout separately. Here, the averaged values for the juvenile samples are reported to reflect the background genetic composition of trout populations in the study area.

ESTIMATION OF SEA TROUT MOVEMENTS

Sea trout movements were estimated by comparing genetic characteristics of sea trout captured at a given fish trap with juveniles sampled upstream of the trap. The averaged individual admixture coefficient of the 11 genetic clusters have been compared between juveniles (assumed to represent the genetic composition of the river) and sea trout (including potential vagrants and strayers) using a Dirichlet regression implemented in the R package DirichletReg (Maier 2015). Identical genetic cluster composition between juveniles and sea trout would indicate sea trout migration into their river of origin, while significant difference in genetic cluster composition would indicate sea trout movements between rivers, which may be further characterised by the differing genetic cluster.

ESTIMATION OF EFFECTIVE DISPERSAL

Assuming that only sea trout can move between basins separated by the marine environment, gene flow between basins can only be caused by sea trout effective dispersal. To assess if observed sea trout movements translate into effective dispersal, the recent migration rate was estimated between Nives, Nivelle and Bidasoa juvenile trout populations. These populations were selected because they are the only one to be involved in sea trout movements, whether as population of origin or destination (*see* Results). BayesAssNM version 1.0 (Jehle *et al.,* 2005) was used to estimate recent migration rates between all pairs of these three populations over the last two generations. The NM implementation of BayesAss was chosen because it assumes that no immigrant individual is included in the samples (Jehle *et al.,* 2005). It corresponds to the present situation since only juvenile genotypes, that cannot be immigrants themselves, were included in the analysis. Three independent runs using different random seed numbers and consisting of a burn-in of 100000 followed by 100100000 iterations recorded every 200 steps were performed. Convergence of the analyses was checked using Tracer program version 1.6 (Rambaut,. 2014) to insure reliable results. Mean and 95% confidence interval of migration rates between all pairs of populations and non-migration rates for the three populations are reported.

RESULTS

After removing all but one of the full sib individuals (51 in total), the baseline genotypic dataset used for subsequent analyses consisted of 506 juveniles from the Bay of Biscay rivers (or '*in group*'), 40 individuals that were used as intraspecific '*out-group*' (including 12 individuals from the Ebro, 10 from the Leyre and 18 from the Brittany and Normandy populations), and 36 *Salmo salar* individuals used as interspecific '*out-group*' (Table 1). A total of 615 sea trout individuals were successfully genotyped (110 from the Nivelle, 55 from the Nives, 302 from the Gave d'Oloron and 148 from the Gave de Pau) and were included in subsequent analyses (Table 1).

Genetic distances between populations show a hierarchical structure with *Salmo salar* group being the most differentiated from the other *Salmo trutta* populations (Figure 2). Within *S. trutta*, the Ebro river population is the most divergent group (Figure 2) in accordance with its Mediterranean drainage basin location. This contrasts with the Atlantic drainage basin that characterises all other populations. Among Atlantic populations, position in the genetic distance tree (based on analysis of the juvenile samples) clearly mirrors population geography, with populations located at the north of the study area (Leyre, Brittany & Normandy and Garonne) being grouped together (Figure 2) and populations from the upper part of the Adour drainage basin (Upper Adour, Gave d'Oloron and Gave de Pau) clustering closely together and sharing one common branch of the tree. Populations from the Lower part of the Adour drainage basin (Lower Adour and Nives) group (Figure 2) with the southernmost populations (Spanish and French coastal rivers). Sea trout sampled in the Gave d'Oloron and Gave de Pau are closely related to juvenile groups from the same river (Figure 2). However, sea trout from Nivelle and Nives have intermediate genetic characteristics between the juvenile group from their sampling location (French coastal rivers and Nives, respectively) and those of the Spanish coastal rivers (Figure 2).

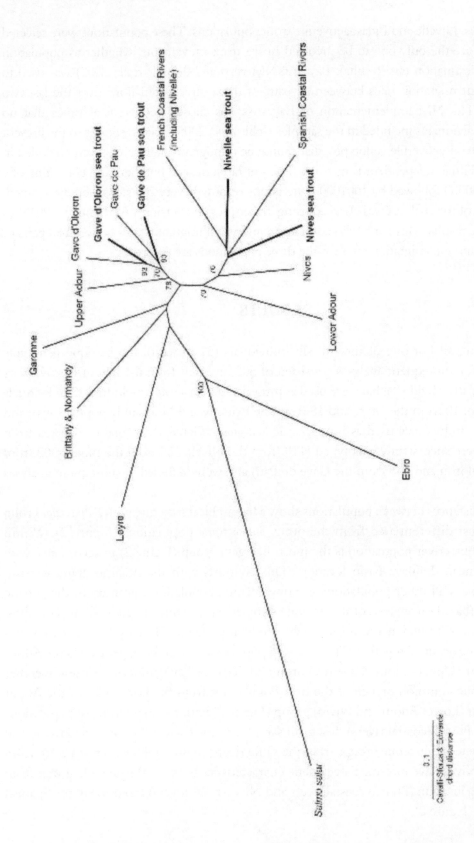

Figure 2. Phylogenetic neighbour-joining tree computed using chord distances (Cavalli-Sforza & Edwards, 1967) between trout juveniles populations and sea trout populations (highlighted in bold). Bootstrap values over locus were obtained using 10000 resampling, and are shown for the most confident nodes (nodes supported in at least 70% of the replicates).

The genotypes of individual samples were distributed across the eleven Structure clusters. *S. salar* and Ebro *S. trutta* constitute distinct genetic clusters; clusters 11 and 10 respectively (Figure 3). The Garonne is mostly composed of genetic cluster 8, and Leyre of cluster 9, while the Brittany and Normandy populations contained a mixture of clusters 8 and 9. The Upper Adour drainage basin (Upper Adour, Gave de Pau and Gave d'Oloron) shows a mixture of clusters 5, 6 and 7. The Lower Adour and Nives, as the two populations from the Lower Adour drainage basin, are divided between clusters 3 and 4. In the most southerly populations, genetic cluster 2 predominates in French coastal rivers, while the Spanish coastal rivers are mainly represented by cluster 1 (Figure 3). It should be noted that no genetic clusters are specific to a single population (with the exception of cluster 11 from *S. salar*) and conversely, some populations show a mixture of several genetic clusters in significant proportions. Two notable results follow from this analysis of the population genetic structure in Bay of Biscay trout populations. Firstly, the lower and upper parts of the Adour drainage basin do not show the same genetic cluster composition despite all these populations occupying the same basin and thus sharing the same estuary. Secondly, juvenile populations in the Adour drainage basin and French coastal rivers (including the Nivelle) show little or no sign of genetic influence from Spanish coastal rivers.

While juveniles should be representative of the population where they were sampled (as they cannot have dispersed over sea and their short life span have limited their freshwater migration), sea trout captured in a particular river could originate either from the same (homing movement) or from a different river (vagrancy and straying). For the Nivelle, Nives, Gave

Populations \ clusters	cl1	cl2	cl3	cl4	cl5	cl6	cl7	cl8	cl9	cl10	cl11
Spanish Coastal Rivers	0.52	0.14	0.11	0.05	0.03	0.03	0.04	0.04	0.02	0.02	0.00
French Coastal Rivers	0.08	0.76	0.03	0.03	0.01	0.01	0.02	0.02	0.02	0.01	0.00
Nives	0.06	0.04	0.47	0.16	0.06	0.06	0.06	0.04	0.02	0.02	0.00
Lower Adour	0.07	0.04	0.19	0.39	0.06	0.03	0.03	0.07	0.08	0.04	0.00
Gave d'Oloron	0.02	0.03	0.04	0.06	0.31	0.25	0.17	0.07	0.04	0.02	0.01
Gave de Pau	0.02	0.02	0.05	0.06	0.21	0.13	0.21	0.08	0.08	0.14	0.00
Upper Adour	0.01	0.03	0.06	0.10	0.06	0.09	0.22	0.24	0.17	0.02	0.00
Garonne	0.01	0.02	0.02	0.02	0.03	0.04	0.05	0.73	0.06	0.02	0.00
Leyre	0.02	0.02	0.02	0.02	0.01	0.02	0.02	0.20	0.60	0.08	0.00
Brittany Normandy	0.03	0.05	0.02	0.02	0.03	0.04	0.07	0.41	0.33	0.02	0.00
Ebro	0.02	0.01	0.04	0.01	0.03	0.02	0.02	0.01	0.01	0.84	0.00
Salmo salar	0.00	0.00	0.00	0.00	0.02	0.01	0.01	0.00	0.00	0.01	0.94

Scale

0.00
0.10
0.20
0.30
0.40
0.50
0.60
0.70
0.80
0.90
1.00

Figure 3. Genetic composition of Biscay Bay trout populations estimated as the proportion of each of the 11 Structure's genetic clusters (cl1 to cl11) obtained by averaging individual admixture coefficient within populations (excluding sea trout genotypes).

d'Oloron and Gave de Pau, both juvenile and sea trout samples are available making it possible to compare their genetic cluster composition and to assess potential sea trout movements between populations. The Nivelle juvenile baseline sample is mostly composed of genetic cluster 2 while sea trout captured in this river show a similar level of genetic clusters 1 and 2 (Figure 4a). Notably, the proportion of the genetic cluster 1 typical of the Spanish coastal rivers (Figure 3) is significantly higher and conversely genetic cluster 2 is significantly lower, than the background genetic composition of the river (Figure 4a), indicating the movement of sea trout from Spanish coastal rivers into the Nivelle. Similarly, sea trout genetic cluster composition from Nives significantly differs from the baseline population as they show much higher proportion of cluster 1 from Spanish coastal rivers and a lower proportion of cluster 3 characteristic of the Nives (Figure 4b), indicating the movement of sea trout from Spanish coastal rivers into the Nives as well. By contrast, sea trout captured in the Gave d'Oloron and Gave de Pau do not show any difference of genetic composition with juveniles from the river where they were captured (Figures 4c & 4d), indicating strong tendency for homing movement.

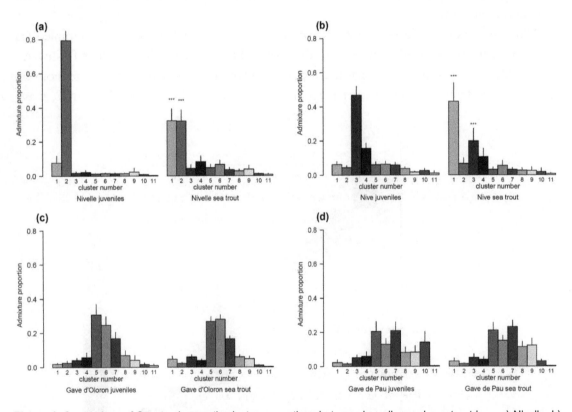

Figure 4. Comparison of Structure's genetic cluster proportions between juveniles and sea trout in: – a) Nivelle, b) Nives, c) Gave d'Oloron and d) Gave de Pau. Differences in genetic cluster proportions in sea trout as compared to juveniles were tested using a Dirichlet regression, three stars (***) indicating significant differences in cluster proportions at a 0.001 error level.

Analyses of recent migration rates (i.e. sea trout movements between basins followed by reproduction also termed effective dispersal) by BayesAssNM between Bidasoa (the closest and largest Spanish coastal river), Nivelle and Nives show a very restricted pattern of gene flow between the three populations (Table 2). The only significant migration with subsequent successful reproduction was found to occur from Nivelle into Bidasoa with an average migration rate of 0.17 (confidence interval: 0.09 – 0.24) and meaning that between 9% and 24% of trout that reproduced yearly in the Bidasoa originated from the Nivelle (by straying) over the last two generations. All other migration rates are not significantly different from zero (Table 2) indicating that trout that reproduced in Nivelle and Nives in the last two generations originated from their natal river (by homing).

Table 2: Recent migration rate (m) estimated by BayesAssNM and their 95% confidence intervals (*in brackets*). Immigrant source populations are listed in the column header (= From) and receiving population are listed in the first column (= Into). Numbers refer to migration rates (*off-diagonal*), i.e. the fraction of the individuals in the receiving population that are migrants derived from each potential source population; and non-migration rates (diagonal). Migration rates significantly different from zero are indicated in bold.

Into \ From	Bidasoa	Nivelle	Nives
Bidasoa	**0.81 (0.73-0.90)**	**0.17 (0.09-0.24)**	0.02 (0.00-0.06)
Nivelle	0.00 (0.00-0.01)	**0.99 (0.97-1.00)**	0.01 (0.00-0.02)
Nives	0.01 (0.00-0.02)	0.01 (0.00-0.02)	**0.99 (0.96-1.00)**

DISCUSSION

In population genetics, dispersal is often viewed as a step-by-step process (Coltman 2005). Consequently, in species exhibiting high rate of dispersal, we intuitively expect geographically close populations to be genetically closely related. However, dispersal is generally constrained spatially and/or temporally by availability of linking corridors, barriers to migration and other factors that limit or enhance the probability of dispersal in one particular direction. As freshwater fish species are subjected to spatial constraints caused by the dendritic shape of their freshwater habitat, there are only rare instances of passive terrestrial dispersal (*e.g.* Incagnone *et al.*, (2015), the best known being river capture. Populations occupying distinct river systems are thus supposed to be disconnected unless they move, in whole or part, from their native river to another through the sea. However, *S. trutta* being a plastic species, with conspecifics being either freshwater residents or sea-run migrants, can potentially contribute significantly to gene flow between river systems.

SEA TROUT NORTHWARD VAGRANCY

Along the Atlantic coast, and particularly in the South of the Bay of Biscay, sea trout are common and promote resilience of endangered small populations of trout, as reported previously in Asturias (Ayllon *et al.,* 2006). Our results demonstrate unambiguously that, despite their high dispersal potential, sea trout migration patterns and gene flow in this part of the Bay of Biscay is non-random. The general trend observed here is that sea trout movement is largely driven by a homing behavior, as observed in the two Gaves and to a lesser extent in Nivelle and Nives, but it is not the only kind of movement detected in our study. Surprisingly, near the coast and up to 30 kilometres inland, we find evidence for the presence of Spanish sea trout. The vagrancy of Spanish sea trout appears widespread, at least in the downstream parts of the Nives and Nivelle rivers. Such a northerly migration was reported previously for sea trout following tagging for French sea trout from the Bresle and Orne rivers entering the English Channel (Euzenat *et al.,* 1991) and for Polish sea trout from the Vistula entering the Baltic Sea (Skrochowska, 1969; Bartel *et al.,* 2010). By contrast, further to the north, a dominant southerly migration prevailed among Swedish sea trout entering in the Bothnian Sea beyond latitude 62.5° N (Degerman *et al.,* 2012).

NON-SIGNIFICANT SEA TROUT STRAYING

Given the abundance of Spanish sea trout in Nivelle and Nives rivers, the absence of contemporary gene flow from Spanish coastal rivers is very surprising. This implies that Spanish sea trout rarely reproduce in these systems or, if they do, their offspring do not survive. At present, it is impossible to state which sea trout actually spawn in the Nives and the Nivelle. An answer to this question would require conducting sea trout tagging experiments throughout the spawning season together with genetic assignments. Overall, however, it is concluded that straying with subsequent gene flow is almost non-existent in all the four French migration corridors studied over the period.

The Bidasoa exhibits an unexpected high rate of emigration from the Nivelle population. Such a gene flow could putatively result from sea trout dispersal. Unfortunately, sea trout entering Bidasoa were not included in our genetic survey preventing the comparison of their genetic cluster composition with that of the juveniles of the same river. Alternatively, the detected gene flow could have an anthropogenic origin, the Bidasoa having been extensively restocked after a major pollution incident in the 1970s (Anon. 1991b), initially with trout of French origin (Anon. 1991a). In the absence of additional information or samples, we cannot state definitively when and how that southerly gene flow took place.

IMPLICATIONS FOR CONSERVATION AND MANAGEMENT

The possible occurrence within any river of sea trout of non-native origin reinforces the adoption of a precautionary approach when selecting parent fish as broodstock for any programme of supportive rearing and stocking. This will require establishing beforehand if all the sea trout potentially available as parent broodstock are from the same population as the resident fish.

ACKNOWLEDGEMENTS

This study was financed by the French National Agency for Water and Aquatic Environments (ONEMA), the Conseil Général des Pyrénées Atlantiques and the French Minister of Education and Research. The authors thank MIGRADOUR, MIGADO, the French Federations and Associations of Angling (departments 40, 64, 65), the Parc Naturel Régional des Landes de Gascogne, the Parc National des Pyrénées, the Gestión Ambiental de Navarra, the technical environmental consultant ECOGEA, as well as fish farms (Peillen, Cauterets, Lées Athas, Viviers de Sarrance) for their help in fish sampling.

REFERENCES

Adam, G., Barracou, D., Ben Khemis, P., Cuende, F-X., Gayou, F., Jalibert, F., Masson, A., Marty, S. & Reverdy, H. (2009). PLAGEPOMI 2008-2012 : plan de gestion des poissons migrateurs Adour et cours d'eau côtiers. COGEPOMI Adour et cours d'eau côtiers, France 7 pp.

Alberto, F. (2009). MsatAllele 1.0: An R Package to Visualize the Binning of Microsatellite Alleles. *Journal of Heredity*, **100** (3), 394-397.

Anderson, E.C. & Dunham, K.K. (2008). The influence of family groups on inferences made with the program Structure. *Molecular Ecology Resources*, **8** (6), 1219-1229.

Anon. (1991a). Politiques de repeuplement en Navarre. In: Truite commune pyrénéenne: Génétique et repeuplement. Recueil des interventions et conclusiions. Agence Régionale pour l'Environnment de Midi-Pyrénées. Journée Technique Internationale., Oronoz (Navarre), 26 Novembre, 1991. pp 181 – 182.

Anon. (1991b). L'établissement piscicole «Saint François d'Assise» Oronoz-Mugaire. In: Truite commune pyrénéenne: Génétique et repeuplement. Recueil des interventions et conclusions. Agence Régionale pour l'Environnment de Midi Pyrénées. Journée Technique Internationale, Oronoz (Navarre). 26 Novembre 1991, pp 103 – 106.

Antunes, A., Faria, R., Johnson, W.E., Guyomard, R. & Alexandrino, P. (2006). Life on the edge: The long-term persistence and contrasting spatial genetic structure of distinct brown trout life histories at their ecological limits. *Journal of Heredity*, **97** (3), 193-205.

Aurelle, D. & Berrebi, P. (2001). Genetic structure of brown trout (*Salmo trutta* L.) populations from south-western France: data from mitochondrial control region variability. *Mol Ecol*, **10** (6), 1551-1561.

Aurelle, D., Cattaneo-Berrebi, G. & Berrebi, P. (2002). Natural and artificial secondary contact in brown trout (*Salmo trutta*, L.) in the French western Pyrenees assessed by allozymes and microsatellites. *Heredity*, **89**, 171-183.

Ayllon, F., Moran, P. & Garcia-Vazquez, E. (2006). Maintenance of a small anadromous subpopulation of brown trout (Salmo trutta L.) by straying. *Freshwater Biol*, **51** (2), 351-358.

Baglinière, J-L., Ombredane, D. & Marchand, F. (2001). Critères morphologiques pour l'identification des deux formes (rivière et mer) de truite (*Salmo trutta*) présentes sur un même bassin. *Bulletin Français de la Pêche et de la Pisciculture* (357-360), 375-383.

Berg, O.K. & Berg, M. (1987). Migrations of sea trout, *Salmo trutta* L., from the Vardnes river in Northern Norway. *Journal of Fish Biology*, **31** (1), 113-121.

Cavalli-Sforza, L.L. & Edwards, A.W.F. (1967). Phylogenetic analysis. Models and estimation procedures. *American Journal of Human Genetics*, **19** (3. Pt 1), 233-257.

Coltman, D.W. (2005). Evolutionary genetics – Differentiation by dispersal. *Nature*, **433** (7021), 23-24.

Cortey, M., Vera, M., Pla, C. & Garcia-Marin, J.L. (2009). Northern and Southern expansions of Atlantic brown trout (*Salmo trutta*) populations during the Pleistocene. *Biological Journal of the Linnean Society*, **97** (4), 904-917.

Degerman, E., Leonardsson, K. & Lundqvist, H. (2012). Coastal migrations, temporary use of neighbouring rivers, and growth of sea trout (*Salmo trutta*) from nine northern Baltic Sea rivers. *ICES Journal of Marine Science*, **69** (6), 971-980.

Elliott, J.M. 1994. *Quantitative ecology and the brown trout*. Oxford University Press, Oxford, 264 pp.

Estoup, A., Largiader, C.R., Cornuet, J.M., Gharbi, K., Presa, P. & Guyomard, R. (2000). Juxtaposed microsatellite systems as diagnostic markers for admixture: an empirical evaluation with brown trout (*Salmo trutta*) as model organism. *Mol Ecol*, **9** (11), 1873-1886.

Etheridge, E.C., Harrod, C., Bean, C. & Adams, C.E. (2008). Continuous variation in the pattern of marine v. freshwater foraging in brown trout Salmo trutta L. from Loch Lomond, Scotland. *J Fish Biol*, **73** (1), 44-53.

Evanno, G., Regnaut, S. & Goudet, J. (2005). Detecting the number of clusters of individuals using the software STRUCTURE: a simulation study. *Mol Ecol*, **14** (8), 2611-2620.

Falush, D., Stephens, M. & Pritchard, J.K. (2003). Inference of population structure using multilocus genotype data: Linked loci and correlated allele frequencies. *Genetics*, **164** (4), 1567-1587.

Gauthey, Z., Freychet, M., Manicki, A., Herman, A., Lepais, O., Panserat, S., Elosegi, A., Tentelier, C. & Labonne, J. (2015). The concentration of plasma metabolites varies throughout reproduction and affects offspring number in wild brown trout (*Salmo trutta*). *Comparative Biochemistry and Physiology, Part A: Molecular & Integrative Physiology*, **184**, 90-96.

Jehle, R., Wilson, G.A., Arntzen, J.W. & Burke, T. (2005). Contemporary gene flow and the spatio-temporal genetic structure of subdivided newt populations (*Triturus cristatus*, *T. marmoratus*). *Journal of Evolutionary Biology*, **18** (3), 619-628.

Jensen, A.J., Diserud, O.H., Finstad, B., Fiske, P. & Rikardsen, A.H. (2015). Between-watershed movements of two anadromous salmonids in the Arctic. *Canadian Journal of Fisheries and Aquatic Sciences*, **72** (6), 855-863.

Jensen, J.L.A. & Rikardsen, A.H. (2012). Archival tags reveal that Arctic charr Salvelinus alpinus and brown trout Salmo trutta can use estuarine and marine waters during winter. *J Fish Biol*, **81** (2), 735-749.

Jones, O.R. & Wang, J. (2010). COLONY: a program for parentage and sibship inference from multilocus genotype data. *Molecular Ecology Resources*, **10** (3), 551-555.

King, T.L., Eackles, M.S. & Letcher, B.H. (2005). Microsatellite DNA markers for the study of Atlantic salmon (*Salmo salar*) kinship, population structure, and mixed-fishery analyses. *Mol Ecol Notes*, **5** (1), 130-132.

Nall, G.H. (1930). *The life of the sea trout*. Seeley, Service & Company Limited, London, Great Britain, 335 pp.

Masson, S., Lepais, O., Manicki, A., Prévost, E. & Chat, J. (2017). Disentangling individual movement between populations from effective dispersal in the facultative andronomy of Salmo trutta.L. *Ecology of Freshwater Fish*. [*In press.*]

O'Reilly, P.T., Hamilton, L.C., McConnel, S.K. & Wright, J.M. (1996). Rapid analysis of genetic variation in Atlantic salmon (*Salmo salar*) by PCR multiplexing of dinucleotide and tetranucleotide microsatellites. *Canadian Journal of Fisheries and Aquatic Sciences*, **53**, 2292-2298.

Page, R.D.M. (1996). TreeView: An application to display phylogenteic trees on personal computors. Computer Applications in the Biosciences, 12 (4), 357 – 358.

Pratten, D. & Shearer, W. (1983). Sea trout of the North Esk. *Aquaculture Research*, **14** (2), 49-65.

Presa, P. & Guyomard, R. (1996). Conservation of microsatellites in three species of salmonids. *Journal of Fish Biology*, **49** (6), 1326-1329.

Pritchard, J.K., Stephens, M. & Donnelly, P. (2000). Inference of population structure using multilocus genotype data. *Genetics*, **155** (2), 945-959.

Rodriguez-Ramilo, S.T. & Wang, J. (2012). The effect of close relatives on unsupervised Bayesian clustering algorithms in population genetic structure analysis. *Molecular Ecology Resources*, **12** (5), 873-884.

Sakamoto, T., Okamoto, N. & Ikeda, Y. (1994). Rapid Communication – Dinucleotide Repeat Polymorphism of Rainbow-Trout, Fgt2. *Journal of Animal Science*, **72** (10), 2765-2765.

Sakamoto, T., Okamoto, N. & Ikeda, Y. (1996). Application of PCR primer pairs from rainbow trout to detect polymorphisms of CA repeat DNA loci in five confamilial species. *Fisheries Science*, **62** (4), 552-555.

Schöffmann, J., Sušnik, S. & Snoj, A. (2007). Phylogenetic origin of *Salmo trutta* L 1758 from Sicily, based on mitochondrial and nuclear DNA analyses. *Hydrobiologia*, **575** (1), 51-55.

Skrochowska, S. (1969). Migrations of the sea-trout (*Salmo trutta* L.) brown trout (*Salmo trutta* M. *fario* L.) and their crosses III. Migrations to, in and from the sea. *Polskie Archivum Hydrobiologii*, **16** (2), 149-180.

Slettan, A., Olsaker, I. & Lie, O. (1995). Atlantic Salmon, *Salmo-Salar*, Microsatellites at the Ssosl25, Ssosl85, Ssosl311, Ssosl417 Loci. *Animal Genetics*, **26** (4), 281-282.

Snoj, A., Marić, S., Bajec, S.S., Berrebi, P., Janjani, S. & Schöffmann, J. (2011). Phylogeographic structure and demographic patterns of brown trout in North-West Africa. *Molecular Phylogenetics and Evolution*, **61** (1), 203-211.

Toonen, R.J. & Hughes, S. (2001). Increased throughput for fragment analysis on an ABI PRISM (R) automated sequencer using a membrane comb and STRand software. *Biotechniques*, **31** (6), 1320-1324.

Wang, J. & Santure, A.W. (2009). Parentage and Sibship Inference From Multilocus Genotype Data Under Polygamy. *Genetics*, **181** (4), 1579-1594.

ELECTRONIC REFERENCES

Langella, O. (1999). Populations, Version 1.2.30. *Available from URL*: http://bioinformatics.org/~tryphon /populations/#ancre_telechargement.

Maier, M.J. (2015). DirichletReg: Dirichlet Regression in R. R package version 0.6-2. *Available from: URL*: http://dirichletreg.r-forge.r-project.org/.

Rambaut, A., Suchard, M.A., Xie, D. & Drummond, A.J. (2014). Tracer v1.6. *Available from:* http://beast. bio.ed.ac.uk/Tracer.

370

Feeding ecology of sea trout in the Irish Sea

W. ROCHE[1], N. MILNER[2], C. DAVIES[2], S. SHEPHARD[1], J. KING[2],
J. COYNE[1], P. GARGAN[1] & R. HUGHES[2]

[1] Inland Fisheries Ireland, Citywest Business Campus, Dublin 24, Ireland.
[2] Bangor University, Bangor, Gwynedd LL57 2DG, Wales.

ABSTRACT

The marine feeding ecology of sea trout (*Salmo trutta* L.) and information on the prey species they consume is fundamental to understanding the factors likely to influence their distribution, migration and growth in the marine environment. This paper presents stomach content analysis from 991 marine-caught sea trout, sampled from around the Irish Sea, in littoral and offshore pelagic habitat. Frequency of occurrence and percentage composition by weight were used to compute an index of prey importance. Fish, which was the major dietary component, was dominated by two components, sand eels (*Ammodytes* spp.) and sprat (*Sprattus sprattus* L.). Sand eels were the most prevalent with percentage occurrence and percentage abundance by weight of 56% and 62%, respectively, followed by sprat at 28% and 18% respectively. Spatial and ontogenic variation was observed and pelagic feeding fish, which were almost exclusively feeding on sprat, demonstrated significantly higher feeding intensity compared to inshore feeding fish. Identifying the keystone prey species contributes to identification and understanding of the distribution of important sea trout habitats and, in the longer term, to development of enhanced management and conservation strategies for sea trout and its marine habitat, their prey and associated habitat types.

Keywords: *Salmo trutta*; Irish Sea; marine feeding: diet, pelagic.

INTRODUCTION

Following migration from freshwater into estuarine or marine waters, both inshore and offshore, sea trout typically remain at sea for a few months up to several years (Went,

1962; Pratten & Shearer, 1983; Jonsson, 1985, Klemetsen *et al.*, 2003). Migration between freshwater and the marine environment is regarded as an adaptive life-history strategy where sea trout can utilise optimal habitat to access more food, which ultimately enhances their growth, fecundity and fitness (Thorstad *et al.*, 2015). Feeding opportunities at sea, where productivity and consequently food availability is higher than in freshwater, particularly in temperate latitudes, confers these advantages on migrants (Gross *et al.*, 1988).

In the marine environment, sea trout can inhabit estuaries, inshore waters (Klemetson *et al.*, 2003) and coastal waters (Rikardsen & Amundsen, 2005). One of the major factors that influences their distribution at sea is their feeding and/or migration strategies (Rikardsen *et al.*, 2006). Migration into the marine environment introduces sea trout to a range of different physical habitats in an ecosystem that is markedly different from freshwaters (Rikardsen & Amundsen, 2005; Jensen & Rikardsen, 2008). The majority of studies on the feeding ecology of sea trout at sea have focussed on inshore areas (e.g. Pemberton, 1976; Fahy, 1983, 1985; Gronvik & Klemetsen, 1987; Lyse *et al.*, 1998; Knutsen *et al.*, 2001, 2004; Rikardsen *et al.*, 2006; 2007a). Pelagic feeding has been investigated by Rikardsen & Amundsen (2005) who used a surface trawl to sample offshore waters. Other studies infer feeding behaviour from sea trout tagged with depth and temperature tags (Sturlaugsson & Johannsson, 1996; Sturlaugsson & Johannsson, 2015; Rikardsen *et al.*, 2007b) while some accounts are available from sea trout taken in offshore commercial drift net fisheries targeting Atlantic salmon *(Salmo salar* L.) in Ireland (Fahy, 1981) and from sea trout fisheries in the Irish Sea (Fahy, 1981; 1983). Small sample size and relatively narrow sampling windows are features of several of these studies as noted by Rikardsen *et al.*, (2007a). Trout are known to be opportunistic feeders in both freshwater and marine environments (Elliott, 1997; Klemetsen *et al.*, 2003; Rikardsen & Amundsen, 2005). While sea trout have been shown to feed primarily on fish at sea, their diet can also include high proportions of invertebrate prey such as polychaetes, crustaceans and insects (Pemberton, 1976; Fahy, 1985; Gronvik & Klemetsen, 1987; Knutsen *et al.*, 2001; Rikardsen & Amundsen, 2005). Rikardsen *et al.*, (2006) observed seasonal variation in diet with fish species (herring, sand eel and capelin) comprising the majority during the warmer summer months while crustaceans made up the majority of food items at other times of the year.

Baseline knowledge of their feeding ecology and the types of prey species they consume is central to understanding how sea trout utilize the marine environment. This knowledge will contribute to identification and understanding the distribution of important sea trout habitats likely to influence migration routes and timing, predator distribution, in addition to offering environmental conditions suitable for growth. Furthermore, it is likely to contribute to understanding the distribution of different stocks and variety of sea trout life histories. This study aimed to describe the marine feeding ecology of sea trout, both inshore and offshore, on a relatively extensive spatial scale, within the Irish Sea.

METHODS

STUDY AREA

The Irish Sea, where the marine sampling effort was mainly focussed, is a north-south orientated channel which is approximately 300km in length. With a surface area of 47,000 km^2 (Howarth, 2005) it is largely shallow. In general, depths range from 20-100m over the greater extent of the basin, but a deeper channel, exceeding 100m, extends north-south from the central part of the Irish Sea and reaches a maximum depth of 315m in Beaufort's Dyke (off the Scottish/Northern Ireland coast). The coastline of the Irish Sea study area exceeds 4,000 km in length. For this study the marine sampling area (which included the south coast of Ireland) was divided into 30 discrete marine sampling zones (MZ01-MZ30) (Figure 1). Only data from sea trout feeding in the Irish Sea are referred to in this paper. The mean annual sea surface temperature (SST), from M2 buoy (53.48008N, -05.42508W; Integrated Marine Observations (IMOS)) located in the central area of the Irish Sea, is 11.5°C (range 8.1-15.9), based on hourly data for 2012 provided by the Marine Institute (of Ireland). Salinity ranged from 34 to 34.8 PSU (ICES data for the December to March period in 1960-2000) and decreases from south to north (Young & Holt, 2007). Lower values (range 31.8- 33.8 PSU) are observed in the northeast of the Irish Sea where minimum values are recorded in inshore waters extending from Solway to Liverpool Bay.

SAMPLING STRATEGY

The sampling strategy covered both inshore and offshore waters. Inshore sampling was primarily shore-based and entailed a range of different techniques. All inshore sampling was generally confined to waters < 500m from shore. Offshore sampling was confined to pelagic trawling. Sampling was mainly undertaken in 2010-2012 between March and October in each year. No sampling was carried out in the central portion of the Irish Sea. A small number of fish (15) from summer 2007 and 2008 were included in the total sample. Three discrete sampling areas, comprising groups of marine sampling zones, were selected for inshore sampling: Area 1 (east coast of Ireland from Wexford to south of Strangford Lough), Area 2 (outer and inner Solway District of Southwest Scotland, Northwest England and the north coast of Wales), Area 4 (west and South Wales, Isle of Man). Area 3, which comprised (offshore) pelagic trawl sampling sites (Dundalk Bay outer, southwest Scotland, Isle of Man, and Lancashire) where sea trout were captured, was sampled in August 2011 only. Area 1 included MZ04 – MZ08, Area 2 included MZ09 – MZ13, Area 3 comprised offshore segments of MZ07, MZ13, MZ29, MZ30 and Area 4 included MZ14 – 18 and MZ23-24 (Figure 1). Several sites were sampled within each Marine Zone.

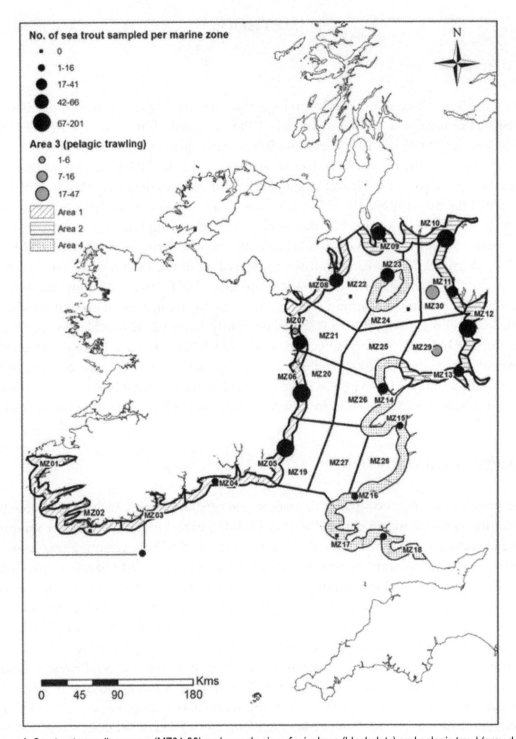

Figure 1. Sea trout sampling zones (MZ01-30) and sample sizes for inshore (black dots) and pelagic trawl (grey dots) samples. Areas 1, 2, 3 & 4 consisting of groups of Marine Zones are denoted by hatching. Area 1 is the east coast of Ireland; Area 2 is Scotland, Solway, Nth England and Nth Wales coast; Area 3 comprises pelagic zones sampled by trawling; Area 4 is the Isle of Man and west Wales. MZ25, 26 & 27 were not sampled.

SAMPLING METHODS

Inshore

Three generalised types of net fishing gear (gill nets, draft nets and stake nets) captured the majority of fish. For inshore sampling, a multi-mesh survey gill net, designed to sample for trout across a broad size range of the population from post-smolts up to larger multi-spawners (based on methods in O'Grady, 1981), was used at sites throughout the study area as the preferred sampling method. This consisted of 6 x 10m panels of 0.4 gauge monofilament with different mesh sizes (57, 76, 79, 102, 123 & 140mm full stretched mesh); total length 60m when mounted. Each panel was 30.5 meshes deep except 57mm at 40.5 meshes deep: which was the only panel depth available. Floating and benthic types were used, but waters sampled were generally shallow (< 2m depth). These nets were deployed perpendicular to the shore, often at low water and usually at dusk, and fished up to and through each high tide. Soak times were generally short (< 4hrs fishing). Alternative sampling methods, including different forms of netting, were added from year 2 because of the low CPUE values recorded for multi-mesh gill net sampling in Year 1.

Existing or previously used commercial methods, other netting techniques and sea angling were amongst the many methods used to satisfy the primary objective of obtaining samples. A total of 28 different gears were utilised which included draft, gill, stake, haaf, seine, drift and coastal type nets. Angling yielded a small sample of fish and sea trout were also collected from fish screens on a cooling-water intake at Heysham 2 Power station in Lancashire and from two small localised marine fish kills. Two of the more effective sampling methods are described below. A site-specific draft net was used on the east coast of Ireland (76 mm full-stretched monofilament mesh of 60 meshes deep x 100m). This was deployed by boat and fished perpendicular to shore (ends held by boat crew and shore crew) from point A to point B with the tide for a distance of ≥ 500m. The net was closed at point B by coming ashore before it was manually hauled to shore. Sampling using this method was generally conducted at night under relatively calm conditions. In Scottish waters, samples were selected randomly from several commercial stake net fisheries (including fisheries in the Fleet, Annan and Nith estuaries). The typical stake net is 400m in length, mesh size ≥ 90mm stretched mesh, suspended on tall stakes, which extends seaward, perpendicular to the shore, for a prescribed distance, with pockets (or fish courts) along the net to trap the fish.

Offshore

Surface trawling, which had been previously been successful in other salmonid coastal sampling programmes (Rikardsen *et al.*, 2004; Sheehan *et al.*, 2011), was the only nominated offshore sampling method. Due to constraints in available sampling time and budget, trawling was conducted in a limited number of locations and potential areas for trawling excluded marine zones over the deep central trough in the Irish Sea (ICES VIIa). A modified mid-water trawl

(Swan Net Gundry Ltd), designed for the SALSEA project, was used. The headline was fitted with a plastic floating collar and the trawl was fished at surface level. A transducer mounted to the headline monitored fishing depths and general net activity. The trawl was fished from a 23 m trawler (500 KW), and maximum trawl speeds were up to 5 knots depending on tidal conditions and wind speed. At the start and finish of each trawl, GPS location, time and trawl speed were recorded along with surface temperature, salinity and water depth. Owing to regulatory constraints trawl sampling from a large vessel (>10m) is limited to areas outside the 6 nautical mile (nm) fisheries limit in England and Wales and outside designated Special Areas of Conservation (SACs). A second series of tows was carried out from a smaller vessel (<10 m) which can operate inside the 6 nm limit in several areas off the south Wales coast using a mid-water sprat trawl (77 m long x 9.2 m deep) in September and October 2012. This trawl was modified for the second set of trawls by fitting a plastic floating collar to fish at surface level. No sea trout were captured by trawling in South Wales.

DATA COLLECTION

Fish were generally retrieved within a short time of encountering the sampling gear and were usually alive. Each was dispatched by a method appropriate to catch type and within regulatory guidelines and placed in a labelled individual plastic bag and frozen whole. Eighteen samples of frozen sea trout tissue (head and gut only) from individual fish were provided by fish dealers from commercial fisheries in Wales (all from MZ13).

Fork-length (Lf) to the nearest mm and wet-weight (Wf) to the nearest gram were recorded for *freshly* caught (*f*) sea trout when feasible. All sea trout were stored at -18°C and subsequently *thawed* (*t*), measured (fork-length Lt) and weighed (Wt) in the laboratory. A correction factor ($Lf = 1.0157 \, Lt + 4.8084$ and $Wf = 1.0235Wt + 10.925$) was applied to forklengths and weights from thawed samples (Lt and Wt respectively) where no fresh lengths and weights were available. Fresh (or converted thawed to fresh) lengths and weights are used in the text below. Fish were assigned to one of four length-groupings, *Group 1* = 125-249 mm, *Group 2* = 250-349 mm, *Group 3* = 350-550 mm and *Group 4* = > 550 mm, for the analysis.

Whole stomachs were cut from the body cavity between the oesophagus and the pyloric sphincter. Any prey items in the buccal cavity (protruding from the stomach into the mouth) were collected, retained and counted as part of the stomach contents. Total stomach wetted-weight, including contents, was recorded to 0.01g. Prey items were identified to species level where possible, and the numbers of each were recorded where discernible. In some fish, the advanced state of digestion prevented counting of individual prey items. Where stomach content was unidentifiable (other than the remains of teleost fish) it was classified as '*Other Food*'. The wetted weights (W) of each prey type/group were recorded to 0.01g. Stomach wall opacity was classified as 'thick-walled' or 'thin-walled' for a subsample of fish.

DATA & STATISTICAL ANALYSIS

Four metrics (a-d) were used to determine the importance of various food groupings. The frequency of occurrence and relative abundance of different prey types were calculated for the whole survey area (Amundsen *et al.*, 1996).

The percentage of occurrence (= %*Fo*) (Hyslop, 1980) and the percentage abundance by weight (= %*W*) of prey type (*i*) were described by the following equations:

(a) $\%Fo = (N_i/N) \times 100$
(b) $\%W_i = (\Sigma W_i / \Sigma W_t) \times 100$

where: N_i is the number of sea trout with prey *i* in their stomachs, N is the total number of sea trout with stomach contents. W_i is the stomach content (by weight in grams) composed by prey *i*, and W_t is the total stomach content (*t*) by weight for all stomachs with food.

Feeding intensity was described by the percentage of fish that were feeding and their stomach fullness (*Fw*) (Rikardsen *et al.*, 2006) by:

(c) $Fw = $ (total stomach content weight g/whole fish weight)$\star 100$.

An Index of Importance (*IOI*), which combined %*Fo* and % W_i (Gray *et al.*, 1997), was used to rank dietary importance:

(d) $IOI_i = 100 \star HI_i / \Sigma_{i=t} HI$

where: $HI_i = \%Fo_i + \%W_i$

Prey composition, expressed as weight (g) of food item, was explored with ordination techniques applied using the vegan package (Oksanen *et al.*, 2016) in R. Non-metric multi-dimensional scaling (NMDS) was used to map Bray-Curtis dissimilarity in prey composition onto ordination space. The analysis examined the effects of fitting different variables (as vectors), including sampling area (Areas 1–4), location (MZs), season (Spring, Summer, Autumn & Winter), month, year, sampling method, fish length grouping and sex, on to the ordination. The contribution of given prey species to Bray-Curtis dissimilarity in the stomach contents of sampled sea trout was assessed using the 'simper' function in vegan.

RESULTS

A total of 991 stomachs were analysed from sea trout captured in the Irish Sea between 2007 and 2012. Sampling effort was extensive in inshore zones (Figure 1) whereas offshore pelagic sampling by trawl was confined to disparate sites in the western, northern and southern

Table 1. Numbers of sea trout sampled, ranked by generalised sampling method.

Sampling Gear	No. fish sampled	% of total	Marine sampling zone
Draft net	388	39.2	MZ04 – MZ08
Gill net	207	20.9	MZ05, MZ06, MZ09-MZ16, MZ18, MZ23
Fish screen/fish kill	123	12.4	MZ12, MZ14, MZ16, MZ23
Stake net	99	10.0	MZ09, MZ10
Trawling	71	7.2	MZ05, MZ07, MZ13, MZ29, MZ30
Angling	30	3.0	MZ03, MZ13
Haaf net	32	3.2	MZ10
Seine net	18	1.8	MZ13, MZ14
Drift net	14	1.4	MZ01, MZ07, MZ10, MZ11
Unknown	6	0.6	MZ09, MZ15, MZ18
Coastal net	3	0.3	MZ09, MZ10
Total	*991*	*100*	

Irish Sea (Figure 2). 82.5% of all samples were taken by four generalised net types: draft nets (39.2%), gill nets (20.9%), fish screens/fish kills (12.4%) and stake nets (10%) (Table 1). Sea trout were taken in four (MZ07, MZ13, MZ29, MZ30) of the ten zones sampled by trawling (Figure 2) which accounted for 7.2% of the total sample. The largest number of samples was taken in summer (June-August) in 2010 /2011 and spring (March -May) in 2012, when fish in the 350-550 mm length range dominated catches. This size range made up 57.7% of the total over the entire period (Table 2 & Figure 3) and this dominance may have reflected mesh size selectivity as larger mesh sizes ($\geq$ 90mm) were a feature of the most successful (and frequently used) net sampling methods. Mean sea trout fork-length (Lf- all samples) was 385mm (range 128-760mm) and mean weight (Wf) was 845g (range 29.0-6070g). Trawl sampled fish were small relative to the overall sample; mean Lf averaged 237 mm (range 150-397 mm) and all were immature. Of the 991 sea trout, 722 (72.9%) were female, 247 (24.9%) were male and 21 (2.2%) were either of undetermined sex or were not examined. The majority (84%) of stomachs available for analysis were from sea trout caught between March and August.

STOMACHS WITH FOOD

Of the total of 991 sea trout examined, 45.3% of stomachs were empty and 54.7% contained food (Table 2 & Figure 4). Seasonally, apart from 2010, the number of stomachs with food (including trawl sample) was highest in spring (2011 and 2012) and then declined up to autumn where it was consistently low in all years (2010–2012) (Table 2). The proportions of stomachs with content tended to increase with fish size although fish >550 mm were lowest with 30.5% holding food (Figure 4).

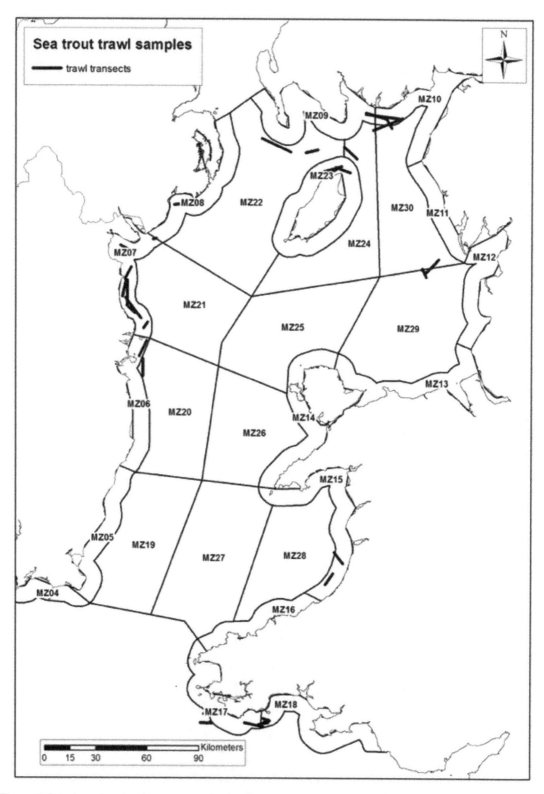

Figure 2. Pelagic surface trawl survey sampling locations

Table 2. Sea trout sample (n=991) showing percentage of stomachs with food (n=542), by year, season and length grouping (mm).

Year	Capture Season	Fish Length Group (mm)				Season Unknown	No. Fish In season	% with food
		125-249	250-349	350-549	>550			
2007	Summer	5	7	0	0	0	12	75.0
2008	Spring	0	0	1	2	0	3	33.3
2010	Spring	3	4	51	4	0	62	58.1
	Summer	1	24	83	9	0	117	77.8
	Autumn	1	7	22	2	0	32	31.3
	Winter	0	0	0	0	16	0	-
2011	Spring	7	15	79	3	0	104	63.5
	Summer	54	60	124	14	0	252	56.7
	Autumn	0	6	9	2	0	17	35.3
	Winter	0	0	0	0	13	0	-
2012	Spring	73	22	105	4	0	204	78.4
	Summer	1	10	59	9	0	79	43.0
	Autumn	0	2	23	5	0	30	3.3
	Winter	3	6	16	2	23	27	70.4
Column Totals		148	163	572	56	52	991	54.7

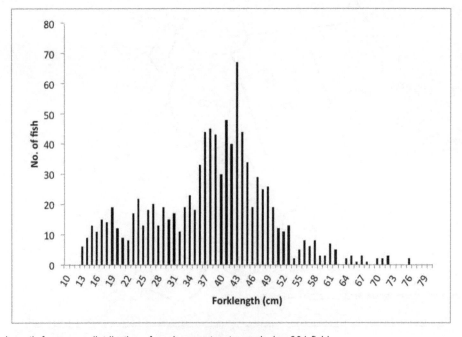

Figure 3. Length-frequency distribution of marine sea trout sample (n= 991 fish).

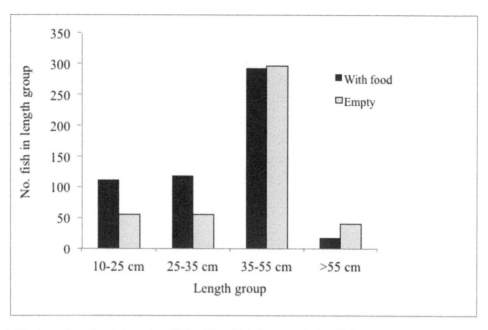

Figure 4. Numbers of sea trout stomachs with food from Irish Sea sample (n = 991) by ranked length groups. Includes all trawl sampled fish (n = 69), sampled in August 2011 ranging from 19-30 cm in length, where 54 (76%) of stomachs contained food.

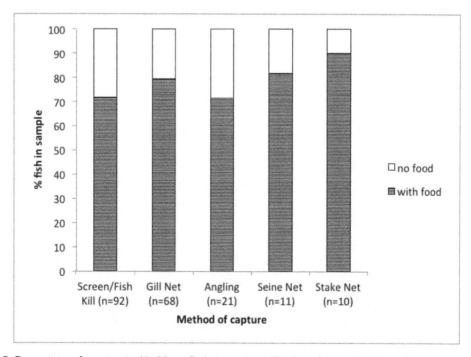

Figure 5. Percentage of sea trout with thin-walled stomachs, indicative of recent feeding when captured (n=222). Regurgitation likely where no food recorded.

REGURGITATION

Between 10 and 28.6% of a subsample of 222 sea trout captured using five different sampling methods, had empty, but nevertheless distended 'thin-walled' stomachs (Figure 5). Similar descriptions for empty stomachs from pike (*Esox lucius* L.) and perch (*Perca fluviatilis* L.) (Treasurer, 1988) were considered to be indicative of some degree of post-capture food regurgitation for samples collected using gill nets. Although there was evidence of regurgitation in the current study, no significant difference was observed between sampling methods ($\chi^2 = 4.326$, df=4, p>0.05) which meant that stomach content data could be pooled.

PREY ITEMS

The stomachs of 542 sea trout contained food and seven different prey categories were identified (Table 3). The sand eels were the most frequently recorded food item occurring in 55.7%*Fo* of stomachs. Sprat had the second highest frequency of occurrence (28.04%) followed by unidentified teleosts (21.8%).

Table 3. Prey items recorded in 542 sea trout stomachs from the Irish Sea, grouped by prey categories (n = number of stomachs with prey item; %Fo = percentage frequency occurrence; %*IOI* = percentage index of importance).

Prey category	*Species*	*No*	*% Fo*	*Total prey weight (W) (g)*	*Total % prey weight W(g)*	*% IOI*
Polychaeta		2	0.37	2.75	0.06	0.19
Other inverts.		23	4.24	5.86	0.13	1.92
Crustacea	*Crangon crangon/ Palaemon serratus*	3	0.55	7.01	0.16	0.31
	Brachyura sp.	2	0.37	0.83	0.02	0.17
	Amphipoda sp.	26	4.80	6.49	0.15	2.17
Pelagic teleosts	*Sprattus sprattus*	152	28.04	773.90	17.46	20.00
	Clupea harengus	8	1.48	351.50	7.93	4.14
	Scomber scombrus	1	0.18	41.83	0.94	0.50
	Unidentified clupeids	3	0.55	13.79	0.31	0.38
Ground-fish	*Ammodytes* sp.	302	55.72	2,724.15	61.47	51.51
	Taurulus bubalis	2	0.37	2.40	0.05	0.19
	benthic fish	1	0.18	2.40	0.05	0.10
Unidentified	Teleost remains	118	21.77	351.27	7.93	13.05
	Other material	48	8.86	147.80	3.33	5.36
Totals		691	127.49	4,431.98	100	100

PREY CATEGORY RICHNESS

All teleosts contributed 96.15% of the total diet by weight (%W) over the period comprising mainly of sand eels (61.5%) and sprat (17.46%) (Table 3). Minor constituents included polychaetes (0.06 % W), crustacea (0.32), other invertebrates (0.13) and unidentified 'other material' (3.33). Applying an Index of Importance (*IOI*) (Gray *et al.*, 1997) showed that sand eels dominated (51.1%), followed by sprat (20.0%) and unidentified teleosts (13.1%) (Table 3). Herring (*Clupea harengus* L.) and amphipods also feature, with respective IOIs of 4.14% and 2.17%. Sprat dominated stomach contents of trout from the pelagic trawl samples (98.26%W) (Table 4).

Table 4. Prey items recorded in 54 trawl caught sea trout with food.

Prey category	Species	No.	% Fo	Total Prey weight (W)(g)	Total % prey weight (W)(g)	% IOI
Pelagic teleosts	*S. sprattus*	54	100	215	98.26	96.46
Ground-fish	*Ammodytes* sp.	1	1.85	0.85	0.38	1.08
Unidentified teleosts	Remains	2	3.7	2.96	1.35	2.46
Total		57	105.5	218.81	100	100

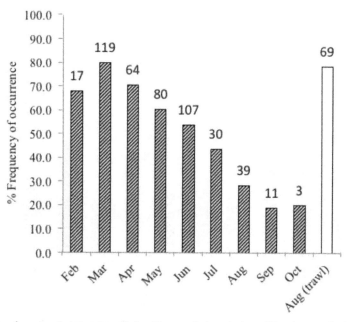

Figure 6. Percentage of sea trout stomachs with food by month from inshore/littoral zones (hatched bars) and August pelagic trawl sample (clear bar) from around the Irish Sea. Number of stomachs examined displayed over bars.

STOMACH FULLNESS & FEEDING INTENSITY

The percentage of sea trout stomachs with food from inshore/littoral waters reduced steadily from March to October (Figure 6). Peaking in March at 79.9%, fewer stomachs contained food by month with a continual decrease in summer months up to the lowest in September/October combined (mean 19.5%). In contrast, 78.3% of stomachs from offshore pelagic fish taken by trawling in a single August sampling event contained food (Figure 6). Pelagic sea trout (trawl sampled fish) had a significantly higher feeding intensity (stomach fullness $Fw = 2.53$) compared to fish in inshore/littoral areas (monthly range 0.65-1.84) (Figure 7) (ANOVA: $F_{1,536} = 48.1$, $p<0.01$).

FEEDING BY LENGTH GROUP

Within the four sea trout fork-length groupings teleosts (i.e. sand eels, sprat, herring, mackerel and other fish) dominated diet, where they comprised 91-97.5 %W of all prey categories (Table 5). Dietary species preference was significantly different between length groupings (NMDS, p < 0.005)(Table 6); partitioning by species showed that sprat dominated at 86.25% by weight in smaller sea trout (i.e. Group 1 length category 125-249 mm size) and were less prevalent in all larger length groupings, comprising only 1.24% abundance in the largest fish (Group 4 – fish >550 mm). Sand eels replaced sprat as the dominant food for fish in the 250–349 mm and 350–550 mm length ranges, comprising 59% and 74% respectively, and were less prominent at

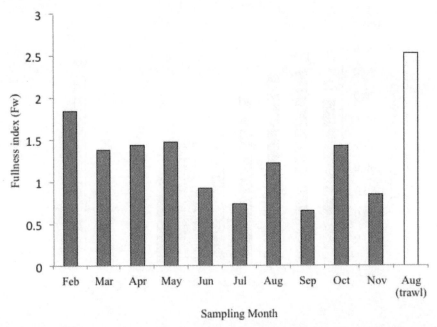

Figure 7. Mean stomach fullness index (Fw) for sea trout by month for inshore/littoral areas (mean Fw = 1.25) and August trawl sample (Mean Fw = 2.55).

Table 5. Percentage abundance of food item by weight (%*W*) in sea trout forklength (cm) categories.

Food item	Length Gp 1 125-249 mm	Length Gp 2 250-349 mm	Length Gp 3 350- 549 mm	Length Gp 4 > 550 mm
Sand eels	7.45	58.97	73.92	36.02
Sprat	86.25	27.38	14.95	1.24
Herring	0.00	0.00	1.25	37.49
Mackerel	0.00	0.00	0.00	4.96
Other fish & remains	1.67	11.04	7.34	11.43
Amphipods	2.21	0.25	0.01	0.00
Other Crustacea	0.10	1.20	0.03	0.00
Polychaetes	0.00	0.00	0.10	0.00
Other	2.31	1.16	2.40	8.86
Total %	*100*	*100*	*100*	*100*
Total % contribution of teleosts to diet	95.37	97.39	97.46	91.14

Table 6. Correlation between fitted environmental covariates and non-metric multidimensional scaling (NMDS) ordination of prey composition in sea trout stomachs. Samples from 2007 and 2008 were excluded from the analysis due to small sample size (n=15); four fish with body weight >5000g were excluded as outliers.

Covariance	R^2	p
Area (1, 2, 3 & 4)	0.0147	0.029*
Marine Zone	0.0404	0.192
Season (S, S, A & W)	0.0043	0.112
Year	0.0047	0.322
Month	0.0384	0.076
Sampling method	0.0085	0.510
Length grouping	0.0640	0.001***
Sex	0.0007	0.956

36% in the diet of larger fish in the >550 mm group. Herring featured only in the diet of larger fish (> 350 mm) and contributed almost 38% of total stomach content by weight in fish of >550 mm, where mackerel comprised almost 5%. Fish/fish remains contributed 1.67-11.43% of total diet and was dominated by fish remains where advanced digestion resulted in a lack of family/species differentiation.

Minor dietary constituents included crustacea (mainly amphipods) and polychaetes. Crustacea were prevalent in smaller fish up to 350 mm while polychaetes were an insignificant food item. Sea trout in the 125-150 mm length group were primarily feeding on amphipods (Figure 8) which were substantially less prevalent in larger fish. Fish (sprat) contributed approximately 33% of the diet of the smallest sea trout (125-150 mm) and a predominantly fish-based diet was evident for all fish > 150 mm where fish exceeded 80% of stomach content for all length groups (Figure 8).

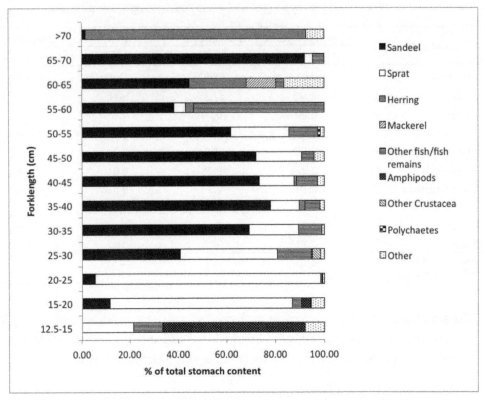

Fig. 8. Composition of diet by percentage weight (%W) within discrete length groupings (cm).

SPATIAL FEEDING PATTERN

Fish dominated diet by weight in inshore zones (mean 92.1 %W, range 45.9-100%) and constituted 100% of diet from all trawl sampled zone sites (Figure 9). Sand eels were prevalent in feeding fish from inshore zones sampled that included the east coast of Ireland, the Isle of Man and zones along the English and Welsh coast (Figure 9). On average sand eels comprised 52.6%W from feeding fish at all 14 inshore zones. Sprat were less common in samples (mean occurrence of 22.3%) and mainly from fish in MZ07 (east coast of Ireland), MZ09 (Scotland coast/Solway, MZ11 (England coast) and north Wales (MZ13). Other fish comprised 11.12% (mean) and dominated in MZ23 (Isle of Man) only. Sprat comprised 98.3%W of diet in trawl samples.

'Area' (1, 2, 3 & 4) was significantly correlated with ordinations of sea trout prey composition by weight (NMDS, p<0.05). No other tested covariates were significantly correlated (Table 6). Bray-Curtis dissimilarity in prey composition between tested pairs of areas was consistently explained by weight of sprat and sand eels consumed, except for the comparison between Areas 1 (east coast of Ireland) and 4 (west and South Wales, Isle of Man), where stomach content in the former included greater weights of unidentified 'remains' (Table 7).

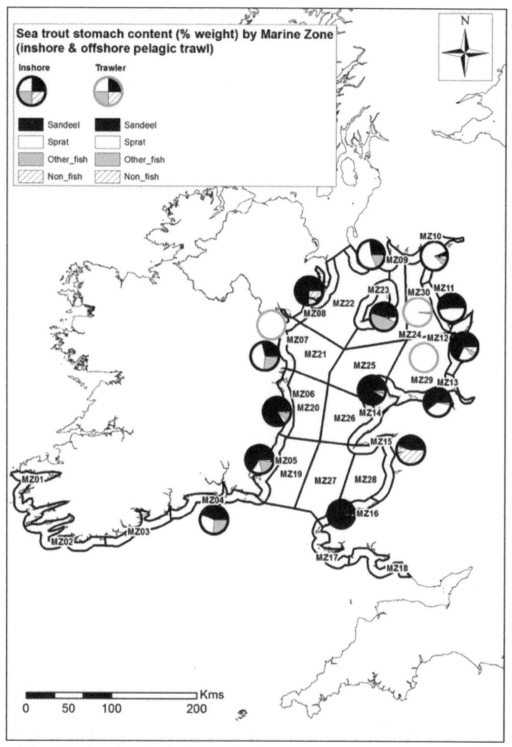

Figure 9. Proportion of prey items (sand eels, sprat, other fish and invertebrates (non-fish)) by weight for total sample by Marine Zone. MZ29 and MZ30 are trawl samples. Area 1 = MZ04 to MZ08, Area 2 = MZ09 to MZ13, Area 3 = MZ29 & MZ30 & trawled fish in MZ07, Area 4 = MZ14 to MZ18, MZ23 to MZ24.

Table 7. Cumulative contributions of given prey items to at least 80% of Bray-Curtis dissimilarity in stomach contents between tested pairs of Irish Sea areas.

Comparison	Influential species	% Contribution	Cumulative Contributions %
Areas 2:1	Sand eels	0.589	0.589
	Sprat	0.223	0.812
	Teleost remains	0.120	0.932
Areas 2:4	Sand eels	0.540	0.540
	Sprat	0.212	0.752
	Teleost remains	0.062	0.814
Areas 2:3	Sprat	0.758	0.768
	Sand eels	0.148	0.916
	Teleost remains	0.055	0.971
Areas 1:4	Sand eels	0.644	0.644
	Teleost remains	0.100	0.744
	Sprat	0.086	0.830
Areas 1:3	Sand eels	0.481	0.481
	Sprat	0.401	0.882
	Teleost remains	0.082	0.964
Areas 4:3	Sand eels	0.483	0.480
	Sprat	0.377	0.860
	Teleost remains	0.039	0.899

DISCUSSION

This work represents the first large scale seasonal study of sea trout diet in the Irish Sea (situated between 52° and 54°N) and complements previous studies in temperate latitudes (Pemberton, 1976; Fahy, 1983, 1985) and several from higher latitudes (minimum > 57°N up to the Arctic Circle) (Grønvik & Klemetsen, 1987; Lyse *et al.*, 1998; Knutsen *et al.*, 2001, 2004; Rikardsen *et al.*, 2005, 2006, 2007a). The current study also provides a contemporaneous comparison of inshore littoral versus offshore pelagic diet, albeit confined to one sampling month. Data on diet of pelagic sea trout are limited although it has been studied in June and July in northern Norway by Rikardsen & Amundsen (2005).

Fish was the dominant prey item in sea trout from the Irish Sea and this is consistent with other studies (Grønvik & Klemetsen, 1987; Knutsen *et al.*, 2001, 2004; Rikardsen & Amundsen, 2005; Rikardsen *et al.*, 2006, 2007a; Knudsen *et al.*, 2011). Migratory trout in the Irish Sea, irrespective of size, adopt a diet with a high fish content on entry into marine waters; fish comprised >80%*W* of diet in trout >150mm FL. An increase in the prevalence of fish in sea trout diet with increasing size is well known (Pemberton, 1976; Fahy, 1985; Rikardsen *et al.*, 2007a); in the present study, smaller fish > 125 mm, likely 1+ year old fish, were piscivorous. Pemberton (1976) stated that smolts in the 150-180mm size range were not sufficiently large to feed on fish but Fahy (1985) and Rikardsen *et al.* (2007a) found substantial percentages of fish in post- smolts > 150mm length. Larval fish dominated Atlantic salmon smolt diet in Norwegian fjords, where average smolt forklength ranged from 119-154 mm (Rikardsen *et al.*, 2004). Although piscivory has been documented occasionally in 0-group trout, possibly to reduce competition with fish in the same size range, Sanchez-Hernandez *et al.* (2013) note that it is generally first manifested in trout in the 20-30cm range. Rikardsen *et al.* (2007a) found that sea trout, sampled between June and August in a Norwegian fjord, were fully piscivorous at ≥250 mm, which they attributed to the local abundance of herring larvae, and indicative of dietary selectivity. Early adoption of a fish diet at post-smolt stage and full piscivory (>80%*W*) in older fish, as observed for sea trout in the Irish Sea, is a highly beneficial feeding strategy because of the high energy value of marine prey, particularly fish (Rikardsen *et al.*, 2004). The current study highlighted the importance of smaller pelagic species like sand eels and sprat in sea trout diet in inshore and offshore habitats. Sand eels, which are partly pelagic, were the most prevalent prey, occurring in over 50% by weight of all stomachs with food; other studies also recorded a high prevalence of sand eels in sea trout (Grønvik & Klemetsen, 1987; Rikardsen *et al.* 2007a) and salmon post-smolt (Rickardsen *et al.*, 2004) diet. Sprat was the second most frequently recorded dietary item (28% of all samples) and, while it was a feature in a small number of studies (Fahy, 1983; Pemberton, 1976; Knutsen *et al.*, 2001), prevalence was lower. While herring was an important component in studies in Norwegian waters (Grønvik & Klemetsen, 1987; Rikardsen *et al.*, 2006, 2007a) a low frequency occurrence was noted in Irish Sea trout diet where it was only recorded in larger sea trout (>350mm length) and dominated diet (%*W*) in fish >550 mm. Seasonal abundance and availability, and prey size are likely to influence diet and the high prevalence of herring in sea trout diet from Area 4 (Isle of Man and mid-Wales) (Figure 10) most likely reflects the availability of herring in this part of the Irish Sea, and supports the characterisation of sea trout as opportunistic feeders (Elliott, 1997; Klemetsen *et al.,* 2003; Rikardsen & Amundsen, 2005).

In contrast to other studies diet diversity in the Irish Sea was limited. Invertebrates (including Crustacea and Polychaetes) comprised <5% *IOI*, (Grey *at al.,* 1997) and were a minor constituent. Only in smaller post-smolts (125-150mm) were Crustacea in any way prominent whereas Crustacea and polychaetes were important dietary elements in fish of all sizes in other studies (Rikardsen *et al.*, 2006, 2007; Knutsen *et al.*, 2001). In their review, Thorstad *et al*, 2016 noted that polychaetes and terrestrial insects may contribute frequently to sea trout diet in estuarine and inshore habitats, whereas fish are prominent in the pelagic diet of sea trout. The prevalence of fish in sea trout diet in inshore sites and offshore pelagic sites observed in the current study may indicate a preference for fish as prey, where available, irrespective of feeding location.

The feeding intensity of littoral trout (as indicated by the proportion of stomachs with food by month), peaked in spring and tapered off in summer months and was lowest in early winter months, a pattern also observed by Pemberton (1976). Knutsen *et al.,* (2001) attributed such feeding intensity in spring, by smolts on entry into marine waters and by adults that had

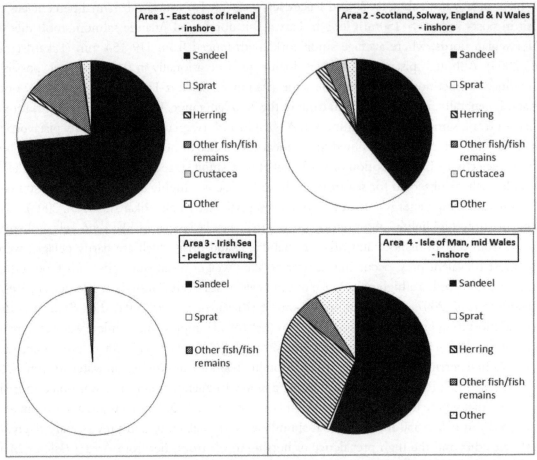

Figure 10. Diet composition by 'Area' by weight (%W). Area 1 n=272, Area 2 n=145, Area 3 n=56 & Area 4 n=69.

spawned the previous autumn/winter returning to sea, to a heavy feeding strategy which would likely have restored lowered energy levels.

Differences in the proportions of the main food items, sand eels and sprat, were observed in sea trout from inshore zones (Figure 10), but the major contrast was the dominance of sprat in the diet of sea trout in the offshore pelagic zone (Area 3). Sea trout in the marine environment mainly tend to occupy the upper 1–3 m range in the water column (Lyse *et al.*, 1998; Rikardsen *et al.*, 2007a). The response of sea trout to the apparent abundance of sprat in the pelagic zone, where this prey species dominated the trawl sample by-catch, was a highly selective diet (>98% *W* sprat) focussed on a spatially and temporally abundant food source. The prevalence of sprat in trawl caught sea trout from three discrete sites (grouped as Area 3) (Figure 9), demonstrated a consistent feeding strategy within the pelagic zone. Coupled with the highest level of stomach fullness documented over this study (Figure 7), this was further evidence that pelagic sea trout, all small immature fish, were feeding opportunistically. This was further emphasized by the high percentage of stomachs with food compared to inshore feeding fish (Figure 6) and characterised the highly intensive nature of feeding observed for pelagic sea trout. The similarities between observations made by Rikardsen & Amundsen (2005) and this study support the proposition that smaller sea trout use the pelagic zone during their migration where suitable prey is available. Eldoy *et al.* (2015) found that all size classes of sea trout were likely to undertake long-distance migrations (i.e. >10 km from river mouth) into pelagic waters. However, other studies (Jensen *et al.*, 2014; Knutsen *et al.*, 2001) recorded that larger sea trout migrated longer distances which they related to enhanced feeding opportunities on pelagic fish. While the current study suggests a size-related feeding strategy the potential effect of methodological limitations of trawling, particularly the likely differential capacities of larger sea trout to evade capture by trawl, must be acknowledged. This could be tested by undertaking further studies of pelagic trout using enhanced trawling methods to determine and assess the distribution and feeding of larger sea trout in offshore habitats.

Sea trout diet varied with size as reported by Knutsen *et al.* (2001). Selection of prey is dependent on predator size, where features such as mouth gape is a limiting factor (Wankowski, 1979). Consequently, apart from some specialist feeders, prey size tends to increase with the increased size of the predator. Food preference progressed from smaller to larger prey such as sand eel and sprat in larger fish. The larger prey items, such as mackerel or herring, were found only in the stomachs of sea trout > 350 mm in length (Table 5). The selection of larger prey items as sea trout grow represents a more cost–effective feeding strategy because less relative energy is required to hunt a small number of larger prey species than a large number of smaller prey items. Hislop *et al.* (1991) showed that sprat have a higher calorific value per mean length of fish compared to sand eels; but such variation is inconsequential in relation to the variability of prey abundance which appears to be a more important influence on foraging selection and efficiency in an opportunistic feeder like sea trout.

Overall, sand eels were the most prevalent food of sea trout in the Irish Sea, possibly reflecting their abundance relative to sprat, although high quality distribution and abundance data are lacking. However, a geographical separation of prey consumption was noted from north to south. Sea trout in inshore waters of Dundalk Bay (MZ07), the Solway coast (MZ09 & 10), around North West England (MZ11), North Wales (MZ13) and in the pelagic zones, had ingested proportionally higher quantities of sprat compared to other areas where sand eels were the dominant prey item. This separation of prey consumption was loosely associated with known sand eel habitat types. Observed sand eel distribution was not, however, obviously related with presence in sea trout diet at the low resolution of available sand eel survey data. In contrast, the occurrence of sprat in the diet was closely linked with their observed distribution (Heessen *et al.*, 2015; ICES, 2015). In that context the significant 'Area' effect on diet may be due primarily to the spatial distribution of prey species. It is possible that seasonal variation of prey abundance affected diet. For example, although sand eels comprised the majority of the sea trout diet around North Wales (Figure 9), some sprat were found in sea trout stomachs during the winter months when they are known to become abundant in coastal waters in other parts of the Irish Sea (Molloy, 1967; Plirú *et al.*, 2012).

The Irish Sea ecosystem has attracted less attention than areas such as the North Sea, with less collation and integration of existing data (ICES, 2008). Data on distribution of key prey species in the Irish Sea are sparse and unsuitable in terms of undertaking robust spatial or temporal comparisons on availability to predators. Nonetheless, time-series survey indices (trawl catch rate) for the Celtic Sea Ecoregion (Heessen *et al.*, 2015), which includes the Irish Sea, showed that sand eels and sprat average abundance from 2010-2012 was relatively high which was consistent with the dietary preferences of sea trout observed over the course of this study. As keystone prey species both are an important components of the marine trophic web upon which sea trout, other marine fish and bird species depend and should be a focus for monitoring. Improved survey data has emerged for the Irish Sea which is likely to support development of scientific advice for sprat (ICES, 2015). However, detailed monitoring of sandeels requires specialised gear types and sampling effort (Greenstreet *et al.*, 2010; Heessen *et al.*, 2015) with consequent demands on sampling resources.

This study provides new information on the marine diet of sea trout and specifically alludes to the potential value of exploring the relationship between the spatial distribution of preferred prey species and their partial coincidence with prey habitat types. Clearly, more systematic, stratified and spatially extensive data on prey availability, marine habitats and the nature and extent of linkages in the sea trout food web would greatly improve understanding of sea trout marine ecology and their response to wider ecosystem changes.

ACKNOWLEDGEMENTS

Staff at Inland Fisheries Ireland, Bangor University, the Environmental Agency, Natural Resources Wales, Dept. of Environment, Food and Agriculture, Isle of Man, Nith District Salmon Fisheries Board (NSFB), Galloway Fisheries Trust (GFT), River Annan District Salmon Fishery Board (ASFB) and Buccleuch Estate (Border Esk) are acknowledged for their considerable efforts in collecting marine samples. Thanks are also due to commercial fishermen, particularly the crews of trawlers Iuda Naofa and Emily Rose, and anglers for sampling and/or providing samples. The project was part-funded under the Ireland-Wales Territorial Co-operation Programme 2007-2013 (INTERREG 4A). Additional funding, provided by the River Annan District Salmon Fishery Board, the Nith District Salmon Fishery Board and the Galloway Fisheries Trust, is gratefully acknowledged.

REFERENCES

Amundsen, P-A., Gabler, H-M. & Staldvik, F.J. (1996) A new approach to graphical analysis of feeding strategy from stomach contents data – modification of the Costello (1990) method. *Journal of Fish Biology*, **48**, 607-614.

Eldøy SH, Davidsen JG, Thorstad EB, Whoriskey F, Aarestrup K, Næsje TF, Rønning L, Sjursen AD, Rikardsen AH, Arnekleiv JV (2015) Marine migration and habitat use of anadromous brown trout (*Salmo trutta*). *Canadian Journal of Fisheries Fish & Aquatic Sciences* **72**:1–13

Elliott, J.M. (1997). Stomach contents of adult sea trout caught in six English rivers. *Journal of Fish Biology,* **50,** 1129-32.

Fahy, E. (1980b). Prey selection by young trout fry (Salmo trutta). *Journal of Zoology,* **190,** 27-37.

Fahy, E. (1981). Sea-trout and their fisheries from the Dublin Fishery District. *Fisheries Bulletin No. 5.* Dublin, 13 pp.

Fahy, E. (1983). Food and gut parasite burden of migratory trout Salmo trutta L. in the sea. *The Irish Naturalists' Journal,* 11-8

Fahy, E. (1985). Feeding, growth and parasites of trout, *Salmo trutta*, from Mulroy Bay, an Irish sea lough. *Irish Fisheries Investigations Series A,* **25,** 3-12.

Gray A.E, Mulligan T.J. & Hannah, R.W. (1997). Food habits, occurrence and population structure of the bat ray, *Myliobatis californica*, in Humboldt Bay, California. *Environmental Biology of Fishes,* **49,** 227–238.

Greenstreet, S. P. R., Holland, G. J., Guirey, E. J., Armstrong, E., Fraser, H. M. & Gibb, I. M. 2010. Combining hydroacoustic seabed survey and grab sampling techniques to assess "local" sandeel population abundance. ICES *Journal of Marine Science,* **67**: 971–984.

Grønvik, S. & Klemetsen, A. 1987. Marine food and diet overlap of co-occurring Arctic charr *Salvelinus alpinus* (L.), brown trout *Salmo trutta* L. and Atlantic salmon *S. salar* L. off Senja, N. Norway. *Polar Biology,* **7,** 73–177.

Gross, M.R., Coleman R.M. & McDowall R, M. (1988) Aquatic productivity and the evolution of diadromous fish migration. *Science,* **239,** 1291–1293.

Heessen, H.J.L., Daan, N. and Ellis J. R (eds.) (2015) Fish Atlas of the Celtic Sea, North Sea and Baltic Sea. Wageningen Academic Publishers, The Netherlands. ISBN: 978-90-8686-266-5

Hislop, J.R.G, Harris, M.P. and Smith, J.G.M. (1991) Variation in the calorific value and total energy content of the lesser sand eel (Ammodytes marinus) and other fish preyed on by seabirds. *Journal of Zoology,* **224,** 501-507

Howarth, M. J (2005) Hydrography of the Irish Sea. SEA6 Technical Report, POL Internal Document 174. Report to Department of Trade and Industry, United Kingdom.

Hyslop, E.J. (1980). Stomach content analysis—a review of their methods and their applications. *Journal of Fish Biology,* **17**:411–429

ICES. (2008) Report of the Working Group for Regional Ecosystem Description 25-29 Feb 2008 Copenhagen. ICES CM2008/ACOM:47.

ICES. 2015. Report of the Herring Assessment Working Group for the Area South of 62°N (HAWG), 10-19 March 2015, ICES HQ, Copenhagen, Denmark. ICES M 2015/ACOM: 06.850 pp.

Jensen, J.L.A., Rikardsen, A.H., Thorstad, E.B., Suhr, A.H., Davidsen, J.G. & Primicerio, R. 2014. Water temperatures influence the marine area use *Salvelinus alpinus* and *Salmo trutta. Journal of Fish Biology* **84,** 1640–1653. doi:10.1111/jfb. 12366

Jensen, J.L.A. & Rikardsen, A.H. (2008). Do northern riverine anadromous Arctic charr Salvelinus alpinus and sea trout Salmo trutta overwinter in estuarine and marine waters? *Journal of Fish Biology* **73**, 1810-8

Jonsson, B. (1985). Life History Patterns of Freshwater Resident and Sea-Run Migrant Brown Trout in Norway. *Transactions of the American Fisheries Society,* **114**, 182-94.

Klemetsen, A., Amundsen, P.A., Dempson, J.B., Jonsson, B., Jonsson, N., O'Connell, M.F. & Mortensen, E. (2003). Atlantic salmon Salmo salar L., brown trout Salmo trutta L. and Arctic charr Salvelinus alpinus (L.): a review of aspects of their life histories. *Ecology of Freshwater Fish,* **12**, 1-59.

Knudsen, R., Amundsen, P-A. and Rikardsen, A. H. (2011), Individual feeding specialisation of a naïve vs. veteran predators. *Ecology of Freshwater Fish*, **20**, 522–528.

Knutsen, J.A., Knutsen, H., Olsen., E.M. & Jonsson, B. (2004). Marine feeding of anadromous *Salmo trutta* during winter. Journal of Fish Biology, 64, 89-99.

Knutsen, J.A., Knutsen, H., Gjøsæter, J. & Jonsson, B. (2001). Food of anadromous brown trout at sea. *Journal of Fish Biology* **59**, 533-43.

Lyse, A.A., Stefansson, S.O. & Fernö, A. (1998). Behaviour and diet of sea trout post-smolts in a Norwegian fjord system. *Journal of Fish Biology,* **52**, 923-36.

Milner, N.J., Elliott, J.M., Armstrong, J.D., Gardiner, R., Welton, J.S. & Ladle, M. (2003). The natural control of salmon and trout populations in streams. *Fisheries Research,* **62**, 111-25.

Molloy, J. (1967). Irish Sprats and Sandeels. *Irish Fisheries Investigations* Series B (Marine) No 2. Fisheries Division, Department of Agriculture and Fisheries,) Dublin. 18pp

O'Grady, M.F. (1981) Some direct gillnet selectivity tests for brown trout populations. *Irish Fisheries Investigations,* Series A (Freshwater), No. 22, 9pp.

Plirú, A., van der Kooij, J., Engelhard, G. H., Fox, C. J., Milligan, S. P., and Hunter, E. 2012. Sprat feeding behaviour, selective predation, and impact on plaice egg mortality. – *ICES Journal of Marine Science*, 69: 1019–1029

Pemberton, R. (1976). Sea trout in North Argyll sea lochs: II. diet. *Journal of Fish Biology* **9**, 195-208.

Pratten, D. J. & Shearer, W. M. (1983), Sea Trout of the North Esk. *Aquaculture Research*, **14**, 49–65.

Rikardsen, A.H. & Amundsen, P.A. (2005). Pelagic marine feeding of Arctic charr and sea trout. *Journal of Fish Biology,* **66**, 1163-6.

Rikardsen, A. H., Haugland, M., Bjørn, P. A., Finstad, B., Knudsen, R., Dempson, B., Holst, J. C., Hvidsten, N. A. & Holm, M. (2004). Geographical differences in marine feeding of Atlantic salmon post-smolts in Norwegian fjords. *Journal of Fish Biology* **64**, 1655–1679. doi: 10.1111/j.1095-8649.2004.00425.x

Rikardsen, A.H., Amundsen, P-A., Knudsen, R. & Sandring, S. (2006). Seasonal marine feeding and body condition of sea trout (*Salmo trutta*) at its northern distribution. *ICES Journal of Marine Science,* **63**, 466-75.

Rikardsen, A.H., Dempson, J.B., Amundsen, P.A., Bjørn, P.A., Finstad, B. & Jensen, A.J. (2007a). Temporal variability in marine feeding of sympatric Arctic charr and sea trout. *Journal of Fish Biology,* **70**, 837-852.

Rikardsen, A.H., Diserus, O.H., Elliott, J.M., Dempson, J.B., Sturlaugsson, J. & Jensen, A.J. (2007b). The marine temperature and depth preferences of Arctic charr (*Salvelinus alpinus*) and sea trout (*Salmo trutta*), as recorded by data storage tags. *Fisheries Oceanography,* **16**, 436-46.

Sánchez-Hernández, J., Servia, M.J., Vieira-Lanero, R., Cobo, F. 2013. Ontogenetic Dietary Shifts in a Predatory Freshwater Fish Species: The Brown Trout as an Example of a Dynamic Fish Species. In: *New Advances and Contributions to Fish Biology*.(Hakan Türker. Ed.). InTech, 51000 Rijeka, Croatia. ISBN 978-953-51-0909-9

Sheehan, T. F., Renkawitz, M. D. and Brown, R. W. (2011). Surface trawl survey for U.S. origin Atlantic salmon *Salmo salar*. *Journal of Fish Biology,* **79**: 374–398.

Sturlaugsson, J. & Johannsson, M. (1996). Migratory Pattern of wild sea trout (Salmo trutta L.) in SE-Iceland recorded by data storage tags. *ICES CM 1996/* M: 5, 16 pp.

Sturlaugsson, J. & Johannsson, M. (2015). Migration study of wild sea trout (Salmo trutta L.) in SE-Iceland: Depth movements and water temperature recorded by data storage tags in freshwater and marine environment. *Proceedings of Fifth European Conference on Wildlife Telemetry.* Strasbourg, France, 25-30 August 1996, 12pp.

Thorstad E.B., Todd C.D., Uglem, I., Bjørn, P.A., Gargan, P.G., Vollset, K.W., Halttunen, E., Kålås, S., Berg, M. & Finstad, B (2015) Effects of salmon lice *Lepeophtheirus salmonis* on wild sea trout *Salmo trutta*—a literature review. *Aquacult Environ Interact,* 7, 91-113Thorstad, E.B., Todd, C.D., Uglem, I., Bjorn, P.A., Gargan, P. G., Vollset, K.W., Halttunen, E., Kålås, S., Berg, M. & Finstad, B. (2016) Marine life of the sea trout. *Marine Biology.* **163**, 47. doi:10.1007/s00227-016-2820-3

Treasurer, J. W. (1988). Measurement of regurgitation in feeding studies of predatory fishes. *Journal of Fish Biology,* **33**, 267–271.

Went, A.E.J. (1962). Irish Sea Trout: A Review of Investigations to Date. *Scientific Proceedings of the Royal Dublin Society*, Series A. 10, 265-298.

Wankowski, J.W.J. (1979) Morphological limitations, prey size selectivity, and growth response of juvenile Atlantic salmon*, Salmo salar*. *Journal of Fish Biology.* **14**, 89-100.

ELECTRONIC REFERENCES

Oksanen, J., Blanchet, F.G., Kindt, R., Legendre, P., Minchin, P.R., O'Hara, R.B., Simpson, G.L., Solymos, P., Henry, M., Stevens, H. & Wagner, H. (2016). vegan: Community Ecology Package. R package version 2.3-3. *Available from:* https://CRAN.R-project.org/package=vegan

R Core Team (2015). R: A language and environment for statistical computing. R Foundation for Statistical Computing, Vienna, Austria. URL. *Available from:* https://www.R-project.org/.

Migration behaviour of sea trout (*Salmo trutta, L.*) in a large sub-arctic river system: evidence of a two-year spawning migration.

P. ORELL[1], J. ERKINARO[1], T. KANNIAINEN[1] & J. KUUSELA[2]

[1]*Natural Resources Institute Finland, P.O.B. 413, FI-90014 Oulu, Finland.*
[2]*Natural Resources Institute Finland, Nuorgamintie 7, FI-99980 Utsjoki, Finland.*

ABSTRACT

The migratory behaviour and in-river dispersal of sea trout (*Salmo trutta* L.) was investigated in the large subarctic River Teno, Northern Fennoscandia, by tagging 154 individuals with radio transmitters over three consecutive years. Two clearly different migratory groups were observed consisting of either immature migrants or spawning migrants. Most immature sea trout ascended the lower reaches (≤70 km) of the river in late summer and remained for a long overwintering period (~8-10 months) with only limited movements. A return migration to the estuarine feeding grounds took place in late May and June. By contrast, most spawning migrations of mature trout took two years: with upstream migration starting in late summer, followed by a long and stationary overwintering phase in the main stem and then a further continuation of their upstream migration next spring and summer. Spawning areas were exclusively located in small tributaries and streams, including the uppermost headwaters some 300 km from the estuary. Spent sea trout (= kelts) descended from the tributaries to the main stem soon after spawning for overwintering and their seaward migration then took place the next spring. Both the telemetry results and scale reading indicated that most repeat spawning occurred biennially. Fishing was targeted at sea trout throughout the Teno system at different migration phases. Exploitation of the spawning migrants occurred during three consecutive seasons and was occasionally very high.

***Keywords*:** sea trout; River Teno; management; migration; overwintering; radio telemetry.

INTRODUCTION

Within its natural distribution range, the brown trout (*Salmo trutta*) displays both resident and anadromous forms (Klemetsen *et al.*, 2003; Jonsson & Jonsson, 2006). Resident trout spend their life in fresh water, where they may spend their entire life in small streams, or they may move between their natal rearing sites and different lakes and sections of river within the same catchment (*c.f.* Jonsson & Jonsson, 2011). The life cycle of anadromous migratory trout (= sea trout) consist of juvenile phase in its natal river followed by smoltification and downstream migration to feeding areas in the estuary/sea before returning to its natal river of origin for spawning (Klemetsen *et al.*, 2003; Jonsson & Jonsson, 2011). In some rivers, immature sea trout may migrate from the sea to overwinter in fresh water and then return to their marine feeding areas the following spring (Jonsson, 1985; Berg & Berg, 1989; Thomsen *et al.*, 2007). This movement between fresh water and marine habitats may occur repeatedly before maturation. In the southern parts of their distribution area, sea trout can attain maturity after only one summer in the sea (.0+), while most individuals in the north spend 2 – 3 summers at sea before maturing and returning to fresh water to spawn (Jonsson & L'Abée-Lund, 1993).

Both immature and mature sea trout usually return to fresh water in summer and autumn (Jonsson, 1985), although individual sea trout in some rivers may ascend throughout the year (Jonsson & Jonsson, 2011). In large rivers, upstream migration of mature trout may occur many months before spawning, whereas fish in small streams may ascend shortly before spawning (Klemetsen *et al.*, 2003); which usually takes place with falling temperature between September and December depending on the geographical location and environmental conditions of the particular system (Jonsson & Jonsson, 2011). Spawning requirements of brown trout are generally similar to those of Atlantic salmon, *Salmo salar*, but with trout more frequently spawning in tributaries and smaller streams (Milner *et al.*, 2006; Louhi *et al.*, 2008).

The general life cycle and the migratory behaviour of sea trout has been extensively studied and is quite well documented for most of the species distribution area (*see* Harris & Milner, 2006; Jonsson & Jonsson, 2011). However, only limited knowledge is available from populations inhabiting the northernmost parts of the distribution area (Berg & Berg, 1989; Berg & Jonsson, 1990; Jensen & Rikardsen, 2012). This knowledge gap is particularly evident for large river systems because most of the earlier studies were conducted in small or medium sized rivers (e.g. Jonsson, 1985; Berg & Berg, 1989; Aarestrup & Jepsen, 1998; Finstad *et al.*, 2005; Jensen & Rikardsen, 2012). In the northern part of their range, where human impacts on catchments and rivers are generally less than in the south, vital salmonid populations still exist in their natural surroundings making them important reference systems. These northern rivers may sustain potentially important sea trout populations with unique, but yet undefined, life-history characteristics that may have significant implications for their conservation and pro-active management.

The main aims of this study were to investigate the in-river migration behaviour and dispersal of both immature and mature sea trout in the large River Teno system in the most northerly part of their natural distribution range in Northern Europe and also to determine the location of the spawning areas and rates of exploitation in this vast river system with a very large sympatric Atlantic salmon population complex (Vähä *et al.*, 2007; 2008) and diverse rod and net fisheries (Niemelä, 2004).

STUDY AREA AND METHODS

STUDY AREA

The sub-arctic River Teno (= Tana in Norwegian) is a border river between Finland and Norway (70° N, 28° E) that drains into the Barents Sea through the Tana Fjord (Figure 1). The system has a drainage area of 16,386 km² and the uppermost headwater extends 350 km from the river mouth. The Teno watershed represents one of the last remaining large Atlantic salmon and sea trout rivers. It contains an abundant and virtually pristine catchment area with more than 1,200 km of main river and tributaries accessible to migrating adult salmonids (Niemelä *et al.*, 2005). Annual estimated catches from the various fisheries range between 60-250 tonnes for salmon and between 2-10 tonnes for sea trout (Natural Resources Institute Finland, *unpublished data*). Because of the northerly location of the Teno system, the environmental conditions are extreme. Ice covers the river for about 6-7 months from October/November until May and is followed by spring floods in May and early June with flows occasionally exceeding 3,000 m³/s (mean annual discharge c.200 m³/s). Water temperatures vary considerably: during the winter (October to early May), they are constantly <1° C, but may occasionally exceed 20° C during summer (June-August). Polar-day conditions prevail over 2.5 months from mid-May until the end of July with 24 hours of sunlight.

CATCHING AND TAGGING

Sea trout (n =154) were caught and tagged in three different areas at different phases of their migration between 2011 and 2013 (Figure 1 & Table 1). The mean length of tagged trout was 49.3 cm ranging from 33.5 cm to 78.0 cm. The mean river age was 5.3 years, with most individuals (89%) smolting at an age of four to six years. The mean sea-age (number of sea-summers) of unspawned (maiden) sea trout (n =107) at tagging was 1.8 years (range 0-4 years). In addition to these maiden fish, 41 repeat spawners with up to three previous spawning marks on their scales and 5 freshwater resident trout were also tagged.

A majority of the fish (n =110) were caught on their feeding grounds at the estuary (=river mouth) of the Teno between early June and mid-August. A further 33 fish were caught from

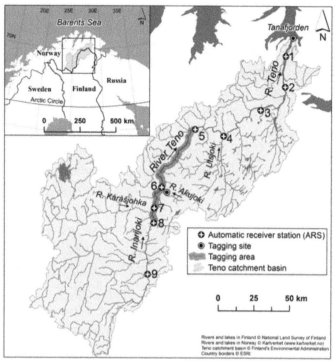

Figure 1. The River Teno system showing the locations of the three tagging sites/areas and the nine automatic receiver stations (ARS) used in this study.

Table 1. Numbers of sea trout tagged, with mean and range of length (mm) and weight (g) of tagged fish from different capture sites in 2011-2013. [*Fish were not weighed in 2011.*]

Year	Tagging Site	No. Fish Tagged	Length of Fish (mm)		Weight of fish (g)	
			Mean	*Range*	*Mean*	*Range*
	Estuary	32	436	335 - 615	n/d	n/d
2011	Main Stem	6	453	465 - 690	n/d	n/d
	Akujoki	5	524	420 - 654	n/d	n/d
	Estuary	40	494	380 - 655	1226	500 - 3450
2012	Main Stem	14	564	470 - 780	1850	700 - 5100
	Akujoki	6	517	435 - 620	1425	700 - 2200
2013	Estuary	38	478	365 - 715	1108	450 - 2900
	Main Stem	13	540	465 - 650	1715	1000 - 2850

the overwintering areas in the upper-mid reaches of the Teno main stem (135 – 222 km from the estuary) between late-May and mid-June and 11 fish were caught from the tributary River Akujoki (192 km from the estuary: catchment area 193 km²) between June and September before the start of the spawning season (Figure 1). In the Teno estuary, all fish were caught by rod-and-line, whereas in the Teno main stem tagging area a proportion of the trout were caught with drift nets and in the River Akujoki all fish were captured by gill nets. After capture, fish were placed in a holding cage close to the catching area for 1-24 hours before tagging.

All sea trout were tagged internally to avoid a possible increase in the fishing mortality linked to external tagging (Rikardsen & Thorstad, 2006) by their capture in the extensive net fisheries operating in the Teno system. After the settling period, each anaesthetised (buffered MS-222-solution, <100 mg/1) fish was placed ventral side up in a plastic tube specially designed for tagging purposes before a 20 – 30 mm longitudinal incision was made in the middle of the fish between the pectoral and abdominal fins. The transmitter (Advanced Telemetry Systems Inc., model F1580, weight 3.9 g in air, battery capacity 440 days or model F1835, weight 14.0 g in air, battery capacity 600 days) was inserted into the fish and a hypodermic needle was inserted c. 25 mm caudally from the incision to run the transmitter antenna out of the body cavity. The incision was closed with one or two non-absorbable polyamide monofilament sutures (Ethicon, model EH7798H 2-0; or Ethicon EH7794H 3-0) with a secure surgical stitch (triple-throw). All fish were also tagged with external plastic tipped dart tags (Hallprint Pty Ltd, model PDL) below the dorsal fin. Total length (measured from tip of nose to tip of tail) of the tagged fish was measured to the nearest 0.5 cm, weight was measured to the nearest 50 g and a scale sample was taken for age and growth analysis. The whole tagging procedure lasted 2.0–2.5 min per fish. Tagged fish were placed in a holding cage for 15-30 min to recover from tagging before releasing them into the river. No tagging mortality occurred prior to release and all individuals appeared vigorous and active when released.

TRACKING OF FISH

Tracking of the tagged fish was undertaken at a series of automatic receiver stations (ARS) and by manual tracking. An ARS consisted of an automatic data-logging receiver (ATS model R4500S, 140-144 MHz) connected to either a 6-element or 9-element Yagi antenna. ARSs were installed and maintained at nine fixed locations (Figure 1) throughout the study period (27th May 2011 – 15th October 2014). The lowermost ARS (no. 1: *see* Figure 1) was situated slightly above the tidal limit (15 km from the estuary) and the other ARSs were positioned at biologically and/or logistically relevant sites in areas close to large rapids and tributary outlets with easy access and available electricity. Overall, the nine ARSs were positioned at distances of 15 – 265 km from the estuary; the two uppermost loggers (nos. 8 – 9) were installed on the banks of the major headwater tributary, the River Inarijoki (Figure 1).

Manual tracking of the tagged trout was conducted on weekly basis during the most important migration period between late May and early October by driving a car along the streamside roads. During the winter, manual tracking occurred mainly on monthly basis. Transmitter signals were recorded by ATS receivers (models R4000 and R4500S) connected to a 6-element Yagi antenna mounted on top of the car. In addition to car-based manual tracking, aerial tracking was conducted before and during spawning time in the River Inarijoki and its tributaries (see Figure 1) between late August and mid-September 2012 and 2013. Manual tracking was employed to obtain additional information on fish behaviour, dispersal and fate and to confirm the observations recorded by automatic receiver stations.

RESULTS

SPAWNING MIGRATION AND SPAWNING AREAS

The tracking data on fish tagged in different areas and at different phases of migration clearly established that the Teno sea trout showed a two-year spawning migration (Figure 2). Typically, upstream migration started from the estuarine feeding area in late summer, followed by a long and stationary overwintering period in the Teno main stem, a subsequent continuation of the upstream spawning migration the following spring-summer until the final spawning in early autumn (Figure 2). Only one sea trout in a small tributary of the lower Teno (the Ruossajohka, some 42 km from the estuary) showed any indication of a "normal" spawning migration by spawning in the same year that it started its upstream migration. By contrast, another sea trout heading into the same tributary exhibited a two-year spawning migration, with a stationary overwintering period in the Teno main stem close to the tributary outlet (Figure 3).

The direct tracking data and observations of sea trout disappearing from the Teno main stem and re-appearing after spawning time both showed the spawning areas in the Teno system were exclusively located in small tributaries, including the uppermost headwaters some 300 km from the estuary. No indication of spawning in the main stem was evident. This was also evident for the large headwater tributary, the River Inarijoki, as all tracked individuals in this area (n = 10) were located in small tributaries of the Inarijoki by aerial tracking before and during the spawning time.

The behaviour of tagged fish showed that spawning generally occurred between late August and mid-September (Figure 4). Soon after spawning, spent trout (= kelts) descended from their spawning streams and overwintered in the larger headwater tributaries or in the Teno main stem. This was then followed by a return migration to the estuarine feeding areas in late spring and early summer of the following year (Figure 4). Telemetry tracking data indicated that repeat spawning occurred only biennially (*see* Figure 2 B: behaviour of kelts) although scale reading of repeat spawners also suggested an annual spawning behaviour. However, scale reading proved extremely difficult and the results may be unreliable (*c.f.* Berg & Jonsson, 1990).

WINTERING MIGRATION OF IMMATURE TROUT

In this study, an immature migrant was defined as a fish ascending from the estuary to the

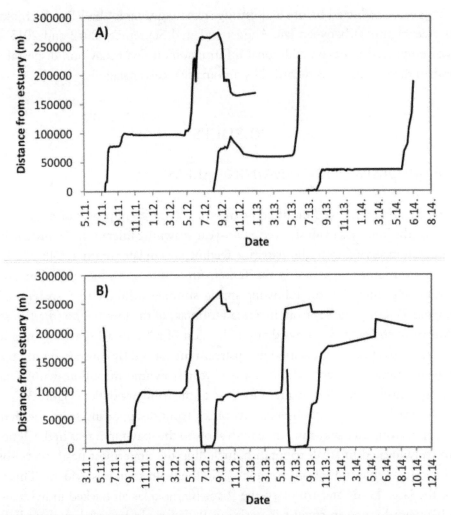

Figure 2. Spawning migratory behaviour of three sea trout tagged in the estuarine feeding area (A) and three sea trout tagged in the upper middle reaches of the Teno main stem (B). Two of the sea trout tagged in the estuary (tagged in 2012 and 2013) were caught by fishermen during their second year of spawning migration. The Teno main-stem fish were tagged as kelts and the plots show their downstream migration, feeding migration in the estuary and their subsequently repeated two-year spawning migration. Date indicates month and year.

lower Teno main stem that did not exhibit any signs of migration into either the tributaries or continuing upstream migration after overwintering in the main river. These immature (*maiden*) trout undertook overwintering migrations into fresh water by ascending the lower reaches of the Teno main stem in late summer and autumn (Figure 5), followed by a long overwintering period (~8-10 months) with little or no subsequent movement and then a return migration to the estuarine feeding grounds next spring (Figure 5). The overwintering areas were situated below the first large section of fast rapids some 70 km upstream from the estuary, with most of the fish overwintering 15 – 40 km from the estuary.

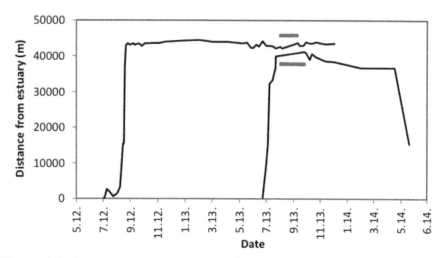

Figure 3. Migratory behaviour of two sea trout spawning in the lower Teno tributary (Ruossajohka) in 2013. The fish tagged in 2012 undertook a two-year spawning migration and fish tagged in 2013 one-year spawning migration. The trout tagged in 2013, however, was not actually located from the Ruossajohka, but it was estimated to have ascended there based on tracking data from the Teno main stem. The short grey lines indicate the estimated tributary stay. Date indicates month and year.

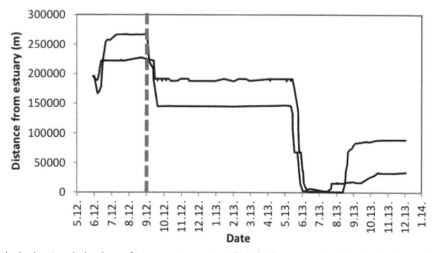

Figure 4. Typical migratory behaviour of two spent sea trout (kelts) after spawning. The dashed grey line indicates approximate spawning time. The graph also shows feeding migration in the estuary and the beginning of a new spawning migration for both individuals. Date indicates month and year.

EXPLOITATION RATES

The estimated overall exploitation rate of tagged sea trout was 27.9% (43/154 sea trout recaptured) over the entire study period (2011-2014). However, this represents a minimum estimate because not all the fish caught were reported. A large proportion of sea trout (44%)

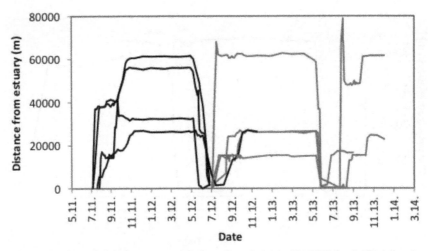

Figure 5. Migratory behaviour of eight immature wintering migrants tagged in 2011 (n=4, black lines) and 2012 (n=4, grey lines). Date indicates month and year.

either disappeared before the transmitter battery died or were assumed 'dead' (showing no movement over a long time), and a number of these fish may have been captured but not reported. The potential exploitation rates for sea trout in the Teno system may be very high. This is supported by the estimated exploitation rates for spawning migrants tagged in the estuary (46%, n =13), and for kelts tagged in the River Akujoki (60%, n =5) and in the Teno main stem (50%, n =6). These spawning migrants were estimated to have been recaptured during their first (n =1) or second year (n =5) spawning migration, and 5 of 6 kelts tagged in Akujoki and Teno main stem were caught from the estuarine feeding area.

All 20 reported sea trout recaptured in the Teno estuary were caught by rod-and-line fishing, whereas fish recaptured in the river itself were caught by both nets (55%, n =12) and rods (41%, n =9), and one (4%) sea trout was caught by an unknown method. Only one tagged fish was caught outside the river or its estuary. This was in the Tana Fjord by a fyke net, located some 15 km outside the estuary.

DISCUSSION

This extensive and long-term radio-tracking programme clearly demonstrated that the River Teno sea trout exhibit a two-year spawning migration. To our knowledge, this is a unique migratory strategy for sea trout that has not been reported elsewhere. The upstream migration and spawning of sea trout normally take place in the same year, with upstream migration occurring from few months to few days before the spawning period and generally commencing earlier in large rivers than in small rivers (Klemetsen et al., 2003; Finstad *et al.*, 2005; Jonsson & Jonsson, 2011). In the Teno system the spawning migration starts 12-13 months prior to spawning and this is followed by an overwintering period of 9-10 months by the spawned kelts: a total freshwater residency period of >20 months before returning to the estuary. A similar two-year spawning migration and overwintering of spent fish in fresh water is known for Atlantic salmon in some of the Kola Peninsula rivers (Whoriskey *et al.*, 1996), located quite close to the Teno system.

The ecological basis and possible fitness advantages of this atypical two-year spawning migration are not entirely clear. This pattern of behaviour may be connected in part to the reduced hypo-osmoregulatory capacity of trout in the sea when water temperatures are low (*see* Thomsen *et al.*, 2007). In these circumstances, upstream migration to overwinter in fresh water might be advantageous for spawning migrants. The River Teno catchment is situated in the far north of Europe (70°N) with very low water temperatures over a long period between autumn and spring. Furthermore, because of the long distance of up to 300 km to the upstream spawning areas in the Teno system, sea trout may use the first migration year and the period of overwintering to be closer to their natal streams. This strategy decreases the length of migration required in the second year and promotes further upstream migration during optimal flow conditions, possibly assisting the fish to reach the smaller spawning streams in due course. However, this hypothesis does not explain the two-year spawning migration of sea trout reproducing in the lower Teno tributaries, such as observed in the River Ruossajohka, located 42 km upstream from estuary. It might still be advantageous to overwinter in fresh water, but to continue staying for the summer in the Teno main stem instead of returning to the estuarine feeding area seems exceptional and counter-intuitive. The brown trout, however, is a particularly plastic species and can readily move between different feeding habitats (Klemetsen *et al.*, 2003; Jonsson & Jonsson, 2011), and anadromous brown trout may feed in fresh water (Jonsson & Gravem, 1985). In this respect, the Teno main stem may offer suitable feeding opportunities for the few summer months before the spawning period, although no information about the feeding of brown trout in this area is available. However, when combined with a presumably lower predation pressure than in the estuary, such as seals, cod and other large predatory marine fish (Svenning *et al.*, 2005), a long pre-spawning residence in fresh water might be a beneficial tactic.

In addition to the evident two-year spawning migration, the data also indicated one possible example of a one-season spawning migration to a small tributary of the lower part of the system, the River Ruossajohka. This behaviour may, however, be logical as this tributary is located close to the estuary and, therefore, could favour a shorter one-year spawning migration. It is possible that sea trout spawning in different tributaries with varying distances from the estuary would adopt different migratory strategies, with a one-year spawning migration occurring in the lower Teno tributaries and a two-year migration in the middle and upper Teno tributaries. Overall, the telemetry tracking data from the lower Teno tributaries were rather scarce, possibly limiting our ability to detect spawning migrants from these areas, so that the proportion of one-year spawning migrants may have been underestimated. Unfortunately, it was not possible to undertake aerial tracking in this part of the Teno.

Telemetry tracking verified that spawning areas of sea trout in Teno system are exclusively located in tributaries and sub-tributaries, including the uppermost headwaters c. 300 km from estuary. The use of tributaries and small streams for spawning is particularly common for sea trout in rivers with sympatric salmon populations (Milner *et al.*, 2006). Earlier data from diving counts in the Teno reveal that the spawning areas of sea trout and salmon overlap in many tributaries but that sea trout also reproduce in very small streams where salmon are absent (Orell, *unpublished data*). The use of headwater streams for spawning by sea-run trout is also supported by Gründler (2009) who reported that stable isotope analysis revealed significant proportions (70-80%) of sea trout in samples of the adult catch originated from the upper Teno and its tributaries.

The post spawning behavior of sea trout was similar with that observed for salmon spawning in the small tributaries of the Teno, including a rapid descent from their natal streams to larger main stems and overwintering there until the following spring (Orell, *unpublished data*). Difficult overwintering conditions, such as ice formation, low water levels, in small streams probably make it more beneficial for sea trout to descend to the Teno main stem where deep, slow flowing pools are readily available as suitable wintering areas. Overwintering of sea trout kelts in fresh water in the Teno accords with observations from other northern rivers (Berg & Berg, 1989; Jonsson & Jonsson, 2011); although new studies have revealed that trout from small northern rivers can also migrate to the sea soon after spawning (Jensen & Rikardsen, 2012). This is probably because of harsh winter conditions in their potential riverine habitats and suggests that the benefits of staying in such freshwater habitats during winter might be outweighed by the benefits of feeding in saltwater during the same period (Rikardsen *et al.*, 2006). In the Teno system, with its suitable freshwater wintering habitat, especially for the headwater sea trout populations that are a long distance away from the estuary feeding area, this strategy is probably not a feasible option.

As with spawning migrants, immature migrants also ascended the Teno main stem for overwintering, and this behaviour seems to be a common phenomenon in sea trout, especially in northern rivers (Jonsson, 1985; Berg & Berg, 1989; Klemetsen *et al.*, 2003), although more complex wintering patterns with estuarine and sea residency have been recently documented from some northern rivers (Rikardsen *et al.*, 2006; Jensen & Rikardsen, 2012). Overwintering in fresh water suggests that the benefits of feeding in saltwater may be outweighed by the benefits of returning to fresh water after the summer in the sea (Rikardsen *et al.*, 2006). In addition to possible hypo-osmoregulatory problems in cold seawater (Thomsen et al., 2007), the generally safer freshwater habitat (Rikardsen *et al.*, 2004), combined with decreasing growth rates towards autumn, may explain the riverine overwintering pattern of the Teno sea trout in that survival may be optimized by moving into fresh water. There is also some anecdotal evidence on super-cooling water and frazil ice formation in the Teno estuary area, which, in combination with the lowered salinity tolerance of trout in cold saltwater, may be one reason for avoiding the estuary during winter.

The time spent in the estuarine feeding area was considerable short (c.2 months) for both spawning and immature migrants, but it is in accordance with observations form a North Norwegian river where the annual feeding migration of sea trout lasted on average 68 days (Berg & Berg 1989). They also showed that extended stay in the feeding area resulted in only minor increase in length (Berg & Berg, 1987). This phenomenon indicates that the Teno sea trout are able to produce both maiden fish and recondition fish (kelts) in a short time in the estuarine feeding area. The Teno estuary supports an abundant population of lesser sand eel (*Ammodytes marinus*), which is the main prey of sea trout (Svenning et al., 2005), enabling fast growth of trout. It is, however, evident that growth increment (length) of repeat spawning sea trout between two spawning migrations is normally very small at c. 1-3 cm (Orell, *unpublished data*).

The estimated total exploitation of the tagged sea trout in the Teno system over the entire study period was moderate (27.9%), but it is evident that not all the fish captured were reported. The ascending spawning migrants and their descending kelts were heavily exploited, possibly because of their long period of river residence. The spawning migrants are exploited over three consecutive fishing seasons; starting with their upstream migration in year 1, continuing during their continued upstream migration in year 2 and then during their downstream descent to the estuary as post-spawned kelts in year 3. Consequently, the cumulative mortality rate can be high, especially for fish spawning in the headwaters, which have to migrate long distances and face tens of passive fishing gears (weirs and gill nets), drift netting and intensive rod fishing throughout their migration route (Niemelä *et al.*, 2006). Much of the exploitation of sea trout in the estuarine feeding area results from targeted rod and line fisheries. In the Teno main stem, sea trout are mainly captured as a by-catch of the rod and net fisheries for salmon. Only one tagged sea trout was captured outside the River Teno or its estuary. This may indicate that feeding is mostly concentrated into the estuarine area. However, the marine feeding behaviour of the Teno sea trout and their possible dispersal within the fjord and in the open sea is not well known and merits a specific study.

Overall, the status and conservation of the sea trout populations in the Teno is largely dependent on salmon management schemes as the only fishery specifically targeting sea trout is operated over a short time period by rod fishermen in the estuarine area. As the life cycle of Teno sea trout appears to take place mainly within the Teno and its estuary, its management needs in the fjord and at sea do not necessarily have a significant role in the conservation of sea trout. However, development of a new management strategy with stricter regulations for the Teno salmon fishery is underway and should be in operation in 2017. This should also benefit conservation of the sea trout populations. In addition, the current legal minimum size limit of 25 cm for Teno sea trout should be increased to 40-50 cm to secure the maturation of a significant proportion of sea trout before harvest in the rod and net fisheries and to increase its value, especially within the feeding area of the Teno estuary.

ACKNOWLEDGEMENTS

We would like to thank Velimatti Leinonen, Arto Koskinen and the other field staff of the Natural Resources Institute Finland for their dedication and hard work during catching, tagging and tracking of the Teno sea trout. Narve Johansen from Tanavassdragets fiskeforvalting (TF), Mika Linna and local fishermen helped considerably throughout the study, many thanks to all. Audun Rikardsen and Jenny Jensen from University of Tromsø also deserve thanks for helping with the Norwegian research permits. Finally we would like to thank the two referees for their valuable comments to improve the text. This study was partly funded by the Finnish Ministry of Agriculture and Forestry.

REFERENCES

Aarestrup, K. & Jepsen, N. (1998). Spawning migration of sea trout (*Salmo trutta* (L)) in a Danish river. *Hydrobiologia*, 371/372, 275–281.

Berg, O. K. & Berg, M. (1987). The seasonal pattern of growth of the sea trout (*Salmo trutta* L.) from the Vardnes river in northern Norway. *Aquaculture* **62**, 143-152.

Berg, O. K. & Berg, M. (1989). The duration of sea and freshwater residence of the sea trout, *Salmo trutta*, from the Vardnes River in northern Norway. *Environmental Biology of Fishes*, **24**, 23-32.

Berg, O. K. & Jonsson, B. (1990). Growth and survival rates of the anadromous trout, *Salmo trutta*, from the Vardnes River, northern Norway. *Environmental Biology of Fishes*, **29**, 145-154.

Finstad, A. G., Økland, F., Thorstad, E. B. & Heggberget, T. G. (2005). Comparing upriver spawning migration of Atlantic salmon *Salmo salar* and sea trout *Salmo trutta*. *Journal of Fish Biology*, **67**, 919-930.

Gründler, S. A. (2009). Investigating different migration patterns of *Salmo trutta* (l.) in the Teno River system using stable isotope analyses. MSc Thesis. University of Jyväskylä, 39 pp.

Harris, G. & Milner, N. (*Eds.*) (2006). *Sea Trout: Biology, Conservation & Management*. Proceedings of the 1st International Sea Trout Symposium, July 2004, Cardiff, Wales, UK. Blackwell Publishing, Oxford, 499 pp.

Jensen, J. L. A. & Rikardsen, A. H. (2012). Archival tags reveal that arctic charr *Salvelinus alpinus* and brown trout *Salmo trutta* can use estuarine and marine waters during winter. *Journal of Fish Biology*, **81**, 735-749.

Jonsson, B. (1985). Life history patterns of freshwater resident and sea-run migrant brown trout in Norway. *Transactions of the American Fisheries Society*, **114**, 182-194.

Jonsson, B. & Gravem, F. R. (1985). Use of space and food by resident and migrant brown trout. *Environmental Biology of Fishes*, **14**, 281-293.

Jonsson, B. & L'Abée-Lund, J. H. (1993). Latitudinal clines in life history variables of anadromous brown trout in Europé. *Journal of Fish Biology*, **43** (Suppl. A), 1-16.

Jonsson, B. & Jonsson, N. (2006). Life history of the anadromous trout *Salmo trutta*. In: *Sea Trout: Biology, Conservation & Management* (Graeme Harris & Nigel Milner. *Eds.*). Proceedings of the 1st International Sea Trout Symposium, July 2004, Cardiff, Wales, UK. Blackwell Publishing, Oxford, 196-223.

Jonsson, B. & Jonsson, N. (2011). Ecology of Atlantic salmon and brown trout: habitat as a template for life histories. *Fish & Fisheries Series* 33. Springer, London, 708 pp.

Klemetsen, A., Amundsen, P.-A., Dempson, J.B., Jonsson, B., Jonsson, N., O'Connell, M.F., Mortensen, E. (2003). Atlantic salmon *Salmo salar* L., brown trout *Salmo trutta* L., and Arctic charr *Salvelinus alpinus* (L.): a review of aspects of their life histories. *Ecology of Freshwater Fish*, **12**, 1–59.

Louhi, P., Mäki-Petäys, A. & Erkinaro, J. (2008). Spawning habitat of Atlantic salmon and brown trout: General criteria and intragravel factors. *River Research and Applications*, **24**, 330-339.

Milner, N. J., Karlsson, L., Degerman, E., Johlander, A., MacLean, J. C. & Hansen, L-P. (2006). Sea trout (*Salmo trutta* L.) in European salmon (*Salmo salar* L.) rivers. In: *Sea Trout: Biology, Conservation & Management* (Graeme Harris & Nigel Milner. *Eds.*). Proceedings of the 1st International Sea Trout Symposium, July 2004, Cardiff, Wales, UK. Blackwell Publishing, Oxford, 139-153.

Niemelä, E. (2004). Variation in the yearly and seasonal abundance of juvenile Atlantic salmon in a long-term monitoring programme. Methodology, status of stocks and reference points. Acta Universitatis Ouluensis A 415, Oulu, Finland. 54 pp.

Niemelä, E., Erkinaro, J., Julkunen, M. & Hassinen, E. (2005). Is juvenile salmon abundance related to subsequent and preceding catches? Perspectives from a long-term monitoring programme. *ICES Journal of Marine Science*, **62**, 1617-1629.

Niemelä E., Erkinaro, J., Julkunen, M., Hassinen, E., Länsman, M. & Brørs, S. (2006). Temporal variation in abundance, return rate and life histories of previously spawned Atlantic salmon in a large subarctic river. *Journal of Fish Biology*, **68**, 1222–1240

Rikardsen, A. H., Thorpe, J. E. & Dempson, B.(2004). Modelling the life-history variation of Arctic charr. *Ecology of Freshwater Fish*, **13**, 305-311.

Rikardsen, A. H. & Thorstad, E. B. (2006). External attachment of data storage tags increases probability of being recaptured in nets compared to internal tagging. *Journal of Fish Biology*, **68**, 963-968.

Rikardsen, A. H., Amundsen, P-A., Knudsen, R. & Sandring, S. (2006). Seasonal marine feeding and body condition of sea trout Salmo trutta at its northern distribution. *ICES Journal of Marine Science*, **63**, 466–475

Svenning, M. A., Borgstrøm, R., Dehli, T. O., Moen, G., Barrett, R. T., Pedersen, T. & Vader, W. (2005). The impact of marine fish predation on Atlantic salmon smolts (*Salmo salar*) in the Tana estuary, North Norway, in the presence of an alternative prey, lesser sandeel (*Ammodytes marinus*). *Fisheries Research*, **76**, 466-474.

Thomsen, D. S., Koed, A., Nielsen, C. & Madsen, S. S. (2007). Overwintering of sea trout (*Salmo trutta*) in freshwater: escaping salt and low temperature or an alternate life strategy? *Canadian Journal of Fisheries and Aquatic Sciences*, **64**, 793-802.

Vähä, J. P., Erkinaro, J., Niemelä, E. & Primmer, C. R. (2007). Life-history and habitat features influence the within-river genetic structure of Atlantic salmon. *Molecular Ecology*, **16**, 2638–2654.

Vähä, J. P., Erkinaro, J., Niemelä, E. & Primmer, C. R. (2008). Temporally stable genetic structure and low migration in an Atlantic salmon population complex: implications for conservation and management. *Evolutionary Applications*, **1**, 137–154.

Whoriskey, F.G., Kuzhmin, O. & Goodhart, D. (1996). Monitoring of sports fishing catches of Atlantic Salmon (*Salmo salar* L.) of the Ponoi River, Russia to document population characteristics. *Polish Archives of Hydrobiology*, **43**, 167–177.

Using stable isotopes to assess the distribution of reproduction by migratory and resident *Salmo trutta* within river systems: some complicating factors

R. A BRIERS[1], R. N. B .CAMPBELL[2], K. GALT[2], M. WALTERS[3] & J.HOLMES[1].

[1]*School of Applied Sciences, Edinburgh Napier University, Sighthill Campus, Edinburgh, EH11 4BN, Scotland.*
[2]*The Tweed Foundation, Drygrange Steading, By Melrose, Roxburghshire, TD6 9DJ, Scotland.*
[3]*Moray Firth Trout Initiative, c/o Kyle of Sutherland Fisheries Trust, Dornoch Road, Bonar Bridge, Sutherland, IV24 3EB, Scotland.*

ABSTRACT

Understanding the distribution of spawning resident and migratory trout in a river system is important for fishery management. In most cases this information is lacking or only partial, and mostly derived from surveys of breeding adults. Stable isotope analysis of fry provides an alternative method by which to determine the relative importance of different areas for migratory and resident fish breeding. The ratios of carbon and nitrogen stable isotopes in fish tissue vary predictably between offspring from different forms; sea trout typically show higher abundance of the heavier stable isotopes of both elements. These are passed to their offspring, allowing distinction at this phase. Here we show the results from applying this technique to two different river systems; the Gala Water tributary of the River Tweed and tributaries of the River Deveron. Although it is generally possible to distinguish migratory and resident offspring, interpretation is complicated by considerable isotopic variation within river systems. This may be linked to the influence of freshwater feeding, catchment-scale land-use patterns and isotopic variation in adults. In order to maximise the utility of stable isotope-based techniques in fisheries management, these factors need to be more fully understood.

Keywords: *Salmo trutta*; stable isotope analysis; migration, catchment; population composition; reproduction.

INTRODUCTION

Migratory and resident forms of trout *Salmo trutta* L. are commonly found within the same river system and, with complex and overlapping distributions, there is also commonly extensive interbreeding between the two forms (Charles *et al.*, 2005). The distribution and abundance of reproduction by migratory and resident forms of trout and other salmonids is thought to be influenced by physical conditions within rivers and the difficulty of migrating distances upriver (Bohlin *et al.*, 2001; Kristensen *et al.*, 2010; Berejikian *et al.*, 2013) but patterns of distribution are often complex. Understanding the distribution of reproduction of the two forms is important for fishery management: for example to ensure that migratory access is maintained and that important breeding areas are protected. A number of different techniques have been employed to help distinguish between migratory and resident fish, given that phenotypic characteristics are not always reliable. These include the assessment of strontium levels in scales, eggs or otoliths (Rieman *et al.*, 1994; Howland *et al.*, 2001; Koksvik & Steinnes 2005; Kristensen *et al.*, 2010), carotenoid profiles (Youngson *et al.*, 1997; Briers *et al.*, 2013) and stable isotope ratios (McCarthy & Waldron, 2000; Curry, 2005; Briers *et al.*, 2013). These techniques can be used on both adult fish and eggs/offspring. The presence of adults is not necessarily indicative of the reproductive contribution to any particular area unless spawning is observed. Ideally each assessment should be based on the characteristics of the population of offspring that are contributing to the next generation. Stable isotope ratios are increasingly widely used in a variety of contexts within ecology and environmental management, including tracking migration of species (Brattström *et al.*, 2010) and distinguishing trophic characteristics (Eloranta *et al.*, 2014). Studies of both trout and other salmonids have used stable isotope ratios to distinguish the offspring from migratory and resident fish and to determine the relative proportions of the different forms within populations (Doucett *et al.*, 1999; Charles *et al.*, 2004; Curry, 2005; Charles *et al.*, 2006; Jardine *et al.*, 2008). The use of the stable isotope ratios can provide valuable information in the context of fisheries management, particularly when combined with other information such as surveys of juvenile abundance and assessment of adult populations. The aim here, through work undertaken within the River Deveron and River Tweed (specifically the Gala Water tributary) in Scotland, is to highlight some significant issues in the interpretation of stable isotope information that need to be given careful consideration to avoid potential mis-interpretation of the data provided.

BASIS OF THE METHOD AND SAMPLING

The ability to distinguish between the offspring of migratory and resident individuals is based on relatively predictable differences in the relative amounts of the heavier stable isotopes of carbon and nitrogen, namely ^{13}C and ^{15}N. Stable isotope ratios are generally expressed in terms of delta values (δ) in units of parts per thousand (‰). These represent the ratio of the heavier to lighter isotope within the sample relative to the ratio of a standard. In the case of ^{13}C this is a marine fossil, the Pee Dee Belemnite, and for ^{15}N it is atmospheric N. In both cases, migratory trout have a greater abundance of the heavier isotope than resident fish within their tissues. This is linked to the greater abundance of both forms in marine systems in comparison to freshwaters (Peterson & Fry, 1987; McCarthy & Waldron, 2000). The stable isotope ratios of the eggs deposited reflect the characteristics of the spawning females and thus have similar stable isotope ratios to the adult tissues. This difference is retained by young fry, although the distinction gradually reduces due to freshwater feeding within a matter of months (Doucett *et al.*, 1999; Briers *et al.*, 2013).

Samples can be obtained from young fry either by taking a sample of tissue, typically the white muscle, or by fin clippings. Only a small amount of tissue is required for analysis (typically 0.6 – 0.8 mg dry weight depending on the equipment used) so fin clippings, particularly from the adipose fin, can provide a non-destructive method of characterisation of fish (Hanisch *et al.*, 2010). For small fry however, the mass of the adipose fin may be insufficient to allow analysis (Thornton *et al.*, 2015), thus requiring destructive sampling. There are also differences between isotope ratios of fin clippings and those of muscle, particularly for the adipose fin in terms of carbon isotope ratios, mostly due to its high lipid content (Graham *et al.*, 2013). Recent studies have also found variation in stable isotope ratios even within individual fins (Hayden *et al.,* 2015). Therefore, to reduce the influence of inter-tissue variability in isotope ratios, it is generally preferable to use a consistent tissue type for characterisation. As indicated above, samples are dried and then prepared for analysis of stable isotope ratios in an Isotope Ratio Mass Spectrometer (IRMS). Characterisation can be undertaken from fresh, frozen or preserved samples, although prolonged preservation, and the preservative used, may influence stable isotope ratios to some extent (Kelly *et al.*, 2006; Vizza *et al.*, 2013).

EXAMPLES OF USE IN POPULATION CHARACTERISATION

RIVER DEVERON

The first example is based on analysis of fry from ten sites within the River Deveron system which flows directly into the Moray Firth, North-East Scotland. The freshwater sampling sites were chosen to represent a range of different potential population characteristics. Some sites were chosen as 'reference' sites with known characteristics based on previous fishery information and others, notably a number of coastal streams, were chosen specifically to provide information on the characteristics of the population to aid fishery management. Details of each of the sampling sites are given in Table 1 and the location of the sites in Figure 1.

At each site, ten fry (standard length 5-8cm) were sampled in August 2013 and analysed for stable isotope ratios of both carbon and nitrogen. Following analysis, values were plotted on a dual isotope biplot to visualise the differences in stable isotope ratios between fry from different sites (Figure 2).

Table 1. Characteristics of the sites sampled in the River Deveron system.

Burn / River	Location	Easting	Northing	Notes
Burn of Boyne	Bridge of Tilly Naught	359887	860962	Coastal burn
Tore Burn	Upstream of Nethermill	383857	865520	Coastal Burn – with gravel bar at mouth
Water of Philorth	Rathen	399586	860759	Coastal burn
King Edward		370741	857789	Thought to be a sea trout burn
Upper Blackwater	Allt Daimh	333369	828008	Well studied brown trout population
Upper Deveron	Charach Water	336079	831183	Trout burn off upper Deveron
Isla	Crooksmill	342492	851422	Downstream of Keith
Isla	Auchindachy	340685	847509	Upstream of Keith – above various barriers
Upper Bogie	Burn of Craig	344659	825208	Above impassable waterfall = brown trout reference
Bogie	Kirkney Water	358850	833579	Below barrier

The patterns shown by the fish at the Deveron sites demonstrate clearly the distinction between migratory and resident fish in terms of stable isotope ratios. The most obvious difference is shown between the reference resident population (Upper Bogie, above an impassable waterfall) and the fish at the Burn of Boyne and Water of Philorth sites, which represent offspring from entirely migratory reproduction. The results for the Tore Burn are a good example of where the technique can be used to support or reject other information about the population and inform management. This site is another coastal stream, but one which has a large gravel bar situated across the mouth of the river which was thought could act as an impediment to migration. The stable isotope results would support this interpretation, as the values for all fish sampled at this site would tend to indicate that the reproduction is solely derived from resident fish. The results for the two sites on the Isla tributary (Crooksmill and Auchindachy) are also informative. The lower site at Crooksmill would appear to be dominated by the progeny of migratory fish whereas the site at Auchindachy, which is above a series of in-stream barriers, has a distinctly different isotope composition, one that is intermediate between the two extremes.

Interpretation of 'intermediate' isotope ratio values such as these is not straightforward. For some sites that fall into this 'intermediate' zone, a wide spread of values that spans the range of values those which are characteristic of both forms would tend to suggest mixed reproduction. Often values within a site will fall into two separate clusters, representing migratory and resident offspring and allowing proportions of the different forms within the site to be estimated (Charles *et al.*, 2004; Curry, 2005). Separation may not always be so marked however, leading to some potential ambiguity in interpretation (such as those observed in fish obtained at King Edward Burn).

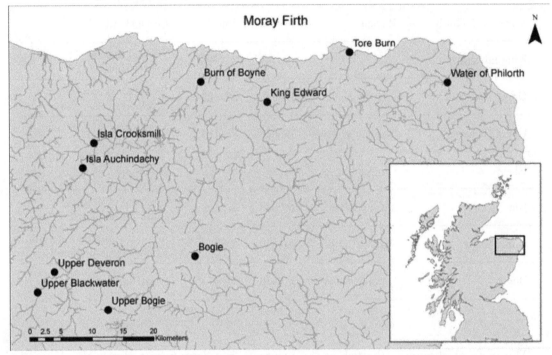

Figure 1. Map of sites sampled within the River Deveron system. Inset map shows location of study area within Scotland. © Crown Copyright and Database Right 2016, Ordnance Survey (Digimap licence).

Most previous studies have sampled fry more or less immediately after emergence. Sampling of very early stages may not always be practical due to field conditions; most standard fisheries surveys are undertaken later in the year, once the fish have been active in freshwater for several months. In this case the fry were sampled in August, by which time the influence of freshwater feeding on stable isotope ratios is likely to be evident (Jardine *et al.*, 2008; Briers *et al.*, 2013), leading to less marked distinction between offspring of different sources and the consequent ambiguity evident at some of the sites. The composition of the food consumed is likely to influence the rate and extent of change in isotope values of the young fish (Thornton *et al.*, 2015), along with other factors such as individual variation in metabolism (Heady & Moore 2013) and prevailing environmental conditions such as temperature.

For offspring of migratory fish, although the isotopic variation between marine and freshwater ecosystems is the basis of the technique employed, there is also evidence, at least for Atlantic salmon (*Salmo salar* L.), that migration to different sea feeding areas also leads to variation in stable isotope values (Dempson *et al.*, 2009; MacKenzie *et al.*, 2012). It is a reasonable assumption that similar patterns may be evident in migratory trout, if fish returning to breed in a particular river may have spent time at sea feeding in different areas and thus have distinct stable isotope values, could further complicate interpretation. Given the known wide variation in stable isotope ratios of adult trout, even within a single waterbody (Etheridge *et al.*, 2008), a better understanding of the extent and nature of variation in ratios in adult migratory trout returning to breed would be highly beneficial.

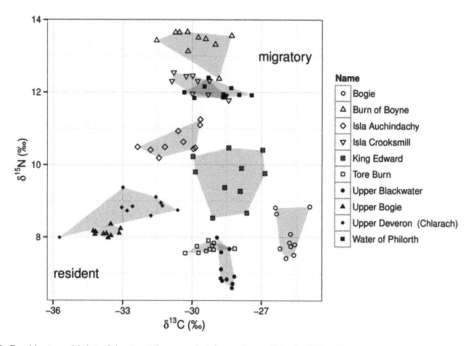

Figure 2. Dual isotope biplot of the trout fry sampled from sites within the River Deveron.

GALA WATER, RIVER TWEED

The second example is drawn from sites on the Gala Water tributary of the River Tweed in the Scottish Borders and forms part of an ongoing larger, catchment-wide characterisation. Sampling was similar to that undertaken in the Deveron; ten fry were sampled from each site in August 2013. The first useful comparison to draw is between isotope values for both river systems overall (Figure 3). From this it is clear that the overall pattern of variation in stable isotope ratios is similar between the two river systems. This is not always the case however, as comparison of the values given here with values obtained from other rivers and lakes shows wider ranges of variation in young stages of trout in both isotopes considered (McCarthy & Waldron, 2000; Charles *et al.*, 2006). Therefore it is not possible to give stable isotope ratios that are 'characteristic' of resident or migratory fish; the values vary between waterbodies and can only be interpreted relative to each other in the context of the system under study.

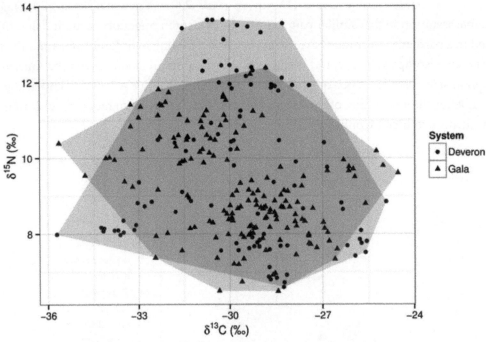

Figure 3. Dual isotope biplot of all fish sampled from the River Deveron and Gala Water.

For the Gala Water, there are much more strongly overlapping ranges of values between sites (Figure 4) compared to that shown in the Deveron sites, even if the overall range of variation is similar to the Deveron. It is still possible to distinguish populations where reproduction is predominantly or entirely derived from either resident or migratory forms (e.g. Site 17 for migratory fish), but the majority appear to be mixed populations where both forms appear to be contributing to recruitment. Previous work on the Gala Water (Holmes, 2015), showed an inconsistent relationship between the relative contribution of sea trout spawning activity with either distance upstream from the mouth of the river; or altitude. This would suggest that other, more local, factors may also be important in determining the location of sea trout spawning sites.

What is evident from Figure 4 is that there is clustering of sites into two fairly distinct groups in the opposite axis of variation to that typical of the overall resident-migratory distinction. When these sites are mapped (Figure 5), it is clear that the groups relate to areas of the river catchment with contrasting land-use patterns, suggesting a potentially strong influence of catchment on overall variation in both isotopes. Most notable is the strong distinction between the cluster of sites at the top left of Figure 4, which are in an area which drains mostly pasture and those towards the bottom right, which drain areas of mostly moorland and natural grassland land use. There were significant differences in both isotope ratio values between these two groups (Welch's t-test, δ^{15}N: $t = 14.75$, $df = 131.76$, $p<0.0001$, δ^{13}C: $t = 7.06$, $df = 111.32$, $p<0.0001$), with pasture sites having lower δ^{13}C and higher δ^{15}N values than moorland/grassland sites.

Previous work has shown that δ^{15}N values in particular within entire aquatic food webs

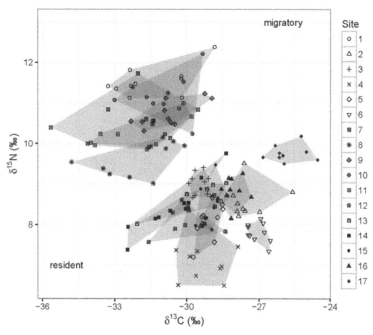

Figure 4. Dual isotope biplot of the trout fry sampled from sites within the Gala Water.

are influenced by the nature of run-off from the catchment (Anderson & Cabana, 2005; Moore *et al.*, 2014). [13]C isotope ratios in terrestrial vegetation also vary in relation to land-use e.g. Hobson (2007) and therefore the isotopic characteristics of detritus entering and being incorporated into the aquatic food web are also likely to vary. This may influence both the isotope values of resident adult fish, which are the passed on to the offspring, and also the rate and extent of temporal change in isotope characteristics of fry from either source (Briers *et al.*, 2013) through variation in isotopic characteristics of their food and differences in growth rates driven by variation in the overall productivity of the rivers (Jonsson *et al.*, 2011).

KEY ISSUES

The aim of this study was to explores some of the issues that need to be taken into consideration when using stable isotope techniques to provide information on the composition of offspring populations. Previous work on relatively small numbers of sites and using very early stages have generally found fairly clear-cut differences between resident and migratory offspring of trout and other salmonids (Doucett *et al.*, 1999; Charles *et al.*, 2004; Curry, 2005; Charles *et al.*, 2006; Jardine *et al.*, 2008; Briers *et al.*, 2013). This study highlights that there may commonly be a considerable amount of variation between the stable isotope ratios of fish found at different sites, even populations that are consistently derived from either migratory or resident reproduction. Drawing a distinction between offspring from resident and migratory females using stable

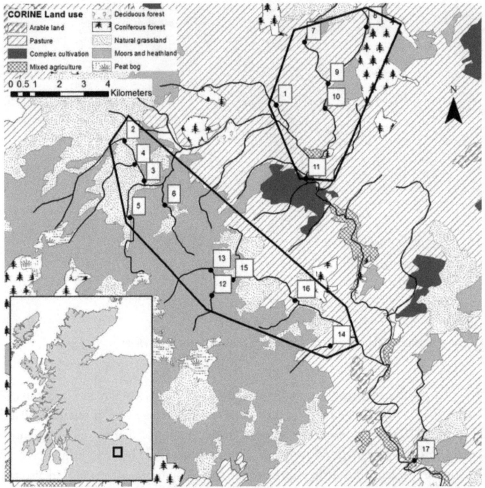

Figure 5. Map of the sites sampled within the Gala Water and the predominant land-use in different parts of the catchment. Inset map shows location of study area within Scotland © Crown Copyright and Database Right 2016, Ordnance Survey (Digimap Licence). Land-use data derived from CLC 2012 Corine Land Cover Classification © European Environment Agency, Copenhagen, 2013.

isotope analysis is therefore not always straightforward without an understanding of the extent and pattern of variation in stable isotope ratios within the river under consideration. The most significant influences are summarised below:

Influence of Sampling Time and Freshwater Feeding

There are quite rapid temporal changes in isotope values following emergence (Curry, 2005) as maternal resources become used up and offspring stable isotope ratios begin to reflect those of local freshwater food sources (Briers *et al.*, 2013). The small size and rapid growth of fry at this stage mean that stable isotope ratios change more rapidly than in larger fish. Sampling during the very early stages of post-emergence is therefore best for enabling maximum distinction, but may be subject to practical limitations. Interpreting the stable isotope ratios of larger fry requires consideration of the effects of freshwater feeding, which may also vary between sites depending on diet, individual variation in physiology and environmental influences such as temperature and catchment productivity (see below).

Effect of Catchment Characteristics

The characteristics of the river catchment in terms of land-use can have an important influence on both the extent and nature of temporal change in stable isotope ratios, through influences on productivity, growth and also the overall carbon and nitrogen stable isotopic characteristics of fish populations at different sites, due to effects at the level of the entire food web. Given that the extent of difference, particularly in nitrogen stable isotopes (Cole *et al.*, 2004; Anderson & Cabana, 2005; Diebel & Vander-Zanden, 2009) can be linked to land-use characteristics, most notably agricultural impacts, it may prove possible to 'correct' stable isotope values for land-use influences, although this awaits further development.

Variation in Adult Stable Isotope Ratios

This has a potentially strong influence on the stable isotope ratios of progeny from both resident and migratory fish. For migratory trout, few data exist on variation in stable isotope ratios of adults in relation to marine feeding areas but it is reasonable to assume that similar patterns will be shown as have been found for Atlantic salmon *Salmo salar* L. (Dempson *et al.*, 2009; MacKenzie *et al.*, 2012). The stable isotope ratios of adult trout are known to vary along a continuum between typical resident and migratory values, even within a single waterbody (Etheridge *et al.*, 2008) and this may reflect both marine feeding and variation relating to catchment influences.

CONCLUSION

In summary, while stable isotope analysis of offspring provides a potentially powerful technique for assigning fry to the progeny of resident or migratory females, in order to make most effective use of the technique for fishery management or other purposes, the potential role of the sources of variation highlighted above need to be considered and accounted for when drawing interpretation from surveys and analysis of young stages.

ACKNOWLEDGEMENTS

A number of people assisted in the fieldwork, preparation and analysis of the samples discussed here; in no particular order: Iain Reid, Viora Weber, Ian Martin and Nora Washbourne. The analysis was supported by funding and donations of time from the Atlantic Salmon Trust, the Wild Trout Trust, the Deveron, Bogie and Isla River Trust, the Deveron Salmon Fishery Board, NERC and Edinburgh Napier University. Stable isotope analysis was undertaken at the NERC Stable Isotope Facility in East Kilbride; thanks are due to Rona McGill and Jason Newton for assistance and advice.

REFERENCES

Anderson, C. & Cabana, G. (2005). $\delta^{15}N$ in riverine food webs: effects of N inputs from agricultural watersheds. *Canadian Journal of Fisheries and Aquatic Science* **62**, 333–340.

Berejikian, B. A., Campbell, L. A., Moore, M. E. & Grant, J. (2013). Large-scale freshwater habitat features influence the degree of anadromy in eight Hood Canal *Oncorhynchus mykiss* populations. *Canadian Journal of Fisheries and Aquatic Science* **70**, 756–765.

Bohlin, T., Pettersson, J. & Degerman, E. (2001). Population density of migratory and resident brown trout (*Salmo trutta*) in relation to altitude: evidence for a migration cost. *Journal of Animal Ecology* **70**, 112–121.

Brattström, O., Bensch, S., Wassenaar, L. I., Hobson, K. A. & Åkesson, S. (2010). Understanding the migration ecology of European red admirals *Vanessa atalanta* using stable hydrogen isotopes. *Ecography* **33**, 720–729.

Briers, R. A., Waterman, J. O., Galt, K. & Campbell, R. N. B. (2013). Population differentiation and temporal changes of carotenoid pigments and stable isotope ratios in the offspring of anadromous and non-anadromous trout *Salmo trutta*. *Ecology of Freshwater Fish* **22**, 137–144.

Charles, K., Guyomard, R., Hoyheim, B., Ombredane, D. & Baglinière, J-L. (2005). Lack of genetic differentiation between anadromous and resident sympatric brown trout (*Salmo trutta*) in a Normandy population. *Aquatic Living Resources* **18**, 65–69.

Charles, K., Roussel, J-M. & Cunjak, R. A. (2004). Estimating the contribution of sympatric anadromous and freshwater resident brown trout to juvenile production. *Marine and Freshwater Research* **55**, 185-191.

Charles, K., Roussel, J-M., Lebel, J-M., Baglinière, J-L. & Ombredane, D. (2006). Genetic differentiation between anadromous and freshwater resident brown trout (*Salmo trutta* L.): insights obtained from stable isotope analysis. *Ecology of Freshwater Fish* **15**, 255–263.

Cole, M. L., Valiela, I., Kroeger, K. D., Tomasky, G. L., Cebrian, J., Wigand, C., McKinney, R. A., Grady, S. P. & da Silva, M. H. C. (2004). Assessment of a $\delta^{15}N$ isotopic method to indicate anthropogenic eutrophication in aquatic ecosystems. *Journal of Environment Quality* **33**, 124-132.

Curry, R. A. (2005). Assessing the reproductive contributions of sympatric anadromous and freshwater-resident brook trout. *Journal of Fish Biology* **66**, 741–757.

Dempson, J. B., Braithwaite, V. A., Doherty, D. & Power, M. (2009). Stable isotope analysis of marine feeding signatures of Atlantic salmon in the North Atlantic. *ICES Journal of Marine Science* **67**, 52–61.

Diebel, M. W. & Vander Zanden, M. J. (2009). Nitrogen stable isotopes in streams: effects of agricultural sources and transformations. *Ecological Applications* **19**, 1127–1134.

Doucett, R. R., Hooper, W. & Power, G. (1999). Identification of anadromous and nonanadromous adult brook trout and their progeny in the Tabusintac River New Brunswick, by means of multiple-stable-isotope analysis. *Transactions of the American Fisheries Society* **128**, 278–288.

Eloranta, A. P., Nieminen, P. & Kahilainen, K. K. (2014). Trophic interactions between introduced lake trout (*Salvelinus namaycush*) and native Arctic charr (*S. alpinus*) in a large Fennoscandian subarctic lake. *Ecology of Freshwater Fish* **24**, 181–192.

Etheridge, E. C., Harrod, C., Bean, C. & Adams, C. E. (2008). Continuous variation in the pattern of marine v. freshwater foraging in brown trout *Salmo trutta* L. from Loch Lomond Scotland. *Journal of Fish Biology* **73**, 44–53.

Graham, C. T., Harrison, S. S. & Harrod, C. (2013). Development of non-lethal sampling of carbon and nitrogen stable isotope ratios in salmonids: effects of lipid and inorganic components of fins. *Isotopes in Environmental and Health Studies* **49**, 555–566.

Hanisch, J. R., Tonn, W. M., Paszkowski, C. A. & Scrimgeour, G. J. (2010). $\delta^{13}C$ and $\delta^{15}N$ signatures in muscle and fin tissues: nonlethal sampling methods for stable isotope analysis of salmonids. *North American Journal of Fisheries Management* **30**, 1–11.

Hayden, B., Soto, D.X., Jardine, T.D., Graham, B.S., Cunjak, R.A., Romakkaniemi, A. & Linnansaari, T. (2015). Small tails tell tall tales – intra-individual variation in the stable isotope values of fish fin. *PLoS ONE* **10**, e0145154.

Heady, W.N. & Moore, J.W. (2013). Tissue turnover and stable isotope clocks to quantify resource shifts in anadromous rainbow trout. *Oecologia* **172**, 21-34.

Hobson, K. A. (2007). An isotopic exploration of the potential of avian tissues to track changes in terrestrial and marine ecosystems. In: *Stable Isotopes as Indicators of Ecological Change*, pp. 127–144. Elsevier BV.

Holmes, J. (2015). Investigating the distribution of nonanadromous (freshwater-resident) and anadromous (sea-run migratory) brown trout (*Salmo trutta*) from the Gala Water tributary of River Tweed through stable isotope ratio analysis. MSc Thesis, Edinburgh Napier University

Howland, K. L., Tonn, W. M., Babaluk, J. A. & Tallman, R. F. (2001). Identification of freshwater and anadromous Inconnu in the Mackenzie River system by analysis of otolith strontium. *Transactions of the American Fisheries Society* **130**, 725–741.

Jardine, T. D., Chernoff, E. & Curry, R. A. (2008). Maternal transfer of carbon and nitrogen to progeny of sea-run and resident brook trout (*Salvelinus fontinalis*). *Canadian Journal of Fisheries and Aquatic Science* **65**, 2201–2210.

Jonsson, B., Jonsson, N. & Ugedal, O. (2011) Production of juvenile salmonids in small Norwegian streams is affected by agricultural land use. *Freshwater Biology* **56**, 2529-2542.

Kelly, B., Dempson, J. B. & Power, M. (2006). The effects of preservation on fish tissue stable isotope signatures. *Journal of Fish Biology* **69**, 1595–1611.

Koksvik, J. I. & Steinnes, E. (2005). Strontium content of scales as a marker for distinguishing between sea trout and brown trout. *Hydrobiologia* **544**, 51–54.

Kristensen, E. A., Closs, G. P., Olley, R., Kim, J., Reid, M. & Stirling, C. (2010). Determining the spatial distribution of spawning by anadromous and resident brown trout *Salmo trutta* L using strontium content of eggs collected from redds. *Ecology of Freshwater Fish* **20**, 377–383.

MacKenzie, K. M., Trueman, C. N., Palmer, M. R., Moore, A., Ibbotson, A. T., Beaumont, W. R. C. & Davidson, I. C. (2012). Stable isotopes reveal age-dependent trophic level and spatial segregation during adult marine feeding in populations of salmon. *ICES Journal of Marine Science* **69**, 1637–1645.

McCarthy, I. D. & Waldron, S. (2000). Identifying migratory *Salmo trutta* using carbon and nitrogen stable isotope ratios. *Rapid Communications in Mass Spectrometry* **14**, 1325–1331.

Moore, J. W., Lambert, T. D., Heady, W. N., Honig, S. E., Osterback, A.-M. K., Phillis, C. C., Quiros, A. L., Retford, N. A. & Herbst, D. B. (2014). Anthropogenic land-use signals propagate through stream food webs in a California, USA, watershed. *Limnologica – Ecology and Management of Inland Waters* **46**, 124–130.

Peterson, B. J. & Fry, B. (1987). Stable isotopes in ecosystem studies. *Annual Reviews in Ecology and Systematics* **18**, 293–320.

Rieman, B. E., Myers, D. L. & Nielsen, R. L. (1994). Use of otolith microchemistry to discriminate *Oncorhynchus nerka* of resident and anadromous origin. *Canadian Journal of Fisheries and Aquatic Science* **51**, 68–77.

Thornton, E. J., Hardy, R. W. & Quinn, T. P. (2015). Experimental determination of the limits of using stable isotopes to distinguish steelhead and rainbow trout offspring. *North American Journal of Fisheries Management* **35**, 810–817.

Vizza, C., Sanderson, B. L., Burrows, D. G. & Coe, H. J. (2013). The effects of ethanol preservation on fish fin stable isotopes: does variation in C:N Ratio and body size matter? *Transactions of the American Fisheries Society* **142**, 1469–1476.

Youngson, A. F., Mitchell, A. I., Noack, P. T. & Laird, L. M. (1997). Carotenoid pigment profiles distinguish anadromous and nonanadromous brown trout (*Salmo trutta*). *Canadian Journal of Fisheries and Aquatic Science* **54**, 1064–1066.

Assessment and Recruitment Status of Baltic Sea Trout Populations

S. PEDERSEN[1], E. DEGERMAN[2], P. DEBOWSKI[3]
& C. PETEREIT[4].

[1]Technical University of Denmark, DTU Aqua, National Institute for Aquatic Resources, Section for Freshwater Fisheries and Ecology, Silkeborg, Denmark.
[2]Swedish University of Agricultural Sciences, Institute of Freshwater Research, Pappersbruksallén 22, SE-702 15 Örebro, Sweden.
[3]Inland Fisheries Institute, Department of Migratory Fishes, Rutki 49, 83-330 Zukowo, Poland.
[4]GEOMAR Helmholtz Centre for Ocean Research Kiel, Evolutionary Ecology of Marine Fishes, Düsternbrooker Weg 20, 24105 Kiel, Germany.

ABSTRACT

Sea trout populations in the Baltic Sea area are assessed using a newly developed model. In this model, recruitment status is assessed from the observed density of 0+ parr and the estimated maximum possible densities under different habitat conditions. Values are then adjusted for differences in climate and river magnitude across the Baltic Sea. The population trend is assessed by regression of the recruitment status against time. The present status of trout populations in different areas and countries varies significantly. In the catchments draining into the northern part of the Baltic Sea, populations are weak and strongly affected by sea fisheries targeting other species. Population status is also poor in the southeastern part of the Baltic. In the Gulf of Finland, populations have in general been increasing and are close to their optimum. In the south-west, the status is variable in Germany, but close to optimum in Denmark, Poland and Sweden, in spite of an apparent decrease in later years in Denmark and Sweden.

Keywords: *Salmo trutta*; sea trout; Baltic Sea; modelling; recruitment; habitat; stock assessment.

INTRODUCTION

The brown trout (*Salmo trutta*) has its natural distribution in Northern and Western Europe from the White Sea to the Mediterranean, including the entire Baltic Sea (MacCrimmon & Marshall, 1968). The anadromous form, called 'sea trout', migrate from their natal rivers or streams to the sea where they forage until reaching sexual maturity after which they return to their native rivers to spawn (Klemetsen *et al.,* 2003).

The Baltic Sea (Figure 1) is the largest brackish sea in northern Europe with a surface area of 394,000 km². Salinity varies between 1 ppt in the north to 20 ppt at the Danish Straits where the Baltic Sea connects to the North Sea via the Kattegat. The brown trout is widespread in catchments draining into the Baltic Sea, with an estimate of approximately 630 populations containing anadromous sea trout, with about half of these retaining their original wild populations (ICES, 2015). Releases of hatchery-reared trout have a long history in the Baltic. In 2014, some 3.3 million smolts, 518,000 eggs, 3.2 million alevins, 4.7 million fry, 221,000 0+ summer parr and 355,000 older trout were stocked (ICES, 2015).

Migration patterns of the sea trout in the Baltic Sea vary between stocks, with some sea trout making relatively short coastal migrations while others undertake long-distance migrations into the open sea (Aro, 1989, Degerman *et al.,* 2012; Svärdson & Fagerström, 1982; Bartel *et al.,* 2001; Bartel *et al.,* 2010; Hantke, 2010; Hantke *et al.,* 2011). Coastal migration seems to be

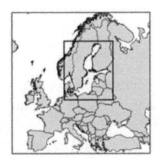
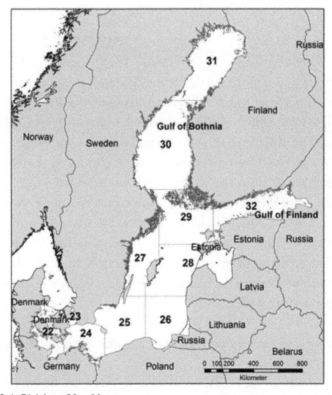

Figure 1. The Baltic Sea showing ICES Sub-Divisions 22 – 32.

more frequent in northern stocks than in southern stocks, where some populations exhibit longer migrations into the open sea. In all sea areas, movement into neighboring areas during feeding migration was observed (Aro, 1989). Sea trout from outside the Baltic are also reported to migrate into the Baltic (Pedersen *et al.,* 2006).

The sea trout is subject to both commercial and recreational fishing. Offshore fishing for salmon increased significantly in the 1950s (Karlsson & Karlström 1994) and sea trout migrating into the open sea were caught by the commercial fishery as a by-catch. Sea trout are also caught in coastal fisheries either as the primary target species or as a by-catch.

During the period 2012-2014, the commercial catch averaged 237 metric tonnes (in ICES Sub-Division (SD) 22-32), which was about one third of the catch for one decade earlier (ICES, 2015). The magnitude of the recreational catch (both fixed gear and sport fishing) is presently uncertain in most countries, but it exceeded the commercial catch significantly in recent years. In 2014, the recreational catch in SD 22-32 was estimated to be 171 tonnes (ICES, 2015). This did not include a Danish catch of 521 tonnes (DTU Aqua: *unpublished*).

The first data on average densities trout fry and parr from some Baltic rivers began to be available, together with some landing statistics, in the 1980s. Some information on the status of populations was collected by the Working Group on Baltic Salmon & Sea Trout (WGBAST) operating under the auspices of the International Council for the Exploration of the Seas (ICES) in the 1980s (ICES, 1985), and was included in the annual ICES assessments from 1987 (ICES, 1987). However, scarcity of data limited the opportunities for assessment and attention focused initially on recorded adult catch, and the impact of stocking. Later, the results from tagging experiments (migration, growth) were reported and, throughout the 1980s and 1990s, the amount of available information gradually increased: including smolt estimates, number of spawners from fish counters and traps and the numbers of populations and their status. The first indication of a low status in sea trout populations appeared in 1990 in the northern part of the Baltic (ICES, 1990). From 1993 to 2011, assessment consisted of 'expert evaluation' of reported catches, densities, number of streams with trout populations and possible reasons for the poor status of some populations. Interest in sea trout populations increased, partly because of increased knowledge about the fate of sea trout in areas with weak populations. This stimulated increased activity, initially resulting in the *"Baltic Sea Trout Workshop"* (Heinemaa *et al.*, 2007) and later, under the auspices of ICES, the *"Study Group on Data Requirements and Assessment Needs for Baltic Sea Trout"* (SGBALANST) (ICES, 2008 & 2009; 2011). In parallel with the ICES Study Group, the HELCOM Salar Project (HELCOM, 2011) was also convened under the auspices of HELCOM. Independent of these initiatives, the *"Workshop on Baltic Sea Trout"* (Pedersen *et al.*, 2012) focused on specifying the management implications of issues affecting sea trout populations negatively. Based on the results from ICES (2011), assessment became model-based for the first time in 2012 and, again, in 2015.

The assessment of a species usually includes both biological data, such as recruitment, age structure, growth and other information from the fisheries such as catch, fishing effort, yield and gear. Various mathematical computations based on monitoring data are usually used to produce a quantitative estimate of the status of the populations in question (Hilborn & Walters, 1992). The ultimate purpose of these assessments is to provide advice on the management of the stock or stocks.

Assessment of salmonid populations is often focused on the freshwater stages, particularly parr abundances (ICES, 2013). Generally, these include density estimates at specific sites fished in consecutive years during the late summer or autumn months. Longer time-series of densities may provide an index of population strength over time and provide an estimate of population status.

Observed densities of salmonid populations in fresh water have been expanded to enumerate entire populations by stratified sampling in sections with a different topography (run, rapid, pool). This is then extrapolated to the entire river system and used to provide estimates of smolt runs (Baglinière *et al.,* 1988; 1993).

HABSCORE is a more advanced method used to evaluate the status of salmonid populations that uses a stepwise multiple regression analysis of population size against stream habitat variables. It brings in habitat quality and provides information on its utilization (Milner *et al.,* 1998; Cowx & Fraser, 2003). The variables used in HABSCORE include mean depth, width, shade, substrate composition and embeddedness, flow and discharge (Barnard & Wyatt, 1995; Milner *et al.,* 1998).

Another method, PHABSIM, models the influence of flow and stream velocities relative to habitat (depth and substrate) (Milhous *et al.,* 1989). The model quantifies the availability of different habitat types using Weighted Usable Area (WUA) and Habitat Suitability Values (HSVs) at different discharges for the variables of depth, velocity and substrate and from these predicts fish abundance.

In the ICES SGBALANST study group, the data available for the construction of a method for assessment were identified and it was the task of the study group to develop an assessment model based on this data (ICES, 2008; 2009). The simple model was constructed as a mean of comparing the abundance of young trout, essentially recruitment between years and areas, and to relate the status to an estimated maximum recruitment.

The objectives of the present paper are: 1) to present the latest version of a model developed for trout assessment in the Baltic Sea area, b) to describe the status of sea trout in the Baltic and c) to discuss possible improvements to the model.

METHODS

MODEL CONSTRUCTION

The prerequisites for development of an assessment model were that it should: 1) utilize data already being collected in order to have a low cost and provide access to a time-series of data, 2) be transparent in order to estimate quality, 3) evaluate the strength of populations in relation to their potential strength, 4) compare areas/regions, and 5) show how populations of sea trout developed over time.

The screening of the quantitative data available across the Baltic identified that data from monitoring parr densities by electro-fishing in the streams were available from almost all countries. Since habitat variables were also available from the monitoring sites, it was decided to focus on this information as a basis for the construction of a model.

The number of young salmonids in a given area of streambed depends on number of spawners (Baglinière *et al.*, 2005), combined with the survival of offspring, which will depend on habitat quality. It should therefore be feasible to compare electrofishing survey densities between sites if spawning fish have had access to sufficient suitable spawning areas near the sites investigated and information on habitat quality is incorporated into the model used.

HABITAT CLASSIFICATION

To enable comparison of habitat quality between sites, countries and geographic regions the classification of habitats needs to be on a standardized basis. Available habitat information from the sites monitored included *dominant substratum, water velocity, average depth, wetted width, shade and slope*. In some countries, information on river slope was not available.

Depending on the value of each variable, a score between 0 and 2 was assigned, with 0 representing poor conditions and 2 representing the best conditions. Scores assigned for each variable were based on published values (Heggenes, 1988; Heggenes & Saltveit, 1990; Heggenes & Borgstrøm, 1990; Heggenes *et al.*, 1991; Mäki-Petäys *et al.*, 1997; Armstrong *et al.*, 2003; Conallin *et al.*, 2014) for habitat preference and suitability and also, in part, on shade and wetted width (E. Degerman & B. Sers, *(unpublished data)*; Debowski & Radtke, 1998) and expert opinion from within the study group (Table 1).

For routine surveys of fish densities, the water velocity and substrate are generally registered in descriptive terms rather than actual measurements. Water velocities are usually assigned to at least one of the following classes: 1) quiet or slow (corresponds to approx. < 20 cm s^{-1}),

Table 1. Habitat score values for different habitat variables.

Variable	*Habitat score*		
	0	*1*	*2*
Water velocity (m sec^{-1})	< 0.2	> 0.7	$0.2 - 0.7$
Substrate diameter (mm)	< 0.2	$0.2 - 2$ and > 200	$2 - 200$
Average depth (m)	> 0.5	$0.3 - 0.5$	< 0.3
Wetted width (m)	> 10	$6 - 10$	<6
Shade (%)	<10	10-20	>20
Slope of section (%)	<0.2 and >8	0.2-0.5 and 3-8	0.5-3

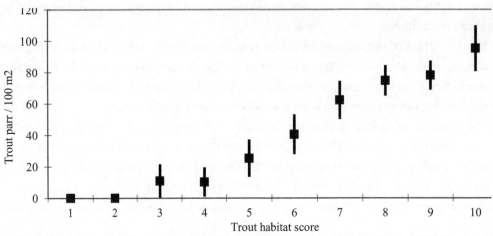

Figure 2. Observed average densities (and standard error) of 0+ trout from 1,833 Danish electro-fishing occasions relative to Trout Habitat Score 0 – 10.

2) moderate (20 – 70 cm s⁻¹) or 3) fast (> 70 cm s⁻¹), and substrate assigned to the following classes: 1) fine (< 2mm), 2) gravel (2-100 mm), 3) stone (100-200 mm) or 4) boulder/bedrock (>200 mm).

The Trout Habitat Score (THS) is then simply the addition of score values for each variable (c.f. Shirvell, 1989) as *THS = substrate +velocity + depth + width +shade + slope,* resulting in THS scores ranging from 0 to a maximum of 12 (or 0 – 10 where information on slope is not available). As an example of the outcome, observed average densities for each THS from 1,833 Danish electro-fishing occasions are presented in Figure 2. For simplicity, and in order to make the assessment more robust, the individual THS values are grouped into *THS classes* (Table 2).

RECRUITMENT STATUS

The maximum possible densities for each THS class need to be known to assess the status of individual populations relative to populations with maximum possible recruitment. Since these values were not available, the highest observed densities in the Baltic Sea area were used

Table 2. Grouping of THS values into THS classes.

THS Class	Maximum THS	
	10	12
0	THS < 5	THS < 6
1	THS = 5 – 6	THS = 6 – 8
2	THS = 7 – 8	THS = 9 – 10
3	THS = 9 – 10	THS = 11 – 12

instead. These were selected from rivers with 'good' water quality in accordance with the EU Water framework directive and from these the three best years after 2000 were chosen. As far as was possible, the sites selected in the rivers were not to be negatively affected by fishing, migration obstacles or pollution according to 'expert judgment'. If a shorter time series was available, only the best year was selected: except where the density was below 10 0+ trout/100 m² for sites with stream width < 5 m or where the density of trout was 5 0+ trout/ 100 m² for sites where stream width was between 5 – 15 m. At sites with stream width > 15 m, at least one 0+ trout/100 m² had to be present for the site to be included in the reference data set. Sites that were stocked with trout were included in this selection.

Densities of trout vary with both climate and the size of the river (ICES, 2009). To correct for variation in these factors, a relationship was established by a multivariate linear regression (Barnard & Wyatt, 1995). The variables: Log_{10} (wetted width), longitude, latitude, average air temperature, THS class (0-3) were entered, with Log_{10} (0+ density) as dependent variable. This resulted in the relationship:

(1) Log_{10} (0+ density) = 0.963 – (0.906 log_{10} (width)) + (0.045 airtemp) – (0.037 longitude) + (0.027 latitude) + (0.033 THS); (r^2 = 0.50, Anova; $F_{2.254}$ = 51.8, p<0.001).

This was used to assess the maximum predicted densities for all monitored sites. Recruitment status was then calculated for each assessment site (*see below*) as the average of:

(2) Recruitment status = [observed Log_{10} (0+ density +1) / maximum Log_{10} (0+ density + 1)] ★ 100 %.

For comparing rivers or larger regions, the mean of the recruitment status was calculated. The ICES Sub-Divisions (Figure 1) were adopted as assessment units. This numerical model is used to identify areas and assessment units where recruitment status was below expected levels. Additional information was incorporated into the final assessments which included: a) observed number of adult spawners (from fish ladders, fish counters or by video monitoring), b) reports of river catches as an index of spawning runs, c) recapture pattern (time and gear) of tagged smolts, d) expert knowledge on local fishing intensity and e) information on smolt numbers.

The goodness of fit of trends over the latest available 5-year periods (2010-2014 or 2009-2013) were calculated for each site as Pearson's r value using bivariate correlation between recruitment status and year to give values ranging from -1 to +1. This does not give the magnitude of trends, but the direction and a quantitative value of how distinct the trend is.

RESULTS

In the southwest Sub-Division (SD 22-25; Denmark, Germany, Poland, Sweden), abundances of 0+ parr were generally high with averages between 38-205 trout /100 m². However, while

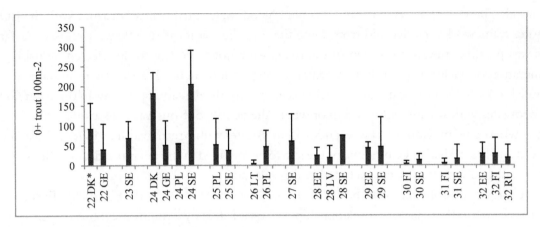

Figure 3. Average densities (and standard error) for the time period 2012 – 2014 by ICES Sub-Division and Country (Standard deviation) (DK = Denmark, EE = Estonia, FI = Finland, GE = Germany, LT = Lithuania, LV = Latvia, PL = Poland, RU = Russia, SE = Sweden). *Site partly in Sub-Division 21.*

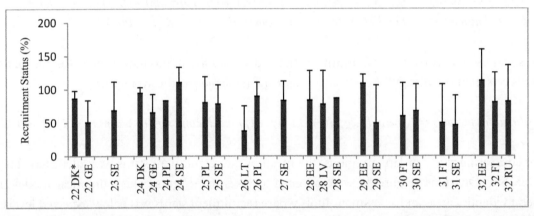

Figure 4. Recruitment status (with standard error) for the time period 2012-2014 by ICES Sub-Division and Country (Standard deviation) (DK = Denmark, EE = Estonia, FI = Finland, GE = Germany, LT = Lithuania, LV = Latvia, PL = Poland, RU = Russia, SE = Sweden). * Site partly in Sub Division 21

recruitment status was about or above 80 % in SD 22-25 (Denmark, Poland, Sweden), it was only just over 50 % in SD 22 and 65 % in SD 24 in Germany (Figures 3 & 4 and Table 3). The trend in German populations was unknown and for the remaining countries there were clear reductions in both Danish and Swedish streams (SD 22 & 23); but with some improvement at one Danish site in SD 24 (Figure 5).

In the southeast (SD 26), there were huge differences between Poland and Lithuania. In Poland the recruitment status was high with average densities of almost 50 0+trout /100 m^2 and recruitment status was close to 100 % compared with Lithuania with an average 0+ density of 5.4/100m^2 and a recruitment status below 40 % (Table 3). Any trend in recruitment status was not detected in these countries.

Table 3. Recruitment status and density (No/ 100 m²) for 0+ trout by ICES Sub-Division & Country for 2012–2014. N = number of sites, S.D.= Standard deviation, C.V.= Coefficient of variation. * Some Danish sites in Sub-division 21.

Sub-Division	Country	Recruitment					Density			
		N	Status	S.D.	95% CL	C.V.	N/100 m⁻²	S.D.	95% C.L.	C.V.
22*	Denmark	10	87.3	10.6	6.5	0.1	93.1	64.6	31.7	0.7
-	Germany	48	51.8	31.9	9.0	0.6	41.4	63.6	18.0	1.5
23	Sweden	33	100.0	26.4			69.4	42.2	29.2	0.6
24	Denmark	2	95.3	7.7	10.6	0.1	182.5	52.5	72.8	0.3
-	Germany	45	65.9	26.7	7.8	0.4	51.9	60.7	17.7	1.2
-	Poland	1	84.0				55.0			
-	Sweden	5	111.1	22.1	19.3	0.2	205.3	85.5	74.9	0.4
25	Poland	52	81.0	38.2	10.4	0.5	52.9	65.4	17.8	1.2
-	Sweden	10	79.0	27.8	17.3	0.4	38.3	51.1	31.7	1.3
26	Lithuania	190	38.6	36.7	5.2	1.0	5.4	7.9	1.1	1.5
-	Poland	9	90.4	20.3	13.3	0.2	47.6	40.3	26.3	0.8
27	Sweden	33	84.1	28.1	9.6	0.3	61.8	67.3	23.0	1.1
28	Estonia	14	84.6	43.2	22.6	0.5	25.6	19.2	10.1	0.8
-	Latvia	24	78.4	49.6	19.9	0.6	19.7	29.2	11.7	1.5
-	Sweden	1	87.5				75.5			
29	Estonia	2	109.3	12.9	17.9	0.1	44.2	13.7	19.0	0.3
-	Sweden	12	49.9	56.2	31.8	1.1	47.3	73.8	41.7	1.6
30	Finland	6	60.4	48.9	39.2	0.8	4.9	5.7	4.6	1.2
-	Sweden	16	68.2	39.5	19.3	0.6	14.2	13.8	6.8	1.0
31	Finland	9	50.4	57.1	37.3	1.1	6.3	9.9	6.4	1.6
-	Sweden	19	47.0	43.6	19.6	0.9	17.3	34.5	15.5	2.0
32	Estonia	54	113.6	46.0	12.3	0.4	29.8	26.4	7.0	0.9
-	Finland	21	81.2	44.0	18.8	0.5	29.9	39.1	16.7	1.3
-	Russia	18	82.4	53.7	24.8	0.7	19.7	31.5	14.5	1.6

The average abundance of trout was relatively high in the central part of the Baltic (SD 27-29) for Sweden, Estonia, Latvia), with average densities between 19.7 and 75.5 trout/100 m². Recruitment status was above approximately 80 %, except in Sweden in SD 29 where the status was variable, but averaged only 50 % (Table 3), and the trend was negative (Figure 5).

In the north, in the Gulf of Bothnia (SD 30 & 31), densities varied considerable between Sweden (14.2–17.3/100m²) and Finland (4.9–6.3/100m²), and the recruitment status was relatively low (47–68 %) (Table 3). Improvement over time in most populations was modest, except in the one river in Finland (Figure 5).

In the Gulf of Finland (SD 32), the average abundance varied from 20–30 0+ parr/100 m² and the recruitment status was above 80 %. For all three countries in the area, the improvement was positive (Figures 3-5 & Table 3).

In general, the average densities and recruitment levels were associated with considerable variation (high standard deviation), both between sites (Table 3) and also between years at most sites (*data not presented in this paper*).

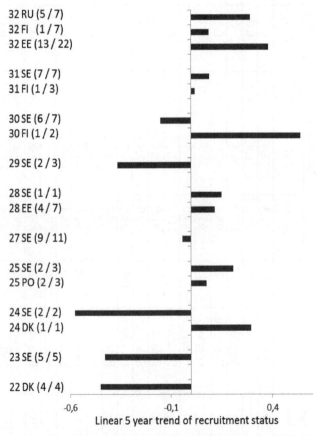

Figure 5. Five year trend in Goodness-of-Fit (Pearson's r) of recruitment status by ICES Sub-Division and Country (DK = Denmark, EE = Estonia, FI = Finland, GE = Germany, LT = Lithuania, LV = Latvia, PL = Poland, RU = Russia, SE = Sweden). (Number of rivers / Number of sites). Only sites with a time series of at least 5 years shown. Total number of streams was 66 with 95 sites.

DISCUSSION

There were large temporal variations in recruitment status between years, especially in small streams. One obvious explanation, although by far not the only one, for such variation is variation of the spawning population between years. Counts of spawners in 4 smaller German streams showed variable numbers of spawners (a 3-fold variation of between approximately 800 and 2,300 fish in the Hellbach system (SD 22) for the period 2009-2014) (Hantke, 2015). In the larger Polish River Slupia, the number of spawners counted varied from approximately 3,500 and 7,300 fish between 2006–2014 (ICES, 2015). In the River Pirita in Estonia (at the outlet into SD 32), the smolt run and ascending spawners are counted. The smolt run over the period 2008 – 2014 has varied between a few hundred to approximately 2,500 fish. In 2014 and 2015, only 19 and 121 spawners respectively were counted in this river (Martin Kesler, *pers. comm.*).

There were large differences in recruitment status in different regions in the Baltic. Several factors may be responsible, but the ascending numbers of spawners seems to be the ultimate factor. In the Bothnian Bay, spawners are counted in a number of large Swedish rivers (Kalix, Pite, Åby, Byske, Rickleån and Ume-Vindelälven). Up to year 2000, the number of ascending spawners was below 100 in all rivers. They then increased to approximately 200 fish, but after a few years numbers fell again except in the River Kalix, where the number remained stable until 2013 and then increased to approximately 300 (ICES, 2015). In contrast to these rivers, the River Pite showed a steady improvement in the spawning run from year 2000, increasing to approximately 850 sea trout in 2014. After taking the size of these rivers into consideration, the populations were well below what could be expected when compared with much smaller rivers in Poland and Germany. There are indications that the increased number of spawners is related to decreased fishery exploitation. A long time series of catches in the River Kalix and in the Swedish part of the River Torneälven shows gradually decreasing catches from approximately 3 tonnes in the early 1960s to a few hundred kilograms in the 1970s. Catches have been very low in later years, indeed almost non-existent, partly a result of fishing restrictions and low population abundance. Catches in the neighboring River Kalix showed a similar trend, although the decline started in the late 1960s.

The recruitment status of sea trout populations in the Gulf of Bothnia is very low, especially in the northern area (SD 31). This is at least partly a result of the sea trout exploitation in the sea and confirms previous findings (ICES, 1990, Jutila *et al.*, 2006; Lundquist *et al.*, 2006; Degerman, 2012). Signs of progress have been observed in some areas that probably result from the introduction of fishing regulations with an increased minimum size of trout and restrictions on net fishing. Sea trout in the area mature at a sea-age of 3-5 years at a length of greater than 65 cm (Atso Romakaniemi, *pers. comm.*; Jutila *et al.*, 2006) and only a small proportion of adults survive to this age and size due to high fishing mortality. The status of the populations in this area was identified as 'critical' from the 1980s (ICES, 1990; Jutila *et al.*, 2006 & 2012; Lundquist *et al.*, 2006). In the Gulf of Finland, there is concern over the low number of spawners and small number of smolts in the River Pirita, which has already been referred to, even though populations have typically increased in the area.

In the central part of the Baltic, the status of the sea trout populations appears to be close to optimal.

In the southeast, populations in Lithuania are very low. This may be associated with both poor conditions in the streams and / or a high fishing mortality (Kontautas & Kesminas, 2012). The vast majority of the entire reported catch (2,400 sea trout) was taken as a by-catch in the Curonian Lagoon. This shows that recruitment status may detect a problem but not the cause of that problem.

In the southwestern part of the Baltic, the status in some German streams is relatively low. The reason for this is unclear and any trend cannot be detected because no time-series of electro-fishing monitoring data is available before 2012 (Petereit *et al.*, 2013). However, one reason could be poor quality of spawning habitats (Dierksmeyer & Brunotte, 2009); but it is also known that sea trout are caught in local coastal fisheries. Although the trend in recruitment status has been negative in Denmark and Sweden, population status remains high.

In summarizing population status and trends, it is evident that fishing pressure is potentially the major factor causing low status.

One limitation of the recruitment status approach is that it is not possible to provide an estimate of smolt production. However, such estimates are calculated in most countries from electro-fishing data and estimated survival from the pre-smolt to smolt stages. Thus, for example, the total smolt output from Lithuania was estimated at between 34,000 and 45,000 fish during the period 2012-2014 (ICES, 2015). The future development of the recruitment status model should include an assessment of smolt production from electro-fishing data and habitat surveys (*see* Höjesjö *et al.,* 2017b).

Another problem is in distinguishing between resident and anadromous spawners. It is technically possible to distinguish between the offspring of resident and anadromous female parents by chemical analysis of the strontium/calcium ratio (Kalish, 1990; Limburg, 1995, Taal *et al.,* 2014). However, analyzing the huge number of samples that would be required might be impracticable. Better information on the general nature and importance of the relative contributions of trout of freshwater resident and anadromous parentage to the juvenile trout population might be feasible from detailed studies in index streams and from direct monitoring of adults at spawning time.

Transporting models between streams and areas is problematic (Shirvell, 1989; Barnard & Wyatt, 1995). However, the basic preference for the physical variables of velocity, depth and substrate has been found to be constant (at least for salmon) across a range of different stream types (Morantz *et al.,* 1987; Shirvell & Dungey, 1983). The present model was developed and applied across a large and relatively diverse area and therefore should not suffer this constraint.

It has been suggested that trout population estimates from electro-fishing operation should only be carried out in small to medium-sized river systems with catchment sizes below about

1,000 km² (ICES, 2009; 2011). In the larger rivers in the Baltic area, juvenile populations may be dominated by salmon with trout confined to smaller streams (ICES, 2009; Milner *et al.*, 2007). Sea trout often spawn in the many smaller tributaries of larger rivers, so that there are potentially thousands of streams and rivulets that might need to be monitored. However, our results indicate that population status is generally quite similar in larger geographical regions, possibly reflecting regional fishing pressure. This indicates the possibility of using a number of Index Rivers to establish recruitment status for sea trout.

There was a positive relationship between density and habitat quality in general and at densities below maximal. This could be because individual territories in a given area will vary in quality so that territories are gradually occupied in sequence according to their quality as densities increase with the better territories occupied first. The sizes of territories will be influenced by a large number of interacting variables (Finstad *et al.*, 2011; Heggenes, 1996), including the availability of food and cover. Density independent variation is, therefore, likely to have considerable influence on the actual fish densities.

The recruitment status is particularly sensitive for populations with low densities, making it useful for the assessment, for which it was constructed through detection of populations at seriously low status. However, since sea trout populations often vary temporally in a cyclic manner, poor status for shorter time period may not provide the true status for the overall population. This is, on the other hand, counteracted through the assessment of larger assessment units that may integrate environmental and fisheries dependent conditions of the spawning population.

The use of data collected routinely in countries around the Baltic Sea as the basis for the model makes this approach cost effective. By grouping THS *score values* into THS *class intervals,* the approach is likely to become more robust. Smaller differences in assigning precise score values in the included variables should be less influential when estimating final assessments of status. In the basic data recorded in the field, both substrate and velocity were derived from descriptive classes and then assigned to class intervals. The grouping of THS *score values* into THS *class intervals* is also likely to help balance the possible effect from lack of inter-calibration between teams of field workers in different countries.

Being based on a combined set of habitat variables that have been either measured or classified on site, the assessment should be more accurate compared to the evaluation of just trout parr densities, possibly combined with parameters such as river run type, width or stream order.

The THS is constructed as a sum of scores, where each component has a value adding to the habitat score. Certainly, some components may be more important than others, e.g. stream width, which often have a high impact on trout juvenile abundance (ICES, 2009). A high score of a less important variable could potentially, but not necessarily, compensate for a low score of a more important variable. Certainly it would be possible to parameterize the THS by giving each component a different weight, most simply with a multiple linear regression. It was felt that such an approach may not be so applicable on a wider geographical scale. This should however be tested in the future development of THS when a larger data set is available.

When calculating the predicted maximum densities THS was used together with stream width, air temperature, latitude and longitude. Air temperature, longitude and latitude are all proxies for other variables that are more difficult to measure, e.g. overall ecosystem productivity (increasing from north to south), species richness (increasing from east to west) a shift from oceanic to continental climate and different fishing patterns within the Baltic (ICES, 2008 & 2009). Identifying more relevant environmental drivers is essential if the approach shall be expanded outside the Baltic area, and also essential for a better understanding of major drivers of trout productivity.

It should be noted that all field measurements were collected without inter-calibration between field workers and that, therefore, the precise assignment of scores might vary somewhat between countries.

Apart from the ability of the suggested relationship between recruitment of young fish and the biomass of spawners to assess and compare the status of both adjacent and more distant sites, the development of THS should enable the identification of local or even in-stream factors responsible for low recruitment status, such as barriers to upstream migration. Sites with high THS would be expected to show high levels of recruitment. By taking into account the large variability between years (*see above*); this should facilitate identification of those sites where recruitment status was significantly below the expected and regional means. Thus, recruitment status and THS may be useful techniques in both detecting large-scale and small-scale problems in recruitment. We suggest that even when more sophisticated models of stock-recruitment are developed, recruitment status and THS may be a valuable tool in sea trout stock management. There is still considerable scope for development and improvement of this model approach. Precision is expected to increase with both a longer time-series of data and more sites, and performance might be improved by the inclusion of more relevant variables: such as distance from sea, elevation, migration obstacles, cover, flow variability, and water chemistry. There should also be a greater focus on obtaining estimates of smolt production in the future development of the approach.

ACKNOWLEDGEMENTS

We wish to thank all members of the ICES Salmon and Trout Assessment Working Group (WGBAST) for supplying data for the assessment of trout and for critical and fruitful discussions. Christoph Petereit was funded by the Federal-Fishing Fund "Fischereiabgabe" Schleswig-Holstein, co-financed by the European Fisheries Fund (EFF), granted by the Ministry of Energy, Agriculture, the Environment and Rural Areas of Schleswig-Holstein and by GEOMAR in the framework of the four projects "Sea Trout Literature study, ParrQuant, VariParr & SMARRT (30/ SH305E)".

REFERENCES

Armstrong, J. D., P. S. Kemp, G. J. Kennedy, M. Ladle, & N. J. Milner. (2003). Habitat requirements of Atlantic salmon and brown trout in rivers and streams. *Fisheries Research,* **62**: 143-170.

Aro, E. (1989). A review of fish migration patterns in the Baltic. *Rapports et procès-verbaux des réunions / Conseil permanent international pour l'exploration de la mer,* **190,** 72-96.

Baglinière, J-L., G. Maisse, A. Nihouarn, J. P. Porcher, & P. M. Le Gloanec. (1988). Comparison of two methods for the estimation of the natural production of Atlantic salmon smolts (*Salmo salar* L.). *Bulletin Francais de la Peche et de la Piscicultur,* **308,** 24-34.

Baglinière, J-L., G. Maisse, & A. Nihouarn. (1993). Comparison of two methods of estimating Atlantic salmon (*Salmo salar*) wild smolt production. In: Production of Juvenile Atlantic Salmon, *Salmo salar,* in Natural Water (R. Gibson & R. Cutting, (*Eds.*). *Canadian Journal of Fisheries and Aquatic Sciences.* **118,** 189-201.

Baglinière, J-L., F. Marchand, & V. Vauclin. (2005). Inter-annual changes in recruitment of the Atlantic salmon (*Salmo salar*) population in the River Oir (Lower Normandy, France): relationships with spawners and in-stream habitat. *ICES Journal of Marine Science,* **62**: 695-707.

Barnard, S. & Wyatt, R.J. (1995). An analysis of predictive models for stream salmonid populations. *Bulletin Francais de la Peche et de la Pisciculture,* **337-339,** 277-282.

Bartel, R., Ikonen, E. & Auvinen, H. (2001). Differences in migration pattern and growth of Polish and Finnish sea trout (*Salmo trutta* L.) released in the same areas. *Archives of Polish Fisheries* **9,** 105-122.

Bartel, R., Pachur, M. & Bernas, R. (2010). Distribution, migrations, and growth of tagged sea trout released into the Vistula River. *Archives of Polish Fisheries,* **18,** 225-237.

Conallin, J., E. Boegh, M. Olsen, S. Pedersen, M. J. Dunbar, & J. K. Jensen. (2014). Daytime habitat selection for juvenile parr brown trout (*Salmo trutta*) in small lowland streams. *Knowledge and Management of Aquatic Ecosystems* 413, 09. DOI: 10.1051/kmae/2014006.

Cowx, I. & Fraser, D. (2003). Monitoring the Atlantic Salmon. Conserving Natura 2000 Rivers. Monitoring Series No. 7, English Nature, Peterborough. 35 pp

Debowski, P. & G. Radtke. (1998). Density and growth of young brown trout (*Salmo trutta* L.) in streams of Northern Poland versus habitat attributes *Archives of Polish Fisheries,* **45**: 77-89.

Degerman, E. (2012). Status of sea trout stocks in the Swedish part of the Baltic Sea 1990-2010 assessed from recruitment data and spawner counts. In: *Workshop on Baltic Sea Trout.* (S. Pedersen., P. Heinimaa & T. Pakarinen. *Eds.*). Helsinki, Finland, 11-13 October 2011. DTU Aqua Report No 248-2012. National Institute of Aquatic Resources, Technical University of Denmark, 95 pp.

Degerman, E., Leonardsson, K. & Lundquist, H. (2012). Coastal migrations, temporary use of neighbouring rivers, and growth of sea trout (*Salmo trutta*) from nine northern Baltic Sea rivers. *ICES Journal of Marine Science,* **69,** 971-980.

Dirksmeyer, J. & E. Brunotte. (2009). Sediment textures and hydrogeomorphological characteristics of salmon and sea trout spawning habitats in Germany – a contribution to river ecology. *Zeitschrift für Geomorphologie,* **53,** 319-334.

Finstad, A.G., Armstrong, J.D., & Nislow, K.H. (2011). Freshwater Habitat Requirements of Atlantic Salmon. In: *Atlantic Salmon Ecology.* (Ø. Aas., S. Einum., A. Klemetsen. & J. Skurdal. *Eds.*). Blackwell Publishing Ltd, 67-87.

Hantke, H. (2015). Bestandserfassung der Meerforelle (*Salmo trutta* L.) in drei ausgewählten Fließgewässern M-V durch videooptische Zählungen und Markierungsversuche sowie eine darauf basierende Abschätzung des Gesamtbestandes in der Mecklenburger Bucht. Verein Fisch und Umwelt Mecklenburg-Vorpommern, Jahresheft 2014/2015, 56 pp. *[In German.]*

Hantke, H. (2010). Erste zusammenfassende Ergebnisse der Markierungen von Meerforellen (*Salmo trutta*) mit DST-GPS Tags zur Ermittlung der horizontalen und vertikalen Wanderung im Bereich der Ostsee. Verein Fisch und Umwelt Mecklenburg-Vorpommern, Jahresheft 2009/2010: 29-45. *[In German.]*

Hantke, H., Jennerich, H-J. & Schulz, N. (2011). Optimierung des Bestandsmanagements für Meerforellen (*Salmo trutta trutta* L.) in den Küstengewässern Mecklenburg-Vorpommerns durch Ermittlung vertikaler und horizontaler Wanderwege. *Beiträge zur Fischerei in Mitteilungen der Landesforschungsanstalt für Landwirtschaft und Fischerei Mecklenburg-Vorpommern* **45**, 1-11. *[In German with English Abstract.]*

Heggenes, J. (1988). Substrate preferences of brown trout fry (*Salmo trutta*) in artificial stream channels. *Canadian Journal of Fisheries and Aquatic Sciences,* **45**: 1801-1806.

Heggenes, J. (1996). Habitat selection by brown trout (*Salmo trutta*) and young Atlantic salmon (*S. salar*) in streams: Static and dynamic hydraulic modelling. *Regulated Rivers: Research & Management,* **12**: 155-169.

Heggenes, J., A. Brabrand, & S. J. Saltveit. (1991). Microhabitat use by brown trout, *Salmo trutta* L. and Atlantic salmon, *S. salar* L., in a stream: A comparative study of underwater and river bank observations. *Journal of Fish Biology,* **38**: 259-266.

Heggenes, J. & R. Borgstrøm. (1991). Effect of habitat types on survival, spatial distribution and production of an allopatric cohort of Atlantic salmon, *Salmo salar* L., under conditions of low competition. Journal of Fish Biology, **38**: 267-280.

Heggenes, J. & S. J. Saltveit. (1990). Seasonal and spatial microhabitat selection and segregation in young Atlantic salmon, *Salmo salar* L., and brown trout, *Salmo trutta* L., in a Norwegian river. Journal of. Fish Biology, **36**: 707-720.

Heinimaa, P., E. Jutila, & T. Pakarinen. (2007). Baltic Sea Trout Workshop, 31.5.-2.6.2006, Kalatutkimuksia – Fiskundersökningar 410. Helsinki. 69 pp

HELCOM. (2011). Salmon and Sea Trout Populations and Rivers in the Baltic Sea – HELCOM assessment of salmon (*Salmo salar*) and sea trout (*Salmo trutta*) populations and habitats in rivers flowing to the Baltic Sea. *Baltic Sea Environment Proceedings* No. 126A. 39 pp.

Hilborn, R., & C. J. Walters. (1992). Quantitative Fisheries Stock Assessment Choice, Dynamics and Uncertainty. Chapman and Hall, 559 pp.

Höjesjö, J., Nilsson, N., Degerman, E., Halldén, A. & Aldvén, D. (2017b). Calculating smolt production of sea trout from habitat surveys and electrofishing: pilot studies from small streams in Sweden. In: *Sea Trout: Science & Management*. Graeme. Harris. *Ed.*). Proceedings of the 2nd International Sea Trout Symposium, October 2015, Dundalk, Ireland, Troubador, 458–469.

ICES. (1985). Report of the Baltic Salmon and Trout Assessment Working Group, Copenhagen, 11-16 April 1987, C.M. 1985/Assess:14. 55 pp.

ICES. (1987). Report of the Baltic Salmon and Trout Assessment Working Group, Copenhagen, 9-15 April 1987, C.M. 1987/Assess:21. 51 pp.

ICES. (1990). Report of the Baltic Salmon and Trout Assessment Working Group, ICES C.M. 7 – 14 March 1990. 1990/Assess: 21. 85 pp.

ICES. (2008). Report of the Study Group on data requirements and assessment needs for Baltic Sea trout [SGBALANST], By Correspondence, December 2007 – February 2008. ICES CM 2008/ DFC:01. 74 pp.

ICES. (2009). Report of the Study Group on Data Requirements and Assessment Needs for Baltic Sea Trout (SGBALANST), 3–5 February 2009, Copenhagen, Denmark. ICES CM 2009/DFC:03. 97 pp.

ICES. (2011). Study Group on data requirements and assessment needs for Baltic Sea trout (SGBALANST), 23 March 2010 St. Petersburg, Russia, By correspondence in 2011. ICES CM 2011/SSGEF:18. 54 pp.

ICES. (2012). Report on the Classification of Stock Assessment Methods developed by SISAM. ICES CM 2012/ACOM/SCICOM:01. 15 pp.

ICES. (2013). Report of the Workshop on Sea Trout (WKTRUTTA), 12–14 November 2013, ICES Headquarters, Copenhagen, Denmark. ICES CM 2013/SSGEF:15. 243 pp.

ICES. (2015). Report of the Baltic Salmon and Trout Assessment Working Group (WGBAST), 23-31 March 2015, Rostock, Germany. ICES CM 2015\ACOM:08. 362 pp.

Jonsson, N., B. Jonsson, & L. P. Hansen. (1998). The relative role of density-dependent and density-independent survival in the life cycle of Atlantic salmon *Salmo salar*. *Journal of Animal Ecology,* **67**: 751-762.

Jutila, E., A. Saura, I. Kallio-Nyberg, A. Huhmarniemi, & A. Romakkaniemi. (2006). The status and exploitation of sea trout on the Finnish coast of the Gulf of Bothnia in the Baltic Sea. In*: Sea Trout: Biology, Conservation & Management.* (Graeme Harris & Nigel Milner. *Eds.*). Proceedings of the 1st International Sea Trout Symposium, July 2004, Cardiff, Wales. Blackwell Publishing. 128-138

Jutila, E., T. Pakarinen, J. R. Saur, V. Vähä, & A. Huhmarniemi. (2012). Status of sea trout populations in Finland. In: S. Pedersen, P. Heinimaa, & T. Pakarinen (Eds.). *Workshop on Baltic Sea Trout.* 11-13 October 2011, Helsinki, Finland. DTU Aqua Report No 248-2012. National Institute of Aquatic resources, Technical University of Denmark. 95 pp.

Kalish, J. M. (1990). Use of otolith microchemistry to distinguish the progeny of sympatric anadromous and non-anadromous salmonids. *Fishery Bulletin,* **88**: 657-666.

Karlsson, L. & Ö. Karlström. (1994). The Baltic salmon (*Salmo salar* L.): its history, present situation and future. *Dana,* **10**: 61-85.

Klemetsen, A., Amundsen, P-A., Dempson, J.B., Jonsson, B., Jonsson, N., O'Connell, M.F. & Mortensen, E. (2003). Atlantic salmon *Salmo salar* L., brown trout *Salmo trutta* L. and Arctic charr *Salvelinus alpinus* (L.): a review of aspects of their life histories. *Ecology of Freshwater Fish,* **12**, 1-59.

Kontautas, A. & V. Kesminas. (2012). Sea trout in Lithuania. In: *Workshop on Baltic Sea Trout., 11-13 October 2011, Helsinki, Finland*. (S. Pedersen, P. Heinimaa, & T. Pakarinen. *Eds*). DTU Aqua Report No 248-2012. National Institute of Aquatic Resources, Technical University of Denmark. 95 pp.

Limburg, K. E. (1995). Otolith strontium traces environmental history of sub-yearling American shad *Alosa sapidissima. Marine Ecology Progress Series,* **119**, 25-35.

Lundquist, H., S. M. McKinnell, S. Jonsson, & J. Östergren. (2006). Is stocking with sea trout compatible with the conservation of wild trout (*Salmo trutta* L.)? In: *Sea Trout: Biology, Conservation & Management*. (Graeme. Harris, & Nigel Milner. *Eds*.). Proceedings of the 1st International Sea Trout Symposium, July 2004, Cardiff, Wales. Blackwell Publishing. 356-371.

MacCrimmon, H.R. & Marshall, T.L. (1968). World Distribution of Brown Trout, *Salmo trutta. Journal of the Fisheries Research Board of Canada*, **25**, 2527-2548.

Mäki-Petäys, A., T. Muotka, A. Huusko, P. Tikkanen, & P. Kreivi. (1997). Seasonal changes in habitat use and preference by juvenile brown trout, *Salmo trutta*, in a northern boreal river. Canadian Journal of Fish and Aquatic Science, **54**, 520-530.

Milhous, R.T., Updike, M.A., & Schneider, D.M. (1989). Physical Habitat Simulation System Reference Manual – Version II. Instream Flow Information Paper No. 26. U.S. Fish & Wildlife Service Biological Report 89(16), 404 pp.

Milner, N. J., J. M. Elliott, J. D. Armstrong, R. Gardiner, J. S. Welton, & M. Ladle. (2003). The natural control of salmon and trout populations in streams. *Fisheries Research,* **62**: 111-125.

Milner, N.J., Karlsson, L., Degerman, E., Johlander, A., MacClean, L.P. & Hansen, L-P. (2007). Sea Trout (*Salmo trutta* L.) in European Salmon (*Salmo salar* L.) Rivers. *In:. Sea Trout: Biology, Conservation & Management*. (Graeme Harris & Nigel Milner *Eds.*). Proceedings of the 1st International Sea Trout Symposium, July 2004, Cardiff, Wales. Blackwell Publishing Ltd, Oxford. 139-156

Milner, N. J., R. J. Hemsworth, & B. E. Jones. (1985). Habitat evaluation as a fisheries management tool. *Journal of Fish Biology*, **27A**: 85-108.

Milner, N.J., Wyatt, R.J., & Broad, K. (1998). HABSCORE – applications and future developments of related habitat models. *Aquatic Conservation-Marine and Freshwater Ecosystems*, **8**, 633-644.

Morantz, D. L., R. K. Sweeney, C. S. Shirvell, & D. A. Longard. (1987). Selection of Microhabitat in Summer by Juvenile Atlantic Salmon (*Salmo salar*). *Canadian Journal of Fisheries and Aquatic Sciences,* **44**: 120-129.

Pedersen, S., Heinimaa, P. & Pakarinen, T. (*Eds.*). (2012). *Workshop on Baltic Sea Trout 11-13 October 2011,Helsinki, Finland*. DTU Aqua Report No 248-2012. National Institute of Aquatic Resources, Technical University of Denmark. 95 pp.

Pedersen, S., R. Christiansen, & H. Glüsing. (2006). Comparison of survival, migration and growth in wild, offspring from wild (F1) and domesticated sea-run trout (*Salmo trutta* L.). In: *Sea Trout: Biology, Conservation & Management*. (Graeme. Harris & Nigel Milner *Eds*). Proceedings of 1st International Sea Trout Symposium, July 2004, Cardiff, Wales. Blackwell Publishing. 377-388.

Petereit, C., Reusch, T. B. H., Dierking, J. & Hahn, A. (2013). Literaturrecherche, Aus-und Bewertung der Datenbasis zur Meerforelle (*Salmo trutta trutta* L.): Grundlage für ein Projekt zur Optimierung des Meerforellenmanagements in Schleswig-Holstein. GEOMAR Report N. Ser. 010. 158 pp. 10.3289/GEOMAR_REP_NS_10_2013. http://oceanrep.geomar.de/21919/ . (*In German*)

Shirvell, C. S. (1989). Habitat Models and their Predictive Capability to Infer Habitat Effects on Stock Size. In: *Proceedings of the National Workshop on Effects of Habitat Alteration on Salmonid Stocks.* (C. D. Levings, L. B. Holtby & M. A. Henderson. *Eds.*). Canadian Special Publication of Fisheries & Aquatic Sciences **105,**

Shirvell, C. S. & R. G. Dungey. (1983). Microhabitats chosen by brown trout for feeding and spawning in rivers. *Transactions of the American Fisheries Society,* **112**: 355-367.

Svärdson, G. & Fagerström, Å. (1982). Adaptive differences in the long-distance migration of some trout (*Salmo trutta* L.) stocks. Report from the Institute of Freshwater Research, Drottningholm, **60,** 51-80.

Taal , I., M. Kesler, L. Saks, M. Rohtla, A. Verliin, R. Svirgsden, K. Jürgens, M. Vetemaa & T. Saat. (2014). Evidence for an autumn downstream migration of Atlantic salmon *Salmo salar* (Linnaeus) and brown trout *Salmo trutta* (Linnaeus) parr to the Baltic Sea. *Helgoland Marine Research,* 68, 373-377.

Perspectives on sea trout stocks in Sweden, Denmark & Norway: monitoring, threats and management

J. HÖJESJÖ[1], D. ALDVÉN[1], J. G. DAVIDSEN[2], S. PEDERSEN[3] & E. DEGERMAN[4].

[1]*Department of Biology and Environmental Sciences, University of Gothenburg, Box 463, 405 30 Göteborg, Sweden.*
[2]*NTNU University Museum · Department of Natural History, Trondheim, Norway.*
[3]*Technical University of Denmark, DTU Aqua – National Institute for Aquatic Resources, Section for Freshwater Fisheries & Ecology, Vejlsøvej 39, DK – 8600 Silkeborg, Denmark,*
[4]*Swedish University of Agricultural Sciences, Institute of Freshwater Research, Pappersbruksallén 22, SE-702 15 Örebro, Sweden.*

ABSTRACT

An overview of the status, monitoring and management of sea trout populations in Denmark, Norway and Sweden is presented and discussed. The sea trout is one of the most important species for the recreational fishery in this region and it is therefore important to regulate and manage stocks in ways that are sustainable. Electro-fishing is clearly the most important tool for monitoring the status and wellbeing of stocks. In a few systems, counts of adult spawners and smolt counts are also carried out, often as a by-product of salmon monitoring. Biological reference points based on stock-recruitment relationships are rare. Establishing such reference points is difficult due to the great complexity and variability of sea trout´s life cycle and the large number of streams and rivers entailed.

Keywords: *Salmo trutta;* sea trout; stock status; monitoring, Denmark; Norway; Sweden.

INTRODUCTION

Brown trout (*Salmo trutta* L.) became established in Scandinavia soon after the last ice age and the species now occurs as both resident freshwater populations in lakes and streams or as anadromous (*sea trout*) populations that migrate to sea to feed and grow before returning to freshwater to spawn. Although not directly threatened as a species, its status differs between geographical regions and knowledge of the present stocks in Scandinavia is incomplete (Pedersen *et al.*, 2012: ICES WKTRUTTA, 2013). The migratory life history of sea trout within different freshwater and marine environments creates difficulties in the assessment of its population status and the identification of any bottlenecks in production. A further complication in assessing stock status is that many populations exhibit partial anadromy with only a variable proportion of the population migrating to sea (Bohlin *et al.*, 2001).

There is currently no standard methodology for assessing and comparing the status of populations between countries in this region although, historically, juvenile abundance was mainly determined by repeated electro-fishing surveys to monitor juvenile densities from selected sites in smaller streams (Bohlin et *al.*, 1989; ICES WGBAST, 2015). The overall stream density can then be extrapolated using models that incorporate calculated habitat-specific densities of trout assessed within each discrete habitat type. A model has been developed recently (Trout Habitat Score), that compares the observed densities of young-of-the-year (0+) parr to maximum potential parr densities after taking into account river size, climate, geographic location and habitat quality (Pedersen *et al.*, 2016). The assessment of abundance and mortality of adults in the sea is much more demanding and monitoring has been based mainly on catch data obtained from either commercial or recreational fishermen, where accurate and complete information is generally scarce. In addition to electro-fishing surveys, the number of out-migrating smolts is also monitored with traps in a relatively few rivers. ICES (WKTRUTTA, 2013) recognized that the marine phase contained the largest knowledge gaps, including such apparently simple biological metrics as survival, marine residence time and adult return rates.

There are 4 index rivers in Sweden, 2 in Norway and none in Denmark where the number of both out-migrant smolts and returning adult spawners is monitored continuously using traps and automatic fish counters; mainly for Atlantic salmon (*Salmo salar*). These index rivers are usually relatively wide and, as such, do not represent ideal habitats for sea trout. This may result in the under-estimation of juvenile parr densities so that they provide a less precise assessment of their sea trout stocks (ICES SGBALANST, 2009).

Consequently, data is generally lacking throughout Scandinavia to establish accurate biological reference points for rivers where stock-recruitment relationships are established: especially for sea trout. The overall aim of this paper is, therefore, to provide an overview of the present knowledge of population status and structure of sea trout in Sweden, Denmark and Norway.

MATERIALS AND METHODS

SWEDEN

Data on juvenile sea trout densities and size are available from the Swedish Electrofishing Register (SERS), which collects annual data from standardized electrofishing surveys (Bergquist *et al.*, 2014) throughout Sweden. Juvenile sea trout parr abundance (0+ and >0+) is calculated by successive removals (Bohlin *et al.*, 1989).

Any temporal changes in the density of different year-classes were analysed using a linear regression analysis (SYSTAT). To investigate any difference in the development of the sea trout stock due to climate, the data were divided into three regions: 1) northern Sweden (average air temperature -2 to 2 °C for 65 sites), 2) central Sweden (3-6 °C for 107 sites) and 3) southern Sweden (7-8 °C for 199 sites) and the average abundance of sea trout within a specific time-period was compared with the overall abundance for the whole period to assess any temporal changes within a region.

DENMARK

Regular monitoring of trout populations are undertaken by routine electro-fishing surveys in most Danish rivers approximately every 7-8 years by DTU Aqua. Approximately 7000 sites are monitored and from these approximately two-thirds are electro-fished. Results from the surveys by DTU Aqua are published in river-specific reports (*see* www.aqua.dtu.dk). Smolt runs are irregularly monitored by traps as part of specific projects, often including PIT tagging of emigrating smolts. In the same rivers adult returns are usually monitored at PIT reader stations.

NORWAY

The only national register related to abundance of sea trout is the collection of catch reports from freshwater recreational fisheries (*see Statistics Norway* www.ssb.no). However, these catches are generally under-reported, especially in smaller watercourses with poor administration of the licensed fisheries. Catch returns are obligatory from professional sea and freshwater fishermen. A new national register for biological and environmental data collected during environmental assessments, including densities of juvenile sea trout, is under construction (http://vannmiljo. miljodirektoratet.no), but only limited information on sea trout is available to date. Several institutions (e.g. NTNU University Museum, Norwegian Institute of Nature Research, Uni Research) undertake regular surveys to assess 0+ and older parr densities by electro-fishing from late summer to early autumn and visual counts are made of the numbers of spawning fish in many salmon rivers by observations on foot, from boats or by drifting divers. Smolt runs are monitored with Wolf traps in two index rivers or occasionally (typically for 1 – 5 years) by rotary screw traps, PIT tag antennae, submerged video cameras or other temporarily installations. Returning adults are counted in Wolf traps in the index rivers or occasionally (typically for 1-5 years) by PIT tag antennas, submerged video cameras or other temporary installations.

RESULTS AND DISCUSSION

SWEDEN

The coastline of Sweden is approximately 2,400 km long (386,000 km including all bays and capes on the mainland) and extends over a broad latitudinal gradient from the border with Finland in the east (N 68°) to the border with Norway in the west (N 55°). Sea trout occur all along this coast with at least 800 individual rivers and streams supporting sea trout populations (Degerman *et al.*, 2011), although the total number is unknown. The abundance of juvenile sea trout was monitored by electro-fishing from the 1970s (5,581 surveys at 371 sites and 217 streams were undertaken between 1985 – 2014) and the electro-fishing data from 411 streams was reported to the Baltic Marine Environment Protection Commission (Degerman *et al.*, 2011).

Overall, sea trout parr abundance was higher in small streams and rivers compared with larger rivers where Atlantic salmon may be more abundant (Figure 1). Brown trout parr are more littoral than salmon parr so that a smaller proportion of the habitat is suitable for trout in wider rivers (*c.f.* Eklöv, 1998). This indicates that sea trout monitoring should focus on smaller rivers and ICES SGBALANST (2009) suggested that monitoring of sea trout parr should be carried out in rivers with catchments of less than 1,000 km^2 (which corresponds to a median wetted-width of about 25 m in Sweden).

Due to the longitudinal gradient along the coastline, average yearly air temperature in the region ranges from -2 °C to +8 °C (Swedish Meteorological & Hydrological Institute, SMHI). This alone may explain a large proportion of the observed differences in parr densities from cold to warm regions where there was an average one hundred-fold increase in densities of

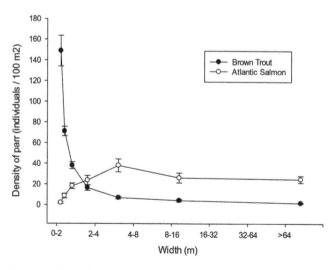

Figure 1. Average abundance (estimated numbers of 0+ and 1+ salmon and sea trout parr/100 m^2 with 95% confidence interval) in suitable habitat versus stream width from electrofishing on 18,643 occasions in Sweden.

trout fry and parr (0+, >0+) between the two extremes with medians of 0.5 parr/100 m² at -2 °C compared with 53 fry and parr/100m² at 8 °C.

Nevertheless, there has been a general improvement in sea trout parr abundance in northern Sweden (average air temperature -2 to 2 °C) and central Sweden (3-6 °C) compared with a significant decline in southern Sweden (7-8 °C) (Figure 2). This agrees with the general pattern in the Baltic (ICES, 2015).

This negative trend of juvenile abundance does not necessarily reflect an overall decline in the population of sea trout in Scandinavia. Generally, sea trout abundance in the sea in Sweden, Denmark and the Skagerrak coast of Norway does not appear to have decreased based on anecdotal reports and an increased tendency of anglers to target their fishing effort at sea trout in these areas. This would not be the case if sea trout stocks had declined. Aldvén *et al.,* *(in prep)* showed that in several systems on the west coast of Sweden the densities of >0+ sea trout parr decreased significantly in number but increased in length at the same time as the density of 0+ remained at a stable level. Sea trout smolts within this region have significantly decreased in size over the period to indicate an earlier age at smoltification resulting in an increased number of 1+ smolts migrating to the sea. It is likely that these changes are driven by climate changes since Aldvén *et al., (in prep.)* also detected an effect of increased temperature on both 0+ and smolt sizes. Climatic conditions encountered during the embryonic development can influence later life-history traits, such as smolt size in anadromous salmonids (Jonsson & Jonsson, 2009) and temperature affects metabolic processes and growth in fishes (Wootton, 1999). The time of fry emergence, parr growth rates and smolt emigration (Connor *et al.*, 2002)

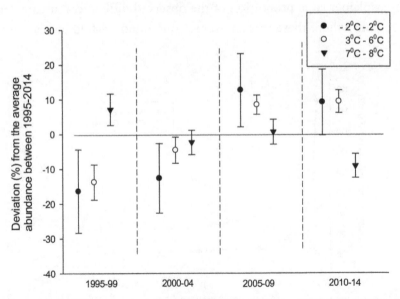

Figure 2. Mean abundance of sea trout parr (all year classes) expressed as deviation from the average (0) between 1995-2015 in three different climate regions (mean air temperature -2 to 2, 3 – 6 and 7 – 8 °C) during four periods (1995-99; 2000-04; 2005-09 and 2010-2014).

reflects the strong effect of water temperature. Correlation studies in the Norwegian River Imsa suggested that warmer and wetter winter before hatching resulted in the better growth of offspring in the subsequent first year of life so that a higher proportion of the cohort became 1-year old smolts (Jonsson *et al.*, 2005).

Only 7 rivers in Sweden monitor the number of out-migrating smolts (Mörumsån, Vindelälven, Rickleån, Torneälven, Högvadsån, Åvaån and Himleån). These are mainly targeted at Atlantic salmon and only one, the Högvadsån on the west coast of Sweden, has any long-term data on the number of out-migrating sea trout smolts. Data from this system since the 1960's also strongly shows an overall increase in the number of out-migrating smolts (p<0.001, t = 6.35; N = 32) since the number of smolts has increased threefold between the 1960s and 2010s (Figure 3). In agreement with the overall data from southern Sweden, there was also an overall decrease in the density of 1+ parr (p<0.001, t = -4.20, N = 34) while the density of 0+ fish remained constant (p = 0.294, t = 1.11, N = 34) (Figure 3). The density of salmon exhibited a similar trend, with the densities of 0+ parr remaining unchanged, although a trend of decline was observed (p = 0.098, t = -1.70, N = 34). The density of >0+ salmon significantly decreased (p<0.001, t = -3.72, N = 34). There was no significant negative correlation between the abundance of salmon and trout for any of the year classes: suggesting a limited effect of interspecific competition (p>0.1).

In general, additional information on the number of spawners, spawning pits, catch statistics

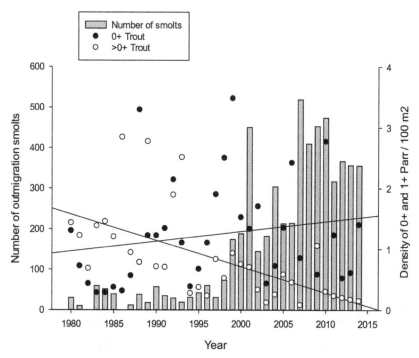

Figure 3. The number of out-migrating smolts (bars) caught in the trap and the density of 0+ (black dots) and >0+ trout parr (white dots) from electrofishing at eight sites between 1979 -2014 in River Högvadsån, Sweden.

or other population characteristics is sparse in this region; with only limited information available from Rivers Selångersån, Åvaån, Själsöån and Nybroån.

DENMARK

The coastline of Denmark is 7,314 km long. The number of sea trout streams has increased from 176 in 1960 to 406 in 2012. The densities of 0+ trout have increased significantly from 20.8 fish/100m² in the 1980s to 59.7 fish/100m² in the 2010s (p=0.003, t=3,09, N=59): but with large regional differences. Densities of both 0+ and >0+ parr are generally higher in the eastern part of the country (and partly also in north Jutland), with the highest average densities of 0+ observed on Bornholm (Figure 4). The high densities on Bornholm relate to stream gradient and the absence of fine sediment (sand) in the streams together with sufficient spawning gravel to ensure that recruitment is optimal in most streams. Similarly, densities of older trout (>0+) are between 20–35/100m² on Bornholm, between 15–20/100m² in eastern Jutland, but below 10 trout/100 m² in all other locations (Figure 5).

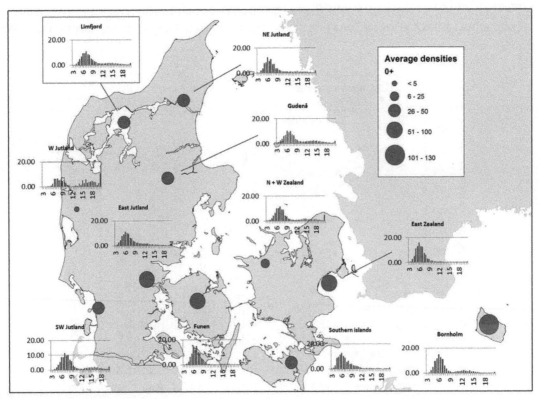

Figure 4. Mean densities and length (cm) distributions (%) of 0+ trout in late summer in larger geographical areas of Denmark (data from the period between 2008 and 2014). Values for western Jutland do not include any of the larger streams in the area.

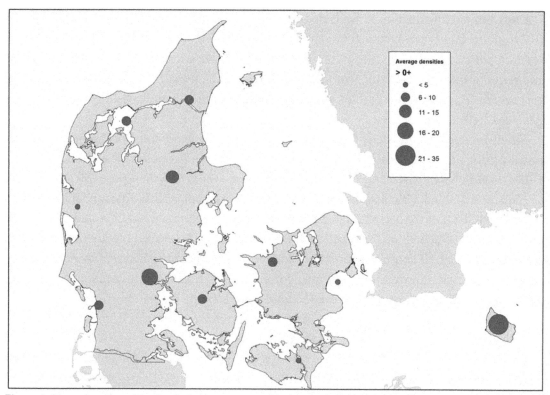

Figure 5. Mean densities of trout > 0+ in larger geographical areas in Denmark (data from the period between 2008 and 2014). Values for western Jutland do not include any of the larger streams in the area.

It is currently estimated that the natural smolt production in Denmark is about 600,000, having increased from some 200,000 in the 1980's. The reason for this increase was initial improvements in water quality, followed by improved accessibility and the restoration of spawning opportunities (by the addition of gravel). In addition, fishing restrictions introduced over the period have improved the situation for sea trout, particularly in the sea. The increase in production (at least in the Baltic area) has slowed down in recent years, possibly because most of the easier (smaller scale) restoration and improvement programmes were completed. The current level of production is still much below potential, with populations limited by heavy sediment erosion and transport, existing barriers and in those areas with slow flowing water upstream of those barriers where fish passage facilities were inserted but where the reservoir impoundments were maintained. In addition, artificial lakes constructed in the lower part of streams in order to remove nitrogen have resulted in severe smolt losses (Olsson *et al.*, 2009); Boel et *al.*, 2013; Kristensen *et al.*, 2014), as does avian predation by cormorants (*Phalacrocorax carbo sinensis*) (Jepsen *et al.*, 2014).

The usual smolt age is between 1 and 3 years, mostly around 1.8 years, but precise data are only available from the River Karup from 1997–1999 which showed a smolt age range of 1.8–2.2 years (Pedersen, unpublished data).

449

Only limited information is available on smolt production from traps. A point estimate in 2012 from the highly productive River Krobæk in southern Zetland (length 8.9 km, catchment area 11.6 km²) was as high as 30 smolt/100 m² of productive stream bed (Henriksen, 2012). A time series of 8 years is available from the small River Læså (length 15 km, catchment area 52 km²) on the island Bornholm. This showed a range in annual smolt production of between 2,000 and 16,000 fish.

Smolt production in eastern Jutland, Funen, most of Zealand and Bornholm is estimated annually using a fixed percentage of the young-of-the-year (0+) trout surviving to smoltification of 10% (*unpublished empirical data*). If trout are stocked into the rivers, their potential contribution to production is added. Calculations are based on the most recent available data and the number is reported to ICES. For the period 2002–2014, the estimated production has increased significantly (p<0.001, t = 10.7, coeff. = 15.3): although the production has levelled off since 2010 (Figure. 6) (Pedersen, 2015). The reason for this change in improvement is believed to result from a reduction in habitat improvement work after completion of all the 'easy' restoration programmes and because further improvements would require a significantly higher effort.

Estimates of the number of spawners are rare and limited to estimates from various projects. The calculated numbers (from mark-recapture) are reported in Table 1. In River Karup, the sea age of spawners in 2000 was between 1-6 years (average 3.2 years) and 45 % of all females were repeat-spawners that had previously spawned on 1-4 occasions (Pedersen, *unpublished data*).

Population changes in absolute number are not available, but river catches may be used as a proxy to reflect population changes. Reported catches from two rivers on the east coast of Jutland and the Karup (a tributary of the Limfjord) suggest that populations of sea trout have

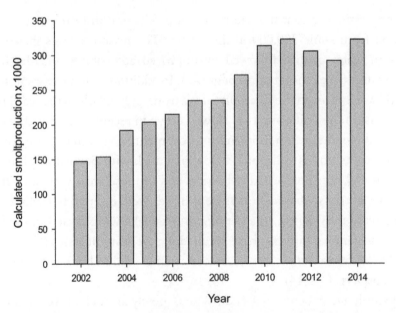

Figure 6. Calculated production of smolts in eastern Jutland, Funen, most of Zealand and Bornholm (Danish parts of ICES subdivisions 22-25).

Table 1. Estimated number of spawners based on mark-recapture data in 7 different streams. Source: a) Sivebæk, F. & Jensen, A.R. (1997); b) Henriksen, P.W. (2014a); c) Stig Pedersen (*unpublished*).

River	Year / period	N (95%, min max)	Length (km)
Brede Å (west Jutland)[a]	mid 1990s	1864 (1409-2319)	48
Ribe Å (west Jutland)[a]	mid 1990s	4597 (2899-6295)	71
Sneum Å (west Jutland)[a]	mid 1990s	472 (314-630)	37
Vidå (west Jutland)[a]	mid 1990s	429 (281-598)	69
Tuse Å (Zealand)[b]	1998/1999	610 (491-729)	12
Tuse Å (Zealand)[b]	2012/2013	1034 (593-2000)	12
Karup Å (Jutland)[c]	1996/1997	9074 (6316-14377)	78

increased (Figure 7). However, it should be noted that catch reports in recent years are likely to be more complete than in previous years and that reporting was made mandatory in one of the larger fishing associations on the Karup in 2010. This may explain much of the sharp increase from that date. Fishing intensity in all the rivers is not likely to have increased by much over the period so that the increases in the rivers Vejle and Kolding may reflect an actual increase in population size.

NORWAY

The coastline of Norway is 25,148 km long and extends over a broad latitudinal gradient from the Skagerrak (N 56°) in the south on the border with Sweden and Denmark to the Barents sea in the north (N 71°) on the border with Russia. As in Sweden and Denmark, sea trout populations occur all along this coast. In Norway, trout populations are doing better in the south compared with the northern, western and central parts (Figure 8). A total of 1,106 streams support wild populations of which 137 are threatened or vulnerable and 21 stocks have been lost, (www.miljodirektoratet.no/no/ Tema/Arter-og-naturtyper/ Villaksportalen/).

The number of rivers with reported catches has increased over time and there are now regulations that have improved the catch statistics. From 1980, fishing with salmon traps and nets was prohibited in most rivers except the Numedalslågen and in the county of Finnmark. The average fishing season has decreased and, for the last few years, catch quotas of one to three fish per person in a 24-hour period were introduced. When comparing the two periods 1993-1996 and 2011-2014, catches from Norwegian rivers and from permanent fishing gear in coastal areas, have declined by 24–77 % except in the most northern areas. The exact causes for the general decrease in the Norwegian sea trout populations are unknown. High impacts of sea lice (*Lepeophtheirus salmonis*) from aquaculture are likely to represent a major threat in some regions (Thorstad *et al.*, 2015) and ecosystem changes and fish diseases

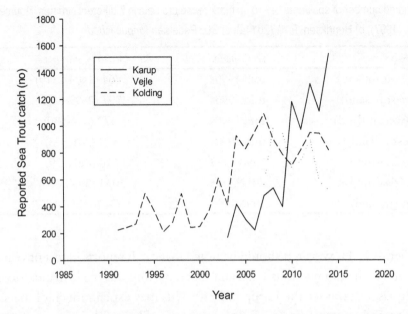

Figure 7. Reported river catches (number of sea trout) from sport fishermen between 1991 and 2013 from River Vejle, Kolding and Karup.

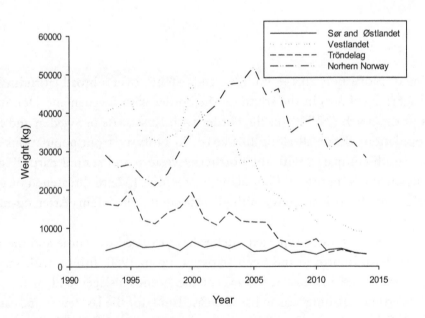

Figure 8. Catch statistics of sea trout from Norwegian rivers and permanent fishing gear in coastal areas in four Norwegian regions from 1993-2014. Angling catches at sea are not included in the catch statistics. It should also be noted that during this period new regulations have influenced the catch effort (i.e. restrictions on fisheries and reduced effort where populations have declined), but data on catch per unit effort from sea trout fisheries are not available. (*Source:* Statistics Norway).

may also have a negative impact on the populations. However, it is difficult to evaluate these trends since the quality and reliability of the catch statistics is unknown and they may differ between watercourses. No information exists about differences in the levels of exploitation between populations when captured at sea and the catch from recreational coastal fishing is not reported (Anon., 2015). Coastal recreational fisheries have increased over the last five years, especially in the Skagerrack on the southern coast of Norway, which may influence the size of local populations.

Yearly-based beach seine net surveys indicate that the number of sea trout along the coast of Skagerrak has increased since 1950 (Espeland & Knutsen, 2014). In the River Imsa, western Norway, all sea trout moving between the river and the sea were counted from 1976. Marine survival from smolt migration to adult return has decreased significantly to about 25% over the period 1976-2005 (Jonsson & Jonsson, 2009). Long-term data from river Stjørdalselva, central Norway, between 1990 and 2013 (Figure 9) suggests that overall abundance of both 0+ and >0+ sea trout has decreased, but that the extent of decline differs between different parts of the river (Arnekleiv *et al.*, 2014).

In River Halselva, Northern Norway, no decrease in marine survival was found over the period 1994-2007 (Jensen *et al.*, 2015). On average, 17.3% (range 8.2%–25.4%) of the sea trout returned to the river to overwinter later the same summer of the year that they emigrated as smolts, while a total of 26.6% (range 11.9%–37.4%) were recaptured in the fish trap in the river or elsewhere up to 8 years after their first return from the sea.

CONCLUSIONS & IMPLICATIONS FOR MANAGEMENT

The data from the three countries provides a somewhat incomplete and heterogeneous picture of sea trout stock status: probably reflecting both the plasticity of the sea trout as a species and the lack of a common and standardized method to assess the stock, except for electrofishing surveys. In general terms, smolt production has increased in both Sweden and Denmark, probably because of extensive restoration work in rivers and improved access to spawning habitats. Data from Sweden and Norway also suggests a potential shift in age of smoltification from mainly 2-year old smolts to a larger proportion of 1-year old smolts since the densities of >1+ parr have decreased in the rivers at the same time as the number of smolts increased. This trend should be investigated in more systems and its potential implications examined in relation to life-history variables, such as growth at sea, age at maturity and spawning success. In Norway, good statistics are lacking and the trends are not uniform. Data from beach seine net surveys along the Skagerrak coast suggests that number of sea trout has increased whereas catches in Norwegian rivers and along the coast using permanent fishing gear have decreased.

To some extent, most streams in these regions have been subject to modification, such as logging, hydropower generation, removal of meanders, deepening, construction of barriers

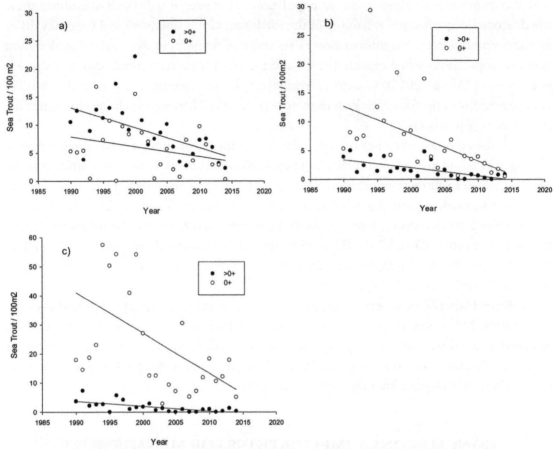

Figure 9. Yearly number of estimated densities of juvenile trout >0+ and 0+ per 100 m² at three zones in the regulated River Stjørdalselva.

and (in Sweden and southern Norway) by acidification, resulting in poorer living conditions and reduced, or even complete loss, of spawning potential. Furthermore, these former activities have increased the nature and extent of erosion, resulting in strongly elevated loads of fine sediment that reduce spawning success. Additional threats in the streams may include predation (cormorant, heron, otter), occasional pollution events (principally from agriculture), illegal fishing at river outlets and areas closed to fishing around river outlets, recreational and professional net fishing and angling. The current estimate of the harvest by the recreational fishery in the Baltic Sea area (Sub-Division 22 – 25) is between 225 – 350 tons, of which 90% relates to the angling catch. Many damage mitigation schemes were completed over the last 20 years, most notably the addition of spawning material, often done by NGO's. Public activities, currently carried out under the EU Water Framework Directive are the principal driver for river improvement works: although such work is limited in rivers used for hydropower generation in Sweden. Some regulation of the cormorant population in Denmark occurs by reducing breeding success and attempts are made to reduce freshwater foraging by cormorants in some locations where vulnerable or threatened species are present, such as grayling (*Thymallus thymallus*) and salmon.

An understanding of how habitat quality influences recruitment is generally poor and any Biological Reference Points (BRPs) where both electro-fishing data and smolt migration data exists are lacking. Ideally, BRPs should be established using similar principles as for salmon index rivers where the stock-recruitment relationship may be extrapolated to other rivers. However, establishing valid stock-recruitment relationships for sea trout populations may be much more difficult than for salmon due to the greater complexity and variability of the sea trout's life cycle and the large number of trout rivers entailed. Hence, stock-recruitment relationships may only be applicable for a very limited number of rivers with similar characteristics or in the same geographical region. It is probable that larger number of index studies in different streams along a north-south gradient over a decade is needed to thoroughly address and understand the many factors affecting the population dynamics of sea trout.

ACKNOWLEDGEMENTS

This study was supported by the Interreg Project 'MarGen'. We are grateful to everyone involved with the biotope and electrofishing surveys.

REFERENCES

Anon. (2015). Status of Norwegian salmon populations in 2014. Norwegian Scientific Advisory Committee for Atlantic Salmon Management.

Arnekleiv, J. V., Kjærstad, G., Rønning, L., Davidsen, J. G. & Sjursen, A. D. (2014). Studies on freshwater biology in the river Stjørdalsvassdraget in 2009-2013. – NTNU Vitenskapsmuseet naturhistorisk rapport 2014-3: 1-82.

Bergquist, B., Degerman, E., Petersson, E, Sers, B., Stridsman, S. & S. Winberg, (2014). Aqua reports 2014:15. Standardiserat elfiske i vattendrag – en manual med praktiska råd. Sveriges Lantbruksuniversitet, Drottningholm, 165 pp. (Code of practice for electrofishing. *In Swedish*)

Boel, M., & A. Koed. (2013). Smolttabet i Årslev Engsø: En sammenligning af den nydannede engsø i 2004 og den etablerede engsø i 2011. DTU Aqua-rapport nr. 260-2013. Institut for Akvatiske Ressourcer, Danmarks Tekniske Universitet, 37 pp.

Bohlin T., Hamrin S., Heggberget T.G., Rasmussen G. & Saltveit S.J. (1989). Electrofishing theory and practice with special emphasis on salmonids. *Hydrobiologia*, **173**, 9-43.

Bohlin, T., Pettersson, J. & E. Degerman. (2001). Population density of migratory and resident brown trout (Salmo trutta) in relation to altitude: evidence for a migration cost. Journal of Animal Ecology, **70**, 112-121.

Connor, W.P., Burge, H.L., Waitt, R. & Bjornn. (2002). Juvenile life history of wild fall chinook salmon in the Snake and Clearwater rivers. *North American Journal of Fisheries Management,* **22**, 703-712

Degerman, E., Andersson, M., Häggström, H. & J. Persson. (2011). Salmon and sea trout populations and rivers in Sweden – HELCOM assessment of salmon (*Salmo salar*) and sea trout (Salmo trutta) populations and habitats in rivers flowing to the Baltic Sea. Baltic Sea Environment Proceedings no. 126B, 110 pp.

Eklöv, A. (1998). The distribution of brown trout (Salmo trutta L.) in streams in southern Sweden., Doctoral thesis. University of Lund, iSBN-91-7105-092-2, 26 pp.

Henriksen, P.W. (2012). Smoltudvandringen fra Krobæk i 2012. Undersøgelsen er udført af Limno Consult for Næstved Kommune.(*In Danish – Smolt migration from the stream Krobæk*).

Henriksen, P.W. (2014). Havørredbestandene på Sjælland, Møn og Lolland – Falster. Status og udviklingspotentiale Del 1, 2014. Projekt udført for Fishing Zealand af Limno Consult. [*In Danish: 'Seatrout populations on Zealand, Møn and Lolland – Falster. Status and potential for improvement'.* Part 1. 2014. Project for Fishing Zealand. Lomno Consult. Xxpp?

ICES. 2009). Report of the study group on data requirements and assessment needs for Baltic trout (SGBALANST). ICES CM 2009/DFC:03. 97 pp.

ICES. (2013). Report of the Workshop on Sea Trout (WKTRUTTA), 12–14 November 2013, ICES Headquarters, Copenhagen, Denmark. ICES CM 2013/SSGEF:15. 243 pp.

ICES, (2015). Report of the Baltic Salmon and Trout Assessment Working Group (WGBAST), 23-31 March 2015, Rostock, Germany. ICES CM 2015\ACOM:08. 362 pp.)

Jensen, A. J., Diserud, O. H., Finstad, B., Fiske, P. & Rikardsen, A. H. (2015). Between-watershed movements of two anadromous salmonids in the Arctic. *Canadian Journal of Fisheries and Aquatic Sciences* **72**, 855-863.

Jepsen, N, Skov, C., Pedersen, S.& Bregnballe, T., (2014). Betydningen af prædation på danske ferskvandsfiskebestande – en oversigt med fokus på skarv. DTU Aqua-rapport nr. 283-2014. Institut for Akvatiske Ressourcer, Danmarks Tekniske Universitet. 78 pp.

Jonsson, N., Jonsson, B., & Hansen, L.P., (2005). Does climate during embryonic development influence parr growth and age of seaward migration in Atlantic salmon (*Salmo salar*)? *Canadian Journal of Fisheries and Aquatic Sciences,* **62**(11), 2502–2508.

Jonsson, B. & Jonsson, N. (2009). Migratory timing, marine survival and growth of anadromous brown trout Salmo trutta in the River Imsa, Norway. *Journal of Fish Biology,* **74**, 621-638.

Kristensen, M., A. Koed, & J. S. Mikkelsen. (2014). Egå Engsø – tab af havørredsmolt i en Vandmiljøplan II-sø, DTU Aqua-rapport nr., 276-2014.

Pedersen, S. (2015). National report to WGBAST. (ICES. 2015. Report of the Baltic Salmon and Trout Assessment Working Group (WGBAST), 23-31 March 2015, Rostock, Germany. ICES CM 2015\ ACOM:08. 362 pp.)

Pedersen, S., Heinimaa, P. & T. Pakarinen (*Eds.*). (2012). Workshop on Baltic sea trout. Helsinki, Finland, 11-13 October 2011. DTA Aqua report no. 248, 95 pp.

Pedersen, S., Degerman, E., Debowski, P. & Petereit. (2017). Assessment and recruitment status of Baltic sea trout populations. In *Sea Trout: Science & Management.* (Graeme Harris. *Ed.*). Proceedings of the 2nd International Sea Trout Symposium. October 2015. Dundalk, Ireland. *[Troubador and pps at page-proof stage]*

Sivebæk, F. & Jensen, A.R. (1997). Laksefiskene og fiskeriet i vadehavsområdet – Supplerende undersøgelser. Samarbejdsprojekt mellem Danmarks Fiskeriundersøgelser, Ribe Amt og Sønderjyllands Amt. DFU-rapport nr. 40b-97.

Thorstadt, E.B., Todd, C.D., Uglem, I., Bjørn, P.A., Gargan, P.C., Vollset, K.W., Halttunen, E., Kålås, S., Berg, M & Finstad, B. (2015). Effects of salmon lice *Lepeophtheirus salmonis* on wild sea trout *Salmo trutta* – a literature review. *Aquaculture Environmental Interactions*, **7**, 91–113.

Wootton, R. J. (1999). Ecology of teleost fishes. Dordrecht: Kluwer Academic Publishers, 133-145.

ELECTRONIC REFERENCES

Espeland, S. H. & Knutsen, H. (2014). Report on the beach seine survey in Oslofjord, 2014, 15 pp. *Available at:* https://www.imr.no/filarkiv/2014/12/31-2014_strandnot_indre_oslofjorden _2014.pdf/ nb-no

Calculating smolt production of sea trout from habitat surveys and electrofishing: pilot studies from small streams in Sweden

J. HÖJESJÖ[1]., N. NILSSON[2], E. DEGERMAN[3], A. HALLDÉN[4] & D. ALDVÉN[1].

[1]*Department of Biology and Environmental Sciences – University of Gothenburg, Box 463, 405 30 Göteborg, Sweden.*
[2]*Jönköpings fiskeribiologi AB, Gjuterigatan 9,553 18 Jönköping, Sweden.*
[3]*Swedish University of Agricultural Sciences, Institute of Freshwater Research, Pappersbruksallén 22, SE-702 15 Örebro, Sweden.*
[4]*Länsstyrelsen i Jönköpings län, 551 86 Jönköping, Sweden.*

ABSTRACT

The status of sea trout populations is often monitored using electrofishing in streams, which normally only gives information on recruitment at a few selected sites. More robust information on actual smolt production or the size of the spawning stocks is needed for fishery management purposes. Estimating this with traps or automatic fish counters is often laborious work affected by high flow events or malfunctioning equipment making the data unreliable. Here we present two methods for combining electrofishing with habitat surveys to give an estimate of the smolt production. The SBS-method (Swedish Biotope Survey) is based on a standardized method of quantifying the trout habitat together with a model to estimate smolt production using the mean density of >0+ trout parr (pre-smolt) in autumn. The method was designed for streams with a mean smolt age of two years. It requires estimates of survival over winter and during smolt migration along with the proportion of juveniles likely to become smolts at 2 years of age. A simple model is also presented where the smolt output is calculated as 30% of the density of >0+ sea trout and after applying a migration loss during migration. Both methods give acceptable estimates, but the actual smolt output may deviate in certain years because of climatic events (high or low flows) during the winter or episodic pollution incidents.

Keywords: *Salmo trutta*; brown trout; Sweden; electro-fishing surveys; habitat surveys; smolt production.

INTRODUCTION

The brown trout (*Salmo trutta* L.) is an important and iconic species that is, perhaps, one of the most genetically and phenotypically diverse of all vertebrates. It is widely distributed throughout its present natural range in the North Atlantic, where it generally co-exists alongside its congeneric relative, Atlantic salmon (*Salmo salar*), in those rivers and streams with unobstructed access to the sea.

It is able to exists as two distinct forms in response to conditions prevailing in the freshwater environment, either as resident trout that complete their entire life history in freshwater or as anadromous trout (= *sea trout*) that spend their early juvenile life in freshwater (*as parr*) before undergoing a physiological, morphological and behavioural transformation that pre-adapts them to life in saltwater. They then migrate to sea (*as smolts*) to feed and grow before returning to freshwater to spawn in their natal river of origin.

Although sea trout and salmon exhibit similar life histories, there are important differences. The salmon is an 'obligate migrant' that rarely establishes resident populations in freshwater, while the brown trout is a 'facultative migrant' that exhibits partial anadromy where variable proportions of the juvenile trout either migrate to sea or remain as residents in freshwater (Svärdson, 1982). These proportions are not fixed, and they may vary widely between different rivers and in different years.

All salmon producing nations in the North Atlantic have agreed that salmon stocks should be conserved by the adoption of measures to ensure that an adequate number of adult spawners enter each river to optimise annual production and smolt yields (NASCO,1998). This is broadly based on a number of stock-recruitment models (Ricker, 1954) and the assumptions that *a*) the number of fish produced in the next generation (= recruitment) is related to the number of returning adult fish in the previous generation (= stock) and *b*) that the production of juvenile fish depends largely on the quality of the available freshwater habitat and the density dependent processes operating in the early life stages (Gibson, 1993; Elliot, 1994; 2001).

Various measures have now been adopted to conserve and maintain salmon stocks based on science-based 'Conservations Limits'. However, a parallel approach to the conservation of sea trout stocks is more complicated by the spatial and temporal differences in the incidence of partial anadromy, variability in the expression of life history and practical difficulties in distinguishing the fraction of the juvenile trout population that is destined to become anadromous sea trout until they undergo the smolt transformation. Consequently, the management of sea trout stocks is currently achieved largely by default as an incidental by-product of measures to protect and conserve salmon stocks (Walker, *et al.*, 2006). There is, therefore, a clear need for a better understanding of the complex relationship between the availability of freshwater trout habitats and juvenile recruitment and their interplay with different life history strategies and the production of sea trout smolts.

Armstrong et al., (2003) reviewed the extensive research into the preference for, and utilisation of, different habitats by salmonids and several attempts have been made to model the abundance, density or biomass of juvenile *S. trutta* based on habitat characteristics (Belaud *et al.*, 1989; Baran *et al.*, 1996; Lek *et al.*, 1996; Jutila *et al.*, 1999; Maeki-Petaeys *et al.*, 1999). HABSCORE is one of the habitat evaluation methods most frequently used in England & Wales. It is a system based on a series of empirical statistical models that relate population size and fish density to observed combinations of site and catchment features at a site and catchment scale (e.g. Milner *et al.*, 1993, 1998). Another method, PHABSIM (Physical HABitat SIMulation) is a procedure to transport spawning targets between rivers, fisheries classification and habitat evaluation for habitat restoration purposes (Bovee, 1982; Milhous *et al.*, 1989; Dunbar *et al.*, 2002). This model quantifies the availability of different habitat types using Weighted Usable Area (WUA) at different flow discharges and incorporates the suitability of each habitat to species and age preferences for depth, velocity and substrate. These 'suitability values' are then used to create habitat utilization indices (HSI) that quantify the relative suitability of all habitat variables (*c.f.* Bovee, 1982 Moir *et al.*, 2005). PHABSIM, and others in the suite of Instream Incremental Flow Methodologies (Dunbar *et al.*, 2002; Armstrong & Nislow, 2012) are primarily used for environmental impact assessments, rather than routine population assessment, as they require considerable amounts of data.

The status of trout populations in fresh water in Sweden is generally assessed and monitored using standardized electrofishing by successive removals (Bohlin *et al.*, 1989). Reference stream sections are usually sampled in consecutive years to provide data on density that are comparable between years. To obtain a more accurate assessment of the population it is necessary to categorize and then divide the whole stream into proportions (areas) of suitable habitats for spawners and for 0+ fish and older fish. The overall density of trout within each year-class can then be extrapolated using models that incorporate habitat specific densities of trout assessed within each discrete habitat type.

Because there are numerous trout rivers and streams along the Swedish coastline, the Swedish Biotope Survey (SBS) was developed as an alternative habitat survey technique (Halldén *et al.*, 2002). This categorises five parameters, namely a) water habitat, b) the riparian zone, c) migration obstacles, d) tributaries and e) road crossings, in uniform segments of the river (the smallest unit allowed is 30 m , but this may extend to kilometres if the river habitat and the riparian zone are uniform). The largest river system mapped so far is the River Emån, where approximately 800 km were surveyed and where a total of 317 artificial obstacles to migration were found and 14% of the river length was classed as heavily channelized (County Board of Jönköping, 1999). Because the field data gathered is quite comprehensive and represents a large temporal and spatial variation, a 'light' version of SBS is used that is focused on trout habitat only. Here, the habitat quality relating to both spawning areas and to suitable habitat for both parr and large trout is assessed and ranked on a scale ranging from Category 0 (= no substrate/ wrong velocity) to Category 3 (= several suitable areas/ optimal velocity and shade).

ICES (2013) proposed that Index Rivers should be established in Baltic streams with sufficient annual monitoring of juvenile recruitment (by electro-fishing surveys) and numbers of migrating smolts (by trapping programmes) to assess and establish representative stock-recruitment curves. Stock parameters could then be transferred to other rivers without these data based on a habitat classification system. Ideally, the stock-recruitment relationship should be known. However, there are only five rivers in Sweden (Högvadsån, Åvaån, Kävlingeån, Mörrumsån and Vindelälven) where both the number of spawners and the smolt run is monitored and opportunities for validation are rare. For these 5 rivers, adult counts are determined by trapping the ascending sea trout or by an automatic counter (Vindelälven), while smolt numbers are monitored in Wolf traps (Högvadsån, Åvaån, Kävlingeån) or with rotary screw traps (Vindelälven). However, the efficiency of smolt traps is often low in rivers with high flows, resulting in uncertain estimates and a lack of sufficient and reliable data for sea trout stock-recruitment modelling. Furthermore, three of the monitored rivers are larger salmon rivers where the juvenile rearing habitat of sea trout is difficult to quantify. Consequently, the calculation of sea trout smolt production from electro-fishing data depends on reliable estimates of parr densities, available spawning and parr rearing habitat, and mortality during smolt migration. Such data are generally lacking and recent national smolt production estimates are not available.

The overall aims of this paper are: a) to establish if a combination of the full SBS-model and electrofishing from representative habitats can be used to assess smolt production and b) if this assessment can be simplified further by using a fixed percentage for survival between different life stages of trout and the costs of migration between habitats. The full SBS-model was tested on the Rivers Åvaån and Knipån, two small streams in Sweden, and the simple model was validated on the Rivers Himleån, Kävlingeån and Åvaån.

MATERIAL AND METHODS

SBS-MODEL

The light version of the SBS was used in Sweden (Nilsson *et al.*, 2010) as a basis for modelling sea trout smolt production by combining SBS of the whole stream with electrofishing at representative habitats. Firstly, the 0+, 1+ and >1+ year classes are identified from length distribution and auxiliary equations: with the largest 1+ trout (in mm) identified from the length of the largest 0+ trout x 1,557 – 0,059 x Julian date + 43,185 (Degerman *et al.*, 2010). Secondly, the abundance of different year classes at available electrofishing sites is estimated. In the model, the trout densities in each of the four habitat categories have a fixed proportional relationship with each other and the best habitat category used is as a reference with maximum (100 %) densities of trout. Densities for all habitat categories can then be calculated and extrapolated, even if empirical data are available from only one category of habitat. The model then incorporates assessments of winter mortality, degree of smoltification, a spawning habitat compensation and a migration mortality. Firstly, predicted winter mortality (from 40 – 60 % for 0+ parr and from 50 – 70 % for >0+ parr) and degree of smoltification (3 – 10 % for 0+ parr and 90 – 99 % for >0+ parr) are brought in to the model to generate an estimate of smolts production within each category of habitat. Secondly, a spawning habitat compensation value is introduced to correct for the overestimated smolt production which was observed when the model was initially validated (Nilsson *et al.*, 2013). Depending on the quality of the spawning habitat, the predicted number of smolts produced is multiplied by a factor of 0.25 – 1. Thirdly, a migration mortality is added of 0 – 75 % per km depending on habitat quality and flow characteristics as follows: habitat class 0 = 10 – 17% km^{-1}, class1 = 3 – 12% km^{-1}, class 2 = 3 – 12%, class 3 = 0-5% km^{-1} and lakes = 25-75% km^{-1} (Nilsson *et al.*, 2010; Halldén *et al.*, 2002). Finally, the calculations of the predicted smolt production are repeated 100 times with random values within limits for winter mortality, degree of smoltification and migration mortality (= bootstrapping) in order to obtain a distribution of the predicted smolt production. Figure 1 outlines the inputs to a possible model for calculating smolt production.

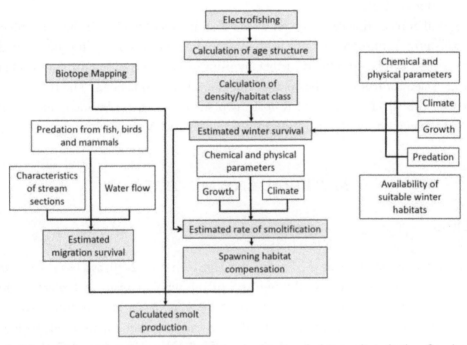

Figure 1. Schematic description of a possible model showing how to calculate smolt production. Grey boxes refer to different investigations or calculations within the Swedish Biotope Survey model. White boxes are factors affecting the outcome of the assessments (Modified after Nilsson *et al.*, 2010).

SIMPLE MODEL

Bohlin *et al.*, (1989) suggested that smolt production in streams on the Swedish west coast, where the majority of smolts are 2-years old, may be predicted from 0.30 x abundance of >0+

trout parr. Aldven *et al.,* (2015) added a migration mortality of 0–12% (average 3%) per km in running sections of the stream. In the southern part of Sweden, the average smolt age is about 1.5–2 years compared with 3–4 years in the northern part. It is stressed that the following data are from rivers with an average smolt age of 2 years.

RESULTS

SBS-MODEL

Good evidence on whether the relationships used are valid is rare, and some conflicting results were reported. In the River Åvaån (2.5 km in length and with a long data set), smolt production was quantified using a smolt trap and the numbers were then compared with predicted production using the SBS-model over nine years (Figure 2). In five of these years, the mean deviation from those predicted by the model was -12 %, but the model overestimated the actual production (by between 89 % and 750 %) in the remaining four years (Nilsson *et al.,* 2010; Nilsson *et al.,* 2013). However, the smolt trap was flooded for more than one week during the smolt runs in 2003 (9 days), 2005 (10 days) and 2006 (17 days), making the estimates of the smolt runs unreliable. Furthermore, an agriculture discharge to the river Åvaån occurred in the summer of 2007 resulting in a fish mortality (Nilsson *et al.,* 2010). The smolt production model has also been validated in River Kävlingeån where the accuracy was within ± 25% for

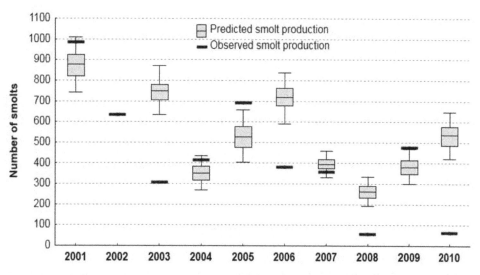

Figure 2. The predicted smolt production using the SBS-model and the observed number of smolts in the smolt trap in the river Åvaån. Grey boxes display the median values with the lower and the upper quartiles, while the error bars display the minimum and maximum values. The predicted smolt production in 2002 could not be calculated because no electro-fishing occurred in 2001.

two out of six years: but the model underestimated the actual production by 31-67 % for the remaining four years (Nilsson *et al.,* 2013).

SIMPLE MODEL

In the Åvaån (approximately 2.5 km long and with a rearing habitat of only 0.38 hectare) the number of eggs deposited was 2,040/100 m² rearing habitat (range 61 – 4,381/100 m²) in 1998 – 2014. Smolt production averaged 10 smolts/100 m², resulting in a survival from egg to smolt of 0.49%. The average densities of 0+ trout at electrofishing sites were 99.1/100 m² (SD 75.5) for 0+ trout and 22.8/100m² (SD 15.7) for >0+ trout. The smolt production was 44% of the density of >0+ trout parr (72% of the smolts are 2 year olds). The migration mortality within the stream should be negligible for this short river.

In longer streams with extensive lentic habitats, the mortality may be higher. Aldvén *et al.,* (2015) worked with a smolt trap in River Himleån (about 32 km in length) over two years. They used available electrofishing data and an existing estimate of the area of parr habitat together with an estimated 30% of >0+ trout becoming smolts and a mean mortality of 3% per km. This resulted in an overestimate of the actual smolt production of trout and salmon of 18 and 19% in consecutive years. This discrepancy may have resulted from the over-representation of the better quality parr habitats in the electro-fished sites to give an overestimation of parr densities for the whole river.

In the Kävlingeån (length 49 km), the average number of smolts trapped between 1998 – 2013 was 2,500. The rearing area is about 15 hectares, giving a smolt production of 1.7/100 m². The average density of >0+ trout parr was 4.4/100 m² (for a mean of 154 fishing occasions at 56 sites), and smolt production was 38% of the >0+ density. The average distance to the smolt trap from sampled sites was 12 km. Application of the suggested mean mortality of 3% per km (Aldven *et al.,* 2015), and taking into account of the average distance of 12 km from survey sites to trap, would give a smolt production of 3.1/100 m². However, from field experiments, Nilsson *et al.,* (2013) suggested a mean mortality of 3 – 12% in the habitat class (Class 1) that was dominant in the Kävlingeån. Using the mean mortality of 7.5% would, instead, result in a smolt estimate of 1.7 smolt/100 m² and would correspond exactly with the number obtained from the smolt trap.

DISCUSSION

Although ranging from very accurate to providing an overestimate of as much as 750 %, it can be argued that, with reliable smolt traps that operate at all river flow levels, the SBS-model will provide a generally acceptable and cost effective alternative for assessing smolt production. The results presented here show that although the estimates for individual years may deviate considerably from measured smolt production, the mean production estimates for a number of years are quite reliable. The deviating years, when pre-smolt (>0+ trout parr) production and the resulting number of smolts did not correlate, was linked to climatic events during the late autumn to spring. Although extreme high flows may facilitate smolt migration, they also make trap counts unreliable (Aldvén *et al,.* 2015, Baglinière *et al.,* 1993). The spring flow situation may also affect the number of migrating smolts (Jonsson & Jonsson, 2002) and stochastic events, such as the pollution fish-kill in Åvaån in 2007, also affected the results. Furthermore, the underestimates for certain years in the River Kävlingeån may be linked to favourable conditions for smolt migrations in those years (*see* Olsson et al., 2009). The simple models cannot predict the weather, but it can provide a good estimate of the expected smolt run as a mean over a number of years.

Generally, there are relatively few rivers worldwide that have long-term data on stock-recruitment relationships for sea trout (*but see* Elliot & Elliot, 2006, Poole *et al.,* 2004 and Euzenat *et al.,* 2006). None of these studies, to our knowledge, have tried to correlate habitat characteristics with densities of parr at representative habitat and with smolt production. However, Baglinière & Champignuelle (1986) used a similar method to ours to estimate 0+ and 1+ parr densities of Atlantic salmon parr in representative habitats along with winter survival in relation to size, age and state of maturity. Their model was validated over five years using a smolt trap in the French River Oir and the numbers of fish migrating as 1+ yearling smolts as estimated by the habitat method were not significantly different to those obtained from trapping. However, the number of 2-year old smolts (2+) estimated from the habitat method was significantly higher than evaluated by trapping (Baglinière *et al.,* 1993).

Subject to further evaluation, the SBS-model could be adopted as an important tool for identifying and prioritizing the need for habitat restoration work and the removal of barriers to movement in certain rivers. By including smolt age in the model, it may be transported to other regions. The differences between the predicted smolt production from the SBS-model and the actual number of smolts observed highlights the need for more high quality background data, including both electrofishing and biotope surveys, to increase the accuracy of the smolt production model. In addition, site specific investigations of winter mortality, degree of smoltification and migration mortality in those catchment areas where the SBS-model is applied is also likely to reduce the discrepancies. A mortality rate of over 50% is rare, but has been reported for smolts migrating through wetlands with high number of avian predators and/or pike (Aarestrup *et al.,* 2014, Aldvén *et al.,* 2015). There is, therefore, a need to validate the SBS-model in more rivers and over longer periods of time. It is also important to consider that the model has been developed for 2-year old smolts and that, with an increasing temperature and at lower latitude, it is plausible that the age of smoltification will decrease (Byrne *et al.,* 2004). Consequently, the model should also be validated on a gradient from north to south and for coastal to elevated streams in order to capture the inherent variability and flexibility present in sea trout streams.

Another major complication is the unknown contribution of resident freshwater trout to sea trout production in populations exhibiting partial migration. This is partly due to the difficulties in distinguishing between parr of resident, migrant or mixed parentage and it is not possible to transport accurately a sea trout stock-recruitment relationship between rivers without this information.

The simple models presented here also gave quite reliable results; but by using only the observed density of >0+ pre-smolt parr, they may overestimate smolt production if migration mortality is not taken into account: especially in long rivers with large lentic section and lakes. In small streams, where greater variations in the magnitude and timing of different river flows may be expected between years than for larger systems, models of smolt production may be unreliable for any single year, but they are, nevertheless, more cost-effective than operating smolt traps. However, the *actual* smolt production of a stream in any single year is seldom of greater management importance than the *expected* mean smolt production from all the small sea trout rivers and streams in a region. Consequently, simple smolt production models may be sufficient for practical management purposes. However, as noted above, there is still a need to establish stock-recruitment relationships in several more index streams.

ACKNOWLEDGEMENTS

This study was supported by the Interreg Project 'MarGen'. We are grateful to everyone involved with the biotype and electrofishing surveys.

REFERENCES

Aldvén, D., Degerman, E. & Höjesjö, J. (2015). Environmental cues and downstream migration of anadromous brown trout (*Salmo trutta*) and Atlantic salmon (*Salmo salar*) smolts. *Boreal Environment Research* **20** (1), 35–44.

Aarestrup, K., Baktoft, H,, Koed, A,, del Villar-Guerra, D. & Thorstad, E.B. (2014) Comparison of the riverine and early marine migration behaviour and survival of wild and hatchery-reared sea trout *Salmo trutta* smolts. *Marine Ecology Progress Series* **496**, 197–206.

Armstrong, J.D., Kemp, P.S., Kennedy, G.J., Ladle, M. & Milner, N.J. (2003). Habitat requirements of Atlantic salmon and brown trout in rivers and streams. *Fisheries Research,* **62**, 143–70.

Armstrong, J. D., and K. H. Nislow. (2012). Modelling approaches for relating effects of change in river flow to populations of Atlantic salmon and brown trout. *Fisheries Management and Ecology* **19**, 527–536.

Baglinière, J-L., Maisse, G. & Nihouarn, A. (1993). Comparison of two methods of estimating Atlantic salmon (*Salmo salar*) wild smolt production. *In*: Production of Juvenile Atlantic Salmon, Salmo salar, in Natural Waters. (R. J. Gibson & R. E. Cutting. *Eds*). *Canadian Special Publication of Fisheries and Aquatic Sciences,* **118**, 189-201.

Baglinière, J-L & Champigneulle, A. (1986) Populations estimates of juvenile Atlantic salmon *(Salmo salar)* as indices of smolt production in the River Scorff, Brittany. *Journal of Fish Biology.* **29**, 467-482.

Baran, P., Lek, S., Delacoste, M. & Belaud, A. (1996). Stochastic models that predict trout population density or biomass on a mesohabitat scale. *Hydrobiologia,* **337**, 1–9.

Belaud, A., Chaveroche, P., Lim, P. & Sabaton, C. (1989). Probability-of-use curves applied to brown trout *(Salmo trutta fario* L.) in rivers of southern France. *Regulated Rivers: Research & Management,* **3**, 321–36.

Bohlin, T., Hamrin, S., Heggberget, T. G., Rasmussen, G. &. Saltveit, S. J. (1989). Electrofishing – Theory and Practice with special emphasis on salmonids. *Hydrobiologia* **173**, 9-43.

Bovee, K. D. 1982. A guide to stream habitat analysis using the Instream Flow Incremental Methodology. Instream Flow Information Paper 12. U.S.D.I. Fish and Wildlife Service, Office of Biological Services. FWS/OBS-82/2, 248 pp.

Byrne, C. J., Poole, R., Dillane, M., Rogan, G., & Whelan, K. F. (2004). Temporal and environmental influences on the variation in sea trout *(Salmo trutta* L.) smolt migration in the Burrishoole system in the west of Ireland from 1971 to 2000. *Fisheries Research,* **66** (1), 85-94.

County board of Jönköping, 1999. Biotopkartering Emån 1998. Meddelande från Länsstyrelsen, Rapport nr 1999:20, 315 pp. (*In Swedish*)

Degerman, E., Sers, B. & K. Magnusson (2010). Hur stora är årsungar och Fjolårsungar vid elfiske? Mimeographed report, Swedish Electrofishing Register, 8 pp. (*In Swedish*),

Dunbar, M.J., Ibbotson, A.T., Gowing, I.M., Mcdonnell, N., Acreman, M. & Pinder A. (2002) Ecologically Acceptable Flows Phase III: Further validation of PHABSIM for the habitat requirements of salmonid fish. Final R&D Technical Report (Project W6-036). Environment Agency and CEH (project C00962), 137 pp + appendices.

Elliott, J.M. (1994). Quantitative Ecology and the Brown Trout. Oxford University Press, Oxford, 286 pp.

Elliott, J.M. (2001). The relative role of density in the stock–recruitment relationship of salmonids. *In: Stock, Recruitment and Reference Points: Assessment and Management of Atlantic Salmon.* (Prevost, E. & Chaput, G. *Eds.*). INRA, Paris, 25–66.

Elliott, J. M., & Elliott, J. A. (2006). A 35-year study of stock-recruitment relationships in a small population of sea trout: assumptions, implications and limitations for predicting targets. *In: Sea Trout: Biology, Conservation and Management.* (Graeme Harris & Nigel Milner. *Eds*). Proceedings of the 1st International Sea Trout Symposium. July 2004, Cardiff, Wales, 257-278.

Euzenat, G., Fournel, F., & Fagard, J. L. (2006). Population dynamics and stock–recruitment relationship of sea trout in the River Bresle, upper Normandy, France. In: *Sea Trout: Biology, Conservation and Management.* (Graeme Harris & Nigel Milner. *Eds.*). Proceedings of the 1st International Sea Trout Symposium, July 2004, Cardiff, Wales, UK. Blackwell Publishing, Oxford, 307-323.

Gibson, R.J. (1993). The Atlantic salmon in freshwater: spawning, rearing and production. Reviews in *Fish Biology and Fisheries,* **3**, 39–73.

Halldén, A, Liliegren, Y & Lagerkvist G. (2002). Biotopkartering – vattendrag, metodik för kartering av biotoper i och i anslutning till vattendrag. Länsstyrelsen i Jönköpings Län. Meddelande 2002:55. (*In Swedish*), 86 pp

ICES. 2013. Report of the Workshop on Sea Trout (WKTRUTTA), 12–14 November 2013, ICES Headquarters, Copenhagen, Denmark. ICES CM 2013/SSGEF:15, 243 pp.

Jutila, E., Ahvonen, A. & Laamanen, M. (1999). Influence of environmental factors on the density and biomass of stocked brown trout, *Salmo trutta* L., parr in brooks affected by intensive forestry. *Fisheries Management and Ecology*, **6**, 195–205.

Jonsson, N., & Jonsson, B. (2002). Migration of anadromous brown trout *Salmo trutta* in a Norwegian river. *Freshwater Biology*, **47** (8), 1391-1401.

Lek, S., Belaud, A., Baran, P., Dimopoulos, I. & Delacoste, M. (1996). Role of some environmental variables in trout abundance models using neural networks. *Aquatic Living Resources*, **9** (01), 23-29.

Maki-Petays, A., Muotka, T., Huusko, A., Tikkanen, P., Kreivi, P. (1997). Seasonal changes in habitat use and preference by juvenile brown trout, Salmo trutta, in a northern boreal river. Canadian Journal of Fisheries and Aquatic Sciences, **54**, 520–530.

Milhous, R. T., M. A. Updike, and D. M. Schneider. (1989) Physical habitat simulation system reference manual. Version 2. BIOLOGICAL, **89** (16), 403pp

Milner, N.J., Wyatt, R.J. & Scott, M.D. (1993) Variability in the distribution and abundance of stream salmonids, and the associated use of habitat models. *Journal of Fish Biology*, **43A**, 103–119.

Milner, N.J., Wyatt, R.J. and Broad, K.(1998) HABSCORE – applications and future developments of related habitat models. *Aquatic Conservation: Marine and Freshwater Ecosystems*, **8**, 633-644.

Moir, H. J., Gibbins, C. N., Soulsby, C. & Youngson, A. F. (2005). PHABSIM modelling of Atlantic salmon spawning habitat in an upland stream: testing the influence of habitat suitability indices on model output. *River research and applications*, **21** (9), 1021-1034.

NASCO. (1998) Agreement on the adoption of a precautionary approach. *Report of the fifteenth annual meeting of the Council*, Edinburgh. NASCO, 167–72 pp.

Nilsson, N, Degerman, E, Andersson H C, & Halldén A. (2010). Uppdatering av modell för beräkning av öringsmoltproduktion. Länsstyrelsen i Stockholms län, 32 pp. (*In Swedish*)

Nilsson, N., Degerman, E., Eklöv, A, Andersson, H.C. & Halldén, A. (2013). Validering av modell för beräkning av öringsmoltproduktion i Kävlingeån, 1999-2005, och Åvaån, 2010. Del 3 i Vättern-FAKTA no: 4, 104 pp. (*In Swedish*)

Olsson, I.C., Eklöv, A. & E. Degerman, (2009). Effects of wetlands and power plants on migration of sea trout (*Salmo trutta* L.) smolt and eel (*Anguilla anguilla* L.). Rapport Länsstyrelsen i Skåne län, no. 36, 61 pp. (*In Swedish.*)

Poole, W. R., Dillane, M., DeEyto, E., Rogan, G., McGinnity, P., & Whelan, K. (2006). Characteristics of the Burrishoole sea trout population: census, marine survival, enhancement and stock recruitment, 1971–2003. In: *Sea Trout: Biology, Conservation & Management*, (Graeme Harris & Nigel Milner. *Eds*). Proceedings of the 1st International Sea Trout Symposium. July 2004, Cardiff, Wales, 279-306.

Ricker, W.E. (1954) Stock and recruitment. *Journal of the Fisheries Research Board of Canada*, **11**, 559–623.

Svärdson, G., and Å. Fagerström. (1982) Adaptive differences in the long-distance migration of some trout (*Salmo trutta* L.) stocks. *Report-Institute of Freshwater Research, Drottningholm* (Sweden), **60**, 51-80.

Walker, A.M., Pawson, M.G. & Potter. (2006). Sea Trout Fisheries Management: Should we follow the Salmon? In: *Sea Trout: Biology, Conservation & Management.* (Graeme Harris & Nigel Milner. *Eds*). Proceedings of the 1st International Sea Trout Symposium. July 2004, Cardiff, Wales, UK. Blackwell Publishing, Oxford, 466-479.

Observations on sea trout stock performance in the rivers Dee, Tamar, Lune & Tyne (1991-2014): The contribution of 'Index River' monitoring programmes in England & Wales to fisheries management

I.C. DAVIDSON[1], R.J. COVE[1], R.J. HILLMAN[2], P.S. ELSMERE[2], N. COOK[3] & A. CROFT[4].

[1]Natural Resources Wales, Chester Road Buckley, Flintshire CH7 3AJ, Wales.
[2]Environment Agency, Sir John Moore House, Victoria Square, Bodmin, Cornwall, PL31 1EB, England.
[3]Environment Agency, Tyneside House, Skinnerburn Road, Newcastle Business Park, Newcastle Tyne & Wear, NE4 7AR, England.
[4]Environment Agency, Lutra House, Dodd Way, Off Seedlee Road, Walton Summit, Preston Lancashire, PR5 8BX, England.

ABSTRACT

Among the 80 principal sea trout rivers in England and Wales (E&W) only five, the Tyne, Tamar, Fowey, Dee and Lune, currently provide annual run estimates from the operation of resistivity fish counters and/or adult traps. Four of these rivers, the Dee, Tamar, Lune and Tyne, are considered as 'Index Rivers' because they also routinely collect biological information, for example on the age and size composition of returning fish. This information is required to identify individual generations of fish and track the structure and dynamics of populations through time. In addition to adult stock monitoring, the index programmes also include routine electrofishing surveys for juvenile trout and an assessment of fishery performance by the collection of rod catch and effort statistics. Trapping is also undertaken on the Dee and Tamar each spring to evaluate smolt output and return rates by mark-recapture.

This paper aims to demonstrate how the detailed and long term data sets generated by index river monitoring can provide unique insight into the biology of sea trout populations and their response to environmental change. It also highlights the current and potential future use of these data to inform and improve stock assessment and management across E&W.

Keywords: index rivers, Salmo trutta L., sea trout, abundance, growth, marine survival.

INTRODUCTION

Very few European rivers support intensive monitoring programmes for sea trout (*Salmo trutta,* L.) aimed at collecting long-term data sets on stock abundance and composition at key life stages (WKTRUTTA, 2013). These programmes are essential to understanding population processes, stock biology and the influence of environmental factors. As such, they are a prerequisite to better management decision making.

The pioneering study of Elliott on the sea trout of the Black Brows Beck, a small sub-catchment of the River Leven, England (e.g. Elliott, 1994; Elliott & Elliott, 2006) is perhaps the best known example of this type of long-term investigation. Other well known, whole-catchment, monitoring programmes include those on the Burrishoole system, Ireland (Poole *et al.*, 2006) and Bresle river, France (Euzenat *et al.*, 2006).

Elsewhere in England and Wales (E&W), a network of monitored rivers, developed over the years by the Environment Agency, Natural Resources Wales, and predecessor organisations, provide Returning Stock Estimates (RSEs) for salmon and, in a few cases, sea trout as well (Figure 1). Currently, RSEs for salmon are reported for nine rivers in E&W: namely the Tyne, Test, Itchen, Hampshire Avon, Frome, Tamar, Fowey, Dee and Lune, with time-series ranging from 10 years (2006-2015) on the Avon to 28 years (1988-2015) on the Test and Itchen (Cefas, Environment Agency & Natural Resources Wales, 2015a & 2015b). On all of these rivers, RSEs are obtained from the operation of resistivity fish counters except on the Dee, where trapping and mark-recapture methods are used. An additional programme on the River Kent (1990-2010) is no longer active.

On six of these rivers, the Tyne, Tamar, Fowey, Dee, Lune and Kent, RSEs have also been obtained for sea trout using the methods described above. However, the time-series of data tend to be shorter than those for salmon: ranging from 25 years (1991-2015) on the Dee to 12 years on the Tyne (2004-2015).

Since its start in 1991, the Dee has been considered an 'index' monitored river for both salmon and sea trout because, alongside the provision of RSEs, the programme includes operation of an upstream trapping facility (at Chester Weir) to sample and obtain biological data (e.g. on age, size, sex, etc.) from returning fish (Davidson *et al.*, 1996, Davidson *et al.*, 2006). Combining these two sets of information allows the structure and dynamics of populations to be explored through the partitioning of RSEs into year class components. This includes exploration of stock and recruitment relationships (Davidson *et al., 2017)* as well as the examination of patterns and trends in biological characteristics and links to abundance, survival and environmental change.

Other index monitored rivers, the Tyne, Tamar and Lune, were developed from 2004 onwards when upstream traps were operated alongside existing resistivity fish counters to collect biological data. In the case of the Tyne, trapping was later replaced by a fishery and broodstock based sampling programme (Environment Agency, 2008 and 2012).

In addition to adult stock monitoring, the index programmes also include routine electrofishing surveys for juvenile salmonids and an assessment of fishery performance from the collection of rod catch and effort statistics. On the Dee and Tamar, downstream trapping is also undertaken each spring to evaluate smolt output and return rates by mark-recapture.

This paper presents some of the results from the index rivers to date – focussing on the Dee as the longest running programme. It compares patterns and trends in sea trout RSEs, explores associations between marine growth, survival and Sea Surface Temperature (SSTs), and describes observations from the Dee on spawner numbers and juvenile recruitment in both sea trout/trout and salmon. The paper aims to demonstrate how the detailed and long term data sets generated by index river monitoring can provide unique insight into the biology of sea trout populations and their response to environmental change. It also highlights the current and potential future use of these data to inform and improve stock assessment and management across E&W.

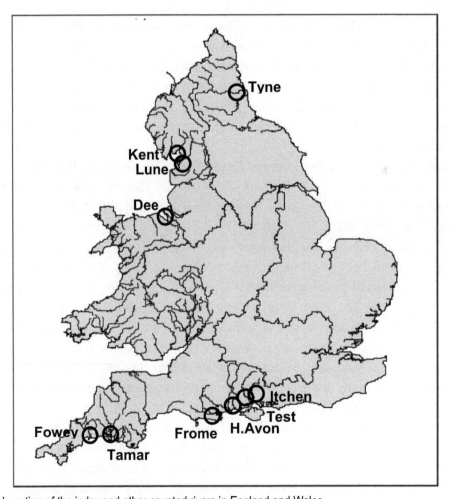

Figure 1. Location of the index and other counted rivers in England and Wales

METHODS

RSES AND BIOLOGICAL DATA

The location of the index and other counted rivers in E&W is shown in Figure 1 with summary details on the former given in Table 1. As noted above, the programmes on the Tyne, Tamar and Lune are reliant on the operation of resistivity fish counters for the provision of RSEs for sea trout and salmon. On the Dee, RSEs are based on trapping and mark-recapture.

Partial upstream traps, co-located with these fish counters, have been used to sample adult sea trout and salmon and collect biological information (e.g. on age and size composition), including the data on sea-age and fork-length (measured to the nearest millimetre) presented here. On the Tyne, the trap sampling programme has since been replaced with a rod fishery/broodstock sampling programme.

Biological data are also used alongside fish length and counter signal size relationships and video validation methods to identify and apportion species at counted sites. On the Tyne, this includes the use of side-view underwater video footage (Environment Agency, 2008 and 2012 provide further details).

Table 1. Adult counter and trap details for the index rivers

Detail	Tyne	Tamar	Dee	Lune
Site name	Riding Mill	Gunnislake Weir	Chester Weir	Forge Weir
NGR	NZ 027 619	SX 435 713	SJ 408 658	SD 516 648
Facilities	Counter & upstream trap	Counter & upstream trap	Upstream tarp	Counter & upstream trap
Distance from head of tide.	11 km	at head of tide	at head of tide	4 km
Counter operation	2004 onward	1994 onward	-	1989 onward
Trap operation	2004 – 2007*	2003 onward	1991 onward	2004 onward
Mean sea trout RSE 2010 - 2014	23,080	10,624	15,077	8,001**
Mean salmon RSE 2010 - 2014	16,025	4,467	4.423	5,381

Adult trapping programme replaced by a fishery and broodstock sampling programme.
*** Sea trout RSE significantly underestimates the .0+ stock component.*

SMOLT TRAPPING AND RETURN ESTIMATES

Rotary Screw Traps (E.G. Solutions: http://home.teleport.com/~egs/) are operated in spring (April-May) on the Tamar and Dee to sample downstream migrating sea trout and salmon smolts at lower main river/tributary locations. Trapping is partial and discontinuous but is designed to cover the main emigration period and provide a sample of fish broadly representative of the run as a whole. Captured fish are adipose fin clipped and/or tagged with Coded Wire

Tags (Northwest Marine Technology: http://www.nmt.us/products/cwt/cwt.shtml) in order to obtain estimates of smolt output and return rate using mark-recapture methods. This relies on the use of the upstream trapping facilities on these systems to screen for returning tagged fish and provide appropriate raising factors from trap efficiency calculations.

SEA SURFACE TEMPERATURE (SST) DATA

Associations between marine growth, smolt return rate and Sea Surface Temperature (SST) are explored here to examine how the latter, as one of the more widely available physical measures in the marine environment, might be linked (directly or indirectly) to biological variability. The SST data used were downloaded from the European Space Agency SST Climate Change Initiative website (http://www.esa-sst-cci.org/PUG/map.htm) and were expressed as monthly means for ~25km x ~25km grids, covering the period 1993-2010. SST data were obtained for two transects of 9 sampling points – one transect each for the Tamar and Dee. Each transect ran ~10km parallel with the coast, with the sampling points spaced ~20km apart and the middle sampling point located opposite the estuary mouth of the rivers in question. The transect for the Tamar ran from Torquay to west of Falmouth and the transect for the Dee extended from Anglesey to Grange-Over-Sands.

SPAWNING ESCAPEMENT AND JUVENILE ABUNDANCE

Time-series of egg deposition estimates for sea trout and salmon are examined for the Dee alongside associated (whole catchment scale) abundance estimates for trout and salmon fry (0+ fish). Egg deposition estimates were derived from RSEs and biological data on the size, sex composition (primarily judged from external characteristics), fecundity (from standard size-fecundity relationships, e.g. Solomon, 1994) and, in the case of .0+ sea trout (Davidson *et al.*, 2006), the maturity of returning fish. Likely in-river losses (e.g. resulting from the intervening rod fishery) were factored into these estimates.

Indices of fry abundance were obtained from timed (5-minute) electrofishing surveys (after the method of Crozier and Kennedy, 1994) targeting more than 80 fixed sites annually. Fry counts from these sites (expressed per 100m2 of river sampled) were raised to standing stock indices based on (i) accessible wetted area estimates for the sections of river they were considered representative of, and (ii) incorporating estimates of sampling efficiency obtained from quantitative electrofishing surveys at sites with similar physical characteristics (e.g. channel widths).

A Ricker (1954) stock-recruitment (SR) relationship was fitted to the time-series of data for the Dee on sea trout egg deposition (stock) and trout fry abundance indices (recruits). The SR curve was fitted using non-linear regression methods described in Davidson *et al.* (2017).

RESULTS

ADULT RETURNS

The time-series of RSEs for the index and other counted rivers in England & Wales that provide run estimates for both sea trout and salmon are shown in Figures 2a and 2b respectively. These six river systems are broadly representative of the geographical spread of sea trout and salmon rivers in E&W.

Long-term average run estimates for sea trout on these rivers ranged from ~4,000 fish on the Kent to ~25,000 on the Tyne, with average returns on the remaining rivers of ~9,000–11,000 fish. For west coast rivers, much of the returning run of sea trout consists of .0+ fish (= *finnock*) weighing roughly 1lb or 0.45kg. For example, an average of 63% of the RSE on the Tamar and 82% on the Dee comprised these smaller .0+ fish.

For salmon, long-term average run estimates were always less than for sea trout on the same river system. Estimates ranged from ~800 fish on the Fowey to ~15,000 fish on the Tyne with returns of ~2,000–7,000 fish on the remaining rivers.

There were notable differences in the patterns of return for these two species over the time-series. For example, among close neighbouring rivers, sea trout RSEs on the Lune and Kent showed similar declining trends whereas on the Tamar and Fowey the patterns of return appeared quite different – with the improved returns on the Fowey seeming to share more in common with the distant Dee than the adjacent Tamar (Figure 2a).

In contrast, for salmon, the patterns of return among stocks appeared more consistent and were generally characterized by a period of peak abundance in mid-2000 followed by marked decline, in many cases to levels at or close to all-time minimums.

MARINE GROWTH

Among the biological details recorded from adult sea trout sampled on the index rivers, size at return (as length and weight) is among the most widely available metrics. Time-series of mean length data for .0+ and .1+ maiden sea trout and .0+SM+ and .1+SM+ previous spawners are shown in Figure 3 for all four index rivers. Pearson correlation analysis indicated marked upward trends (P<0.05) in length at return for Dee .0+SM+ fish, .1+ fish and .1+SM+ fish over the 24 year time-series. This contrasted with the Lune, where trends in length at return were negative (P<0.05) for .0+SM+ fish and .1+ fish over the shorter 9-year period. In all other cases, trends in lengths were not significant (P≥0.05). [Note that annual means based on sample sizes of <5 fish were excluded from these analyses.]

Growth increments, based on mean length at return in year n and n+1, were calculated for separate cohorts of Dee and Tamar sea trout between two stages as: a) .0+ to .0+SM+, and b) .1+ to .1+SM+. Only in the case of Dee .0+ to .0+SM+ fish was a significant (upward)

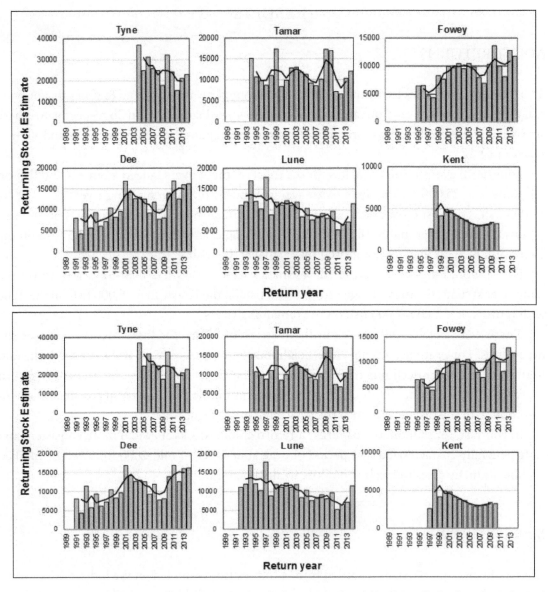

Figure 2. Time-series of Returning Stock Estimates for *a*) sea trout (*top*) and *b*) salmon (*bottom*) on the index and other counted rivers in England and Wales (1991-2014). Solid line indicates rolling 3-year mean.

trend apparent (P<0.001): equivalent to an average additional growth increment of 2.3 mm per year over the 20-year time-series.

Similarly, for Dee .0+ sea trout, back-calculated growth increments available for the smolt stage to the .0+ stage (measured from the last freshwater annulus to the scale edge) also showed a significant upward trend (P=0.025) over the time-series: equivalent to an average additional growth of 0.9 mm per year.

Growth increments for all these stages (Figure 4) were positively correlated with Sea Surface Temperatures (SSTs) recorded ~10km offshore and corresponding to periods when the life stages of interest were most likely to be present in coastal waters (readings averaged along a 120km transect centred around the mouth of the river in question). However, only in the case of back-calculated growth increments for Dee sea trout for the smolt to .0+ stage was the correlation statistically significant (r = 0.746; P = 0.001).

3a) = .0+ and .0+SM+ fish:

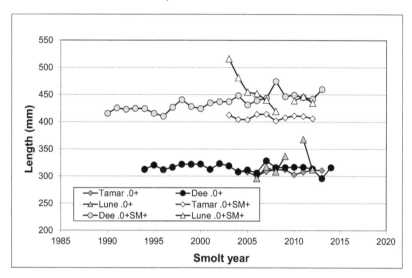

3b) = .1+ and .1+SM+ fish

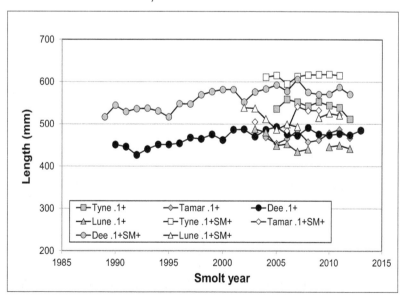

Figure 3. Mean length at return for *a)* maiden (.0+ and .1+) and *b)* previous spawning (.0+SM+ and .1+SM+) sea trout on the Tyne, Tamar, Dee and Lune, 1992-2014.

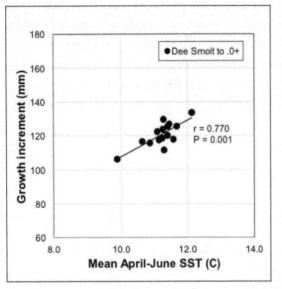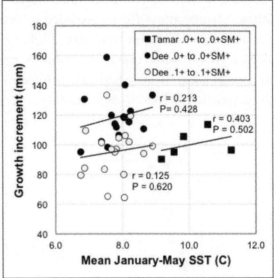

Figure 4. Correlations (Pearson coefficients = r) between growth increment and coastal Sea Surface Temperature (SST) for sea trout returning as .0+, 0+SM+, and .1+SM+ fish. Trend lines shown.

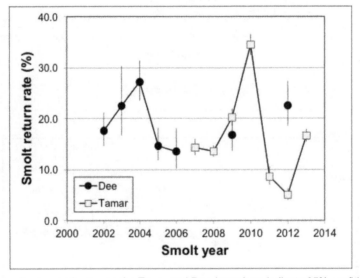

Figure 5. Sea trout smolt return estimates on the Tamar and Dee (error bars indicate 95% confidence limits).

MARINE SURVIVAL

Smolt return rates (a proxy for marine survival) estimated from Coded Wire Tagging and recapture programmes on the Tamar and Dee are shown in Figure 5 (gaps in the time-series for the Dee correspond to years when numbers of fish recaptured were too small to produce reliable return estimates). Average return estimates (for all maiden fish) were similar on the

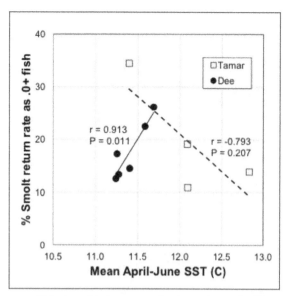

Figure 6. Correlations (Pearson coefficients = r) between smolt return rates on the Tamar and Dee (.0+ fish only) and coastal Sea Surface Temperatures (SSTs). Trend lines shown

two rivers at 16% (range 5 – 35%) on the Tamar and 19% (range 14 – 27%) on the Dee, with return estimates showing a high degree of year-on-year variability on both rivers.

Return rates (for .0+ fish only) were significantly positively correlated with March-June SSTs on the Dee (r = 0.913; P = 0.011), but were negatively correlated (but not significantly so) on the Tamar (r = -0.793; P =0.207) (Figure 6).

FRESHWATER GROWTH

In contrast to the positive trends in marine growth evident for post-smolt stages, examination of data from the Dee indicated no evidence of similar upward trends in freshwater growth for the juvenile pre-smolt stages (Figure 7). Growth indicators for juveniles were measured either as (a) observed mean lengths of ~1+ trout sampled from late summer electrofishing surveys at fixed sites on three Dee tributaries or (b) back-calculated lengths at river age 2 (measured to the second freshwater annulus) for fish returning as .0+ or .1+ maidens.

SPAWNING ESCAPEMENT AND JUVENILE ABUNDANCE

Figure 8 shows standing stock indices of trout and salmon fry abundance on the Dee (derived from electrofishing surveys) alongside egg deposition estimates relevant to each year class of fry.

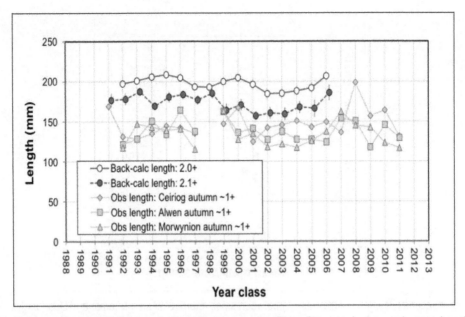

Figure 7. Freshwater growth indicators for juvenile trout on the River Dee as a) observed mean lengths of ~1+ fish sampled from late summer electrofishing surveys on the Ceiriog, Alwen and Morwynion tributaries or b) back-calculated lengths at river age 2 for fish returning as .0+ or .1+ maidens.

The most recent years in these time-series are notable because of the marked increase in trout fry abundance, with estimates in 2014 and 2013 the two highest recorded. This coincided with a period when egg deposition estimates for sea trout were also among the highest to date. In contrast, salmon returns on the Dee have been declining in recent years with egg deposition and fry abundance estimates among the poorest on record (Figure 8).

Figure 9 shows a Ricker (1954) stock-recruitment curve fitted to the sea trout egg deposition and trout fry standing stock data sets .This suggests that current levels of sea trout spawning on the Dee are approaching carrying capacity – equivalent to ~10 million eggs at Smax (or the average number of eggs required to maximise fry production).

DISCUSSION

At the time of publication of the proceedings of the first International Sea Trout Symposium (Harris & Milner, 2006), three out of four of the index river programmes in E&W had barely begun. A decade later, these programmes are still young in terms of the use of traps or other means to collect biological information, and so have covered only a few generations of returning fish (although, in some cases, they may have produced counter derived RSEs for sea trout for many years). Hence, it would be premature at this stage to expect them to provide the essential long-term data sets required to explore in detail the dynamics and biological characteristics of populations and their responses to environmental change. (That said, elsewhere in these

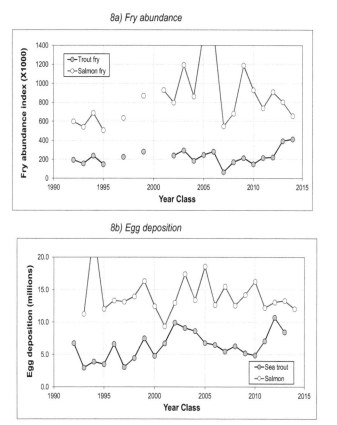

Figure 8. Time-series, by year class, of *a)* electrofishing indices of trout and salmon fry abundance on the Dee along with *b)* estimates of egg deposition from adult returns.

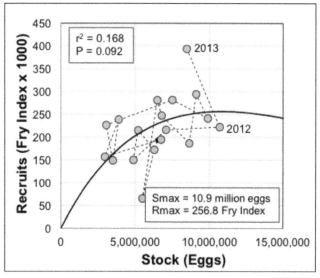

Figure 9. Ricker stock-recruitment curve fitted to Dee sea trout egg deposition and trout fry recruitment indices; 1992-2103. Where (i) Smax is the stock size resulting in maximum recruitment (Rmax) and (ii) data points for the 2012 and 2013 recruitment years are indicated.

proceedings, tentative stock and recruitment relationships have been derived for the index rivers by Davidson *et al.,* 2017 to explore and develop procedures for generating Biological Reference Points for sea trout on all the principal rivers in E&W.)

Accordingly, this paper draws particularly on the findings from the Dee as the longest running of the index river programmes, and primarily serves to illustrate where these intensive and long-term monitoring programmes can provide insight into areas of the sea trout life cycle where our knowledge is lacking. Developing an understanding in these areas is often essential to the process of refining and improving our fisheries and environmental management for *Salmo trutta* L.

The marine phase of the sea trout life cycle is one such area where there are significant knowledge gaps (Milner *et al.*, 2006). The growth, maturation and survival of fish at sea can be expected to drive much of the observed variation in the abundance, size and age composition of returning fish and so these factors are linked to both the success of fisheries and the contribution of spawners (eggs) to the progeny of the next generation. The associations explored in this paper between growth, survival and Sea Surface Temperature (SST) provide only a superficial examination of these factors, but highlight a potentially informative approach which has been used to examine similar questions about the growth and survival of Atlantic salmon (*Salmo salar*, L.) at sea (Friedland *et al.*, 1998 & 2000).

Indeed, using this type of approach on sea trout may prove more informative than it has for salmon given that marine migrations for sea trout are less extensive and so the area of sea to be 'searched' for associations between growth, survival and SST (or other relevant environmental variables such as plankton production; Beaugrand & Reid, 2012), is more constrained. This is particularly so for west coast populations dominated by .0+ fish where most individuals will spend only a few months in coastal waters from late spring to early summer and so are unlikely to journey far from their natal river. This may explain why, in this study, the association between (April-June) SST and the (back-calculated) post-smolt growth increment of Dee fish returning at age .0+ was by far the strongest of the relationships explored (Figure 4).

Similarly, associations with smolt return estimates (a proxy for marine survival) and SST were also strong (and positive) for this sea age group on the Dee, although less strong (and negative) for Tamar fish (Figure 5). These opposing trends hint at a possible optimum temperature or temperature-linked factor (perhaps growth related) associated with survival. Clearly, further data would be required to confirm such a relationship and, indeed, explore how similar mechanisms might influence the survival and growth of .1+ or .2+ maiden fish that remain at sea and forage more widely throughout the year and so can be expected to experience a wider range of temperatures and other environmental conditions.

Improving our understanding of the marine environment, its fine scale complexity, and how sea trout utilise and interact with that environment, e.g. in terms of migration routes (Potter *et al.*, 2017) or habitat use (Launey *et al.*, 2017), is essential if stocks are to be adequately protected at sea and spatial differences in stock performance better explained. The need for this information has perhaps never been greater given (i) the growth in development (proposed and implemented) of marine renewable schemes for tidal and off-shore wind power generation and (ii) the largely unknown effects of climate change (e.g. WKTRUTTA, 2013). Local and broader scale changes to the marine environment associated with both factors have uncertain and potentially adverse consequences for migratory species such as sea trout and salmon, as well as for the wider marine ecosystem. The more we can discover about sea trout in the sea the more effective our management response is likely to be e.g. in terms of controlling development or mitigating for adverse impacts. Exploring the links between marine growth, survival and SSTs (or other environmental variables) is an important part of the process of developing understanding (see e.g. Milner *et al.,* 2017), with the index rivers playing a key role as the only routine source of the required biological data in E&W.

On the River Dee, the general increase in sea trout returns over the last 25 years (Figure 2) has coincided with a period of improved marine growth rates for some sea age groups (Figure 3). It is unclear if these two factors are related because insufficient data are available at present for meaningful exploration of growth-mediated survival hypotheses. Over the same period, the freshwater growth of juvenile trout has remained relatively stable (or declining) (Figure 7). This suggests that a more favourable marine environment, in particular, may have been a key factor influencing improved sea trout returns.

In any event, the outcome appears to have been record levels of trout fry recruitment on the Dee in the last few years with the population approaching carrying capacity – as shown from a Ricker stock-recruitment relationship with sea trout egg deposition as the stock variable (Figure 9). This is in sharp contrast to the picture for salmon in recent years, where spawner and fry numbers have been in decline. Consequently, levels of interaction between largely sympatric populations of trout and salmon are likely to have changed over the time-series and (like the marine phase of the sea trout life cycle) warrant closer investigation. Again, the index rivers are invaluable in this context as the only rivers in E&W providing RSEs and biological data for both *Salmo trutta*, L. and *Salmo salar* L

Index river monitoring for sea trout (and salmon) plays an important and often unparalleled role in helping to fill many of the knowledge gaps that challenge fisheries scientists and managers. Much of the focus of this paper has been on the marine phase of the sea trout life cycle where there are many 'unknowns' and growing pressures: e.g. from the development of marine renewables or climate change. Here, the exploration of links between index river data on growth and survival, and environmental factors such as SSTs, is providing valuable insight into the marine life of sea trout.

Equally, the index programmes provide unique levels of detail on the freshwater phase of the lifecycle, from estimates of numbers of returning adults, to measures of fishery performance, levels of spawning escapement and egg deposition, and information on subsequent juvenile recruitment.

These separate outputs are frequently used in population modelling (e.g. the Ricker egg-to-fry SR curve presented here) as well as in other developments which have generic application e.g. in stock assessment. For example, Davidson *et al.,* (2017) utilise index river data in models to estimate angling exploitation rates and derive measures of stock and recruitment from catch data. These form part of procedures to generate SR curves and associated Biological Reference Points across the full range of sea trout rivers. Index river data are also used in these procedures to check the validity of model outputs.

All these examples serve to illustrate the unique contribution index river monitoring in E&W can, and does, make to further our understanding of sea trout biology and to developing tools and techniques to facilitate stock assessment and management in the widest sense.

ACKNOWLEDGEMENTS

We would like to thank all individuals from the Environment Agency, Natural Resources Wales and predecessor organisations who have contributed to the collection and processing of the data presented here. We also acknowledge the support of Cefas for the smolt trapping programmes conducted on the Tamar and Dee over the years and are particularly grateful for the assistance of Cefas staff in this work.

REFERENCES

Beaugrand, G. & Reid, P.C. (2012). Relationships between North Atlantic salmon, plankton, and hydroclimatic change in the Northeast Atlantic. *ICES Journal of Marine Science* (2012), **69** (9), 1549-1562.

Crozier, W.W. & Kennedy, G.J.A. (1994). Application of semi-quantitive electrofishing to juvenile salmonid stock surveys. *Journal of Fish Biology*, 45, 159-164.

Davidson, I.C., Cove, R.J., Milner, N.J. and Purvis, W.K. (1996) Estimation of Atlantic salmon (*Salmo salar*, L.) and sea trout (*Salmo trutta*, L.) run size and angling exploitation on the Welsh Dee using mark-recapture and trap indices. In: *Stock Assessment in Inland Fisheries*. (I.G. Cowx. *Ed*.). Fishing News Books, Oxford Blackwell Science, 293-307.

Davidson, I.C., Cove, R.J. & Hazlewood, M.S. (2006). Annual variation in age composition and abundance of sea trout returning to the River Dee at Chester, 1991-2003. In: *Sea Trout: Biology, Conservation and Management*. (Graeme Harris & Nigel Milner. *Eds*.). Proceedings of the 1st International Sea Trout Symposium, Cardiff, July 2004. Blackwell Publishing, Oxford, 257-278.

Davidson, I.C., Aprahamian, M.W., Peirson, G., Hillman, R.J., Cook, N., Elsmere, P.S., Cove, R.J. & Croft, A. (2017). Catch and stock based Biological Reference Points for sea trout in England and Wales: A comparison of methods and critical examination of their potential application to stock assessment and management. In: *Sea Trout: Science & Management*. (Graeme Harris. *Ed*.) Proceedings of the 2nd International Sea Trout Symposium, October 2015, Dundalk, Ireland. *(Troubador & pages later)*.

Environment Agency, (2008). Index river monitoring for salmon and sea trout. A progress report on the monitoring programmes on the Tyne, Tamar, Dee & Lune; July 2008. Environment Agency Report GEWA 108BOTB-E-E.

Environment Agency, (2012). Index river monitoring for salmon and sea trout. Second joint report on the monitoring programmes on the Tyne, Tamar, Dee and Lune. Environment Agency Report, August 2012.

Elliott, J.M. (1994). Quantitative Ecology and the Brown Trout. Oxford University Press, Oxford, xi +286p.

Elliott, J.M. & Elliott, J.A. (2006). A 35-year study of stock and recruitment relationships in a small population of sea trout: Assumptions, implications and limitations for predicting targets. In: *Sea Trout: Biology, Conservation and Management.* (Graeme Harris & Nigel Milner. *Eds.* Proceedings of the 1st International Sea Trout Symposium, July 2004, Cardiff, Wales. Blackwell Publishing, Oxford, 257-278.

Euzenat, G., Fournel, F. & Fagard, J-L. (2006). Population dynamics and stock-recruitment relationships for sea trout in the River Bresle, Upper Normandy, France. In: *Sea Trout: Biology, Conservation and Management.* (Graeme Harris & Nigel Milner. *Eds.*). Proceedings of the 1st International Sea Trout Symposium, July 2004, Cardiff, Wales. Blackwell Publishing, Oxford, 307 – 320.

Friedland, K.D., Hansen, L.P. & Dunkley, D.A. (1998). Marine temperatures experienced by post-smolts and the survival of Atlantic salmon (*Salmo salar*, L.) in the North Sea area. *Fisheries Oceanography*, **7**: 22-34.

Friedland, K.D., Hansen, L.P., Dunkley, D.A., & MacLean, J.C. (2000). Linkage between ocean climate, post smolt growth, and survival of Atlantic salmon (*Salmo salar*, L.) in the North Sea area. *ICES Journal of Marine Science*, **57**: 419-429.

Harris, G.S. & Milner, N.J. (2006). *Sea Trout: Biology, Conservation and Management.* (Graeme Harris & Nigel Milner. *Eds.*). Proceedings of the 1st International Sea Trout Symposium, July 2004. Cardiff, Wales. Blackwell Publishing, Oxford, 499 pp.

Launey. S., Quéméré, E., Fagard, J-L. & Baglinière, J-L. (2017*)*. Sea does matter: Seascape heterogeneity influences coastal migration tactics and population connectivity in brown trout *(Salmo trutta L.)*. In: *Sea Trout: Science & Management.* (Graeme Harris. *Ed.*). Proceedings of the 2nd International Sea Trout Symposium, October 2015, Dundalk, Ireland *(Troubador and pages later)*

Milner, N.J., Harris, G.S., Gargan, P., Beveridge, M., Pawson, M.G., Walker, A. & Whelan, K. (2006). Perspectives on sea trout science and management. In: *Sea Trout: Biology, Conservation and Management.* (Graeme Harris & Nigel Milner. *Eds.).* Proceedings of the 1st International Sea Trout Symposium, July 2004, Cardiff, Wales. Blackwell Publishing, Oxford, 480-490.

Milner, N., Potter, E., Roche, W., Tysklind, N., Davidson, I., King, J., Coyne, J. & Davies, C. (2017). Variation in sea trout (*Salmon trutta*, L.) abundance and life histories in the Irish Sea. In: Sea Trout: Science & Management. (Graeme Harris. Ed.). Proceeding of the 2nd International Sea Trout Symposium, October 2015, Dundalk, Ireland. (*Troubador & pages later*)

Poole, W.R., Dillane, M., DeEyto, E., Rogan, G., McGinnity, P. & Whelan., K. (2006). Characteristics of the Burrishoole sea trout population: Census, marine survival, enhancement and stock-recruitment relationship, 1971-2003. In: *Sea Trout: Biology, Conservation and Management.* (Graeme Harris & Nigel Milner. *Eds.*) Proceedings of the 1st International Sea Trout Symposium, July 2004, Cardiff, Wales. Blackwell Publishing, Oxford, 279-306.

Potter, E., Campbell, R., Sumner, K. & Marshall, S. (2017). Marine migrations and distribution of sea trout from rivers in Great Britain. In: *Sea Trout: Science & Management*. (Graeme Harris. *Ed.*). Proceeding of the 2nd International Sea Trout Symposium, October 2015, Dundalk, Ireland. (*Troubador & ages later*)

Ricker, W.E. (1954). Stock and recruitment. *Journal of the Fisheries Research Board of Canada,* **11**:559-623.

Solomon, D.J. (1994). Sea trout investigations. Phase I – Final Report. R&D Note 318, National Rivers Authority. 434-440.

WKTRUTTA (2013). Report of the Workshop on Sea Trout (WKTRUTTA). ICES WKTRUTTA Report 2013, 12-14 November 2013, ICES Headquarters, Copenhagen, Denmark. SCICOM Steering Group on Ecosystem Functions, ICES CM 2013/SSGEF: 15, Ref. WGBAST, WGRECORDS, SCICOM.

ELECTRONIC REFERENCES

Cefas, Environment Agency & Natural Resources Wales (2015a). Annual assessment of salmon stocks and fisheries in England and Wales 2014: Standing report on methods, approaches and wider stock conservation and management considerations. *Available at:* https://www.gov.uk/government/uploads/system/uploads/attachment_data/file/437977/BackgroundSalmonReport-2014.pdf

Cefas, Environment Agency & Natural Resources Wales (2015b). Annual assessment of salmon stocks and fisheries in England and Wales 2014: Preliminary assessment prepared for ICES, March 2015. *Available at:* https://www.gov.uk/government/uploads/system/uploads/attachment_ data/file/450982/SalmonAssessmentReport-2014-finalrevised.pdf

The collection of catch statistics from the recreational rod fisheries in England & Wales

R. EVANS[1] & G. HARRIS[2]

[1]Natural Resources Wales, Ty Cambria, 29 Newport Road, Cardiff CF24 0TP, Wales.
[2]FishSkill Consultancy Ltd., Cathedine, Bwlch, Brecon, Powys, LD3 7PZ, Wales.

ABSTRACT

The collection of an annual record of the rod catch by salmon and sea trout anglers in England & Wales has been a common practice by different management agencies for almost 100 years to provide a measure of the performance of recreational fisheries and an index of the status and wellbeing of the fish stocks. In the absence of supplementary data on run-strength obtained directly from suitably located fish counters and permanent trapping stations on all but a very few rivers, rod catch statistics represent the only alternative source of readily available management information for the majority of rivers in the British Isles. The now standard approach to the collection of rod catch statistics from the 80 principal salmon and sea trout fisheries in England & Wales over the 21-year period from 1994 – 2014 is described in terms of their consistency, comparability and routine use a fishery management tool. Some of the general features of the current approach in E&W are compared with the process of collecting rod catch data in Scotland and Ireland.

Keywords: catch statistics; rod fisheries; England & Wales; sea trout, salmon.

INTRODUCTION

Although catch records were variously collected by different management bodies from the recreational (rod) fisheries and commercial (net) fisheries in England & Wales for many years over the last century, it is only since 1994 that a standard and uniform approach was adopted throughout the entire region. Key stages in the evolution of the current approach were:

- Salmon Act 1865 provided a power to establish local 'Fishery Districts' to protect salmon and sea trout fisheries and to introduce a requirement for every participant in the rod and net fisheries to possess a fishing licence. Some 53 Fisheries Boards were established by 1894 covering 75% of England & Wales.
- The Salmon and Freshwater Fisheries Act 1923 provided powers to introduce a byelaw requiring a compulsory catch return for salmon and sea trout by individual anglers.
- River Boards Act 1948 merged the former Fishery District Boards into 32 River Boards covering all regions of England & Wales.
- Water Resources Act 1963 merged the former River Authorities into 27 River Authorities.
- Salmon & Freshwater Fisheries Act 1972 added the power to require the submission of a 'Nil' return of catch and to stipulate the nature of the information required in the catch return.
- Water Act 1973 incorporated the River Authorities into 10 Regional Water Authorities.
- Salmon & Freshwater Fisheries Act 1975 imposed a general duty to '*maintain improve and develop*' fisheries on the Regional Water Authorities.
- Water Act 1989 combined the 10 Water Authorities into a single National Rivers Authority for England & Wales.
- Environment Act 1996 established the Environment Agency for England & Wales.

Background information on the evolution of the current fisheries management structure over the last century is provided by Ayton (1998) and Harris (2014). This chronicles the progressive integration of a large number of small, single-function, catchment-based bodies into a single, large, multifunctional body with extensive powers and resources and a clearly defined central fishery remit covering all regions of England and Wales.

Russell *et al.*, (1995) compiled a database of all the available catch records published by various management organisation from 1951 – 1990 to establish a single authoritative historical benchmark for future reference. This covered the period when local fisheries management was the responsibility of the River Authorities, through to the establishment of Regional Water Authorities and then to the creation of a single National Rivers Authority for all regions of England & Wales. Each of these organisations had variously collected and reported catch statistics for their respective regions in very different ways at different times over the 40-year period of the record. Consequently, there was little consistency, continuity or comparability between not only different administrative regions but also different rivers within a region. Some of the smaller rivers were not included and it was not until the 1970s that the catch return system was expanded to cover sea trout in most regions. Thus, different organisations had collected, collated and reported catch returns for all, or just some, of their rivers in different ways that included:

- Catches provided by the individual owners of sections of private fishing. These were generally restricted to only the more important salmon rivers.
- Catches provided by local fisheries inspectors based on diary records, often combined with

'intelligence' from other local sources.

- Annual catch returns obtained directly from anglers and, because of the low number of returns submitted, then 'adjusted' by additional information from local bailiffs reports and/ or by a factor based on an arbitrary judgement of whether a season had been 'better' or 'worse' than the previous year.
- Different rod licence structure occurred. Some regions did not require a catch return for sea trout and a few regions did not require any form of mandatory catch return for either salmon or sea trout.
- There was no commonality in the data collection or reporting format between regions and details were normally limited to the total number of fish caught and their total weight for the year.

While most organisations published an annual report of catches, these appeared intermittently in different formats. In several regions, the catches for 'minor' rivers, or rivers sharing a common estuary, were combined with a neighbouring major river or produced as an aggregated total for a district. In some years, commercial net catches were combined with rod catches for a district or region.

THE IMPORTANCE OF CATCH STATISTICS

In the absence of accurate assessments of run-strength based on direct counts from reliable and suitably located fixed traps and counting stations in England & Wales (Davidson *et al.*, 2017a), it is inevitable that essential management information on stock status and wellbeing for whole river systems will continue to depend on indirect assessments of fishery performance provided by catch returns from the rod fisheries.

Harris (1986) identified the two principal limitations on the rod catches (for salmon) as an index of stock abundance over the early part of the historical record as: a) variable reporting procedures and b) incomplete and inaccurate catch returns. However, it was argued that rod catch statistics could provide a reasonably robust measure of actual fishery performance over time subject to four principal criteria:

- They were collected on a consistent basis using the same standard methodology.
- The return of catch was as accurate and complete as possible.
- Fishing effort was known.
- The record was continuous over time.

Notwithstanding the ongoing debate about the nature of any direct link between rod catch and stock as a reliable indicator of stock abundance (Shearer, 1986; Shelton, 2002), catch statistics have a range of basic management applications:-

- They provide a basic index of the performance of a fishery and are a measure of the outcome of past fishery management actions.
- They contribute to determining the market value of a fishery when bought and sold.
- They form a basis for calculating claims in the Civil Courts for compensation for the loss of economic value and enjoyment of the fisheries if damaged by the actions of a third party.
- They contribute in promoting the economic benefit of angling tourism within a region.
- They are used in environmental impact and risk assessments on major projects to determine the nature and extent of the requirement for mitigation and/or any remedial action to protect fisheries.
- They 'spotlight' negative trends in the pattern of catches over time and, as such, are often the first 'alarm signals' indicating a management problem that may require further investigation and possible management action.
- They are an important element in calculating exploitation rates when an independent assessment of run-strength is available from direct counts provided by trapping or counting programmes, or from assessments based on mark-and-recapture studies.
- They provide information on exploitation (harvest) as an input into the calculation of science-based Conservation Limits for salmon
- They are used to determine trends in catch-per-unit-effort as an alternative to Biological Reference Points for assessing the status of sea trout fisheries.

THE CATCH DATA RECORDING SYSTEM

The current approach to the collection of catch records from the recreational rod fisheries in England & Wales is based on a dual system of statutory licensing and mandatory catch returns from each individual angler fishing for salmon and sea trout in any year. Following the introduction of a common rod licence structure and a mandatory requirement to submit a catch return, this system has been in place since 1994 without material change.

The Rod Licensing System

All anglers fishing with rod-and-line in E&W must possess a valid rod licence. This applies to all inland fish species but excludes marine fish species. Separate licence categories are available for migratory salmonids, non-migratory trout and freshwater ('*coarse*') fish species for periods covering a full season, 8 days or a single day: with different rates of licence duty applying to each class and category and with concessionary rates available on the cost of season licenses for retirement pensioners, juvenile and disabled anglers. [*Full details available from*: http://www.gov. uk/fishing-licences/buy-a-fishing-licence . Rod licences can be obtained directly from most local branches of the Post Office and by application online. While there is no limit on the number of licences available for angling in any year, the owners of individual fisheries normally

490

restrict the number of anglers granted access to the fishing in order to prevent overfishing, overcrowding and to maintain the enjoyment of the angling experience.

The income from the annual sale of rod licences for migratory fish over the last 5 years has ranged from £1.03 – £1.6 million and is used to support the discharge of the statutory fishery functions of the Environment Agency and Natural Resources Wales.

The rod licensing system provides an invaluable database in supporting the catch return system. It records:

- The category and class of licence issued to each angler.
- The name and address of each angler, with the national postcode identifying if they are 'local' or 'non-resident' to a particular geographical region.

This customer database also provides an effective means for direct communication with each angler on any new initiatives to protect stocks, promote fisheries and has been used as a foundation for questionnaire surveys on socio-economic importance and value of the fisheries, targeted fishing effort and angler perspectives on the status of the fisheries.

Catch Returns System

Every angler licensed to fish for salmon and sea trout must submit a return of catch after the expiry date of the licence: either at the end of the year for full season licences or within 7 days for short-term licences. A standard catch return form is issued to each angler when the licence is purchased and is then followed by the issue of a formal *'reminder notice'* after the end of the season. In order to increase the rate of submission of returns, a second reminder notice is issued to those anglers who purchased a licence online. A Freepost address is supplied for returning the form or a catch return may be now filed on-line. Failure to submit a catch return is an offence. [The catch return form is bilingual for those anglers obtaining their licence in Wales.] The details required on the catch return form are:

- The name of each river fished. [Season licence holders may often fish several different rivers in a year.]
- The number of fishing trips (days or part-days) made each month on each named river.
- The number of each species of fish caught on each fishing trip.
- The date (day/month) of capture.
- The weight of each fish caught to the nearest 1 lb.
- Whether the fish was released or harvested (killed) after capture.
- The method of capture (fly, spinner or bait).
- The number of fish caught before or after 16th June as a means of identifying early running MSW 'spring' salmon.
- A *'Nil,* return is required if an angler did not fish that year or fished but caught no fish.

491

- Because of the large number of 0SW sea trout (finnock or whitling) of less than 1lb weight that may be caught by some anglers, these fish are recorded separately as the total number caught in each month.

The annual catch records are collected, collated and retained in a central database after checking by local managers to identify any apparent anomalies and inconsistencies. The catch records for each of the 80 'principal migratory fisheries are then published each year and released into the public domain as the series of 'Salmonid & Freshwater Fisheries Statistics for England & Wales' produced by the Environment Agency since 1990. [*Available at*: http://www.gov.uk/government/collections/salmonid-and-freshwater-fisheries-statistics.] The catch returns from individual anglers are treated as confidential and only the aggregated catch data for whole river systems is released into the public domain.

Submission Rates

The number of rod licences and the proportion of catch returns submitted each year from 1994 is shown in Figure 1 for the Welsh Region. Similar analyses show that the average response rates in the Northeast and Northwest Regions of England were very similar at 65%. They then increased to 73.0% in Southwest of England and were highest in Wales at 80.9% over the same period. The higher response rate for Wales, where a very similar catch return reminder system had been in place since 1976, probably reflects the greater familiarity by anglers with the catch return process and reminder system and a greater general awareness of the importance of catch returns in the management of *their* fisheries than in other regions.

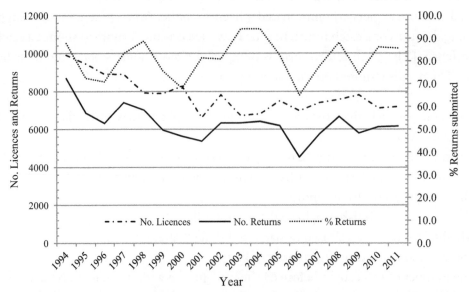

Figure 1. Annual number of rod licences issued, number and proportion of catch returns submitted for the Welsh Region (1994 – 2011).

Catch Return Reminders

The crucial importance of issuing a formal notice at the end of the season to remind anglers to submit their catch returns was a key factor in improving the accuracy of the annual catch record (Harris, 1986). This practice was first introduced by the former Welsh Water Authority in 1976 and then subsequently adopted for all regions of England & Wales from 1994.

Harris (1986) reported that the initial (unprompted) response rate from the 19,000 – 22,000 Welsh licence holders between 1976-1982 ranged from just 28 – 33% across all licence categories (season, week & day). The issue of a first reminder notice at the end of the season to anglers who failed to submit an unprompted return increased the response rate by a further 22 – 38% to provide an overall rate of return of 55 – 66%. The impact of the reminder system on improving the accuracy of the catch return system is evidenced for 1997 when the Water Authority issued 21,284 angling licences.

The unprompted catch return rate at the end of the season from 5,765 anglers (27%) was 9,108 salmon and 9,200 sea trout. The issue of a first reminder notice to the 15,589 anglers who had not submitted a return at the end of the season generated an additional response of 36% from an additional 7,687 anglers who reported an extra extra 1,262 salmon and 5,007 sea trout. The overall return rate for the year from the 13,453 anglers that submitted a return was 63% for a final total of 10,371 salmon and 14,207 sea trout. The reminder system therefore increased the annual rod catch by 14% for salmon and 54% for sea trout.

Significantly, whereas the response rate from holders of a full season licence was 68% overall, the return rate from day licence holders was lower at 48%; suggesting that less frequent, casual, anglers are less likely to submit a return – even after receiving a reminder. The Environment Agency (2010) stated the belief that the annual catch return and reminder system now records over 80% of all migratory salmonids caught in England & Wales.

SCOPE OF DATABASE.

There are 80 'principal' rivers in England & Wales that support significant local sea trout and salmon rod fisheries (Evans & Harris, 2017). For each of these rivers, the central database now contains a continuous 21-year time series of directly comparable catch records with the same level of detail. The following examples are given to illustrate the breadth and depth of the information available under the general headings of:

- The total annual reported catch.
- Annual fishing effort and catch-per-unit-effort.
- Size distribution of catch
- Catch-and-Release Rates
- Method of capture.

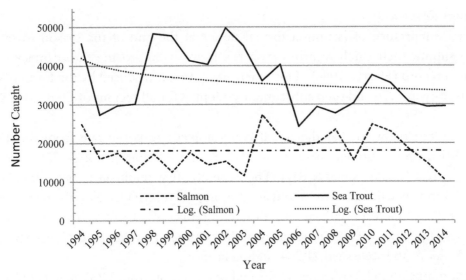

Figure 2. Aggregated mean annual catch of sea trout and salmon for all Regions of England & Wales (1994 – 2014).

Total Annual Catch

The 21-year record of the annual catch of sea trout and salmon for all 80 rivers in England & Wales (Figure 2) shows large fluctuations over short time periods and a general and steady decline in catches for both species: notably from 2002 for sea trout and from 2005 for salmon. The lack of any clear synchronicity in the inter-annual peaks and troughs for sea trout and salmon suggests either different factors affecting survival and return rates in the sea and/or different factors affecting the performance of the fisheries after their return to freshwater.

Harris & Winstone (1990) observed that aggregated catches for the rivers in a large geographical region can mask very real differences between regions and for different rivers within a region. This is illustrated at a regional level in Figure 3[A-B] and at a local level in Figure 4[A-B].

The 14 rivers of the English Northwest Region (Figure 3[A]) all border the northern part of the Irish Sea. The catch trend for salmon has been relatively stable over the period, but with a sharp decline from 2004, while the sea trout catch shows a steady decline over the last 4 years. By contrast, the sea trout catch has declined steadily from 2002 and then improved again from 2006. The annual pattern of increase and decrease in catches for the two species are not synchronised in later years. This contrasts with the pattern of catches for the 6 rivers of the English Northeast region bordering the North Sea (Figure 3[B]). Catches of both sea trout and salmon showed a steady general trend of increase over the period, with annual peaks and troughs broadly synchronised and a sharp decline for sea trout from 2010 and salmon from 2011.

Figure 4[A-B] compares the pattern of catches from the Afon Dyfi in West Wales and the Afon Tywi in Southwest Wales. Both are major sea trout fisheries, with the Dyfi flowing into the

Irish Sea and the Tywi into the adjacent Celtic Sea. The Tywi is also a significant salmon fishery. Salmon catches have fluctuated widely in the Tywi and Dyfi (Figure 4^A), with both rivers showing a steady decline over the period that was most evident over the last 4 years. The most recent assessment of stock status (Ian Davidson – *pers comm.*) places both rivers in the *At Risk* category for salmon. By contrast, different patterns emerge in the trend of sea trout catches (Figure 4^B), with the Dyfi being relatively stable while the Tywi shows steady decline that is most apparent over the last 10 years. The Tywi is currently classified as *Probably not at Risk* and the Dyfi as *Not at Risk* for sea trout.

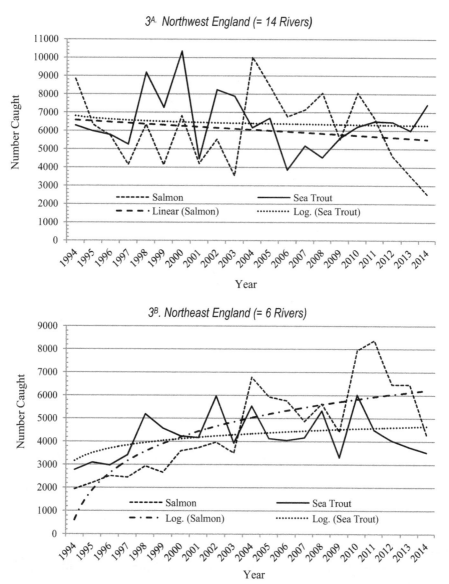

Figure 3^{A-B}. Aggregated mean annual catch of sea trout and salmon for a) English Northwest region and b) the English Northeast Region (1994 – 2014).

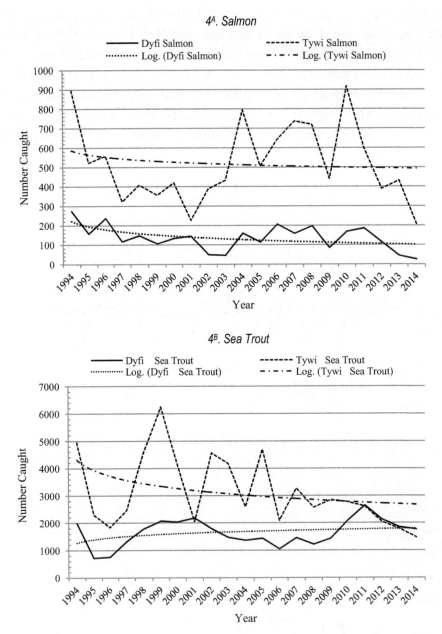

Figure 4 [A-B]. Aggregated mean annual catch of salmon and sea trout from a) Dyfi and b) Tywi in Wales (1994 – 2014).

Fishing Effort & CPUE

The number of the available fish caught during the rod fishing season will depend initially on the number of anglers participating in a fishery and their collective fishing effort over the season. Other factors, principally weather and river flow conditions may modify their fishing success, but the central premise is that any decline in fishing effort will cause a reduced

Table 1. Rod fishing effort, reported catch and CPUE for 22 rivers in Southwest England (1994 – 2014).

Year	Number of Days Fished in year*	Mean No. Days fished per angler	Reported Rod Catch		Reported Catch Per Rod Day fished	
			Salmon	Sea Trout	Salmon	Sea Trout
			No.	No.		
1994	41,100	10.47	5,213	11,525	0.127	0.280
1995	35,362	10.41	2,554	6,842	0.072	0.193
1996	32,307	10.98	2,681	6,941	0.083	0.215
1997	38,809	11.8	2,372	7,088	0.061	0.183
1998	32,145	9.63	2,919	8,418	0.091	0.262
1999	25,479	9.31	1,881	9,668	0.074	0.379
2000	22,272	9.62	2,487	6,472	0.112	0.291
2001	18,342	8.53	1,396	9,019	0.076	0.492
2002	25,030	9.62	1,737	8,253	0.069	0.330
2003	23,103	9.01	1,266	9,344	0.055	0.404
2004	24,496	8.91	2,799	6,570	0.114	0.268
2005	22,144	9.71	1,725	7,291	0.078	0.329
2006	17,510	9.14	1,802	4,590	0.103	0.262
2007	19,864	8.47	2,071	4,259	0.104	0.214
2008	22,573	7.5	2,686	4,353	0.119	0.193
2009	20,009	7.19	1,648	7,194	0.082	0.360
2010	23,206	9.34	2,628	7,578	0.113	0.327
2011	24,008	9.39	2,402	6,216	0.100	0.259
2012	20,482	9.08	2,027	4,849	0.099	0.237
2013	18,385	8.08	1,085	6,379	0.059	0.347
2014	16,221	7.96	799	5,047	0.049	0.311
Mean	*24,897*	*9.25*	*2,199*	*7,043*	*0.088*	*0.292*

*Day = full day or part-day.

catch: and *vice versa*. The introduction of fishing effort data into the catch return system was a significant innovation in understanding and interpreting changes in the long-term pattern of catches within and between different rivers and regions. It also allows the calculation of catch-per-unit-effort (CPUE) as a further measure of annual fishery performance and angling success. This term is used here as the mean number of fish caught by an angler on any one fishing trip over the season.

Table 1 shows the reported fishing effort, rod catch of sea trout and salmon and CPUE expressed as the average number of each species caught by an angler on any one fishing trip. Overall fishing effort has decreased by 60% from the start to the end of the period and is reflected by a decrease in the rod catch by 85% for salmon and by 57% for sea trout over the same period.

When fishing effort is compared with CPUE (Figure 5), an apparent paradox emerges where a decline in effort resulted in an increase of 11% in the average number of sea trout caught by

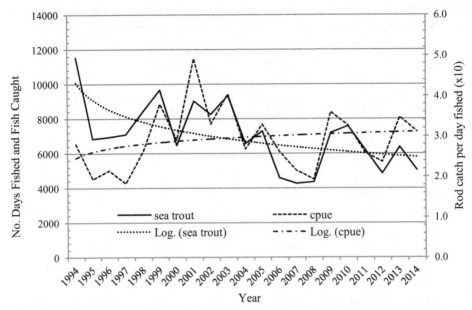

Figure 5. Reported rod catch of sea trout and angler CPUE for the 22 Rivers in Southwest England (1994 – 2014).

anglers on each fishing trip compared with a decrease of 60% for salmon. This may be explained in part by the reduced disturbance created by fewer anglers fishing repeatedly through the same sections of water and reduced competition for the more popular and productive 'taking places' within the fishery. Sea trout usually occupy the shallower, quieter sections of water than salmon and are easily scared in daylight, particularly in the smaller and narrower rivers most typical of Southwest England. Another factor may be the increased fishing effort now targeted specifically at sea trout rather than salmon over the year (Harris & Evans, 2017).

In the absence of Conservation Limits and their alternative for sea trout of Biological Reference Points (Davidson *et al.*, 2017a; Davidson *et al.*, 2017b), an analysis of fishing effort and catch to give a measure of CPUE is now employed in England and Wales to provide an index of sea trout fishery performance (Miran Aprahamian – *pers comm.*). This compares the mean angler CPUE for the current year with the trend in CPUE over the preceding 10 years to identify any pattern of decline. Each river is allocated into one of four risk categories; namely *Not at Risk, Possibly at Risk, Probably at Risk* and *At Risk*. Unlike CLs for salmon, this 'Performance Index' is not predictive and its sole purpose is to provide an 'early warning' of a problem that may require management action to prevent a further, persistent decline. The most recent assessment of sea trout fishery status for the 2015 season (Ian Davidson – *pers. comm.*) indicates that, for 32 'principal' sea trout rivers in Wales, 7 are *At Risk* and 9 *Probably at Risk*. This compares with none *At risk* and 11 *Probably at Risk* for the 44 principal sea trout rivers in England. It is relevant to note that the many of the rivers in these two risk categories are all short, 'minor streams' with only marginal stocks of salmon (Harris & Evans, 2017).

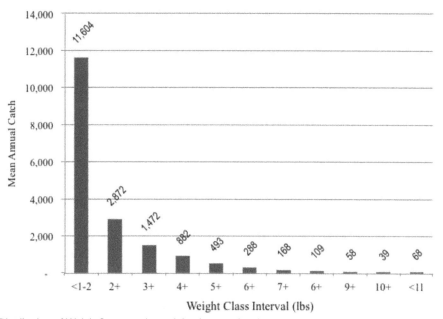

Figure 6. Distribution of Welsh Sea trout by weight classes showing aggregated mean numbers of fish in each class (1994 – 2011).

Size Distribution

The annual catch indicates the performance of the fishery in quantitative terms only. Information on the composition of the catch in qualitative terms can assist in identifying a declining stock from a breakdown of the size range of the catch.

Figure 6 provides a breakdown showing the average number of sea trout in a range of different weight classes for all Welsh rivers over a 21-year period. Fish in the 1-2 lb weight class will represent .0SW immature finnock and those finnock on their 2nd return to the river. Larger size classes will contain a mixture of .1SW and .2SW maidens and repeat spawners, with repeat spawners dominating the larger size classes for most rivers other than in the Northeast of England (Harris, 2002).

Any assessment of stock health and fishery performance should also take into account its existing and future reproductive potential. Larger fish can utilise areas of larger spawning gravel than smaller fish to make greater use of the available spawning gravels within a catchment. They also produce more eggs. This may be particularly important with sea trout where the spawning population contains a significant proportion of fish that are multiple repeat spawners that have increased in size (and fecundity) after each return trip to sea to feed and grown between each spawning. These repeat spawning sea trout can contribute a disproportionate larger number of eggs over their lifetime relative to their actual numbers (Solomon, 1995; Harris, 2002; Harris 2006).

Any decline in the proportions of the larger sizes of sea trout in the catch may indicate an increased mortality of kelts and/or an increased level of selective in-river exploitation by the rod fisheries for larger fish (*see* Table 2 below). Irrespective of any decline in the number of fish caught, a significant decrease in the representation of the larger range groups of fish in the rod catch would be cause for concern. It should be noted that while the total quantity of fish caught may not indicate a management problem, a decrease in the size range of fish within that catch could represent a real problem. This is a particular problem with sea trout, where the annual run of 0SW finnock can vary enormously between years and may mask an underlying trend of decline in the larger size groups of sea trout (Davidson *et al.*, 2006).

Table 2. Number and proportions of sea trout caught-and-released in different weight groups of sea trout for Welsh Region (2005).

Weight Group	Fish Caught	Fish Released	Fish Retained	Release %
<1 lb	7,138	5,486	1,652	76.9
>1 - <2 lb	2,408	1,163	1,245	48.3
>2 - <4 lb	2,653	1,005	1,648	37.9
>4 - <8 lb	1,271	441	830	34.7
>8 - < 12 lb	206	87	119	42.3
> 12 lb	44	20	24	45.0
Total	*13,720*	*8,202*	*5,518*	*59.8*

Catch and Release (C&R)

Information on the number and proportions of fish that were either harvested by anglers or released immediately after their capture is central to an initial assessment of the impact of regulatory measures intended to increase the escapement of fish into the spawning population by maintaining the levels of exploitation at sustainable levels for the wellbeing of future stocks.

Figure 7[A-B] shows the number of sea trout and salmon caught and their catch-and-release rates for all rivers in England & Wales over the last 21 years. The release rates for both species have increased steadily over the period, from just 13.6% to 77.5% for salmon and 38.6% to 79.3for sea trout. This broadly reflects the success of various initiatives to promote catch-and-release as a sporting ethic and to an increased general awareness within the angling community of the need to reduce rates of exploitation in order to safeguard future stocks.

Although C&R is now compulsory on a few rivers where salmon stocks are assessed as *At Risk,* and all rod caught salmon taken before 16 June each year must be released to protect early running MSW 'spring' fish, the higher rates of release for sea trout result mainly from voluntary constraints imposed by the owners or tenants of the fisheries or otherwise adopted by individual anglers as a personal code of conduct.

The data on C&R release can be cross-referenced to information on the size of each fish caught to determine any evidence of selective exploitation by the rod fishery. Table 2 shows a

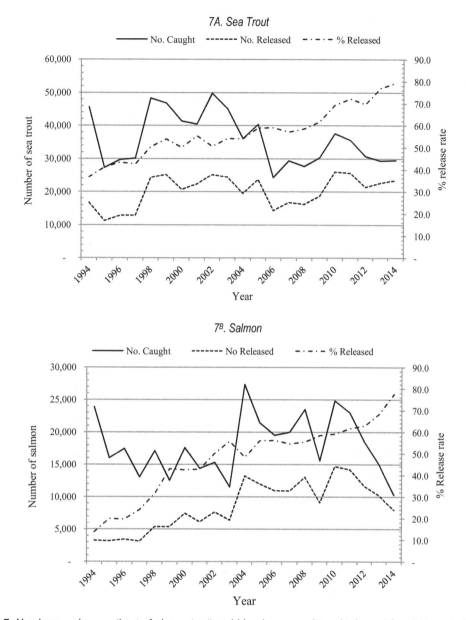

Figure 7. Numbers and proportions of a) sea trout and b) salmon caught-and-released for all rivers in England & Wales (1994 – 2014).

breakdown for 2005 where the harvest and release rates are given for different weight classes of sea trout. The highest release rate of 76.9% occurs with the smallest sea trout of <1lb. It then decreases through the large size groups, with the highest rates of harvest occurring in the medium sized weight groups of >2 – 8 lbs weight before increasing again in the 2 largest size groups. The higher rates of return for the smallest and the two largest weight groups accords with recommendations of Harris (2006) for the adoption of maximum and minimum size limits for the return of immature 0SW finnock and/or the larger 'specimen' sea trout with the greatest fecundity and lifetime egg yield.

Method of Capture

Angling for migratory fish in E&W is restricted by local byelaws to the use of fly, spinner or bait. Other byelaws, combined with less permissive voluntary regulations imposed by fishery owners, may add further restrictions on spinning and/or bait fishing at certain times of the year, at certain river levels and on certain sections of a river. Their purpose is to maintain an adequate spawning escapement by regulating the level of exploitation to within 'safe limits'.

Information on the number of fish caught by different capture methods (Figure 8) may be used in conjunction with trends in annual catch to review the impact of existing regulations and the need for additional measures to increase spawning escapement by improving the benefits of catch-and-release.

Among other regulatory options, this might entail measures to improve the subsequent survival of released fish by requiring the use of barbless or circle hooks when bait fishing, limiting the number of hooks attached to certain types of spinning lures or, as implemented on the Wye and Taff from 2007, a total ban on all bait fishing throughout the season.

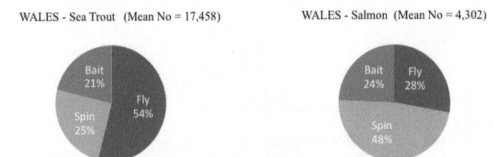

WALES - Sea Trout (Mean No = 17,458)   WALES - Salmon (Mean No = 4,302)

Figure 8. Method of angling capture of sea trout & salmon in Welsh Rivers (1994 – 2014.

OTHER REGIONS OF THE BRITISH ISLES

There is also a long history of collecting rod catch data from the many more migratory fisheries in Scotland and in the Republic of Ireland, where different approaches have been adopted at various times.

Scotland

The fisheries legislation on Scotland differs in a number of important respects to other countries in the British Isles. The most relevant difference here is that there is no system of licensing for the rod or net fisheries. Although a mandatory return of annual catch is required, this is obtained directly from the owners of the private fisheries instead of from individual anglers.

Details of individual owners are held on a central database that is updated regularly when fisheries are sold to another owner. In 2009, this database contained details of 2,940 separate fishery owners. The annual catch return is submitted on a standard catch return issued for completion by each owner, their agents or the tenants of the fishery. In recent years, this was issued in September for completion and return by December. A reminder notice is issued if a return had not been submitted on time and this is then followed by a second reminder to remaining non-respondents. About 90% of returns are submitted each year. Failure to submit a catch return is an offence.

The standard catch return form requires the owner to provide the following basic information:

- The total number and weight of salmon and sea trout caught each season.
- The number and weight of fish caught in each month of the fishing season.

Since 1994, the rod fishery owners were required to provide separate information on the number of fish harvested (= killed) and the number of fish returned alive to the fishery immediately after capture and, since 2004, separate information on the catch of small sea trout (known locally as herling or finnock) was also required.

The system has been in place since 1952 without material change and as such represents the longest time series of broadly consistent and comparable data in the British Isles. However, it provides no information for any river system on: a) the weights of individual fish, b) the method of capture and, more importantly, c) the number of participants in the fisheries or their individual and combined fishing effort.

DAFS (1984) have published a digest of the available catch records for the period 1952 – 1981. No detailed annual report and breakdown of catch statistics is currently produced to parallel those for England & Wales and the Republic of Ireland. A brief summary of the National catch by the rod and net fisheries is published annually by the Scottish Government in a series of 'Topic Notes' covering salmon (No. 68) and sea trout (No. 69). [*Available at*: http://www.gov.scot/Topics/marine/science/ publications/stats/SalmonSeaTroutCatches]

Republic of Ireland

There is a longstanding system of mandatory rod licensing and mandatory catch returns for individual salmon and sea trout anglers in the Republic of Ireland. However, the catch return system was lightly enforced. No catch return reminder system was adopted and therefore, the proportion of returns submitted was <5% in most regions (Fahy, 1985). Therefore, a different system was adopted using reports from local fisheries inspectors' estimates of the number and weight of fish caught based on personal observation and supplementary information from local sources. Apart from being opportunistic and subjective, this system was restricted to the more important salmon fisheries within a region and did not include many of the less productive salmon fisheries or the many small fisheries dominated by sea trout.

In response to serious concern about the decline in salmon fisheries throughout the

Irish Republic, a series of radical regulatory measures was introduced from the early 2000s to protect salmon stocks. This included the introduction of an innovative 'Carcass Tagging & Logbook Recording Scheme' in 2001 for anglers (and netsmen) to replace the previous data collection process. This was expanded to include all rivers and was significantly improved by the inclusion of information on anglers' fishing effort, the weight of individual fish, the number of fish harvested (killed) or released and the method of capture. While this new system closely parallels that adopted in E&W for salmon, this is not so for sea trout because the logbook recording scheme does not require details of any fish of <16 cms in length. As such, it excludes details of all 0SW finnock, and most repeat spawning finnock, which *represent greatest proportion* of the sea trout run into most Irish rivers (Went, 1962, Fahy, 1978).

Following the introduction of the carcass tagging and logbook recording scheme in 2001, catch statistics are now published in the annual series of 'Wild Salmon and Sea Trout Statistics Reports' (*Available at*: http://www.fisheriesireland.info/salmon.salmonstats.htm).

DISCUSSION

The 21-year record of catch statistics now provides a broadly consistent and comparable database for each of the 80 principal migratory fish rivers in England & Wales that is unprecedented in its scope. As such, it provides a growing 'treasure chest' of management information that can be cross referenced and interrogated over a range of in-depth questions about the performance and characteristics of the fisheries at a local and regional level. It can also be cross-referenced to other central databases: including those on rainfall and river flow levels, water quality, regional parr monitoring surveys, land-use management and climate change, to help understand and interpret trends in the pattern of catches within and between rivers and regions over time and their possible causes.

The angling community represents a wide cross section of individuals with varying levels of commitment to their sport, different levels of skill and different degrees of interest in the future management of the fisheries. The available evidence suggests that those anglers who fish most often catch most fish and are more likely to submit a catch return than those who fish occasionally and catch few fish or no fish. Therefore, it is probable that there is a natural 'ceiling' to proportion of anglers likely to submit an annual return of catch beyond which any attempts to improve the catch return rate above the present rate of 70-80% overall are likely to be costly and relatively unproductive.

It is clearly vital that the database should be as complete, accurate and consistent as possible if it is to serve as a reliable index for making valid comparisons of changes in fishery performance from one year to the next over time. Three key points are relevant in this important context:

1. The current system of issuing annual catch return reminders to every angler at the end of

the fishing season should be continued and refined so that they are issued at the same time each year,

2. A routine *'quality assurance'* check should be undertaken each year to monitor the stability of the catch return system as reliable index of performance and to identify any shifts in annual response rates that may affect the validity of any comparisons between different years,

3. The process of engagement with the angling community should be continued to maintain a general awareness about the importance of their individual catch returns to the future management of their fisheries.

ACKNOWLEDGEMENTS

We thank staff of the Environment Agency, Natural Resources Wales and Marine Science Scotland for their support in updating the historical catch records to 2014 and for generating supplementary data used in some of the figures and tables.

REFERENCES

Ayton, W.J. (1998). Salmon Fisheries in England & Wales. Atlantic Salmon Trust. Blue Book. Pitlochry. 48 pp.

DAFS (1984). The Scottish Salmon Catch Statistics 1952 – 1981, Department of Agriculture & Fisheries for Scotland. (*In 2 volumes*), 140 pp & 82 pp.

Davidson, I.C., Cove, R.J. & Hazelwood, M.S. (2006). Annual Variation in Age Composition, Growth and Abundance of Sea Trout Returning to the River Dee at Chester, 1991 – 2003. In: *Sea Trout: Biology, Conservation & Management*. (Graeme Harris & Nigel Milner. *Eds*.). Proceedings of the 1st International Sea Trout Symposium. July 2004, Cardiff, Wales. Blackwell Publishing, 76 – 87.

Davidson. I., Aprahamian, M., Peirson, G., Hillman, N., Cook, P., Elsmere, P. Cove, R. & Croft, A. (2017a). Catch and stock based Biological Reference Points for sea trout in England & Wales: A comparison of methods and a critical examination of their potential application to stock assessment and Management. In: Sea Trout: Science & Management. (Graeme Harris, *Ed*.). Proceedings of the 2nd International Sea Trout Symposium. 20 – 22 October 2015, Dundalk, Republic of Ireland. *(insert publisher & pps)*

Davidson, I., Cove, R., Hillman, R., Elsmere, P., Cook, N. & Croft, A. (2017b). Observations on sea trout stock performance in the Rivers Dee, Tamar, Lune & Tyne (1991-2014). The contribution of 'Index River' monitoring programmes in England & Wales to fisheries management. In: *Sea Trout: Science & Management*. (Graeme Harris, *Ed*.). Proceedings of the 2nd International Sea Trout Symposium. 20 – 22 October 2015, Dundalk, Republic of Ireland. *(insert publisher & pps)*

Fahy, E. (1978) Variation in some biological characteristics of British sea trout (*Salmo trutta*. L.). *Journal of Fish Biology*, 13, 123 – 138.

Fahy, E. (1985). Child of the Tides: a sea trout handbook. Dublin, Glendale Press. 188 pp.

Harris, G.S. (1986). The Status of Exploitation of Salmon in England & Wales. In. *Atlantic Salmon: Planning for the Future*. (Derek Mills & David Piggins. *Eds.*). Proceedings if the Third International Atlantic Salmon Symposium. 21-23 October 1986, Biarritz, France. Croom Helm, London, 69 – 89.

Harris, G.S. (2002). Sea Trout Stock Descriptions: The structure & Composition of Adult Sea Trout Stocks from 16 Rivers in England & Wales. R&D Technical Report W224. Environment Agency Bristol, 94 pp.

Harris, G. (2006). A Review of the Statutory Regulations to Conserve Sea Trout Stocks in England and Wales. In: *Sea Trout: Biology Conservation & Management*. (Graeme Harris & Nigel Milner. *Eds.*). Proceedings of the 1st International Sea Trout Symposium, July 2004, Cardiff, Wales. Blackwell Publishing, 441-456.

Harris, G.S. (2014), Fisheries and Society. In: *What have fish ever done for us?* Proceedings of the 43th Annual Conference. (Phil Hickley. *Ed.*). Institute of Fisheries Management, October 2013, Cardiff, Wales, 16 – 29.

Harris, G.S. & Winstone, A.J. (1990). The sea trout fisheries of Wales. In: *The sea trout in Scotland*. (M.J. Picken & W.M. Shearer. *Eds.*). Proceedings of a Symposium at the Dunstaffnage Marine Research Laboratory, June 1987, 25 – 33.

Russell, I.C., Ives, M.J., Potter, E.C.E., Buckley, A.A. & Duckett, L. (1995). Salmon and migratory trout statistics for England & Wales, 1951 – 1990. Fisheries Research Data Report No. 38. Ministry of Agriculture, Fisheries & Food, Directorate of Fisheries Research, Lowestoft, 252 pp.

Shelton, R. (2002). The Interpretation of Rod and Net Catch Data. Proceedings of a Workshop at the Centre for Fisheries and Aquaculture Science, Lowestoft, 6 – 7 November 2001 Atlantic Salmon Trust, Pitlochry. 103 pp.

Shearer, W.M. (1986). Relating Catch Records to Stocks. In: *Atlantic Salmon: Planning for the Future*. (Mills, D. & Piggins, D. *Eds.*). Proceedings of the Third International Atlantic Salmon Symposium. 21-23 October 1986. Croom Helm, London, 256 – 274.

Solomon, D.J. (1995). The Sea Trout in England and Wales. R&D Report 25. National Rivers Authority, Bristol, 102 pp.

Assessment of the increased mortality risk and population regulating effect of sea lice (*Lepeophtheirus salmonis*) from marine salmon farms on wild sea trout in Ireland and Scotland

P.G. GARGAN[1], S. SHEPHARD[1] & C. MACINTYRE[2].

[1]*Inland Fisheries Ireland, 3044 Lake Drive, City West Business Campus, Dublin 24, Ireland.*
[2]*Argyll Fisheries Trust, Cherry Park, Inveraray PA32 8XE, Scotland.*

ABSTRACT

Infestation of wild sea trout with sea lice from marine salmon farms can result in mortality or premature return to freshwater and drive changes in population structure and population regulating effects. Sea trout with varying levels of sea lice infestation have been sampled in Ireland since 1991 and in Scotland since 1997. These sea trout time series are used to express observed sea lice infestation rates (number of lice per gram body mass (n g^{-1})) at local and national scales in relation to the mortality risk thresholds used to assess potential impacts on wild salmonids from salmon aquaculture in Norway. Analysis of a large international sea trout dataset from Ireland (N = 7,461) and Scotland (N = 16,758) reveals levels of lice infestation on sea trout that imply increased mortality risk in the early years of monitoring in both countries. Lice loads on sea trout have reduced in recent years, likely reflecting improved lice control and changes in salmon farming practice. Population-level increase in risk of mortality or compromised seawater growth or reproduction, inferred from lice infestation rate, was estimated for individual sites. Results reveal that the likely sea trout population regulating effect of sea lice varies among locations; many sites recorded lice levels likely to result in strong regulating effects over a prolonged period, particularly in the west of Ireland. The Norwegian risk assessment framework for marine salmon aquaculture is discussed in relation to the results of lice infestation recorded on sea trout in Ireland and Scotland.

Keywords: sea trout, salmon farms, sea lice, mortality risk, population regulating effect.

INTRODUCTION

Marine salmon farming has expanded significantly over the past two decades, particularly along the west coast of Norway and Scotland, and annual production has now reached 1.3 million tonnes and 180,000 tonnes respectively in both countries. The scale of salmon farming has been much lower in Ireland with an estimated annual production in the range of 12-30,000 tons since the 1990's. The development of salmon aquaculture in all three countries coincided with observations of premature return of sea trout (*Salmo trutta*) to freshwater with heavy lice infestation, a marked reduction in sea trout rod catches and changes in sea trout population structure, (Anon., 1995; Birkeland, 1996; Birkeland & Jakobsen, 1997; Butler & Watt, 2002, Gargan *et al.*, 2003, Poole *et al.*, 1996). Soon after lice infested sea trout were observed returning to freshwater in Ireland, sampling of rivers began in 1991 to determine if this phenomenon was widespread; sea trout post-smolts were recorded in all rivers sampled with infestations of sea lice, predominantly juvenile lice, indicating recent transmission (Tully, Poole & Whelan, 1993). Monitoring programmes to assess the level of lice infestation on sea trout began on the west coast of Scotland in 1997 and along the western coast of Norway in 1992 (Jakobsen *et al.*, 2002).

After migrating to sea, sea trout remain feeding and growing in coastal waters where salmon farms are situated and may therefore be especially vulnerable to salmon lice infestation (Thorstad *et al.*, 2015). Research has shown that in salmon aquaculture bays in springtime the majority of caligid copepod nauplii arise from ovigerous sea lice infesting farmed salmon (Tully & Whelan, 1993; Butler, 2002; Heuch & Mo, 2001). Gargan *et al.*, (2003) demonstrated a statistical relationship between lice infestation on sea trout and distance to the nearest salmon farm over a 10-year period, with highest infestations and variation in infestation seen close to fish farms. A similar relationship for lice infestation and distance to salmon farms was seen in Scottish (Butler & Watt, 2002; Mackenzie *et al.*, 1998) and Norwegian studies (Anon., 1997; Birkeland & Jakobsen, 1997; Bjørn *et al.*, 2001). Middlemas *et al.*, (2013) also demonstrated a link between salmon farms and sea lice burdens on sea trout in the west of Scotland, with the maximum range of effect of lice predicted by a critical threshold model at about 31 km. Gillibrand & Willis (2007) developed a sea lice dispersal model that showed that infective sea lice levels peaked 7–12 km seawards of the source and Serra-Llinares *et al.*, (2014, 2016) also found that wild fish seem unaffected by the direct lice infection pressure imposed by salmon farms at a distance >30km.

Previous studies in all three countries have described the level of lice infestation on sea trout in salmon aquaculture areas (e.g. Tully *et al.*, 1999; Gargan *et al.,* 2003; Birkeland & Jakobsen, 1997; Bjørn *et al.*, 2001; Bjørn & Finstad, 2002, Mackenzie *et al.*, 1998; Urquhart *et al.*, 2010) and some studies have undertaken an assessment of mortality risk of lice infestation. Gargan *et al.*, (2003) calculated the proportion of sea trout with lice loads indicative of causing physiological problems and osmoregulatory disturbances (Bjørn & Finstad, 1997) and found that the proportion of sea trout exceeding this threshold declined with distance from a salmon farm. Middlemas *et al.*, (2013) also developed a critical threshold model to examine the effect on sea trout of lice from salmon farms over a large special scale along the west coast of Scotland and used the critical lice threshold of 13 mobile lice per trout shown in laboratory studies (Wells *et al.*, 2006) to indicate the proportion of trout subject to physiological stress and potential death from sea lice infestation. They found a significant relationship between infestation and distance to the nearest farm, with the probability of sea trout having critical lice burdens being highest close to salmon farms.

More recently, Taranger *et al.*, (2014) developed a range of lice infestation rate indicators causing physiological stress in sea trout, and developed a first generation lice index that estimates increased sea trout mortality risk due to sea lice infestation. A risk spectrum like this provides an excellent context for evaluating both mortality risk and possible fitness impacts of lice infestation. In the present analysis, the effect of sea lice infestation rate of individual sea trout (number of lice per gram body mass ($n\ g^{-1}$)) at local and national scales is expressed for the first time in relation to the mortality risk thresholds as proposed by Taranger *et al.*, (2014). The sum of the increased mortality risks of individual sea trout in different "*infection classes*" in a sample was then used to calculate a population-level increase in risk of mortality or compromised seawater growth or reproduction (reflecting the distribution of the intensity of salmon lice infections of the different individuals sampled, as described by Taranger *et al.*, 2014). The risk was further scored according to the system proposed by Taranger *et al.* (2012a) for assessment of lice-related increased mortality risk at the population level.

MATERIALS AND METHODS

SAMPLING

Annual monitoring of sea trout, primarily by gill netting in estuaries over the May/June period, was undertaken at 50 locations around the Irish coast over the period 1991-2015 (N= 7,461). A detailed description of the sampling strategy in Ireland is outlined in Gargan *et al.*, (2003). Gargan *et al.*, (2003) included only post-smolt sea trout (<26cm) in their analysis, whereas all sea trout available over the period have been included in the present analysis. The majority of sea trout sampling along the Scottish west coast used sweep nets at sea at 55 locations, primarily during the May/July period over the period 1997-2015 (N= 16,758). A detailed description of the sampling in Scotland is given by Middlemas *et al.*, (2013).

Sea trout lice load is calculated as the number of lice per gram body mass ($n\ g^{-1}$) for individual sea trout. There were some missing weight values (notably for Scottish data before 2010). Missing weight values were estimated from log-transformed length-weight relationships from the entire dataset for each country. Taranger *et al.*, (2014) developed a first generation salmon lice risk index based on post-smolt sea trout <150g and larger sea trout >150g. In the entire Irish and Scottish dataset, 83% of sea trout were <150g and so the lice-related mortality risk bands for sea trout <150g are used in the present analysis of the entire dataset. Were the Taranger *et al.*, (2014) risk bands for sea trout >150g to be applied, the assessment of risk of mortality would apply at a lower lice level.

LICE INFESTATION RATES

The salmon lice risk index (Taranger *et al.* 2012) was applied. This index estimates the increased risk of individual mortality due to salmon lice infection (Table 1). This is referred to as a *"traffic-light system"* for sustainable salmon farming, using quantitative data on sea lice infection on wild salmonids as an indicator metric. The "traffic light system" described here is based on counting lice on salmon farms and modelling total emissions of lice larvae in a geographical area and is used as a warning indicator that predicts the risk of sea lice infestation on wild salmonids. Follow up assessment of sea lice on wild salmon and sea trout are used to verify and calibrate the system.

Table 1. Risk categories of sea lice-related sea trout mortality (number of lice per gram body mass (n g^{-1}) for individual sea trout) from Taranger *et al.*, (2012).

Lice/g sea trout	Risk Category	Lice related sea trout mortality
>0.3 lice g^{-1}	High	100%
0.2 – 0.3 lice g^{-1}	Medium	50%
0.1 – 0.2 lice g^{-1}	Low	20%
<0.1 lice g^{-1}		0%

The sum of the increased mortalities of individual sea trout for the different "infection classes" in a sample was then used to calculate the population-level increase in mortality risk, or compromised seawater growth and/or reproduction, reflecting the distribution of the intensity of salmon lice infections for the individuals sampled (Taranger *et al.*, (2014). The risk was further scored according to the system proposed by Taranger *et al.*, (2012) to assess lice related increased mortality risk at the population level (Table 2): where there is a) a low probability of having a population regulating effect when <10% of fish have >0.1 lice per gram fish weight, b) an intermediate probability of between 10% – 30% of fish have more than 0.1 lice per gram of weight, and c) a high probability of a negative effect if >30% of the sample have 0.1 lice per gram of fish weight. At individual locations, sample size was N ≥ 3. However, 75% of Scottish samples had a sample size of ≥17 sea trout and 75% of Irish samples had a sample size of ≥ 7 sea trout.

Table 2. Regulating effect of mortality risk to population status at different levels of lice infestation.

Increased Mortality Risk at Population Level	Population Regulating Effect
>30%	High
10%-30%	Intermediate
<10%	Low

RESULTS

IRELAND

Temporal trends in increased sea trout mortality risk

In order to provide greater insight into lice infestation, the Irish dataset was separated into rivers <30km and >30km from salmon farms. Results show that the increased mortality risk due to salmon lice infections for sea trout within 30km of salmon farms was at the 100% risk level (Taranger *et. al.*, 2014) in every year over the period 1991-2005 except 1994 (Figure 1). The risk of increased mortality decreased over the period 2006-2010 but still remained at the 50% risk level. The lowest recorded risk of increased sea trout mortality was seen in 2011, after which the risk of increased mortality increased again to the 50% level. For sea trout sampled >30km from salmon farms there was no risk of increased mortality due to sea lice infection over the period 1991-2015, albeit with two exceptions when the risk rose to 20% (2002) and 50% (2014). Sampling of Irish rivers distant from salmon farms was generally discontinued in the early 2000's.

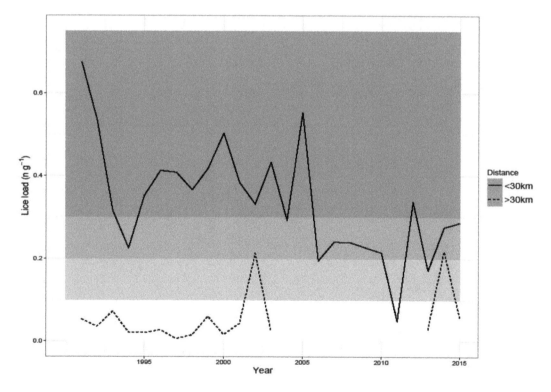

Figure 1. Lice infestation rates for sea trout in Irish rivers close to salmon farms (<30km) and distant from salmon farms (>30km). The risk bands are from Taranger *et al.*, (2014). The clear band is associated with 0% mortality, light grey band with 20% lice-related mortality, the medium grey band with 50% mortality and the dark grey band with 100% mortality.

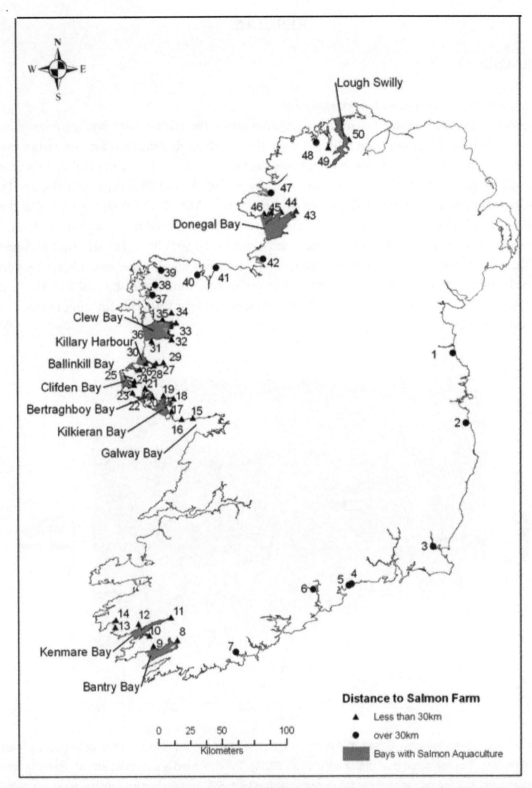

Figure 2. Location of rivers sampled for sea trout around the Irish coast. The general locations of bays with salmon aquaculture are shown.

Table 3. The population-level increase in mortality risk due to salmon lice infections at individual Irish locations. A <10% increase in mortality risk is described as low (= clear), a 10-30% increase in mortality risk is intermediate (= grey) and >30% increase in mortality risk is described as high (= black).

A. Rivers located <30km from salmon farms

Bay	No.	River	1991	1992	1993	1994	1995	1996	1997	1998	1999	2000	2001	2002	2003	2004	2005	2006	2007	2008	2009	2010	2011	2012	2013	2014	2015
Bantry Bay	8	Coomhola			10			0																			
Bantry Bay	9	Adrigole			50	75	77	0			66																
Kenmare Bay	10	Owenshaugh			82	39	34	64	4		29		75	23		52											
Kenmare Bay	11	Roughty			52	28	1	3	0		1																
Kenmare Bay	12	Sneem			49	39	5	9	0		12		64			8											
Kenmare Bay	13	Currane	64	15	6	1	1		5		0		0														
Kenmare Bay	14	Inny		55	13	6	0				1		0														
Galway Bay	15	Spiddal			39	17	0																				
Galway Bay	16	Crumlin				14	5			33																	
Cashla Bay	17	Costello	44	37	65	0		33	44	33	40	0	0			7			19		0						
Kilkieran Bay	18	Furnace				75	37	80	51	62	73	83	0	38	0												
Kilkieran Bay	19	Invermore			77	94	59	85	82	86	82	95	75			55	11		28	80	67	83		20		25	
Bertraghboy Bay	20	Gowla	83	15	92	20			29	73	76	43	0			40	75	0		66		14				33	
Bertraghboy Bay	21	Ballynahinch	88	7	59				66	80		18					25	8									
Bertraghboy Bay	22	Bertraghboy Bay															90	0									
Bertraghboy Bay	23	Cama			0	38																					
Clifden Bay	24	Ardbear						17	46	67	38	38	23														
Clifden Bay	25	Clifden	55	70		59	0	39	17	16																	
Ballinakill Bay	26	Dawros	60	53	35	29	38	10	46	31	38	18	28	40	19	27	53	16	21	50		69	0		29	56	75
Killary Harbour	27	Killary	67	34					64							30	21	34									100
Killary Harbour	28	Culfin				0		46	89	3	12																
Killary Harbour	29	Erriff	56		53	25		44	88	38	22	45	37	1		46	15	87	64	32	100		0		12		23
Killary Harbour	30	Delphi			23	12	54	60			100	54				53	65	100			91				44		
Clew Bay	31	Bunowen	33				24	9																			
Clew Bay	32	Belclare	10			6	31																				
Clew Bay	33	Newport			75	0		0			53	44			54		46	72	38	46	34		33		46		
Clew Bay	34	Burrishoole			79						95	0						96									
Clew Bay	35	Owengarve	0	65	75	7		57	40	12	46	32	2			34	54	40	70								
Clew Bay	36	Inner Clew Bay											21														
Donegal Bay	43	Eske			21	0		71	14	16	24	47	19	33	52	35	26			38	29	12	8	0		28	0
Donegal Bay	44	Eany			9	5		32	13	75	45	44	64	49	67	67	8			0	0	14	23	18		0	46
Donegal Bay	45	Oily			65	6																					
Donegal Bay	46	Stragar			41	1	15																				
Lough Swilly	49	Leannan			16			26	29		0	0		14		43		36	10	7	9	48	5	0	13		36	5
Lough Swilly	50	Crana			33		45	25	61	5	69	20	54	37	52		38	15	85	30	29	53	1	53	7

B. Rivers located >30km from salmon farms

Bay	No.	River	1991	1992	1993	1994	1995	1996	1997	1998	1999	2000	2001	2002	2003	2004	2005	2006	2007	2008	2009	2010	2011	2012	2013	2014	2015
East / South Coast	1	Nanny			12																						
East / South Coast	2	Dargle			22		40	24																			
East / South Coast	3	Slaney			0																						
East / South Coast	4	Tay			0		2			0																	
East / South Coast	5	Colligan			0					5	0		5		0												
East / South Coast	6	Bride			0		0																				
East / South Coast	7	Argideen		3	7		0	0	1	4																	
Tullaghan Bay	37	Owenduff						9	10	0		8	1		26	1											
Tullaghan Bay	38	Owenmore			33		0	0		0		1	23	6		0											
North Mayo/Sligo	39	Glenamoy			0					0	0		1														
North Mayo/Sligo	40	Palmerstown			0	0	0	0		0	0																
North Mayo/Sligo	41	Bunree			0																						
North Mayo/Sligo	42	Drumcliffe	8	0	24				0	0		26															
Loughros More Bay	47	Owenea			7	0	0	0	1			0	0		14		0										
Sheep Haven Bay	48	Lackagh			0	0		2	0	0		3															

Increased mortality risk at the population level in individual rivers / bays

The location of rivers sampled for sea trout lice infestation around the Irish coast is shown in Figure 2. The increased mortality risk due to salmon lice infections at the population level in individual Irish bays is given in Table 3. For Bantry Bay and Kenmore Bay, there was a high risk of sea trout mortality at many sites in the early 1990s. In the south Connemara region, the estimated increase in sea trout mortality due to lice infestation was high for most years in the 1990s in Cashla Bay, Kilkieran Bay and Bertraghboy Bay. From 2000, the increased risk of mortality generally was low in Cashla Bay, and generally alternated between moderate and high for Kilkieran and Bertraghboy Bays. For three bays in north Connemara (Clifden, Ballinakill and Killary), the risk of increased mortality was generally moderate to high over the 1991 to 2000 period, after which the risk of high mortality fluctuated in Ballinakill Bay and remained high in Killary harbour up to 2008. The risk of increased mortality in Clew Bay rivers was generally high for all years. For two bays with salmon aquaculture in Donegal (Donegal Bay and Lough Swilly), risk of increased mortality from lice infection was generally high over the 1995-2002 period after which risk in increased mortality decreased in Donegal Bay. For the rivers sampled in bays distant from salmon aquaculture (East/South coast, Tullaghan Bay, North Mayo/Sligo, Loughros More Bay and Sheep Haven Bay), the risk of increased mortality due to sea lice infestation was predominantly low, with a small number of samples in the intermediate category and two sites in the high risk category. After 2003, sea trout sampling was largely confined to rivers close to salmon farms and the risk of high mortality was generally less evident than during the early period of sampling in the 1990s.

SCOTLAND

Temporal trends in increased sea trout mortality risk

For the Scottish dataset, there were insufficient rivers located >30km from salmon farms to separate the data as undertaken for the Irish data. The increased mortality risk of sea trout due to salmon lice infections was in the 50-100% risk category (Taranger *et. al.*, 2014) for much of the 1997-2001 period (Figure 3). Over the period 2002-2008, the risk of lice-related sea trout mortality decreased and generally was in the 20% risk category, after which the risk of lice-related mortality further decreased.

Increased mortality risk at the population level in individual rivers/bays

The locations of sweep netting sites sampled for sea trout on the Scottish west coast are shown in Figure 4. Although the overall risk of mortality to sea trout reduced over time, the data demonstrate that certain areas had moderate to high risk of mortality (Table 4). The estimated increase in mortality at the population level due to lice infestation was generally low to moderate for West Southerland locations (Table 4). For marine sampling locations in Wester Ross, some sweep netting sites (Dondonnell) recorded a high risk of mortality at the population levels for the majority of years while other locations recorded high risk in individual years. Sampling in Skye began only in 2011 and mortality risk varied across all three categories. Locations in Lochaber recorded a varying risk of mortality from lice infection, with Camus na Gaul recording the highest risk of mortality. Marine locations in Argyll exhibited all three categories of increased mortality risk, with a trend towards greater risk in mortality in rivers sampled since 2011. Locations sampled in the Outer Hebrides reflected all three risk categories up to 2010, after which marine netting sites generally were in the low to intermediate risk category.

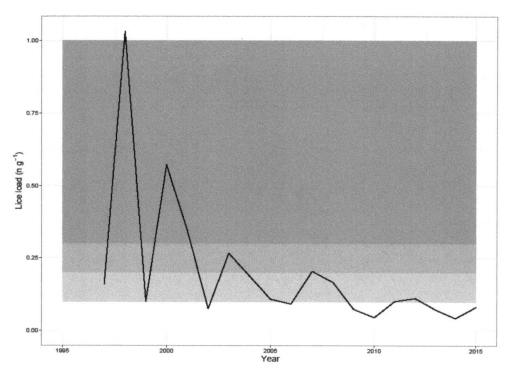

Figure 3. Lice infestation rate for sea trout in Scotland. The risk bands are from Taranger *et al.*, (2014). The clear band is associated with 0% mortality, the light grey band with 20% lice-related mortality, the medium grey band with 50% mortality and the dark grey band with 100% mortality.

DISCUSSION

Analysis of this large Irish data set of sea lice levels on sea trout (N=7,461) over a 25-year period provides evidence of increased mortality risk for sea trout within 30km of salmon farms due to salmon lice infections. This risk of increased mortality was at the 100% level for the first fifteen years of monitoring, though this risk subsequently decreased over the most recent decade. Increased mortality risk, or compromised seawater growth or reproduction, at the population level was recorded at the majority of sites close to salmon farms in Ireland during the early 1990s. Embayments with the highest risk of mortality included Kilkieran Bay, Bertraghboy Bay, Killary harbour and Ballinakill Bay. These findings contrasted with Irish sites sampled for lice infestation >30km from salmon farms, where little risk of increased mortality due to lice infestation was estimated. Gargan *et al.*, (2003) also recorded a significant negative relationship between sea trout survival and the level of lice infestation and concluded that it was reasonable to assume that infections of sea lice were a major contributor to increased marine mortality of sea trout observed since the late 1980's in the west of Ireland. This conclusion is supported by the results of the present analysis. Marine survival of Burrishoole sea trout between 1971-1987 ranged from 11.4% to 32.4% (Poole *et al.*, 1996). Gargan *et al.*, (2003) showed marine survival to have fallen markedly

515

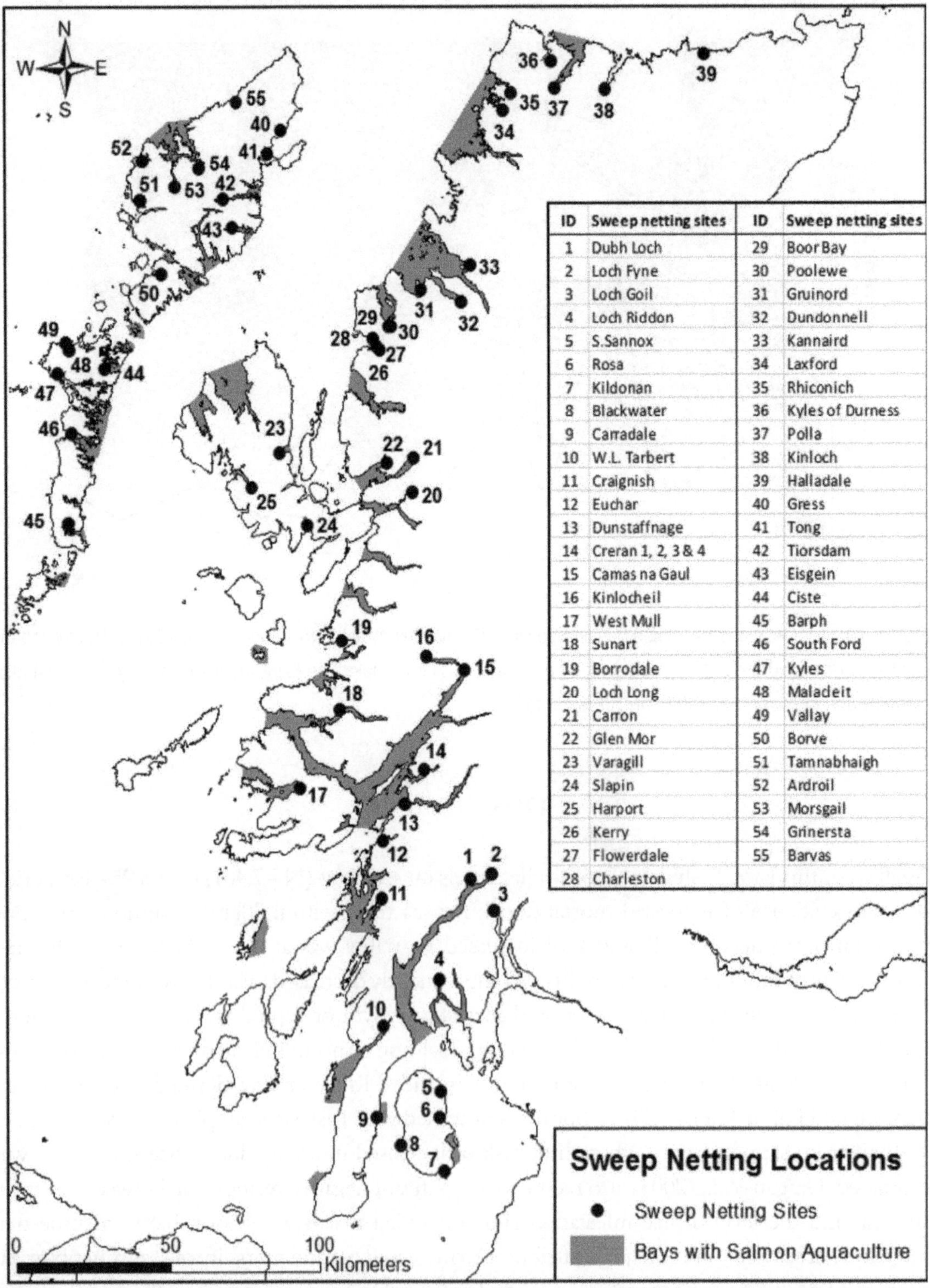

ID	Sweep netting sites	ID	Sweep netting sites
1	Dubh Loch	29	Boor Bay
2	Loch Fyne	30	Poolewe
3	Loch Goil	31	Gruinord
4	Loch Riddon	32	Dundonnell
5	S.Sannox	33	Kannaird
6	Rosa	34	Laxford
7	Kildonan	35	Rhiconich
8	Blackwater	36	Kyles of Durness
9	Carradale	37	Polla
10	W.L. Tarbert	38	Kinloch
11	Craignish	39	Halladale
12	Euchar	40	Gress
13	Dunstaffnage	41	Tong
14	Creran 1, 2, 3 & 4	42	Tiorsdam
15	Camas na Gaul	43	Eisgein
16	Kinlocheil	44	Ciste
17	West Mull	45	Barph
18	Sunart	46	South Ford
19	Borrodale	47	Kyles
20	Loch Long	48	Maladeit
21	Carron	49	Vallay
22	Glen Mor	50	Borve
23	Varagill	51	Tamnabhaigh
24	Slapin	52	Ardroil
25	Harport	53	Morsgail
26	Kerry	54	Grinersta
27	Flowerdale	55	Barvas
28	Charleston		

Figure 4. Location of sweep netting sites sampled for sea trout on the Scottish west coast. The general locations of bays with salmon aquaculture are shown.

Table 4. The population-level increase in mortality risk due to salmon lice infections at individual Scottish locations. A <10% increase in mortality risk is described as low (= clear), a 10-30% increase in mortality risk is intermediate (= grey) and >30% increase in mortality risk is described as high (= black).

Region		Location	1997	1998	1999	2000	2001	2002	2003	2004	2005	2006	2007	2008	2009	2010	2011	2012	2013	2014
Argyll	1	Dubh Loch					14	5	9	1	4	0	3	6	5					
Argyll	2	Loch Fyne									3	0	4	4	2			1	1	0
Argyll	3	Loch Goil																49	1	35
Argyll	4	Loch Riddon									37	2	8	1	7			50	0	33
Arran	5	S.Sannox											10	0						
Arran	6	Rosa											0		27					
Argyll	7	Kildonan	38	50	80	20	8						0							
Arran	8	Blackwater							38	88		0	34							
Argyll	9	Carradale											6	0	6			0	0	1
Argyll	10	W.Tarbert											24	71	13					
Argyll	11	Craignish												33	0					
Argyll	12	Euchar								50		1	18	15	3					
Argyll	13	Dunstaffnage						47	34	17	17	16	77	10	51		14	3	54	0
Argyll	14	Creran1								2										
Argyll	14	Creran2							5	0	25	2	90		7					
Argyll	14	Creran3									64				0					
Argyll	14	Creran4							29	0	17	2	49	9	22					
Lochaber	15	Camus na Gaul							75	1	54	0	45	2	15	6	51	0	48	0
Lochaber	16	Kinlocheil			23	0	26		33	0	18	0	13	0	1	6	9	14	12	0
Argyll	17	West Mull							8	5	1	0	11	0	16					
Lochaber	18	Sunart										56		93	0	19				
Lochaber	19	Borrodale															10	0	3	
Wester Ross	20	Loch Long											53							
Wester Ross	21	Carron												15	0	4				
Wester Ross	22	Glen Mor					56	34	4	3		22								
Skye	23	Varagill																		
Skye	24	Slapin															14		16	35
Skye	25	Harport															11		5	
Wester Ross	26	Kerry											11	28	7					
Wester Ross	27	Flowerdale													6		22	0	0	0
Wester Ross	28	Charleston												7						
Wester Ross	29	Boor Bay	16	6	22	0			90		13		45	0	19	11	0	22	0	
Wester Ross	30	Poolewe						14	85	0	0	0	43							
Wester Ross	31	Gruinard	26	34	22	8														
Wester Ross	32	Dundonnell	49	83	67	94	80	31	33	14	0	6	44	66		76				
Wester Ross	33	Kannaird	79		0							30	21				47	37	42	24
West Sutherland	34	Laxford	5		3	12	2	1	7	6	1	13	3	20	1	1	55	1	30	0
West Sutherland	35	Rhiconich			0	6														
West Sutherland	36	Kyle of Durness									38			1	2	1				0
West Sutherland	37	Polla			5	7	0	0	3	13	1	22	0	5	4	2	4	0	0	0
West Sutherland	38	Kinloch																	0	1
West Sutherland	39	Halladale										100			47					
Outer Hebrides	40	Gress									0	0	0	0						
Outer Hebrides	41	Tong													0		0	0	9	9
Outer Hebrides	42	Tiorsdam								82		43	97	100	18					
Outer Hebrides	43	Eisgean												28		0	14	19	12	
Outer Hebrides	44	Ciste										80	32	17						
Outer Hebrides	45	Barph										62	78	56						
Outer Hebrides	46	South Ford																		
Outer Hebrides	47	Kyles											21				14	0	0	18
Outer Hebrides	48	Malacleit															10	1	11	14
Outer Hebrides	49	Vallay									5									
Outer Hebrides	50	Borve						0				10	9	0	0		7	31	5	2
Outer Hebrides	51	Tamnabhaigh											1							
Outer Hebrides	52	Ardroil											0		0					
Outer Hebrides	53	Morsgail											100							
Outer Hebrides	54	Grimersta						93	15	70		53	48		0	0				
Outer Hebrides	55	Barvas											22	0	33					

517

below these historical levels and to be negatively related to mean lice abundance on sea trout. The present findings of a high risk of sea trout mortality close to marine salmon farms in Ireland for the first fifteen years of sea lice monitoring on wild sea trout also is consistent with the observed collapse in sea trout rod catches in the Irish Connemara district around 1989-1990 (Whelan & Poole, 1996; Gargan *et al.*, 2006), which coincided with the development of salmon aquaculture in estuaries during the mid-1980s, and was linked to salmon lice infestation on sea trout (Tully & Whelan, 1993; Tully *et al.*, 1999; Gargan *et al.*, 2003).

It is apparent from the present results that there was not sufficient control of sea lice on marine salmon farms in Ireland to prevent lice infestation and a high risk of sea trout mortality at many sites over the period when monitoring of sea trout began in 1991 until the mid-2000's. While the extent of sampling was more restricted after 2006, the data indicate that the increased mortality risk for individual sea trout and at the population level fell over the most recent decade. The establishment of sea lice protocol limits on salmon farms in Ireland from 2001, a change in salmon farm practice of moving to single generation sites in the mid 2000's and a general reduction in lice levels on farms over recent years is likely to have contributed to this result. However, results for a small number of individual sites continued to show high risk of sea trout mortality in certain years.

The increase in mortality risk of sea trout (N= 16,758) due to salmon lice infections in Scotland was moderate to high for the first five years of monitoring and decreased subsequently. Fewer sites were sampled prior to 2002, constraining the assessment of the increased mortality risk at the population level, but a high risk was recorded at approximately 50% of monitored sites. The increased risk of sea trout mortality in the early years of sampling in Scotland is consistent with studies on sea trout decline linked to sea lice infestation from salmon farms. In Scotland, unprecedented declines in sea trout rod fisheries were recorded throughout the west coast region during the late 1980's (Walker, 1994; Northcott & Walker, 1996) and the collapse in sea trout rod catch and a change in population structure of the River Ewe sea trout rod catch reported from 1988 was linked to salmon lice epizootics following the establishment of marine salmon farms near the river mouth (Butler & Walker, 2006). Middlemas *et al.*, (2013) found a significant relationship between lice infestation on sea trout and distance to the nearest farm along the Scottish West coast, with the probability of sea trout having critical lice burdens being greatest close to salmon farms. Over the most recent decade, the risk of lice-related sea trout mortality at the individual and population level generally has decreased at Scottish sites. The introduction of single generation sites in Scotland has been in place since 2001 and likely contributed to the more recent reduction in risk of lice-induced sea trout mortality.

Overall, there was a lower lice-related mortality risk for sea trout sampled in Scotland in comparison to fish sampled in Ireland. This difference may be partly explained by sampling location and sampling method. Irish sea trout were captured in inner estuaries or river mouths and had returned prematurely from the sea, whereas the majority of sea trout in the Scottish samples were captured in sweep nets at sea. Premature return of lice infested sea trout to freshwater has been reported in Ireland since lice epizootics have been recorded (Whelan, 1991; Tully & Whelan, 1993) and subsequently also in Scotland (Butler & Walker, 2006; Hatton-Ellis *et al.*, 2006). Bjørn *et al.*, (2001) found that sea trout and arctic char that returned prematurely to freshwater had higher relative infection intensities than fish caught at sea at the same time, and commented that premature return to freshwater of the most heavily infected fish may therefore be triggered to ameliorate the physiological consequences of the infection (Bjørn & Finstad, 1997; Finstad *et al.*, 2000). Bjørn *et al.*, (2001) further comment that most records of sea lice on sea trout are for fish returning prematurely to hyposaline or freshwater conditions (Tully *et al.*, 1993; Birkeland, & Jakobsen, 1997; Tully *et al.*, 1999). This may confer a biased indication of the lice infestation in the total sea-going population because it presumed that the most heavily infested fish return to freshwater (Birkeland & Jakobsen, 1997) and these fish may die before being sampled. If this is so, sampling methods targeting fish at sea alone might reduce observations of the highest intensity infestation levels (Lester *et al.*, 1984). While sampling location may explain to some degree the lower lice related mortality risk observed for sea trout sampled in Scotland, this is not the case for all Scottish samples as some fish were captured in more estuarine locations.

The majority of west of Ireland sea trout populations are dominated by immature finnock (Went, 1962; Fahy, 1985) followed by one sea winter fish and then smaller numbers of maiden sea age groups and previous spawners. O'Farrell *et al.*, (1989) assessed the contribution of the various sea age groups to egg deposition in a west of Ireland catchment and demonstrated that sea trout ≥ 35cm (one and two sea-age fish) make the greatest contribution (76% of all ova) to egg deposition. Butler & Walker (2006) concluded that the combination of reduced abundance, size, longevity and hence frequency of spawning probably had a major influence on total egg deposition of sea trout in the Ewe catchment in western Scotland. The moderate to high risk of increased marine mortality of sea trout at the population level from sea lice infestation observed on the west coasts of Ireland and Scotland seen in the present study is likely to have resulted in loss of older sea age groups and typical population age-structure over time and a reduction in overall egg deposition. Studies in both countries (Poole *et al.*, 1996; Gargan *et al.*, 2006; Butler & Walker, 2006) have documented such changes which emphasise the need for adequate lice control on salmon farms for maintenance of viable sea trout populations.

The "Strategy for an environmentally sustainable aquaculture industry" in Norway (Anon, 2009) states that no disease, including lice, should have a regulatory effect on wild fish. The monitoring of salmon lice infection of wild salmonids is an important verification of whether this goal is achieved, and whether the measures taken are appropriate and sufficient (Taranger *et al.*, 2014). The "traffic light system" described here is used as a warning indicator that predicts the risk of sea lice infestation on wild salmonids based on counting lice on salmon farms and modelling total emissions of lice larvae in a geographical area. Subsequent census of sea lice on wild salmon and sea trout are used to verify and calibrate the model. This first generation measurement of risk assessment of salmon lice and wild salmonids (Taranger *et al.*, 2012b) and further presented in a recent report (Karlsen *et al.*, 2016) will be used as a starting point for the Norwegian Government for controlling and regulating salmon farming. While this management structure is still under development in Norway, the "traffic-light system" will offer a measure for estimating sustainability in salmon farming that could also be applied to Ireland and Scotland in the coming years.

ACKNOWLEDGEMENTS

The Irish sea trout samples were provided by the staff of Inland Fisheries Ireland River Basin Districts (formerly the Central and Regional Fishery Boards). Samples were also provided by Dr Russell Poole, Marine Institute. Scottish sea trout samples were collected by the Fishery Trusts & Boards, namely Argyll Fisheries Trust, Lochaber Fisheries Trust, Wester Ross Fisheries Trust, Skye Fisheries Trust, West Sutherland Fisheries Trust, Outer Hebrides Fisheries Trust. We are grateful to Dr Bengt Finstad, Norwegian Institute for Nature Research, for helpful contributions to the overall manuscript.

REFERENCES

Anon. (1995). Report of the Sea Trout Working Group, 1994, Department of the Marine, Dublin. 254 pp.

Anon. (1997). Report of the Workshop on the Interactions between Salmon Lice and Salmonids, Edinburgh, Scotland, UK. 11-15 November 1996. ICES CM 1997/M: 4, Ref. F. 204 pp.

Anon. (2009). Strategy for an Environmentally Sustainable Norwegian Aquaculture Industry (*in Norwegian*). Ministry of Fisheries and Coastal Affairs, Oslo, Norway, 34 pp.

Birkeland, K. (1996). Consequences of premature return by sea trout (*Salmo trutta*) infested with the salmon louse (*Lepeophtheirus salmonis* Krøyer): migration, growth, and mortality. *Canadian Journal of Fisheries and Aquatic Sciences.* **53** 2808-2813.

Birkeland, K. & Jakobsen, P.J. (1997). Salmon lice, *Lepeophtheirus salmonis*, infestation as a causal agent of premature return to rivers and estuaries by sea trout, *Salmo trutta*, juveniles. *Environmental Biology of Fishes* **49**, 129-137.

Bjørn, P.A. & Finstad, B. (1997). The physiological effects of salmon lice infection on sea trout post smolts. *Nordic Journal of Freshwater Research* **73**, 60-72.

Bjørn. P.A. & Finstad, B. (2002). Salmon lice, *Lepeophtheirus salmonis* (Krøyer), infestation in sympatric populations of Arctic char, *Salvelinus alpinus* (L.), and sea trout, *Salmo trutta* (L.), in areas near and distant from salmon farms. *ICES Journal of Marine Science* **59**, 131-139.

Bjørn, P.A., Finstad, B. & Kristoffersen, R. (2001). Salmon lice infection of wild sea trout and Arctic char in marine and freshwaters: the effects of salmon farms. *Aquaculture Research* **32**, 947-962.

Butler, J.R.A. (2002). Wild salmonids and sea louse infestations on the west coast of Scotland: sources of infection and implications for the management of marine salmon farms. *Pest Management Science*, **58**, 595-608.

Butler, J.R.A. & Watt, J (2003). Assessing and managing the impacts of marine salmon farms on wild Atlantic salmon in Western Scotland: Identifying priority rivers for conservation. In: *Salmon at the Edge* (D. Mills, *Ed*.). Proceedings of the 6th International Atlantic Salmon Symposium, Edinburgh, UK, July 2002. Atlantic Salmon Trust/Atlantic Salmon Federation. 93-118.

Butler, J.R.A. & Walker, A.F. (2006). Characteristics of the sea trout *Salmo trutta* (L.) stock collapse in the River Ewe (Wester Ross, Scotland), in 1988-2001. In: *Sea Trout Biology, Conservation & Management*. (Graeme Harris & Nigel Milner, *Eds*). Proceedings of the 1st International Sea Trout Symposium, July 2005, Cardiff, Wales, 45-59.

Gargan, P.G., Tully. O. & Poole, W.R. (2003). The relationship between sea lice infestation, sea lice production and sea trout survival in Ireland, 1992-2001. In: *Salmon at the Edge*. (Mills, D. Ed.). Proceedings of the 6th International Atlantic Salmon Symposium, Edinburgh, UK, July 2002. Atlantic Salmon Trust/Atlantic Salmon Federation, 119-135.

Gargan, P.G., Poole, W.R. & Forde, G. (2006). A review of the status of Irish sea trout stocks. In: *Sea Trout Biology, Conservation & Management*. (Graeme Harris & Nigel Milner, N. *Eds*.). Proceedings of the 1st International Sea Trout Symposium, July 2005, Cardiff, Wales, 25-44.

Gillibrand, P.A. & Willis, K.J. (2007). Dispersal of sea louse larvae from salmon farms: modelling the influence of environmental conditions and larval behaviour. *Aquatic Biology*, 1, 63−75.

Heuch, P.A, & Mo, T.A. (2001). A model of salmon louse production in Norway: effects of increasing salmon production and public management measures. *Diseases of Aquatic Organisms* 45, 145-152.

Jakobsen, P.J. Birkeland, K., Grimnes, A., Nylund, A. & Urdal, K. (1992). Undersøkelser av lakselus-infeksjoner på sjøaure og laksesmolt i 1992. (Investigations of salmon lice infections on sea trout and salmon smolts in 1992). Report from the Zoological Museum, September. Department of Ecology, University of Bergen, Bergen. 38 pp.

Karlsen, Ø., Finstad, B., Ugedal., O. & Svåsand, T. (2016). Kunnskapsstatus som grunnlag for kapasitetsjustering innen produksjonsområder basert på lakselus som indikator (A status of knowledge as a basis for capacity adjustment in production areas based on sea lice as an indicator). Report from the Institute for Marine Research No.14-2016 (ISSN 1893-4536 online), 137 pp.

Mackenzie, K., Longshaw, M., Begg, G.S. & McVicar, A.H. (1998). Sea lice (Copepoda: Caligidae) on wild sea trout (*Salmo trutta* L.) in Scotland. *ICES Journal of Marine Science* 55, 151-162.

Middlemas, S.J., Fryer, R.J., Tulett, D. & Armstrong, J.D. (2013). Relationship between sea lice levels on sea trout and fish farm activity in western Scotland. *Fisheries Management & Ecology*, 20, 68-74

Northcott, S.J. & Walker, A.F. (1996). Farming salmon, saving sea trout: a cool look at a hot issue. In: *Aquaculture and sea lochs*. (Black, K.D. *Ed*.). The Scottish Association for Marine Science, Dunstaffnage, 72-81.

Poole, W.R., Whelan, K.F., Dillane, M.G., Cooke, D.J. & Matthews, M. (1996). The performance of sea trout, *Salmo trutta* L., stocks from the Burrishoole system western Ireland, 1970-1994. *Fisheries Management & Ecology*, 3, 73-92.

Serra-Llinares, R.M., Bjørn, P.A., Finstad, B., Nilsen, R., Harbitz. A., Berg, M. & Asplin, L. (2014). Salmon lice infection on wild salmonids in marine protected areas: an evaluation of the Norwegian 'National Salmon Fjords'. *Aquaculture Environment Interactions* 5, 1-16.

Serra-Llinares, RM., Bjørn, P.A., Finstad, B., Nilsen, R. & Asplin, L. (2016). Nearby farms are a source of lice for wild salmonids: a reply to Jansen *et al.,* 2016. *Aquaculture Environment Interactions* **8**, 351–356.

Taranger, G.L., Svåsand, T., Kvamme, B.O., Kristiansen, T.S. & Boxaspen, K.K. (2012a). Risk assessment of Norwegian aquaculture [Risikovurdering norsk fiskeoppdrett] (*In Norwegian*). Fisken og havet, særnummer 2-2012, 131 pp.

Taranger G. L., Boxaspen, K. K., Madhusn, A. S. & Svasand, T. (*Eds.*) (2012b). Suggested first generation method for environmental impact indicators with respect to genetic influences from farmed salmon to wild salmon and the impact of sea lice from farmed fish on wild salmon populations (*in Norwegian*). Fisken og Havet 13-2012.

Taranger, G.L., Karlsen, Ø., Bannister, R.J., Glover, K.A., Husa, V., Karlsbakk, E., Kvamme, B.O., Boxaspen, K.K., Bjørn, P.A., Finstad, B., Madhun, A.S., Craig Morton, H. & Svåsand, T. (2014). Risk assessment of the environmental impact of Norwegian Atlantic salmon farming. *ICES Journal of Marine Science* **72**, 997-1021.

Thorstad, E. B., Todd, C. D., Uglem, I., Bjørn P. A., Gargan, P. G., Vollset K. W., Halttunen, E., Kålås S., Berg, M. & Finstad, B. (2015). Effects of salmon lice *Lepeophtheirus salmonis* on wild sea trout *Salmo trutta*—a literature review. *Aquaculture Environment Interactions* **7**, 91–113.

Tully O, & Whelan, K.F. (1993). Production of nauplii of *Lepeophtheirus salmonis* (Krøyer) (Copepoda: Caligidae) from farmed and wild salmon and its relation to the infestation of wild sea trout (*Salmo trutta* L.) off the west coast of Ireland in 1991. *Fisheries Research* **17**, 187-200.

Tully, O., Poole, W.R. & Whelan, K.F. (1993). Infestation parameters for *Lepeophtheirus salmonis* (Krøyer) (Copepoda: Caligidae) parasitic on sea trout, *Salmo trutta* L., off the west coast of Ireland during 1990 and 1991. *Aquaculture and Fisheries Management* **24**, 545-557.

Tully, O., Gargan, P., Poole, W.R. & Whelan, K.F. (1999). Spatial and temporal variation in the infestation of sea trout (*Salmo trutta* L.) by the caligid copepod *Lepeophtheirus salmonis* (Krøyer) in relation to sources of infection in Ireland. *Parasitology* **119**, 41-51.

Urquhart, K., Pert, C.C., Fryer, R.J., Cook, P., Weir, S., Kilburn, R., McCarthy, U., Simons, J., McBeath, S.J., Matejusova, I. & Bricknell, I.R. (2010). A survey of pathogens and metazoan parasites on wild sea trout (*Salmo trutta*) in Scottish waters. *ICES Journal of Marine Science* **67**, 444-453.

Walker A, F. (1994). Sea trout and salmon stocks in the Western Highlands. In: *Problems with sea trout and salmon in the Western Highlands*. Atlantic Salmon Trust, Pitlochry, Perthshire, 6-18.

Wells, A., Grierson, C.E., MacKenzie, M., Russon, I.J., Reinardy, H., Middlemiss, C., Bjørn, P.A., Finstad, B., Wendelaar Bonga, S.E., Todd, C.D. & Hazon, N. (2006). Physiological effects of simultaneous, abrupt seawater entry and sea lice (*Lepeophtheirus salmonis*) infestation of wild, sea-run brown trout (*Salmo trutta*) smolts. *Canadian Journal of Fish and Aquatic Sciences* **63**, 2809-2821.

Whelan, K.F. & Poole, W.R. (1996). The sea trout stock collapse, 1989-1992. In: *The Conservation of Aquatic Systems*. (J. Reynolds. *Ed.*). Proceedings of a Seminar held on 18-19 February 1993. Royal Irish Academy, 101–110.

Sea Trout and Tidal Power: Challenges and Approaches

A. TURNPENNY, R. HORSFIELD & J. WILLIS,

THA Aquatic Ltd, The Lodge, Dean Hill Park, West Dean, Salisbury, SP5 1EY, United Kingdom.

ABSTRACT

Tidal power from hydrokinetic or tidal range turbines has the potential to kill or injure fish that move into their flow path. For diadromous fish, this is exacerbated where the turbines are sited near to migration routes into rivers. For sea trout in particular, risk may be higher than for other diadromous species, owing to their coastal residence during the marine phase, though formal evidence on the extent of their marine dispersion remains limited. New techniques based on individual-based models (IBM) of fish behaviour are being used to predict encounter rates with tidal turbines. Combined with established models for predicting fish injury rates associated with turbine passage, a scientific framework exists for assessing the potential fish losses associated with tidal power schemes. However, these are just tools and they must be underpinned by scientific data and corroborated by expert opinion, with the weighting on the former, and appropriately audited for quality assurance. In this paper we review the modelling methods and consider the level of detail and complexity in sea trout behaviour 'rules' required to develop a satisfactory assessment. We illustrate it with a case study from the proposed Swansea Bay tidal lagoon scheme, identifying areas of debate and knowledge gaps. Ongoing sea trout tracking studies in coastal waters will help to close these gaps but we will also consider what further information would strengthen the behaviour models.

Keywords: sea trout, tidal power, turbine mortalities, migratory behaviour, individual-based modelling, hydrodynamic models.

INTRODUCTION

The development of tidal range energy schemes around Britain's coastline has been mooted for many years, but may soon become a reality. In June 2015, the Secretary of State issued a Development Consent Order (Swansea Bay Tidal Generating Station Order 2015) for the construction and operation of a tidal lagoon generating scheme in Swansea Bay, South Wales. It still awaits its Marine Licence from Natural Resources Wales' Marine Licensing Team. Other larger lagoons are being considered for the Severn Estuary and other high-tidal-range areas of the British coast (http://www.tidallagoonpower.com/).

The proposed Swansea lagoon differs from tidal barrage schemes such as those at La Rance in Brittany (Le Mao, 1985) or at Annapolis in the Bay of Fundy, Nova Scotia (Dadswell & Rulifson, 1994), in that the tidal lagoon sea wall does not directly impede any rivers. The footprint of the scheme falls between the mouths of the River Tawe to its west and the Rivers Neath and Afan to its east (Figure 1). Nonetheless, the proposal has caused controversy among stakeholders and observers, some of whom are concerned that the proximity of the scheme to the mouths of these rivers is likely to interfere with migratory patterns of diadromous species and damage stocks. Sea trout (*Salmo trutta* L.) have become a particular focus of concerns since, unlike Atlantic salmon, they are known to remain and forage in coastal waters as post-smolts and adults once they have left their natal rivers, and may re-enter and re-leave rivers sporadically to forage prior to spawning runs (Solomon, 1995). The developers, Tidal Lagoon (Swansea Bay) plc (TLSB), have had to draw on innovative modelling and assessment methods to put this scheme into the planning process, and would be required to provide intensive fish monitoring and, if necessary further mitigations, in an iterative process that would continue for many years after the scheme is commissioned. In this paper, we consider the particular case of sea trout.

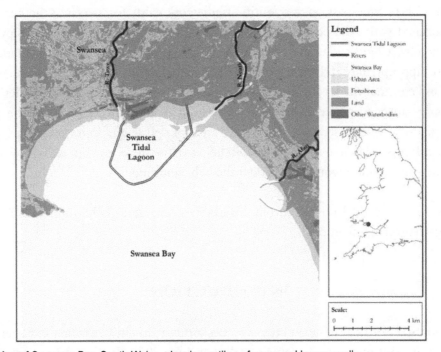

Figure 1. Map of Swansea Bay, South Wales, showing outline of proposed lagoon walls.

THE PROPOSED SWANSEA BAY TIDAL LAGOON

The proposed lagoon would have an enclosed area of 1,160 ha, bounded by sea wall of 9.5 km in length. Sixteen axial-flow bulb turbines would operate in a continuous cycle of ebb- and flood-generation, interspersed with periods of turbine pumping (15.3%) and passive sluicing (6.5%) to maximise energy extraction, to give 320MW installed capacity with 14 hours of predictable generation every day. Adjacent to the turbines a bank of eight large rectangular sluice gates would be operated towards the end of each tidal phase to maximise the water available for generation. Each of the 16 turbines would pass flows of up to 430 m^3s^{-1}, with sluice gates releasing combined flows of up to 10,000 m^3s^{-1} over short periods in each tidal cycle. The maximum velocity of flow through the turbine runner reaches 11.2 ms^{-1}; hydraulic modelling shows that the intake velocity to the turbines drops to around 10% of this value at an axial distance of around 30 m from the inlet. While these figures appear very large in engineering terms, they nevertheless represent only a small proportion of the natural tidal flux through Swansea Bay, approximately 4% by volume of the designated Swansea Bay Water Framework Directive water body.

SEA TROUT IN SWANSEA BAY

The three main rivers draining into Swansea Bay each have a modest annual run of sea trout. Sea trout are one of several diadromous species. All species support WFD designation requiring *'no deterioration'*. Over the last decade or so, sea trout in the Swansea Bay rivers have been

Table 1. Sea trout rod catches for rivers draining into Swansea Bay for the years 2001-2011 (source: *Natural Resources Wales*).

Year	Afan	Neath	Tawe
2001	166	673	373
2002	103	782	424
2003	162	400	272
2004	168	532	173
2005	153	393	372
2006	63	298	153
2007	158	487	243
2008	161	317	144
2009	120	492	242
2010	112	493	426
2011	142	444	196
Mean	137	483	274

monitored primarily in terms of rod catch data, which has indicated an average catch of less than 900 fish per year across all three rivers (Table 1). Modal length recorded from historical fish trap data at Panteg on the R. Tawe was around 55 cm (range 35-75 cm: Table 2).

Table 2. Example of STRIKER™ v.4 output for fixed-speed Swansea Turbine operating at 67 rpm at a tidal height of 2.75m above Chart Datum during ebb-tide generation. The example is for adult sea trout and uses a length-frequency distribution obtained from sea trout trapping on the R. Tawe at Panteg. The figures show the break-down into relative contributions of strike, shear and pressure-related injury for each size class and (emboldened figure, bottom-right) injury rate across all size classes. Note: all injuries are assumed to lead to mortality.

Fish Length (cm)	Predicted Injuries Due to:				Length Frequency	Net Injury Rate
	Strike	Shear	Pressure	Compound		
35	4.3%	1.1%	0.3%	5.7%	8%	0.45%
45	6.0%	1.1%	0.3%	7.3%	21%	1.53%
55	7.7%	1.1%	0.3%	9.0%	50%	4.49%
65	9.4%	1.1%	0.3%	10.7%	19%	2.04%
75	11.3%	1.1%	0.3%	12.5%	2%	0.25%
85	13.1%	1.1%	0.3%	14.3%	0%	0.00%
	Predicted injury rate at 2.75 m operating head, ebb generation					**8.76%**

POTENTIAL RISKS FROM SCHEME OPERATION

Although impacts on fish can arise from all stages of the scheme, from construction to eventual decommissioning, the types of impact associated with stages other than operation would be common to all types of marine construction schemes, e.g. arising from port and harbour development, and are therefore not particular to tidal lagoon schemes but no other such developments incorporate turbines. Further discussion of these non-specific impacts will therefore not be offered here.

While the Swansea Bay Environmental Statement examines operational-phase effects associated with various environmental changes, such as noise emissions from turbines and risk of stranding within the lagoon as the tide ebbs, the effects that have given rise to most concern are those associated with passage of fish through the turbines and sluices, and disruption of smolt migrations and adult spawning migrations. Key questions addressed in the Environmental Statement for the scheme in respect of diadromous species were therefore ones such as:-

"What is the likelihood of fish encountering the turbines during migrations?"

"What is the expected injury rate for those fish that pass through the turbines?"

"How many times on average can a fish be expected to pass through a turbine as a result of tidal flux?"

"What is the net mortality risk to fish of these fish-turbine interactions?"

For the purposes of the impact assessment, the worst-case was always assumed, namely that there was no avoidance of the turbines by fish and that any injury resulted in death of the fish. Consideration of fish movements within the hydrodynamic model of tidal currents in Swansea Bay also allowed prediction of the most likely migration path swathes based on modelled changes to river odour (olfactory) trails in scheme operational scenarios.

INJURY RISK IN TURBINES AND SLUICES

A risk of injury to fish caused by passage through turbines has been known since the origins of hydroelectric generation. Von Raben (1957) first presented a probabilistic model for estimating the injury rate of fish passing through a turbine, based on the concept of 'water-length'. He defined the term water-length as the length of a water path that can pass through a turbine after one turbine runner blade has passed and before the next arrives during its rotational cycle. This is influenced by the number of turbine blades, the runner rotation rate, the velocity of flow through the turbine and the angle at which the turbine guide-vanes direct the flow towards the runner blade leading edge. Simply put, a fish that is aligned with the flow will be struck by one or more blades if its length exceeds the water-length, but has some probability of escaping blade-strike if it is shorter than water-length or in a more favourable alignment.

The simple Von Raben (1957) type of analysis based on blade strike probability has been elaborated in many later studies. These recognise that injuries can arise from other stress factors, including the hydrostatic and hydrodynamic pressure changes that fish experience as they pass through the turbine intake, runner and draft tube, along with turbulence, hydraulic shear and cavitation effects. They can also become exposed to crushing and scissor-action if they become caught between the end of the turbine blade and the turbine housing, and collision with guide vanes, stay vanes and other static structural elements of the turbine (Solomon, 1988). Until the early 1990s, other more subtle injury types, such as gas embolisms, swim bladder rupture and internal haemorrhaging were attributed to these types of causes but only as a general complex of injuries. In the late 1980s, renewed interest in developing a UK tidal power programme led the Severn Tidal Power Group (STPG) to commission more detailed studies, including topical reviews by Solomon (1988) and Davies (1988), and a laboratory programme in which the separate effects of strike impacts, pressure flux, cavitation and hydraulic shear were investigated for a range of species common in the Severn Estuary, including the migratory salmonids (Turnpenny *et al.*, 1992; Turnpenny, 1998; Turnpenny & Everard, 1999). The outputs from this work allowed the relative effects of different stressors to be understood and development of the first STRIKER™ turbine fish injury model for non-tidal turbines (Turnpenny *et al.*, 2000). Ploskey & Carlson (2004) reviewed the performance of various fish/blade strike models against field observations, including those cited above used in the Severn work, and found that in all cases predicted probabilities of blade strike exceeded observed injury and mortality rates, while trials with a prototype turbine gave predictions that were within 4% of observed immediate salmonid fish survival rates. Other North-American workers (e.g. Čada, 1997; Deng *et al.*, 2005) built on the UK research and further investigated effects of hydraulic shear stress and pressure flux on fish, enabling the development of the latest STRIKER™ v.4 model, developed specifically for assessment of tidal range turbines.

STRIKER™ v.4 was used to predict turbine passage injury rates for the Swansea scheme under all operating conditions – flood and ebb generation, pumping and turbine sluicing (free-wheeling). Table 2 shows example outputs from a single model run based on a 4-bladed fixed speed turbine option. Table 3 integrates results over all tidal conditions and operational states, based on design operational curves, predicting 2.9% mortality risk for sea trout smolts, and 8.7% for adults, for each time they pass through a turbine for this design option.

Table 3. STRIKER™ v.4 figures for sea trout smolt and adults integrated over full tidal range of ebb generation

Life Stage	*Ebb Tidal Conditions – Net Operating Head (m)*									
	1.25	*1.75*	*2.25*	*2,75*	*3.25*	*3.75*	*4.25*	*4.75*	*5.25*	***Full Range***
Smolt	3.3%	3.2%	2.9%	2.9%	2.9%	2.8%	2.8%	2.8%	2.9%	**2.90%**
Adult	10.5%	9.9%	8.5%	8.8%	8.6%	8.4%	8.4%	8.4%	8.5%	**8.70%**

INDIVIDUAL-BASED MODELLING OF TURBINE ENCOUNTERS

The use of Individual Based Models (IBMs) for predicting turbine encounters was first used within the Severn Tidal Power Strategic Environmental Assessment (Willis & Teague, 2014), and similar models have been proposed for investigating impacts of marine renewable sites in Scotland (Guerin *et al.*, 2014). No other type of model has yet been proposed for this purpose and in the Swansea case there has been no fundamental disagreement about the model type, but finding agreement on the scope of the model and the validity of the data used to inform it has proved more challenging. Regulator and stakeholder engagement at Swansea has highlighted the importance of early discussion of IBM model scope and data sources to ensure that relevant species, life-stages, behavioural habits and environmental characteristics are adequately captured.

IBMs in the Swansea application use as their foundation an underlying water model, in which virtual fish are influenced by the tidal water movements (Willis, 2011). The Danish Hydraulic Institute Mike 21™ hydrodynamic model used by ABPmer for Swansea Bay was primarily intended for modelling coastal processes associated with the scheme, and its use within the fish IBMs was secondary, making its use highly cost-effective. The behaviour of fish within the IBM is simulated by treating them as particles in the water model that have specific capabilities defined by parameters, and specific behaviours defined by rules. Parameters are capabilities of a single animal such as swimming speed, and rules are instructions such as 'follow an odour trail', or 'avoid shallow water'.

IBMs focus on the individual fish at a particular point in its life cycle, where there can be relative certainty about motivations, sensitivity to stimulus, cognitive capability and therefore resulting behaviour. The intention is to use the minimum plausible model to reflect the key features of the real system that is being modelled. All superfluous elaboration of parameters and rules is avoided, which makes interpretation more tractable. The models represent the implications of known science combined with expert opinion about a limited set of parameters and rules; they are not an attempt to model the full richness of an animal or its habitat. It is important to make clear statements about what aspects of behaviour are covered or not covered within the model scope, and for the purposes of environmental impact assessment, to assess the degree of uncertainty the unrepresented behaviours represent. When calibrated against real fish behaviour data obtained e.g. by telemetry, these uncertainties are expressed as randomness or 'tortuosity' within the observed relative to predicted fish movements.

In the adult sea trout IBM developed for Swansea, the life-cycle point considered is the brief period of inshore spawning migration towards its natal river. No attempt was made to model a coastal residency component, although this was identified within the environmental assessment as a limitation of the model that would preferably be addressed in future tidal power applications. The general salmonid model of homing towards the natal river set out by Pascal & Quinn (1991) and Quinn (2011) hypothesises that navigation at long distances away from the river is mediated via geomagnetic cues, and that at some point within a few tens of kilometres from the river mouth, the returning adult uses olfaction to detect the odour of its natal river in the form, it is presumed, of soluble or particulate compounds. Thereafter, the fish tracks the odour trail by trial and error along an increasing concentration gradient towards its source. Since the dispersion of the odour trail is controlled by water movement, it is reasonable to assume that the water model can mimic the odour plume trajectory and the IBM then only requires a simple rule of turning inwards along a concentration gradient to follow it. However, the model also recognises that this plume-tracking is imperfect and the fish's orientation at each model step is bounded by an error distribution. The result is that by applying the same rule to the same odour trail, a swathe of possible paths results, all defined by the error distribution attached to the navigation term (Figure 2.). The error distribution itself forms part of the model calibration, and can only be derived from empirical data obtained by observing the tortuosity of a sample of real fish tracks, usually from telemetry studies. In practice, the error distribution derived from observed track tortuosity can be regarded as a catch-all for non-modelled behaviours. These would include, for example, changes of direction when the fish is diverted by a threat or an opportunity that crosses its path.

Parameters such as migration swimming speed are also obtained from observational data and similarly are represented in terms of mean values with associated standard deviations. The standard used, following international IBM protocols (Willis, 2011) involves 10,000 instantiations of the model (i.e. 10,000 virtual fish), each with parameter values drawn at random from the prescribed distributions as a Monte Carlo process. It should be evident that in order to use fish tracking observations to derive these parameters, it is first necessary to subtract the water movements from the active fish swimming movements, which requires a water model mimicking the exact tidal conditions in which the fish observations take place. The fish tracking observations also need be detailed in terms of fish position and time of observation, and can only be obtained by active tracking from a moving boat or within a fixed two-dimensional hydrophone array where fish position versus time can be automatically determined.

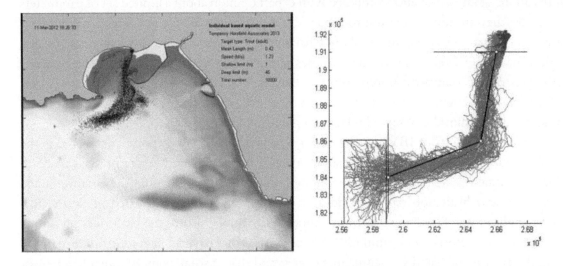

Figure 2. Graphical outputs from the IBM. The left-hand plot shows a frozen frame from the model animation in which the black dots represent the 10,000 virtual sea trout adults as they home towards the R. Tawe and interact with the scheme. The right-hand plot illustrates a tortuosity analysis in which 100 virtual fish tracks have been generated using field-derived data on swim speed and tortuosity assuming the fish are attempting to follow the heavy black ground line.

MODEL CALIBRATION, VALIDATION AND RESULTS

Detailed tracking observations on sea trout adults and smolts have not been available to this point and most of the European scientific literature deals with observations of Atlantic salmon (Table 4), which were used to calibrate the model. It may be surprising to some that although there have been numerous published accounts of salmon tracking, few are based on following the tracks of individual fish in situations where the underlying water movements can be accurately estimated to allow their subtraction. Thus, the available calibration data are actually rather limited, something which will need to be addressed by the industry in the near future if adequate environmental assessments are to be undertaken. However, studies listed in Table 4 provided the calibration data used for both salmon and sea trout models in the Swansea study, including a single instance of an historical salmon smolt track in Swansea Bay which provided some confirmation that the swimming speed and tortuosity calibrations were appropriate. Further tracking studies have been commissioned by TLSB to supplement these data.

Table 4. IBM model characteristics for Swansea sea trout model.

Life History Segment	Sea Trout Smolt	Sea Trout Adult
Model Feature	Seaward migration from natal Rivers	Inward migration to natal river
Initialisation zone	Point initialization in river mouth	Uniform random distribution across olfactory trail 'gateway' zone for Swansea Bay
Initialisation times	Uniform random distribution 4 hours each side of spring tide	Uniform random distribution 8 hours each side of spring high tide
Navigational mode	Outward trail follow	Inward trail follow
Key Salmonid References	Aprahamian *et al.*, (1998); Bendall *et al.*, (2005); Bertmar, (1979); Claridge *et al.*, (1986); Davidsen *et al.*, (2013); Hansen & Quinn, (1998); Quinn, (2011); Moore *et al.*, (1998); Stabell, (1992).	

Table 5 summarises the predicted turbine encounter rates and repeat turbine passes, i.e. those fish that pass through once and are not killed and so may pass again more than once. The STRIKER™ v.4.0 model allocates a kill probability each time a fish encounters a turbine, yielding the Turbine Mortality figures shown in Table 5. Predicted mortality rates are very small for out-migrating smolts (0.13 ± 0.04%) and somewhat greater for inward-migrating adults (2.18 ±0.15%) owing to their larger size and strike injury probability.

Table 5. Modelled turbine encounter rates, turbine passes and predicted turbine mortalities using IBM and STRIKER v.4.0 models for Swansea Lagoon scheme.

Life-History Stage	No. Encountering Turbines	Turbine Passes	Repeat Turbine Passes	Turbine Mortality %	
				Mean	Std Error
Adult	2297	3974	1.73	2.18	0.15
Smolt	283	563	1.99	0.13	0.04

NON-SPAWNING-RELATED MOVEMENTS

The feature that distinguishes sea trout from Atlantic salmon within the behavioural modelling realm is their longer residence within coastal waters, potentially increasing their exposure risk to lagoon operational effects. A simple IBM could mimic this behaviour based on a combination of marine current advection and a random walk. If one were to consider a fixed sea area around the lagoon which represented the home range of the stock, and knew the average density of adults within that area and their mean swimming speed (±standard error), the model would compute the probability per unit time of sea trout encountering the turbines and sluices.

Unlike the spawning migration case, attrition of the stock would persist for the entire duration of marine residence. Thus, if the home range was limited to within a small distance from the lagoon (e.g. a few tens of kilometres), the attrition rate might be injuriously high. On the other hand, if the stock dispersed more widely, chance encounters with the lagoon could be negligible. At the time of writing, neither the population density of adult sea trout nor the home range could be estimated reliably and thus there was no evidence base for establishing a model for this life stage. Other studies reported within this Symposium throw further light on the matter, and it will be valuable to attempt such a model as and when more information becomes available for dispersion in the marine phase.

The simple spatial-use model described above forms a structured basis for investigating important aspects of fish behaviour but may need additional rules to achieve realism, since it ignores any reactive behaviours to environmental cues. For example, fish are known to map their environment, and salmonids have been shown to exhibit spatial learning to improve foraging (Braithwaite *et al.*, 1996; Braithwaite, 1998; Braithwaite & de Perera, 2006). In doing so, they no doubt at the same time both memorise good feeding locations, which may include areas around turbines where injured or disorientated fish are easy prey, as observed at La Rance tidal barrage (Le Mao, 1985), and learn to avoid hazards associated with them through associated noise, turbulence, etc.. A good example is that of adult bass (*Dicentrarchus labrax*), which can regularly be seen feeding on small fish entrapped in the seawater cooling intakes of certain UK power stations (Turnpenny *et al.*, 2010), but very rarely are they themselves drawn in. The complexity of the model needed to represent these behaviours will be better understood once the scheme is operating and monitoring, including tracking work, is taking place

OTHER CONCERNS

During discussions with regulators, anglers and other interested parties, various questions have been raised. Some of these are briefly addressed below.

EFFECTS OF FISH MOVEMENT IN GROUPS

It has been suggested that fish moving in groups (e.g. schooling smolts or returning adults) may behave differently from the individual fish that are typically tracked to provide model calibration data. IBMs are well suited to modelling schooling in fish (Willis, 2008). Recent research by Berdahl *et al.* (2014) has demonstrated that the navigation efficiency of both Pacific (*Oncorhynchus* spp.) and Atlantic salmon is improved when fish migrate in large groups and hypothesised that collective navigation is based on consensus, resulting in reduced standard error of navigation efficiency. Within our salmonid IBMs, this would imply that measurements of navigation error based on tortuosity of individual fish tracks would tend towards overestimation, making turbine encounters appear more likely to occur. In practice, given the small annual runs of migratory salmonids in the Swansea Bay rivers the collective navigation effect may be small enough to ignore. A second effect of schooling may be to increase day-to-day variability in turbine mortality through clumping, although long-term means would be expected to remain the same.

EFFECTS OF STRONG WATER CURRENTS AROUND THE TURBINES

Another concern has been that powerful currents associated with the intake and discharge of water via the turbines and sluices would push fish off their navigational course. This is an interesting concept as current discontinuities are perhaps of paramount importance to fish in their lifetime (e.g. Belkin *et al.*, 2014). There is no evidence of migrating salmon being inconvenienced or delayed by strong currents acting as barriers to their natal rivers, although one would expect there to be much evidence if this did occur. On the contrary, there are many natural analogues to fish contending with strong tangential currents in natural coastal water bodies. Swansea Bay itself provides an excellent example as the normal tidal flow around the Mumbles Head is just such a high speed jet perpendicular to the entrance of the Tawe, visualised in the Project's water models. The water speed from west to east in the flooding spring tide can cause a jet of water about 1 km wide to be travelling at a maximum of around 1.2 ms^{-1}, for about 5-10 km. The fastest jet exiting from the turbines reduces in speed from about 2 ms^{-1} at about 100 m from the turbines to about 1 ms^{-1} within around 1500 m of the turbines. To put these speeds into perspective, the most energetically efficient and presumed most comfortable speed for adult salmonids in a marine environment is about 1 body length per second, while in the extreme, adult salmon can maintain swimming speeds of up to 5-7 ms^{1} over several 100 m (Quinn, 2011). The fact that adult salmonids do presently return to the Tawe is evidence that they are not inconvenienced by this type of water movement; quite the contrary, it is well within what they would expect to encounter as part of their natural environment.

INTERFERENCE OF THE LAGOON WITH THE OLFACTORY TRAIL

Based on the odour-trail model, the likelihood of fish entering the lagoon is expected to increase if the odour trail is drawn into the lagoon, thus attracting fish. The numerical model predicts that the erroneous signal emanating from the lagoon is at maximum around 4% and on average around 1% of the odour trail and, therefore, the distraction should be minimal.

IBM MODEL SENSITIVITY

Owing to the large number (10^5) of instantiations within each model run, sensitivity analysis is essentially built-in, since any instability would become apparent from the extreme cases drawn from the parameter distributions. However, more formal sensitivity analyses are the norm in modelling and so are presented here. The purpose of such analyses is to ensure that outputs of the models (in this case, turbine encounters and mortality) are not unduly influenced by small changes in input values. Table 6 shows the findings of analysis performed for sensitivity of sea trout IBM to swim speed and navigational error ('determination' or 'det') parameters. In each case, the value of the test parameter is varied ±1 standard deviations while other parameters are held constant. This was considered by some observers to be too narrow a range and future cases may benefit from considering wider variations. The final pair of sensitivity tests was on the navigational frequency parameter. This governs how often (on average) a fish is able to get good navigational information and thus realign itself to the olfactory trail or other target it has. It is also a measure of uncertainty but at a different range of scales to the determination parameter above. This parameter was changed by one step up and one down. The columns to the right-hand side of the table show how changing each of the parameter values affects the predicted mortalities. The results demonstrate that the model is sensitive to variation in the primary parameters in a way that is logical and smooth, without apparent thresholds or extreme sensitivity.

MONITORING AND MITIGATION

As Tidal Lagoon Swansea Bay is the first European example of a tidal generating lagoon, there is still much to be learnt about potential effects on fish, including sea trout. The importance of ongoing scientific investigation and monitoring is fully recognised and a comprehensive Adaptive Environmental Management Plan (AEMP) is being developed in consultation with

Table 6. IBM analysis of sensitivity to changes in swim speed (±1 standard deviation), navigational (determination) error (±10%) and number of steps between navigation decisions (±1 step).

Parameter		Life stage	
		Smolt	Adult
Swim speed ms^{-1}	*Mean*	0.28	0.52
	SD	0.02	0.02
Determination	*×π per step*	0.3	0.2
Navigational frequency	*No. of steps*	4	5
Predicted mortality %	*Mean*	0.13	2.18
	SD	0.04	0.15
Mortality -speed %	*-1 SD*	0.12	2.62
	+1 SD	0.13	1.84
Mortality - Determination %	*-10%*	0.11	1.76
	+10%	0.13	2.68
Mortality - Step %	*-1 Nav.*	0.14	1.72
	+1 Nav.	0.12	2.55

regulators and stakeholders. It will include a framework for monitoring fish, including passage through the turbines using hydro-acoustic counting methods and validation by turbine tailrace netting, as well as fish tracking in the vicinity of the scheme and in-river stock monitoring. If fish mortalities exceed agreed regulatory limits, or stocks are seen to decline persistently following scheme commissioning, the AEMP will be adapted as necessary to identify causes and apply additional mitigation. As a key mitigation for sea trout and other species, the Development Consent Order requires the fitting of acoustic fish deterrents (AFDs) at the turbine entrances, as is now considered best practice at coastal power station cooling water intakes (Turnpenny *et al.*, 2010). A second focus for mitigation is the design of the turbines themselves. Technical advances even since the initial planning of the scheme, including the introduction of the first large-scale variable speed turbines with only three blades, have at the same time increased turbine efficiency over a wide range of tidal states and substantially reduced fish risk factors (Table 7). Over the 120-year lifetime of the project, further technical advancements will no doubt allow further improvements, as is happening all the time in the conventional river hydropower sector.

The required monitoring plans for any tidal lagoon generating scheme are challenging on the large scale in the hostile marine or estuarine environments involved and will require developers to undertake significant testing and refinement. Hydro-acoustic monitoring methods, although now well advanced, provide limited capacity to discriminate the types of fish passing and can sample only limited volumes and need to be trialled within the specific environs of such projects to see what can realistically be achieved. Tailrace netting on this scale is also likely to prove difficult. The Electric Power Research Institute (EPRI, 1997) reviewing similar (but inland) applications in the USA concluded that tailrace fish-netting was safely and successfully deployed on turbine flows of up to 70 m^3s^{-1}, a figure well below the 430m^3s^{-1} turbine flow proposed for Swansea, and it is likely on that basis that only 10-15% of the flow could be sampled. Sub-sampling is not in itself a problem but the level of sampling required to meet statistical objectives will need to be established. Fish tracking of sufficiently fine spatial resolution and with statistically robust numbers of subjects to inform

Table 7. Comparison of STRIKER v.4.0™ predicted turbine passage injury rates for sea trout smolts and adults from Swansea Bay rivers for a fixed-speed 4-bladed axial flow bulb turbine versus that for a new-design 3-bladed variable speed turbine.

Sea Trout Life stage	Direction of Generation	Predicted Through-Turbine Injury Rate	
		4-bladed Fixed Speed Turbine Option	*3-bladed Variable Speed Turbine Option*
Smolt	Ebb	2.90%	1.57%
	Flood	3.52%	0.98%
Adult	Ebb	8.70%	6.90%
	Flood	9.28%	4.25%

and calibrate IBMs will be both physically and technically challenging and costly and will require a strong level of commitment by developers. Tidal lagoon power generation raises many issues for fish and fisheries but probably no other species offers as many challenges as the sea trout, as witnessed by the complex and often unpredictable behaviours reported at the 2nd International Sea Trout Symposium (Harris, 2017). It is important that modelling, assessment and monitoring activities make full use of this emerging scientific knowledge and that knowledge gaps are identified. Some initial thoughts on potential areas that would merit investigation are presented below:

- *Seascape and feeding*: Types of offshore substrate most likely to be favoured as feeding grounds for post-smolt and likely to favour near-shore residency. Sea trout exiting and possibly adults returning to rivers may elect to spend time near-coastal waters if there is an abundant food supply. Key prey fish species for sea trout in the Irish Sea include sand eel (*Ammodytes* and *Hyperoplus* spp.) and sprat (*Sprattus sprattus*) (Roche *et al.*, 2016). Preferred substrate particle size is estimated by Holland *et al.*, (2005) to be between 0.25 to 2 mm. Sprat, a pelagic species is however not substrate dependent. Other studies have shown that sea trout in coastal waters will feed opportunistically on a wide variety of fish and invertebrate species (Knutsen *et al.*, 2001) and therefore any highly productive area might prove attractive. Habitat changes that may be caused by the development need also to be considered in this context.
- *Hydrodynamics*: sea trout smolts exiting rivers might be more likely to linger in near-shore areas if conditions were not hydrodynamically challenging. Little is known about specific hydrodynamic preferences of sea trout, but Weihs's (1973) general principle that fish tend to swim at volitional speeds close to an energetically efficient optimum is likely to apply. Weihs (*loc.cit.*) reported an optimum fish cruising speed of, typically, around 1 body-length per second. This could act in favour of tidal lagoon site selection, as by definition they will be in high-energy tidal areas.
- *Attraction/avoidance of turbine draw zones*: the assessment for Swansea assumed that sea trout (and other fish species) approaching the turbines in the generating flow will pass through the turbines and be subject to injury risk as estimated by the STRIKER™ model. However, observations on behaviour of other fish have demonstrated avoidance of accelerating flows at hydroelectric intakes and other water intake openings, e.g. in Atlantic salmon and American shad, *Alosa sapidissima* (Haro *et al.*, 1998) and European eel, *Anguilla anguilla* (Piper *et al.*, 2015). This principle is recognised in Environment Agency guidance on bypass entrance design (Turnpenny & O'Keeffe, 2005). Understanding any such effect in sea trout would lead to more effective modelling.
- *Distribution:* estimating the proportions of post-smolts remaining close to the river mouth and local coast versus those dispersing further offshore is critical to being able to assess the fraction of the population vulnerable to lagoon entrainment; also the duration for which any life-stage remains within the locality. Knowing patterns of distribution will also help to

inform lagoon and turbine siting decisions. This information will benefit from collation of existing knowledge from targeted fish surveys, incidental and target catches in commercial fisheries and sea angling records, and from genetic studies; *c.f.* King *et al.,* (2016). The establishment of fixed acoustic telemetry arrays, combined with tagging of realistically large numbers of out-migrating post-smolts would however provide the best indication of post-smolt activity in the immediate area of a lagoon project.

- *Non-local stocks*: use of the coastal zone as migration pathways/temporary feeding locations by fish from other regions (evidence of temporary/seasonal mixed stocks).

- *River Migration*: timing and pattern of entry into rivers of origin by upstream adult migrants in relation to river flows (floods and drought) and the extent of influence of olfactory plumes.

- *Predators*: predation on seaward migrating post-smolts by piscivorous seabirds, marine mammals and fish causes high mortalities under natural conditions. Dieperink *et al.,* (2002) reported highest predation losses in sea trout and Atlantic salmon smolts during the first 9 hours after estuarine entry, declining rapidly thereafter, with Atlantic salmon suffering 3-4 times higher predation losses than sea trout. This short period of elevated risk may have been partly associated with salinity change and may be dependent on fish size, with lower risk in larger individuals. Predators are known to congregate in the vicinity of tidal barrages, such La Rance, Brittany (Le Mao, 1985), and may increase predation risk. This risk could be particularly high with turbines located close to a river mouth where smolts could still be in this vulnerable phase, and so turbine positioning may be critical in this respect. Once any tidal lagoon scheme becomes operational, it will be possible to gain a better understanding of predation effects through predator observation, telemetry studies and gut analysis of predatory fish.

- *Non-lethal impacts*: In the impact assessment for the Swansea project, any fish predicted by the STRIKER model to be injured as a result of turbine passage was counted as a mortality, although laboratory studies of simulated tidal power turbine passage (Turnpenny *et al.,* 1992) demonstrated the potential for recovery in some cases. Assuming 100% mortality is therefore the conservative option in this respect. A further uncertainty, however, is the potential for fish that have passed through the turbine to be uninjured but disorientated to the extent that vulnerability to predation is increased. Although turbine tailraces may appear to be unpromising sites for acoustic telemetry to monitor detailed behaviour of fish exiting turbines, range-testing trials at a hydroelectric plant in the USA (Ingraham *et al.,* 2014) indicate that such studies are likely to be feasible.

ACKNOWLEDGEMENTS

We are indebted to Gill Lock of Tidal Lagoon [Swansea Bay] plc (TLSB) for constructive comments on the manuscript and to TLSB for funding the work described in this paper.

REFERENCES

Aprahamian, M.W., Jones, G.O. & Gough P.J. (1998). Movement of adult Atlantic salmon in the Usk estuary, Wales. *Journal of Fish Biology*, **53**, 221-225.

Bendall, B., Moore, A. & Quayle, V. (2005), The post-spawning movements of migratory brown trout *Salmo trutta* L. *Journal of Fish Biology*, **67**, 809–822.

Bertmar, G. (1979). Home range, migrations and orientation mechanisms of the river Indalsalven Trout, *Salmo trutta* L. Swedish. *Institute of Freshwater Research Drottningholm Rep*, **58**, 5-26.

Braithwaite, V.A., Armstrong, J.D., McAdams, H.M. & Huntingford, F.A. (1996). Can juvenile Atlantic salmon use multiple cue systems in spatial learning? *Animal Behaviour*, **51**, 1409-1415.

Braithwaite, V. A. (1998). Spatial memory, landmark use and orientation in fish. In: *Spatial Representation in Animals.* (Healy, S. *Ed.*). New York, NY, Oxford University Press, 86-102.

Braithwaite, V. A. & de Perera, T. B. (2006). Short-range orientation in fish: how fish map space. *Marine & Freshwater. Behavior & Physiology*, **39**, 37-47.

Claridge, P. N., Potter, I. C. & Hardisty, M. W. (1986). Seasonal changes in movements, abundance, size composition and diversity of the fish fauna of the Severn Estuary. *Journal of the Marine Biological Association of the United Kingdom*, **66**, 229-258.

Čada, G.F. (1997). *The development of biological criteria for the design of advanced hydropower turbines.* US Department of Energy, Idaho Operations Office, Report No. DOE/ID/10578.

Dadswell, M.J. & Rulifson, R.A. (1994). Macrotidal estuaries: a region of collision between migratory marine animals and tidal power development. *Biological Journal of the Linnaean Society*, **51**, 93-113.

Davidsen, J. G., Rikardsen, A. H., Thorstad, E. B., Halttunen, E., Mitamura, H., Præbel, K. & Skarðhamar, J., *et al.*, (2013). Homing behaviour of Atlantic salmon (*Salmo salar*) during final phase of marine migration and river entry. *Canadian Journal of Fisheries and Aquatic Sciences*, **70**(5), 794-802.

Davies, J.K. (1988). A review of information relating to fish passage through turbines: Implications to tidal power schemes. *Journal of Fish Biology*, **33** (suppl. A), 111-126.

Deng, Z., Guensch, G.R., McKinstry, C.A., Mueller, R.P., Dauble, D.D. & Richmond, M.C. (2005). Evaluation of fish-injury mechanisms during exposure to turbulent shear flow. *Canadian Journal of Fisheries and Aquatic Sciences*, **62**, 1513–1522.

Dieperink, C., Bak, B.D., Pedersen, L-F., Pedersen, M.I. & Pedersen, S. (2002). Predation on Atlantic salmon and sea trout during their first days as postsmolt. *Journal of Fish Biology*. **61**, 848–852.

Electric Power Research Institute. (1997). Guidelines for hydro turbine fish entrainment and survival studies. EPRI Report No. TR-107299. (*Authors*: Amaral, S.V. & Winchell, F.C.), EPRI, Pala Alto, California, USA.

Guerin, A. J., Jackson, A. C., Bowyer, P. A. & Youngson, A. F. (2014). Hydrodynamic models to understand salmon migration in Scotland. The Crown Estate, 116 pages. ISBN: 978-1-906410-52-0.

Harris, G.S. (2017). Sea Trout: Science & Management, Proceeding of the 2nd International Sea Trout Symposium, October, 2015, Dundalk, Ireland. *[Troubador & pp at page-proof stage*

Hansen LP, & Quinn TP. (1998). The marine phase of the Atlantic salmon (*Salmo salar*) life cycle, with comparisons to Pacific salmon. *Canadian Journal of Fisheries and Aquatic Sciences.* **55**(S1): 104-118.

Haro, A, Odeh M., Noreika, J., Castro-Santos, T. (1998). Effect of water acceleration on downstream migratory behavior and passage of Atlantic salmon smolts and Juvenile American shad at surface bypasses. *Transactions of the American Fisheries Society,* **127**, 118–127.

Holland, G.J., Greenstreet, S. P. R., Gibb, I. M., Fraser, H. M., & Robertson, M. R. (2005). Identifying sandeel *Ammodytes marinus* sediment habitat preferences in the marine environment. *Marine Ecology Progress Series*, **303**, 269–282.

Ingraham, J.M., Deng, Z.D., Martinez, J.J., Trumbo, B.A., Mueller, R.P. & Weiland, M.A. (2014). Feasibility of Tracking Fish with Acoustic Transmitters in the Ice Harbor Dam Tailrace. *Science Report 4*, 4090; DOI:10.1038/srep04090.

King, R.A., Stockley, B., Hillman, R., Elsmere, P. & Stevens, J.R. (2017). Managing mixed stocks of sea trout (*Salmo trutta* L.) straying between rivers sharing a common estuary in southwest England: a genetic approach. In: *Sea Trout Science & Management*. (G.S. Harris *Ed.*). Proceeding of the 2nd International Sea Trout Symposium, October, 2015, Dundalk, Ireland. *[Troubador & pp at page-proof stage]*

Knutsen, J.A., Knutsen, H., Gjosaeter, J. & Johnson, B. (2001). Food of anadromous brown trout at sea. *Journal of Fish Biology,* **59**, 533-543.

Le, Mao, P. (1985). Peuplements piscicole et teuthologique du bassin maritime de la Rance: impact de l'aménagement marémoteur. PhD thesis, École Nationale Supérieure Agronomique, Rennes, France.

Moore A., Ives S., Mead T.A. & Talks, L. (1998). The migratory behaviour of wild Atlantic salmon (*Salmo salar* L.) smolts in the River Test and Southampton Water, southern England. *Hydrobiologia,* **371/372**, 295–304.

Pascal, M.A. & Quinn, T.P. (1991). Evaluation of alternative models of the coastal migration of adult Fraser River sockeye salmon (*Oncorhynchus nerka*). *Canadian Journal of Fisheries and Aquatic Sciences,* **48**(5), 799-810.

Piper, A.T, Manes, C., Siniscalchi, F., Marion, A., Wright, R.M. & Kemp, P.S. (2015). Response of seaward-migrating European eel (*Anguilla anguilla*) to manipulated flow fields. *Proceedings of the Royal Society Series B,* **282**, Issue 1811.

Ploskey, G.R. & Carlson, T. J. (2004). Comparison of blade-strike modelling results with empirical data. Pacific *Northwest National Laboratory, Report* No. PNNL-14603, 36 pp.

Potter, E.C.E. (1985). Salmonid migrations off the North East coast of England. *Proceedings of the Institute of Fisheries Management 16th Annual study Course, 16-19 Sept. 1985 York University*, 124-141

Quinn, T. P. (2011). *The behavior and ecology of Pacific salmon and trout*. Vancouver, University of British Columbia Press.

Roche, W., Milner, N., Davies, C., King, J., Coyne, J., Gargan, P. & Hughes, R. (2016). Feeding ecology of sea trout in the Irish Sea. In: Sea Trout: Science & Management. (G.S. Harris. *Ed.*). Proceedings of the 2nd International Sea Trout Symposium, October 2015, Dundalk, Ireland. *[Insert publisher/pages at page-proof stage.]*

Solomon, D.J. (1988). Fish Passage through Tidal Energy Barrages. *Technical Report for Energy Technology Support Unit: Harwell, UK*, 1988, ETSU TID4056.

Solomon, D.J. (1995). Sea trout stocks in England & Wales. *National Rivers Authority R&D Report 25*, National Rivers Authority, Bristol, 102 pp.

Stabell, O.B. (1992). Olfactory control of homing behaviour in salmonids. *In:* Hara, T (ed.) *Fish Chemoreception*. London, Chapman and Hall, 249-270.

Turnpenny, A.W.H. (1998). Mechanisms of Fish Damage in Low-Head Turbines: An Experimental Appraisal. In: *Fish Migration and Fish Bypasses*, (M. Jungwirth, S. Schmutz, & S. Weiss. *Eds.*). Fishing News Books, Blackwell Publishing, Oxford, United Kingdom, 300-314

Turnpenny, A.W.H., Davis, D.M., Fleming, J.M., & Davies, J.K. (1992). Experimental Studies Relating to the Passage of Fish and Shrimps Through Tidal Power Turbines. Unpublished Report, National Power plc, Fawley, Hampshire, United Kingdom.

Turnpenny, A.W.H., Clough, S. Hanson, K.P., Ramsay, R. & McEwan, D. (2000). Risk Assessment for Fish Passage Through Small, Low-Head Turbines. *Final Report.* Energy Technical Support Unit, Harwell, United Kingdom.

Turnpenny, A.W.H. & Everard, J.K. (1999). Can cavitation injure fish? In: *Innovations in Fish Passage Technology* (Odeh, M. *Ed.*). American Fisheries Society. ISBN 1-888569-17-4, 197-205.

Turnpenny, A.W.H., Coughlan, J., Ng, B., Crews, P. & Rowles, P. (2010). Cooling water options for the new generation of nuclear power stations in the UK. *Science Report SC070015/SR*, Environment Agency, Bristol, 214 pp.

Turnpenny, A.W.H. & O'Keeffe, N. (2005). Best practice guide for intake and outfall fish screening. The Environment Agency *Science Report SC030231,* Bristol, UK.

Weihs, D. (1973). Optimal fish cruising speed. *Nature,* **245** (Sept.7): 48-50.

Willis, J. (2008). Simulation model of universal law of school size distribution applied to southern bluefin tuna (*Thunnus maccoyii*) in the Great Australian Bight. *Ecological Modelling,* **213,** 33–44.

Willis, J. (2011) Modelling swimming aquatic animals in hydrodynamic models. *Ecological Modelling,* **222,** 3869-3887.

Willis, J. & Teague, N.N. (2014). Modelling fish in hydrodynamic models: an example using the Severn Barrage SEA. In: *International Fish Screening Techniques* (A.W.H. Turnpenny & A. Horsfield, *Eds.*). Southampton: WIT Press, 179–190.

ELECTRONIC REFERENCES

Belkin, I.M., Hunt, G.L., Willis J. (2014). Fronts, Fish, and Predators. Deep Sea Research Part II: Topical Studies in Oceanography. *Available online* 23 July 2014, ISSN 0967-0645, http://dx.doi.org/ 10.1016 /j.dsr2.2014.07.009.

Berdahl, A., Westley, P. A., Levin, S. A., Couzin, I. D., & Quinn, T. P. (2014). A collective navigation hypothesis for homeward migration in anadromous salmonids. *Fish and Fisheries.* DOI: 10.1111/ faf.12084

The impact of a small hydropower scheme on the migratory behaviour of sea trout (*Salmo trutta L.*) smolts in the River Frome, southern England

A. MOORE[1], R. LAURIDSEN[2], L. PRIVITERA[1] & W.R.C. BEAUMONT[2]

[1]*Centre for Environment, Fisheries and Aquaculture Science, Lowestoft Laboratory, Pakefield Road, Lowestoft, Suffolk, NR33 0HT, UK.*
[2]*Game and Wildlife Conservation Trust, Salmon & Trout Research Centre, The River Laboratory, East Stoke, Wareham, Dorset, BH20 6BB, UK.*

ABSTRACT

The migratory behaviour of emigrating sea trout (*Salmo trutta*) smolts was monitored in relation to a small low head hydropower scheme on the River Frome, southern England. The majority of the smolts, tagged with miniature acoustic transmitters bypassed the hydropower scheme with only 2.4% of the fish moving downstream through the turbine. No mortalities were recorded in the fish passing through the turbine; but their physical condition is not known. Movement of the smolts was nocturnal within freshwater and occurred during elevated river flows. There was no apparent delay in the movement of the smolts at the turbine intake or at the adjacent weir. Migration of all smolts through the estuary of the River Frome was nocturnal and migration into the sea occurred at all states of the tide. Survival of the sea trout smolts was high during the transition from the fresh to the marine environments.

Keywords: sea trout; smolts; River Frome; hydropower; migration; acoustic telemetry.

INTRODUCTION

In 2009, as the result of concerns over climate change, the UK was set a mandatory target to achieve 15% of its energy consumption from renewable sources by 2020 (EU, Directive 2009/28/EC 2009). Hydropower was identified as one of the means of achieving this target and this has led to renewed interest in the construction of small low-head run-of-river hydroelectric schemes. These schemes are usually located on existing in-channel structures, such as weirs and mills where the fall of water is often < 5 m. In the UK, there are estimated to be about 26,000 locations where a hydropower turbine could be constructed and produce electricity (Environment Agency, 2010). However, very little is understood regarding the impact of such run-of-river schemes on fisheries and the freshwater ecosystem, particularly at the catchment level (Robsen *et al.*, 2011). Previous studies, have suggested that the construction and operation of larger high-head run-of-river hydropower schemes may result in a number of environmental impacts. These include, changes in fish population structure, habitat alterations, loss of crucial spawning and nursery habitat, loss of biological diversity, modifications to water quality and hydrological regimes, barriers to fish migration and disruption of longitudinal connectivity (Bunt *et al.*, 1999; Marchetti & Moyle, 2001; Moser *et al.*, 2002; Trussart *et al.*, 2002, Robertson *et al.*, 2004; O'Connor *et al.*, 2006; Fette *et al.*, 2007; Habit *et al.*, 2007; Poulet, 2007; Murchie *et al.*, 2008; Lucas *et al.*, 2009). There are now concerns that the small hydroelectric schemes may also cause similar environmental problems and that any impacts may potentially lead to changes in fish population dynamics (Nislow *et al.* 2011). These small hydroelectric schemes may cause direct mortalities to fish (e.g. where fish encounter turbines) (Calles *et al.*, 2010; Muir *et al.*, 2001) and/or indirect mortalities (e.g. where delays to migration make fish more vulnerable to predation).

However, one of the major concerns is the cumulative impacts of a series of structures throughout a river basin on diadromous fish species that need free passage during their seaward migration to the marine feeding/spawning grounds and during their subsequent return to the freshwater feeding/spawning grounds Diadromous species of particular concern in the UK are the Atlantic salmon (*Salmo salar* L.), sea trout (migratory form of *Salmo trutta* L.) and European eel (*Anguilla anguilla* L.), although lampreys (*Lampetra fluviatilis*, *L. planeri* and *Petromyzon marinus*), shad (*Alosa fallax* and *A. alosa*) and smelt (*Osmerus eperlanus*) may also be impacted depending upon the location of the scheme within the river catchment. Many other freshwater species such as cyprinids, percids and pike also exhibit potadromous migratory behaviour, which may be disrupted by riverine structures (Lucas & Frear, 1997; Bolland *et al.*, 2008; Nunn *et al.*, 2010). Although single hydropower schemes are considered less likely to have major impacts on fish populations within a river system as a whole, the cumulative effects of more than one scheme can be potentially more ecologically damaging. Paquet & Witmer (1985) have previously detailed the occurrence and variety of cumulative impacts, which include delays in fish migration (Holbrook *et al.*, 2009), fish mortality at impoundments, losses of fish spawning and rearing habitats (Hall *et al.*, 2011) and losses of adult fish due to blocked migration, as well as issues threatening water quality, invertebrates and aquatic plants. Previous work in France has also concluded that it is bad management practice to plan the construction of more than a very limited number of small-scale hydropower stations on a single river (Larinier, 2008). However, existing structures such as weirs may also impede fish passage and the construction of a hydropower scheme with the requirement for a new or improved fish pass to meet fish passage legislation may also benefit diadromous fish (Fraser *et al.*, 2015).

The present study investigated the impact of a small hydropower scheme on the migratory behaviour of sea trout smolts as they emigrated through the freshwater section of the River Frome and entered the marine environment at the exit of Poole Harbour. In particular, the research examined the delay to migration at the intake of the hydropower scheme and the effects of passage through the turbine on the subsequent temporal and spatial migration of the fish in the river and estuary.

MATERIALS AND METHODS

STUDY SITE

The River Frome is located in southern England (Figure 1). It rises in the Dorset Downs at Evershot and travels approximately 70 km to the tidal limit at Wareham Bypass Bridge. The catchment area is 181 square miles (454 km²) (see Westlake *et al.* 1972 for detailed description). At Wareham, the River Frome flows into Poole Harbour via the Wareham Channel. Poole Harbour is a bar built estuary occupying an area of approximately 38 km² at high water springs, of which 54% is intertidal. Water depths throughout the estuary are generally < 2 m above chart datum. The estuary is micro-tidal, with a tidal range of 1.8 m on springs and 0.6 m on neaps at Poole Quay. The tidal regime is characterised by a prolonged "double" high water that can sustain water levels above mean tide level for 16 out of every 24 hours (Humphreys, 2005). The strongest tidal currents (around 2.0 ms^{-1}) occur at the entrance to the harbour with maximal currents in the main channel of approximately 0.5 ms^{-1}.

FISH CAPTURE AND ACOUSTIC TRACKING SYSTEM

The study was carried out over a two-year period during the smolt runs of 2013 and 2014. Between the 10th and 15th April 2013 and 28th March and 23rd April 2014, migrating sea trout smolts were captured using an eel rack 16.8 km above the tidal limit of the river (SY877818). In 2013, thirty sea trout smolts (mean length ± S.E. = 182.2 ± 5.94 mm and mean weight ± S.E. = 72.19 ± 6.59 g) were trapped after dark; usually during periods of elevated river flow (Mean flow ± S.E. = 8.29 ± 0.29 m³s^{-1}; 2014 mean daily flow ± S.E. = 10.27 ± 0.56 m³s^{-1}). In 2014, 51 sea trout smolts (mean length ± S.E. = 212.7 ± 3.90 mm and mean weight ± S.E. = 105.32 ± 5.59 g) were again trapped at night during similar flow conditions (mean daily flow ± S.E. = 10.27 ± 0.56 m³s^{-1}). In 2014, the smolts were significantly larger than in 2013 (length t= 4.475, 79 d.f. p < 0.001; weight t=847.000, p < 0.001). Individual fish were anaesthetised with 2 phenoxy ethanol (0.4 ml l^{-1}) and a miniature coded acoustic transmitter (Model V6-4H Vemco, Halifax, Nova Scotia, Canada) operating at a frequency of 180 kHz, was surgically implanted into the peritoneal cavity as originally described by Moore *et al.*, (1990). The transmitters measured 16.5 mm x 6 mm in size and had a projected battery life of 57 days. All smolts were subjected to minimal handling and allowed to recover fully following surgery before being released back into the river, normally within 5-10 minutes. The subsequent movements of the tagged smolts were monitored using 180 kHz VR2W submersible acoustic receivers (Vemco, Halifax, Nova Scotia, Canada) positioned at strategic positions around Bindon Mill and extending to the exit of Poole Harbour. The acoustic receivers were placed at 4 locations: 1) upstream of the weir at the Game and Wildlife Conservation Trust, East Stoke Laboratory, 2) the tidal limit in Wareham, 3) the saline limit of the river, at the entrance of the Poole Harbour and 4) at the exit of Poole Harbour (Figure 1).

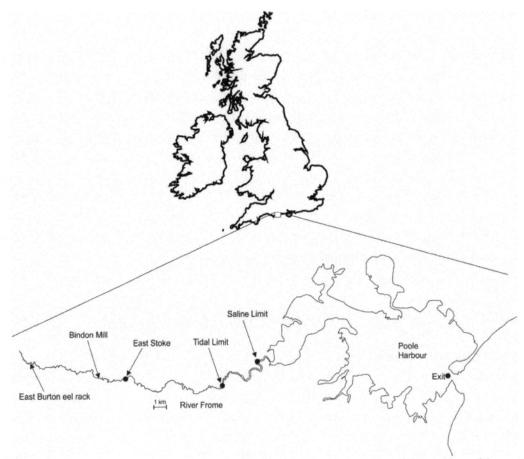

Figure 1. Map of the River Frome showing the capture site of the sea trout smolts and the positions of the acoustic receivers (●).

HYDROPOWER SCHEME

The hydropower scheme is situated at Bindon Mill (SY 869855) on the River Frome, 11.4 km above the tidal limit of the river. The turbine is a 2.2 metre diameter Archimedes screw

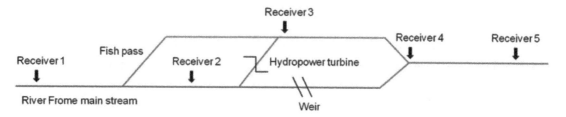

Figure 2. Schematic diagram of the River Frome around the hydropower scheme at Bindon Mill showing the positions of the acoustic receivers.

generating up to 16.5 kW from a flow of 2,100 lsec^{-1} over a head of 1.2 metres. A schematic diagram of the river at Bindon Mill is shown in Figure 2. Five VR2W receivers were placed upstream and downstream of the turbine to determine by which route the migrating smolts bypassed the structure or whether they passed through the turbine (Figure 2). During 2013, the turbine operated continuously: except for a 48-hour period between the 14-16 April, when the turbine was turned off. This was to determine whether the operation of the turbine had an impact on the behaviour of migrating smolts as they approached the turbine and their subsequent route downstream. During 2014, the turbine operated continuously. Smolts that were detected at the receiver located immediately upstream of the turbine (HP2) and then subsequently at the receiver located immediately downstream of the turbine (HP3) within a 5 minute period were considered to have migrated through the turbine. Fish detected only at HP3 may have moved down through the fish pass and are not included in any analyses of turbine passage. A receiver was not located in the adult fish pass due the high turbulence and reduced detection range.

STATISTICAL ANALYSES

The downstream migration of tagged smolts detected by the acoustic receivers located around the hydropower scheme and throughout the river and Poole Harbour were analysed using circular statistical methods, testing if the movement of smolts was random with respect to time of day and state of tide using the Rayleigh test ('*r*' value) (Batschelet, 1981). The value of *r* is a measure of angular dispersion and, in this respect, can be used to determine if the movement of the fish is directed in relation to time of day or to a specific period within the tidal cycle. An *r* value of 0 means uniform dispersion whilst a value of 1 means complete concentration in one direction or time of day/tidal cycle. All analyses were carried out using the Oriana software (Kovach, 2011). Comparisons between years were carried out using a t-test and, if the Normality Test (Shapiro-Wilk) failed, a Mann-Whitney Rank Sum Test was undertaken. High water at Wareham Quay has been used as a reference time for all analyses of movement within tidal waters.

RESULTS

In 2013, 27 tagged smolts were detected downstream of the hydropower scheme at the receiver located at East Stoke. One smolt had migrated through the turbine whilst it was operational, and 21 smolts moved over the adjacent weir. No fish migrated through the turbine when it was not operating. A further 5 smolts migrated through a small side stream located 650 metres above the turbine and which re-entered the River Frome upstream of the East Stoke receiver. This was the first record of smolts using this channel to migrate seawards. In 2014, 44 tagged smolts were detected at East Stoke. One smolt had migrated through the turbine, whilst 43 smolts moved over the weir. No sea trout smolts were detected moving downstream through the side stream.

The arrival of all smolts at the hydropower scheme was strictly nocturnal, with mean times of detection at 23:50 (2013) and 23:14 (2014) (Figure 3). In both years, there was no period of residency above the turbine intake before the two smolts entered the turbine; with fish being detected at the downstream Receiver 3 between 3 and 4 minutes after detection at the upstream Receiver 2 (Figure 2). In both years, there was also no delay in migrating smolts negotiating the weir. The mean time ± S.E. taken for smolts to migrate between Receiver 2 and Receiver 5 in 2013 was 2.47 ± 0.964 min (n=19) and in 2014 was 3.00 ± 1.036 min (n=11). The movement of smolts in relation to the hydropower scheme occurred during periods of elevated river flow (2013, mean daily flow ± S.E. = 8.08 ± 0.38 $m^3 s^{-1}$; 2014, mean daily flow ± S.E. = 10.05 ± 0.35 $m^3 s^{-1}$).

In 2013, the smolt that migrated through the turbine was last recorded at East Stoke two hours later but was not recorded at the tidal limit or any of the receivers located within Poole Harbour. In 2014, the smolt that entered the turbine was subsequently recorded passing the receiver located at the exit of Poole Harbour and entering the marine environment. The time of passage between the hydropower scheme and the marine environment was 79 h 06 min. There was insufficient data to undertake a comparison of the speed of migration between fish that entered the turbine and those that migrated over the weir gates.

The time taken for the groups of smolts that migrated over the weir to reach East Stoke was significantly different between years (2013 = mean time ± S.E. = 1.69 ± 0.59 hours and 2014 = mean time ± S.E. = 4.48 ± 2.14 hours; P = 0.013). The mean times that the smolts were detected 1) upstream and downstream of the hydropower scheme, 2) the tidal limit, 3) the saline limit and 4) the mouth of the estuary in both years of the study are shown in Table 1. In 2013, the movement of smolts continued to be nocturnal and directed in relation to time of day as they migrated past the tidal limit (Figure 4) and subsequently during the emigration through the estuary. However, in 2014 the movement of the smolts through the estuary was random with respect to time occurring during both day and night (Table 1).

In 2013, 23 of the tagged sea trout smolts (76%) were detected by at least one of the receivers located at the exit of the estuary and are considered to have successfully negotiated the estuary and entered the marine environment. In 2014, 39 sea trout smolts (76%) also entered

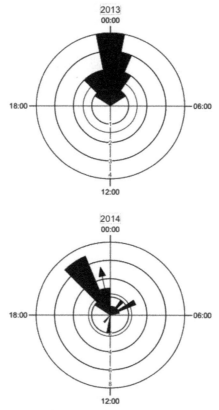

Figure 3. Histogram showing the time of day that the sea trout smolts were detected approaching the hydropower scheme in 2013 and 2014. The histogram provides an indication of the number of smolts at each time. The arrow represents the mean time of detection calculated by vector analysis and its length represents the r value calculated using the Rayleigh test (Batschelet, 1981).

Figure 4. Histogram showing the time of day when the sea trout smolts were detected passing the tidal limit of the river in 2014. The histogram provides an indication of the number of smolts at each time. The arrow represents the mean time of detection calculated by vector analysis and its length represents the r value calculated using the Rayleigh test (Batschelet, 1981).

Table 1. The downstream movements of sea trout smolts at the receivers located upstream and downstream of the hydropower scheme and at the tidal limit, saline limit and estuary mouth in relation to the time of day. The mean times that smolts were recorded passing each site have been calculated from the mean vectors (Batschelet, 1981). The *r* values provide a measure of randomness of movement in respect to time calculated using the Rayleigh test. All times are calculated from the previous 1st High Water measured at Wareham Quay. The value n is the total number of smolts recorded at each of the receivers.

	Upstream		Downstream		Tidal Limit		Saline Limit		Estuary mouth	
	2013	*2014*	*2013*	*2014*	*2013*	*2014*	*2013*	*2014*	*2013*	*2014*
Mean time	23:50	23:14	00:58	23:43	02:21	02:30	03:19	Random movement	05:17	Random movement
r	0.906	0.67	0.870	0.702	0.728	0.669	0.380	0.134	0.425	0.049
p	< 0.0001	< 0.0001	< 0.0001	< 0.0001	< 0.0001	< 0.0001	= 0.04	= 0.467	= 0.014	= 0.906
n	22	35	27	43	24	26	22	43	23	42

Table 2. The movement of sea trout smolts recorded at the receivers located at the saline limit and estuary mouth in relation to the tidal cycle. The mean times that smolts were recorded passing each site have been calculated from the mean vectors (Batschelet, 1981). The *r* values provide a measure of randomness of movement in respect to time calculated using the Rayleigh test. All times are in hours and minutes and calculated from the previous 1st High Water measured at Wareham Quay. The value n is the total number of smolts recorded at each of the receivers.

	Saline Limit		Estuary mouth	
	2013	*2014*	*2013*	*2014*
Mean time	6h 58 min	6 h 23 min	6 h 33 min	4 h 14 min
r	0.545	0.553	0.819	0.721
p	< 0.0001	< 0.0001	< 0.0001	< 0.0001
n	25	43	20	42

the marine environment (Lauridsen *et al.*, 2016). In 2013 and 2014 movement past the saline limit and entry into the estuary occurred on an ebbing tide (Table 2). The migration out of the estuary in both years was also non-random with respect to the tidal cycle and occurred predominantly on an ebbing tide (Figure 5).

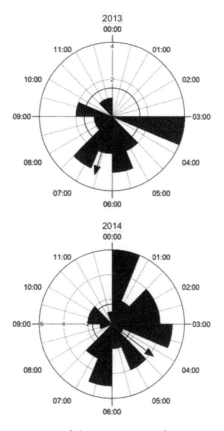

Figure 5. Histogram showing the movement of the two groups of sea trout smolts emigrating into the coastal environment in relation to the tidal cycle in 2013 and 2014. The histograms provide an indication of the number of smolts at each time. The arrow represents the mean time of detection calculated by vector analysis and its length represents the r value calculated using the Rayleigh test (Batschelet, 1981). The histogram shows the time in hours after the previous 1st HW at Wareham Quay.

DISCUSSION

The hydropower scheme on the River Frome appeared to have a minimal impact on the emigrating sea trout smolts. During the two years of the study, only two smolts moved downstream through the turbine: with 97% bypassing the scheme either within the main river channel or through a small side stream not previously known to be used by migrating smolts. Two fish did pass through the turbine and a single fish was subsequently recorded migrating into Poole Harbour. However, the second smolt was not recorded at the tidal or saline limit during the rest of the study and the effect of turbine passage is not known. Passage of smolts through hydropower turbines have previously been shown to result in physical damage and high mortalities. Causes of mortality for smolts passing through turbines are generally the result of mechanical damage: such as grinding or collisions with moving parts of the turbine, pressure-induced damage, shearing action damage due to passage through areas of extreme turbulence and cavitation damage (Ruggles, 1980; Mont´en, 1985; Larinier, 2008). The mortality risk increases with increasing fish length (Mont´en, 1985; Ferguson *et al.*, 2008; Larinier, 2008) but is highly dependent upon the turbine type and operational procedures. There have been relatively few studies on the effects of Archimedes screw hydropower turbines (ASHT) on salmon smolts, but the turbine is considered to be more 'fish friendly' than other designs. Pressure induced and cavitation damage is considered negligible, with the most likely causes of damage to fish being mechanical as a result of blade strikes and grinding. A single study on salmon smolts in the UK noted that mechanical damage to smolts was between 1% and 3% and fish suffered scale loss of between 5% and 10% (Fishtek, 2007). Studies on Archimedes lifts and fish pumps with similar screw-type impeller design have also indicated wounds consistent with strike injuries McNabb *et al.*, 2003) or low levels of scale loss in juvenile Chinook salmon (*Oncorhynchus tshawytscha*) (Helfrich *et al.*, 2001). A parallel study on salmon smolts at Bindon Mill indicated that 20% of fish introduced above the turbine and recovered immediately below had significant scale loss (40-70%) considered to be the result of grinding (Moore *et al.*, *in preparation*).

There was no significant delay in the fish moving past the structure or a period of residency above the intake to the turbine in those fish that subsequently moved downstream by this route. Similarly, no significant delays to migrating salmon smolts were noted at Bindon Mill (Moore, *unpublished data*) or a similar hydropower scheme on the River Dart, UK (Fishtek 2007). There was also no apparent delay to the fish moving downstream through the hatches located on the adjacent weir. These results are different to other reported studies where river structures have been shown to significantly delay smolt migration and, in some cases, lead to increased vulnerability to predation (Jepsen *et al.*, 2000; Aarestrup *et al.*, 1999; Aarestrup & Koed, 2003; Serrano *et al.*, 2009). It is considered that in the present study the migration of the fish during periods of high flows within the river assisted the fish in moving rapidly pass the hydropower structure and was the predominant factor in reducing the potential impact of the scheme on the fish. However, consideration should be given to the impact of these structures during periods of low flow.

The general migratory behaviour of sea trout smolts in the River Frome was very similar to that reported previously in other rivers and estuaries in England and Wales (Moore & Potter, 1994; Moore *et al.*, 1998a; Russell *et al.*, 1998) and is similar to salmon smolt migration (Moore *et al.*, 1995; Moore *et al.*, 1998b). The nocturnal migration is generally considered to be predator avoidance behaviour (Solomon, 1978; Moore *et al.*, 1995), although there is often a seasonal change in the pattern of smolt migration with the later running fish moving both day and night: a behaviour that would ensure that the majority of the smolts entered the marine environment at the optimum time (Moore *et al.*, 1995; McCormick *et al.*, 1998).

In conclusion, the present study indicated that the hydropower scheme on the River Frome appeared to have a minimal impact on emigrating sea trout smolts. However, it is accepted that generic assessments of individual hydropower schemes may be misleading and that the potential impact of a scheme may be dependent upon its location on the existing structure, the efficacy of the fish pass and its position within the river catchment. Where there are concerns that a scheme may impact on emigrating smolts, then simple mitigation measures can be implemented, including ceasing operation of the turbine for the duration of the smolt run and ceasing operation at night or at critical flows that initiate the movement of smolts. The movement of larger fish such as salmon and sea trout kelts and emigrating silver European eels (*Anguilla anguilla*) will need to be determined together in respect of any effects resulting from turbine passage in order to manage and conserve populations of diadromous fish.

ACKNOWLEDGEMENTS

The study was funded by the UK Government's Department for Environment, Food and Rural Affairs (Defra) and carried out in collaboration with the Game and Wildlife Conservation Trust (GWCT). The authors are particularly grateful to L.J. Scott (GWCT) and Wilfrid and Sally Weld (owners of Bindon Mill) for his very kind assistance and tolerance in allowing the study to be sited on their property. In 2013, the tagging procedure was carried out under a Project Licence (PPL 70/7588) held by Andrew Moore under the Home Office The Animals (Scientific Procedures) Act 1986 and in 2014 under Project Licence PPL 30/2732 held by William Beaumont.

REFERENCES

Aarestrup, K., Jepsen, N., Rasmussen, G. & Økland, F. (1999). Movements of two strains of radio tagged Atlantic salmon, *Salmo salar* L., smolts through a reservoir. *Fisheries Management and Ecology* **6**, 97–107.

Aarestrup, K. & Koed, A. (2003). Survival of migrating sea trout (*Salmo trutta*) and Atlantic salmon (*Salmo salar*) smolts negotiating weirs in small Danish rivers. *Ecology of Freshwater Fish* **12**, 169–176.

Batschelet, E. (1981). Circular statistics in Biology. London, Academic Press. 371 pp.

Bolland, J.D., Cowx, I.G. & Lucas, M.C. (2008) Movements and habitat use of wild and stocked juvenile chub, *Leuciscus cephalus* (L.), in a small lowland river. *Fisheries Management and Ecology* **15**, 401-407.

Bunt, C.M., Cooke, S.J., Katopodis, C. & McKinley, R.S. (1999). Movement and summer habitat of brown trout (*Salmo trutta*) below a pulsed discharge hydroelectric generating station. *Regulated Rivers Research & Management* **15**, 395-403.

Calles, O., Olsson, I.C., Comoglio, C., Kemp, P.S., Blunden, L., Schmitz, M. & Greenberg, L.A. (2010). Size-dependent mortality of migratory silver eels at a hydropower plant, and implications for escapement to the sea. *Freshwater Biology* **55**, 2167 – 2180.

Environment Agency (2010). Mapping hydropower opportunities and sensitivities in England and Wales. Environment Agency Report, 74 pp.

Ferguson, J. W., Ploskey, G. R., Leonardsson, K., Zabel, R. W. & Lundqvist, H. (2008). Combining turbine blade-strike and life cycle models to assess mitigation strategies for fish passing dams. *Canadian Journal of Fisheries and Aquatic Sciences* **65**, 1568 – 1585.

Fette, M., Weber, C., Peter, A. & Wehrli, B. (2007). Hydropower production and river rehabilitation: A case study on the Alpine river. *Environmental Modelling and Assessment* **12**, 257-267.

Fishtek (2007). Fish monitoring and live fish trials. Archimedes screw turbine, River Dart. Phase 1 report: live fish trial, smolts, leading edge assessment, disorientation study, outflow monitoring. Fishtek Consulting, Okehampton, UK.

Fraser, D., Palmer, S. & Stewart-Russon, I. (2015). Cumulative effects of hydropower schemes on fish migration and populations. Environment Agency Project SC120078/R1, Environment Agency, Bristol 81 pp.

Habit, E., Belk, M.C. & Parra, O. (2007). Response of the riverine fish community to the construction and operation of a diversion hydropower plant in central Chile. *Aquatic Conservation* **17**, 37-49.

Hall, C.J., Jordaan, A. & Frisk, M.G. 2011. The historic influence if dams on diadromous fish habitat with a focus on river herring and hydrological longitudinal connectivity. *Landscape Ecology* **26**, 95-107.

Helfrich, L.A., Liston, C.R., Mefford, M. & Bark, R. (2001). Survival and injury of splittail and Chinook salmon passed through a large Hidrostal pump. *North American Journal of Fisheries Management* **21**, 616-623.

Holbrook, C.M., Zydlewski, J., Gorsky, D., Shepard, S.L. & Kinninson, M.T. (2009). Movements of prespawn adult Atlantic salmon near hydroelectric dams in the Lower Penobscot River, Maine. *North American Journal of Fisheries Management* **29**, 495-505.

Humphreys, J. (2005). Salinity and tides in Poole harbour: Estuary or lagoon? *In The Ecology of Poole Harbour. Proceedings of Marine Science*, Vol. 7 (Humphreys, J & May, V. *Eds.*), 195-203.

Jepsen, N., Pedersen, S. & Thorstad, E. (2000). Behavioural interactions between prey (troutsmolts) and predators (pike and pikeperch) in an impounded river. *Regulated Rivers: Research and Management* **16**, 189–198.

Kovach, W.L. (2011). *Oriana – Circular Statistics for Windows, ver. 4*. Kovach Computing Services, Pentreath, Wales, UK.

Larinier, M. (2008). Fish passage experience at small-scale hydro-electric power plants in France. *Hydrobiologia,* **609**, 97–108.

Lauridsen R., Moore, A., Gregory, S.D. Beaumont, W.R.C., Privitera, L. & Kavanagh, J.A. (2017). Migration behaviour and loss rate of smolts in the transitional zone between freshwater and saltwater. In*: Sea Trout: Management & Science, (*Graeme Harris. *Ed..). Proceedings of the 2nd International Sea Trout Symposium*. October 2015. Dundalk, Ireland.*[Inset pp at page-proof].*

Lucas, M.C., Bubb, D.H., Jang, M.H., Ha, K. & Masters, J.E.G. (2009) Availability of and access to critical habitats in regulated rivers: effects of low-head barriers on threatened lampreys. *Freshwater Biology* **54**, 621-634.

Lucas, M.C. & Frear, P.A. (1997) Effects of a flow-gauging weir on the migratory behaviour of adult barbel, a riverine, cyprinid. *Journal of Fish Biology* **50**, 382-396.

Marchetti, M.P. & Moyle, P.B. (2001) Effects of flow regime on fish assemblages in a regulated California stream. *Ecological Applications* **11,** 530-539.

McCormick, S.D., Hansen, L.P. Quinn, T.P. & Saunders, R.L. (1998). Movement, migration, and smolting of Atlantic salmon (*Salmo salar*). Canadian Journal of Fisheries and Aquatic Sciences 55 (Supplement 1), 77-92.

McNabb, C.D., Liston, C.R. & Borthwick, S.M. (2003). Passage of juvenile Chinook salmon and other fish species through Archimedes lifts and hidrostal pump at Red Bluff, California. *Transactions of the American Fisheries Society* **132,** 326-334.

Mont´en, E. (1985). Fisk och turbiner. Om fiskars m¨ojligheter att oskadda passera genem kraftverksturbiner. Stockholm: Vattenfall.

Moore, A. Russell, I.C. & Potter, E.C.E. (1990). The effects of intraperitoneally implanted dummy acoustic transmitters on the physiology and behaviour of Atlantic salmon parr. *Journal of Fish Biology* 37, 713-721.

Moore, A. & Potter, E.C.E. (1994) The movements of sea trout smolts through the estuary of the River Avon, Southern England. *Fisheries Management and Ecology* **1**, 1-14.

Moore, A., Potter, E.C.E., Milner, N.J. & Bamber, S. (1995). The migratory behaviour of wild Atlantic salmon smolts in the estuary of the River Conwy, North Wales. *Canadian Journal of Fisheries and Aquatic Sciences.* **52** (9), 1923-1935.

Moore, A., Stonehewer, R., Kell, L.T., Challiss, M.J., Ives, M. Russell, I.C. Riley, W.D. & Mee, D.M. (1996). The movements of emigrating salmonid smolts in relation to the Tawe barrage, Swansea. In: *Barrages: Engineering Design & Environmental Impacts.* (N. Burt & J. Watts eds.) HR Walingford Ltd. John Wiley & Sons Ltd., 409-417.

Moore, A., Ives, M., Scott, M. & Bamber, S. (1998a). The migratory behaviour of wild sea trout (*Salmo trutta* L.) smolts in the estuary of the River Conwy, North Wales. *Aquaculture* **168**, 57-68.

Moore, A., Ives, S., Mead, T.A. & Talks, L. (1998b). The migratory behaviour of wild Atlantic salmon (*Salmo salar L.*) smolts in the River Test and Southampton Water. *Hydrobiology* **371/372**, 295-304.

Moser, M.L., Ocker, P.A., Stuehrenburg, L.C. & Bj0rnn, T.C. (2002). Passage efficiency of adult Pacific lampreys at hydropower dams on the lower Columbia River, USA. *Transactions of the American Fisheries Society* **131**, 956-965.

Muir, W.D., Smith, S.G., Williams, J.G. & Sandford, B.P. 2001. Survival of juvenile salmonids passing through bypass systems, turbines, and spillways with and without flow detectors at Snake River dams. *North American Journal of Fisheries Management* **21**, 135-146.

Murchie, K.J., Hair, K.P.E., Pullen, C.E., Redpath, T.D., Stephens, H.R. & Cooke, S.J. (2008). Fish response to modified flow regimes in regulated rivers: Research methods, effects and opportunities. *River Research &Applications* **24**, 197-217.

Nislow, K. H., Hudy, M., Letcher, B. H. & Smith, E. P. (2011). Variation in local abundance and species richness of stream fishes in relation to dispersal barriers: implications for management and conservation. *Freshwater Biology 56,* 2135-2144.

Nunn, A.D., Copp, G.H., Vilizzi, L. & Carter, M.G. (2010). Seasonal and diel patterns in the migrations of fishes between a river and a floodplain tributary. *Ecology of Freshwater Fish* **19**, 153-162.

O'Connor, J.P., O'Mahony, J.M. & Glenane, T.J. (2006) Some impacts of low and medium head weirs on downstream fish movement in the Murray-Darling basin in southeastern Australia. *Ecology of Freshwater Fish* **15**, 419-427.

Paquet, P.J & Witmer, G.W. (1985). Cumulative impacts of small hydropower developments: an overview of the issues. In: Symposium on Small Hydropower and Fisheries. Denver, Colorado. 343-345.

Poulet, N. (2007) Impact of weirs on fish communities in a piedmont stream. *River Research & Applications* **23**, 1038-1047.

Robertson, M.J., Pennell, C.J., Scruton, D.A., Robertson, G.J. & Brown, J.A. (2004). Effect of increased flow on the behaviour of Atlantic salmon parr in winter. *Journal of Fish Biology* **65**, 1070-1079.

Ruggles, C. P. (1980). A review of the downstream migration of Atlantic salmon. *Canadian Technical Report on Fisheries and Aquatic Sciences* **952**, 1–39.

Russell, I.C., Moore, A., Ives, S., Kell, L.T., Ives, S. & Stonehewer, R.O. (1998). The migratory behaviour of juvenile and adult salmonids in relation to an estuarine barrage. *Hydrobiology.* **371/372**, 321-333.

Serrano, I., Rivinoja, P., Karlsson, L. & Larsson, S. (2009). Riverine and early marine survival of stocked salmon smolts, *Salmo salar* L., descending the Testebo River, Sweden. *Fisheries Management and Ecology* **16**, 386–394.

Solomon, D. J. (1978). Migration of smolts of Atlantic salmon (*Salmo salar* L.) and sea trout (*Salmo trutta* L.) in a chalkstream. *Environmental Biology of Fishes* **3**, 223-229.

Robson, A., Cowx, I.G. & Harvey, J.P. (2011). Impact of run-of-river hydro-schemes upon fish populations: Phase 1 Literature Review, SNIFFER Report WFD114, August 2011, 71pp.

Trussart, S., Messier, D., Roquet, V. & Aki, S. (2002) Hydropower projects: a review of most effective mitigation measures. *Energy Policy* **30**, 1251-1259.

Looking Ahead: Management Priorities for Sea Trout

K. WHELAN[1], G. HARRIS[2], N. MILNER[3], E. POTTER[4], I. LLEWELYN[1]
& C. GALLAGHER[5]

[1]Atlantic Salmon Trust, 11 Rutland Square, Edinburgh EH1 2AS, Scotland.
[2]Fishskill Ltd., Greenacre, Cathedine, Bwlch, Brecon, Powys LD3 7PZ, Wales.
[3]Apem Ltd., c/o Bangor University, School of Biological Sciences, Deiniol Road, Bangor, Gwynedd LL57 2UW, Wales.
[4]Cefas, Pakefield Road, Lowestoft, Suffolk NR33 OHT, England.
[5]Inland Fisheries Ireland, 3044 Lake Drive, Citywest Business Campus, Dublin 24, Ireland.

ABSTRACT

Progress in the science and management of sea trout since the 1st International Sea Trout Symposium in 2004 is reviewed in the context of subsequent developments. The contribution of recent workshops, collaborative investigations, advances in technology and emerging eco-political drivers for the sustainable management of the resource and its associated fisheries is discussed. Those major topic areas of strategic importance that are common to most sea trout producing countries in Europe are identified where future investigations are required to reduce uncertainties and improve management capability and efficacy. Strategic management priorities for future investigation in key topic areas are identified.

Keywords: Sea Trout; science; research; management; developments, key topics; future studies.

1. INTRODUCTION

The over-arching aim of the 1st International Sea Trout Symposium held in Cardiff in 2004 was to raise the profile of sea trout and to address a long history of neglect so that it was no longer overlooked or considered as only of secondary importance relative to its more prestigious and co-dwelling relative, the Atlantic salmon. The Symposium undoubtedly succeeded in advancing this objective across many areas of applied research; as evidenced by the 30 formal papers presented at this 2nd Symposium and by other related developments. There is now increased recognition of the role of sea trout in sustaining recreational and/or commercial fisheries against the background of declining salmon stocks, in the growing popularity of sea trout as a chosen target species and also as a model species for scientific study of evolutionary processes and environmental responses. However, there has been less progress in the direct management of sea trout stocks, and our increased understanding of sea trout biology and behaviour has yet to be fully integrated into the way sea trout stocks are managed at a local, national and international level.

This concluding chapter considers progress in addressing the principal recommendations of the 1st Symposium (Section 2). It outlines significant developments since the 1st Symposium (Section 3). It then identifies the main management issues, concerns and opportunities that have emerged over the intervening period and summarises our strategic management priorities for future investigations (Section 4). In doing so, we have not confined ourselves to only those developments that were considered at this 2nd Symposium and we have ranged more widely across several topic areas to ensure that other significant management needs and priorities are also identified for future action.

2. THE 1st INTERNATIONAL SEA TROUT SYMPOSIUM

The principal recommendations from the 1st Symposium in 2004 are listed below to provide a background perspective on subsequent developments and progress in sea trout science and management over the intervening period. A fuller account is given in Chapter 34 of the published 'Book of Proceedings' (Harris & Milner, 2006). They were:

1. To explore how genetic and environmental factors interact in determining the incidence of the sea-going migratory habit.
2. To develop an understanding of the stock-recruitment process in trout, including interactions with other species, particularly salmon, in a wide range of stream types.
3. To gain a better description and understanding of trout life tables, stock structures and life history strategies in different geographical regions and to determine the temporal stability in stock structure and composition.
4. To understand the genetic and ecological consequences of stocking on anadromy in trout and to develop and promote stocking practices that are protective of wild sea trout and are operationally effective.
5. To improve the relationships among habitat availability, quality and trout production and life histories, which needs to consider catchment scale connectivity of habitats, spawning distribution and population dispersal.
6. To develop BRP-based assessment and appropriate catchment management.
7. To refine estimates of the socio-economic value of sea trout and brown trout fisheries and consider their potential for sustainable development.

8. To investigate the distribution, movements and feeding migrations of post-smolts and adults in estuarine and coastal waters and to examine the influence of marine environmental factors on sea trout growth, maturation and survival in freshwater and the sea.

9. To understand better the effects of fishing on sea trout stocks, particularly the impacts of selective exploitation of the larger (mainly female) fish.

3. DEVELOPMENTS SINCE 2004

Several organisations have held meetings or other events to consider a range of different topics and issues relating directly or indirectly to various aspects of sea trout management in a particular local context. Since many of these specific local issues were also relevant in a broader generic context, they are included in the following summary of strategic developments and future management priorities.

3.1 EUROPEAN UNION PROJECTS

The 1st Symposium stimulated the development of three major trans-national projects relevant to sea trout management under the auspices of the EU Interreg Programme. They each entailed hitherto unprecedented levels of cross-border cooperation between different state agencies and other stakeholder interests and were: 1) the Celtic Sea Trout Project (2010 - 2013), 2) the Atlantic Aquatic Resource Conservation Project (2007–2013), and 3) the Living North Sea project (2009–2012).

Whereas the Celtic Sea Trout Project was essentially a science programme based solely on sea trout, setting it in the context of marine ecosystems and in seeking to engage with the wider fisheries community, the two other EU Interreg projects included both sea trout and other diadromous fish species and were more generally focussed on the practical and operational management of the fisheries resource in an integrated ecosystem context.

3.1.1 Celtic Sea Trout Project (CSTP)
The CSTP (http://celticseatrout.com/) focused on the many sea trout rivers bordering the Irish Sea and adjacent Celtic Sea within the separate fisheries jurisdictions of England, Wales, Scotland, Republic of Ireland and the Isle of Man. Its specific objectives were linked directly to the recommendations of the 1st Symposium. They were: 1) to map and describe the sea trout fisheries in rivers and coastal waters, examining opportunities for development, 2) to map the marine distribution of sea trout and describe genetic variation and stock structuring, 3) to describe the marine ecology (feeding, growth, survival) and life-table features, 4) to describe and model freshwater production based on river habitat, 5) to model life history variation and responses (catchment scale) and marine environmental variation, 6) to develop

and promote a network of awareness and activity in protecting sea trout fisheries and their conservation, and to develop and disseminate management advice based on improved understanding.

The project generated seven of the formal papers presented at this Symposium by Prodöhl *et al.* (2017); Milner *et al.* (2017); Harris & Evans (2017); Potter *et al.* (2017a & 2017b); Roche *et al.* (2017) and Evans & Harris (2017). CSTP (2016) provides a detailed technical report on all aspects of the project.

3.1.2 Atlantic Aquatic Resources Conservation Project (AARCP)

The AARCP included regions within England, Ireland, France, Spain and Portugal and involved studies of sea trout and other diadromous fish species in several of these areas and, *inter alia*, it produced a genetic map of sea trout populations in Southern England (http://aarcproject.org). The overall objective was to investigate sustainable, integrated, water resources management using anadromous fish species as an indicator of success and point of linkage between trans-boundary socio-economic issues and drivers.

Two papers from this project were presented at this symposium by Launey *et al.* (2017) and King *et al.* (2017).

3.1.3 Living North Sea Project (LNSP)

The LNSP included partners in France, Belgium Holland, Germany, Denmark, Norway, Sweden, Scotland and England. It considered sea trout with the aim of using Sustainable Coastal Zone Management tools for the principal diadromous species of the North Sea (http://www.living-north-sea.eu/about/). It also included a number of studies of sea trout stocks in the North Sea area, including investigations of migratory behaviour in estuaries, the effects of barriers and genetic stock identification.

3.2 ATLANTIC SALMON TRUST (AST)

The AST sponsored the first workshop dedicated specifically to sea trout, held in North Wales in 1984 (Le Cren, 1985) and co-sponsored the 1st Symposium some 20 years later. It convened a specialist Workshop in 2011 to review progress since the 1st Symposium and to provide further advice to research funders, scientists and managers. The workshop report (Atlantic Salmon Trust, 2011) recommended the development of programmes of research into factors that influence trout life history choices, in particular anadromy, together with the ways that climate change might affect them, and supported investigations into the utilisation of estuaries, small streams, intertidal and coastal habitats by sea trout at all life stages. It also highlighted the need to give greater attention to the significance of small streams in the production and recruitment of sea trout (*see* 4.7).

3.3 INTERNATIONAL COUNCIL FOR THE EXPLORATION OF THE SEA

The International Council for the Exploration of the Sea (ICES) has organised a number of expert group meetings on sea trout in the past (e.g. ICES, 1994; 1999) and convened the 'Workshop on Sea Trout' (WKTRUTTA) in 2012 to review and report on progress with research and investigations since the 1st Symposium. Topics considered included: 1) population genetics, 2) migratory routes, 3) anadromous/non-anadromous population interactions and 4) habitat preferences and life history understanding. It also identified remaining critical knowledge gaps for priority research on potential threats to sea trout populations: including the development of Biological Reference Points (BRPs), cumulative impact of migratory barriers, marine survival issues and climate change. The Workshop report (ICES, 2013) noted that sea trout research had increased significantly across several major topic areas since 2004, principally into genetics, the processes governing anadromy and in marine movements and ecology.

A second ICES Workshop on Sea Trout (WKTRUTTA2) took forward some of the recommendations from WKTRUTTA and incorporated the results of a Workshop on '*The Use of Sea Trout Population Models in Stock Assessment and Management*' that was held in conjunction with the 2nd Symposium (ICES, 2017). Its principal aim was to review different approaches for modelling sea trout populations, assessing the status of sea trout stocks and investigating the impacts of natural and anthropogenic factors. It was also specifically tasked to provide a review of current monitoring methods, initiate work to develop Biological Reference Points (BRPs) or alternative methods for assessing the status of sea trout populations and to recommend how this work could be progressed (see 4.5). This work will be taken forward by a special Working Group now scheduled to report in 2019.

3.4 THE 2nd SEA TROUT SYMPOSIUM

This 2nd Symposium was intended to maintain the momentum in sea trout science and management generated by the 1st Symposium. Its main aims were: to promote the wider application of an evidence-based approach to the future management and exploitation of sea trout in ways that are sustainable in response to modern threats and pressures, to identify those existing and new gaps in our knowledge that limited our management ability, to identify those topic areas where the existing knowledge base was sufficient to undertake appropriate management action and to promote closer working links between fishery scientists and managers. Particular emphasis was given to the major topic areas previously identified as management priorities at the 1st Symposium of genetic stock identification, marine movements and ecology and stock assessment and monitoring.

4. PRIORITY TOPICS FOR FUTURE MANAGEMENT & RESEARCH

This section outlines the key management and research priorities to be addressed within the next decade. Initially based on progress since the 1st Symposium in 2004, its scope and focus is extended to give wider coverage to the research gaps and management challenges faced by sea trout populations in both the freshwater and the marine environments.

It should be noted that any future investigations into the marine environment on the scale and duration required to fill critical gaps in our current knowledge would be expensive to undertake in terms of the combined costs of equipment, routine maintenance, data analysis and staffing. There is, therefore, a clear need for much closer liaison between scientific disciplines, agencies and regulators as co-operating partners in the selection of sites and methods most likely to generate the maximum amount of information from any single study. They should take account of the lessons learned from previous work and the need to gather essential site-specific information on the environmental factors required to interpret the results from future marine and freshwater investigations.

4.1 LIFE HISTORY VARIATION

An understanding of life history variation and life history strategies is fundamental to managing sea trout. The interplay between the stocks of migratory fish and residents in any given water, and how the relative abundance of the two forms of trout is regulated by genetics and environment, is at the very core of the challenges facing those tasked with managing sea trout populations.

Life histories of sea trout are the population-specific outcomes of anadromy, growth, maturation and reproduction. Through their simple metrics of abundance, size and age structures, they convey also the basic nature of the stocks and fisheries of primary concern to managers and stakeholders. In these abbreviated forms, sea trout life histories are reported routinely in statistics from most countries: albeit with highly contrasting levels of rigour (*see* 4.6). If managers wish to know how sea trout fisheries might respond to environmental or fishing pressures, it is essential to describe and understand trout life histories. This basic tenet of fisheries science still struggles for recognition in sea trout research and management. If generally accepted, it would influence stock assessment and monitoring practices far more than at present.

Recent years have seen life history characterisation begin to improve, and it was one of the 1st Sea Trout Symposium's recommendations (see Elliott and Elliott, 2006; Jonsson & Jonsson, 2006). Further advances have been made since then (Cucherousset *et al.*, 2010; Tysklind *et al.*, 2015; Milner *et al.*, 2017) or are now in hand (see ICES 2013; ICES, 2017). The three priority issues in this respect that have emerged since this over-arching topic was discussed at the 1st Symposium are:

1. *How to model sea trout populations.*

   The various forms of life history models, from conventional life tables through matrix age/stage based models to individual based models, were reviewed by ICES (2013, 2017). A key application of such models lies in the development of biological reference points (BRPs). To be most useful, they need to refer to populations in the strict sense of reproductive units experiencing broadly common environmental pressures. This is generally impracticable and, in practice, most assessments refer at best to whole river catchments, often comprising multiple populations. It raises the problem of sampling design to minimise the potential masking effect of many populations. The degree to which this is important is currently unknown because the required intensive studies have not yet been carried out: although some basic understanding of the potential complexity of this variation is available (e.g. Cucherousset *et al.*, 2010). The description and understanding of life history variation between rivers and regions is a demanding research requirement.

2. *How to describe better sea trout "population" life histories.*

   Problems of data coherence across regions and countries resulting from the variation in intensity and detail of sea trout monitoring are considered later in this chapter (*see* 4.5 & 4.6) and we consider here the importance of the methods for describing age-specific and stage-specific structures. Index rivers are generally monitored in sufficient detail, but this is not so for the majority of rivers - particularly the smaller rivers dominated by sea trout rather than salmon. Size data from catch records can provide valuable data on stock composition and spatial and temporal variation in life histories (Tysklind *et al.*, 2015; CSTP, 2016; Milner et al., 2017). Full life history analyses of age structures are required, and this entails scale reading, at least on a subset of representative rivers (*see* 4.6.2).

3. *How to interpret life history analysis for management.*

   Life history models can appear highly complex and this, along with their extensive data demands, may explain why their formal use is limited in much freshwater fisheries assessment and decision-making. To encourage their wider use, we recommend that case studies are undertaken to demonstrate the benefits of such an approach, particularly as it applies to assessing harvest /conservation strategies and their impacts on overall egg deposition and the subsequent relative abundance of the migratory component of the stock. For example, the management application of growth studies relates to the role that growth or energetics might play in the onset of anadromy or maturation (time and size of adult returners), and how changing size affects reproductive behaviour and timing. A proper understanding of the potential of life history modelling and its limitations could provide a guiding principle for future stock assessment, monitoring and management. Some issues, such as climate change, will exert their effect through life history adjustments and present major challenges; but the life history approach will at least offer a framework to assemble explanations and interpretations of the available data, and over time, to assess the likely consequences of environmental changes in the hydrology of catchment and the temperature/flow regimes.

The all-embracing nature of '*Life Histories*' can appear too broad to be manageable unless it is carefully partitioned. Nevertheless, it represents an overarching strategic approach and, with appropriate modelling, provides a unifying analytical framework for the many study topics that fall within its scope.

Management Priority.

➤ Commission separate case studies to demonstrate the management benefits of sea trout life history investigations, particularly their applications for assessing harvesting and conservation strategies and their impacts on overall egg deposition and the subsequent relative abundance of the anadromous and resident components of the stock.

4.2 UNDERSTANDING ANADROMY

Anadromy is just one of a continuum of different life history strategies that *S. trutta* L. can adopt. Nevertheless, '*going to sea*' is the defining characteristic of sea trout, and improving our understanding of it is likely to remain a focus of sea trout research. From the latest review of the available information presented at the 2nd Symposium (Ferguson *et al.*, 2017), it is evident that our understanding of the reason why some juvenile brown trout migrate to sea (to become sea trout) and why others may remain in freshwater for their entire life history (as resident trout) has progressed a long way since this key topic was considered at the 1st Symposium (Ferguson et al., 2006). However, our understanding of the link between genetics and the environment in controlling and then modifying the expression of facultative anadromy or freshwater residency in *S. trutta*, and the wide variability in the life histories strategies of sea trout from different geographical regions and river types, requires continued investigation (*see* 4.1).

Management Priority.

➤ Implement a series of structured investigations to improve our understanding of the link between genetics and the environment in controlling and modifying the expression of facultative anadromy or freshwater residency in *S. trutta* and the wide variability in the expression of life histories strategies of sea trout from different geographical regions and river types.

4.3 GENETIC STUDIES

The development and wider application of techniques for identifying genetic differences in populations of *S trutta* has now established and clarified differences within and between stocks in different geographical regions and rivers in several parts of Europe: notably the Irish

Sea (Prodöhl *et al.*, 2017), Southern England (King *et al.*, 2016 & 2017), the English Channel (Quéméré *et al.*, 2016; Launey *et al.*, 2017), the Rhine and Meuse Delta (Ensing *et al.*, 2017), Norway (Hogvaard *et al.*, 2006) and various parts of the Baltic Sea (ICES, 2013).

The Irish Sea study (CSTP, 2016; Prodöhl, *et al.*, 2017) was the largest and most comprehensive Genetic Stock Identification (GSI) study on *S. trutta* undertaken for any discrete geographical region to date. A genetic baseline based on juvenile trout samples from 100 different rivers bordering the Irish Sea established the existence of nine major, genetically distinct, phylogeographic groups of sea trout.

Although genetic studies now provide a clearer picture of differences in stock structures in several regions, our knowledge of the nature and extent of genetic diversity in sea trout stocks throughout much of Europe remains incomplete. ICES (2013) suggested that the long-term management objective should be the step-wise compilation of a map of the genetic profile of all known European sea trout rivers, including those regions not studied to date. However, this will not be a quick and simple task because of the very large (but still unknown) number of rivers entailed and the considerable resources required to collect and then analyse the baseline juvenile trout samples.

Management Priorities.
  ➤ Improve and strengthen existing regional databases by incorporating juvenile trout samples from those rivers not included in original sampling programmes: principally the minor sea trout rivers and small coastal streams.
  ➤ Review existing methodologies and protocols for obtaining juvenile trout samples to ensure that they are representative of the river stock.
  ➤ Assess the accuracy of each database by validating the reliability of assignments against samples of smolts and/or kelts obtained from within the same catchment.
  ➤ Investigate the practicalities of merging existing genetic databases.
  ➤ Collaborate in the creation of a common database and map of the genetic profile of all known sea trout rivers in Europe as an ultimate objective.

4.4 MIXED STOCK FISHERIES

A topic that has received little attention to date is the occurrence and impact of mixed stock fisheries where sea trout are exploited as a by-catch with other diadromous or marine fish species (*see* 4.8). In the latter context, this may be a significant (but unquantified) concern in regions where sea trout feed mainly in coastal and near-shore waters (*see* 4.8.1.) and in those regions where the resumption of commercial netting remains a potential threat.

Tagging studies over the last 150 years have indicated the widespread mixing of sea trout stocks in coastal waters and estuaries (Potter *et al.*, 2017; Aldvén & Davidsen, 2017). This is now well established by the use of Genetic Stock Identification techniques (*see* 4.2). Microchemistry and isotopic analyses also offer methods of stock identification, although this approach is less reliable than genetics techniques because of the masking effects of background geochemistry (Veinott *et al.*, 2012; CSTP, 2016; Briers *et al.*, 2017).

The Celtic Sea Trout Project (CSTP, 2016) included an extensive investigation of migratory behaviour and stock mixing covering the well-defined and discrete geographical region of the Irish Sea. It provided a genetic baseline for 100 rivers bordering the Irish Sea and over 1,000 adult fish caught in offshore and coastal waters were assigned back to their local regions of origin. This confirmed that sea trout derived from rivers within the national jurisdiction of six national administrations overlapped and ranged throughout the entire region, although the majority of any given stock tended to remain local to their natal river.

A parallel investigation in Southwest England (King *et al.*, 2016; 2017) identified the occurrence of a commercial net fishery based on mixed stocks of sea trout (and salmon) from three rivers sharing a common estuary. It also identified a mixed stock rod fishery in the lower freshwater sections of two of those rivers, where a significant proportion of the annual rod catch consisted of straying by temporary residents (*'vagrants'*) from other neighbouring rivers. However, these vagrants were thought not to spawn in their non-natal rivers. Chat *et al.* (2017) also reported a high incidence of non-spawning vagrancy in France, and Ensing & Breukelaar (2017) allude to a similar phenomenon in the Rhine.

The adoption of international agreements and related national policies to control exploitation of mixed stocks of salmon during their marine feeding and return migrations to spawn in their natal rivers throughout the North Atlantic (NASCO, 2009 & 2014) resulted in the introduction of various regulatory measures to close many interceptory and known mixed stock fisheries and to manage most others to protect the weakest of the contributing salmon stocks. The overall management objective should be to provide sea trout with the same degree of regulatory protection now afforded to salmon during their marine phase and then to extend that protection to include coastal feeding sea trout (*see* 4.8.1).

Management Priorities.

➢ Investigate the occurrence of mixed stocks of sea trout and mixed-stock sea trout fisheries in coastal, estuarine and fresh waters and assess their potential impact on the management of single stock fisheries.

➢ Particular attention should be given to determining the rivers of origin of coastal feeding sea trout and their possible exploitation as a by-catch in fisheries for marine fish species.

4.5 STOCK ASSESSMENT & MONITORING

The second ICES Workshop on Sea Trout (WKTRUTTA2) reviewed progress in developing and applying population models for the assessment and management of sea trout stocks. It highlighted the lack of information on a large proportion of the yet unknown number of European sea trout stocks (possibly in excess of 2,000) and initiated the development of a definitive database of available information, including estimates of the relative abundance of sea trout and salmon in each river. It reported that sea trout are not considered to be of any significant importance and value when compared with co-dwelling Atlantic salmon in many European countries. Consequently, core data on catch and fishing effort varied in both coverage and quality between regions, and although juvenile monitoring took place in all countries, the sampling programmes were often not well structured or consistent over time. The group also compiled information on 34 *Index River* stocks. Although these stocks were more intensively monitored, only a few provide sufficient data for the development of detailed population models.

Different approaches for modelling sea trout populations and developing BRPs were considered in detail, and the Workshop discussed whether models of sea trout populations needed to take account of the contribution of resident fish. Because much of the variability in migratory life-history strategies may be related to environmental conditions, it was likely that the contribution of resident fish to future recruitment could change over time. It concluded, ideally, that stock-recruitment models for sea trout should attempt to include the resident population where anadromy occurs. Nevertheless, this may be difficult due to lack of data. Additionally, several studies have shown that resident fish make only a small contribution to egg deposition in many rivers (CSTP, 2016; Kennedy *et al.*, 2017). For these stocks, research to date therefore suggested that it was reasonable to develop population models based solely on their migratory component.

The Workshop considered a number of approaches for modelling sea trout populations and reviewed the stock-recruitment (SR) relationships established for the few extensively monitored Index Rivers. While these relationships provided the best method for establishing BRPs similar to those used for salmon, it concluded that they were unlikely to provide an adequate and reliable basis for transferring BRPs to the very many other sea trout stocks because of the greater complexity and variability in trout life history strategies. Consequently, two alternative approaches for establishing transportable BRPs that seemed to show the greatest potential for widespread application were identified (ICES, 2017). The first used catch data to develop *pseudo-stock-recruitment relationships*; and thereby establish BRPs in the conventional way (Davidson *et al.*, 2017a). The second was based on the '*Trout Habitat Score*' developed for Baltic sea trout stocks (Höjesjö *et al.*, 2017). This used historic electrofishing data on juvenile trout densities to establish a relationship between the habitat quality, defined by a small number of physical characteristics, and the expected pristine juvenile abundance. A special ICES Working Group was established to investigate and develop these approaches in detail. It is scheduled to report in 2019.

There are relatively few rivers subject to routine in-depth monitoring using fixed traps and electronic counting stations. In the absence of robust data on run-strength, run-timing and stock structure for the majority of rivers in most regions, and the likelihood that the development of transportable BRPs for sea trout will have only limited management application, some alternative means of assessing the status and well-being of individual sea trout stocks will be required for routine management purposes for the majority of European rivers (*see* 4.6).

Management priorities.

> ➢ Continue the current work on Index River monitoring, stock recruitment modelling and the development of river specific Biological Reference Points (BRPs).
> ➢ Extend routine Index River monitoring programmes to include a representative sub-sample of the many smaller catchments that are more typical of the majority of sea trout rivers in most regions.
> ➢ Further develop and assess methodologies for establishing transportable BRPs or alternative indicators of stock status for individual rivers.
> ➢ Investigate the nature and extent of straying into freshwater by sea trout from other rivers and assess its potential impact on the reliability of stock assessments based on fish traps, counters and angler catch records.

4.6 MANAGEMENT STATISTICS

An understanding of life history variation and life history strategies is fundamental to managing sea trout populations (*see* 4.1). This is dependent on the collection of fishery statistics relating to stock abundance, fish size, age structures, catch and harvest of the individual populations.

4.6.1 Catch Records

Catch statistics represent the most basic information required for the management of sea trout stocks and their associated fisheries. ICES (2013; 2017) noted the marked differences in the requirements for collecting catch data for sea trout in European countries. A special Workshop on '*Sea Trout Rod Catch and Effort Data*' reviewed current approaches for the collection of catch and effort statistics from recreational fisheries for sea trout in UK and Ireland (AST, 2015). Both observed that the quality of data on sea trout fisheries was very variable and that, catch returns are not required at all in some countries.

One notable exception to this general data limitation applies in England & Wales. Evans & Harris (2017) describe the long history of mandatory catch records for the recreational rod fishery that currently provides a unique 21-year time-series of reasonably robust and highly detailed record of annual rod catches that is broadly consistent and comparable for each of the 80 principal salmon and sea trout rivers in the region. In addition to the total annual catch, it also provides important information relevant to life history modelling and stock assessment (Milner *et al.*, 2017) and a wide range of different management needs. Davidson *et al.* (2017a) described how, in the continued absence of sea trout BRPs, these catch and effort data were used to develop a '*Sea Trout Fishery Performance Index*' based on the trend of increase or decrease in angler catch-per unit effort as one readily available means in England & Wales of using rod fishery performance to gauge stock status.

Rod catch data serves two principal related purposes, firstly as a measure of fishery performance and secondly as indices of in-season run strength which, subject to certain qualifications, can be equated with stock size. They can also provide information on stock structure and run-timing and can be used to obtain scale samples from anglers for ageing, subsequent GSI studies and as important inputs for population models to support management (ICES, 2017). Since the current data collection process, and the legislative framework that supports it, varies significantly between the various jurisdictions, it was concluded (Atlantic Salmon Trust, 2015) that no single system for improving catch and effort data was currently feasible in all regions. Accordingly, it recommended the development of appropriate systems in each jurisdiction that take account of local conditions and factors.

Management Priorities.
- ➢ Establish a working group to investigate the future feasibility of obtaining robust, consistent and comparable records of annual catch and fishing effort from all fisheries, both marine and fresh water, and to provide guidance on 'best practice' in generating a robust time series of annual catch statistics that include data on fishing effort.
- ➢ Obtain more comprehensive and reliable data on sea trout catches and fishing effort by different types of fishing in those regions where they are currently lacking or deficient.

4.6.2 Stock Structure & Composition

Scale reading and morphometric analysis is a valuable method for describing stock age structures, migratory behaviours and reproductive schedules. However, it is difficult to achieve consistency of scale interpretation across readers and regions (Solomon, 1995; Harris, 2002; CSTP, 2016; ICES, 2017). If scale reading is to become a routine part of stock assessment, it should be managed through training, method development and quality control. The complementary use of techniques such as image analysis, microchemistry, stable isotope analysis, coupled with marked-and-recaptured fish of known ages, would greatly improve interpretation. In several countries, issues of fish welfare and the licensing of procedures will need to be considered within the broader strategy for monitoring and assessment.

There are useful historical accounts of how to interpret sea trout scales by Nall (1930) and Went (1962) and recent manuals (Elliott & Chambers, 1996; CSTP, 2016) have attempted to standardise interpretation and nomenclature for the British Isles. A feature of sea trout is the spatial variation in scale characteristics for the same life stage, possibly reflecting local environments, geographies and life histories. Therefore, to complement proposals for common stock assessment, it would be useful to develop sea trout scale reading guidelines to cover a wider geographical range of river and marine habitats: such as those developed for salmon (ICES, 2011).

Management priorities.

➢ Undertake a critical review of historic scale reading investigations in each sea trout producing region of Europe in a similar form to the earlier review for England & Wales.

➢ Initiate a structured programme of scale reading investigations on a representative number of rivers of different types, in each region, to provide a contemporary description and benchmark reference on the structure and composition of sea trout stocks.

➢ Consider the adoption of a representative sub-sample of regional Index Rivers where scale reading investigations are undertaken annually to monitor temporal changes in stock structure and the effects of climate change on age structure, growth and life history expression.

➢ Produce a pan-European *Sea Trout Scale Reading Guidance Manual* to improve consistency and accuracy in the interpretation of age and life history of sea trout by workers in different regions.

➢ Investigate complementary techniques to improve the accuracy of scale reading by using microchemistry, stable isotope analysis and comparisons with fish of known age and life history from mark-recapture studies.

4.7 IMPORTANCE OF SMALL STREAMS

The importance of safeguarding the aquatic environment and the availability, distribution and quality of suitable trout spawning and nursery habitat in small streams and in the minor tributaries of larger rivers generally favoured by sea trout was a key recommendation from the 1st Symposium. This has since received more detailed consideration in the British Isles at a Workshop under the heading '*Small Streams: Contribution to populations of trout and sea trout*' (IBIS. 2012).

The need to achieve compliance with the requirements of the EU Water Framework Directive (WFD) since its introduction in 2000 triggered a major investment by individual Member States to address a long history of environment degradation to freshwater ecosystems. This included: a) the removal or easement of physical barriers to upstream migration, b) improvements in water quality, c) physical improvements to spawning nursery areas, d) protection and reinstatement of the riparian corridor and bank-side cover, e) better regulation of land management practices and f) greater control over water abstractions and inter-catchment water transfers. Nevertheless, many of the first and second order tributaries and small coastal streams are often not included by respective Governments under the WFD as '*significant water bodies*' and, although in part assessed by the various authorities in European countries, they fall outside the regulatory and reporting provisions and so they remain vulnerable to adverse environmental impacts. These streams account for two-thirds to three-quarters of the total length of waterways in the Europe and they are often located in remote locations where routine monitoring is, at best, uncommon. It was suggested (IBIS, 2012) that fuller use of the UK-Environmental Observation Directive to encourage 'Citizen Science' projects to study the environment (http://www.ukeof.org.uk/) could be used to promote the effective use of volunteers from local communities to undertake routine inspection and monitoring surveys of small tributary streams to supplement the limited coverage provided by the statutory agencies. The Atlantic Salmon Trust recently pioneered a scheme within the UK and Ireland to recruit and train volunteers in characterising and monitoring small streams, both in the upper reaches of rivers and in coastal areas (http://www. atlanticsalmontrust.org/small-streams-course/).

Issues relevant to sea trout and brown trout conservation in the catchments of small coastal streams (in contrast to minor tributary sub-catchments of larger rivers) were considered by Whelan (2014). It was noted that these streams contributed to the range of genetic diversity in sea trout by supporting populations that may be specially adapted to their often extreme freshwater environments. Their small catchment areas may also make them particularly vulnerable to long-term damage from climate change impacts, changes in land-use and short-term, episodic events (floods, droughts and pollution). It was noted that although their individual contribution to the production of adult fish may be low, their collective contribution to mixed stocks of sea trout in the sea may be significant (CSTP, 2016) and they may be important to some regions in supporting recreational and commercial fisheries in coastal waters. Research on salmonids in small coastal streams is more advanced in the Baltic and in North America: where work has been ongoing for many years (Landergren, 1998; 2001, and Quinn *et al.*, 2006).

The need to bring together experts from a wide range of disciplines to address the general deterioration of Small Water Bodies (SWBs) was one of the drivers behind the organisation of the *'Expert Workshop on Small Water Courses'* by Cefas in 2014, with the aim of bringing together specialists with a wide range of knowledge and experience relating to small water courses to discuss their function and management. This initiative then led to the formation of the *'Expert Group on Small Water Bodies'* which was tasked to: 1) develop and maintain a network of scientific experts on small water bodies, 2) provide a forum on SWBs among experts, stakeholders and other interest groups, 3) to discuss emerging issues on SWBs and consider possible responses, 4) to review ongoing research on SWBs, 5) to identify gaps, improve coordination and collaborate in the development of new proposals, and 6) to advise funding agencies on research needs. Building on the work of Biggs *et al.* (2016), this group is compiling a major report on SWBs in the UK and Ireland which will review ecological functioning, anthropogenic degradation and options for restorative action.

Management Priorities.
  ➢ Determine the importance of small tributary streams to sea trout production in Index River catchments.
  ➢ Incorporate small stream surveys into routine stock assessment programmes in all monitored catchments.

> ➤ Progress the development and extension to other areas of routine monitoring programmes utilising volunteers from within local communities to inspect the status of minor tributaries and small coastal streams as a pragmatic and cost effective means of reporting damaged and vulnerable spawning and nursery areas and prioritising those healthy streams in need of continuing surveillance.

4.8 THE MARINE PHASE

Our understanding of many aspects of the migratory behaviour and ecology of sea trout during their marine feeding phase has increased significantly in recent years to the extent that this critical phase in the life history of sea trout can no longer be described a 'black-hole' of knowledge (Harris & Milner, 2006; Launey *et al.*, 2017; Milner *et al.*, 2017). Recent advances in hydro-acoustic telemetry, microchemistry and techniques of Genetic Stock Identification (GSI) of adult fish caught at sea have helped to fill the many gaps in our knowledge and indicated the future direction for more structured regional and transnational studies directly linked to specific management questions.

4.8.1 Movement & Migration

The reviews of historical data on conventional tagging (mark-recapture) and other studies (Potter *et al.*, 2017a); Aldvén & Davidsen, 2017), combined with the growing body of information on GSI studies from other regions (*see* 4.3), have established that sea trout from different regions often exhibit quite different migratory behaviour during the marine phases of their life cycle. The comprehensive review by Potter *et al.* (2017) of some 60 disparate tagging studies from 50 rivers and coastal locations over the last 150 years in Great Britain provides a clearer perspective on the range of variability in migratory behaviour between geographical regions. Three general patterns of behaviour were identified as: 1) smolts in the fjordic loch systems in the west and northwest of Scotland remaining predominantly in the sea lochs and nearby river systems, 2) fish from the Scottish East coast to the north of the Forth and most regions of England & Wales (other than from the northeast of England) spreading out from their natal river and undertaking fairly short migrations, usually of <150 km, and often entering other neighbouring rivers, and 3) fish from the Tweed and rivers on the northeast coast of England making directed long distance migrations into the southern North Sea.

Aldvén & Davidsen, (2017) similarly noted that, while some adult sea trout from rivers entering the Baltic may make long-distance migrations of >1,000 km, the feeding movements of post-smolt sea trout are predominantly restricted to more local coastal areas and they may also enter the estuaries and freshwater sections of other rivers to feed and/or overwinter. Clearly, parallel reviews of historical tagging studies from other geographical regions would help complete a broader picture and indicate the need for further investigations.

Differences in the observed migratory behaviour of geographical stocks may reflect inherent differences in their genetic stock structure linked to their evolutionary origins and selection pressures in their local marine and freshwater environments. Anthropogenic pressures, including selective exploitation by various fisheries while at sea, may also affect the nature of these differences.

The coastal feeding habit of adult sea trout in all areas studied to date poses a range of important management questions that require further investigation. They include:

- What proportion of sea trout from any one river adopt a coastal feeding habit?
- Do coastal feeding sea trout remain in the general vicinity of their rivers of origin, or do they range more extensively along the coastline?
- Do coastal feeding sea trout from neighbouring rivers within a region overlap to form mixed stock aggregations of feeding fish?
- To what extent is the pattern of migratory behaviour influenced by genetic differences between stocks and then by environmental factors such as seascape, tidal transport, sea temperature and the spatial and temporal availability of prey species?
- Do recovering kelts exhibit the same pattern of feeding movements and behaviour in the sea as post-smolts?
- Are coastal feeding sea trout more likely to return to fresh water to spawn as 0SW fish than other older post-smolts?
- What is the influence of sea temperature and growth rate in determining the onset of sexual maturity and the time of first return to freshwater of maiden fish?

Any future investigations into the marine movements and migrations of sea trout on the scale and duration required to fill critical gaps in our current knowledge will be expensive to undertake and sustain because of the costs of capital equipment, routine maintenance, data analysis and staffing. There is, therefore, a clear need to select sites that are most likely to generate the maximum amount of information from any one study and to take into account the lessons learned from previous work on the best use of available technology and the site-specific information on environmental factors required to interpret the results. Careful consideration and planning should be given to promoting joint projects entailing cross-border co-operation and a shared responsibility for the costs of major, long-term projects. Whenever possible, future tracking studies should include both salmon and sea trout, and objectives regarding both species should be included in the original programme design.

Management Priorities.

➤ Critically review the results from past tracking studies on the movements and migrations of sea trout in different geographical regions to identify key knowledge gaps and so further the development of a coordinated and structured programme of investigations into the coastal feeding movements of sea trout in different regions and different types of coastal seascape based on past experience and available new technologies.

571

> ➢ Obtain more detailed local information on the marine movements and distribution of coastal feeding sea trout from a range of different river types in regions where such information is currently limited or lacking and make optimum use of those catchments already equipped with the necessary infrastructure.
> ➢ Recognise the importance of cross-border cooperation in tracking sea trout movements between different management jurisdictions.

4.8.2 Ecology & Feeding

Baseline knowledge of the feeding behaviour and distribution of post-smolt sea trout is fundamental to our understanding of how they utilise their marine environment. It contributes to our understanding of how to identify the location of important feeding habits likely to influence migration routes, along with those environmental conditions suitable for growth and the onset of sexual maturity and, therefore, the pattern and timing of adult return to freshwater.

Roche *et al.* (2017) reported the findings of an extensive investigation into the marine diet and feeding behaviour and behaviour of sea trout in the Irish Sea that supplemented the limited information from other regions. An examination of the stomach contents and diet of 991 fish from both coastal and offshore waters established that the principal prey consisted of sand eels (*Ammodytes* spp.) followed by sprat (*Sprattus sprattus*). They noted that our knowledge of the marine ecology and distribution of sea trout would benefit from more systematic and spatially extensive investigations of prey availability, marine habitats and the nature and extent of linkages in the sea trout food web. This would advance our understanding of their response to wider ecosystem and climate change impacts and provide an evidence base for the integrated management and regulation of the marine environment to benefit both marine feeding sea trout and their prey species within the provisions of the European Marine Strategic Framework Directive.

Management Priorities.
> ➢ Identify and classify those seascape and related habitat features providing significant feeding opportunities for post-smolt sea trout and kelts.
> ➢ Investigate the seasonal feeding behaviour and distribution of fish of different sea-age groups and sizes and the influence of sea temperature and marine currents on the distribution of feeding fish and their prey species.
> ➢ Investigate the ecology, habitat preferences and factors affecting the abundance, survival and distribution of the individual major prey species.

4.9 THE IMPORTANCE OF ESTUARIES

The need for a better understanding and overall perspective about the importance of estuaries was identified as an emerging theme and priority topic area (Atlantic Salmon Trust, 2011). The estuary transition zone is widely recognised as a potentially hazardous period in the life-cycle of sea trout and salmon that may represent a critical bottleneck affecting the survival of smolts and their subsequent return as adults (Levings, 2016).

The characteristics of rivers estuaries can vary widely. Different permutations of key features may apply to any given location in relation to their length, width, depth, slope, salinity, tidal range and intrusion, topography, biotope and freshwater input. Most studies to date have focussed on the movement of salmon and sea trout smolts in rocky, deep fjordic estuary inlets. By comparison, similar studies on other types of estuary, such as the large sandy estuaries more common along the open, low-lying coastline in many other parts of Europe, have been neglected (Aldvén & Davidsen, 2017; Middlemas *et al.*, 2017). In some locations, estuaries may represent important foraging areas for adult fish (Orell *et al.*, 2017) and in others they may be important in providing overwintering refuge areas under extreme conditions (Degerman *et al.*, 2012; Sturlauggson, 2017).

A better understanding is required about the importance of the estuary transition zone in the successful two-way passage of sea trout between freshwater and marine environments and how spatial and temporal differences in environmental conditions in estuaries with different physical characteristics influence the patterns of smolt movement and survival. This should also include consideration of the physiological status of individual smolts (Aldvén *et al.*, 2017).

Whenever possible, subsequent investigations on fish passage and survival through estuaries should extend outside the headland to link with investigations into adjacent coastal movements.

Management priorities.

➢ Critically review the results of previous studies on the estuarine movements and survival of smolts to inform future studies by identifying the significant gaps in our knowledge about different estuary types, the influence of local conditions on observed behaviours and the technologies now available to support future studies.

➢ Investigate the passage of smolts through those open, shallow and non-fjordic types of estuary common to many regions and incorporate detailed information on their physical characteristics and the physiological status of the smolts when interpreting the findings.

4.10 MARINE RENEWABLES

The generation of electrical power in Europe from renewable sources has traditionally concentrated on in-river hydroelectric power schemes, but the focus has more recently shifted to the use of land-based and offshore wind farms. In high tidal energy regions, such as parts of the UK and Ireland, there is also an increased exploration of the construction of estuary barrages, coastal lagoons and tidal stream turbines. There is also longer-term research on the use of open ocean wave energy as source of electrical power (http://www.seai.ie/Renewables/Ocean_Energy_OLD/Galway_Bay_Test_Site/).

573

The proposed development of the Swansea Bay Tidal Lagoon Power Project (Turnpenny *et al.*, 2017) is the precursor to a number of similar proposals around the coastline of Wales and Northwest England at locations where there are extensive and important sea trout and salmon fisheries. Perhaps more than anything else, this pioneer project has highlighted the urgent need for robust and reliable information about the migratory behaviour and coastal feeding residence periods of sea trout in the vicinity of each scheme. This potential new threat also raises novel questions about how river specific odour trails orientate fish to their natal streams, the swimming speed and avoidance behaviour of different sizes of fish in the vicinity of the turbines, and the likelihood of fish becoming entrapped within the lagoons, along with a range of other issues about the potential local impact of each scheme on stocks sea trout and other diadromous and marine fish species. The impact assessment requires understanding of coastal ecology, behaviour and robust life history based population models, which are still lacking for sea trout, to translate the proximate impacts into population and stock responses. Consideration of these and other unknowns need to be incorporated into the mandatory Environmental Impact Assessment (EIA) as an essential pre-requisite for obtaining a construction licence from the statutory regulator. There is currently very limited information to assess the potential impact of each scheme on local stocks resulting in great uncertainty in the outcomes. It is clear that, more generally within Europe, we need to assess how the revision of the EU Review of the Environmental Impact Assessment Directive can be put to best use in protecting migratory fish populations (http://ec.europa. eu/environment/eia/review.htm). Such studies are costly and they currently fall between regulators, governments and developers without being adequately coordinated or funded by any one interest group. This is a significant constraint on progress and a strategic national approach is warranted.

Management Priorities.

- ➢ Acknowledge the important differences in the patterns of life history expression, marine migrations, distribution and feeding behaviour of sea trout in different geographical regions and the potential risks of transporting information between regions for use in Environmental Impact Assessments.
- ➢ Obtain a deeper understanding of the generic factors, both intrinsic and extrinsic, likely to influence the impact of each scheme on local stocks of sea trout and their prey species.
- ➢ Make proposals for strategic funding at a national level for coordinated research into marine energy schemes and for the adoption of effective monitoring programmes before, during and after their construction.

4.11 AQUACULTURE IMPACTS

Data were presented at the 1st Sea Trout Symposium showing the impact of intense infestation with sea lice from salmon farms on the survival rates of sea trout in Ireland (Gargan *et al.*, 2006). At the 2nd Symposium, Gargan *et al.* (2017) provided an updated assessment of the increased mortality risk and population regulating effect of sea lice (*Lepeophtheirus salmonis*) from marine salmon farms on wild sea trout in Ireland and Scotland and compared their results with data from Norway. The development of salmon aquaculture in all three countries coincided with observations of the premature return of sea trout to freshwater with heavy lice infestation, a marked reduction in sea trout rod catches and changes in sea trout population structure.

Gargan *et al.* (2017) describe a significant statistical relationship between lice infestation on sea trout and distance to the nearest salmon farm and a similar relationship for lice infestation and distance to salmon farms from Scotland and Norway. Research to date has shown that the zone of impact from sea lice, emanating from salmon farms, is within 30km and that sea trout are unaffected by the direct lice infection pressure imposed by salmon farms at distances >30km. They also found a high risk of sea trout mortality close to marine salmon farms in Ireland for the first fifteen years of sea lice monitoring on wild sea trout. This result was consistent with the observed collapse in sea trout rod catches in the Irish Connemara district in 1989-1990 and with the expansion of salmon aquaculture in west of Ireland estuaries during the mid-1980s. They argue that there was not sufficient control of sea lice on marine salmon farms in Ireland to prevent lice infestation and a high risk of sea trout mortality at many sites over the period when monitoring of sea trout began in 1991 until the mid-2000s. Although the extent of sampling was more restricted after 2006, the data indicate that the increased mortality risk for individual sea trout at the population level fell over the most recent decade. The establishment of sea lice protocol limits on salmon farms in Ireland from 2001, a change in the salmon farming practice of moving to single generation sites in the mid 2000's and a general reduction in lice levels on farms over recent years, is likely to have contributed to this result. However, results for a small number of individual sites continued to show high risk of sea trout mortality in certain years.

A broad range of studies over the past 25 years has provided convincing evidence of impacts from sea lice emanating from salmon farms on sea trout, both at an individual and at a population level (Thorstad *et al.*, 2015 and Gargan *et al.*, 2016). To combat such impacts, Gargan *et al.* (2017) describe the assessment methodology recently developed by Taranger *et al.* (2014) in Norway and known as the *traffic light system*. The 'Strategy for an environmentally sustainable aquaculture industry in Norway' (Anon, 2009) states that no disease, including lice, should have a regulatory effect on wild fish. The monitoring of salmon lice infection of wild salmonids is an important verification of whether or not this goal was achieved, and if the measures taken to minimise its impact are appropriate and sufficient.

The *traffic light system* is used as a warning indicator that predicts the risk of sea lice infestation on wild salmonids based on counting lice on salmon farms and modelling total emissions of lice larvae in a geographical area. Subsequent counts of sea lice on wild salmon and sea trout are used to verify and calibrate the model. This first generation measurement of risk assessment of salmon lice and wild salmonids (Taranger *et al.*, 2012 & Karlsen *et al.*, 2016) will be adopted

575

as a starting point by the Norwegian Government to control and regulate sea lice emissions from salmon farms. While this management structure is still under development in Norway, the *traffic light system* offers a method for controlling the level of sea lice impacts from salmon farming that could also be applied to other countries over the coming years.

Management Priorities.

> ➢ Develop specific management strategies to combat sea lice infestations from salmon farms for each site in line with best international practice, such as the Norwegian traffic light system.
> ➢ Ensure that strategies to reduce or eliminate sea lice impacts are also monitored effectively to establish if sea trout populations are recovering because of these actions.
> ➢ Ensure that future developments are only located at ecologically sustainable sites.
> ➢ Undertake focused studies to assess the best options for restoring and increasing stocks in areas where they are critically endangered due to the impacts of aquaculture and habitat loss: including 'restorative' stocking programmes on a controlled basis.

4.12 CLIMATE CHANGE

Climate change is an over-arching concern affecting the future approach to management and monitoring for all fish, particularly diadromous species that traverse contrasting marine and freshwater habitats. Long term changes in sea trout stock features in the Irish Sea have been attributed in part to increasing sea water temperature, although changes in freshwater are also important (Davidson *et al.*, 2016; CSTP, 2016; Milner *et al.*, 2017). Among other things, there is now, and will continue to be, a need for greater emphasis on monitoring changing conditions in the marine environment. Broad patterns of climate change are well established in marine ecosystems (Phillipart *et al.*, 2011; Edwards *et al.*, 2013) and in freshwater (Walsh & Kilsby, 2007; Orr *et al.*, 2014). Their consequences for anadromous fish are less clear, although there have been important reviews since the last Sea Trout Symposium (e.g. Graham & Harrod; 2009; Jonsson & Jonsson, 2009; Elliott & Elliott, 2010; ICES, 2017) and now a rapidly expanding literature.

Climate change is of particular relevance to the many smaller sea trout rivers and tributary spawning areas that are vulnerable due to their faster reaction times, instability and stochastic variability. In this respect, consideration should be given to extending existing long-term monitoring programmes on Index Rivers to incorporate environmental indicators of climate change (principally, water temperature, rainfall and river flows, coupled with temperature and productivity changes in the relevant marine habitats, in order to establish their links to stock characteristics such as a) smolt yield, b) returning adult run-strength run-timing, c) smolt age and sea age structure and d) growth rate. This would also help to interpret temporal changes and trends in the proportions of juveniles adopting either an anadromous or a resident life history. Future studies incorporating the downscaling of global climate models to assess the likely future impacts of various water discharge and temperature scenarios on such smaller catchments could prove particularly important (Fealy *et al.*, 2013).

Sea trout are dependent upon ecosystem functioning throughout their marine phase and this is changing with climate (Beaugrand & Reid, 2003). The production of keystone prey species, such as sandeel and sprat, is crucial to sea trout and to marine fish and bird species, but is not monitored effectively.

Management priorities.

➤ Initiate a comprehensive programme on '*Life History Optimisation in Trout in a Changing Environment*' to explore the factors that influence the life history strategies that trout may adopt and the ways that climate change might affect them.

➤ Review the adequacy of existing programmes for monitoring the impact of climate change on anadromous fish, their associated fisheries and ecosystems in freshwater and marine habitats.

➤ Develop an integrated regional network of carefully selected catchments to routinely monitor environmental conditions and the quantitative and qualitative structure and composition of their individual stocks more comprehensively.

➤ Investigate the application of the global climate model downscaling approach to establish a series of likely climate change scenarios appropriate for sea trout waters.

➤ Identify and evaluate appropriate adaptive river restoration and climate change mitigation practices.

4.13 ECONOMIC VALUE

Although assessing the economic value of sea trout fisheries and the broader ecosystem services environmental value of sea trout as a sentinel environmental species was not discussed at the Symposium, it remains an important gap area in the overall management of sea trout populations. It was repeatedly noted that sea trout, through their ubiquity and use of multiple aquatic habitats, are a potentially important keystone sentinel species of environmental quality. This is a role that remains undervalued and yet to be fully explored.

The need to obtain estimates of the value of sea trout fisheries and their economic contribution to regional communities was one key recommendation from the 1st Symposium that was again repeated by Atlantic Salmon Trust (2011) and ICES (2013) but which has not been progressed. It was agreed that this information would help raise the general profile and importance of the sea trout to provide a stronger justification for future investment in the protection and management of the fisheries in many regions where sea trout were regarded as being of secondary importance to salmon (Harris & Milner, 2006; ICES, 2017). However, interest in sea trout has increased since the 1960s as salmon abundance has declined, both qualitatively and quantitatively, to the point where many stocks are considered to be '*at risk*', '*threatened*' or '*endangered*'. In some countries, this has led to the introduction of progressively more robust regulatory measures to conserve future salmon stocks, including the closure of rod and net fisheries and the introduction of compulsory catch-and release for rod fisheries on an increasing number of rivers. This has raised awareness of the importance of the sea trout as an alternative target fish in sustaining the social and economic value of the fisheries, particularly on the very many smaller rivers where salmon runs were never abundant (Harris & Evans, 2017).

However, progress in commissioning the necessary economic studies is frustrated by practical constraints for two principal reasons. Firstly, the practical difficulties inherent with previous methodologies in separating the expenditure (and derived economic benefit) targeted directly at fishing for sea trout as opposed to other species of fish (principally salmon) over the same fishing season (O'Reilly & Mawle, 2006; Harris & Evans, 2017). Secondly, the marked differences between countries in the nature and extent of various forms of fishing, the number of the fisheries, the limited and variable data on the number of participants in those fisheries and problems in identifying individual fishermen in the absence of an effective system of licensing or registration and/or a system of mandatory catch returns.

Management Priorities.

➢ Recognise the longstanding need for authoritative estimates of the importance and value of sea trout fisheries in generating income and employment in local communities, especially in more remote and economically deprived locations, as justification for their fuller consideration in the development of locally based Catchment and River Basin Management Plans.

➢ Establish a working group of appropriate specialists (including economists) to define acceptable and valid measures for assessing economic benefit and to develop a standard methodology (or methodologies) for evaluating the contribution of different types of recreational and commercial fishing in different regions.

➢ Consider the development of a basic survey "toolkit" for general use by stakeholder interest groups wishing to undertake site-specific surveys on the economic value and benefit of discrete local fisheries.

5. GENERAL CONCLUSION

Sea trout science has seen useful progress in the last 20 years in many strategic topic areas, although not at a uniform rate throughout its geographical range. This has succeeded in increasing the potential to manage stocks by a better understanding of their structuring and likely responses to environmental change and other pressures. Nevertheless some key actions remain, particularly in relation to monitoring, life history modelling, population dynamics and fisheries assessments. The fundamental question about the balance between residency and anadromy requires the simultaneous integration of genetics, evolutionary biology and ecology across freshwater and marine habitats. There is also a continuing need for better dialogue amongst managers, scientists and the public on common management aims for the species. This Symposium and the other discussions mentioned above have gone some way towards achieving this. Such discussions remain at the heart of what modern ecosystem-based fishery management is about because they validate, sharpen and then focus the collective effort across all sectors of society.

It is hoped that the management priorities listed here will provide a basis for tackling these core knowledge gaps but, as we have seen in the past, sea trout research and applied management initiatives need authoritative and influential champions at both a national and international level. In this respect, ICES and EIFAC have a key role to play in formulating and agreeing management and research priorities and recommending best practice for migratory fish species. This will enable state agencies and third sector groups to compete for the funding required to implement best management practice and to undertake prioritised programmes of research on key indicator species such as the sea trout.

REFERENCES

Aldvén, D. & Davidsen, J.G. (2017). Marine Migrations of sea trout (*Salmo trutta*). (2017). In: *Sea Trout: Science & Management* (Graeme Harris. Ed.). Proceedings of the 2nd International Sea Trout Symposium, 20-22 October 2015, Dundalk, Ireland. Troubador, 267-276..

Aldvén, D., Závorka, L. Aarstrup, K & Höjesjö. J. (2017). Migration pathways in a fjord of two populations of *Salmo trutta* L.) sea trout smolts In: *Sea Trout: Science & Management* (Graeme Harris. Ed.). Proceedings of the 2nd International Sea Trout Symposium, 20-22 October 2015, Dundalk, Ireland. Troubador, 277-291.

Anon. (2009). Strategy for an Environmentally Sustainable Norwegian Aquaculture Industry (*in Norwegian*). Ministry of Fisheries and Coastal Affairs, Oslo, Norway, 34 pp.

Beaugrand, G & Reid, P.C. (2003). Long-term changes in phytoplankton, zooplankton and salmon related to climate change. Global Change Biology, **9**, 801-817.

Biggs, J., von Fumetti, S. & Kelly-Quinn, M. (2017). The importance of small water bodies for biodiversity and ecosystem services: implications for policy makers. *Hydrobiologia*. January 2017. DOI: 10.1007/s10750-016-3077-z

Briers, R., Campbell, R., Galt, K., Walters, M. & Holmes, J. (2017). Using stable isotopes to assess the distribution and reproduction by migratory and resident *Salmo trutta* within river systems: some complicating factors. In: *Sea Trout: Science & Management.* (Graeme Harris. *Ed.*). Proceedings of the 2nd International Sea Trout Symposium, 20-22 October 2015, Dundalk, Ireland. Troubador, 410–422.

Chat, J., Masson, S., Manicki, A., Geraud, F., Rives, J., Lange, F., Huchet, E., Coste, P., Aymes, J-C. & Lepais, O. (2017). Do sea trout promote interbasin Connectivity between populations? In: *Sea*

Trout: Science & Management. (Graeme Harris. *Ed.*). Proceedings of the 2nd International Sea Trout Symposium, 20-22 October 2015, Dundalk, Ireland. Troubador, 354–370.

Cucheroussett, J., Ombredane, D., Charles, K., Marchand, F. & Baglinière, J-L. (2005). A continuum of life history tactics in a brown trout (*Salmo trutta*) Population. *Canadian Journal of Fisheries and Aquatic Sciences* **62**, 1600–1610.

Davidson, I.C., Hazelwood, M.S & Cove, R.J. (2006). Predicted growth of juvenile trout and salmon in four rivers in England and Wales based on past and possible future temperature regimes linked to climate change. In: Sea Trout: Biology, Conservation and Management. (Graeme Harris & Nigel Milner. *Eds*). Proceedings of the 1st International Sea Trout Symposium. July 2004, Cardiff, Wales. Blackwell Publishing, Oxford, 410–414.

Davidson, I., Aprahamian, M., Peirson, G., Hillman, R., Cook, N., Elsmere, P., Cove, R. & Croft, A. (2017a). Catch and stock based Biological Reference Points for sea trout in England & Wales: a comparison of methods and critical examination of their potential application to stock assessment and management. In: *Sea Trout: Science & Management.* (Graeme Harris. *Ed.*). Proceedings of the 2nd International Sea Trout Symposium, 20-22 October 2015, Dundalk, Ireland. Troubador, 129–152.

Davidson, I., Cove, R., Hillman, R., Elsmere, P., Cook, N. & Croft, A. (2017b). Observations on sea trout stock performance in the Rivers Dee, Tamar, Lune & Tyne (1991-2014). The Contribution of Index River monitoring programmes in England & Wales to fisheries management. In: *Sea Trout: Science & Management.* (Graeme Harris. *Ed.*). Proceedings of the 2nd International Sea Trout Symposium, 20-22 October 2015, Dundalk, Ireland. Troubador, 470–486.

Degerman, E., Leonardsson, K. & Lundqvist, H. (2012). Coastal migrations, temporary use of neighbouring rivers, and growth of sea trout (*Salmo trutta*) from nine northern Baltic Sea rivers. *ICES Journal of Marine Science*, **69**, 971-980.

Edwards, M., Bresnan, E., Cook, K., Heath, M., Helaouet, P., Lynam, C., Raine, R. & Widdicombe, C. (2013) Impacts of climate change on plankton. Marine Climate Change Impacts Partnership: Science Review. *MCCIP Science Review* 2013, 98-112.

Elliott, J.M. & Elliott, J.A. (2006). A 35-Year Study of Stock-Recruitment Relationships in a Small Population of Sea Trout; Assumption. Implications and Limitations for Predicting Targets. In: *Sea Trout: Biology, Conservation and Management.* (Graeme Harris & Nigel Milner. *Eds*). Proceedings of the 1st International Sea Trout Symposium. July 2004, Cardiff, Wales. Blackwell Publishing, Oxford, 257–278.

Elliott, J.M. & Chambers, S. (1996). A Guide to the interpretation of sea trout scales. National Rivers Authority, R&D Report 22. National Rivers Authority, Bristol, 63 pp.

Elliott J. M. & Elliott, J. A. (2010) Temperature requirements of Atlantic salmon *Salmo salar*, brown trout *Salmo trutta* and Arctic charr *Salvelinus alpinus*: predicting the effects of climate change. *Journal of Fish Biology* **77**, 1793–1817.

Ensing, D. & Breukelaar, A. (2017). Genetic structure and tracking of sea trout (*Salmo trutta* L.) in the Rhine and Meuse estuary in the Netherlands. In: *Sea Trout: Science & Management.* (Graeme Harris. *Ed.*). Proceedings of the 2nd International Sea Trout Symposium, 20-22 October 2015, Dundalk, Ireland. Troubador, 253–266.

Evans, R. & Harris, G.S. (2017). The collection of sea trout and salmon statistics from the recreational rod fisheries in England & Wales. In: *Sea Trout: Science & Management.* (Graeme Harris. *Ed.*). Proceedings of the 2nd International Sea Trout Symposium, 20-22 October 2015, Dundalk, Ireland. Troubador, 487–506.

Fealy, R. (2013). Deriving probabilistic based climate scenarios using pattern scaling and statistically downscaled data. A case study application from Ireland. *Progress in Physical Geography,* **37** (2), 178–205.

Ferguson, A. (2006). Genetics of sea trout, with particular reference to Britain and Ireland. In: *Sea Trout: Biology, Conservation & Management of Sea Trout.* (Graeme Harris & Nigel Milner. Eds.). Proceedings of the 1st International Sea Trout Symposium, 7-10 July 2004, Cardiff, Wales. Blackwell Publishing, 157–182.

Ferguson, A., Reed, T., McGinnity. P. & Prodöhl, P. (2017). Anadromy in brown trout (*Salmo trutta* L.): A review of the relative roles of genes and environmental factors and the implication for management. In: *Sea Trout: Science & Management* (Graeme Harris *Ed.*). Proceedings of the 2nd International Sea Trout Symposium, 20-22 October 2015, Dundalk, Ireland. Troubador, 1–40.

Gargan, P.G., Shephard, S. & C. Macintyre, C. (2017) Assessment of the increased mortality risk and population regulating effect of sea lice (*Lepeophtheirus salmonis*) from marine salmon farms on wild sea trout in Ireland and Scotland. In: *Sea Trout: Science & Management.* (Graeme Harris. *Ed.*). Proceedings of the 2nd International Sea Trout Symposium, 22-22 October 2015. Dundalk, Ireland. Troubador, 507–522.

Gargan, P.G., Kelly, F.L., Shephard, S. & Whelan, K.F. (2016) Temporal variation in sea trout *Salmo trutta* life history traits in the Erriff River, Western Ireland. *Aquaculture Environment Interactions,* Vol. **8**: 675–689,

Gargan, P.G., Poole, W.R. & Forde, G. (2006). A review of the status of Irish sea trout stocks. In: *Sea Trout Biology, Conservation & Management.* (Graeme Harris & Nigel Milner, N. *Eds.*). Proceedings of the 1st International Sea Trout Symposium, July 2005, Cardiff, Wales, 25-44.

Graham, C.T. & Harrod, D.C. (2009). Implications of climate change for the fishes of the British Isles. *Journal of Fish Biology,* **74**, 1143–1205.

Harris, G.S. (2002). Sea Trout Stock Descriptions: The Structure & Composition of Adult Sea Trout Stocks from 16 Rivers in England & Wales. R&D Technical Report W224, Environment Agency, Bristol, 93 pp.

Harris, G.S. & Evans, R. (2017). The relative importance of sea trout and salmon to the recreational rod fisheries in England & Wales. In: *Sea Trout: Science & Management.* (Graeme Harris. *Ed.*). Proceedings of the 2nd International Sea Trout Symposium, 20-22 October 2015, Dundalk, Ireland. Troubador, 185–204.

Harris, G.S. & Milner, N.J. (2006). *Sea Trout: Biology, Conservation & Management.* Proceeding of the 1st International Sea Trout Symposium. 7-10 July 2004, Cardiff, Wales. Blackwell Publishing, 499 pp.

Hogvaard, K., Skaala, Ø. & Nævdal, G. (2006). Genetic differentiation among sea trout, *Salmo trutta* L., populations from western Norway. *Journal of Applied Ichthyology,* **22** (1), 57-61.

Höjesjö, J., Nilsson, N., Degerman, E.,Halldén, A. & Aldvén, D. (2017) Calculating smolt production of sea trout from habitat surveys and electrofishing: pilot studies from small streams in Sweden. In:

Sea Trout: Science & Management (Graeme Harris *Ed.*). Proceedings of the 2nd International Sea Trout Symposium, 20-22 October 2015, Dundalk, Ireland. Troubador, 458–469.

ICES. (1994). Report of the Study Group on Anadromous Trout (SGAT), 28-31 August 1994, Trondheim, Norway. ICES CM 1994/M:4, ANACAT. 80 pp.

ICES. (1999). Report of the Study Group on Sea Trout (SGST), by correspondence. ICES CM/1999/G: 10, 11 pp

ICES. (2011) Report of the Workshop on Age Determination of Salmon (WKADS), 18
20 January 2011, Galway, Ireland. ICES CM 2011/ACOM: **44**, 67 pp.

ICES. (2013). Report of the Workshop on Sea Trout (WKTRUTTA), 12-14 November 2013. ICES Headquarters, Copenhagen, Denmark. ICES CM 2013/SSGEF: 1.5, 243 pp.

ICES. (2017). Report of the Workshop on Sea Trout 2 (WKTRUTTA2), 2 - 5 February 2016, ICES Headquarters, Copenhagen, Denmark. ICES CM 2016/SSGEPD: 20, 121 pp.

ICES. (2017). Report of the Workshop on Potential Impacts of Climate Change on Atlantic Salmon Stock Dynamics (WKCCISAL). ICES WKCCISAL Report 2017 ICES ADVISORY COMMITTEE. ICES CM 2017/ACOM:39.

Jonsson, B. & Jonsson, N. (2006). The Life History of Anadromous Trout *Salmo trutta*. In: *Sea Trout: Biology, Conservation & Management of Sea Trout*. (Graeme Harris & Nigel Milner. *Eds.*). Proceedings of the 1st International Sea Trout Symposium, 7-10 July 2004, Cardiff, Wales. Blackwell Publishing, 196-223.

Jonsson, B. & Jonsson, N. (2009). A review of the likely effects of climate change on anadromous Atlantic salmon Salmo salar and brown trout *Salmo trutta*, with particular reference to water temperature and flow. *Journal of Fish Biology*, **75**, 2381–2447.

Karlsen, Ø., Finstad, B., Ugedal., O. & Svåsand, T. (2016). Kunnskapsstatus som grunnlag for kapasitetsjustering innen produksjonsområder basert på lakselus som indicator. (A status of knowledge as a basis for capacity adjustment in production areas based on sea lice as an indicator). Report from the Institute for Marine Research No.14-2016 (ISSN 1893-4536 online), 137 pp.

Kennedy, T.J., Crozier, W.W. Rosell. R., Allen, M. & Prodöhl, P. (2017). Trout recruitment, production and ova seeding requirements on a small coastal river: A case study from the Shimna River, Northern Ireland. In: *Sea Trout: Science & Management* (Graeme Harris *Ed.*). Proceedings of the 2nd International Sea Trout Symposium, 20 - 22 October 2015, Dundalk, Ireland. Troubador, 153–166.

King, R.A., Hillman, R., Elsmere, P., Stockley, B. & Stevens, J.R. (2016). Investigating patterns of straying and mixed stock exploitation of sea trout, *Salmo trutta*, in rivers sharing a common estuary in south-west England. *Fisheries Management & Ecology*, **23**, 376–389.

King, A., Stockley, B., Hillman, R., Elsmere, P. & Stevens, J. (2017). Managing stocks of sea trout (*Salmo trutta* L.) straying between rivers sharing a common estuary in Southwest England: a genetic approach. In: *Sea Trout: Science & Management* (Graeme Harris. *Ed.*). Proceedings of the 2nd International Sea Trout Symposium, 20-22 October 2015, Dundalk, Ireland. Troubador, 308–327.

Landergren, P. (2001). Survival and growth of sea-trout parr in fresh and brackish water. *Journal of Fish Biology* **58** (2), 591–593.

Landergren, P. & Vallin, L. (1998). Spawning of sea-trout *Salmo trutta* L. in brackish waters - lost effort or successful strategy? *Fisheries Research*, **35**, 229-36.

Launey, S., Quémére, E., Fagard, J-L. & Baglinière, J.L. (2017). Sea does matter: seascape heterogeneity influences coastal migration tactics and population connectivity in brown trout (*Salmo trutta* L.). In: *Sea Trout: Science & Management* (Graeme Harris *Ed.*). Proceedings of the 2nd International Sea Trout Symposium, 20-22 October 2015, Dundalk, Ireland. Troubador, 53–68.

Le Cren, E.D. (1985). Sea Trout. Proceedings of the Atlantic Salmon Trust Workshop. Plas Menai, 24-26 October 1984, 42pp.

Levings, C. (2016) *The Ecology of Salmonids in Estuaries around the World: Adaptations, Habitat and Conservation.* University of British Columbia Press, Vancouver. 2016. ISBN 978-0-7748-3173-4.

Middlemas, S., Stewart, D., Henry, J., Wyndham, M., Ballantyne, L. & Baum, D. (2017). Dispersal of post-smolt Atlantic salmon and sea trout within a Scottish sea loch system. In: *Sea Trout: Science & Management* (Graeme Harris. *Ed.*). Proceedings of the 2nd International Sea Trout Symposium, 20-22 October 2015, Dundalk, Ireland. Troubador, 339–353.

Milner, N.J., Potter, E., Roche, W., Tysklind, N., Davidson, I., King, J. & Davies, C. (2017). Variation in sea trout (*Salmo trutta*) abundance and life histories in the Irish Sea. In: *Sea Trout: Science & Management* (Graeme Harris. *Ed.*). Proceedings of the 2nd International Sea Trout Symposium, 20-22 October 2015, Dundalk, Ireland. Troubador, 96–128.

Milner, N.J., Harris, G.S., Gargan, P., Beveridge, M., Pawson, M.J., Walker, A. & Whelan, K. (2006). Perspectives in Sea Trout Science and Management. In: *Sea Trout: Biology, Conservation & Management of Sea Trout.* (Graeme Harris & Nigel Milner. *Eds.*). Proceedings of the 1st International Sea Trout Symposium, 7-10 July 2004, Cardiff, Wales. Blackwell Publishing, 480-490.

Nall, G.H. (1930). *The Life of the Sea Trout: Especially in Scottish Waters.* Seeley, Service & Co., 335 pp.

NASCO. (2009). Guidelines for the Management of Salmon Fisheries. NASCO Council Document CNL(09)43. Edinburgh, 8 pp.

NASCO. (2014). Implementation Plan for the period 2013-2018 – EU–UK (England & Wales). (Updated 1 December 2014). NASCO Council Document CNL (14)71, Edinburgh, 27 pp.

O'Reilly, P.O. & Mawle, G.W. (2006). An Appreciation of the Social and Economic Value of Sea Trout in England & Wales In: *Sea Trout: Biology, Conservation & Management of Sea Trout.* (Graeme Harris & Nigel Milner. Eds.). Proceedings of the 1st International Sea Trout Symposium, 7-10 July 2004, Cardiff, Wales. Blackwell Publishing, 457–465.

Orell, P., Erkinaro, T., Kanniainen, T. & Kuusela, J. (2017). Migration behaviour of sea trout (*Salmo trutta*.L.) on a large sub-arctic river system: evidence of a two year spawning migration. In: *Sea Trout: Science & Management.* (Graeme Harris. *Ed.*). Proceedings of the 2nd International Sea Trout Symposium, 20-22 October 2015, Dundalk, Ireland. Troubador, 396–409.

Orr, H.G., Simpson, G.J., des Clers, S., Watts, G., Hughes, M., Hannaford, J., Dunbar, M.J., Cédric, I. & Laizé, L.R. (2015). Detecting changing river temperatures in England and Wales, *Hydrological Processes,* **29** (5), 752–766.

Pedersen, S., P. Heinimaa, & T. Pakarinen. (Eds.). (2012). Workshop on Baltic Sea Trout, Helsinki, Finland, 11-13 October 2011. DTU Aqua Report No 248-2012. National Institute of Aquatic Resources, Technical University of Denmark. 95 pp.

Philippart, C.J.M., Anadón, R., Danovaro, R., Dippner, J.W., Drinkwater. K.F., Hawkins S.J., Oguz, T., O'Sullivan, G. & Reid, P.C. (2011). Impacts of climate change on European marine ecosystems. Observations, expectations and indicators. *Journal of Experimental Marine Biology & Ecology*, **400**, 52–69.

Potter, E.; Campbell, R.; Sumner, K. & Marshall, S. (2017a). Marine migrations and distribution of sea trout from rivers in Great Britain. In: *Sea Trout: Science & Management*. (Graeme Harris. *Ed*.). Proceedings of the 2nd International Sea Trout Symposium, 20-22 October 2015, Dundalk, Ireland. Troubador, 205–227.

Potter, E., Beraud, C., Bacon, J., Van der Molen, J. & Van Leeuwen, S. (2017b). Simulation of movements of sea trout post-smolts in the Irish and Celtic Seas. In: *Sea Trout: Science & Management*. (Graeme Harris. *Ed*.). Proceedings of the 2nd International Sea Trout Symposium, 20-22 October 2015, Dundalk, Ireland. Troubador, 228-252.

Prodöhl, P., Antoniacomi, A., Bradley, C., Carlsson, J., Carvalho, G.R., Coughlan, J., Coyne, J., Cross, M.C., Davies, C.A., Dillane, E., Gargan, P., Hynes, R., McGinnity, P., Milner, N., Reed, T., Roche, W., Taylor, M., Tysklind, N. & Cross, T.F. (2017). Population genetics and genetic stock identification of anadromous *Salmo trutta* from the Irish Sea and Adjacent area, using microsatellite DNA loci. In: *Sea Trout: Science & Management*. (Graeme Harris. *Ed*.). Proceedings of the 2nd International Sea Trout Symposium, 20-22 October 2015, Dundalk, Ireland. Troubador, 69–97.

Quéméré, E., Baglinière, J-L., Roussel, J-M., Evanno, G., McGinnity, P. & Launey, S. (2016). Seascape and its effect on migratory life-history strategy influences gene flow among coastal brown trout (*Salmo trutta*) populations in the English Channel. *Journal of Biogeography*, **43**, 498–509.

Quinn, T.P. & Myers, K.W. (2006). Patterns of anadromy and migrations of Pacific salmon and trout at sea. In: *Sea trout: biology, conservation and management*. (Graeme Harris & Nigel Milner. *Eds*.), Proceedings of the 1st International Sea-Trout Symposium, Cardiff Wales, July 2004. Oxford. Blackwell, 11-24.

Roche, W., Milner, N., Davies, C., Shephard, S., King, J., Coyne, J., Gargan. P. & Hughes, R. Feeding Ecology of sea trout in the Irish Sea. In: *Sea Trout: Science & Management* (Graeme Harris. *Ed*.). Proceedings of the 2nd International Sea Trout Symposium, 20-22 October 2015, Dundalk, Ireland. Troubador, 371–395.

Sturlaugsson, J. (2017). The marine migration and swimming depth of sea trout (*Salmo trutta* L.) in Icelandic waters. In: *Sea Trout: Science & Management*. (Graeme Harris. *Ed*.). Proceedings of the 2nd International Sea Trout Symposium, 20-22 October 2015, Dundalk, Ireland. Troubador, 328–338.

Solomon, D. (1995). Sea Trout Stocks in England & Wales. R&D Report 25. National Rivers Authority, Bristol, 102 pp.

Taranger, G.L., Karlsen, Ø., Bannister, R.J., Glover, K.A., Husa, V., Karlsbakk, E., Kvamme, B.O., Boxaspen, K.K., Bjørn, P.A., Finstad, B., Madhun, A.S., Craig Morton, H. & Svåsand, T. (2014). Risk assessment of the environmental impact of Norwegian Atlantic salmon farming. *ICES Journal of Marine Science* 72, 997-1021.

Taranger G. L., Boxaspen, K. K., Madhusn, A. S. & Svasand, T. (Eds.) (2012). Suggested first generation method for environmental impact indicators with respect to genetic influences from farmed salmon to wild salmon and the impact of sea lice from farmed fish on wild salmon populations (*in Norwegian*). Fisken og Havet 13-2012.

Thorstad, E.B., Todd, C.D., Uglem, I., Bjørn, P.A., Gargan, P.G., Vollset, K.W., Halttunen, E., Kålås, S., Berg, M. & Finstad, B. (2015). Effects of salmon lice *Lepeophtheirus salmonis* on wild sea trout *Salmo trutta*—A Literature Review. *Aquaculture Environment Interactions*, **7**, 91–113.

Turnpenny, A., Horsefield, T. & Willis, J. (2017). Sea trout and Tidal Power: Challenges and Approaches. In: *Sea Trout: Science & Management*. (Graeme Harris. *Ed.*). Proceedings of the 2nd International Sea Trout Symposium, 20-22 October 2015, Dundalk, Ireland. Troubador, 323–540.

Tysklind, N., Carvahlo, G.R. & Milner, N.J. (2015). Population Dynamics analysis of sea trout populations around the Celtic and Irish Seas. Report to the Atlantic Salmon Trust. AST, Perth, 56pp.

Veinott, G., Westley, P. A. H., Warner, L. & Purchase, C.F. (2102) Assigning origins in a potentially mixed-stock recreational sea trout (*Salmo trutta*) fishery. *Ecology of Freshwater Fish*, **21**, 541–551.

Walsh, C.L. & Kilsby, C.G. (2007). Implication of climate change on flow regime affecting Atlantic salmon. Hydrobiology & Earth Sciences Discussions. European Geosciences Union, 2007 11(3), 1127–1143.

Whelan, K.F. (2014). Sea Trout Populations in Small Coastal Streams. *Biology and Environment. Proceedings of the Royal Irish Academy,* Vol. **114B**, No. 3, 199 - 204.

Went. A.E.J. (1962). Irish sea trout, a review of investigations to date. *Scientific Proceedings of the Royal Society of Dublin*, 1A, No. 10, 265-296.

ELECTRONIC REFERENCES

Atlantic Salmon Trust (2011). Report of the Sea Trout Workshop, Bangor, Wales, 9 – 10 February 2011. Available at: http://www.environmentdata.org/archive/ast:141

Atlantic Salmon Trust. (2015). Report of a workshop on sea trout rod catch and effort data. 11-12 March 2015. Plas Menai, Bangor. *Available at*: http://www.environmentdata.org/archive/ast:143

CSTP. (2016). Celtic Sea Trout Project – Technical Report to Ireland Wales Territorial Co-operation Programme 2007-2013. (Milner, N., McGinnity, P. & Roche, W. *Eds*.). (INTERREG 4A). 850 pp. [Online] Dublin, Inland Fisheries Ireland, 850 pp. *Available at*: http://celticseatrout.com/downloads/technical-report/

IBIS. (2012). Small Streams: Contribution to populations of trout and sea trout. Report of the Workshop held in Carlingford, Co. Louth, Ireland, 27–28 November, 2012. *Available at*: http://seatroutsymposium.org/wp-content/uploads/2014/10/small_streams_report_final_.pdf